INTERPRETING THE MMPI-3

INTERPRETING THE MMPI-3

YOSSEF S. BEN-PORATH and
MARTIN SELLBOM

University of Minnesota Press
Minneapolis
London

Copyright 2023 by the Regents of the University of Minnesota

All rights reserved. No part of this publication may be reproduced, stored in a retrieval system, or transmitted, in any form or by any means, electronic, mechanical, photocopying, recording, or otherwise, without the prior written permission of the publisher.

Published by the University of Minnesota Press
111 Third Avenue South, Suite 290
Minneapolis, MN 55401-2520
http://www.upress.umn.edu

ISBN 978-1-5179-1248-2 (hc)

A Cataloging-in-Publication record for this book is available from the Library of Congress.

Printed in the United States of America on acid-free paper

The University of Minnesota is an equal-opportunity educator and employer.

32 31 30 29 28 27 26   10 9 8 7 6 5 4 3 2

To Auke Tellegen—
mentor, colleague, friend.

Contents

List of Tables — xi
List of Figures — xiii
Preface and Acknowledgments — xvii

PART I. FOUNDATIONS

1 Historical Foundations of the MMPI-3: The MMPI and MMPI-2 — 3
   The Original MMPI — 3
   The MMPI-2 — 24
   Toward the MMPI-2-RF — 37

2 Transitioning to the MMPI-3: The MMPI-2-RF — 39
   A First Step: The Restructured Clinical (RC) Scales — 39
   Developing the Restructured Clinical (RC) Scales — 44
   Appraisals of the Restructured Clinical (RC) Scales — 55
   Completing the MMPI-2-RF — 59
   The MMPI-2-RF Substantive Scales — 60
   The MMPI-2-RF Validity Scales — 72
   Appraisals of the MMPI-2-RF — 96
   Toward the MMPI-3 — 99

3	Developing the MMPI-3	101
	Preliminary Research	102
	Development Samples and Instruments	104
	Scale Development	107
	The MMPI-3 Scales	113
	The MMPI-3 Norms	117
4	The MMPI-3 Validity Scales	135
	Applicability of the MMPI-2-RF Literature	135
	Are Validity Scales Needed?	137
	Psychometric Findings With the MMPI-2-RF/MMPI-3 Validity Scales	139
	Two Functions of the Scales	152
5	The MMPI-3 Substantive Scales	157
	Higher-Order (H-O) Scales	158
	Restructured Clinical (RC) Scales	164
	Specific Problems (SP) Scales	198
	Personality Psychopathology Five (PSY-5) Scales	222
	Mapping the MMPI-3 Onto Contemporary Psychopathology Models	229
6	Diversity-Sensitive Assessment With the MMPI-3	239
	Literature Review	240
	MMPI Translations and International Adaptations	257
	MMPI-3 Features That Enhance Diversity-Sensitive Assessment	261
	Future Directions	265

PART II. APPLICATIONS

7	Administering and Scoring the MMPI-3	269
	Administering the MMPI-3	269
	Scoring the MMPI-3	275
	Computer-Generated MMPI-3 Reports	276

8	Interpreting the MMPI-3 Validity Scales	333
	Threats to Protocol Validity	333
	Interpretive Guidelines	340
	Case Illustrations	354
9	Interpreting the MMPI-3 Substantive Scales	381
	Higher-Order (H-O) Scales	383
	Restructured Clinical (RC) Scales	385
	Specific Problems (SP) Scales	393
	Personality Psychopathology Five (PSY-5) Scales	415
10	Interpreting the MMPI-3: Recommended Framework and Process	421
	Using the MMPI-3 Interpretation Worksheet	421
	Case Example	446
11	MMPI-3 Case Studies	461
	Ms. A: Chronic Fatigue Syndrome	461
	Mr. B: ADHD or Mania?	471
	Mr. C: Severe Personality Disorder	483
	Mx. D: A Case of Social Communication Deficits	494
	Ms. E: A Bariatric Surgery Candidate	504
	Mr. F: A Spinal Cord Stimulator Candidate	513
	Ms. G: Psychological Sequela of Head Trauma	522
	Ms. H: Personality Disorder or Complex PTSD?	532
	Mr. I: A Case of Diminished Responsibility?	543
	Mr. J: A Police Candidate	554
	Ms. K: Neuropsychological Assessment of a Spanish Speaker	570
	Notes	579
	References	581
	Index	633

Tables

Table 3.1.	The MMPI-3 Scales	114
Table 3.2.	Percentile Equivalents of Uniform T Scores	132
Table 5.1.	Corresponding PSY-5 Scales, AMPD Trait Domains, and ICD-11 Trait Qualifier Domains	235
Table 8.1.	MMPI-3 Validity Scales: Threats to Protocol Validity and Confounds	339
Table 8.2.	Cannot Say (CNS) Score Interpretation	341
Table 8.3.	CRIN (Combined Response Inconsistency) Interpretation	342
Table 8.4.	VRIN (Variable Response Inconsistency) Interpretation	343
Table 8.5.	TRIN (True Response Inconsistency) Interpretation	343
Table 8.6.	F (Infrequent Responses) Interpretation	346
Table 8.7.	Fp (Infrequent Psychopathology Responses) Interpretation	347
Table 8.8.	Fs (Infrequent Somatic Responses) Interpretation	348
Table 8.9.	FBS (Symptom Validity Scale) Interpretation	349
Table 8.10.	RBS (Response Bias Scale) Interpretation	350
Table 8.11.	L (Uncommon Virtues) Interpretation	352
Table 8.12.	K (Adjustment Validity) Interpretation	353
Table 9.1.	Emotional/Internalizing Dysfunction (EID) Interpretation	384
Table 9.2.	Thought Dysfunction (THD) Interpretation	385
Table 9.3.	Behavioral/Externalizing Dysfunction (BXD) Interpretation	386
Table 9.4.	Demoralization (RCd) Interpretation	387
Table 9.5.	Somatic Complaints (RC1) Interpretation	388
Table 9.6.	Low Positive Emotions (RC2) Interpretation	390
Table 9.7.	Antisocial Behavior (RC4) Interpretation	391
Table 9.8.	Ideas of Persecution (RC6) Interpretation	392

Table 9.9.	Dysfunctional Negative Emotions (RC7) Interpretation	393
Table 9.10.	Aberrant Experiences (RC8) Interpretation	394
Table 9.11.	Hypomanic Activation (RC9) Interpretation	395
Table 9.12.	Malaise (MLS) Interpretation	397
Table 9.13.	Neurological Complaints (NUC) Interpretation	397
Table 9.14.	Eating Concerns (EAT) Interpretation	398
Table 9.15.	Cognitive Complaints (COG) Interpretation	399
Table 9.16.	Suicidal/Death Ideation (SUI) Interpretation	400
Table 9.17.	Helplessness/Hopelessness (HLP) Interpretation	401
Table 9.18.	Self-Doubt (SFD) Interpretation	401
Table 9.19.	Inefficacy (NFC) Interpretation	402
Table 9.20.	Stress (STR) Interpretation	403
Table 9.21.	Worry (WRY) Interpretation	403
Table 9.22.	Compulsivity (CMP) Interpretation	404
Table 9.23.	Anxiety-Related Experiences (ARX) Interpretation	405
Table 9.24.	Anger Proneness (ANP) Interpretation	405
Table 9.25.	Behavior-Restricting Fears (BRF) Interpretation	406
Table 9.26.	Family Problems (FML) Interpretation	407
Table 9.27.	Juvenile Conduct Problems (JCP) Interpretation	408
Table 9.28.	Substance Abuse (SUB) Interpretation	409
Table 9.29.	Impulsivity (IMP) Interpretation	409
Table 9.30.	Activation (ACT) Interpretation	410
Table 9.31.	Aggression (AGG) Interpretation	411
Table 9.32.	Cynicism (CYN) Interpretation	412
Table 9.33.	Self-Importance (SFI) Interpretation	413
Table 9.34.	Dominance (DOM) Interpretation	414
Table 9.35.	Disaffiliativeness (DSF) Interpretation	414
Table 9.36.	Social Avoidance (SAV) Interpretation	415
Table 9.37.	Shyness (SHY) Interpretation	416
Table 9.38.	Aggressiveness (AGGR) Interpretation	417
Table 9.39.	Psychoticism (PSYC) Interpretation	418
Table 9.40.	Disconstraint (DISC) Interpretation	418
Table 9.41.	Negative Emotionality/Neuroticism (NEGE) Interpretation	419
Table 9.42.	Introversion/Low Positive Emotionality (INTR) Interpretation	419
Table 10.1.	Recommended Framework and Sources of Information for MMPI-3 Interpretation	422

Figures

Figure 3.1.	MMPI-2-RF Scores of MMPI-3 Normative Sample Men and Women—Validity Scales	123
Figure 3.2.	MMPI-2-RF Scores of MMPI-3 Normative Sample Men and Women—Higher-Order and Restructured Clinical Scales	124
Figure 3.3.	MMPI-2-RF Scores of MMPI-3 Normative Sample Men and Women—Somatic/Cognitive and Internalizing Scales	124
Figure 3.4.	MMPI-2-RF Scores of MMPI-3 Normative Sample Men and Women—Externalizing, Interpersonal, and Interest Scales	125
Figure 3.5.	MMPI-2-RF Scores of MMPI-3 Normative Sample Men and Women—Personality Psychopathology Five Scales	125
Figure 3.6.	Spanish-Language MMPI-3 Normative Sample Scored Using English-Language MMPI-3 Norms—Validity Scales	128
Figure 3.7.	Spanish-Language MMPI-3 Normative Sample Scored Using English-Language MMPI-3 Norms—Higher-Order and Restructured Clinical Scales	128
Figure 3.8.	Spanish-Language MMPI-3 Normative Sample Scored Using English-Language MMPI-3 Norms—Somatic/Cognitive and Internalizing Scales	129

Figure 3.9.	Spanish-Language MMPI-3 Normative Sample Scored Using English-Language MMPI-3 Norms—Externalizing and Interpersonal Scales	129
Figure 3.10.	Spanish-Language MMPI-3 Normative Sample Scored Using English-Language MMPI-3 Norms—Personality Psychopathology Five (PSY-5) Scales	130
Figure 3.11.	Prototype Distribution Serving as Target in the Derivation of the Uniform T Scores	132
Figure 5.1.	HiTOP and MMPI-3 Scale Mapping	234
Figure 7.1.	Mr. J's MMPI-3 Score Report	278
Figure 7.2.	Mr. J's MMPI-3 Score Report With Comparison Group Data	293
Figure 7.3.	Mr. J's MMPI-3 Interpretive Report for Clinical Settings	305
Figure 8.1.	MMPI-3 Score Report Validity Scales Profile Showing Nonresponding	355
Figure 8.2.	MMPI-3 Score Report Validity Scales Profile Showing Nonresponding	356
Figure 8.3.	MMPI-3 Score Report Validity Scales Profile Showing Combined Inconsistent Responding	357
Figure 8.4.	MMPI-3 Score Report Validity Scales Profile Showing Variable Inconsistent Responding	359
Figure 8.5.	MMPI-3 Score Report Validity Scales Profile Showing Variable Inconsistent Responding	360
Figure 8.6.	MMPI-3 Score Report Validity Scales Profile Showing Fixed, Content-Inconsistent True Responding	361
Figure 8.7.	MMPI-3 Score Report Validity Scales Profile Showing Fixed, Content-Inconsistent False Responding	363
Figure 8.8.	MMPI-3 Score Report Validity Scales Profile Showing a Highly Elevated F Score Reflecting Overreporting	364
Figure 8.9.	MMPI-3 Score Report Validity Scales Profile Showing an Elevated Fp Score Reflecting Overreporting of Severe Psychopathology	365
Figure 8.10.	MMPI-3 Score Report Validity Scales Profile Showing Highly Elevated F and Fp Scores	367
Figure 8.11.	MMPI-3 Score Report Validity Scales Profile Showing a Moderately Elevated F Score	368
Figure 8.12.	MMPI-3 Score Report Validity Scales Profile Showing an Elevated Fs Score Reflecting Overreporting of Somatic Symptoms	369
Figure 8.13.	MMPI-3 Score Report Validity Scales Profile Showing an Elevated FBS Score and a Moderately Elevated RBS Score	371

Figure 8.14.	MMPI-3 Score Report Validity Scales Profile Showing an Elevated RBS Score and a Moderately Elevated FBS Score	372
Figure 8.15.	MMPI-3 Score Report Validity Scales Profile Showing Highly Elevated Scores on All Overreporting Scales	373
Figure 8.16.	MMPI-3 Score Report Validity Scales Profile Showing an Elevated L Score	374
Figure 8.17.	MMPI-3 Score Report Validity Scales Profile Showing an Elevated K Score With a Low L Score	376
Figure 8.18.	MMPI-3 Score Report Validity Scales Profile Showing Elevated L and K Scores	377
Figure 8.19.	MMPI-3 Score Report Validity Scales Profile Showing Elevated F and L Scores Reflecting Overreporting While Claiming Uncommon Virtues	378
Figure 8.20.	MMPI-3 Score Report Validity Scales Profile Showing a Valid Protocol	379
Figure 10.1.	MMPI-3 Interpretation Worksheet	423
Figure 10.2.	MMPI-3 Interpretation Worksheet With Completed Validity Scales Page	428
Figure 10.3.	MMPI-3 Score Report Validity Scales Profile	429
Figure 10.4.	Ms. N's MMPI-3 Score Report	431
Figure 10.5.	Ms. N's Completed MMPI-3 Interpretation Worksheet	438
Figure 10.6.	Mr. I's MMPI-3 Score Report	447
Figure 10.7.	Mr. I's Completed MMPI-3 Interpretation Worksheet	454
Figure 11.1.	Ms. A's MMPI-3 Score Report	463
Figure 11.2.	Mr. B's MMPI-3 Score Report	473
Figure 11.3.	Mr. C's MMPI-3 Score Report	485
Figure 11.4.	Mx. D's MMPI-3 Score Report	496
Figure 11.5.	Ms. E's MMPI-3 Score Report	506
Figure 11.6.	Mr. F's MMPI-3 Score Report	515
Figure 11.7.	Ms. G's MMPI-3 Score Report	524
Figure 11.8.	Ms. H's MMPI-3 Score Report	534
Figure 11.9.	Mr. I's MMPI-3 Score Report	545
Figure 11.10.	Mr. J's MMPI-3 Police Candidate Interpretive Report	555
Figure 11.11.	Ms. K's MMPI-3 Score Report	571

Preface and Acknowledgments

The various iterations of the MMPI have been a mainstay of psychological assessment for over eight decades. Among the factors contributing to the inventory's longevity have been the availability of an unparalleled empirical literature and comprehensive texts written to integrate this literature and guide users of the test. Published in 1960, Grant Dahlstrom and George Welsh's *MMPI Handbook* was the first such resource, setting the standard for future efforts with subsequent versions of the test. Jack Graham's and Roger Greene's MMPI-2 texts, and Bob Archer's guide to using the MMPI-A carried this tradition forward with subsequent editions of the MMPI. The predecessor to this volume, Ben-Porath's *Interpreting the MMPI-2-RF*, was written to serve a similar function for the restructured version of the inventory, and it serves as the foundation for the current guide to using the MMPI-3.

The intended audience for this book includes graduate students learning about the test and how to best use it, scholars interested in the MMPI literature, and practitioners seeking to optimize use of the MMPI-3 in their assessments. Part I canvasses the historical, conceptual, and empirical foundations of the MMPI-3. In chapter 1, we review the historical foundations of the inventory, beginning with development and publication in 1943 of the original MMPI, followed by the first comprehensive revision of the test that produced the MMPI-2 in 1989. In chapter 2, we describe the rationale and process used for the second comprehensive revision of the test, culminating in the 2008 publication of the MMPI-2-RF. Because the restructured form serves as the foundation for many features of the MMPI-3, we discuss the restructuring process and the resulting instrument in considerable detail. In chapter 3, we describe the process and outcome of developing the MMPI-3. A critical element of the MMPI-3 development plan was that revisions of MMPI-2-RF scales would be implemented in a manner that would allow MMPI-3 users to rely on the extensive MMPI-2-RF literature (as of this writing, amounting to over 560 peer-reviewed publications). This literature is reviewed in detail in chapters 4 and 5, which cover, respectively, the MMPI-3 Validity and Substantive Scales. A particular emphasis in chapter 5 is to highlight how the MMPI-3 scales are anchored in contemporary psychopathology literature. In chapter 6, the final foundational chapter, we discuss diversity-sensitive assessment with the MMPI-3. We review the extensive literature on use of the MMPI instruments with diverse groups within the United States. Adaptations of the inventory for use in other languages and cultures are discussed and recommended practices for conducting diversity-sensitive assessments with the MMPI-3 are presented.

Part II of this book covers MMPI-3 applications. In chapter 7, we describe standard procedures for administering and scoring the test. Chapters 8 and 9 provide interpretive guidelines for the MMPI-3 Validity and Substantive Scales, respectively. In chapter 10, we describe and illustrate the recommended framework for writing an MMPI-3 interpretation, and in chapter 11 we provide a series of cases studies from mental health, medical, forensic, and public safety settings.

Several individuals made important contributions to this book, for which we are very thankful. Melissa Halozan and Maria Cimino provided extensive administrative assistance during its writing. David Corey, David McCord, and Antonio Puente provided very helpful reviews of an initial draft of the book. Katie Nickerson and Alicia Gomez, at the University of Minnesota Press, provided essential guidance and support throughout the writing process. We also thank our families for their steadfast support.

INTERPRETING THE MMPI-3

Part I
Foundations

Historical Foundations of the MMPI-3

The MMPI and MMPI-2

The MMPI item pool, assembled by Hathaway and McKinley (1943) and augmented for the MMPI-2 by Butcher and colleagues (1989), was a mainstay of psychological assessment for 8 decades, a testament to the richness and clinical utility of the MMPI instruments. However, the original MMPI Clinical Scales, constructed in the late 1930s using then state-of-the-art methods, did not conform to modern psychometric standards. To address this shortcoming, Professor Auke Tellegen, of the University of Minnesota, initiated a revision of the Clinical Scales shortly after the MMPI-2 was published. Tellegen's development of the MMPI-2 Restructured Clinical (RC) Scales (Tellegen et al., 2003) became the first phase of a project to modernize the MMPI-2, which resulted in the MMPI-2-RF (Restructured Form), the starting point for development of the MMPI-3.

To set the stage for chapters discussing the rationale for and methods used to develop the MMPI-2-RF and MMPI-3, this chapter begins with a review of the original MMPI, outlining the conceptual and empirical foundations of the test, major milestones in its development and use as a clinical assessment device, and the role it played in some important developments in assessing personality and psychopathology. The MMPI Restandardization Project and its product, the MMPI-2, are described next, including discussion of both the major accomplishments and limitations of the revision.

THE ORIGINAL MMPI

As detailed by Dahlstrom (1992), the MMPI was published during a period of increasing skepticism concerning the utility of self-report personality inventories (e.g., Landis & Katz, 1934; Landis et al., 1935). The two major instruments in use at the time, the Bernreuter Personality Inventory (Bernreuter, 1933) and the Humm–Wadsworth Temperament Scales (Humm & Wadsworth, 1935), were viewed as overly transparent and, as a result, subject to manipulative distortion. They were also considered too narrow in scope to serve as omnibus measures of psychopathology. Thus, Hathaway and McKinley (1940) sought to "create a large reservoir of items from which various scales might be constructed in the hope of *evolving* [emphasis added] a greater variety of valid personality descriptions than are available at the present time" (p. 249). It is noteworthy that as early as 1940, Hathaway and McKinley viewed their initial efforts at scale development as a starting point for what they hoped would be an evolving instrument.

Theoretical Foundations

The scale construction method that Hathaway and McKinley adopted was clearly empirical, but it is a mistake to view the development of the MMPI as atheoretical. The inventory was assembled in a medical setting, to be used as a screening instrument for the detection of psychopathology. The test authors relied on an existing model of psychopathology and were influenced by behavioral and psychodynamic thinking as well as by the psychometric knowledge and experience of their time.

When compiling the candidate test items, Hathaway and McKinley (1940) were guided by psychiatric practices of the 1930s:

> The individual items were formulated partly on the basis of previous clinical experience. Mainly, however, the items were supplied from several psychiatric examination direction forms, from various textbooks of psychiatry, from certain of the directions for case taking in medicine and neurology, and from the earlier published scales of personal and social attitudes. (p. 249)

In selecting targets for scale development, Hathaway and McKinley followed the diagnostic classification system of the 1930s, which was a derivative of the descriptive system developed by Kraepelin (1921). Kraepelinian nosology, which allowed for reliable diagnoses of disorders such as hysteria, schizophrenia, and manic depression, supplied the model for the initial designation of MMPI scales, and a combination of behavioral, psychodynamic, and psychometric thinking characterized early theoretical writings on the test. All three elements are found in Meehl's (1945a) article "The Dynamics of 'Structured' Personality Tests," written in response to a critique of self-report personality inventories that faulted them for relying on the assumption that test items must always have the same meaning for different individuals. While agreeing that this assumption was unsupported, Meehl asserted that it was also unnecessary for tests such as the MMPI:

A "self-rating" constitutes an intrinsically interesting and significant bit of verbal behavior, the non-test correlates of which must be discovered by empirical means. Not only is this approach free from the restriction that the subject must be able to describe his own behavior accurately, but a careful study of structured personality tests built on this basis shows that such a restriction would falsify the actual relationships that hold between what a man says and what he *is*. (p. 297)

Thus, according to Meehl (1945a), the literal content of the stimulus (item) was unimportant, even irrelevant, and potentially misleading; the empirical correlates of scales composed of item responses should be the sole source for test interpretation. Moreover, Meehl provided examples of MMPI items scored in counterintuitive or nonintuitive directions, laying the foundation for psychodynamically based assumptions:

The complex defense mechanisms of projection, rationalization, reaction formation, etc., appear dynamically to the interviewer as soon as he begins to take what the client *says* as itself motivated by other needs than those of giving an accurate verbal report. There is no good a-priori reason for denying the possibility of similar processes in the highly structured "interview," which is the question–answer personality test. (p. 298)

Here, Meehl appears to equate ambiguous item content with the ambiguous stimuli used in projective testing, which, at that time, was the most common method used in clinical assessments of personality.

Although he provided a theoretical rationale for ignoring item content in test interpretation, Meehl (1945a) was well aware that those who completed the MMPI were attuned to the meaning of test items and might, for a variety of reasons, distort their self-presentation. He recognized that item subtlety or ambiguity could go only so far in preventing such distortions and that other means must also be employed to counter this possibility. The MMPI Validity Scales L and F and the later-added K scale (Meehl & Hathaway, 1946) provided additional psychometric means for detecting, and possibly correcting, the effects of distortion.

In sum, the theoretical foundations of the MMPI included the following:

1. initial development of items and designation of scales based on the then-contemporary Kraepelinian descriptive nosology;
2. treatment of test items as stimuli for behavioral responses, the aggregates of which may have certain empirical correlates, including diagnostic group membership;
3. rejection of content-based test interpretation as overly susceptible to the influences of overt (intentional) and covert (unconscious) distortion; and

4. recognition that, point 3 notwithstanding, test takers do attend to item content and may intentionally or unintentionally respond in a misleading manner, therefore necessitating use of validity scales to assess for response distortion.

Construction of the MMPI

Hathaway and McKinley described the development of several of the original Clinical Scales in a series of articles (Hathaway & McKinley, 1940, 1942; McKinley & Hathaway, 1940, 1942, 1944) compiled in Welsh and Dahlstrom's (1956) *Basic Readings.* Applying a methodology analogous to the one used by Strong (1938) to construct his Vocational Interest Blank, they assembled the scales by contrasting responses of differentially diagnosed patient samples with the responses of a nonclinical sample and, for each of the Clinical Scales, selecting items judged satisfactorily to differentiate the former from the latter. Additional contrast groups were used in constructing some of the scales. The nonclinical sample consisted primarily of visitors to the University of Minnesota Hospital who volunteered to answer the broad list of experimental test items described earlier. They were mostly rural Minnesotans with an average of 8 years of education and employed primarily as skilled and semiskilled laborers and farmers. These individuals served as the normal contrast group for item selection, and their responses were also used to develop norms for the MMPI.

Clinical scale raw scores were calculated for each scale by counting how many items assigned to the scale in question an individual had answered in the keyed direction (True or False), that is, keyed in the direction more often answered by the targeted disorder group (e.g., hypochondriasis) than by the normative sample. These scores were converted into standardized T scores with a mean of 50 and a standard deviation of 10, corresponding to the raw score mean and standard deviation for the normative sample on each given scale.

Subsequent Developments

Despite the care and ingenuity that characterized Hathaway and McKinley's efforts, for many reasons the MMPI never worked as its authors had intended. Attempts to replicate the validity of the Clinical Scales as predictors of diagnostic group membership were only marginally successful for some scales and largely unsuccessful for others (Hathaway, 1960). However, rather than fading away, as had many of its predecessors, the MMPI underwent a substantial transformation. As quoted earlier, Hathaway and McKinley (1940) viewed the initial development of the MMPI as a start, not an end point. Led by Paul Meehl, Hathaway's students and colleagues reinvented the MMPI by directing its use away from the narrow task of differential diagnosis to a considerably broader application.

A Paradigm Shift: Code Types

Although no doubt disappointed by the failure of the test to meet its original goal, early users of the MMPI observed that certain *patterns* of scores tended to recur in the settings in which they practiced, and test takers who produced these combinations shared certain clinical characteristics. Researchers began to shift their focus from scores on individual scales to identifying replicable empirical correlates of these patterns of scale scores. MMPI investigators began to use the term *profile* to refer to the complete set of scores on the Clinical Scales, which now included two later additions, Masculinity/Femininity and Social Introversion, and profile types to identify certain patterns or combinations of scores. Gough (1946), Meehl (1946), and Schmidt (1945) published a series of articles on the utility of certain *profile types* in differential diagnoses. Hathaway (1947) and then Welsh (1948) developed numerical coding systems that provided convenient summaries of the pattern of scores on a profile. This led to the adoption of the term *code type* to designate different classes of profiles.

Within a decade of its initial publication, the prevailing use of the MMPI had changed dramatically. The Kraepelinian nosological model was dropped in favor of a considerably broader and more ambitious goal of describing normal and abnormal personality characteristics. Code types rather than individual scales were viewed as the primary source of information provided by the test. Reflecting this change, the original scale names that corresponded to the Kraepelinian nosological system were modified by using either abbreviations (e.g., Hs for Hypochondriasis) or digits representing their order of appearance in the profile (e.g., Scale 1 for Hypochondriasis). Seeking to advance this transition, Meehl (1956), in his presidential address to the Midwestern Psychological Association, issued a call for an "MMPI cookbook." Researchers were implored to identify a new, clinically useful set of MMPI-based classes and establish their empirical correlates. With the development of an actuarial classification system, test interpretation would involve the simple clerical task of using the scores to identify the individual's type and looking up its empirical correlates in actuarial tables. Investigators responded with several comprehensive efforts to develop such systems (Gilberstadt & Duker, 1965; Marks & Seeman, 1963). Hathaway (1960) summarized this transformation as follows:

> The MMPI began with validity based upon the usefulness of the various diagnostic groups from which its scales were derived. Now the burden of its use rests upon construct validity. Only a small fraction of the published data relating clinical or experimental variables to its scales or profiles can be understood in terms of the original approach. If the validity views of 1941 were the only support for the inventory, it could not survive. What is happening is that the correlations being observed with other variables in normal and

abnormal subjects are filling out personality constructs that emerge, to be in turn tested for their ability to survive. It is significant that constructs, in the general sense of construct validity [Cronbach & Meehl, 1955], can be the forerunners of diagnostic classes. (p. viii)

Further Scale Development

The codebook approach became the primary method for MMPI interpretation. However, soon after the initial publication of the inventory, researchers began creating additional scales from the MMPI item pool. Most early efforts followed the methods of Hathaway and McKinley by using contrasted groups to select items for their scales (Cuadra, 1953; Gough, 1948, 1951; Gough et al., 1951; Williams, 1952). This early work was followed by a profusion of similar studies designed to construct empirically keyed scales for the MMPI. By 1975, volume 2 of the *MMPI Handbook* (Dahlstrom et al., 1975) listed almost as many Supplementary Scales (455) as there were test items. Eventually, the number of Supplementary Scales exceeded the number of test items. In contrast with the 10 Clinical and 3 Validity Scales that were scored from only 383 of the 550 MMPI items, the Supplementary Scales made use of the entire item pool. Most, however, remained obscure and were rarely used in clinical practice.

Another Paradigm Shift: Content-Based Assessment

Although Hathaway and McKinley, for the most part, ignored item content in selecting items for the Clinical Scales, it was not assumed that individuals taking the test would do so. Subsequent scale development efforts sought to take advantage of opportunities (some only perceived, others real) to capitalize on this feature of self-report measures.

WIENER-HARMON SUBSCALES

Recognizing that some MMPI Clinical Scale items appeared much more obviously related in content to the scale on which they were scored than were others, Wiener and Harmon (1946) sought to divide the scales into *obvious* subscales, composed of items whose scoring on a given scale was intuitively clear, and *subtle* subscales, made up of items whose connection to the scale was either unclear or counterintuitive based on the content or scoring direction. Working in a Veterans Administration counseling center, Wiener and Harmon articulated two goals for their efforts: (1) "[to] detect symptoms of emotional disturbance in test-conscious veterans who did not want to indicate them" (p. 7) and (2) "[to distinguish] invalidity on the separate scales of the Multiphasic Inventory" (p. 7). Concealed problems would be indicated when a test taker's subtle subscale score was elevated but the full-scale score was not. Scale-level invalid responding would be detected by contrasting the individual's score on the subtle and obvious subscales within each scale. A significant discrepancy between the two scores would signal either overreporting, if the obvious subscale score was higher, or underreporting, if the subtle subscale score was higher. For these subscales to function as intended, the necessary implicit assumption was that the subtle subscales were no less valid than the obvious subscales and were not (or were less) susceptible to misleading responding.

Wiener (1948) conducted one of the first external validation studies of the subtle and obvious subscales. He compared the obvious and subtle T scores of 100 veterans, half of whom had been successful in school and in on-the-job training. Previous analyses of these data using the full scales indicated that "the MMPI showed consistent but generally insignificant differences favoring the emotional stability of the successful group" (Wiener, 1948, p. 168). In Wiener's new analyses, all five obvious subscales were significantly higher for the unsuccessful group than for the successful group, averaging a 6.5 T-score point difference. Foretelling subsequent findings, none of the subtle subscales discriminated significantly between the two groups. Wiener interpreted these findings as supporting the use of the subtle and obvious subscales because the obvious scales were able to discriminate between the two groups much more successfully than did the full scales. However, these findings failed to provide empirical support for the subtle subscales and should have raised questions from the beginning about the appropriateness of including the subtle items in the full Clinical Scales. On the other hand, they did demonstrate for the first time that using the MMPI item pool for content-based assessment (as represented by the rationally derived obvious subscales) could yield statistically and clinically significant findings.

WELSH FACTOR SCALES

Development of the Welsh factor scales, Anxiety (A) and Repression (R), was another important landmark in the evolution of content-based MMPI interpretation. Welsh (1956) developed these scales to provide measures of two dimensions that appeared repeatedly in factor analyses of the MMPI Clinical Scales. How these scales were constructed is less important for the present discussion than is the way Welsh analyzed them and recommended their use. Prominent among the analyses he reported was a detailed inspection of the item content of each scale; that is, Welsh's recommendations for interpreting scales A and R were guided, to a significant degree, by their content, which he interpreted from a psychodynamic perspective (as evidenced by their labels). This approach, advocated by one of the leading figures in MMPI research, marked a significant departure from the early doctrine of strict empirically based test interpretation.

HARRIS-LINGOES SUBSCALES

Harris and Lingoes (1955) carried out an even more direct attempt to incorporate item content in MMPI interpretation. These authors developed another set of subscales designed to assist in interpreting clinical scale scores by indicating which of several diverse sources of content contributed to an elevated score on a given scale. Harris and Lingoes rationally assigned items on most of the Clinical Scales to content-based subscales. The utility of these subscales was predicated on the assumption that test takers respond in interpretable ways to MMPI item content.

CRITICAL ITEM LISTS

If interpretable item content is relevant to assessing personality and psychopathology, a logical extension is to examine responses to individual items. Grayson (1951) first proposed such an approach and devised a list of 38 items he believed to be indicative of severe psychopathology that should, if answered in the keyed direction, lead the test interpreter to pause and take notice. Grayson generated his list based on a rational inspection of item content. Caldwell (1969) later proposed a similar list of 68 items. Two subsequent lists were developed by Koss and colleagues (Koss & Butcher, 1973; Koss et al., 1976) and by Lachar and Wrobel (1979) based on empirical analyses of item sets nominated by groups of expert judges.

Critical item lists are, in some respects, the most radical of the content-based approaches to MMPI interpretation. The psychometric limitations of individual item responses are well known, chief among them being unreliability. However, developers of these lists did not propose that they be used as psychometric indicators; rather, they were viewed as a useful way for the test interpreter to get the flavor of some of the specific issues of concern to the test taker.

THE WIGGINS CONTENT SCALES

Wiggins (1966) set the standard for rigorous construction of content scales for the MMPI. In providing a rationale for his project, he noted the dearth of attempts to develop content-based scales for the test. He attributed this to the ambivalence, if not the opposition, of the authors of the MMPI toward any deviation from the strict external criteria-based empirical approach to scale construction and interpretation. Wiggins offered cogent arguments favoring development of content-based scales for the MMPI, citing research that had demonstrated equivalence, if not superiority, of content-based measures over empirically keyed ones and the desirability of developing psychometrically sound dimensional means of gauging the information conveyed by the test taker.

Wiggins (1966) began his study by examining the internal consistency of the 26 content-based groupings of the MMPI item pool presented originally (for descriptive purposes) by Hathaway and McKinley (1940). He found some content areas to be promising for further scale-development efforts, whereas others, for a variety of reasons, including a dearth of items, clearly were not. He then set about revising the content categories based on a rational-intuitive analysis followed by additional empirical analyses that yielded a set of 15 content dimensions promising enough to warrant further analyses. Empirical analyses involving the entire item pool of the MMPI eventually yielded a set of 13 internally consistent and relatively independent content scales.

The significance of Wiggins's (1966) efforts cannot be overstated. His methods served as the prototype for all subsequent efforts to develop content-based scales for the MMPI. The psychometric success of his endeavor provided much-needed empirical support for the still-fledgling content-based approach to personality assessment in general and to MMPI interpretation in particular.

VALIDITY SCALES

The development of the MMPI Validity Scales, intended to measure how a test taker approached the instrument, also reflected early recognition that item content could not be ignored. In the same article in which he articulated the theoretical foundations for empirical interpretation of the MMPI, dubbed by Wiggins (1990) "the empiricists manifesto," Meehl (1945a) noted,

> While it is true of many of the MMPI items, for example, that even a psychologist cannot predict on which scale they will appear or in what direction different sorts of abnormals will tend to answer them, still the relative acceptability of defensive answering would seem to be greater than is possible in responding to a set of inkblots. (p. 302)

Picking up on this theme, Meehl and Hathaway (1946) commented later,

> One of the important failings of almost all structured personality tests is their susceptibility to "faking" or "lying" in one way or another, as well as their even greater susceptibility to unconscious self-deception and role-playing on the part of individuals who might consciously be quite honest and sincere in their responses. (p. 525)

The development and routine use of the MMPI Validity Scales were thus predicated on the assumption that test takers respond to item content in meaningful ways.

In summary, although construction of the Clinical Scales was carried out with little or no attention paid to item content, and interpretation based on code types was devoid of any content considerations, MMPI interpreters were provided the means for assessing and considering test takers' content-based responses.

Appraisals of the MMPI and Thoughts About Its Revision

Various methods may be used to appraise the utility of a psychological assessment device, including an examination of how frequently it is used in practice and in research and taking into account scholarly reviews by experts in the field. Consideration of these criteria points to diverging views of the original MMPI.

Clinical Application and Research

Judged by its use in practice and research, the MMPI was clearly well received. In a survey of practicing psychologists in the late 1950s, Sundberg (1961) found that the inventory was by then the most widely used objective measure of personality and psychopathology and was among the most widely used psychological tests. Lubin and colleagues (1971) reported similar findings based on a survey conducted in 1969. Welsh and Dahlstrom (1956) provided a list of 689 papers published through December 1954 that made "more than casual reference to the MMPI" (p. 619). Almost 20 years later, Dahlstrom and colleagues (1975) listed over 5,000 MMPI references compiled through the end of 1973. Together, these data show that by the end of the 1960s, the MMPI had become one of the more widely used and by far the most frequently studied psychological test.

During the period from the 1940s through the 1960s, MMPI investigations contributed significantly to two lines of research: one involving the advance of applied personality assessment, and the other consisting of basic studies of personality and psychopathology. Examples of the former are the introduction and elucidation of a construct validity approach to appraisals of psychological tests (Cronbach & Meehl, 1955), the formulation of and answers to questions about the merits of clinical versus statistical prediction (Meehl, 1954), examination of linear versus configural scoring and interpretation (Goldberg, 1965; Meehl & Dahlstrom, 1960), and studies of the putative influences of response styles on self-report measures of personality and psychopathology (Block, 1965; Edwards, 1964; Jackson & Messick, 1962). The psychopathology studies included research designed to identify the basic building blocks and structures of personality and psychopathology (Welsh, 1956), investigations of the role of personality in physical disease and in somatoform disorder (Hanvik, 1951; Wiener, 1952), studies of the association between personality and criminal conduct (Edwards, 1963), and identification of physiological correlates of psychopathology (Halevy et al., 1965).

These dual tracks of basic and applied MMPI research fostered significant cross-fertilization. Test users were provided the means to incorporate findings of basic research into their clinical assessments, and investigators were given access to a wealth of clinical data enabling relevant research and encouraging theoretical developments that would otherwise have been very difficult to accomplish. However, beginning in the 1960s, MMPI research became increasingly focused on the cookbook approach to test interpretation. As investigators compiled sizable datasets and identified clinically relevant empirical correlates of the code types, MMPI interpretation became focused almost exclusively on these correlates, that is, on criterion validity rather than more broadly on construct validity. Basic researchers, on the other hand, found limited value in the practically convenient but theoretically undeveloped code types and turned instead to alternative measures for studying personality and psychopathology. This schism had unfortunate consequences for both camps. MMPI research became increasingly divorced from developments in the fields of personality and psychopathology, and basic researchers lost access to rich sources of clinical data available on literally hundreds of thousands of individuals tested with the instrument in a broad array of mental health, medical, forensic, and various nonclinical settings.

Scholarly Appraisals

Hathaway's own appraisals of the MMPI might best be characterized as ambivalent. In a foreword to the first edition of Dahlstrom and Welsh's (1960) *MMPI Handbook*, he wrote,

> Our most optimistic expectation was that the methodology of the new test would be so clearly effective that there would soon be better devices with refinements of scales and of general validity. We rather hoped that we ourselves might, with 5 years' experience, greatly increase its validity and clinical usefulness, and perhaps even develop more solidly based constructs or theoretical variables for a new inventory. I doubt now that it is possible to improve the MMPI enough to repay the effort. I am not even sure that we could hold to what validity and usefulness we have. (p. vii)

Hathaway went on to explain that his skepticism stemmed from the absence of a sound alternative to the Kraepelinian nosological system, which was the basis for his work with McKinley in developing the original clinical scales. On a more optimistic note, he observed,

> That the MMPI will be a stepping stone to a higher level of validity I still sincerely hope; I hope too that the new level will soon loom in sight. In the meantime I see it as a stepping stone that permits useful communication at its own level even though the stone is rather wobbly. (p. viii)

Hathaway (1972a) revisited this topic in a brief foreword to the second edition of the *MMPI Handbook*. Writing 12 years after his previous comments were made, he stated,

If another 12 years were to go by without our having gone on to a better instrument or better procedure for the practical needs, I fear that the MMPI, like some other tests, might have changed from a hopeful innovation to an aged obstacle. Do not misunderstand me. I am not agreeing with a few critics who have already called for the funeral and written the epitaph. They have not yet identified what is better. We cannot lay down even a stone-age axe if we have no better one to hew with. (p. xiv)

In a paper titled "Where Have We Gone Wrong? The Mystery of the Missing Progress," Hathaway (1972b) elaborated on these observations and reiterated his view that to a large extent, the lack of progress in refining the MMPI Clinical Scales could be attributed to the absence of an improved (or, for that matter, equally useful) alternative to the Kraepelinian diagnostic system. Hathaway also discussed his disagreement with those who had already eulogized the MMPI, citing as an example a statement by Goldberg (1968, as cited by Hathaway, 1972b) that included the following:

Historically, the MMPI is of the greatest importance to those of us committed to personality assessment. At present, my own belief is that soon it will be little more than an historically interesting instrument. (p. 23)

Hathaway (1972b) responded,

I am not denying a place in history for the MMPI, but Dr. Goldberg's time schedule suggests that it will become historical sooner than I think is likely. Even if it has little more to offer us in research, I fear that the aged MMPI will be tolerated for some time by those concerned with practical problems in psychological evaluation. (p. 23)

Hathaway here conceded that the MMPI was likely to become of increasingly limited interest to basic personality researchers, and even to those investigating applied questions in personality assessment, but predicted that this would not deter practitioners from continuing to use the test until a viable alternative materialized. Hindsight shows that Hathaway's prediction was accurate on all counts.

WHETHER AND HOW TO IMPROVE THE MMPI

Hathaway's (1972b) paper was one of several presented at a conference convened in his honor in 1970 (the Fifth Annual Symposium on Recent Developments in the Use of the MMPI), devoted to consideration of whether the time had come for a revision of the MMPI and, if so, what form it should take. The conference produced an edited volume (Butcher, 1972a) that included most of the presentations and a detailed discussion of the topic by Meehl (1972). Among the most critical commentators were Jane Loevinger and Warren Norman. Although not a participant in this conference, Douglas Jackson, also a critic of the MMPI, had recently weighed in on this topic, and his recommendations are considered here as well.

Loevinger

Advocating the development of measures of theoretically promising constructs, Loevinger (1972) argued,

> There is no substitution for having a psychologist in charge who has at least a first-approximation conception of the trait he wishes to measure, always open to revision, of course, as the data demand. (p. 56)

She rejected Hathaway's view that personality theory had yet to reach a point where it could meaningfully inform the writing and selection of items for a self-report measure of psychopathology. On a related note, and addressing a question raised by several conference contributors, Loevinger observed,

> If a categorical diagnostic decision is the aim of the new test, then quantitative measures are inappropriate. If quantitative traits are to be measured, then discrimination of extreme groups is too crude and inappropriate a method for item selection. (p. 56)

Her own work clearly favored quantitative (i.e., continuous) traits and measures.

A third issue identified by Loevinger (1972) as a critical concern for any MMPI revision was the need to attend to what she saw as a ubiquitous feature of self-report measures: "Every test seems saturated with a method factor that outweighs other kinds of valid variance" (p. 49). Loevinger viewed the already well-established finding that a strong general factor contributed substantial variance to all the MMPI Clinical Scales as evidence of a nuisance variable that was influencing results. She characterized the K correction (discussed later) as a failed attempt to control for this factor (presumably because even K-corrected scores remained heavily saturated with this variable) and advocated that efforts to do so occur at the point of scale construction rather than ad hoc.

Norman

Norman (1972) focused on several conceptual and psychometric problems with the original MMPI Clinical Scales. Conceptually, he argued that the model that guided Hathaway and McKinley in constructing the MMPI was obsolete and no longer relevant to how the test was used:

> Whether or not Kraepelinian nosology was an appropriate system on which to base a psychiatric diagnostic instrument in the early 1940s, its relevance for that purpose in the late 1960s has surely become tenuous at best. In one respect, the MMPI already reflects this shift away from classical terminology by the substitution of numerical designations for the old scale names and by the shift in interpretive emphasis from the original, single scales to profile code types. (p. 64)

Anticipating a possible retort that bootstrapping and the shift from single-scale to code-type interpretation had made it unnecessary to rely on the original model and thus rendered its inadequacies largely irrelevant, Norman (1972) went on to observe,

> Whatever one thinks of the desirability of the original construction of the basic clinical scales (granting the purposes for which they were intended), it is abundantly clear that they are about as inappropriate and maladapted a set as one could imagine for their current uses in profile analysis and interpretation and typal classification system. (p. 64)

He singled out their heterogeneity and the excessively high intercorrelations among them (stemming, to a degree, from item overlap) as the most serious problems with use of the Clinical Scales as configural indicators of meaningful types:

> In brief, linear composites of items which are to be used as the component scales of a profile, the configural properties of which are of potential interest, must each be statistically homogeneous. It would also be desirable from the viewpoint of efficiency for the separate scales to be relatively uncorrelated with one another. And, of course, it would be nice if some interpretation of each component scale based on the content of its items could be given, although that would not be strictly necessary for purposes of diagnosis alone. There is no possible benefit or justification I can think of, however, for keying single responses on two or more of the component scales of such a profile set. (p. 66)

On a related note, Norman (1972) commented on the "general factor of the MMPI," which Loevinger (1972) had viewed as a nuisance variable. Granting that it *might* instead reflect a substantive factor analogous to g in cognitive assessment devices, he noted that the MMPI

> displays a large first factor variously known as "alpha," "A," "ego strength," "social desirability," or "general pathology," depending upon one's predilections. But, in general, with adequate domain sampling of traits and with application to relevant populations a general personality factor seems less likely to appear or to be interpretable than is true in the ability or aptitude area.

When such a factor is present, however, I would argue that clarity of interpretation and meaningfulness of the assessments are likely to be best served by dealing with such a component separately from the others implicit in the residual sources of variation. (p. 82)

Jackson

In contrast to Hathaway's (1960, 1972a, 1972b) pessimistic appraisal, Jackson (1971) argued that progress in the science of personality had been sufficient to allow the replacement of a descriptive model such as the Kraepelinian nosology with a conceptually richer set of targets for scale construction. He advocated that a modern approach to this task entail candidate items written by experts well versed in the science of personality and selection of those items that pass a succession of psychometric hurdles related to enhancing internal consistency and controlling for response styles.

Jackson (1971) argued that the bootstrapping method (described by Cronbach & Meehl, 1955) for enriching the construct validity of scales that were developed based on fallible criteria (e.g., Kraepelinian diagnoses in the case of the MMPI Clinical Scales) may have been necessary at the time the test was developed, owing to limitations of knowledge then, but that this method was no longer needed or justified. In his words, "the ignorance about personality to which Meehl alluded a quarter of a century ago hardly seems a suitable defense at the present time" (Jackson, 1971, p. 232). He singled out the subtle items (discussed earlier) as an example of the detrimental impact of blind empiricism, noting, "most subtle items have been shown to correlate negatively with the rest of the items contained in an MMPI scale, raising the suspicion that they did not belong there in the first place," and he speculated that these items were "present in MMPI scales due to errors in sampling items and subjects in the initial item-selection procedures" (p. 234).

Jackson (1971) was also critical of the nonlinear (categorical) measurement model underlying the MMPI code types, that is, of the notion that they represented true classes or types. He also noted the absence of evidence that configural scoring (e.g., code-type classification or other, even more complex models) improves on methods that rely on "a linear relationship between items and a single underlying latent continuum" (p. 239).

Finally, Jackson (1971) revisited the issue of response styles that he and others had raised earlier as a major criticism of the MMPI. Jackson and Messick (1962), building on the work of Edwards (1957), had proposed that much (if not all) of the variance in MMPI clinical scale scores was attributable to two response styles (rather than substantive sources), termed *social desirability* and *acquiescence*. These investigators factor analyzed MMPI scale scores in a broad range of samples and concluded that two factors accounted for much of the variance in the test. They attributed variance on these factors to the two response styles and cautioned that MMPI scale scores appeared primarily to reflect individual differences on these two dimensions. In an extensive and sophisticated series of analyses, Block (1965) later demonstrated that these two primary MMPI factors actually represented substantive personality dimensions, with meaningful, real-world correlates that could be understood within a theoretical framework rather than as stylistic response tendencies.

Jackson (1971) was unconvinced by Block's (1965) analysis, contending that his finding of meaningful external correlates of the two broad dimensions was not sufficient to rule out that they are primarily nonsubstantive and should, at the very least, be measured separately rather than repeatedly and therefore redundantly. Ignoring Block's detailed theoretical framework for understanding the two dimensions as measures of the constructs *ego control* and *ego resiliency,* Jackson maintained that "if in the tradition of radical empiricism one eschews theoretical or substantive definitions and prefers to rest one's case solely with external correlates, there is, indeed, no basis for distinguishing content from stylistic variance" (p. 241).

Meehl

Responding to an invitation to comment on these and other observations regarding the need for a revision and the methods that might be used, Meehl (1972) revisited his earlier (Meehl, 1945a) justification for a strict empirical approach to MMPI construction and interpretation. He conceded to some of Jackson's criticisms, while holding steadfast on others. Declaring his "'dust-bowl empiricist' paper of 1945" (Meehl, 1972, p. 147) to be "half-right half-wrong" (p. 134), Meehl considered how, with the benefit of 30 years of accumulated knowledge and experience, one might go about revising the MMPI (and whether this would be worth doing). On the matter of the role of theory in test construction and interpretation, he stated,

> I now think that at all stages in personality test development, from the initial phase of item pool construction to a late-stage optimized clinical interpretive procedure for the fully developed and "validated" instrument, theory—and by this I mean all sorts of theory, including trait theory, developmental theory, learning theory, psychodynamics, and behavior genetics—should play an important role. (p. 150)

On the related topic of item subtlety, a key feature of Jackson's (1971) critique, Meehl (1972) indicated,

> I now believe (as I did not formerly) that an item ought to make theoretical sense, and without too much ad hoc explaining of its content or properties. But going in the other direction, I would still argue that if an item has

really stable psychometric (internal and external) properties of such-and-such kinds, it is the business of a decent theory to "explain" its possession of those properties in light of its verbal content. (p. 155)

Meehl's position had evolved from the radical 1945 notion that understanding item content was of no consequence (or a distraction) to a view that allowed for exploratory analyses of a heterogeneous item pool, provided that the items finally selected could be understood within a developing theoretical framework. He thus rejected Jackson's (1971) stance that a fully developed theory must precede and guide all aspects of item writing and selection. However, although he did not state this directly, it is doubtful that Meehl saw much evidence to support the construct validity of the MMPI subtle items, and it is clear that he now rejected the use of items whose contribution to a scale could not be understood.

Responding to Loevinger's (1972) criticism of the use of continuous measures, such as the Clinical Scales, to assess or predict categorical class membership, Meehl (1972) commented,

> I do not see anything inherently absurd about employing quantitative fallible indicators for the probabilistic identification of a taxonic entity, as examples from the genetics of loose syndromes—or, for that matter, the numerous dimensional indicators employed in internal medicine attest. . . . However, the test constructor ought to think through whether, when he constructs a "depression" key, he has in view primarily the assessment of degree (depth of depressed mood) cutting across nosological categories, or whether he wants instead to build an instrument that will classify individuals as belonging, say, to the taxon "endogenous psychotic depression, unipolar type," where the aim is one of minimizing classification errors in a two-category population with specific base rates. In arguing that the investigator should have in mind his preferred substantive views as to the existence of a certain taxonomic entity when proceeding with his psychometric job, I do not deny that the behavior of the test items may itself contribute to the corroboration or falsification of that substantive position. (pp. 151–152)

Meehl's preference for taxonic variables is evident in his development of taxometric methods in a quest to identify psychopathology taxa. However, in his 1972 conjectures about future directions for the MMPI, he considered as open the ultimate question of whether certain psychopathologies were better understood as taxa or as continua (let alone whether one needed to adopt one model entirely to the exclusion of the other) but insisted that an MMPI revision should, at the very least, be guided by a position (subject to revision in response to empirical data) on this fundamental conceptual question.

In response to Norman's (1972) criticism of the continued reliance on the Kraepelinian nosology (an inherently taxonic system) as the basis for developing the Clinical Scales, Meehl (1972) stood firm:

> I cannot refrain from a cautionary comment about Dr. Norman's (otherwise sound and helpful) contribution, where he permits himself the usual psychologist's dogma that the old Kraepelinian nosological categories are not worth anything.... A fair-minded reading of the literature should convince Dr. Norman that the prognostic and treatment-selective power of our major nosological rubrics is at least as good as any "psychodynamic" assessment (by clinical interview) or any existing psychometric device, structured or projective. (p. 157)

Commenting specifically on the assertion that a major problem with the Kraepelinian diagnostic classes is that they are notoriously unreliable, Meehl (1972) first contended that the evidence in support of this assertion is tainted by methodologically flawed research and went on to observe that "psychologists have a tendency to be obsessed with reliability . . . and an insufficient concern for what might be called the intrinsic or qualitative validity of a construct or judgment" (p. 159). Using an example from medicine that he recalled hearing as a student in Hathaway's class 30 years earlier, Meehl noted that although the test–retest reliability of blood pressure measurement (around .65) was substantially lower than that of measuring the width of a patient's wrist (.98), physicians find the former much more relevant to the task of assessment and management of medical conditions.

On the issue of scale heterogeneity and the related topic of the impact of a broad general factor on clinical scale interpretation, Meehl (1972) conceded that

> one difficulty with an unqualified blind criterion keying is that it does not provide even a weak guarantee—unless done in the context of multiple exclusionary criteria along with the positive one—that it is "causally close" to the psychological variable of interest. Example: MMPI scale 4 (Pd = psychopathic deviate) is one of the better validated clinical keys; when its elevation is found together with an elevated 9 (Ma = Hypomania) and a relative absence of either neurotic or psychotic elevations—especially with a normal or supernormal pattern on the "neurotic triad"—it is a pretty powerful identifier of the broadly "sociopathoid" type. But every clinician experienced with the MMPI has learned that, taking the Pd scale alone, there are some important clinical differentiations which we would like to make better than we can. (p. 170)

Expanding on the source of this difficulty and prescribing a potential solution, Meehl (1972) went on to note,

Unfortunately one can achieve a moderate and sometimes rather high elevation on scale 4 without being a sociopath—not surprising when we look at the items scored for this variable. . . . At an increment of 2 or 3 T-score points per raw score item shift, it takes less than 10 items in the combined areas of family strife and "institution troubles" to achieve a score at T = 70. We all recognize today that this kind of thing happens, and is one source of error which we attempt to "correct for" mentally by taking the patient's situation into account as well as looking at the rest of his profile. But it would be nicer if such error were eliminated from the Pd key entirely. As a factor analyst once complained to me during a heated discussion on criterion keying, internal consistency, scale "purity," and related topics, "if you Minnesotans are going to eyeball the profile and do a subjective factor analysis in your head that way, why not let the computer do it better, at the stage of scale construction?" Not an easy argument to answer. (pp. 170–171)

Here Meehl (1972) proposed that criterion keying might be a good starting point for identifying a set of construct-relevant items, to be followed up with additional analyses designed to identify and develop separate measures of homogeneous components of the resulting item pool.

On the related topic of the impact of a general factor, Meehl (1972) noted,

That an item discriminates a criterion "significantly" does not tell us whether it might be discriminating something else even more. And if it happens further that the criterion of interest is correlated with a variable that runs through a whole batch of items, it is possible statistically that I should construct a key which, while admittedly "valid for the criterion," is even more valid for some nuisance variable that got dragged along in the process. (p. 172)

As a corrective, Meehl proposed that criterion keying be augmented by analyses designed to ensure that the items selected for a scale are adequately correlated with the relevant construct and minimally correlated with measures of nonrelevant constructs, including the general factor. To accomplish the former, and in a concession to Jackson (1971), he stated,

It no longer seems sensible to me to oppose internal consistency approaches to empirical criterion keying approaches, especially in light of what I have said above about the necessity of having available an extended and qualitatively "good" network of interlocking "negative criterion" and other psychometric variables, even when we aim to measure only a single important clinical dimension. (p. 174)

Finally, in response to Goldberg's (1965, 1969) evidence against the utility of configural scoring, which Meehl (1972) now appeared to accept at the item level, he equivocated with regard to its implications for scale-level interpretation:

> I doubt that Professor Goldberg wants to maintain that a strong anticonfigural generalization can safely be made at this time, except in the cautious way in which he makes it, that is, there is no satisfactory positive evidence for significant configural effects. I will bravely record my prophecy that with (1) sufficiently large N and (2) adequate criteria, there will be found (3) some significant configural effects in accord with the clinical lore of experienced MMPI users. But it may well be that any such found (while statistically significant) will be so small that they are not worth the trouble. (p. 182)

Summary and Conclusions

The MMPI was developed to fulfill a practical need for an omnibus differential diagnostic instrument. Introducing the test to the medical community, McKinley and Hathaway (1943) stated (using the language of the time),

> Many a medical man has wished for an easily applicable measuring device which would identify and characterize the psychoneurotic patient with a minimum use of the time-consuming interview technique that is conventional in the psychiatric approach. Realizing this problem and desiring to contribute to its solution, we began work in 1937 on the development of an objective personality test which was simple to use, easy to interpret, and conserving of time. (p. 161)

From a practical perspective, Hathaway and McKinley's quest to develop a useful assessment device was clearly successful. Within a decade and a half of its release, the MMPI had become the most widely used self-report measure of psychopathology and personality and among the most widely used of all psychological tests. By the early 1970s, it had become by far the most widely studied assessment device. Hathaway was ambivalent about the instrument. Regretting the lack of further refinement of the MMPI Clinical Scales, which he attributed to the absence of progress in our understanding of psychopathology, he expressed his belief that the MMPI would continue to be used for the foreseeable future because the needs that prompted its development remained. He did not envision a clear path toward the construction of a successor.

Critics such as Goldberg, Jackson, Loevinger, and Norman found fundamental problems with the MMPI. Chief among these was the developers' reliance on dated Kraepelinian nosology. To a retort that this criticism was unwarranted owing to the paradigm shift toward code-type interpretation, these critics would undoubtedly have responded with concerns about the absence of evidence to support configural scoring and interpretation (Goldberg, 1965, 1969), criticism of the code-type approach as (like the Clinical Scales) bereft of any theoretical foundation (Jackson, 1971; Loevinger, 1972), and problems with the Clinical Scales as components of the code types—excessive intercorrelations stemming from a strong general factor and item overlap and excessive heterogeneity represented most egregiously by the inclusion of invalid subtle items on the scales (Norman, 1972).

Meehl (1972) conceded that the radical empirical rationale outlined in his 1945 defense of the MMPI was overstated. In particular, he agreed that sound psychometric practice should include consideration of item content at the various stages of scale development. He also now advocated reliance on statistical analyses, including possibly factor analyses, to control for competing (with the targeted construct) sources of variance at the stage of scale development. Relatedly, he now viewed internal consistency of scales as desirable and heterogeneity as undesirable. In contrast, Meehl remained steadfast in his view that at least some of the constructs of interest in psychopathology were taxonic, and he staunchly defended the utility of the Kraepelinian nosological system as an exemplar of such a model. With respect to the latter, it is noteworthy that six subsequent revisions of the *Diagnostic and Statistical Manual for Mental Disorders* (*DSM-III*, American Psychiatric Association [APA], 1980; *DSM-III-R*, APA, 1987; *DSM-IV*, APA, 1994; *DSM-IV-TR*, APA, 2000; *DSM-5*, APA, 2013; *DSM-5-TR*, APA, 2022) reflected (essentially) a neo-Kraepelinian descriptive model for the classification of psychopathology.

Toward the MMPI-2

The conference held to honor Hathaway's contributions was convened in 1970. In addition to the contributions just reviewed, papers by Butcher (1972b), Dahlstrom (1972), and Campbell (1972) discussed the mechanics of a possible revision of the test. Contributors to this conference, and to the subsequent volume in which these papers appeared (Butcher, 1972a), would likely have found it difficult to reach a consensus on how to go about revising the inventory, though all, for varying reasons, would likely have agreed with the statement that the MMPI needed to be revised.

Complicating matters further, a process or the means for undertaking a revision of the inventory did not exist. The owner of the MMPI, the University of Minnesota, had, through its press, licensed publication rights for the instrument to the Psychological Corporation and lacked a mechanism with which to plan, fund, and oversee any type of revision. However, in the early 1980s, under the leadership of Beverly Kaemmer, later to be appointed manager of the University of Minnesota Press's newly formed Test Division, a major change in the university's role in managing the MMPI made a revision feasible. In 1982, the press, as publisher of the MMPI, licensed National Computer Systems (now Pearson Assessments) to distribute the instrument. As part of this agreement, the university undertook the task of revising the test with funding generated by royalties made possible under the new arrangement. A committee consisting initially of James Butcher, Grant Dahlstrom, and John Graham, joined later by Auke Tellegen, and coordinated by Kaemmer, known as the MMPI Restandardization Committee, initiated and carried out a revision that produced the MMPI-2.

THE MMPI-2

The 1989 publication of a revised version of the MMPI, the MMPI-2 (Butcher et al., 1989), represented the culmination of nearly a decade of research. Among the main objectives for revising the test, reflected in the title, the MMPI Restandardization Project, was an update of the test norms, a task that had not been the focus of the 1970 conference just discussed. The MMPI normative sample was collected in the 1930s and consisted almost exclusively of White, working-class, rural Minnesotans possessing an average of 8 years of education who happened to be visiting friends and relatives at the University Hospital at the time the test was developed. This sample represented well the initial target population for the test, patients receiving services at the hospital, but was no longer adequate as the MMPI became more widely used in a variety of settings throughout the United States.

A second focus of the revision was on problematic MMPI items. The item pool of the inventory had come under considerable criticism over the years. Foremost among these concerns was the inclusion of item content that was no longer (and, in some cases, had never been) clear, relevant, or appropriate for assessing personality and psychopathology (e.g., "drop the handkerchief"). A set of MMPI items singled out as particularly problematic dealt with test takers' religious beliefs and practices. Other controversial items concerned excretory functions and sexual orientation.

In addition, a relatively large set of MMPI items was not scored on any of the Clinical, Validity, or widely used Supplementary Scales. These nonworking items were candidates for deletion and replacement. A final item-level issue was the absence of content dealing with matters relevant to clinical personality assessment (e.g., suicidal ideation, type A behavior, use of drugs such as marijuana, work-related difficulties, and treatment readiness). A trade-off between nonworking and new items was viewed as the appropriate strategy for confronting both problems. The revision of the test was an opportunity to eliminate objectionable items, rewrite others that were worded archaically or contained gender-specific references, and eliminate nonworking items and replace them with items addressing contemporary clinical concerns. In the next sections, the goals, methods, and outcome of the revision are described and then evaluated.

Goals for the Revision

In the 1989 MMPI-2 manual and the writings of the three original committee members (Butcher, Dahlstrom, and Graham), one finds little or no discussion of the proposals by Jackson (1971), Loevinger (1972), Meehl (1972), and Norman (1972) for addressing fundamental problems with the MMPI Clinical Scales. Early on, these committee members made a strategic decision to keep the Clinical Scales essentially intact to allow for continued and unchanged reliance on the reported empirical correlates of code types formed by these scales, which, as discussed previously, had become the primary focus of MMPI interpretation. The Restandardization Committee thus assigned itself two goals: to improve the test and to maintain as much continuity as possible with the original MMPI. Improvement was to be attained by updating the normative base and correcting the item-level deficiencies just noted. Continuity was to be accomplished by minimizing changes to the basic scales, making it possible for test interpreters to continue to rely on decades of accumulated research and clinical experience with these measures.[1]

Methods of Revision

Instruments

The Restandardization Committee's first step was to develop an experimental booklet with which the new normative data would be collected and from which new items could be added to the test. The MMPI-AX was developed by retaining all 550 original MMPI items (although 82 were reworded slightly to correct for archaic or otherwise problematic language), dropping the 16 repeated items that had been added to the test for machine scoring, and writing 154 new, experimental items, candidates for replacing nonworking and objectionable items.

Additional instruments developed for the Restandardization Project included a biographical data form used to collect extensive demographic data on normative and other subjects and a life events form designed to identify participants who had been experiencing extreme stress in the 6 months prior to participating in the project. A subset of those who participated in the normative data collection along with their spouses or live-in partners also completed a modified version of the Katz and Lyerly (1963) Adjustment Scale and Spanier's (1976) Dyadic Adjustment Scale. These were to be used as sources of validity and correlate data for new scales that might be developed.

Participants

The MMPI-2 normative sample (later also used as the normative sample for the MMPI-2-RF) was collected throughout the United States by using a variety of procedures designed to sample the population of individuals with whom the test is used. Over 2,900 individuals completed the test battery. Of these, 2,600 (1,462 women and 1,138 men) produced valid and complete protocols and were included in the normative sample; in addition, the 1,680 members of the normative sample who participated along with their spouses or live-in partners completed the Adjustment Scale and Dyadic Adjustment Scale (mentioned in the previous paragraph). Individual subjects were paid $15 for their participation; couples received $40.

A number of additional clinical and nonclinical datasets were compiled and used in various scale development and validation studies. These included a sample of psychiatric inpatients (Graham & Butcher, 1988), individuals undergoing substance abuse treatment (McKenna & Butcher, 1987), patients at a pain treatment clinic (Keller & Butcher, 1991), college students (Ben-Porath & Butcher, 1989a, 1989b; Butcher, Graham, Dahlstrom, & Bowman, 1990), military personnel (Butcher, Jeffrey et al., 1990), mothers at risk for child abuse (Egland et al., 1991), and participants in the Boston Normative Aging Study (Butcher et al., 1991). Altogether, over 10,000 individuals were tested as part of the Restandardization Project.

Outcome of the Revision

From the 704 items in the AX experimental booklet, 567 were selected for inclusion in the MMPI-2 test booklet; 372 of the 383 items scored on the 13 basic Validity and Clinical Scales of the original MMPI were retained in the MMPI-2; 11 items were deleted owing to objectionable content, but no basic scale lost more than four items, and most scales did not lose any; and 64 of the 82 reworded items were included on the MMPI-2. Ben-Porath and Butcher (1989a) found the revised items to have a negligible impact on the psychometric functioning of the scales on which they were scored. Thus, consistent with the goal of maintaining continuity, the basic validity and Clinical Scales of the MMPI-2 were nearly identical to those of the MMPI. Improvements were made with the introduction of a new set of norms, a new way of calculating MMPI-2 standard scores, new Validity Scales, and the MMPI-2 Content Scales (Butcher, Graham, Williams, & Ben-Porath, 1990).

New Norms

As noted, the MMPI-2 norms were based on the national sample of 2,600 individuals tested for the Restandardization Project. For several reasons, members of the MMPI-2 normative sample produced higher raw scores on the test's Clinical Scales than did their 1930s counterparts. A change in the instructions given to MMPI test takers contributed significantly to this difference. At the time it was developed, the original MMPI was administered by presenting a test taker with each item printed on a separate index card and instructing the individual to sort them into three piles, representing statements that were True, statements that were False, or statements about which they "cannot say" whether the statement was True or False. These instructions, used when the original norms were collected, did not discourage the "cannot say" response option. When MMPI administration shifted from the card form to booklet, the instructions were altered, and item omission was explicitly discouraged. These revised instructions, which had become the standard for MMPI administration, were used in the normative data collection for the MMPI-2. As a result, members of the new normative sample responded to a larger number of the test items than did their counterparts who responded to the original MMPI, thus contributing to the increase in raw scores on the Clinical Scales.

Societal changes over the 40 plus years that separated the two normative data collections also contributed to higher clinical scale raw scores in the MMPI-2 normative sample. These included both real shifts in psychological functioning and a likely greater willingness to admit holding potentially unattractive beliefs and engaging in undesirable behaviors. A final factor potentially contributing to normative changes was the collection of a broader, much more diverse sample than the one used to derive the original MMPI norms.

Regardless of their cause, higher raw scores in the new normative sample resulted in lower T scores based on the new norms. This shift led the Restandardization Committee to lower the cutoff for determining clinically meaningful elevation from a T score of 70 on the MMPI to a T score of 65 on the MMPI-2.

Another potential source of change at the T-score level was the use of uniform T scores with the MMPI-2 (Tellegen & Ben-Porath, 1992). Uniform T scores were developed to correct a fundamental problem with original MMPI T scores. Because the raw-score distributions for the Clinical Scales were differentially skewed, when linear T scores were used (as was the case with the original MMPI norms), the same T-score value did not necessarily correspond to the same percentile for different scales. The lack of percentile equivalence across scales made direct comparisons of T scores on different Clinical Scales potentially misleading. The solution, developed by Tellegen and adopted by the Restandardization Committee, was to compute the average distribution of non-K-corrected raw scores on the eight original Clinical Scales for men and women in the normative sample and then adjust (in the transformation of raw score to T score) the distribution of each of the scales to fit this composite distribution. This approach yielded percentile-equivalent T scores while retaining the skewed nature of the distributions of the Clinical Scales (Tellegen & Ben-Porath, 1992).

Uniform T scores were subsequently adopted for use with the MMPI-2-RF and MMPI-3 and are described in detail in chapter 7.

New Scales

As discussed earlier, the Restandardization Project had two potentially conflicting goals: to improve the instrument and to maintain continuity with its empirical and experiential foundations. Continuity was fostered by leaving the 13 basic Validity and Clinical Scales of the MMPI largely intact. Improvement at the scale level was accomplished primarily through the introduction of 21 new measures, including three new validity scales, the MMPI-2 Content Scales (Butcher, Graham, Williams, & Ben-Porath, 1990), and three supplementary scales, two designed to measure gender roles and one to assess for posttraumatic stress disorder (PTSD).

VALIDITY SCALES

One of the three new Validity Scales, the Back F (F_B) scale, was made up of items that appeared in the latter portion of the test booklet that were endorsed infrequently by the MMPI-2 normative sample. This MMPI-2 scale was designed to detect changes in the test taker's pattern of responding to items that were placed after the first part of the booklet, where nearly all the F scale items were located. All the items required to score the 13 basic MMPI-2 scales were placed among the first 370 items of the MMPI-2 test booklet to facilitate an abbreviated administration of the inventory to individuals deemed incapable of completing the 567-item MMPI-2.

The other two new MMPI Validity Scales were response-inconsistency measures fashioned after similar scales developed by Tellegen for the Multidimensional Personality Questionnaire (MPQ; Tellegen, 1995/2003). Variable Response Inconsistency (VRIN) was designed to detect quasi-random responding by considering test takers' responses to pairs of MMPI-2 items selected through a series of statistical and semantic analyses designed to yield item pairs that were nearly identical or opposite in meaning. The second Inconsistency scale, True Response Inconsistency (TRIN), was designed to detect patterns of indiscriminant fixed responding (True or False) by considering responses to pairs of items, all opposite in meaning, identified in a manner similar to the VRIN item pairs.

THE MMPI-2 CONTENT SCALES

As noted earlier, beginning in the 1950s, content-based considerations gained increasing acceptance as a supplement to the code-type interpretation of scores on the MMPI Clinical Scales. The MMPI-2 Content Scales (Butcher, Graham, Williams, & Ben-Porath, 1990) were developed through a series of rational-conceptual and empirical analyses fashioned after those used by Wiggins (1966) to develop the original MMPI Content Scales. Candidate items were assigned first to potential scales based on a consensus among judges, who conducted a rational examination of the content. Next, a series of statistical analyses was carried out to eliminate items that did not contribute to the internal consistency of a scale and to identify additional item candidates for inclusion that were missed in the first round of rational analyses. The latter were added if found by consensus to be related conceptually to the domain a scale was designed to measure. Final statistical analyses were conducted to eliminate items that contributed to excessively strong intercorrelations between the scales.

This process yielded a set of 15 content scales. As might be expected, some of these scales were similar in composition to those developed by Wiggins (1966). Nearly all the scales included new MMPI-2 items, and some (e.g., Type A Behavior and Negative Treatment Indicators) were composed predominantly of new items.

OTHER SCALES

Three additional scales introduced in 1989 with the MMPI-2 did not fare as well as the new validity and content scales and therefore did not play a role in the development of the MMPI-2-RF (discussed in chapter 2). They included two gender role measures, Gender Role–Masculine and Gender Role–Feminine, and a scale designed to assess symptoms of PTSD, the Schlenger PTSD scale.

Subsequent Developments: The 2001 MMPI-2 Manual

During the decade following its publication, the MMPI-2 was the subject of over 800 journal articles, 70 book chapters, 20 books, and approximately 360 doctoral dissertations. Some research focused initially on comparing clinical scale scores based on the MMPI and MMPI-2 norms. Concerns about possible incongruence between the two sets of norms were resolved after it was determined that if codetype interpretation was limited to well-defined cases, where there was sufficient separation of the scales defining the code type from the remaining Clinical Scales, the two sets of norms yielded comparable Clinical Scales profiles (Graham et al., 1991; McNulty et al., 1998; Tellegen & Ben-Porath, 1993). The focus then shifted to validating the new scales and exploring further scale development based (in part) on the new items in the inventory. The revised edition of the MMPI-2 manual (Butcher et al., 2001) was designed to update interpretive guidelines for some scales, formalize the discontinuation of other scales, and provide guidelines for interpreting several new measures developed during the decade following the revision. The revised manual did not introduce any changes to the norms or item composition of the MMPI-2 scales included in the 1989 manual.

DISCONTINUED SCALES

Two years prior to publication of the 2001 manual, the MMPI-2 publisher, the University of Minnesota Press, decided to discontinue one set of MMPI subscales that had been included in the 1989 manual, the Wiener and Harmon (1946) subtle and obvious subscales. As discussed earlier, empirical support for the validity of the subtle subscales was scant from the beginning. Nonetheless, in the interest of continuity, the Restandardization Committee retained them in the official scoring materials for the test. This sparked renewed effort to study these measures (Timbrook et al., 1993; Weed et al., 1990), which continued to point toward invalidity of the subtle subscales. Given these disconfirmatory results, the Wiener–Harmon subscales were dropped from the MMPI-2. The Schlenger PTSD scale was also dropped from the test and did not appear in the 2001 manual. During the decade following publication of the MMPI-2, it had been found to be largely redundant with the Keane PTSD scale, an original MMPI measure developed by Keane, Malloy, and Fairbank (1984), which remained on the list of Supplementary Scales.

REVISED VALIDITY SCALES PROFILE

The authors of the 2001 manual introduced a significant structural change to the Validity Scales profile. The four original Validity Scales (Cannot Say, L, F, and K) had been augmented, as described earlier, by the F_B, VRIN, and TRIN scales introduced with the 1989 publication of the MMPI-2. In the following decade, two additional validity scales, Infrequency Psychopathology (Fp; Arbisi & Ben-Porath, 1995) and Superlative Self-Presentation (S; Butcher & Han, 1995), had been introduced and validated sufficiently to warrant inclusion among the MMPI-2 validity indicators. The 2001 revisions to the Validity Scales profile placed these scales within a conceptual framework for assessing test protocol validity and presented them in the order in which they were recommended for consideration. This framework also guided construction of the MMPI-2-RF Validity Scales, as described in chapter 2.

THE CONTENT COMPONENT SCALES

Item analyses designed to maximize internal consistency ensured that the MMPI-2 Content Scales would be considerably more homogeneous than the Clinical Scales. Nonetheless, it was possible to parse some of the Content Scales into relatively independent subsets of items. Ben-Porath and Sherwood (1993) constructed the MMPI-2 Content Component Scales to clarify content scale interpretation, much as the Harris–Lingoes subscales were used with the Clinical Scales. The Content Component Scales were derived through a series of principal component and item analyses of each of the content scales separately, resulting in a total of 27 subscales for 12 of the 15 Content Scales. Most scales yielded only two component subscales.

Initial data reported by Ben-Porath and Sherwood (1993) indicated that the Content Component Scales had sufficient within-parent-scale discriminant validity to enable the test interpreter to develop a more refined picture of the test taker's self-portrayal. Subsequent studies (Clark, 1996; Englert et al., 2000) supported the utility of the Content Component Scales in clarifying the interpretation of scores on their parent content scales.

THE PERSONALITY PSYCHOPATHOLOGY FIVE (PSY-5) SCALES

The Personality Psychopathology Five (PSY-5) Scales were a major addition to the MMPI-2, incorporated into the 2001 manual. They had been introduced first by Harkness and colleagues (1995) as measures of a personality psychopathology model developed and described in detail by Harkness and McNulty (1994). Harkness and colleagues (2002) subsequently provided extensive analyses of the psychometric properties of the PSY-5 Scales. Revised versions of the MMPI-2 PSY-5 Scales were incorporated into the MMPI-2-RF, and subsequently, the MMPI-3. A detailed description of the conceptual underpinnings of these scales, their development, and the five constructs is presented in chapter 5.

ADDITIONAL SUPPLEMENTARY SCALES

Three new and one existing scale were added to the MMPI-2 Supplementary Scales profile in the 2001 manual. The three new scales were the Marital Distress Scale (MDS), developed by Hjemboe et al. (1992), and two substance abuse measures: the Addiction Potential Scale (APS) and Addiction Acknowledgment Scale (AAS), developed by Weed et al. (1992). These authors reported initial data indicating that APS and AAS were incrementally valid with respect to the MacAndrew Alcoholism Scale–Revised (MAC-R), a revised version of the scale that was the primary source of information regarding risk for substance abuse on the original MMPI. Similar results were reported by Greene et al. (1992). Follow-up studies (Aaronson et al., 1996; Rouse et al., 1999; Sawrie et al., 1996; Stein et al., 1999; Svanum et al., 1994) supported the utility of AAS in particular as a predictor of substance abuse. Results for APS were more equivocal. Finally, an original MMPI scale that was not included in the 1989 manual, the Cook and Medley (1954) Hostility (Ho) Scale, was added to the Supplementary Scales profile following renewed interest in the scale (Han et al., 1995), given the association between hostility and health problems largely cardiac in nature.

Appraisals of the MMPI-2

Judged by the criteria of frequency of use and research used earlier to evaluate the MMPI, the MMPI-2 was similarly successful despite criticisms expressed initially by some MMPI users who were concerned that the test had changed too much as well as complaints by critics of the original MMPI who found that the test had not changed enough.

INITIAL REACTIONS

Although not without debate, four years after publication of the MMPI-2, the inventory had replaced the original MMPI in most applied settings (Webb et al., 1993). Initial reactions by some psychologists foresaw a different outcome. An article published in the *APA Monitor* under the title "Does the 'New' MMPI Beat the 'Classic'?" (Adler, 1990) began as follows:

> Psychologists have had 9 months to scrutinize the new Minnesota Multiphasic Personality Inventory (MMPI) and some leaders in the field are likening the revised product to "New Coke." They like the classic version better, and they aren't ready to switch. (p. 18)

The article ended with the following prognostication:

> While the final outcome of the MMPI–MMPI-2 debate looks to be a long way off, Irving Gottesman, of the University of Virginia, was willing to hazard a guess: "The consumers will say they prefer the classic Coke," he said. (p. 19)

The primary concern expressed by those quoted in the article related to the representativeness of the new normative sample. It was sparked by data reported in the MMPI-2 manual indicating that members of the normative sample were better educated than the general population. Another concern raised about the new norms (and the uniform T scores in particular) was that deflated T scores distorted the clinical scale code types and, as a result, compromised reliance on the original MMPI code-type literature when interpreting the MMPI-2.

Concerns About Norms

The Restandardization Committee was aware that the MMPI-2 T scores were lower than corresponding scores on the MMPI (for reasons discussed earlier) and lowered the threshold for clinically significant elevation from 70T to 65T accordingly. To address concerns about the relatively high socioeconomic status (SES) of the new normative sample, Pope and colleagues (1993) produced figures illustrating the absence of clinically meaningful differences between the profiles of various SES groups. Schinka and Lalone (1997) later recalculated the MMPI-2 norms basing them on a reduced sample designed to match national SES distributions and concluded that the altered norms were not meaningfully different from the MMPI-2 norms.

To address concerns that the uniform T scores were responsible for the lower scores and, possibly, changed code types, Graham et al. (1991) compared profiles based on uniform versus traditional linear T scores (both derived from the new normative sample) and found that uniform T scores did not substantially alter the pattern or level of scores on the MMPI-2 Clinical Scales profile. Thus, empirical data showed that the relatively high SES standing of the MMPI-2 normative sample and the uniform T scores did not affect the utility of the revised norms.

Code-Type Congruence

Initial concerns about inadequate congruence between code types resulting from the old and new norms were prompted by data reported in the 1989 MMPI-2 manual indicating that the same 2-point code type was found in only two-thirds of cases when the same raw scores were transformed to T scores based on MMPI versus MMPI-2 norms. These concerns were not trivial. As noted earlier, the Restandardization Committee decided not to make meaningful changes to the Clinical Scales, given their goal of maintaining continuity with the original MMPI and, in particular, with its code-type–based interpretation. If, in roughly one-third of the cases, the two sets of norms yielded different code types (as suggested by data in the MMPI-2 manual), which set of empirical correlates (corresponding to which of the two code types) should be used in interpreting the profile? As it turned out, this concern was based on problematic data analyses, including those reported in the 1989 MMPI-2 manual.

The method used to define code types in the analyses reported in the 1989 manual (and later by Dahlstrom, 1992, a member of the Restandardization Committee) yielded highly unstable and thus unreliable code types. A change of 1 T-score point on two scales could lead to an entirely different code-type designation. Because none of the Clinical Scales were perfectly reliable, meaningful code-type classification could not be sensitive to such unreliable changes; rather, a minimal degree of separation between the scales in the code type and the remaining scales on the profile was necessary for the code type to be stable. Graham et al. (1991) conducted analyses that indicated that scales in a code type needed to be at least 5 points higher than the remaining scales in a profile for the code type to be sufficiently stable. Such well-defined code types were also quite stable across the MMPI and MMPI-2 norms.

HELMES AND REDDON (1993)

The strategic decision by the Restandardization Committee to keep the Clinical Scales intact was bound to disappoint those who had earlier called, or agreed with calls, for major changes to, if not a complete overhaul of, the inventory. In a comprehensive review of the MMPI-2, Helmes and Reddon (1993) were critical of nearly all aspects of the revision but, in particular, objected to the decision to retain the Clinical Scales. Helmes and Reddon's (1993) critique included several factual, logical, conceptual, and psychometric errors. Those that pertain to features of the MMPI-2 carried over to the MMPI-2-RF and MMPI-3 are discussed next.

Social Desirability

Helmes and Reddon (1993) criticized the decision to retain the Clinical Scales on the grounds that this perpetuated the problem of "response styles" in the MMPI-2, which they asserted "particularly in regard to *social desirability*, has never been resolved since the mid 1960s" (p. 461). Although they limited their criticism on this topic to the Clinical Scales, Jackson et al. (1997) later extended it to the MMPI-2 Content Scales, which, they concluded, were extremely confounded with stylistic variance, leading the authors to "doubt that the MMPI-2 Content Scales would show acceptable discriminant properties in appropriate studies utilizing multitrait-multimethod designs" (p. 117). In fact, previously published findings (e.g., Ben-Porath, Butcher & Graham, 1991) cited by Helmes and Reddon (1993) had already demonstrated the discriminant properties of the Content Scales in reference to non-self-report criteria. Moreover, as discussed earlier, Block (1965) marshaled compelling evidence that the two broad sources of MMPI variance that Jackson and his colleagues attributed to construct-irrelevant response styles were substantive dimensions of direct relevance to the assessment of personality and psychopathology.

Unbalanced Scale Keying

Helmes and Reddon (1993) were critical of the unequal proportion of True- and False-keyed items on many MMPI and MMPI-2 scales. Advocating instead balanced scoring keys, they asserted that "the major reason for having balanced keying is to control for an acquiescent response style" (p. 462). However, balanced scoring keys do not provide protection from acquiescence or nonacquiescence and may mask such a test-taking approach if it occurs. Consider two 20-item scales, A and B. A is perfectly balanced, with 10 items keyed True and the other 10 keyed False. All 20 items on B are keyed True. If an extremely acquiescent test taker were to answer all 40 A and B items True irrespective of their content, both scale scores would be equally invalid. Moreover, while the resulting raw score of 20 on B would be extreme, and thus potentially alert the interpreter that an unlikely score was attained, a raw score of 10 on A, although equally invalid in this case, would more likely go unnoticed.

Helmes and Reddon (1993) also contended that "low scores on unbalanced scales reduce the amount of possible information that might be obtained if the scales were bipolar" (p. 462) and proposed that on a scale that has items keyed only in one direction, a low score implies the absence of the characteristics measured by the scale. In contrast, with a bipolar scale, a low score implies the opposite of the characteristics measured by the scale. (p. 462)

In fact, balanced scoring keys are neither necessary nor sufficient for developing bipolar measures or scales with informative low scores. Bipolarity is a property of constructs, not scales. Consider the example of two 4-item scales: C, a measure of introversion, and D, a measure of persecutory thinking. C is made up of the following items, all keyed True:

- I prefer to be on my own.
- I rarely go to parties.
- I have very few friends.
- I avoid being the center of attention.

D is made up of the following items, alternatively keyed True and False:

- Someone is out to get me.
- The CIA has never tapped my phone.
- I am being followed.
- I have never been poisoned intentionally.

A test taker with a raw score of zero on C presents as outgoing and extraverted. On the other hand, a test taker with a raw score of zero on D presents as lacking persecutory beliefs. C is an unbalanced scale that assesses a bipolar construct, and D is a perfectly balanced scale that assesses a unipolar construct.

Unequal Scale Lengths

Helmes and Reddon (1993) were also critical of the unequal lengths of MMPI and MMPI-2 scales, asserting,

> Problems when scales within a test are of unequal length arise when one attempts to interpret a profile and to determine if scales are significantly different. It is commonly recognized that one must take into account the reliabilities of the scales in question when one is comparing scales of different lengths (Lord & Novick, 1968), but one should also adjust the reliabilities (using the Spearman–Brown formula) to equate the length of the scales before calculating standard errors or differences between scales. (pp. 462–463)

This assertion is incorrect. All that is necessary to calculate the standard error of the difference between two standardized scale scores are the standard errors of measurement (*SEMs*) of these two scores and the correlation between the two scales.

Moreover, the Spearman–Brown formula establishes a relation between scale length and scale reliability that can imply the desirability of *unequal* scale lengths if comparable reliabilities are desired. Consider the following hypothetical example of two 20-item scales, E and F, with reliability estimates of .85 and .75, respectively. Applying the Spearman–Brown formula, if six items are deleted from E and six items are added to F, it is possible to achieve comparable reliabilities of approximately .80 for both scales with 14 and 26 items, respectively. Requiring equal scale lengths not only is unnecessary but can be counterproductive.

Uniform T Scores

Helmes and Reddon (1993) devoted a section of their critique to the uniform T score transformation that was adopted for the MMPI-2 Clinical and Content Scales and carried over to the MMPI-2-RF and MMPI-3. Tellegen and Ben-Porath (1992) had already provided a detailed description of this transformation and the rationale for its use, discussed in detail in chapter 6. The distinctive function of uniform T scores is to preserve the generally positive skew of the raw-score (and original T-score) distributions of the scales in question while producing distributions that are more similar across scales.

Helmes and Reddon (1993) proposed that "an argument might be made for normalized scores in that there is likely to be a certain number of individuals in a random sample who have some form of psychopathology, thus leading to a positive skew with samples not screened for abnormality" (p. 465). This is precisely the feature of a representative population sample that calls for not using normalization but instead for using the kind of skewness-preserving transformation provided by the uniform T scores. If we assume that the normative sample is indeed essentially a representative sample and not one made up of persons specifically selected for being in good mental health (i.e., a "normal" sample), then, arguably, the expectable occurrences of psychopathology would cause the normative underlying distribution to have a positive skew. In that case, only a skewness-maintaining standardization could preserve the basic metric of the latent dimension, while normalization would distort it (Tellegen & Ben-Porath, 1992).

Conclusions

Judged by the frequency with which the MMPI-2 came to be used in practice and research, the revision was clearly successful. This is particularly true in light of the skeptical reaction of some original MMPI enthusiasts who opined that the test had changed too much and mistakenly predicted that, as a result, the MMPI-2 would fail to replace its classic predecessor. This initial tepid reaction suggests that the strategic decision of the Restandardization Committee to update the test norms and forgo any meaningful changes to the Clinical Scales was wise, insofar as the goal of fostering transition to the MMPI-2 was concerned.

The strategic decision to leave the Clinical Scales essentially unchanged did, however, have negative consequences. As discussed earlier, up until the 1960s, the MMPI played a significant role in basic research in personality and psychopathology and in studies of important applied questions in personality assessment. As concerns about the psychometric soundness of the Clinical Scales mounted, basic researchers lost interest in the MMPI, as did many investigators interested in fostering improvements in applied personality assessment. This schism disadvantaged MMPI users, who could no longer rely on direct links to these lines of investigation, and it was also detrimental to researchers in these areas, who lost access to the wealth of clinically rich data available on the hundreds of thousands of individuals tested yearly with the inventory. The continuity achieved by protecting the Clinical Scales had the negative consequence of maintaining the growing gulf between MMPI-2 users and innovative research in personality and psychopathology.

Nevertheless, successful efforts to link the MMPI-2 to emerging approaches to the measurement and study of psychopathology and personality were carried out. The PSY-5 Scales provided a link to a dimensional model of personality disorder–related psychopathology, which could also be associated with the widely studied five-factor model of personality, and presaged subsequent development of the *DSM-5* alternative model of personality disorders (APA, 2013), discussed in chapter 5. On the applied side, a substantial body of research on the MMPI-2 Content Scales indicated that largely transparent MMPI-2 measures could perform at least as well as the Clinical Scales in assessing psychopathology and personality constructs. Finally, extensive literature was published on applications of new and old MMPI-2 Validity Scales (in particular, VRIN, TRIN, and Fp), providing test users with a firm foundation for assessing a variety of threats to the validity of test protocols.

TOWARD THE MMPI-2-RF

The structural problems with the MMPI-2 Clinical Scales discussed at length by Jackson (1971), Loevinger (1972), Meehl (1972), and Norman (1972), and revisited by Helmes and Reddon (1993), led Auke Tellegen, a member of the Restandardization Committee, to begin exploring ways they might be addressed. This work culminated in the development of the Restructured Clinical (RC) Scales (Tellegen et al., 2003), which was the first step toward the construction of the MMPI-2-RF. A detailed discussion of these structural challenges, the methods used to address them, and the outcome of these efforts to restructure the MMPI are provided in the next chapter.

Transitioning to the MMPI-3

The MMPI-2-RF

Publication of the MMPI-2-RF in 2008 introduced the third and most consequential paradigm shift in the inventory's evolution (the first two—the move away from individual clinical scale to code-type interpretation and incorporation of content-based scale construction and interpretation—were discussed in chapter 1). Adoption of an empirically derived hierarchical dimensional framework, linked to contemporary personality and psychopathology conceptualizations and research (see Sellbom [2019b] and chapter 5 of this book for a detailed discussion of these links), provided MMPI users a more efficient, psychological construct-focused assessment instrument. As this is the foundation upon which the MMPI-3 was constructed, we provide in this chapter a detailed account of development of the MMPI-2-RF.

A FIRST STEP: THE RESTRUCTURED CLINICAL (RC) SCALES

Soon after the MMPI-2 was published, Auke Tellegen, a member of the MMPI Restandardization Committee, began to explore ways to address long-recognized problems with the Clinical Scales. As discussed in chapter 1, the MMPI/MMPI-2 item pool served as a rich source of clinically relevant information for nearly 7 decades. However, significant questions had been raised over the years about the psychometric adequacy of the Clinical Scales, which, for continuity, were left intact in the MMPI-2. Approximately 10 years after Tellegen began this effort, its product, a set of Restructured Clinical (RC) Scales, was added to the inventory. This was the first phase of a comprehensive effort to modernize the test, which ultimately generated the MMPI-2-RF.

Development of the RC Scales played a critical role in construction of the MMPI-2-RF. The procedures Tellegen designed for revising the Clinical Scales were later implemented during development of many of the additional measures included in the MMPI-2-RF. This chapter begins with a detailed discussion of the rationale for revising the Clinical Scales, followed by a description of the methods used to restructure them and a review of the appraisals of the resulting RC Scales. The second part of this chapter describes development of the MMPI-2-RF, which included construction of new Higher-Order and Specific Problems Scales and updates to the MMPI-2 PSY-5 and Validity Scales. The chapter ends with a discussion of appraisals of the MMPI-2-RF.

Why Restructure the Clinical Scales?

Although they contained compelling and informative items, it had long been recognized that, as aggregate measures, the Clinical Scales were not psychometrically optimal. Two primary problems were the higher-than-expected intercorrelations between the scales and the substantial heterogeneity within them.

Excessive Intercorrelations of the Scales

Chief among the identified shortcomings of the Clinical Scales were the higher-than-expected intercorrelations. For example, the correlation between Clinical Scale 7, a measure of emotional dysfunction associated with anxiety, and Clinical Scale 8, designed to assess disordered thinking, averaged around .90 in clinical samples (Tellegen et al., 2003). Although anxiety-related problems and disordered thinking certainly co-occur, epidemiological findings (Buckley et al., 2009) are inconsistent with an 80% co-morbidity rate implied by these correlations. As a second illustration, the correlation between Clinical Scale 2, a measure of depression, and Clinical Scale 4, intended to assess features of psychopathy, averaged approximately .60 in clinical samples (Tellegen et al., 2003). However, depression has generally been found to be either uncorrelated or only modestly associated with measures of psychopathy (Patrick, 2007). In general, correlations between the Clinical Scales often exceeded substantially the known rates of co-occurrence of the phenomena they were designed to assess.

One source of these excessive intercorrelations was item overlap. For example, Clinical Scales 7 and 8 shared 17 items. An extreme example is item 31: "I find it difficult to keep my mind on a task or job." It was not an oversight that this item was keyed True on five of the eight original Clinical Scales (2, 3, 4, 7, and 8). Hathaway's (1956) rationale for allowing item overlap on the Clinical Scales was that the syndromes they targeted had overlapping clinical features:

In some cases, as with Pt and Sc, an arbitrary decision had to be made about the proper amount of overlap. These scales correlate and the syndromes as observed in clinical cases also overlap. It would be undesirable to eliminate this correlation in measurement of syndromes. The correlation was deliberately built in by leaving in each scale certain items that had been observed to be valid for the other syndrome. (pp. 104–105)

It is now recognized that allowing the same item response to contribute variance to more than one measure artificially inflates intercorrelations between item-overlapping scales by introducing correlated measurement error. Item overlap on scales that are analyzed comparatively (e.g., scales plotted on the same profile) is inconsistent with current standards of psychological test construction.

Although clearly a problem, item overlap was not the primary source of the excessive intercorrelations between the Clinical Scales. As discussed later, Demoralization, a construct that in the past had been labeled the *MMPI First Factor, General Maladjustment,* and *Anxiety* among other names, was the primary contributor to this phenomenon. Regardless of their origin, excessive correlations between the Clinical Scales substantially limited their discriminant validities. As correlations between measures of two constructs range higher, it becomes increasingly difficult for those measures to adequately differentiate between the constructs they are intended to assess.

Substantial Heterogeneity of the Scales

A second major source of difficulty with the Clinical Scales was their heterogeneous, overinclusive item content, which significantly attenuated their convergent validities. Like item overlap, heterogeneity was built into the scales intentionally to assess multifaceted syndromes (Hathaway, 1956). However, attempting to assess multifaceted syndromes with heterogeneous, univariate scales is problematic and unlikely to be effective (Nunnally, 1967). Item heterogeneity has the effect of producing ambiguous scale scores. The same score on a heterogeneous scale may reflect very different sets of responses, associated with dissimilar problems, unless the score approaches its maximal value. The adverse impact of MMPI clinical scale heterogeneity was exacerbated by the so-called subtle items.

THE SUBTLE ITEMS

The subtle items, long the focus of MMPI critics (Jackson, 1971; Norman, 1972), are an example of the problem caused by overinclusive item content. As discussed in chapter 1, Meehl (1972), who had previously defended the inclusion of subtle items on the Clinical Scales (Meehl, 1945a), no longer viewed it desirable to include on a scale items whose content could not be understood as relevant to the targeted construct.

Doubts about the subtle items can be traced to data presented by Wiener (1948) in initial support of the Wiener–Harmon subtle and obvious subscales. These data showed that scores on the obvious subscales were more highly correlated with relevant criteria than were scores on the full Clinical Scales. On the other hand, subtle subscale scores were uncorrelated with the criteria in Wiener's study. Taken together, these findings indicated that the subtle items contributed construct-irrelevant variance (i.e., noise) to the full scales and thus attenuated their validities.

Jackson (1971) speculated that many invalid subtle items were included on the Clinical Scales because of sampling error. This is a plausible hypothesis. Hathaway and McKinley had very limited resources when constructing the Clinical Scales. Most of the original criterion samples were quite small (20–50 subjects were available for the development of all but Scale 4), and cross-validation of item selections with independent samples was generally not possible. Moreover, thousands of correlations were calculated by hand in the process of developing the Clinical Scales, creating many opportunities for clerical error.

Weed et al. (1990) tested the random variance hypothesis by replacing the subtle items with items selected randomly from the MMPI-2 to create *pseudo-subtle* subscales. Consistent with the hypothesis that the subtle items, for the most part, contribute random variance or psychometric noise to the Clinical Scales, Weed and colleagues found that pseudo–clinical scale scores, composed of the obvious plus pseudo-subtle subscales, had validities comparable to those found with the actual Clinical Scales.

These findings, indicating that the subtle items were most likely included on the Clinical Scales as a result of random error, coupled with the absence of any consistent evidence of the extratest validity of subtle subscale scores, resulted in the publisher's decision to discontinue their use with the MMPI-2 in 1999. However, the subtle items themselves were not removed from the Clinical Scales and continued to exacerbate the problem of scale heterogeneity.

In sum, excessive intercorrelations, which reduced their discriminant properties, and heterogeneity, which attenuated their convergent validities, were the primary shortcomings that motivated Tellegen to explore a restructuring of the Clinical Scales.

Pre-Restructured Clinical Scale Solutions

It may be instructive to consider how these challenges were met prior to the development of the RC Scales. Two relatively early developments, the shift to code-type interpretation and the introduction of the Harris–Lingoes subscales, provided the primary means for dealing with these problems.

Scale 4 can be used to illustrate the problem and its pre–RC scale solutions. Following in the tradition of the large-scale cookbook studies of the original MMPI, Graham et al. (1999) conducted a comprehensive investigation of the empirical correlates of MMPI-2 scales and code types in a community mental health center. Extratest criterion data, consisting of historical and mental status findings reported by intake workers and ratings provided later by therapists (without access to the MMPI-2 results), served as the criteria. The correlates obtained for Scale 4 included those that would be expected for a measure of so-called psychopathic deviance (e.g., substance abuse, family problems, anger). However, a larger number of correlates, with generally stronger associations with Scale 4, reflected features such as depression, anxiety, insecurity, and pessimism, which would not be expected to correlate with a psychopathy measure.

Examination of the items scored on Scale 4 provides an explanation for these unexpected findings. They included statements such as "I wish I could be as happy as others seem to be" (keyed True [T]), "I have not lived the right kind of life" (T), "I am happy most of the time" (keyed False, [F]), and "These days I find it hard not to give up hope of amounting to something" (T). An explanation of how such items wound up scored on Scale 4 is provided in the subsequent section on defining and capturing the MMPI common factor.

Given the diversity of features associated with higher scores on Scale 4, how was an interpreter to characterize an individual with a clinically significant elevation on the scale? The code types and subscales provided some necessary guidance. If, along with a Scale 4 elevation, the test taker produced a clinically significant elevation on Scale 9, and scores on the remaining scales were substantially lower than those on Scales 4 and 9 (i.e., the test taker produced a well-defined 49–94 code type), the empirical correlates identified by Graham et al. (1999) for the 49–94 code type included impulsivity, narcissism, and problems with authority figures but not the unexpected emotional correlates of Scale 4. For a different test taker who produced the same score on Scale 4 but, rather than having an elevated Scale 9 score, scored high on Scale 2 (thus forming a well-defined 24–42 code type), the correlates reported by Graham and colleagues included depression, anxiety, and feelings of inferiority, and none of the acting-out descriptors were correlated significantly with this code type. Thus, by considering scores on other scales on the profile, the interpreter was able to distinguish between the two very different types of Scale 4 correlates. However, this method for indirect dismantling of heterogeneous scales was hardly an ideal solution.

Moreover, not all MMPI-2 test takers with elevated scores on Scale 4 produced well-defined code types. In such cases, the Harris–Lingoes subscales could be of assistance. For example, the correlates Graham et al. (1999) reported for the Harris–Lingoes subscale Authority Problems (Pd2) included substance abuse, a criminal history, and being described by their therapist as antisocial, but included none of the emotional correlates of Scale 4, whereas the correlates observed for Self-Alienation (Pd5) included depression, anxiety, acute psychological turmoil, and feelings of inferiority, but no acting-out descriptors were associated with this subscale. However, these armchair-constructed measures had their own shortcomings, including overlapping items within subscale sets, subscales for which the highest T scores did not exceed the cutoffs for clinically significant elevation, and, for some, very low reliabilities. Perhaps because of these difficulties, the Harris–Lingoes subscales were never subjected to systematic empirical investigation.

Conclusion

Although the code types and Harris–Lingoes subscales were, in some cases, helpful in meeting the challenges of excessive intercorrelations and heterogeneity, neither approach provided a psychometrically sound solution. As additional Supplementary Scales were added to the MMPI and MMPI-2, they, too, were enlisted in the increasingly complex task of deciphering clinical scale scores. The basic aim of the restructuring process was to revise these scales to provide a more efficient and psychometrically sound solution to the problems just discussed.

DEVELOPING THE RESTRUCTURED CLINICAL (RC) SCALES

Tellegen's first task in attempting to revise the Clinical Scales was to devise a method for doing so. As discussed in chapter 1, critics of the Clinical Scales (Jackson, 1971; Loevinger, 1972; Meehl, 1972; Norman, 1972) had proposed various strategies for addressing the psychometric challenges just described. This section begins with a discussion of the methods available for revising the Clinical Scales, followed by a description of the approach adopted by Tellegen.

Methodological Considerations

Jackson (1971) articulated a detailed formula for creating new Clinical Scales for the MMPI. The first step would involve a theory-informed designation of the targeted constructs. This would be followed by the writing of items guided by theory and then empirical analyses designed to maximize the internal consistency of the developed scales, enhance their convergent and discriminant properties, and minimize the impact of response styles. Norman (1972) and Meehl (1972) offered similar, more narrowly focused recommendations for addressing specific problems but did not propose an overall strategy.

An alternative scale construction approach, based on exploratory factor-analytic techniques, had previously been devised by Cattell (1966), culminating in the development of the 16PF. Applying this methodology to the Clinical

Scales would have involved conducting factor analyses designed to identify the primary sources of variance in the item pool, rotating the resulting factors to simple structure, and retaining items associated uniquely with a single factor.

Tellegen did not share Jackson's optimism that the fields of personality and psychopathology had converged on a consensual set of constructs that could be targeted in a clinical assessment device, let alone a fully delineated theory that could guide item writing or selection. He opted instead to rely on exploratory analyses designed to discover the primary, distinctive sources of Clinical Scale variance and treat the identified dimensions as "open concepts" (Cronbach & Meehl, 1955; MacCorquodale & Meehl, 1948; Meehl, 1978) to be fleshed out conceptually and empirically. Tellegen concluded that Cattell's (1966) dimensional simplification approach to construct identification was inappropriate for the revision of the Clinical Scales because of the very real possibility that factorially pure dimensions might miss important clinical phenomena, that is, those that are rare and/or do not conform to the requirements of simple structure.

Having concluded that the two primary methods used to construct modern self-report inventories (Jackson's and Cattell's) were not appropriate for revising the Clinical Scales, Tellegen had to devise an alternative. He was guided by his experience developing the Multidimensional Personality Questionnaire (MPQ; Tellegen, 1982), a normal personality inventory assembled by exploratory test construction. Tellegen and Waller (2008) chronicle the development of the MPQ through an iterative process over a 10-year period of theoretically informed item writing, followed by data collection, empirically guided construct refinement, new item writing, new data collection, further construct refinement, and so on. A published version of the MPQ (Tellegen et al. 2023) is now available.

Applying the same methodology to a revision of the Clinical Scales was neither feasible nor necessary. It was not feasible because it would have entailed repeated collection of new clinical samples and, in the end, would have produced a set of scales that required new norms and lacked a comprehensive foundation for empirically grounded interpretation. It was unnecessary because the carefully assembled MMPI-2 item pool was available to Tellegen for a revision that would not necessarily require writing additional items. By the time RC scale construction was complete (in the late 1990s), abundant MMPI-2 data were available to help delineate the open constructs assessed by the new scales and establish an empirical foundation for their interpretation.

The methodology adopted for revising the Clinical Scales, described in detail by Tellegen et al. (2003), retained the use of exploratory factor analyses to guide the identification of targets for scale development, while adopting a flexible approach to the process of assembling a revised set of scales from the entire MMPI-2 item pool. As detailed next, it was guided conceptually by the results of Tellegen's prior work on the interrelatedness of mood, personality, and psychopathology.

Scale Development

Development of the RC Scales proceeded in four steps, each designed to accomplish a particular goal and predicated on specified assumptions. To achieve reliable results, empirically based decisions were guided by consistent findings by using four large samples (composed of male and female psychiatric inpatients and male and female substance abuse treatment patients). The first step addressed the primary source of the excessive correlations between the Clinical Scales: demoralization.

Step 1: Defining and Capturing the Common Factor

The existence of a common factor that contributed substantial variance to the MMPI Clinical Scales and, as a result, markedly increased the intercorrelations between them had been recognized for some time. MMPI critics disagreed about whether this was a substantive source of variance (Norman, 1972) or an artifactual response style (Jackson, 1971; Loevinger, 1972). Meehl (1972) argued that regardless of its origin (about which he remained uncertain), any effort to improve the Clinical Scales—in particular, their discriminant validities—required that the common factor be identified and removed.

Tellegen's view on the nature of this common factor was articulated in a chapter devoted to the assessment of anxiety by self-report (Tellegen, 1985):

> It is generally the case that correlations between measures of adjustment tend to be substantial, giving rise to a large—sometimes very large—general demoralization or subjective discomfort factor in such inventories as the MMPI. . . . One challenge in developing new self-report scales is to find ways of *not* measuring this general factor. (p. 692)

Tellegen's observation that an affect-laden common factor—*demoralization*—was responsible for the excessive intercorrelations between the Clinical Scales (and scales on similar measures) was based on his study of the structure of mood (discussed later). The demoralization construct had similarly been implicated as playing a role in the common (i.e., nonspecific) effects of psychotherapy and in creating a common distress factor in psychiatric screening scales.

In the 1960s and 1970s, Jerome Frank became interested in what was then a much-debated issue in the psychotherapy literature: the nonspecific effects of psychotherapeutic interventions. As alternatives to psychodynamic orientations to psychotherapy emerged in the second half of the 20th century, clinicians began to observe, and research later confirmed, that no form of treatment consistently produced better therapeutic outcomes than others. Moreover, common therapeutic outcomes were found regardless of the specific presenting complaints (cf. Strupp, 1973). Frank (1974) postulated that if disparate therapeutic modalities had common results, this might be because they address a problem that is common across patient types and presenting complaints. He labeled this common variable *demoralization* and commented, "of course, patients seldom present themselves to therapists with the complaint that they are demoralized; rather they seek relief for an enormous variety of symptoms and behavior disorders" (p. 271). Frank went on to observe that

> only a small proportion of persons with psychopathology come to therapy; apparently something else must be added that interacts with their symptoms. This state of mind, which may be termed "demoralization," results from persistent failure to cope with internally or externally induced stresses. . . . Its characteristic features, not all of which need to be present in any one person, are feelings of impotence, isolation, and despair. (p. 271)

Thus, according to Frank, demoralization is common across various forms of psychopathology and unique to none. It is what motivates individuals to seek treatment, and its amelioration, regardless of the therapeutic modality employed, is responsible for the common outcomes of different modes of psychotherapy.

To understand the link between Frank's concept of demoralization and Tellegen's conclusion that a similar affectively colored dimension was responsible for the MMPI common factor, it is necessary to revisit how the Clinical Scales were constructed. Recall that the items for each scale were selected by contrasting the responses of a group of patients with a specific disorder (e.g., hypochondriasis) with those of a nonclinical control sample. The same control sample, made up of hospital patients' friends and relatives who were approached in the hospital hallways about volunteering for a research study and agreed to do so, was used in developing each of the scales. Individuals receiving medical or mental health services were excluded from the control sample. Items were assigned to a given Clinical Scale if the proportion of patients responding in the keyed direction differed significantly from the proportion of nonpatients responding to that item. As a result, some of the items selected for each scale described unique features of the targeted disorder (e.g., somatic complaints for the patients with hypochondriasis), whereas others reflected attributes and experiences that would generally differentiate a hospitalized inpatient from a nonpatient cohort (e.g., being upset and feeling demoralized).

Recall from the earlier example that Scale 4 included items keyed to reflect unhappiness, living the wrong kind of life, and giving up. Such statements, seemingly incongruent with psychopathy, can be understood if one considers that many of the diagnosed patients in the development sample for Scale 4, having been arrested and charged with various minor crimes, were hospitalized under court order. When asked (in responding to the item pool used to develop the MMPI) to describe their mood, it is not surprising that they endorsed statements akin to Frank's concept of demoralization.

Other self-report measures have similarly been found to be influenced by a common demoralization factor. Dohrenwend, Shrout, Egri, and Mendelsohn (1980) linked Frank's concept of demoralization to a common general distress dimension found in many psychiatric screening scales. They observed that

> these screening scales measured a dimension of nonspecific psychological distress. . . . The items in these scales are generally associated with affective distress but are not specific to any particular psychiatric disorder. What they measure is analogous in important ways to measures of temperature in physical medicine. . . . Clearly, elevated scores on these scales, like elevated temperature, tell you something is wrong. However, just as in physical medicine, where many diseases are not associated with elevated temperature, a respondent may have serious psychopathology without having an elevated score [on nonspecific distress]. Some of the symptoms described by Frank in his formulation of "demoralization" are very similar to items in these brief screening scales of nonspecific distress. (pp. 1229–1230)

In sum, Tellegen conceptualized the common factor to be a broad, affectively colored construct labeled *Demoralization*. Although the method used to develop the Clinical Scales undoubtedly contributed to the prominence of demoralization in the scales, the identification of Demoralization as a source of common variance in other self-report measures indicates that this problem was not caused exclusively by the criterion keying approach or its specific application by Hathaway and McKinley.

CAPTURING DEMORALIZATION

Having identified Demoralization as the common factor responsible for excessive correlations between the Clinical Scales, Tellegen next sought to develop a measure of this construct, which would be required for the restructuring process. His approach to capturing Demoralization with the MMPI-2 item pool was guided by his and others' work investigating links between mood, personality, and psychopathology.

Watson and Tellegen (1985) reviewed the literature and reanalyzed previously published data on the structure of mood. They concluded that two factors, labeled *Positive Affect* (PA) and *Negative Affect* (NA), could account for a substantial amount of variance in self-reported affective states. PA was described as a bipolar dimension marked by adjectives such as "enthusiastic" and "peppy" on its high end and "dull" and "sluggish" on its low end. NA was described as a bipolar dimension marked by descriptions such as "fearful" and "nervous" on its high end and "calm" and "relaxed" on its low end. Watson and Tellegen noted that an alternative two-factor structure, achieved through a 45° rotation of the factors, could yield bipolar factors they labeled *Pleasantness/Unpleasantness* (PU) and *Strong Engagement/Disengagement* (SD), which had previously been identified in the mood literature. The two-factor structures were not competing models but rather two ways of organizing the same findings.

The two affect dimensions PA and NA were later renamed more descriptively *Positive Activation* and *Negative Activation,* respectively (Watson et al., 1999; Tellegen et al., 1999a, 1999b), without changing the PA and NA abbreviations. In a subsequent empirical hierarchical elaboration of Watson and Tellegen's model, Tellegen et al. (1999a, 1999b) demonstrated that PU, relabeled *Happiness/ Unhappiness,* emerged as a broad bipolar dimension, overarching PA and NA. Tellegen's (1985) conception of this mood dimension, marked at its dysfunctional end by a combination of high NA and low PA and characterized by adjectives such as "sad," "discouraged," and "blameworthy," was the common demoralization component of self-report measures of personality and psychopathology. Furthermore, Frank (1985) stated that "the demoralized person suffers from a sense of failure, a loss of self-esteem, feelings of hopelessness or helplessness, of alienation or isolation" (p. 17). A comparison of Frank's statement with Tellegen's adjectives reveals that two very distinct lines of research (on the structure of mood and nonspecific components of psychotherapy) converged on a remarkably congruent (and similarly labeled) construct.

Tellegen (1985) observed that the mood (state) PA and NA variables had dispositional (trait) counterparts he labeled *Positive Emotionality* and *Negative Emotionality* (abbreviated PEM and NEM, respectively). He conceptualized a high NEM level as a risk factor for anxiety-related psychopathology and a low PEM level as increasing vulnerability to depression, and he reviewed research findings that supported this perspective on the links between personality and psychopathology. Guided by this conceptualization, Tellegen sought to identify MMPI-2 markers of demoralization through a series of principal component analyses of the combined items of Clinical Scales 2 and 7, MMPI-2 markers of depression and anxiety, respectively. These analyses yielded a 23-item measure made up of items keyed to denote features such as unhappiness, a poor self-concept, a sense of being overwhelmed, and a desire to give up. The content of these items provided empirical support for Tellegen's supposition that demoralization represented the MMPI common factor.

With the identification of a theoretically grounded, empirically derived measure of the common factor, it was possible to move on to the next step in RC scale construction.

Step 2: Identifying the Core Components of the Clinical Scales

The second step in developing the RC Scales was to identify a major distinctive core component of each of the Clinical Scales. Tellegen assumed that each scale included items that assess at least one major construct distinct from demoralization. Analyses were conducted to designate the subset of items in each of the Clinical Scales that represented this component.

Following an exploratory scale construction approach, Tellegen conducted separate principal component analyses of the items of each of the 10 Clinical Scales augmented by the 23 demoralization markers identified in Step 1. Two to four components were extracted and rotated for each scale. The solution with the smallest number of components that included a clear demoralization component and an additional component that reflected a separate substantive attribute was selected to identify items that marked the distinctive core component of that scale. Inclusion of the demoralization items allowed Tellegen to identify, in each Clinical Scale, those items that were associated primarily with the common factor and were the primary sources of excessive demoralization variance on that scale. The number of these items ranged from 3 to 32, with a median of 17 items per scale identified as being primarily markers of demoralization on the Clinical Scales. These exploratory analyses resulted in the identification of a set of items that marked a major distinctive component for each of the Clinical Scales.

For Scale 1, a two-component solution identified a demoralization factor, which included the smallest number of items on any Clinical Scale (in this case, 3) identified as measures of this construct. The second component, which loaded on a set of items that described various somatic complaints, was selected as the major distinctive component for this scale.

For Scale 2, a two-component solution included a demoralization factor and a second factor marked by items that, as keyed, identified the absence of positive emotional experiences, or anhedonia, as the major distinctive component of the scale. These findings corroborated Tellegen's (1985) model in which a low level of positive emotions was hypothesized to be a distinctive risk factor for depression.

For Scale 3, a three-component solution identified a demoralization component; a second component very similar to (and made up of several of the same items as) the somatic complaints factor identified for Scale 1; and a third component marked by items keyed on Scale 3 to denote disavowal of cynical beliefs about others. Although the second component was a stronger contributor to the overall score on Scale 3, the third component was selected to represent this scale because the goal of Step 2 was to identify *distinctive* components of the Clinical Scales.

For Scale 4, a three-component solution included a demoralization component; a second factor marked primarily by items that reflect interpersonal suspiciousness; and a third component that loaded on items that describe various antisocial behaviors. Here, too, although the second component accounted for more variance in Scale 4, the third component was selected because the items that best defined the second component were also markers of the major component of Scale 6.

For Scale 5, a four-component solution included a demoralization component; a second component marked by items that describe various aesthetic and literary interests; a third component that consisted of a mixture of items with aggressive, cynical, and extraverted content; and a fourth that loaded on items that describe various mechanical and physical interests. Because a significant body of literature had indicated that Scale 5 included items that mark two distinct components (designated often as measures of traditional feminine and masculine gender roles), items associated consistently with the second and fourth component were selected to represent these two distinctive components of Scale 5.

For Scale 6, a three-component solution identified a demoralization component; a second component made up of items that described various persecutory beliefs; and a third component marked by items that reflected cynical beliefs, many of which were selected to represent the cynicism component of Scale 3. Items associated consistently with the second component were selected to represent the major distinctive component of Scale 6.

For Scale 7, a two-component solution designated a demoralization component and a second component associated with items that describe various dysfunctional negative emotions. This second component was determined to be the major distinctive component of this scale. These findings corroborated Tellegen's (1985) model in which NEM was hypothesized to be a dispositional risk factor for anxiety-related psychopathology.

For Scale 8, a two-component solution included a demoralization component and a second component marked by items that describe various unusual perceptual or thought processes. Items describing these aberrant experiences, on which the second component loaded consistently, were selected to represent the major distinctive component of this scale.

For Scale 9, a two-component solution identified a demoralization component and a second component associated with items that describe overactivation, grandiosity, aggression, and poor impulse control. Items describing these manifestations of hypomanic activation on which the second component loaded consistently were designated to represent the major distinctive component of this scale.

For Scale 0, a two-component solution identified a demoralization component, with the largest number of items of any Clinical Scale loading on this factor (32). A second component was marked by items that (as keyed) reflect various manifestations of low sociability. This component, which included items that describe a lack of interpersonal assertiveness, avoidance of social situations, and discomfort when interacting with others, was designated to represent the major distinctive component of Scale 0.

At the end of Step 2, a subset of the items of each Clinical Scale was selected to represent its major distinctive core component. Eleven distinctive components were identified. As just described, the domain finally identified as representing the distinctive component of a given scale was not always the second major source of variance on that measure. To avoid developing redundant measures and reflecting the flexible scale construction approach described earlier, Tellegen, when designating a distinctive component for each scale, exercised judgment when the same component, often made up of some of the same items, emerged from analyses of more than one scale.

Step 3: Deriving Seed Scales

The next step in developing the RC Scales was designed to optimize their internal coherence and mutual distinctiveness. In keeping with the idea that a set of completely orthogonal scales was unlikely to accurately represent how psychopathology is manifested (i.e., the reality of comorbidity or co-occurring features), Tellegen made no effort in Step 2 to ensure that items selected to represent the major distinctive component of one scale were *completely* independent of items designated to represent the others. However, insofar as optimizing the discriminant validity of the RC Scales was concerned, he considered it undesirable for an item selected to represent the distinctive component of a given scale to be too highly correlated with the major component of another. Analyses undertaken in Step 3 were designed to preclude this possibility while enhancing the internal consistency of the item sets that emerged from Step 2.

A series of analyses was conducted to achieve the desired optimization of internal consistency and distinctiveness for the 11 sets of items identified in Step 2. First, only items with sufficient loadings on the component they were designated to represent were retained. Next, any item that satisfied this criterion for more than one scale was deleted. This yielded 11 nonoverlapping provisional Seed Scales. This procedure was followed by deletion of items that did not correlate sufficiently with their provisional Seed Scale and then deletion of items that did not consistently have higher correlations with their provisional scale than they did with the 10 other provisional measures. A small number of exceptions and the specific statistical criteria used in these analyses are described by Tellegen et al. (2003).

A final analysis conducted in Step 3 produced a 12th Seed Scale representing demoralization. This analysis was designed to accomplish two distinct goals: first, to ensure that undue demoralization variance would not slip back into the RC Scales in the fourth and final step, and second, to facilitate the development of a RC Scale to assess the demoralization construct. Recall (from chapter 1) that critics of the clinical scales differed as to whether the common factor responsible for the excessive clinical scale intercorrelations was substantive (Norman, 1972) or stylistic (Jackson, 1971; Loevinger, 1972), although they agreed that this variable needed to be accounted for in any revision of the scales. Norman (1972) elaborated that if the common factor did indeed represent a substantive construct, it should be measured separately, along with the revised scales. Tellegen's research in the area of mood persuaded him that demoralization is an important, substantive construct worthy of separate measurement. He assembled a Seed Scale to represent this construct by deleting four items from the 23-item set of demoralization markers used in Step 2. The four deleted items were either weakly correlated with a provisional demoralization scale or judged to be redundant in content.

Step 3 yielded 12 Seed Scales made up of relatively small, mutually exclusive subsets of items from the original Clinical Scales. These seeds were used to derive the final RC Scales in Step 4.

Step 4: Deriving the Final Restructured Clinical Scales

The fourth step in deriving the RC Scales was designed to build on the structural changes attained in Steps 1–3 by recruiting items from the entire MMPI-2 item pool for the final set of scales. The goal was to achieve a balance of internal consistency, convergent and discriminant validity, and content representativeness in a set of measures that assesses the major distinctive core components of the Clinical Scales. Four sets of analyses were conducted to accomplish this goal.

Tellegen first calculated correlations between the 567 MMPI-2 items and the 12 Seed Scales in the four samples used throughout this process. An item was added provisionally to an RC scale if (1) its correlation with the seed for that scale was higher than it was with the other 11 Seed Scales, (2) its correlation with that Seed scale was high enough, and (3) its correlations with the remaining Seed Scales were low enough. Tellegen et al. (2003) reported the specific correlation values that were used to satisfy these three criteria, which, by necessity, varied across scales.

Examination of the content of the resulting scales indicated that the items assigned to RC7 and RC9 were too heterogeneous for the targeted constructs (Negative Emotionality and Hypomanic Activation). For each of these scales, Tellegen identified a subset of items whose content unequivocally represented the intended constructs and correlated those subsets with the other items assigned provisionally to that scale. Items that did not correlate sufficiently with the unequivocal subset were deleted from the provisional scales.

Next, for each of the provisional RC Scales, analyses were conducted to identify items that lowered or contributed weakly to internal consistency. Only one item was deleted as a result of these analyses.

Finally, correlations between the items in the provisional restructured versions of Scales 1, 2, 4, 6, 7, and 8 and appropriate external criterion measures were examined. No suitable criterion measures were available for similar analyses of the provisional restructured versions of Scales 3 and 9. These analyses led to a small number of final item assignment changes for the restructured versions of Scales 2, 6, and 8 (detailed by Tellegen et al., 2003).

Step 4 yielded nine RC Scales (RCd and restructured versions of the 8 original Clinical Scales) composed of 192 nonoverlapping items. As noted earlier, final RC Scales were not assembled for Clinical Scales 5 and 0, although the three Seed Scales derived from these two measures were used along with the other nine Seed Scales in the first set of analyses conducted in Step 4. Thus, the final RC Scales were designed to be distinctive from the major components of Scales 5 and 0 as well, although final measures of these constructs were not derived until later in the development of the MMPI-2-RF.

Initial Psychometric Findings

The data used to develop the RC Scales were collected during the MMPI Restandardization Project and could have been used to devise these scales at the same time. However, no data were available at that point to examine the psychometric properties of the resulting measures independently of these samples. By the time the RC Scales were completed, new data were available to evaluate and characterize their psychometric functioning. With several large clinical samples and a diverse array of external criteria, Tellegen et al. (2003) compared the psychometric properties of the RC Scales and original Clinical Scales and found that scores on the considerably shorter restructured scales showed comparable-to-improved reliability, substantial reduction in saturation with demoralization, reduced intercorrelations, comparable-to-improved convergent validity, and improved discriminant validity.

Based on these findings, Tellegen et al. (2003) recommended that the RC Scales be used to help clarify scores on the Clinical Scales. They anticipated that the ultimate role of the new measures would be determined by further research and noted that an abundance of previously collected data were already available for this purpose because all the items scored on the RC Scales were embedded within the MMPI-2. As anticipated, a substantial body of empirical studies of the RC Scales accumulated after they were added to the MMPI-2 in 2003. The findings of these investigations, along with a review of the conceptual and empirical literature related to the constructs assessed by the RC Scales, can be found in chapter 5.

APPRAISALS OF THE RESTRUCTURED CLINICAL (RC) SCALES

Appraisals of the MMPI and MMPI-2 in chapter 1 of this book included consideration of test use and research patterns and scholarly commentary. Because the RC Scales were embedded first within the MMPI-2, it is not possible to determine the extent to which clinicians using the test relied on those scales in interpreting test results. As evidenced by the literature reviewed in chapter 5, a substantial body of empirical research on the RC Scales accumulated within the first few years following their introduction. Before turning to published appraisals, it might be instructive to consider whether and how the restructuring of the Clinical Scales addressed the criticisms and recommendations offered by reviewers of the original MMPI and its revision (discussed in detail in chapter 1).

Loevinger (1972) and Jackson (1971), and later, Helmes and Reddon (1993), were very critical of the absence of a theoretical grounding for the selection of constructs and writing of items for the MMPI Clinical Scales. Although they conceded a lack of sufficient theoretical foundation at the time the scales were developed, Loevinger and Jackson both held that advances in the ensuing 3 decades had remedied this deficiency. They advocated that any effort to revise the scales begin essentially from scratch, targeting theoretically defined constructs for new scale construction. Tellegen's exploratory approach to restructuring the scales was different and more closely matched the recommendations of Norman (1972) and Meehl (1972).

Norman (1972) was very critical of profile interpretation based on scales that were heterogeneous (including invalid subtle items), overlapping, and otherwise highly intercorrelated (owing to a strong common factor). The RC Scales addressed all these concerns. Although not ready to abandon the Kraepelinian nosological system, Meehl (1972) conceded that there were problems caused by scale heterogeneity (including subtle items). He also acknowledged that it is difficult to argue against recommendations to factor analyze the Clinical Scales and identify distinctive components as targets for new scale construction—much the way Tellegen set about identifying the major distinctive core components of the Clinical Scales. The development of a separate measure of the common factor is consistent with the recommendations of Norman (1972) and Meehl (1972), and an emphasis on internal consistency conforms to the recommendations of all four authors.

Tellegen's approach to identifying the common MMPI factor was guided directly by a theoretical model linking personality, mood, and psychopathology—a conceptual framework that remains at the core of contemporary conceptualizations of mood and anxiety disorders. Indeed, all 9 RC Scales can be linked conceptually and empirically to current models of personality and psychopathology (as detailed in chapter 5). Consistent with Loevinger's, Norman's, and

Jackson's recommendations, Tellegen made a clear decision to target continuous rather than taxonic constructs, although, as detailed by Meehl (1972), this does not preclude using the resulting scales to assess categorical phenomena.

Jackson's (1971) concerns about the impact of response styles, repeated later by Helmes and Reddon (1993), were discussed earlier in this chapter (and in chapter 1). As elaborated by Tellegen et al. (2006), a fundamental problem, the confound of psychopathology and undesirability, led Jackson himself to abandon efforts to develop social desirability–free measures of psychopathology. Moreover, because social desirability measures, particularly the one created by Edwards (1957) and favored by Jackson, are themselves heavily saturated with demoralization (after all, demoralization itself is not desirable), empirical findings reported by Tellegen et al. (2006) show that RC scale scores are substantially less correlated with social desirability measures than are the Clinical Scales. Nonetheless, as discussed in the "Negative Appraisals" section later, adherents of a Jacksonian scale construction approach find fault with the failure to control for social desirability in the steps taken to restructure the Clinical Scales.

Published appraisals of the RC Scales can be divided into two general conclusions: positive and negative. As evident in the following review, authors of positive appraisals based their conclusions on data analyses that included external criteria, whereas negative ones were based on beliefs about the nature of constructs assessed by the Clinical Scales or internal analyses limited to correlations between subsets of MMPI-2 items.

Positive Appraisals

Chapter 5 provides a comprehensive review of RC Scale literature. Authors of specific investigations (limited in the following discussion to early studies using datasets not involved in RC scale development and initial validation research) generally concluded that the RC Scales provide psychometrically sound, useful findings in a broad range of assessment types and settings. In mental health settings, Handel and Archer (2008) concluded that their "results generally replicate and support the findings from inpatient samples presented by Tellegen et al. (2003)" (p. 248). In a study of individuals diagnosed with PTSD and various comorbid disorders, Wolf et al. (2008) concluded that

> the RCs demonstrated good psychometric properties and patterns of associations with other measures of psychopathology that correspond to current theory regarding the structure of comorbidity. A notable advantage of the RCs compared with the MMPI-2 [Clinical Scales] was their enhanced construct validity and clinical utility in the assessment of comorbid internalizing and externalizing psychopathology. (p. 340)

In medical settings, based on a comparison of patients with epileptic and pseudononepileptic seizures, Locke et al. (2010) concluded that "RC1 added significant incremental validity to a set of demographic and medical history predictors" (p. 6). Using the same sample, Thomas and Locke (2010) conducted a series of sophisticated analyses of the psychometric properties of RC1 and concluded that "overall, the results indicate that the scale has strong psychometric properties. Clinical researchers and practitioners should feel confident that the RC1 scale accurately assesses the latent construct of somatization for individuals in the impaired range of the distribution" (p. 24).

Based on a study conducted with a clinical sample and a sample of community-dwelling veterans, Simms et al. (2005) concluded that "the results of this study broadly suggest that the RC Scales represent a somewhat successful attempt to improve on weaknesses often associated with the Clinical Scales while clarifying the core constructs of each" (p. 355). Discussing their findings in a study of genetic variation and covariation in the Clinical and RC Scales, Viken and Rose (2007) commented, "from the standpoint of familial aggregation, little was lost by using the much shorter RC Scales . . . Correlations among the basic and Clinical Scales [suggest] success in the RC goal of deriving more distinct and homogeneous scales" (p. 846). Based on their investigation of the RC Scales with a sample of young adults, Osberg et al. (2008) concluded that "the RC Scales demonstrated good convergence with the Clinical Scale counterparts and were more distinctive than the Clinical Scales" (p. 81). Discussing the results of their study of the RC Scales with chronic pain patients, McCord and Drerup (2011) remarked that "the RC Scales have great promise for improving the convergent and discriminant validity of the MMPI" (p. 6). In a forensic setting, commenting on the results of analyses of the RC Scales in a sample of individuals with varying levels of traumatic brain injury (TBI) and effort, Thomas and Youngjohn (2010) concluded that "the MMPI-2 RC Scales can aid in the diagnosis of overreported TBI symptomatology" (p. 1). Reid and Carpenter (2009) concluded that the RC Scales "appear to capture meaningful characteristics of a substantial portion of hypersexual patients" (p. 184).

Negative Appraisals

A special issue of the *Journal of Personality Assessment*, published 3 years after the RC Scales were added to the MMPI-2, included several papers with criticisms of the (then) new measures. Rogers and colleagues (2006) analyzed an archival dataset, and though they were able to replicate many of the scale development steps and findings reported by Tellegen et al. (2003), Rogers et al. (2006) expressed concern that clinically significant elevations on the RC Scales were observed in only half the cases in their sample. However, closer examination of the sample made available to Rogers et al. for their analyses indicated that contrary to what they had been told, it included many job applicants and child custody litigants who would not be expected to produce elevations on measures of psychopathology (Tellegen et al., 2006). Moreover, Tellegen et al. (2006) reported findings showing in multiple clinical and nonclinical samples that the RC Scales did not produce more profiles within normal limits than did the Clinical Scales. One important actual difference between the two sets of scales was that RC Scales profiles very often had smaller numbers of elevated scales, which is consistent with their improved discriminant properties.

Rogers et al. (2006) were also critical of Tellegen et al.'s (2003) failure to "consider adequately Jackson's (1970) second principle [of scale construction] involving suppression of response variance" (p. 145). Tellegen et al. (2006) discussed the rationale for doing so at length and reported findings showing that although this was not a goal of the restructuring effort, scores on the RC Scales are, in fact, less correlated with measures of social desirability than were clinical scale scores.

Nichols (2006) criticized the RC Scales for failing to retain "syndromal fidelity," drifting from the constructs assessed by the original Clinical Scales, and even from the ones targeted by the Seed Scales used in their development; failing to adequately capture the MMPI-2 common factor with the Demoralization scale; and creating new measures that are largely redundant with existing MMPI-2 scales. Tellegen et al. (2006) provided detailed, empirically based responses to all these criticisms and noted the absence of external validity data in Nichols's own analysis, which was based entirely on rational examination of item content and correlations between various subsets of MMPI-2 items.

Briefly, on the topic of syndromal fidelity, Tellegen et al. (2006) acknowledged that the RC Scales in fact were not designed to individually measure complex, multivariate phenomena such as psychiatric diagnoses (a long-recognized major flaw of the Clinical Scales discussed earlier in this chapter) and showed that despite this, the RC Scales generally have substantially higher correlations with diagnoses than the Clinical Scales. Tellegen et al. (2006) also noted that it has long been recognized that psychometric prediction of complex phenomena is best accomplished with multivariate assessment of the different elements of such constructs.

On the topic of construct drift, Tellegen et al. (2006) pointed out that the shift to more narrowly defined constructs was not accidental or haphazard (as implied by the term *drift*) but intentional, and that the constructs assessed by the RC Scales represent the major distinctive core components of the Clinical Scales (delineated in detail in this chapter). Regarding measurement of the MMPI common factor, Tellegen et al. (2006) reported findings showing the superiority of the Demoralization scale (RCd) over the various alternatives Nichols proposed. Finally, regarding redundancy, Tellegen et al. (2006) acknowledged that it was certainly possible that one or more of the RC Scales would be very similar to an already existing MMPI-2 measure and that if this had occurred, those measures could have been adopted instead of any redundant RC Scales. However, this turned out not to be the case. In any event, it is a moot point insofar as the MMPI-2-RF and MMPI-3 are concerned because the scales with which Nichols thought the RC Scales were redundant were not scored on the restructured version of the inventory.

Butcher and colleagues (2006) sought to demonstrate Nichols's point about construct drift by showing that RC3 (Cynicism) did not assess somatic complaints. As would be expected of a scale designed specifically not to measure this construct, Butcher et al. (2006) found that scores on RC3 were not correlated with other MMPI-2 measures of somatic complaints in an eating disorder treatment sample. By most standards, this study would more accurately be viewed as a demonstration of the discriminant validity of RC3 in that the authors found scores on the scale to be unrelated to a construct it was designed explicitly not to measure.

Finally, Caldwell (2006) argued that RC4 represented a good illustration of loss of syndromal fidelity in that it focuses on a considerably narrower construct (antisocial behavior) than its clinical scale counterpart, which was designed to measure psychopathy. Caldwell asserted that as a result, Clinical Scale 4 was a better measure of psychopathy, as operationalized by Hare's (2003) Psychopathology Checklist–Revised (PCL-R) or Psychopathology Checklist–Screening Version (PCL-SV). In contrast with Caldwell's opinion, Sellbom, Ben-Porath et al. (2007) subsequently reported that RC4 substantially outperformed Clinical Scale 4 in predicting PCL-SV scores in a sample of criminal defendants.

In several subsequent publications, some of the authors who were just cited repeated their criticisms of the RC Scales without consideration of the responses that were just noted. The robust literature on the RC Scales summarized in chapter 5 and the widespread adoption of the MMPI-2-RF and subsequently the MMPI-3 indicate that the concerns outlined in this section were neither supported empirically nor consequential in practice.

COMPLETING THE MMPI-2-RF

As reflected in the following quotation from the monograph that introduced them, the RC Scales were not intended to represent all the information available in the very rich MMPI-2 item pool. Rather, as discussed earlier, each restructured scale was designed to assess a major distinctive core component of an original Clinical Scale.

> The introduction of the RC Scales may stimulate additional MMPI-2 scale development. It may prove worthwhile to search for and measure distinctive

core features of important MMPI-2 scales other than the MMPI-2 Clinical Scales, some of which may also be confounded with a strong Demoralization component. Investigations along these lines may lead to additional measures that are incrementally informative beyond the RC Scales. Through such efforts it may be possible eventually to capture the full range of attributes represented by the large body of MMPI-2 constructs with a set of new scales more transparent and effective than those currently available. (Tellegen et al., 2003, pp. 85–86)

The authors' goal in completing the MMPI-2-RF was to produce a comprehensive set of measures representing the clinically significant substance of the entire MMPI-2 item pool.

Five additional sets of scales were developed to complete the MMPI-2-RF. Following previous efforts to identify a broad-based dimensional structure of personality and psychopathology, the MMPI-2-RF authors conducted a series of factor analyses of the RC Scales, which led to the identification of three recognizable broadband dimensions and the construction of Higher-Order Scales to assess them. They also developed more narrowly focused measures related to clinical scale components not captured by the RC Scales, RC scale facets warranting separate measurement, and constructs assessable with the MMPI-2 items not represented directly in either the Clinical or RC Scales. These analyses produced 23 Specific Problems Scales and two Interest Scales. In addition, the authors sought to include in the test measures of the Personality Psychopathology Five (PSY-5; Harkness & McNulty, 1994), a dimensional model of personality disorder features that had already been studied extensively and provided a link to other dimensional models of normal and abnormal personality. Harkness and McNulty revised the MMPI-2 versions of these scales using the 338 items of the MMPI-2-RF to construct the five revised PSY-5 Scales. Finally, the authors sought to build on the solid foundation laid by the MMPI-2 Validity Scales by revising seven of the existing validity measures and adding a new one, yielding a set of eight Validity Scales for the MMPI-2-RF. In 2011, a ninth Validity Scale was added.

THE MMPI-2-RF SUBSTANTIVE SCALES

As with the RC Scales, the starting point for development of many of the additional substantive measures was the existing MMPI-2 scales. The following sections describe the processes followed in developing the remaining Substantive Scales of the MMPI-2-RF. The constructs assessed by the Substantive Scales that have been carried over to the MMPI-3, and the empirical data that support their use are discussed in detail in chapter 5.

Higher-Order Scales

Search for a Structure of Personality

Investigators in the fields of personality and psychopathology have long sought to identify meaningful structural models to provide an organizing descriptive framework for psychological assessment and psychodiagnosis. Empirical efforts to discover such structures were greatly facilitated by Francis Galton's (1888) invention of the precursor to the correlation coefficient and the subsequent refinement of the procedure by his student Karl Pearson (Pearson & Filon, 1898). Heymans and Wiersma (1906) were the first to apply the Galton–Pearson correlational technique to uncover the structure of personality and its association with psychopathology. As detailed by Ben-Porath and Butcher (1991), these investigators constructed a 90-item rating scale and asked approximately 3,000 physicians to apply it to individuals they knew well. Based on correlational analyses of these ratings, the authors identified eight primary character traits they labeled *amorphous, apathetic, nervous, sentimental, sanguine, phlegmatic, choleric,* and *impassioned*. Relying on observations of correlations between the eight primary factors, Heymans and Wiersma (1906) delineated a higher-order structure consisting of constructs labeled *Activity, Emotionality,* and *Primary versus Secondary Function*. These constructs are remarkably similar to broadband personality dimensions that have been labeled *Extraversion/ Positive Emotionality, Neuroticism/Negative Emotionality,* and *Constraint*.

Heymans and Wiersma's (1906) approach, as well as some of their items, were subsequently revised and incorporated in similar efforts by Hoch and Amsden (1913) and Wells (1914), laying the foundation for Woodworth's (1920) Personal Data Sheet, described by Goldberg (1971) as the forerunner of all self-report personality inventories. Goldberg chronicled additional early developments, including those that entailed factor analyses of primary scales, which also yielded higher-order dimensions reminiscent of those first proposed by Heymans and Wiersma (1906).

Modern efforts to delineate the structure of adult personality and psychopathology have proceeded along two primary lines of research. In one, nonclinical measures were used to study the structure of normal personality. The other focused on delineating a higher-order structure of psychopathology measures. Both lines of investigation converged on structures remarkably reminiscent of the ones identified by Heymans and Wiersma (1906).

Wiggins (1968) reviewed efforts to carve out a higher-order structure of normal personality inventories using the major instruments of the time: the Eysenck Personality Inventory (EPI; Eysenck & Eysenck, 1964), the 16PF (Cattell, 1965), the Guilford–Zimmerman Temperament Survey (Guilford, 1959), and the

California Psychological Inventory (CPI; Gough, 1957). He observed, "if consensus exists within the realm of temperament structure, it does so with respect to the importance of the large, ubiquitous and almost unavoidable dimensions of extraversion and anxiety (neuroticism)" (Wiggins, 1968, p. 309). Although the authors of these measures used different terms and occasionally disagreed with each other's interpretations of the results of factor analytic studies (Eysenck, 1977; Guilford, 1977), these dimensions represent two of the three broad domains identified early on by Heymanns and Wiersma (1906): Activity and Emotionality. Their third dimension, Primary versus Secondary Function, was very similar to a third factor in Eysenck's model, Psychoticism (Eysenck & Eysenck, 1975). Eysenck's choice of label for his third factor was misleading. Examination of the content and empirical correlates reveals that this construct represents externalizing proclivities, though Eysenck himself never wavered on his label as he argued that externalizing tendencies were risk factors of psychosis, which he viewed as the extreme manifestation of this personality domain (Eysenck & Eysenck, 1975).

A similar three-factor structure emerged from research on Tellegen's normal personality inventory, the Multidimensional Personality Questionnaire (Tellegen, 1982). The three higher-order factors of the MPQ are labeled *Positive Emotionality, Negative Emotionality,* and *Constraint*. Tellegen and Waller (2008) reported the results of a joint factor analysis of the MPQ, Gough's CPI, and the Eysenck Personality Questionnaire (EPQ), showing that these three measures yield a highly congruent three-factor higher-order structure.

Efforts to delineate the higher-order structure of the MMPI began shortly after publication of the test. Commenting on a problem that plagued most of these studies from their inception, Wiggins (1968) noted, "the dangers implicit in factoring MMPI scales with overlapping items continues to be announced (Adams & Horn, 1965; Shure & Rogers, 1965) and ignored (Slater & Scarr, 1964)" (p. 314). Other sources of difficulty in this endeavor were reliance on the misleading labels of the Clinical Scales and assignment of alternative labels that also failed to accurately characterize the constructs that emerged from these investigations.

Results of these early studies and his own analyses led Welsh (1956) to identify two primary dimensions in the MMPI that he labeled *Anxiety* (A) and *Repression* (R). Examination of the items that Welsh identified as best markers of these two dimensions and his own descriptions of what they assess indicates that Welsh's chosen psychodynamically colored labels were misleading. He described A as "related to disability of a dysthymic and dysphoric nature in which anxiety is prominent" (p. 280) and a low level of R as accompanying "externalized and 'acting out' behavior" (p. 280). Kassebaum et al. (1959) replicated Welsh's findings with a broader set of MMPI scales. They also linked the higher-order dimensions they recovered to findings with other instruments (Eysenck, 1953; Guilford, 1939) and concluded that alternative rotations of the MMPI higher-order factors were consistent with findings on other measures.

Factor analytic studies of the Personality Assessment Inventory (PAI; Morey, 1991) identified similar higher-order dimensions. Using data provided by a large sample of individuals tested in correctional settings, Ruiz and Edens (2008) identified two broad dimensions among the PAI's clinical scales. The authors labeled one dimension *Internalizing,* marked by high loading on measures of anxiety, depression, somatization, schizophrenia, and suicidal ideation, and labeled the second dimension *Externalizing,* marked by high or unique loadings on measures of antisocial behavior, aggression, and drug and alcohol problems. Blais (2010) conducted a joint factor analysis of the PAI and the NEO Personality Inventory–Revised (NEO-PI-R; Costa & McCrae, 1992), a measure of normal personality, in a nonclinical sample and reported finding three broad dimensions reminiscent of the higher-order factors identified in the studies of normal personality inventories just described.

The finding and labeling of the higher-order dimensions of Internalizing and Externalizing link the adult psychopathology literature to a structure identified by Achenbach and Edelbrock (1978) as characterizing child and adolescent psychopathology. These authors observed that two broad-band dimensions, labeled *Overcontrolled/Internalizing Syndromes* and *Undercontrolled/Externalizing Syndromes,* had emerged from several factor analytically based lines of research. The starting point for these investigations was Achenbach's (1966) study of case history data obtained from six hundred 4- to 15-year-old boys and girls treated at inpatient and outpatient facilities. Behavioral problems reported in these case records were rated and factor analyzed, identifying several more narrowly focused constructs (e.g., aggressive behavior, phobias) as well as the two broad-band dimensions just mentioned. Achenbach and Edelbrock (1978) reviewed the results of 15 subsequent studies, conducted by various investigators with different measures and sources (i.e., case histories, self-report, teacher report, and parent report), and found that all identified a similar pair of higher-order dimensions.

A COMMON STRUCTURE OF NORMAL PERSONALITY AND PSYCHOPATHOLOGY

The findings just described point to considerable similarity and overlap in the higher-order dimensions identified with measures of normal personality and psychopathology. Based on a review of a broad body of similar research, O'Connor (2002) concluded that "the dimensional universes of normality and abnormality are apparently the same, at least according to data derived from contemporary assessment instruments" (p. 962). Encouraged by such findings, Markon et al. (2005) sought to delineate the structure of normal and abnormal personality using an integrative hierarchical approach. Based on a meta-analysis of previous investigations of measures of normal and abnormal personality and new analyses conducted with several instruments, these authors concluded that a hierarchical structure, composed of two higher-order dimensions related to

Negative and Positive Emotionality, could account for common variance among these measures. Markon and colleagues also found meaningful subordinate three-, four-, and five-factor structures. Consistent with findings in the normal personality domain, in the three-factor structure, the Negative Emotionality factor bifurcated into one that focuses more specifically on negative emotional experiences and a second disinhibition factor analogous to Tellegen's (1995/2003) higher-order Constraint factor. Further developments in this area and how they relate to the MMPI-3 Substantive Scales are discussed in chapter 5.

In the psychopathology domain, investigators converged on two broad dimensions labeled (following Achenbach & Edelbrock, 1978) *Internalizing* and *Externalizing*. These broadband dimensions were identified as likely responsible for high rates of comorbidity within the two domains (see Krueger & Markon, 2006, for a meta-analysis) and as playing an etiological role in the development of internalizing and externalizing disorders (see Krueger et al., 2021; Watson et al., in press, for reviews). Across the two domains, combinations of internalizing and externalizing dysfunction have also been implicated in the development of complex psychiatric disorders such as posttraumatic stress disorder (PTSD; Miller et al., 2008), psychopathy (Blonigen et al., 2005), and borderline personality disorder (James & Taylor, 2008), and gender differences on the internalizing and externalizing dimensions were found to play a role in gender differences in the prevalence of common mental disorders (Kramer et al., 2008) as well as aggression and violence (Mendez et al., 2021).

A MISSING CONSTRUCT: THOUGHT DYSFUNCTION

Prior to the publication of the MMPI-2-RF in 2008, a factor related to disordered thinking was conspicuously absent from the higher-order dimensions discussed thus far. Although understandable in the context of normal personality inventories, consistent failure of factor-analytic studies of the MMPI/MMPI-2 and PAI to identify a distinctive dimension related to thought dysfunction was puzzling, given the inclusion of relevant measures on both inventories. Subsequent developments in the psychopathology literature (Kotov et al., 2011) identified evidence for a separate thought disorder factor in samples with both sufficient variability (e.g., psychiatric inpatients) and range of indicators for a viable factor to emerge in such analyses (see Kotov et al., 2020, for a review).

In terms of the MMPI specifically, users and investigators have long been cognizant of the need to assess for thought dysfunction with the instrument. Meehl (1946), describing an early system for differential diagnosis based on profile patterns (i.e., code types), distinguished three broad domains of psychopathology assessable with the MMPI, labeled *Psychosis, Psychoneurosis,* and *Conduct Disorder*. His scheme for differentiating between the first two conditions primarily involved the examination of the relative elevations of Clinical Scales 7 and 8.

Thirty years later, Skinner and Jackson (1978) proposed an MMPI-based differential diagnostic model derived from existing code-type systems and concluded that the test is most useful in identifying three broad domains of psychopathology: neurotic, psychotic, and sociopathic. Along similar lines, an effort to develop a shorter version of the MMPI informed by "decades of research and clinical lore" prompted Swanson et al. (1995, p. 362) to construct three scales: Subjective Distress, Acting Out, and Psychosis.

Thus, throughout the test's history, clinicians have either explicitly or implicitly used the MMPI to assess three broad types of psychopathology related to emotional, thought, and behavioral dysfunction (with the emotional domain at times bifurcating into emotional dysfunction and somatization), yet factor-analytic studies of the instrument consistently failed to identify a distinctive thought dysfunction dimension. Given the generalizability of this finding to other measures of abnormal and normal personality, the inadequacies of the MMPI Clinical Scales alone are insufficient to explain this failure. However, these shortcomings made an already complicated task even more difficult.

As just noted, Meehl's (1946) early approach to differentiating neurosis from psychosis (adopted in one form or another in all code-type schemes) involved the examination of the relative elevation of Clinical Scales 7 and 8. Recall from earlier in this chapter that in clinical settings, the correlation between these two scales hovered around .90, making it all but impossible for the two measures to define distinctive higher-order dimensions. Furthermore, considered in the context of the restructuring effort, the saturation of Clinical Scales 8 and 6 with demoralization variance rendered infeasible the discernment of a thought dysfunction–related higher-order dimension. This raised the possibility that improvements introduced with the RC Scales might yield a different outcome. Indeed, in two-factor-analytic studies of the RC Scales, the authors found a clearly differentiated Thought Dysfunction dimension marked by RC6 and RC8 (Hoelzle & Meyer, 2009; Sellbom et al., 2008a). Sellbom and colleagues also identified higher-order dimensions of Internalizing (marked by RCd, RC2, RC7) and Externalizing (marked by RC4 and RC9). Hoelzle and Meyer (2009) identified the same dimensions as well as two more narrowly focused factors marked by single RC Scales (RC1 and RC3, respectively). Tellegen and Ben-Porath (2008/2011) also conducted analyses indicating that the RC Scales conform to a higher-order structure reflective of the long-held code-type-based practice of differentiating between emotional, thought, and behavioral dysfunction. Specifically, these analyses pointed to a clear higher-order structure, with the Emotional/Internalizing domain marked by RCd, RC2, and RC7; Thought Dysfunction by RC6 and RC8; and Behavioral/Externalizing by RC4 and RC9. These domains correspond to the three most commonly occurring clinical scale code types: 27–72, 68–86, and 49–94, respectively.

SUMMARY

Converging lines of research identified two broad domains of psychopathology, internalizing and externalizing, in the child and adolescent psychopathology literature and, subsequently, in studies of adult psychopathology. A three-factor structure, dating back to the early work of Heymans and Wiersma (1906), bifurcates the internalizing domain into Negative Emotionality/Neuroticism and Positive Emotionality/Extraversion. Apart from initial studies of the RC Scales, prior to the publication of the MMPI-2-RF, factor-analytic studies of the MMPI and PAI, as well as general studies of adult psychopathology structure, failed to isolate a Thought Dysfunction domain. However, code-type-based approaches to MMPI/MMPI-2 interpretation long recognized the importance of this domain and the need to differentiate it from emotional dysfunction. Nevertheless, as discussed next, code-types were deficient measures of broad-based *dimensions* of dysfunction.

Developing the Higher-Order (H-O) Scales

RATIONALE AND OBJECTIVES

An inherent problem with code-type-based interpretation is its mutually exclusive nature. By definition, a test taker cannot produce both a 27–72 and a 68–86 code type, yet it is quite possible for an individual to present with significant dysfunction in both these domains. It was the MMPI-2-RF authors' goal to determine whether development of dimensional measures of these higher-order constructs (as defined by the factor structure of the RC Scales) was feasible and would yield scales that conform to expectations for measures of these constructs. To be effective, the resulting measures would need to be only moderately correlated with each other and associated distinctively with a broad range of psychopathology symptoms, personality characteristics, and behavioral proclivities.

METHOD

The combined items of the RC Scales that had been found to be the primary markers of the three higher-order factors (i.e., RCd, RC2, RC4, RC6, RC7, RC8, and RC9) were factor analyzed in the samples used to derive the RC Scales. From each of these item-level analyses, a rotated three-factor solution and corresponding factor scores were obtained. Next, the three factor scores were correlated with each of the 567 MMPI-2 items in each of the derivation samples. Finally, a set of items was identified for each scale by selecting from the MMPI-2 item pool diverse and distinctive item markers associated statistically and conceptually with one, but not the other, two higher-order factors.

OUTCOME

The three resulting scales were labeled *Emotional/Internalizing Dysfunction* (EID), a measure of difficulties in the domain of mood and affect; *Thought Dysfunction* (THD), a measure of disordered thinking; and *Behavioral/Externalizing Dysfunction* (BXD), which assessed problems associated with undercontrolled behavior. For EID, most, but not all, of the items selected were scored on one of the three RC Scales that marked this dimension: RCd, RC2, or RC7. For THD, all the selected items were scored on either RC6 or RC8. All but one of the items selected for BXD were scored on RC4 or RC9.

The three nonoverlapping Higher-Order (H-O) Scales provide dimensional measures related to the basic categorical distinctions provided by the classical MMPI 27–72, 68–86, and 49–94 code types, respectively. However, in contrast with the mutually exclusive nature of code-type-based interpretation, a dimensional measurement model allows for the identification of dysfunction in more than one of these broad domains (indicated by clinically elevated scores on more than one of the H-O Scales) and can provide an indication of the relative prominence of problems, as reflected by the relative elevation of the H-O Scales. The scales also provide a link to the rich and ever-expanding psychopathology literature discussed in chapter 5.

Specific Problems and Interest Scales

Rationale and Objectives

The authors' goal in developing the Specific Problems (SP) and Interest Scales for the MMPI-2-RF was to augment the RC and H-O Scales with measures needed to derive a comprehensive instrument that assessed the broad range of constructs measurable with the MMPI-2 item pool. Several types of constructs were targeted in developing these scales. First, as described earlier, in the process of developing the RC Scales, Tellegen constructed Seed Scales for Clinical Scales 5 and 0, although final RC Scales were not derived for these measures because they did not focus on psychopathology. Development of measures of the distinctive constructs associated with these scales would accomplish the goal of canvassing the full range of domains assessed with the MMPI-2.

A second set of constructs targeted for further scale development emerged from Tellegen's principal component analyses of the original Clinical Scales (Step 2 of deriving the RC Scales, described earlier in this chapter). Several of these analyses identified more than one distinctive component. However, only one was deemed the major distinctive component of a scale and was targeted for the restructuring effort. For example, analyses of Clinical Scale 3 identified distinctive demoralization, somatization, and cynicism components (assessed with

RCd, RC1, and RC3, respectively) as well as a set of items related to social anxiety, a construct not represented by the RC Scales. These excess components of the heterogeneous Clinical Scales were also candidates for further scale development.

A third set of targeted constructs reflected the broader scope of some RC Scales. Although clearly less heterogeneous than the Clinical Scales, some of the MMPI-2/MMPI-2-RF RC Scales were multifaceted, suggesting the potential utility of developing more narrowly focused scales targeting subdomains or facets of these measures. For example, RC4 contained items related to juvenile misconduct, substance abuse, and family difficulties, all of which are related conceptually and empirically to the targeted construct of antisocial behavior, but it may also be helpful to assess each of these constructs separately with more focused scales. RC7 assessed a fairly broad range of dysfunctional negative emotions (related to anxiety, anger, and fear) perhaps also worthy of separate assessment. Thus, RC scale facets that may warrant separate, more narrowly focused assessments were also targeted for further scale development.

A fourth set of constructs considered for further scale development represented clinically significant attributes found in the MMPI-2 item pool but not represented (directly) by either the Clinical or RC Scales. For example, the MMPI-2 item pool included several items that described suicidal ideation or attempts. These items were added to the MMPI-2 as part of the Restandardization Project and therefore were not scored on any of the Clinical Scales. And although current suicidal ideation and recent suicide attempts were found to be associated with scores on RCd, these items were not scored on this scale either. Nevertheless, the MMPI-2-RF authors sought to include them on a possible restructured inventory and explored the development of a scale to do so. To identify similar possibilities, they examined the content of all the scales included in the MMPI-2 manual as well as several prominent research scales. Several of the MMPI-2 Content Component Scales (e.g., Suicidal Ideation) were particularly helpful in this context.

Development

Construction of the SP and Interest Scales followed an iterative process using methods similar to those employed in developing the RC Scales. As was the case with the RC Scales, it was not possible to follow a simple recipe in the analyses for the SP and Interest Scales. Judgment calls were made throughout the process, with an added final step designed to ensure that the resulting measures successfully assessed the targeted constructs.

First, to minimize the contribution of Demoralization variance to scores on the additional measures, a set of items representing each of the targeted constructs was factor analyzed, along with the Demoralization items used in constructing the RC Scales (as described earlier in this chapter). Items with excessive Demoralization loadings were dropped from further analyses. Exceptions were made for scales that targeted constructs related conceptually or empirically to demoralization (e.g., suicidal ideation).

Next, Seed Scales were developed by further deleting from the item lists identified in the first step those that were too highly correlated with any of the other item sets. In a third step, correlations were calculated between the Seed Scales and the 567 items of the MMPI-2 (except those scored on a given scale), and items were added to a scale if they were sufficiently correlated with the seed for that scale, minimally correlated with the other seeds, and related conceptually to the targeted construct. Next, to maximize the reliabilities of the resulting scales, some of which were quite short (owing to the constraints of the item pool), item analyses were conducted with the scales that emerged from the third step, and any item that reduced the internal consistency of a scale was dropped.

Finally, empirical correlates were examined with several available datasets used later in the validation analyses reported in the *MMPI-2-RF Technical Manual*. Only scales for which the authors found meaningful empirical correlates supporting their convergent and discriminant validity were included in the final set of SP and Interest Scales.

Unlike the H-O and RC Scales, development of the SP Scales was an iterative process. The first round of additional scale construction yielded 14 measures. Further examination of the MMPI-2 item domain resulted in the addition of three scales. Preliminary examination of external validity data for the 17 scales provided encouraging findings, and this provisional set of scales was presented at the 40th Annual Symposium on Recent MMPI Research (Tellegen & Ben-Porath, 2005). Based on feedback received from symposium attendees and additional analyses, three more scales were added, yielding a preliminary list of 20 scales designed to complement the RC Scales.

The list of 20 scales, including representative items for each, was sent to 14 expert MMPI-2 researchers and users for review. The experts were informed of the authors' goal of the MMPI-2-RF representing the clinically significant substance of the MMPI-2 item pool with a comprehensive set of psychometrically adequate measures and including in the revised inventory the RC Scales, a revised set of PSY-5 Scales (described later), and possibly the 20 scales described in the materials they received. They were asked whether any of the large number of existing MMPI-2 scales contained clinically significant content that might be lacking adequate representation by the RC, PSY-5, and 20 additional scales. If they answered affirmatively, they were asked to identify the relevant MMPI-2 scales and to describe the item content of the scales in question. MMPI-2 experts Paul Arbisi and Jack Graham also provided very helpful input regarding this preliminary list.

Based on feedback provided by the reviewers and others who subsequently examined the scales, the authors conducted additional analyses that ultimately yielded the set of 25 MMPI-2-RF scales that are the subject of this section.

Outcome

The scales derived by this process were organized according to the areas they assess, with 23 designated as SP Scales and two as Interest Scales. These 25 scales were nonoverlapping and relatively short, and some of the shorter scales yield comparatively low reliability estimates. The extensive empirical correlates for these scales (reported in Appendix A of the *MMPI-2-RF Technical Manual*) provided evidence of validity for all 25 scales, which, as mentioned, was the determining factor in deciding to include them on the instrument.

Although some of the SP Scales could be linked conceptually to facets of the RC Scales, they were not subscales analogous to the Harris–Lingoes or Content Component Scales of the MMPI-2. A critical difference was that most of the SP Scales included items that were not scored on related RC Scales. An important implication of this distinction was that SP scale scores could be interpreted regardless of the test taker's scores on related RC Scales. This feature of the MMPI-3 SP Scales is highlighted in chapter 10 and illustrated in chapter 11. The constructs assessed by these scales and the empirical literature supporting their use are reviewed in chapter 5.

PSY-5 Scales

The Original PSY-5 Model and Scales

RATIONALE, OBJECTIVES, AND DEVELOPMENT

Attempts to develop dimensional models of normal personality and psychopathology were reviewed earlier in this chapter. In the psychopathology domain, this review concentrated on traditional Axis I disorders. Efforts to carve out dimensional structures of personality disorders were also undertaken, and one such program of research led to the development of the PSY-5 model (Harkness & McNulty, 1994). Harkness (1992) described his initial work in this area, intended to develop a dimensional measurement model of personality disorders. In assembling the item pool he used for this purpose, Harkness augmented a list of *DSM-III-R* Axis II criteria with items reflecting psychopathy and normal personality constructs. Thus, in contrast with other five-factor models that had been explored ex post facto as dimensional models of personality disorders (Widiger & Costa, 2002), the PSY-5 constructs originated directly from the clinical criteria for diagnosing these conditions. Abandoning the categorical measurement model embodied in the *DSM-III-R* in favor of a dimensional model of personality disorders was quite novel at the time Harkness began work on this project in the 1980s. Such an approach has been advanced as the *DSM-5* Alternative Model of Personality Disorders (AMPD; APA, 2013), which is discussed in chapter 5.

Harkness (1992) administered to several samples a set of items written to canvass the *DSM-III-R* criteria, Cleckley's (1941) psychopathy descriptions, and Tellegen's (1982) primary normal personality factors. Through application of a series of data-reduction techniques, Harkness and McNulty (1994) converged on a model composed of five underlying factors. They described the first dimension, *Aggressiveness,* as entailing a general disposition to engage in offensive, goal-directed behavior or in instrumental aggression. The second dimension, *Psychoticism,* was described as representing the verisimilitude or accuracy of the individual's inner perceptions of their outer social and object world. The third dimension, *Constraint,* was linked to Tellegen's (1982) similarly labeled higher-order dimension, combining facets of control versus impulsiveness, harm avoidance, and traditionalism. The fourth dimension, *Negative Emotionality/Neuroticism,* related to Tellegen's Negative Emotionality construct and Eysenck's Neuroticism construct (both discussed earlier in this chapter), was characterized as a broad affective disposition to experience negative emotions focusing on anxiety and nervousness. Harkness and McNulty (1994) characterized the fifth dimension, *Positive Emotionality/Extraversion,* as representing a broad disposition to experience positive affect and to seek out and enjoy social experiences, assessed with Tellegen's (1982) Positive Emotionality higher-order dimension.

Recognizing that MMPI-2 measures of the PSY-5 constructs could help provide a conceptually grounded assessment of Axis II disorders, Harkness and colleagues (1995) developed the original set of PSY-5 Scales using a method they termed *replicated rational selection.* Harkness et al. reasoned that because proper functioning of the scales was predicated on test takers' accurate comprehension of their content and its relation to the underlying construct, having laypersons participate in item selection would yield items that were most likely to be properly understood. Lay judges were provided detailed descriptions of the five constructs and were asked to select MMPI-2 items they deemed pertinent to each of the five dimensions. Items selected by the majority of lay judges were assigned to provisional PSY-5 Scales. Harkness and McNulty then deleted some items that, based on their expert review, did not conform to the meaning of the PSY-5 construct for which they had been nominated by the majority of lay judges. In a final step designed to enhance the discriminant validity of the resulting scales, item analyses were conducted, and items that were more highly correlated with a scale other than the one to which they had been assigned provisionally were dropped. Thus, the original PSY-5 Scales were composed entirely of items selected by lay reviewers. Although some additional items were dropped based on expert review or psychometric analyses, none were added to the lists generated by the lay reviewers. In the process of developing the PSY-5 Scales, two constructs, constraint and low positive emotionality/extraversion, were reflected so that higher scores on all the scales would indicate likely dysfunction. The resulting scales and constructs were labeled Disconstraint (DISC) and Introversion/Low Positive Emotionality (INTR).

REVISING THE PSY-5 SCALES FOR THE MMPI-2-RF

The literature just reviewed established the PSY-5 Scales as empirically validated measures linked to a conceptually rich model of personality pathology. Seeking to retain this model in the MMPI-2-RF, Harkness and McNulty were invited to revise the PSY-5 Scales using the reduced, 338-item booklet, and they graciously agreed to do so. Harkness and McNulty (2007) described the revision of the scales as an iterative process involving internal (item scale) and external (item criterion) analyses.

They began by identifying the surviving 96 of the 139 PSY-5 items and went through a series of steps designed to yield revised scales that would provide comparable and possibly improved measures of the PSY-5 constructs. Based on these analyses, 22 of the 96 surviving items were dropped from the revised scales, and 30 items not included on the original measures were added, yielding five nonoverlapping scales composed of 104 items. Harkness and McNulty (2007) compared the original and revised scales and concluded that the new measures showed several improvements, including lower intercorrelations for some and evidence of comparable-to-improved external validity. A review of the literature on the PSY-5 Scales can be found in chapter 5.

Summary

The 42 MMPI-2-RF Substantive Scales were the product of a comprehensive program of research designed to replace the MMPI-2 substantive measures with a complete set of psychometrically adequate measures. Given that no new items appeared on the MMPI-2-RF, existing MMPI-2 datasets could be used by the test authors to report in the *MMPI-2-RF Technical Manual* extensive empirical correlates for the new measures. Investigators were also able to use existing MMPI-2 datasets in MMPI-2-RF research, leading to the accumulation of a substantial body of peer reviewed publications in a short amount of time. This literature is reviewed in chapter 5.

THE MMPI-2-RF VALIDITY SCALES

Validity Scales have been an integral component of the MMPI since its initial publication as the Minnesota Multiphasic Personality Schedule (Hathaway & McKinley, 1942). As implied by their label, these scales were designed to assist the MMPI interpreter in identifying invalid test results. Validity Scales have also served a second purpose: informing the interpreter about a test taker's possible feigning or denial of problems. In chapter 8, we detail a conceptual framework for interpreting the MMPI-3 Validity Scales. The framework is briefly described here, followed by a review of the evolution of the MMPI validity indicators through the MMPI-2-RF, which served as the starting point for developing the MMPI-3 Validity Scales. Chapter 4 covers the empirical research on the MMPI-3 Validity Scales, which consisted in large part of the MMPI-2-RF literature at the time the MMPI-3 was released.

Threats to Protocol Validity

Ben-Porath (2013) described a conceptual framework for understanding and using Validity Scales as measures of protocol validity. The premise underlying this approach is that even if a hypothetically 100% valid self-report measure were available, any given administration of the instrument could nonetheless yield invalid results. Threats to protocol validity fall broadly into two categories that reflect the role of item content in invalid responding: non-content-based and content-based. Important distinctions can be made within each of these categories.

Non-content-based invalid responding occurs when the test taker's responses are not based on an accurate reading and comprehension of the test items. Its deleterious effects on protocol validity are obvious: to the extent that a test taker's responses do not reflect their reactions to the actual items, the responses cannot gauge the individual's standing on the constructs of interest. This invalidating test-taking approach can be divided further into three subtypes: non-responding, random responding, and fixed responding.

Content-based invalid responding occurs when the test taker skews their responses to items and, as a result, creates a misleading impression. This test-taking approach falls broadly into two classes discussed under various labels in the literature. The first has been termed *overreporting, feigning, faking bad, negative response bias,* and *malingering*; the second has been labeled *underreporting, faking good, positive response bias, denial,* and *positive malingering*. Because both types of content-based invalid responding can be generated intentionally and unintentionally, the more neutral descriptive terms *overreporting* and *underreporting* are preferred and used here. Chapter 8 covers these concepts in greater detail.

Assessing Threats to Protocol Validity With the Original MMPI

Regardless of intentionality, content nonresponsiveness, overreporting, and underreporting can produce scale scores that distort the appraisal of a test taker's functioning. Recognizing this inherent limitation of self-report inventories, Hathaway and McKinley (1943) incorporated measures termed *Validating Scores* (later relabeled *Validity Scales*) in the first MMPI manual, noting that "the evaluation of a profile begins with the problem of whether or not the responses of the subject will yield a valid set of scores" (p. 8). Commenting on the relative paucity of efforts by self-report inventory developers to address threats to protocol validity, Meehl and Hathaway (1946) observed,

> It is almost as though we inventory makers were afraid to say too much about the problem because we had no effective solution for it, but it was too obvious a fact to be ignored so it was met by a polite nod. (p. 526)

Acting on this concern, Hathaway and McKinley (1943) incorporated 3 Validity Scales, Cannot Say (then known as the Question Score and abbreviated "?"), L, and F, into the original test. The MMPI was not the first self-report measure to make Validity Scales available to its users. Cady (1923) modified the Woodworth Psychoneurotic Inventory, derived from Woodworth's (1920) original Personal Data Sheet, to assess juvenile incorrigibility and incorporated negatively worded repeated items in the revised inventory to examine respondents' "reliability." Maller (1932) included items that were designed to assess respondents' "readiness to confide" in the Character Sketches measure. Humm and Wadsworth (1935), developers of the Humm–Wadsworth Temperament Scales, incorporated scales designed to identify defensive responding in their measure. Ruch (1942) developed an honesty key for the Bernreuter Personality Inventory (BPI; Bernreuter, 1933), the most widely used self-report inventory prior to the MMPI.

Hathaway and McKinley's (1943) inclusion of Validity Scales on the original MMPI was thus consistent with a growing recognition among test developers of the need to incorporate formal means for assessing and considering threats to protocol validity. As noted, Hathaway and McKinley commented on the need to assess protocol validity in the initial test manual, which included instructions on how to score and interpret the three original Validity Scales. A fourth validity indicator, K, was added to the test in 1946, rounding out the list of original MMPI Validity Scales. Because revised versions of the four original scales remain part of the MMPI-3, their conceptual origins and initial interpretive recommendations are discussed in detail next.

Cannot Say (CNS)

Hathaway and McKinley (1943) described the Question Score (?) as "a validating score consisting simply of the total number of items put in the *Cannot Say* category" (p. 4). This definition pertains to the format used for administering the original MMPI, the *Card Form,* in which each item was printed on a separate index card. Test takers were instructed to sort the cards into three categories, reflecting their response to each item: True, False, or Cannot Say. T-score values were "arbitrarily assigned on the basis of experience and percentile tables rather than on the usual statistical basis" (p. 8). Hathaway and McKinley noted that higher scores on the Cannot Say (CNS) scale were associated with lower scores on the remaining MMPI scales. Foreseeing contemporaneous approaches to confronting the threat of nonresponding, they pointed out that "since the items most often questioned [i.e., answered "cannot say"] make up varying percentages of the total items in each scale, the effect of these items on the scores for the different scales will of course vary from one to another" (p. 8).

Lie (L)

Hathaway and McKinley (1943) introduced the Lie (L) scale as "a validating score that affords a measure of the degree to which the subject may be attempting to falsify [their] scores by always choosing the response that places [them] in the most acceptable light socially" (p. 4). They indicated that construction of this scale was inspired by the work of Hartshorne et al. (1930), whose research on honesty in children involved concocting situations in which the subjects of their investigations were led to believe they could get away with dishonest behavior, when in fact experimenters would be able to record and quantify this conduct. The 15 items selected for the L scale were designed similarly "to detect the person who is lying in the sense of trying to place [themselves] in a highly conventional and socially acceptable light" (Hathaway & McKinley, 1943, p. 8). Responses in the keyed direction reflected uncommon claims of virtue.

As they did for the CNS score, Hathaway and McKinley (1943) devised arbitrary T-score values for L ("based on experience and percentiles" [p. 9]) because the use of uncommonly answered items produced an "extremely skewed distribution of raw scores" (pp. 8–9). They went on to point out that a T score above 70 does not necessarily invalidate the protocol: "The fact that a high L score is likely to accompany a high Hy score does not invalidate the high Hy finding because the hysterical subject frequently seems to believe [themselves] to be more immune to psychological frailties than does the average person" (p. 9). However, Hathaway and McKinley did recommend that a high L score engender a cautious interpretation, although they did not provide any specific recommendations on how such caution was to be exercised.

Hathaway and McKinley's (1943) interpretive recommendations for L reflect two important, related features of the scale: first, they saw the potential that elevated scores could reflect both intentional and (as in their example of a high score on Hy) unintentional underreporting; second, they advised that elevated scores on the Substantive Scales should not be ignored (i.e., deemed invalid) even when test takers produced markedly elevated L scores.

Infrequency (F)

Hathaway and McKinley (1943) labeled this scale the *Validity Score* and indicated that it

> serves as a check on the validity of the whole record. If the F score is high, the other scales are likely to be invalid either because the subject was careless or unable to comprehend the items, or because someone made extensive errors in entering items on the record sheet. (p. 4)

The latter interpretation relates to the considerable potential for error in transcribing the three piles of sorted cards (corresponding to True, False, and Cannot Say responses) onto a record sheet that was then used to score the MMPI scales. Hathaway and McKinley explained that the

> F score is derived from a group of 64 items that have been very infrequently answered in the scored direction by normal persons. All the items are answered in the infrequent direction less than ten percent of the time by normals, and the percentage is but little higher for miscellaneous abnormal subjects. (p. 8)

It is noteworthy that assessment of overreporting is not mentioned in Hathaway and McKinley's (1943) discussion of F. The scale was devised to detect content nonresponsiveness or clerical scoring errors. However, soon after its publication, important alternative interpretations were identified. Meehl and Hathaway (1946) observed,

> From the first it was recognized that F represented several things.... any error in recording, such as mistaking true items for false items and the like, would raise the F score appreciably. Similarly, if a subject could not understand what he was reading adequately enough to make conventional answers to these items, the F score would obviously be higher. It was felt to be axiomatic that this method would eliminate as invalid records of subjects who could not read and comprehend or who refused to cooperate sufficiently to make expected placements.
>
> In addition, however, it was early discovered that schizoid subjects *and subjects who apparently wished to put themselves in a bad light* [emphasis added] also obtained high scores. (pp. 535–536)

Commenting on the first alternative, Meehl and Hathaway (1946) noted that

> the schizoid group obtained high scores because, due to delusional or other aberrant mental states, they said very unusual things in responding to the

items . . . This is referred to as distortion since we feel that an impartial study would not justify the patient's placements. (p. 536)

Thus, Meehl and Hathaway identified unintentional overreporting as a potential source of elevated scores on F.

With respect to intentional overreporting, Meehl and Hathaway (1946) stated:

With the problems of measurement that developed in the armed forces where a subject might be expected frequently to attempt to put himself in a bad light in answering the MMPI, the F score became especially interesting. It was, of course, immediately possible to consider the F score as evidence of this attempt to malinger and obtain fallaciously bad scores on other scales. (p. 537)

They went on to describe the first MMPI malingering study, in which a group of men enrolled in the Army Specialized Training Program "who had completed a considerable portion of their training in psychology" (p. 537) were asked to take the MMPI twice (in a counterbalanced design), once under standard instructions and another time with instructions "to assume that they wished to avoid being accepted in the draft and in order to be rejected they were to obtain adverse scores without giving themselves away" (p. 537). Meehl and Hathaway reported finding that "96 percent of the 'fake bad' records had a raw score F of 15 or more (T > 78), indicating that even these men who were somewhat cognizant of psychological measurement betrayed themselves when they attempted to fake a bad record" (p. 537). The authors concluded:

From this experiment it appeared that F was a very good device for identifying the intentional faking that could be set up in an experimental situation. It still seemed desirable, however, to attempt to separate among the individuals obtaining relatively high F scores who were of the above-described schizoid type or who were simply over pessimistic in their view of themselves, from those who for one reason or another faked a bad score or did not understand the items. (p. 537)

In summary, Meehl and Hathaway (1946) identified three possible threats to protocol validity associated with elevated scores on F: content nonresponsiveness in the form of unintentional random responding, unintentional overreporting, and intentional overreporting.

Correction (K)

The K scale was not included or mentioned in the original MMPI manual. It was formally incorporated into the test material in 1946, with the publication of a supplementary manual, which also introduced the K correction. Although concerns were expressed about the K correction from its inception, the procedure was applied routinely in MMPI interpretation and was carried over to the MMPI-2 when it was published in 1989. The K correction was not included in the MMPI-2-RF, a substantial change that, although consistent with subsequent developments with the MMPI-2, requires a somewhat detailed examination.

THE K CORRECTION

McKinley and colleagues (1948) indicated that the K scale was developed to "correct the scores obtained on the personality variables proper for the influence of attitudes toward the test situation" (p. 20). Nonrelevant sources of variance in the MMPI Clinical Scales were to be removed to improve prediction. The basic idea was that the correction would increase scores on the Clinical Scales in cases of underreporting—producing higher scores that more accurately reflected the individual's psychopathology—and reduce scores on the Clinical Scales in cases of overreporting.

A more detailed account of the rationale for constructing the K scale was articulated by Meehl and Hathaway (1946), who described its development as a suppressor variable designed to correct scores on the Clinical Scales for the effects of invalid responding. Following Horst's (1941) development of the subject, Meehl (1945b) had previously described the function of a potential suppressor variable in psychological testing as one designed "to 'suppress' these components of the independent variable which are not correlates of the criterion" (p. 550). He went on to explain that a useful suppressor variable would be correlated with a predictor (e.g., an MMPI Clinical Scale) but not the criterion it is designed to predict. Removal from the predictor of variance associated with the suppressor (i.e., variance that does not contribute to the prediction task) would leave a residual score (predictor minus suppressor) that is better able to account for variance in the criterion.

Meehl and Hathaway (1946) reported that a scale labeled L6, the precursor to K, was derived by comparing the responses of two samples. The target group comprised 25 men and 25 women receiving treatment at a "psychopathic hospital" who scored 60T or higher on L and had diagnoses indicating that they should have produced abnormal MMPI profiles but instead generated normal-range scores on the Clinical Scales. Their responses were compared with those of men and women in the general group (i.e., the original Minnesota normal participants used to develop the Clinical Scales described in chapter 1). In this manner, 22 items were assigned to L6. Meehl and Hathaway reported that "all of these items showed a percent difference of 30 or more between the criterion cases and the control group, males and females being considered separately" (p. 541), and they observed that "the content of these items would seem to suggest an attitude of denying worries, inferiority feelings, and psychiatrically unhealthy symptoms, together with a disposition to see only good in others as well as oneself" (p. 541).

Meehl and Hathaway (1946) indicated that after selecting the 22 L6 items, they examined several archival records of cases not used in the development of the measure and found that although it was effective as a measure of underreporting and overreporting, the scale "left much to be desired" (p. 542). Specifically, they were concerned that scores on L6 "tended to be low in severe depressive or schizophrenic patient records and thus lead to an underinterpretation in spite of the fact that the patients were very grossly abnormal" (p. 543); low scores on L6, when applied as a correction factor, had the effect of inappropriately lowering scores on the Clinical Scales in cases where test takers were disordered. Because of this effect, Meehl and Hathaway sought to apply a correction to the correction. They did so by identifying eight items found to be insensitive to underreporting or overreporting (reflected in comparable responses in the Army Special Training Program "fake good," "fake bad," and standard instruction samples just described) that differentiated patients diagnosed with depressive disorders or schizophrenia from the general contrast group. The eight correction items were keyed in the direction of the patients' responses and were added to the 22 L6 items to form the K scale.

The final development of the K correction was described by McKinley et al. (1948), who reported on the derivation of the correction weights used in this procedure. The authors explained, "since high K scores represent the defensive or 'fake good' end of the test attitude continuum, the most obvious approach to the problem is to add K (or some function of K) to the raw score on each personality variable, i.e., increase the score in the direction of abnormality" (p. 21). Identifying the proportion of the K raw score to be added involved trial-and-error testing of alternative weights and selection of those that optimized separation between normal individuals and individuals diagnosed with the disorder corresponding to each of the eight original Clinical Scales. For three of the scales (2, 3, and 6), the authors concluded that adding a K correction did not improve prediction. For the remaining five scales, weights ranging from 20% to 100% of the K raw score were selected. Commenting on the weights they derived in this manner, McKinley and colleagues noted that "it must be emphasized that these weights are optimal, within our sample, for the differentiation of largely inpatient psychiatric cases of full-blown psychoneurosis and psychosis from a general Minnesota 'normal' group. For other clinical purposes, it is possible that other [weights] would be more appropriate" (p. 24).

Initial studies, reviewed by Dahlstrom and Welsh (1960), and subsequent ones, reviewed by Dahlstrom and colleagues (1972), did not support the utility of the K correction as a means for improving predictive validity of clinical scale scores. Nevertheless, the K correction was carried over to the MMPI-2 because the code-type research relied on K-corrected clinical scale scores. Subsequent studies shed additional light on the K correction. Barthlow et al. (2002) examined the contribution of the correction to the predictive validity of the Clinical Scales in two outpatient samples and explored whether alternative weights could improve on those that were applied to the scales. They concluded that neither the routine weights nor any other correction ones improved the validity of the Clinical Scales. On the other hand, noncorrected scores were no more valid than corrected ones. By contrast, Detrick et al. (2001) explored correlations between scores on the MMPI-2 Clinical Scales and the Inwald Personality Inventory (IPI; Inwald, 1992), a measure often used in screening candidates for law enforcement positions. Their results indicated a very substantial attenuation of correlations between MMPI-2 scales and relevant IPI scales when the K correction was applied. This effect was most pronounced—essentially removing the predictive validity of the scales—for Clinical Scales 7 and 8, which received the highest weighted K correction, and least prominent for Scale 9, which received the lowest weighted correction.

Based on this body of research, MMPI textbook authors concluded that the K correction does not work. For example, Greene (2011) commented that "there appears to be little empirical data that justifies the use of the K-correction process" (p. 82). Graham (2012) reached the same conclusion. However, both authors agreed with Dahlstrom et al. (1972) that the K correction cannot be abandoned altogether in MMPI-2 interpretation because the preponderance of research establishing the correlates of the Clinical Scales and code types was conducted with K-corrected scores. Because this constraint does not apply to the MMPI-3, no correction weights are applied to the Substantive Scales of the test.

K AS A MEASURE OF UNDERREPORTING

Although intended originally to function only as a correction factor, evidence that the K scale contributed incrementally (beyond L) in identifying underreporting led early on to its addition as the fourth and final Validity Scale of the original MMPI. In the 1951 revised MMPI manual, Hathaway and McKinley noted that in contrast to L, K "is somewhat more subtle and taps a slightly different set of distorting factors. A high K score represents defensiveness against psychological weakness, and may indicate a defensiveness that verges upon deliberate distortion in the direction of making a more 'normal' appearance" (p. 18).

Heilbrun (1961) identified an important caveat for interpreting K scores in nonclinical settings. Following up on concerns raised by McKinley et al. (1948), who observed that individuals with higher educational levels tested in these settings scored above average on K, Heilbrun (1961) found that in nonclinical settings, higher scores on K were associated with better than average levels of adjustment rather than with defensiveness. Smith (1959) had previously reported similar findings.

SUMMARY

Recognizing the inherent susceptibility of self-report measures to misleading responding and scoring errors, Hathaway, McKinley, and Meehl endeavored to develop a set of validity indicators for the MMPI to alert users to potential threats to the validity of individual test protocols. Nonresponding was assessed with the CNS score, although Hathaway and McKinley (1943) recognized that this was a crude measure because the threat to the validity of a given scale was dependent on the percentage of unscorable items on it. The F scale, developed to detect random responding and clerical scoring errors, was found to be an effective overreporting measure as well. However, the authors recognized that in addition to being sensitive to intentional overreporting, elevated scores on F in clinical settings for some individuals reflected genuine symptoms of psychopathology, and for others, they represented the effects of unintentional overreporting. L was developed to detect underreporting—and based on their initial discussions of the scale, it is clear that Hathaway and McKinley perceived the measure to be sensitive to both intentional and unintentional underreporting. Dahlstrom et al. (1972) reiterated this point and observed that certain cultural factors (e.g., being raised in a religious home) were associated with above average scores on L. As with L, Hathaway and Meehl characterized scores on K as reflecting both intentional and unintentional underreporting. Subsequent investigations indicated that in nonclinical settings, higher scores on K were associated with better than average psychological adjustment.

The MMPI-2 Validity Scales

The standard validity indicators, CNS, L, F, and K were carried over to the MMPI-2 in nearly identical form. As discussed, original MMPI norms for these measures were devised arbitrarily by Hathaway and McKinley (1943) for all but the K scale. Although the authors subsequently concluded that these norms "were not appropriately chosen," no changes were made to the MMPI T scores for these scales (Hathaway & McKinley, 1951, p. 12). The Restandardization Committee decided to use the new normative sample to set the norms for the MMPI-2 versions of these measures, which resulted in several substantial changes. Some interpretive recommendations made in the 1989 MMPI-2 manual (e.g., for K) reflected these changes, whereas others (e.g., for L and F) did not. In addition, 4 of the 64 MMPI F scale items were among those dropped for the MMPI-2 owing to objectionable content (as discussed in chapter 1). These items were not replaced, leaving 60 items in the MMPI-2 F scale.

Validity Scales Introduced in the Initial (1989) MMPI-2 Manual

BACK F (F_B)

All the items needed to score the basic MMPI-2 profile (consisting of L, F, K, and the 10 Clinical Scales) were placed in the first 370 items of the test booklet. This was done to facilitate an abbreviated administration of the test for individuals thought to be incapable of completing the full inventory. As a result, no F item appeared in the MMPI-2 booklet after number 361, resulting in no F scale assessment of infrequent responding past that point in the booklet. Consisting of 40 items, the F_B scale was developed to facilitate continued measurement of infrequent responding in the latter part of the test booklet. The cutoff used to select items for F_B was 20% or less of the men and women of the MMPI-2 normative sample. Although no specific interpretive guidelines were provided for the scale, the authors indicated that it could be used "to identify records in which the individual has stopped paying attention to the test items, and has shifted to an essentially random pattern of responding" (Butcher et al., 1989, p. 27). They noted that this would be particularly salient when considering the validity of scores on the Supplementary and Content Scales, presumably because items that appeared in the latter part of the MMPI-2 booklet were scored primarily on those scales.

VARIABLE RESPONSE INCONSISTENCY (VRIN) AND TRUE RESPONSE INCONSISTENCY (TRIN)

The MMPI-2 inconsistent response indicators, VRIN and TRIN, were developed by Tellegen, who had earlier constructed similarly labeled measures for the Multidimensional Personality Questionnaire (MPQ; Tellegen, 1982). Tellegen (1988) conceptualized consistency scales as analogous to measures of aberrant responding used in ability testing to detect "faulty" response patterns (i.e., answering difficult items correctly more often than easier ones). He distinguished between two types of inconsistent responding—same (i.e., items answered True in an inconsistent manner or items answered False inconsistently) and opposite (i.e., items answered True and False inconsistently). Tellegen (1988) described the MPQ VRIN scale as being made up of pairs of items, the content of which "varies greatly from pair to pair but is quite homogeneous within each pair" (p. 631). MPQ TRIN was also made up of item pairs covering different content domains, but the items making up these pairs were very dissimilar in content so that the same response (both True or both False) would be inconsistent. Tellegen reported findings showing that MPQ TRIN was sensitive to both simulated acquiescent (i.e., inconsistent True) and nonacquiescent (i.e., inconsistent False) responding, and VRIN was effective at detecting simulated variable (i.e., randomly inserted True or False) responding. Neither scale was effective at detecting the type of inconsistent responding detected by the other, demonstrating the need for both types of scales for detecting fixed (TRIN) and random (VRIN) responding.

The MMPI-2 versions of VRIN and TRIN were designed to serve the same function as Tellegen's MPQ scales, with three noteworthy variations. As just mentioned, Tellegen sought to ensure content heterogeneity across item pairs to keep scores on the MPQ Inconsistency Scales as free as possible from the effects of individual differences in actual personality traits. For the MMPI, it was thought particularly important that scores on the Inconsistency Scales not be affected by psychopathology. To accomplish this goal, item pairs selected for the MMPI-2 VRIN and TRIN scales, as scored, were required to be correlated below a maximal level with scores on the Clinical Scales. For example, if a TRIN item pair was keyed so that a response of True to both items was inconsistent, that combination of responses, treated like a mini two-item scale, would be selected only if it were minimally correlated with any of the Clinical Scales.

A second variation involved expanding the MMPI-2 version of VRIN to include item pairs that would also qualify for TRIN. Whereas the MPQ version of VRIN included only pairs of items with very similar content, keyed so that opposite responses would be inconsistent, the MMPI-2 VRIN scale also included items with opposite content, keyed so that the same response to the items would be inconsistent. This change was designed to expand the VRIN scale to include a broader range of variable inconsistent responses. It also introduced considerable overlap between the scales, with 10 of the 23 TRIN item pairs also scored on VRIN.

A final modification was designed to accommodate the fact that inconsistency can be asymmetrical. Consider the following hypothetical pair of items:

1. My life is full of stress.
2. I lead a stress-free life.

Responding True to both items would undoubtedly be inconsistent. However, a False response to both is plausible. An individual may experience sufficient stress from time to time to respond False to item 2 but not frequently enough to respond False to item 1. Thus, whereas a True–True response combination would be inconsistent, a False–False response would not.

Item pairs for the MMPI-2 VRIN and TRIN scales were selected after examination of correlations between responses to all possible pairs of items in two large clinical samples. Item pairs with high negative correlations (indicating empirically that the same response to both was uncommon) were candidates for inclusion on both VRIN and TRIN. Item pairs with high positive correlations (indicating empirically that an opposite response to both was uncommon) were candidates for VRIN. To be assigned to these scales, a candidate pair had to be made up of items that were sufficiently highly correlated with each other and minimally correlated (when scored as a mini-scale) with the Clinical Scales across samples. To detect pairs that should be scored asymmetrically, the observed versus expected (based on chance) frequency of each pair of responses was compared. This identified response combinations that were unexpected statistically and would therefore likely be inconsistent. As a final hurdle, any pair of responses that satisfied these statistical criteria had to be judged by both Tellegen and Ben-Porath to be semantically inconsistent as keyed.

This process yielded a VRIN scale made of 67 possible pairs of inconsistent responses and a TRIN scale comprising 23 possible response pairs. Given their novelty as MMPI validity indicators, interpretive recommendations for VRIN and TRIN in the 1989 manual were relatively vague. The scales were described as "expected to complement L, F, and K in unique and useful ways" (Butcher et al., 1989, p. 28) by identifying possible origins of elevated scores on the original Validity Scales.

Validity Scales Incorporated in the Revised (2001) MMPI-2 Manual

As had been the case throughout the MMPI's history, efforts to improve the test, including development of additional Validity Scales, continued following the introduction of the MMPI-2. During the decade after publication of the revised inventory, empirical data on the Validity Scales introduced in the MMPI-2 manual accumulated, and new scales (including new validity indicators) were constructed and tested, leading the University of Minnesota Press to initiate publication of an updated test manual to reflect these advances with the test. In the revised edition of the MMPI-2 manual (Butcher et al., 2001), two validity indicators, Infrequency Psychopathology (Fp) and Superlative Self-Presentation (S), were added to the standard set of validity indicators. These measures and the scales first introduced in 1989 (F_b, VRIN, and TRIN) were incorporated into a reorganized Validity Scales profile corresponding to the conceptual framework outlined at the beginning of this chapter and detailed in chapter 8.

INFREQUENT PSYCHOPATHOLOGY (F_p)

Arbisi and Ben-Porath (1995) developed the Fp scale to address a significant challenge in interpreting scores on the multifaceted F scale. As reviewed earlier, Hathaway and McKinley (1943) developed F to identify protocols compromised by random responding or scoring errors. In their initial publication on the scale, the authors stated, "if the F score is high, the scales are likely to be invalid either because the subject was careless or unable to comprehend the items, or because of extensive errors in entering the items on the record sheet. A high F score has no other known interpretation" (p. 9). The authors soon discovered another possible reason why test takers might produce deviant scores on F and noted that "F scores will validly be somewhat high for certain persons. These are most often of two types: First, some persons who are highly individual and independent . . . second, a number of rather badly neurotic or psychotic subjects obtain high F scores validly" (p. 8). Thus, three nonmutually exclusive factors could contribute to elevated F scale scores: overreporting, random responding, and genuine psychopathology. MMPI users were challenged to distinguish these very different factors in their interpretations.

This challenge became even greater with publication of the MMPI-2, when deriving standard scores for the scale resulted in T scores that were substantially higher than on the original version of the test. This proved to be particularly problematic in settings in which individuals with severe psychopathology were likely to be assessed (e.g., psychiatric inpatient units and facilities). These individuals were now much more likely to produce F scores in ranges that would raise questions about the validity of the protocol and possible symptom overreporting. With the addition of VRIN, MMPI-2 users were able to effectively consider the possible contribution of random responding (both intentional and unintentional) to high F scores, but this still left in place the very substantial confound of genuine psychopathology and overreporting. Arbisi and Ben-Porath (1995) developed the Fp scale to address this challenge.

Using a dataset collected at a Veterans Administration (VA) inpatient unit, Arbisi and Ben-Porath (1995) identified a set of MMPI-2 items answered True or False by 20% or less of individuals in this sample. Using an archival sample of (non-VA) psychiatric inpatients, they found 27 items from the original list that were also answered by 20% or less of the men and women in the second sample. After confirming that all these items were also answered infrequently by the men and women in the normative sample, the authors designated these 27 items for the Infrequent Psychopathology (Fp) scale.

Arbisi and Ben-Porath (1995) next sought to test the new scale empirically, reasoning that to be more effective than F because it is less confounded with actual psychopathology: (1) Fp scores should be lower than F scores in clinical samples and, relatedly, use of comparable cutoffs should result in fewer cases identified as invalid in such samples; (2) scores on Fp should be less correlated with substantive measures of psychopathology than F; (3) greater differences between clinical and nonclinical samples would be found on F than on Fp; (4) Fp should better distinguish psychiatric patients from individuals simulating a "fake bad" approach to the test than F does; and (5) Fp should add incrementally to F in discriminating psychiatric patients from individuals instructed to overreport in responding to the MMPI-2. The authors presented data supporting all these hypotheses (Arbisi & Ben-Porath, 1995).

Following the introduction of Fp, a considerable body of research replicated and expanded on these findings. Based on a meta-analysis of studies of MMPI-2 overreporting indicators, Rogers et al. (2003) concluded that

> the most important clinical finding from the current meta-analysis involves the usefulness of the Fp across settings and diagnoses. The Fp yielded strong effect sizes and comparatively consistent cut scores that appear useful across settings and diagnostic groups. Despite time honored traditions, we recommend the Fp as the primary MMPI-2 scale for the assessment of feigning. (p. 173)

Although encouraging, this appraisal overstated somewhat the potential for using Fp. In some studies, the F scale (Barber-Rioja et al., 2009) or F_B scale (Bagby et al., 2005) were more effective than Fp in detecting overreporting, indicating the advantage of having multiple infrequent response indicators on the MMPI-2.

SUPERLATIVE SELF-PRESENTATION (S)

Noting that L was developed rationally and that K was developed in reference to psychiatric patients, Butcher and Han (1995) designed the S scale "to explore a different approach to assessing some individuals' tendency to proclaim possession of extreme virtue and absence of psychopathology on the MMPI-2 item pool" (p. 28). The authors used a known-groups design to identify items answered differently by college-educated candidates for airline pilot positions when their responses to the test items were contrasted with those of the MMPI-2 normative sample. Airline pilot candidates were chosen because "they present themselves in a superlative manner, claiming to be superior in terms of their mental health and morality than people in general" (Butcher & Han, 1995, p. 28).

Butcher and Han (1995) contrasted the responses of 274 male airline pilot applicants with those of the 1,138 men of the MMPI-2 normative sample and initially identified 52 items with a 25% or greater response frequency difference across the two groups. Two items that lowered the internal consistency estimates for the scale were dropped, resulting in the 50-item S scale. The authors reported that scores on S were quite highly correlated (approximately .80) with K and that the two scales shared nine items. Removal of the nine overlapping items lowered the correlation between the truncated S scale and K to approximately .75. Correlations with L were considerably lower. Butcher and Han also reported that higher scores on S were correlated with positive descriptions of test takers by their spouses. Finally, based on factor analyses of the S scale item pool, Butcher and Han constructed five subscales for S.

Although its authors did not provide data on the utility of S as an underreporting measure, subsequent studies did demonstrate the effectiveness of the scale in this task (Archer et al., 2004; Baer et al., 1995; Bagby et al., 1999; Bagby et al., 1997; Lim & Butcher, 1996; see Baer & Miller, 2002, for a meta-analysis).

Archer et al. (2004) focused specifically on the incremental validity of S (in reference to L and K) and concluded that the S scale "added incrementally to the prediction levels achieved by the optimal combination of L and K scores" (p. 102).

Revised Validity Scale Profile

To reflect the increased role of the validity indicators introduced in the 1989 manual and accommodate the newly included Fp and S scales, the MMPI-2 Validity Scales profile was expanded and reorganized in the 2001 manual. The framework for identifying threats to protocol validity outlined earlier this chapter guided this reorganization.

Because content nonresponsiveness can affect scores on the Substantive Scales as well as on Validity Scales designed to detect content-based invalid responding, the VRIN and TRIN scales were placed first on the profile. The interpretive recommendation emphasized the need to first examine the CNS score for evidence of excessive nonresponding prior to moving on to VRIN and TRIN. The remaining Validity Scales could be interpreted only if significant content nonresponsiveness was ruled out. Interpretive recommendations for VRIN related to the possibility that both intentional and unintentional random responding could contribute to elevated scores on this scale.

The three overreporting indicators F, F_b, and Fp were placed next, with interpretive recommendations emphasizing the need to consider the score on Fp when interpreting elevated scores on F. In addition, interpretive guidelines for F and F_b emphasized the need to consider the setting in which the test was administered. This served as a proxy for incorporating extratest indications of the likely presence of severe psychopathology when interpreting scores on F and F_b by considering their significant confound with psychopathology. Cutoffs for identifying overreporting in clinical settings were set higher than they had been in the 1989 manual based on findings indicating the substantial contribution of psychopathology to elevated scores on these scales. Consistent with Meehl and Hathaway's (1946) caveat that unintentional overreporting stemming from a distorted self-view may also affect scores on F, interpretive recommendations for F and F_b included psychopathology among the possible reasons for elevation, even at the highest cutoff levels.

The three underreporting indicators, L, K, and S were placed next. For these scales as well, different cutoffs were recommended for clinical and nonclinical settings. These differences were designed to reflect the possibility that interpretations other than underreporting (e.g., better than average psychological adjustment in the case of K and S) were more likely to be appropriate in nonclinical settings. The S subscales were also listed in the revised manual, but no scoring keys, T-score conversion tables, or interpretive recommendations were provided for these measures.

Symptom Validity Scale (FBS)

The final component of the MMPI-2 Validity Scales profile was put in place in 2007 with the addition of the Symptom Validity Scale (FBS). The scale was developed to address concerns articulated by Lees-Haley (1989), who observed that although the traditional MMPI overreporting indicator F had proven effective at identifying misrepresentation of severe psychiatric symptoms (e.g., in individuals undergoing insanity evaluations), it seemed implausible to assume that this measure would operate the same, or as effectively, in detecting noncredible responding to the MMPI items by personal injury litigants or other disability claimants. Lees-Haley concluded that simply adjusting the cutoffs on F was insufficient because the types of responses likely to be given by individuals who present with noncredible symptoms in personal injury litigation (e.g., somatic and cognitive complaints) were qualitatively different from overreporting severe psychopathology.

Lees-Haley et al. (1991) developed FBS to address this concern, taking item content into consideration and comparing the responses of personal injury litigants judged (independently of the MMPI-2) to be malingering with those judged not to be malingering. Content-based item selection was guided by the assumption that overreporting in the context of personal injury litigation involves, on one hand, an effort to appear honest and psychologically normal, except for the influence of the alleged cause of injury, while, on the other, avoiding admission of or minimizing preexisting psychopathology or preinjury antisocial behavior. The authors compared raw scores on the FBS generated by various samples, including a group of personal injury claimants judged to be credible, another group of claimants judged to be malingering emotional distress, and several groups of medical patients instructed to simulate various conditions. They concluded that a raw score of 20 optimally separated the credible personal injury litigants from the other groups. Lees-Haley (1992) subsequently compared FBS scores of a sample of personal injury claimants judged to be malingering symptoms of PTSD—if, for example, the triggering traumatic event was insufficient to account for the claimed symptoms—with those of litigants who did not present with malingered symptoms. He concluded that higher raw score cutoffs (24 for men and 26 for women) were needed to optimally differentiate the two groups.

The FBS was the subject of extensive validation research following its introduction. Consistent with the target population for the scale, the majority of participants in these investigations were personal injury litigants seeking compensation for harm resulting from an injury they had sustained. These individuals typically completed the MMPI-2 as part of neuropsychological evaluations, and the criteria used to validate the scale often included the results of performance validity tests, which are used routinely to identify individuals who do not exert adequate effort on cognitive tests in these evaluations. These known-group design studies, which contrast the MMPI-2 scores of individuals who "pass" versus those who score below established cutoffs on performance validity tests, demonstrated that among the MMPI-2 overreporting indicators, FBS performed best in predicting noncredible cognitive symptom presentation (Greve et al., 2006; Nelson et al., 2010; Nelson et al., 2006). Although most studies that established the effectiveness of the scale in predicting noncredible cognitive symptom presentation were conducted with personal injury litigants or disability claimants, this finding was extended to criminal forensic settings as well (Wygant, Sellbom et al., 2007).

THE QUESTION OF FALSE POSITIVES

Concerns about false positives on the FBS led Butcher et al. (2003) to recommend against using the scale in MMPI-2 interpretation. Butcher and colleagues' methodology and conclusions were challenged by several authors (Greiffenstein et al., 2004; Greiffenstein et al., 2007; Greve & Bianchini, 2004; Larrabee, 2007; Lees-Haley & Fox, 2004). Butcher and colleagues' (2003) admonition against use of the scale went unheeded (although it did call attention to the need to use higher cutoffs than the ones proposed initially for use with the scale), as evidenced by a survey of neuropsychologists reported by Sharland and Gfeller (2007) showing that the FBS was among the most widely used measures among all the psychological tests they relied on to detect problematic performance in neuropsychological evaluations. Butcher et al. (2008) repeated Butcher and colleagues' (2003) concerns about false positive findings in general and particularly in women, and cited court rulings that had relied on this information in excluding FBS testimony in three Florida cases. Ben-Porath, Greve et al. (2009) cited empirical findings that contradicted Butcher and colleagues' (2008) assertions and reported new results showing that a very small proportion of individuals with genuine medical problems, even severe ones, score above 28 on FBS. Scores in the 23–28 range less clearly differentiated between individuals presenting with credible versus noncredible symptoms. Ben-Porath, Greve et al. (2009) also presented data showing that there is no correlation between gender and false positive findings on FBS and outlined a number of problems with Butcher and colleagues' (2008) analysis of legal findings about the scale. In addition, Lee et al. (2012) demonstrated in a large forensic disability sample that there was no gender bias for FBS scores in the detection of overreported cognitive complaints.

ADDITION TO THE MMPI-2

The substantial empirical literature documenting the effectiveness of FBS in detecting noncredible somatic and cognitive symptom reporting led the University of Minnesota Press to conduct a review of the scale for possible inclusion on the test. Based on the largely positive results of this review, the scale was added to the standard MMPI-2 materials. Ben-Porath, Graham, and Tellegen (2009) summarized the psychometric literature supporting and guiding use of FBS in

MMPI-2 interpretation and provided interpretive guidelines for the scale. The guidelines they recommended emphasized the need to consider alternative interpretations of FBS at more moderate levels, as overreporting may not be the only explanation in those cases. This caveat is similar to the one included in guidelines for the other overreporting indicators in the 2001 MMPI-2 manual.

Summary

The 10 MMPI-2 validity indicators (CNS and the nine Validity Scales) considerably expanded the measurement of various threats to the validity of a test protocol. Referring to the conceptual framework described in the first part of this chapter, CNS, VRIN, and TRIN were designed to assist in detecting non-responding, random responding (intentional and unintentional), and fixed responding, respectively. F, F_b, Fp, and FBS assessed overreporting, and L, K, and S identified threats related to underreporting. A substantial body of empirical research was available to support the interpretive recommendations developed for the MMPI-2 validity indicators.

The MMPI-2-RF Validity Scales

Protocol validity measures were the last set of scales developed for the MMPI-2-RF. Tellegen and Ben-Porath (2008/2011) approached this process from the perspective that the conceptually and empirically grounded MMPI-2 validity indicators provided a solid framework from which three goals could be accomplished. First, they sought to eliminate item overlap within subsets of scales. Second, the MMPI-2-RF authors wished to address deficiencies, noted earlier, in some of the MMPI-2 Validity Scales. Finally, they sought to canvass the array of threats to protocol validity, delineated in the first part of this chapter, as comprehensively as possible.

Non-Content-Based Invalid Responding Measures

CNS

The impact of nonresponding continued to be assessed with the CNS score, which reflects the number of unscorable responses to the 338 MMPI-2-RF items. Hathaway and McKinley (1943) had observed that the impact of nonresponding could vary dramatically as a function of the proportion of unscorable responses per scale. Computer scoring enabled consideration of the scale-specific impact of nonresponding by providing the Response % statistic, which indicated the percentage of scorable responses to the items of each scale.

VRIN-R AND TRIN-R

The two other types of non-content-based threats, random and fixed responding, continued to be assessed with revised versions of the MMPI-2 VRIN and TRIN scales (VRIN-r and TRIN-r). Tellegen and Ben-Porath (2008/2011) provided a detailed description of the method used to revise these scales. Two primary considerations guided the revision. First, they sought to eliminate the considerable overlap between the MMPI-2 versions of these scales. (Recall that 10 of the 23 TRIN item response pairs were also scored on VRIN.) To accomplish this goal, VRIN-r item pairs were restricted to positively correlated items, whereas TRIN-r item pairs consisted only of negatively correlated items. Second, because they were working with a smaller item pool (338 versus 567 items), the authors used a different approach to reducing the impact of substantive content variance on scores on these scales. The alternative approach used in constructing VRIN-r and TRIN-r generated a broader selection of item pairs to be considered for inclusion in the revised scales.

Item pairs were selected based on statistical and semantic analyses of possible response combinations. A test taker could respond to a pair of items in one of four possible combinations: both True (TT), both False (FF), the first True and the second False (TF), or the first False and the second True (FT). The consistency scale items were composites made up of a specific combination of responses (e.g., TT) to a pair of MMPI-2-RF items. For example, for a TT composite, a True response to both items in a pair added a point to the raw score of the scale on which that composite was scored. Each composite chosen for VRIN-r and TRIN-r had to meet five criteria:

1. The items in a composite had to be sufficiently correlated with each other (positively for VRIN-r, negatively for TRIN-r) in two clinical samples. Rather than require a specific minimal correlation, the authors sought item pairs that were correlated reliably in both samples and met the remaining four criteria. This allowed them to examine a broader range of items than those considered when the VRIN and TRIN scales were constructed for the MMPI-2.
2. The observed frequency of a composite had to be lower than the frequency expected by chance if the two responses making up that composite were independent. For example, if a TT composite occurred in 5% of the cases in a sample, and the expected (by chance) frequency of responding True to both items was 25%, the observed-to-expected ratio would be .20, indicating that this combination of responses was unlikely and therefore indicative of inconsistency. This was also the method used to determine which combination of responses was statistically inconsistent for the MMPI-2 Inconsistency Scales.
3. The combination of responses in a composite had to be judged by the authors to be content inconsistent.

4. The correlation between a composite and a mini-scale made up of the two items scored in the direction they are keyed in the composite was low. This criterion replaced the requirement that composites be minimally correlated with scores on the Clinical Scales. Instead, the authors required that they be minimally correlated with measures (the mini-scales) that were specific to the content of the items in a pair.
5. Neither item in a composite could belong to another composite of the same type. For example, if a given composite consisting of items A and B was scored TT, then neither item A nor item B could be scored TT in a composite with a different item. This criterion was adopted to ensure that an inconsistent True response or False response to a given item could contribute only once to the score on VRIN-r or TRIN-r.

Application of these criteria resulted in the selection of 53 composites for VRIN-r and 26 composites for TRIN-r. Because of the substantially reduced length of the inventory, the revised scales sampled a larger proportion of the item pool for indications of random or fixed responding.

Content-Based Invalid Responding Measures

OVERREPORTING INDICATORS

Four overreporting indicators (revised versions of F, Fp, and FBS) and a new scale—Fs (Infrequent Somatic Complaints)—were included in the initial release of the MMPI-2-RF. A fifth measure, Response Bias Scale (RBS; Gervais et al., 2007), was added in 2011.

Infrequent Responses (F-r)

Two factors led to the restructuring of the MMPI-2 F scale. Several original F scale items, selected because they were answered in the keyed direction by 10% or less of the original normative sample, no longer met this criterion in the MMPI-2 normative sample. In addition, the F_B scale, made up entirely of items answered infrequently by the MMPI-2 normative sample, outperformed both F and Fp in detecting overreporting in some studies (Bagby et al., 2005). Taken together, these findings suggested that a revised F scale, made up of MMPI-2-RF items answered infrequently by the MMPI-2/MMPI-2-RF normative sample, could contribute incrementally to the detection of symptom overreporting.

Two criteria were used in selecting items for F-r. First, the authors reverted to Hathaway and McKinley's (1943) original criterion for infrequent responding and required that candidate items be answered in the keyed direction by 10% or less of both the men and women in the MMPI-2/MMPI-2-RF normative sample. Second, they did not include any item assigned to the revised Fp, FBS,

L, and K scales or to the new Fs scale, which had already been developed. Thus, all F-r items are answered infrequently by the MMPI-2-RF normative sample and were not scored on the other infrequency scales or the revised underreporting indicators. Four F-r items were scored on the subsequently developed RBS.

Infrequent Psychopathology Responses (Fp-r)

The MMPI-2-RF authors' primary goal in revising Fp was to eliminate overlap with other validity indicators. Arbisi and Ben-Porath (1995) did not require that the items selected for Fp be nonoverlapping with existing MMPI-2 Validity Scales. As a result, 14 of the 27 Fp items overlapped with F, and four Fp items overlapped with L. Gass and Luis (2001) suggested that the inclusion of four L items on Fp might compromise the validity of the scale. However, Arbisi and colleagues (2003) demonstrated that, overall, the Fp scale functioned more effectively when the four L items were included. Nevertheless, considering the authors' goal of eliminating overlap among the MMPI-2-RF content-based invalidity indicators, Tellegen and Ben-Porath (2008/2011) dropped the four L items as well as three items assigned to Fs. Correlation analyses indicated that two other Fp items did not function as effectively as the remaining items, while the addition of three items not scored on Fp was found to improve the scale. The resulting 21-item Fp-r scale did not overlap with any of the content-based invalid responding indicators, although it did share items with the subsequently added RBS scale.

Infrequent Somatic Responses (Fs)

Wygant et al. (2004) developed the Fs scale to identify individuals overreporting somatic symptoms. As with F-r and Fp-r, construction of Fs was predicated on the assumption that individuals who report a relatively large number of uncommon symptoms are likely overreporting. To identify uncommon somatic symptom reports, Wygant et al. (2004) applied a methodology similar to the one used by Arbisi and Ben-Porath (1995) when constructing the Fp scale. They examined item response frequencies in three large medical samples. The first scale development sample was from an original MMPI study of approximately 50,000 medical patients tested at the Mayo Clinic in the 1960s, for which item response frequencies had been published (Swenson et al., 1973). The other samples were from two large archival MMPI-2 datasets collected by the test distributor between 1989 and 1998. The first was a general medical sample made up of 2,568 patients, and the second was a sample of 4,590 chronic pain patients.

Item response frequencies were examined in the three samples, and 166 items answered (True or False) by less than 25% of subjects in all three samples (and less than 20% in the MMPI-2 normative sample) were identified as candidates for the Fs scale. Next, Wygant and Ben-Porath examined the content of the 166 items independently and selected items they judged to contain somatic content. Both authors selected the same set of 16 items, and these items made up the Fs scale. The 16 Fs items were excluded from consideration for the other MMPI-2-RF infrequent response indicators; therefore, this scale did not overlap with F-r and Fp-r. Three Fs items appeared on FBS-r, and two were scored on RBS.

Symptom Validity (FBS-r)
Of the 43 items included on the original FBS scale, 30 were retained in the 338-item MMPI-2-RF pool. Analyses reported in the *MMPI-2-RF Technical Manual* indicated that scores on the truncated measure were highly correlated with the original. Thus, no further analyses were conducted, and the 30 remaining items made up FBS-r. One FBS-r item was scored on Fp-r, three were on Fs, and four appeared on RBS.

Response Bias Scale (RBS)
Gervais et al. (2007) developed RBS "to detect negative response bias in forensic neuropsychological or disability assessment settings" (p. 196). The scale consisted of 28 MMPI-2-RF items that discriminated between persons who passed or failed the Word Memory Test (WMT; Green et al., 1996), the Computerized Assessment of Response Bias (CARB; Allen et al., 1997), or the Test of Memory Malingering (TOMM; Tombaugh, 1997) in a sample of 1,151 non-head-injured disability claimants.

The development sample was split into random halves for the purpose of item selection and scale validation. The 28 RBS items were identified through a series of multiple logistic regression analyses. Dichotomous variables representing passing or failing the three criterion measures (based on standard criteria) were regressed on the MMPI-2 item pool. The 28 items selected for RBS were those that appeared commonly as significant predictors in the regression analyses. A small number of RBS items were scored on each of the other overreporting indicators: four on F-r, two on Fp-r, two on Fs, and four on FBS-r.

UNDERREPORTING INDICATORS
MMPI investigators and users have long recognized that detecting underreporting is more difficult than identifying protocols marked by overreporting (Meehl & Hathaway, 1946). As reviewed earlier, the K scale was developed for use as a correction for underreporting after Meehl and Hathaway (1946) concluded that L, the original MMPI underreporting indicator, was inadequate for this task. The S scale (Butcher & Han, 1995) was added to the MMPI-2 based on evidence that it added to L and K in detecting underreporting. In a meta-analysis of the detection of underreporting with the MMPI-2, Baer and Miller (2002) found that two older MMPI underreporting indicators, the Positive Malingering scale (Mp; Cofer et al., 1949) and the Wiggins (1959) Social Desirability (Sd) Scale, outperformed L, K, and S in this task. Given these findings, Tellegen and Ben-Porath (2008/2011) decided to examine the unique (i.e.,

nonoverlapping) items of these five scales as candidates for developing underreporting indicators for the MMPI-2-RF.

The MMPI-2-RF authors conducted factor analyses of this item pool in several samples that included individuals tested in the context of personnel selection, underreporting simulation, and clinical settings. Replicating results of a similar study conducted at the scale level by Bagby and Marshall (2004), the authors consistently found two primary factors in these analyses and constructed two nonoverlapping scales by selecting items that loaded substantially and consistently on one factor without substantial cross-loadings on the other. Labels were assigned to the two scales based on item content, and abbreviations were used to link each MMPI-2-RF underreporting indicator to the MMPI-2 scale with which it shared the most items.

Uncommon Virtues (L-r)

L-r consisted of 14 items, 11 of which were on the original L scale. Two new items came from Sd, and one from Mp. In contrast with the MMPI-2 L scale, for which all 15 items were keyed False, all three new L-r items were keyed True, reducing the likelihood that an extreme score on this scale is an artifact of fixed responding. The label *Uncommon Virtues* characterized the content of the items scored on this scale, which, as keyed, described virtuous behavior in which most individuals were unlikely to engage on a regular basis. Indeed, most of the items were rarely answered in the keyed direction by the MMPI-2-RF normative sample.

Adjustment Validity (K-r)

K-r consisted of 14 items, all of which appeared on the original K scale. Five of these items were also scored on S. One of the K-r items was actually scored in the opposite direction as one of the control items (discussed earlier) on K. The label assigned to K-r characterized its item content, which comprised assertions of good psychological adjustment as keyed.

Summary

The MMPI-2-RF Validity Scales were developed to capitalize on the established strengths of the MMPI-2 Validity Scales while improving their distinctiveness by eliminating most item overlap and expanding their scope with the addition of Fs and RBS. A substantial body of peer-reviewed research (discussed in chapter 5) provided strong support of these scales' utility and further guidance for their use in a broad range of settings. As discussed in the following chapter, the authors' goal for the MMPI-3 was to further build on the solid foundations of the MMPI-2-RF validity indicators by recalibrating the response inconsistency and infrequency scales using modern samples and incorporating new items in most of the MMPI-3 Validity Scales.

APPRAISALS OF THE MMPI-2-RF

Appraisals of the MMPI and MMPI-2 (discussed in chapter 1) and the RC Scales (reviewed earlier in this chapter) included consideration of use patterns, research, and commentary. We consider each of these indicators here for the MMPI-2-RF.

A limited number of surveys published following release of the MMPI-2-RF indicated expanding use of the inventory in several settings. Martin and colleagues (2015) found that the MMPI-2-RF ranked as the most widely used symptom validity measure in a survey of neuropsychologists (36% versus 30% for the MMPI-2). In a follow-up, Schroeder et al. (2016) reported that the MMPI-2-RF was by far the more widely used source of symptom validity indicators among neuropsychology experts (71% versus 29% for the MMPI-2). The MMPI-2-RF was also the most widely used personality inventory in a survey of VA neuropsychologists (Russo, 2018; 36% versus less than 20% for the MMPI-2). Other indications of broadening MMPI-2-RF use included its translation and adaptation in Brazil (Portuguese), Canada (French Canadian), Croatia, Denmark, France, Germany, Italy, Mexico, Norway, Spain, South Korea, Sweden, the Netherlands, and Belgium.

Detailed MMPI-2-RF interpretive guidance was included in updated versions of the three most used MMPI-2 interpretive guides (Friedman et al, 2015; Graham, 2012; Greene, 2011) and in a shorter MMPI-2-RF interpretive guide (McCord, 2018). Setting specific MMPI-2-RF guidance was provided in books written for police and public safety psychologists (Corey & Ben-Porath, 2018) and forensic psychologists (Sellbom & Wygant, 2018). The MMPI-2-RF was the only personality instrument listed among recommended outcome measures in traumatic brain injury research (Wilde et al., 2010), and it was the only version of the test selected for use in the National Football League's settlement with retired players. Finally, the MMPI-2-RF was listed among recommended measures for assessment of child sexual abusers (Chu & Ogloff, 2012); in police preemployment psychological evaluations (Gallo & Halgin, 2011); in differential diagnostic evaluation of individuals with mild traumatic brain injuries (Larrabee & Rohling, 2013); in presurgical evaluations of bariatric patients (Vortuba et al., 2014) and spine surgery patients (Epker & Block, 2014); in evaluation of chronic pain patients (Bruns, 2014); and in psychological assessments in divorce actions (Ackerman et al., 2015).

A sizable body of literature on various elements of the MMPI-2-RF accumulated within a relatively short time. Two factors contributed to this productivity: restriction of the MMPI-2-RF to the existing MMPI-2 item pool, which allowed for MMPI-2-RF studies to be conducted with existing MMPI-2 datasets, and the earlier (2003) publication of the RC Scales, on which a sizable literature accumulated before publication of the MMPI-2-RF. As of this writing, more than 560 peer-reviewed studies reported MMPI-2-RF findings in a broad range of settings, including mental health, medical, forensic, and public safety. This research is reviewed extensively by Sellbom (2019b) and in chapter 5 of this book.

Authors of two major MMPI-2 textbooks (Graham, 2012; Greene, 2011) included appraisals of the MMPI-2-RF in updated editions of their books. After listing advantages and disadvantages of the revised inventory, both authors provided detailed guidelines for its use and interpretation. The advantages they saw in the new version included brevity, ease of interpretation, and links to the contemporary literature on personality and psychopathology. Both cited the loss of information from clinical scale code types as a primary disadvantage for the MMPI-2-RF. However, Graham (2011) noted that "one could argue that code types evolved largely as a way to deal with the heterogeneity of the Clinical Scales and are not necessary because of the homogeneity of the RC Scales and other MMPI-2-RF scales" (p. 414). This issue was discussed earlier in this chapter.

Both authors also noted as disadvantages the absence of certain supplementary MMPI-2 measures. Graham (2011) specifically mentioned in this regard the MacAndrew Alcoholism scale–Revised (MAC-R; MacAndrew, 1965) and the Hostility scale (Ho; Cook & Medley, 1954) (p. 414). A third scale, Ego Strength (Es; Barron, 1953), was discussed in terms of its positive focus on psychological resources (p. 414). However, although these scales were not included, the constructs they assessed could also be measured with the MMPI-2-RF. Examination of Table 3-16 of the *MMPI-2-RF Technical Manual* (Tellegen & Ben-Porath, 2008/2011) indicated that MAC-R scores were most closely associated with the higher-order Behavioral/Externalizing Dysfunction (BXD) scale of the MMPI-2-RF. The Cynicism scale (RC3 on the MMPI-2-RF; CYN on the MMPI-3) measures the cynical hostility component of Ho, which was implicated in increased risk for coronary artery disease. Es was a more heterogeneous scale that did not have a direct parallel in the MMPI-2-RF. However, interpretive recommendations provided in the *MMPI-2-RF Manual for Administration, Scoring, and Interpretation* (Ben-Porath & Tellegen, 2008/2011) identified positive features associated with low scores on several MMPI-2-RF scales that were relevant to this issue.

Greene (2011) added a third disadvantage:

The "MMPI-2" in MMPI-2-RF is a misnomer because the only relationship to the MMPI-2 is its use of a subset of the MMPI-2 item pool, its normative group, and similar validity scales. The MMPI-2-RF should not be conceptualized as a revised or restructured form of the MMPI-2, but as a *new* self-report inventory that chose to select its items from the MMPI-2 item pool and use its normative group. (p. 22)

In this chapter, we have described in detail the procedures followed in restructuring the MMPI-2 and the conceptual and psychometric reasons for doing so. Calling the MMPI-2-RF, which was made up of MMPI-2 items and scored based on MMPI-2 norms, anything but a restructured version of the MMPI-2 would have been in fact misleading.

Greene (2011) went on to advise that "clinicians who use the MMPI-2-RF should realize that they have forsaken the MMPI-2 and its 70 years of clinical and research history, and they are learning a new inventory" (p. 22). Nonetheless, Green provided in his MMPI-2 book detailed recommendations on how to use the MMPI-2-RF—which spanned roughly one-fourth of the text—and included several case studies.

A third author (Butcher, 2011) provided an exclusively negative appraisal of the MMPI-2-RF and recommended against its use. Much of Butcher's appraisal consisted of repeated criticisms of the RC Scales discussed earlier in this chapter. Butcher (2011) did not attend to the substance of responses to these critiques but instead listed several new concerns about the MMPI-2-RF. Pointing out the relatively low reliabilities for some SP Scales, Butcher indicated that they "need to be studied further to determine if they provide consistent and valid predictions" (p. 191). In fact, external correlate data reported in Appendix A of the *MMPI-2-RF Technical Manual* addressed this need and provided evidence of the validity of these measures. The implication of low reliability estimates and the need to consider them in the context of standard error of measurement (*SEM*) statistics were discussed in the reliability section of that manual.

Under the heading "Insufficient Validation," Butcher (2011) asserted that "the majority of the scales incorporated in the MMPI-2-RF are insufficiently validated to provide the practitioner with confidence in assessment" (p. 189). In fact, extensive external correlate data documenting the validity of MMPI-2-RF scale scores were collected in outpatient and inpatient mental health facilities, medical centers, criminal and civil forensic evaluations, and a nonclinical setting. Criterion data used in these analyses included reports by intake staff and therapists, systematic file reviews, and other self-report measures. All told, Appendix A of the *MMPI-2-RF Technical Manual* reported well over 50,000 validity coefficients. A comparable set of validation data had not been compiled in one source and integrated into interpretive recommendations for any other version of the MMPI.

Butcher (2011) also expressed concern about "information loss from the MMPI-2 in the construction of the MMPI-2-RF" (p. 191) and cited as particularly problematic the loss of items related to "work adjustment" and "treatment resistance and attitudes toward mental health treatment" (p. 193). The items alluded to here were scored on two of the MMPI-2 Content Scales (Butcher, Graham, Williams & Ben-Porath, 1990): Work Interference (WRK) and Negative Treatment Indicators (TRT). Examination of Table 3-16 of the *MMPI-2-RF Technical Manual* showed that both these scales were oversaturated with demoralization variance. The distinctive features of the scales were assessed in the MMPI-2-RF with the Inefficacy (NFC) and Helplessness/Hopelessness (HLP) scales, respectively. Butcher asserted that "information on potential problems in treatment planning or resilience for dealing with problems was not available to practitioners on the MMPI-2-RF" (p. 193). However, treatment considerations were included in the interpretive recommendations for most of the MMPI-2-RF Substantive Scales.

Finally, under the heading "Confusion Resulting from Two Forms of the MMPI-2 Producing Highly Different Interpretations," Butcher (2011) remarked that "it is likely that the interpretations and conclusions drawn from the MMPI-2-RF will differ substantially from an MMPI-2 interpretation" (p. 190). This empirical question was not studied systematically in the context of the full MMPI-2-RF. Sellbom, Ben-Porath, McNulty, Arbisi, and Graham (2006) addressed this question with respect to the Clinical and RC Scales. They concluded that the two sets of scales were, in fact, largely congruent. If a Clinical Scale was elevated, in most cases, its restructured counterpart was elevated as well, and vice versa. In the relatively uncommon cases when they were incongruent, the RC Scale scores were likely to be more consistent with extratest findings.

Summary

Within a few years of its 2008 publication, the MMPI-2-RF was used widely in the broad range of psychological assessments conducted in mental health, medical, forensic, and public safety settings. A comprehensive set of empirical correlates reported in the *MMPI-2-RF Technical Manual* and the peer-reviewed literature was available to support and guide use of the test in these settings. Initial appraisals of the MMPI-2-RF by two of the leading MMPI-2 textbook authors led them to include, in the most recent (at the time) editions of their books, discussions of the revised test and detailed interpretive recommendations for its use. A third author, who opposed efforts to modernize the MMPI-2, weighed in against the revised inventory. Widespread adoption of the MMPI-2-RF indicated that MMPI-2 users did not heed this author's admonitions.

TOWARD THE MMPI-3

The MMPI-2-RF represented a major paradigm shift for the instrument. Two issues not addressed with the restructuring project were the need to expand the scope of the MMPI-2-RF item pool (which was constrained by the MMPI-2 item pool from which it was derived) and limitations of using the MMPI-2 normative data, collected in the mid-1980s, to standardize MMPI-2-RF scale scores. These were the primary objectives for developing the MMPI-3.

Developing the MMPI-3   3

The starting point for developing the MMPI-3 was the MMPI-2-RF (Ben-Porath & Tellegen, 2008/2011; Tellegen & Ben-Porath, 2008/2011), which, as detailed in chapter 2, was derived from the MMPI-2 item pool. The MMPI-2-RF authors' decision to limit the restructuring effort to the MMPI-2 item pool made it possible to use a broad range of existing data to develop and extensively validate the restructured inventory. This decision likely contributed to the test's relatively rapid adoption, despite the major paradigm shift discussed in chapter 2—however, it did come with a cost. Of the 567 MMPI-2 items, 460 were written for the original MMPI in the late 1930s and early 1940s, and 107 were written for the MMPI-2 in the early 1980s. The focus of psychological assessment had expanded considerably since most of the MMPI-2-RF items were written. These limitations of the MMPI-2 item pool constrained MMPI-2-RF development. In addition, the MMPI-2-RF standard scores were derived with the MMPI-2 normative sample, which was collected in the mid-1980s. Substantial demographic and experiential changes occurred in the general population of the United States during the more than 3 decades separating collection of the MMPI-2 and MMPI-3 norms. Consequently, the two primary objectives for developing the MMPI-3 were to expand content coverage and update the test norms.

This chapter begins with an overview of research that preceded development of the MMPI-3. The scale-development process and the resulting 52 MMPI-3 scales are then delineated, and the processes used to develop the MMPI-3 English- and Spanish-language norms are described. The chapter concludes with information about the normative samples and derivation of standard MMPI-3 scores. Throughout this chapter, we refer to tables found in the *MMPI-3*

Technical Manual, which serve as a helpful complement to the development information reported here.

PRELIMINARY RESEARCH

In 2012, the MMPI-3 authors embarked on a multiyear program of research designed to explore further development of the MMPI-2-RF. A series of preliminary investigations, conducted with college student samples tested at Kent State University, were carried out to address questions related to the response format of the test, to identify potential item modifications, and to develop and test new item content that might be added to the inventory.[1]

Response Format

The original MMPI and all subsequent versions of the inventory relied on a True/False (T/F) response format. Some recent test developers have instead used polytomous formats, typically providing four response options. Because such a change would affect both existing and new items, preliminary investigations began with a study of the potential benefit of transitioning from the traditional T/F response option to a polytomous one. Finn et al. (2015) reported the results of this research.

The researchers developed an experimental MMPI-2-RF booklet (MMPI-2-RF Booklet 1) composed of the 338 test items, with instructions and an answer sheet for a 4-point polytomous format, with the options consisting of Definitely True, Mostly True, Mostly False, and Definitely False. Finn et al. (2015) reported the results of this study, based on a sample of 406 participants who completed the MMPI-2-RF twice (counterbalanced), once using each response format (standard and polytomous); these participants also completed a battery of measures selected to evaluate the validity of MMPI-2-RF scores as a function of response format.

Internal structural analyses indicated that the addition of response options increased reliability estimates of scale scores, but the effects were small, with a median increase of .06 in coefficient alpha values. Alpha increases were substantially correlated with increases in scale score variances, indicating that the additional variance gained from polytomous response options was largely reliable and reflected either construct-relevant or systematic error variance. Comparisons of scale score validities were conducted next to determine the extent to which these two possibilities (construct-relevant versus systematic error variance) likely accounted for the reliability findings. If the increased reliabilities reflected added construct-relevant variance, this would have been reflected in improved predictive validity.

Differences between correlations with external criteria (i.e., scale score validities) as a function of response format were rarely statistically significant, and the few differences observed did not consistently favor either format. Thus, the modest reliability estimate increases just mentioned generally reflected increased systematic error rather than enhanced validity. On the basis of these analyses, Finn et al. (2015) concluded that there would be no advantage to using a polytomous response format with MMPI items, and the MMPI-3 authors determined that all further preliminary and test development work would be carried out with the traditional T/F format.

Item Modification

Next, possible item content clarifications and simplifications were explored. The MMPI-3 authors reviewed the 338 MMPI-2-RF items to identify any that were awkwardly worded or had overly complicated content that might benefit from simplification. Based on that review, the authors reworded 47 items and developed an alternative MMPI-2-RF booklet (MMPI-2-RF Booklet 2), which included the modified items in place of the MMPI-2-RF versions. A sample of 552 Kent State University students completed both the MMPI-2-RF and MMPI-2-RF Booklet 2, along with a battery of external criterion measures used to compare the validities of MMPI-2-RF scale scores as a function of item wording (original versus modified). Based on item-total correlation analyses for scales that included reworded items and further review of the reworded item content, the authors decided to retain all but four of the modifications. A comparison of scale score validities for the two booklets indicated that the two versions yielded comparably valid scores—an expected finding considering the relatively small number of rewritten items per scale. The remaining 43 modified items were used in all further MMPI-3 preliminary and test development work.

Expanding Test Content

The MMPI-3 authors conducted a comprehensive review of the constructs assessed by the MMPI-2-RF to identify content domains that they and/or experts they consulted thought were missing or insufficiently covered in the test item pool. This process consisted of three components: consultation with MMPI-2-RF experts (12 experienced researchers and test users) to obtain their suggestions for content enhancements, a review of existing psychological tests and diagnostic interviews, and a review of recent literature on the assessment of personality and psychopathology. Based on information gleaned from these sources, the authors identified several areas for potential item enhancement and wrote 135 trial items intended to assess the targeted constructs.

Some of the trial items targeted content entirely missing from the MMPI-2 item pool (e.g., disordered eating), others represented content that was largely absent (e.g., grandiosity, compulsivity, panic), and a third set of items, the largest of them all, was written to enhance existing content areas (e.g., persecutory ideation, self-doubt, stress, worry, intrusive ideation, anger, disaffiliativeness). The trial items were added to the test booklet after the 338 MMPI-2-RF items to form the 473-item MMPI-2-RF Booklet 3.

The MMPI-2-RF and MMPI-2-RF Booklet 3 were administered (counterbalanced) to a sample of 519 Kent State University students who also completed a battery of collateral measures selected to provide validation data for the trial items. Based on item-total correlations and correlations with external criteria, the authors retained 90 of the 135 trial items for further exploration and wrote five additional items to cover some of the content in the 45 trial items they had discarded. These 95 trial items were included in all subsequent data collected for MMPI-3 development.

DEVELOPMENT SAMPLES AND INSTRUMENTS

Samples

Three types of data were collected for the MMPI-3 development project: field, college, and normative. To represent the populations and types of assessments for which the MMPI is used, field data were collected in applied settings: mental health, medical, forensic, and public safety. As detailed next under the Instruments section, test materials and software were created to facilitate collection of actual assessment data (i.e., data collected during the normal course of and used in actual psychological assessments), which would allow for generalizability of findings to applied assessments. In addition to scale development, these data were used for detailed validation analyses and the formation of comparison groups.

College student data were collected at Kent State University. These data were used for initial psychometric analyses that were part of the development process described later in this chapter, as well as detailed validation analyses reported in Appendixes D and E of the *MMPI-3 Technical Manual* (Ben-Porath & Tellegen, 2020b). Although college student data would not be sufficient for validation purposes (which were conducted first and foremost using the just mentioned field data), the ability to administer extensive batteries of established self-report measures to the college student samples made it possible to conduct detailed validation analyses of newly developed or enhanced MMPI-3 scales. In addition, although college student participants do not exhibit the full range of psychological dysfunction observed in clinical samples, this population is by no means psychopathology free.

Normative data were collected for the purpose of creating the English- and Spanish-language normative samples used to derive MMPI-3 T scores included in the *MMPI-3 Manual for Administration, Scoring, and Interpretation* (Ben-Porath & Tellegen, 2020a) and the *MMPI-3 Manual Supplement for the U.S.*

Spanish Translation (Ben-Porath, Tellegen, & Puente, 2020), respectively. Normative data collection procedures and derivation of the English- and Spanish-language normative samples are described later in this chapter.

Specific samples used in the scale development process are listed in Table 2–1 of the *MMPI-3 Technical Manual*. They included an overall composite development sample made up of 500 men and 500 women with valid MMPI-2-RF protocols assessed in mental health (n = 217 men and 217 women), medical (n = 183 men and 183 women), and college (n = 100 men and 100 women) settings. Rather than represent a specific population, the goal for this sample was to obtain adequate item response variability by including a broad range of participants in the analyses used to develop the MMPI-3 Substantive Scales.

The MMPI-3 inconsistency scales were developed using a sample of 1,322 men and 1,322 women who produced valid MMPI-2-RF protocols. This set of analyses required a large, diverse sample to be used in calculating correlational statistics for all possible combinations of MMPI-3 items. The sample included 701 men and 701 women tested as part of preemployment evaluations for public safety positions, 269 men and 269 women assessed at intake at mental health service delivery agencies, and 352 men and 352 women receiving services as medical patients.

To calculate general population item response frequencies for the purpose of updating the Infrequent Responses (F) scale, the authors used a dataset made up of all 1,143 men and 1,242 women tested as part of the normative data collection project. Setting-specific composite samples representing mental health, medical, and public safety sites were used to update other MMPI-3 overreporting and underreporting scales. These included a composite sample of 301 men and 455 women receiving mental health services, 379 men and 512 women assessed in medical settings, and 2,355 men and 714 women assessed as part of a preemployment psychological evaluation for a public safety position. Demographic characteristics of the development samples are reported in Table 2–1 of the *MMPI-3 Technical Manual*.

Instruments

MMPI-2-RF Expanded (MMPI-2-RF-EX)

MMPI-3 development data were collected with the MMPI-2-RF-Expanded (MMPI-2-RF-EX) booklet, which included a brief biographical information questionnaire followed by the 338 MMPI-2-RF items, 43 of which had been rewritten, and then the 95 trial items. The MMPI distributor, Pearson, created the MMPI-2-RF-EX booklets and answer sheets, as well as a special version of its Q® Local scoring and reporting system (Q Local EX) that could be used to score the MMPI-2-RF from an administration of the MMPI-2-RF-EX. This arrangement allowed field sites to score and use the MMPI-2-RF in applied assessments, and it provided the development project real-world assessment data that were used for scale development and the creation of comparison groups as well as the reliability and validity analyses reported in chapter 3 of the *MMPI-3 Technical Manual*. Field sites were provided complimentary MMPI-2-RF scoring in exchange for making the MMPI-2-RF-EX data available for the MMPI-3 development project.

A Spanish version of the MMPI-2-RF-EX was developed to facilitate collection of Spanish-language MMPI-3 norms. The starting point for developing the Spanish-language MMPI-2-RF-EX booklet was the MMPI-2-RF Spanish translation developed for use in the United States. García-Peltoniemi and Azán Chaviano (1993) updated the MMPI Hispania (Garcia et al., 1983; a Spanish translation of the original MMPI) for use with U.S. Spanish speakers. Azan (1989) translated items that had been revised or newly added to the MMPI-2 and conducted a series of comparability analyses that led García-Peltoniemi and Azán Chaviano (1993) to recommend that the Spanish translation of the MMPI-2 be used with the newly collected English-language MMPI-2 norms. Later, an MMPI-2-RF booklet was developed based on the García-Peltoniemi and Azán Chaviano (1993) version of the MMPI-2 Spanish translation. Following these authors' recommendations for the MMPI-2, the MMPI-2-RF English-language norms, derived from the MMPI-2 normative sample, were also used to score the MMPI-2-RF Spanish translation.

Antonio E. Puente, coauthor of the Spanish version of the MMPI-3, led a team that translated the 43 rewritten and 95 trial items included in the MMPI-2-RF-EX. Details of this effort are described in the *MMPI-3 Manual Supplement for the U.S. Spanish Translation* (Ben-Porath et al., 2020). Briefly, the first step was to assemble a team of individuals that would help address the concept of *pan-Spanish*. Considering the multiple backgrounds of Spanish-speaking individuals, the team included Spanish speakers of varying national origins. The goal was to ensure that (1) all words, phrases, and sentences were translated such that the constructs remained the same and (2) to the extent feasible, the version of Spanish that used was pan-Spanish and would not disadvantage a Spanish speaker from any country in Latin America, the Caribbean, or Spain. Two team members translated the items from English to Spanish. That translation was then back-translated by a third team member into English. Next, a bilingual Spanish/English linguist checked the translation and back-translation. Finally, the team discussed any differences between the original English items of the MMPI-3 and the new items in Spanish. A special effort was made to address contemporary Spanish-language usage.

Initial Validation Data

As just discussed, although limited for the purpose of generalizing to clinical settings, college samples make it possible to collect extensive collateral data that cannot be obtained realistically with clinical samples. Preliminary validation analyses were conducted with college sample data for the limited purpose of gauging whether new and substantially revised MMPI-3 scales evidenced sufficient convergent and discriminant validity to support further consideration for inclusion on the MMPI-3. Additional college sample data were later used for detailed validation. Appendix Table A-1 of the *MMPI-3 Technical Manual* provides a list of the collateral measures used for the preliminary and detailed validation analyses with the college sample.

SCALE DEVELOPMENT

Because the extensive reliability and validity data reported in the *MMPI-3 Technical Manual* provide the best information about the utility of the MMPI-3 scales, the development process is described here in general terms, rather than in exhaustive fashion with specific item inclusion decisions spelled out at each step. All empirical analyses were conducted separately by gender, and data-driven decisions were made only if the results replicated across women and men. During MMPI-3 development, the authors sought to enhance the range of the MMPI-2-RF content without increasing the test's length. To add items without lengthening the inventory, the authors eliminated some scales and reduced the length of others. The process that was followed is described next in the order in which development proceeded.

Substantive Scales

The authors' overarching goal for developing the MMPI-3 Substantive Scales was to enhance coverage of underrepresented constructs while ensuring that scores on measures carried over from the MMPI-2-RF to the MMPI-3 retained (at least) their levels of reliability and validity. To accomplish these objectives, and to avoid lengthening the MMPI-3, the authors reduced the number of items on each measure to the minimum needed to preserve its psychometric properties. The goal of not lengthening the inventory during MMPI-3 development was further accomplished by not carrying over some MMPI-2-RF scales to the updated inventory. Specifically, the Gastrointestinal Complaints (GIC) and Head Pain Complaints (HPC) scales were eliminated, although some items scored on these scales were retained on RC1. The MMPI-2-RF Multiple Specific Fears (MSF), Aesthetic/Literary Interests (AES), and Mechanical/Physical Interests (MEC) scales, which had received limited attention in the literature and contained many items not scored on other scales, were discontinued.

Reconstructed Clinical and Specific Problems Scales

MMPI-3 scale development began with the Reconstructed (RC) Scales, which had been carried over without change from the MMPI-2 to the MMPI-2-RF. The authors had considered making some minor modifications during MMPI-2-RF development to enhance the distinctiveness of the Demoralization (RCd), Ideas of Persecution (RC6), Dysfunctional Negative Emotions (RC7), and Hypomanic Activation (RC9) scales, but they decided against revising the RC Scales so shortly after they had been introduced. The authors began the MMPI-3 scale development process by implementing these previously considered changes. Using the composite development sample, the authors then compared the internal consistencies of the revised and original RC Scales and the intercorrelations between them. The authors also compared the convergent and discriminant validities of the two sets of scale scores by using the college sample. Based on these analyses, they decided to implement most of the proposed item composition changes for these scales.

Next, using the composite development sample, the authors conducted item analyses (calculating item-corrected total score correlations and internal consistencies without the item) for the updated set of RC Scales and all the MMPI-2-RF Specific Problems (SP) Scales, seeking to identify items that could be removed without reducing the internal consistencies of the scales. Any item identified as a candidate for deletion was examined for content to make sure its loss would not limit the scope of the remaining item content of the scale. The authors retained items if their removal would have excessively narrowed scale content. This step produced a provisional set of revised RC and SP Scales for which, using the college sample, the authors calculated correlations with collateral criterion measures and compared the resulting validity estimates with those obtained with the MMPI-2-RF versions of these scales. They also compared internal consistency estimates for the revised and MMPI-2-RF versions of the scales using the composite development sample. For the most part, these comparisons indicated comparable psychometric functioning for the shortened and original versions of the RC and SP Scales. In a few instances, the authors decided to reinstate items designated for deletion to achieve this outcome.

Finally, using the composite development sample, the authors calculated correlations between the reduced RC and SP Scales and the 95 trial items with the goal of identifying possible additions to the scales. Items that were discriminantly correlated with a scale (i.e., sufficiently correlated with a given scale but not excessively so with the other scales in a set) were considered for possible addition to that scale. Such items were added if the item content was judged to expand the scope of the scale as intended.

NEW SP SCALES

The MMPI-3 authors next conducted item analyses using the composite development sample examining subsets of trial items that had been designated for possible new scale development. Items that reduced the internal consistency of a proposed scale were removed from further consideration. Scores on the provisionally designated new scales were then correlated with the remaining MMPI-2-RF-EX items with the goal of identifying candidates for addition to these scales. Items sufficiently and discriminantly correlated with the provisional scales were inspected for content and added if they were judged to be relevant to the targeted constructs.

Using the college sample, the authors then calculated correlations between the updated trial scales and collateral measures selected a priori for this task to examine the convergent and discriminant validities of the new scales. For most of the scales, they found evidence of adequate validity. However, a small number of provisional scales did not exhibit sufficient validity evidence and were eliminated from further consideration.

Higher-Order and Personality Psychopathology Five Scales

The starting point for updating the Higher-Order (H-O) Scales was the set of items remaining available for each scale after deleting items from the RC and SP Scales as just described. Using the composite development sample, the MMPI-3 authors conducted analyses intended to identify any items that reduced the internal consistency of the H-O Scale to which they were assigned. None of the remaining items were removed after these analyses. Next, the authors calculated correlations between trial items selected for inclusion on an RC or SP Scale and the H-O Scales. Any item found to correlate discriminantly with an H-O Scale was examined for content and added to that scale if it was judged to be relevant to that domain.

Allan Harkness and John McNulty, authors of the Personality Psychopathology Five (PSY-5) Scales, updated these measures for the MMPI-3. They were provided a list of items from the MMPI-2-RF PSY-5 Scales that were no longer available and the composite development sample, including the available trial items, to conduct analyses aimed at enhancing the scales. Harkness and McNulty updated the PSY-5 Scales for the MMPI-3 based on analyses similar to the ones just described for the H-O Scales.

As a critical final step, before finalizing item assignments for the MMPI-3 Substantive Scales, the authors examined the psychometric comparability of 73 new and 24 rewritten items selected for inclusion on the test, using the bilingual Spanish-English sample described later in this chapter in the section on normative data collection. This sample consisted of 57 individuals proficient in Spanish and English. Item response agreement analyses indicated adequate comparability for most of these items. Items that had less than 80% bilingual response agreement were examined further by calculating item total score correlations and internal consistency with and without the item in both languages. These analyses identified one of the new items as functioning less efficiently in Spanish, and it was not included on the MMPI-3.

Validity Scales

The nine MMPI-2-RF Validity Scales served as the starting point for developing validity indicators for the MMPI-3. Some of the items scored on the MMPI-2-RF versions of these scales were deleted from the MMPI-3 Substantive Scales (as just described). With some exceptions, these items were also deleted from the MMPI-3 Validity Scales. Items that were not deleted are described in this section as the *remaining items* of each validity indicator. Analyses were conducted to guide the addition of new MMPI-3 items to the Validity Scales and, for those composed of empirically selected items (i.e., items selected for inconsistent and infrequent responding), to ensure that all items met the defining selection criteria described next.

Inconsistent Responding Indicators

The method used to construct the MMPI-2-RF Variable Response Inconsistency (VRIN-r) and True Response Inconsistency (TRIN-r) scales (described in chapter 2) was also used to develop the MMPI-3 inconsistent responding indicators. Item pairs were selected based on statistical and semantic analyses of possible response combinations. A test taker can respond to a pair of items in one of four possible combinations: both True (TT), both False (FF), the first True and the second False (TF), or the first False and the second True (FT). The items that make up the inconsistency scales are composites made up of a specific combination of responses to a pair of MMPI-3 items. For example, for a TT composite, a True response to both items in a pair adds a point to the raw score of the scale on which that composite is scored. Each composite chosen for the MMPI-3 VRIN and TRIN scales had to meet five criteria:

1. The items in a composite had to be sufficiently correlated with each other (positively for VRIN, negatively for TRIN) in both the men and the women of the inconsistency scale development sample. Rather than require a specific minimum correlation, the authors sought item pairs that were correlated reliably in both genders and also met the remaining four criteria.
2. The observed frequency of a composite had to be lower than the frequency expected by chance if the two responses making up that composite were

independent. For example, if a TT composite occurs in 5% of the cases in a sample, and the expected (by chance) frequency of responding True to both items is 25%, the observed-to-expected ratio would be .20, indicating that this combination of responses is unlikely and therefore indicative of inconsistency.
3. The combination of responses in a composite had to be judged by the authors to be content inconsistent.
4. The correlation between a composite and a mini-scale made up of the two items scored in the direction they are keyed in the composite was low. Rather than requiring a specific maximal correlation, the authors sought item pairs that were correlated minimally in both genders and met the remaining criteria.
5. Neither item in a composite could belong to another composite of the same type (TT or FF). For example, if a given composite consisting of items A and B was scored TT, then neither item A nor item B could be scored TT in a composite with a different item. In this example, items A and B could potentially be included in a different FF composite. This criterion was adopted to ensure that an inconsistent True response or False response to a given item could contribute only once to the score on VRIN or TRIN.

The sample previously described for composite inconsistency scale development was used to generate (by gender) the statistics for criteria 1, 2, and 4 for all possible combinations of the 335 MMPI-3 items.

After the deletion of the 75 MMPI-2-RF items not carried over to the MMPI-3, the remaining composites of the MMPI-2-RF inconsistent responding indicators VRIN-r and TRIN-r were used as the starting point for developing the MMPI-3 inconsistent response indicators. MMPI-2-RF composites that satisfied the statistical criteria for both the men and the women of the inconsistency scale development sample were retained for the MMPI-3 versions of the scales and augmented by new composites that included some of the items newly added to the inventory. A total of 53 composites were selected for the MMPI-3 VRIN scale and 33 were selected for TRIN.

A new scale, Combined Response Inconsistency (CRIN), consisting of the 86 inconsistent response composites that make up VRIN and TRIN, was created to serve as a general index of inconsistent responding. This index, first introduced with the MMPI-A-RF (Archer et al., 2016) can help identify cases when a test taker intermittently engages in variable and fixed (False and True) inconsistent responding at levels that are insufficient to produce elevated scores on VRIN and TRIN (see chapter 8 for detailed guidance on CRIN score interpretation).

Overreporting Scales

Empirical data were used to guide updates of the three MMPI-2-RF infrequent responding indicators: Infrequent Responses (F-r), Infrequent Psychopathology Responses (Fp-r), and Infrequent Somatic Responses (Fs). The other MMPI-2-RF overreporting indicators—the Symptom Validity Scale (FBS-r) and the Response Bias Scale (RBS), which are not measures of infrequent responding—were not changed for the MMPI-3.

A dataset consisting of 1,127 men and 1,256 women tested for developing the norms for the English-language MMPI-3 was used to update the MMPI-2-RF Infrequent Responses (F-r) scale for the MMPI-3. The criterion used to select F-r items during MMPI-2-RF development was that no more than 10% of both the men and women of the MMPI-2-RF normative sample had responded to the item in the keyed direction. This criterion proved to be too stringent to identify enough general-population infrequent response indicators for the MMPI-3. A cutoff of no more than 15% of both the men and women of the new normative dataset was used instead. Endorsement frequencies (the proportion of individuals who responded to each item in the keyed direction) of F-r items that had not been deleted from the MMPI-2-RF Substantive Scales earlier in the MMPI-3 development were examined first. Items that did not satisfy the 15% criterion were deleted from the scale. The remaining MMPI-3 items were examined next. Any item that satisfied the selection criterion was considered a candidate for addition to the MMPI-3 Infrequent Responses (F) scale, provided the item did not also meet criteria for either of the remaining infrequency scales, in which case it was assigned to the scale for which it had the best content fit or the scale for which it best matched the infrequency criterion.

The composite mental health sample made up of 301 men and 455 women was used to update the MMPI-2-RF Infrequent Psychopathology Responses (Fp-r) scale for the MMPI-3. The criterion used to select Fp-r items for the MMPI-2-RF (and the MMPI-2 Fp items before that) was that no more than 20% of men and women with psychopathology had responded to the item in the keyed direction. To construct the MMPI-3 Infrequent Psychopathology Responses (Fp) scale, the composite mental health sample was used to identify Fp-r items that did not meet this 20% criterion and to replace them with MMPI-3 items that did.

The composite medical sample, consisting of 379 men and 512 women, was used to update the MMPI-2-RF Infrequent Somatic Responses (Fs) scale for the MMPI-3. The criterion used to select the original Fs items for the MMPI-2-RF was that no more than 25% of men and women assessed in the context of medical treatment had responded to the item in the keyed direction. To construct the MMPI-3 Infrequent Somatic Responses (Fs) scale, the composite medical sample was used to identify remaining MMPI-2-RF Fs items that did not meet this criterion and replace them with MMPI-3 items that did.

Underreporting Scales

The composite public safety sample, consisting of 2,355 men and 714 women who underwent preemployment evaluations as candidates for a police officer, correctional officer, firefighter/medic, or emergency dispatcher position, was used in the empirical analyses that guided updates of the MMPI-3 underreporting indicators, Uncommon Virtues and Adjustment Validity. Individuals assessed in the context of preemployment evaluations have an incentive to underreport, unlike those tested for clinical assessment or research purposes. A similar sample was used for updating the MMPI-2-RF underreporting indicators, producing the L-r and K-r scales that were found to be effective underreporting indicators in a range of settings.

To construct the MMPI-3 Uncommon Virtues (L) scale, the MMPI-2-RF Uncommon Virtues (L-r) items were examined first. Items answered in the keyed direction by more than 40% of either the men or women of the composite public safety sample were deleted from the scale because they are not uncommon. This is analogous to using clinical samples to identify infrequent responding. Next, correlations were calculated between a provisional scale made up of the remaining L-r items and the new MMPI-3 items not yet scored on the Uncommon Virtues scale. Items judged to correlate sufficiently with the scale for both the men and women of the composite public safety sample were added to the scale if they were also judged to have content consistent with the reporting of uncommon virtues.

Next, the remaining MMPI-2-RF Adjustment Validity (K-r) items were examined. One item that best met the criteria outlined for the MMPI-3 Uncommon Virtues (L) scale was deleted. Next, correlations were calculated between a provisional scale made up of the remaining K-r items and the new MMPI-3 items not yet scored on the Adjustment Validity scale. Items judged to correlate sufficiently with the scale for both the men and women of the composite public safety sample were added to the scale if they were judged to have content consistent with the reporting of good psychological adjustment.

THE MMPI-3 SCALES

Table 3.1 lists the 52 MMPI-3 scales that resulted from the development process just described. The 10 Validity Scales include the new Combined Response Inconsistency (CRIN) scale, updated versions of VRIN, TRIN, F, Fp, Fs, L, and K, and the FBS and RBS scales, both of which have the same item composition as the MMPI-2-RF versions.

Updated versions of the H-O Scales assess the three broad domains of dysfunction—Emotional/Internalizing, Thought, and Behavioral/Externalizing—described in chapters 2 and 5. The eight RC Scales—Demoralization (RCd),

TABLE 3.1. The MMPI-3 Scales

Validity Scales

CRIN	Combined Response Inconsistency – Combination of random and fixed inconsistent responding
VRIN	Variable Response Inconsistency – Random responding
TRIN	True Response Inconsistency – Fixed responding
F	Infrequent Responses – Responses infrequent in the general population
Fp	Infrequent Psychopathology Responses – Responses infrequent in psychiatric populations
Fs	Infrequent Somatic Responses – Somatic complaints infrequent in medical patient populations
FBS	Symptom Validity Scale – Noncredible somatic and cognitive complaints
RBS	Response Bias Scale – Exaggerated memory complaints
L	Uncommon Virtues – Rarely claimed moral attributes or activities
K	Adjustment Validity – Claims of uncommonly high level of psychological adjustment

Higher-Order (H-O) Scales

EID	Emotional/Internalizing Dysfunction – Problems associated with mood and affect
THD	Thought Dysfunction – Problems associated with disordered thinking
BXD	Behavioral/Externalizing Dysfunction – Problems associated with undercontrolled behavior

Restructured Clinical (RC) Scales

RCd	Demoralization – General unhappiness and dissatisfaction
RC1	Somatic Complaints – Diffuse physical health complaints
RC2	Low Positive Emotions – Lack of positive emotional responsiveness
RC4	Antisocial Behavior – Rule breaking and irresponsible behavior
RC6	Ideas of Persecution – Self-referential beliefs that others pose a threat
RC7	Dysfunctional Negative Emotions – Maladaptive anxiety, anger, irritability
RC8	Aberrant Experiences – Unusual perceptions or thoughts associated with thought dysfunction
RC9	Hypomanic Activation – Overactivation, aggression, impulsivity, and grandiosity

Specific Problems (SP) Scales

SOMATIC/COGNITIVE SCALES

MLS	Malaise – Overall sense of physical debilitation, poor health
NUC	Neurological Complaints – Dizziness, weakness, paralysis, loss of balance, etc.
EAT	Eating Concerns – Problematic eating behaviors
COG	Cognitive Complaints – Memory problems, difficulties concentrating

INTERNALIZING SCALES

SUI	Suicidal/Death Ideation – Direct reports of suicidal ideation and recent attempts
HLP	Helplessness/Hopelessness – Belief that goals cannot be reached or problems cannot be solved
SFD	Self-Doubt – Lack of self-confidence, feelings of uselessness
NFC	Inefficacy – Belief that one is indecisive and inefficacious
STR	Stress – Problems involving stress and nervousness
WRY	Worry – Excessive worry and preoccupation
CMP	Compulsivity – Engaging in compulsive behaviors
ARX	Anxiety-Related Experiences – Multiple anxiety-related experiences such as catastrophizing, panic, dread, and intrusive ideation

TABLE 3.1, continued

ANP	Anger Proneness – Becoming easily angered, impatient with others
BRF	Behavior-Restricting Fears – Fears that significantly inhibit normal behavior

EXTERNALIZING SCALES

FML	Family Problems – Conflictual family relationships
JCP	Juvenile Conduct Problems – Difficulties at school and at home, stealing
SUB	Substance Abuse – Current and past misuse of alcohol and drugs
IMP	Impulsivity – Poor impulse control and nonplanful behavior
ACT	Activation – Heightened excitation and energy level
AGG	Aggression – Physically aggressive, violent behavior
CYN	Cynicism – Non-self-referential beliefs that others are bad and not to be trusted

INTERPERSONAL SCALES

SFI	Self-Importance – Beliefs related to having special talents and abilities
DOM	Dominance – Being domineering in relationships with others
DSF	Disaffiliativeness – Disliking people and being around them
SAV	Social Avoidance – Avoiding and not enjoying social events
SHY	Shyness – Feeling uncomfortable and anxious in the presence of others

Personality Psychopathology Five Scales

AGGR	Aggressiveness – Instrumental, goal-directed aggression
PSYC	Psychoticism – Disconnection from reality
DISC	Disconstraint – Undercontrolled behavior
NEGE	Negative Emotionality/Neuroticism – Anxiety, insecurity, worry, and fear
INTR	Introversion/Low Positive Emotionality – Social disengagement and anhedonia

Somatic Complaints (RC1), Low Positive Emotions (RC2), Antisocial Behavior (RC4), Ideas of Persecution (RC6), Dysfunctional Negative Emotions (RC7), Aberrant Experiences (RC8), and Hypomanic Activation (RC9)—are updated versions of their MMPI-2-RF counterparts. The Cynicism scale (RC3 on the MMPI-2-RF) has been moved to the Externalizing SP Scales for reasons explained later.

The 26 MMPI-3 SP Scales include four Somatic/Cognitive Scales. Malaise (MLS) and Cognitive Complaints (COG) are updated for the MMPI-3, whereas Neurological Complaints (NUC) is unchanged. A new scale, Eating Concerns (EAT), is included in this group because of its conceptual association with somatic symptom reporting. Two MMPI-2-RF scales in this group—Gastrointestinal Complaints (GIC) and Head Pain Complaints (HPC)—did not retain enough items to create revised scales, although some of their remaining items are scored on the Somatic Complaints (RC1) scale.

The 10 MMPI-3 Internalizing SP Scales include updated versions of Suicidal/Death Ideation (SUI), Helplessness/Hopelessness (HLP), Self-Doubt (SFD), Inefficacy (NFC), Anger Proneness (ANP), and Behavior-Restricting Fears (BRF). The

MMPI-2-RF Anxiety (AXY) scale was substantially expanded for the MMPI-3 and is now labeled Anxiety-Related Experiences (ARX). The MMPI-2-RF Stress/Worry (STW) scale was divided into two measures: Stress (STR) and Worry (WRY). A new scale, Compulsivity (CMP), has been added to this group. Owing to limited research supporting its use and the need to accommodate new items, the MMPI-2-RF Multiple Specific Fears (MSF) scale was not carried over to the MMPI-3.

The seven MMPI-3 Externalizing SP Scales include updated versions of Juvenile Conduct Problems (JCP), Substance Abuse (SUB), and Aggression (AGG). The Activation (ACT) scale is unchanged. An updated version of the MMPI-2-RF Family Problems (FML) scale has been moved from the Interpersonal group to the Externalizing group, reflecting its empirical and conceptual associations with the Antisocial Behavior (RC4) scale. An updated version of the MMPI-2-RF Cynicism (RC3) scale has also been moved to the MMPI-3 Externalizing SP Scales, reflecting its empirical associations with an externalizing psychopathology model described and supported by empirical analyses in Appendix B of the *MMPI-3 Technical Manual*. Briefly, this model reflects research indicating that externalizing psychopathology is a higher-order construct that bifurcates into two more specific domains: antagonistic-externalizing and disinhibited-externalizing (see Krueger et al., 2021, for a review). The MMPI-3 externalizing dysfunction domain can conceptually be arranged to measure both disinhibited and antagonistic forms of externalizing. The H-O Scale BXD clearly reflects an externalizing superfactor akin to extant psychopathology work. RC4, RC9, and DISC (discussed later) reflect broader measures of disinhibition, whereas JCP, SUB, and the new IMP scale provide for more specific measurement of such psychopathology components. On the other hand, AGGR (discussed later) is a broader marker of interpersonal antagonism, with AGG and CYN capturing, more specifically, components of callousness, deceitfulness, suspiciousness, and interpersonal aggression/hostility.

The five MMPI-3 Interpersonal SP Scales include updated versions of Disaffiliativeness (DSF) and Social Avoidance (SAV). The Shyness (SHY) scale is unchanged on the MMPI-3. The MMPI-2-RF Interpersonal Passivity (IPP) scale was also updated, including a reversal of its scoring key and a new label—Dominance (DOM). This change was supported by the model (just discussed) reported in Appendix B of the *MMPI-3 Technical Manual,* which led to inclusion of the Self-Importance (SFI) scale in this set. The MMPI-3 Interpersonal Scales capture more specific aspects of interpersonal antagonism but to a far less pervasive degree than the measures included among the Externalizing Scales. SFI is specifically linked to grandiosity and narcissism but to no other antagonistic features; DOM captures domineering behavior; and DSF has been linked to callousness and lack of emotional attachment to others in the context of psychopathic personality traits (Anderson et al., 2020; Sellbom, Ben-Porath et al., 2012).

CYN (formerly RC3 on the MMPI-2-RF) was previously considered an interpersonal scale, because cynicism reflects an attitudinal worldview with significant interpersonal implications. However, conceptually, the content of this scale very much reflects antagonistic ideation, and was, therefore, included among the Externalizing Scales as just described.

The updated versions of the PSY-5 Scales based on the MMPI-3 item pool assess the same dimensional model of personality-disorder–related psychopathology as did the MMPI-2 and MMPI-2-RF versions of these measures. As discussed in chapter 2 and elaborated in chapter 5, these scales provide a link to current dimensional models of personality psychopathology.

Table 2–3 of the *MMPI-3 Technical Manual* reports, for each of the MMPI-3 scales, the number of items on the MMPI-2-RF scale that was the starting point for its development (scales newly developed for the MMPI-3 are marked by a "–"), the number of items on the MMPI-3 version of the scale, and the number of items common to both versions of the scale (for this purpose, rewritten items count as common). Table 2–4 of the *Technical Manual* lists, for each MMPI-3 scale, the total number of items on that scale, the number of original MMPI items that remain unaltered, the number of original MMPI items rewritten for the MMPI-2, the number of items written for the MMPI-2, the number of original MMPI items rewritten for the MMPI-3, the number of MMPI-2 items rewritten for the MMPI-3, and the number of items new to the MMPI-3.

Overall, the 335-item MMPI-3 comprises 220 original MMPI items (48 of which were rewritten for the MMPI-2 or MMPI-3), 43 items written for the MMPI-2 (5 of which were rewritten for the MMPI-3), and 72 new items written for the MMPI-3. Table 2–4 of the *Technical Manual* also shows that most MMPI-3 scales contain some new items. The four scales developed specifically for the MMPI-3—Eating Concerns (EAT; 5/5 new items), Compulsivity (CMP; 8/8), Impulsivity (IMP; 5/6), and Self-Importance (SFI; 7/10)—consist almost entirely of new items. The following scales include at least 25% new items: Behavioral Externalizing Dysfunction (BXD; 6/24 new items), Ideas of Persecution (RC6; 5/14), Hypomanic Activation (RC9; 4/15), Cognitive Complaints (COG; 3/11), Suicidal Death Ideation (SUI; 3/7), Helplessness/Hopelessness (HLP; 3/7), Self-Doubt (SFD; 3/7), Anxiety-Related Experiences (ARX; 10/15), Stress (STR; 3/6), Worry (WRY; 3/7), Anger Proneness (ANP; 4/12), and Disaffiliativeness (DSF; 4/7).

THE MMPI-3 NORMS

Establishing a new nationally representative normative sample was among the primary goals for developing the MMPI-3. As discussed in chapter 2, standard scores for the MMPI-2-RF were derived from the MMPI-2 normative sample, which was collected in the mid-1980s. Demographic and social changes in the U.S. population during the ensuing 35 years highlighted the need for new norms. During this period, the population became substantially more diverse, and the social milieu was markedly altered with the advent of the internet, particularly social media. Inclusion of 72 new items on the MMPI-3 and rewording of 24 existing items also necessitated new norms. Another important goal for the MMPI-3 normative data collection was to collect, for the first time ever, a normative sample for standardizing scores on the U.S. Spanish-language version of the test.

The following sections describe the procedures used to collect normative data for the MMPI-3 and to assemble the English- and Spanish-language normative samples. A discussion of demographic and other characteristics of the MMPI-3 normative samples concludes this chapter.

Data Collection

To collect normative data for the MMPI-3, the publisher retained the services of EurekaFacts, a social science research firm with experience in national data collection projects and expertise in recruiting participants from difficult-to-reach populations, including individuals of Hispanic origins. This capability was deemed particularly important for two reasons. First, to reflect current U.S. demographics, there was a need to substantially increase the proportion of Hispanic individuals in the English-language normative sample. In addition, part of the plan for the MMPI-3 was to collect separate, Spanish-language norms.

Targets for the English-language normative sample were based on U.S. Census Bureau population proportion projections for race/ethnicity and age in the 2020 census (U.S. Census Bureau, 2017). This source did not include 2020 projections for education. Instead, 2020 education distribution targets relied on the reported 2017 education distributions with a correction to adjust these estimates for the projected 2020 age proportions. Proportional targets for race, age, and education are reported respectively in the Tables 2–5, 2–6, and 2–7 of the *MMPI-3 Technical Manual*.

The recruitment targets were provided to EurekaFacts, who devised a plan to collect a sample of 2,300 adults (ages 18 and older), matching these distributions throughout the continental United States. The plan also called for recruiting 300 of these individuals to return for a second session to obtain test–retest data for calculating MMPI-3 score reliability estimates. The research plan included recruiting 625 monolingual, Spanish-speaking adults to complete the Spanish-language MMPI-2-RF-EX to establish Spanish-language norms and 65 bilingual Spanish/English-speaking adults for the purpose of examining the psychometric comparability of any new items considered for inclusion on the MMPI-3. For the bilingual sample, EurekaFacts recruited individuals who spoke Spanish at home while growing up and who were currently attending a postsecondary institution or employed in a predominantly English-speaking environment.

Normative data for the MMPI-3 were collected between September 2017 and December 2018 at nine sites: Chicago, Illinois; Dallas, Texas; New York, New York; Miami, Florida; Minneapolis, Minnesota; San Diego, California; Seattle, Washington; Washington, DC; and a rural region of West Virginia. The last site was included to ensure sufficient representation for individuals living in more rural areas, though such data were also obtained at the other data collection sites.

EurekaFacts staff used three primary methods to recruit potential participants: social media and general advertisement, community-organization–based outreach, and direct recruitment from existing databases. Social media and general advertisement methods employed placement of ads in targeted venues, including specific locations on Facebook and Google, and use of classified advertisements or more general announcements in online and print versions of newspapers. As anticipated, these methods were most successful in recruiting individuals with higher education levels.

Community-organization–based outreach included using databases of individuals, households, businesses and community organizations, independent clubs, and activity-centered groups; posting information on local community sites; contacting community organizations and leaders via email, phone calls, and in-person meetings; and email and phone call efforts to region-specific recruitment centers contracted with EurekaFacts. These methods were most successful in recruiting older adults and Hispanic populations.

Direct recruitment efforts included email and phone calls to individuals listed in databases of people interested in participating in research studies; email and phone calls to lists of individuals obtained from highly reputable commercial vendors that provide direct marketing outreach services; and snowballing referrals from personal and business networks at the time of responding to general appeals or after completing recruitment screening interviews.

EurekaFacts implemented several strategies aimed at maximizing the recruitment of hard-to-reach participants. For identification of ethnic minority participants, the company relied on its ties with community-based organizations throughout the United States, including religious organizations and charities. To effectively reach populations that speak Spanish as their primary language, EurekaFacts worked with organizations that provide adult English-as-a-second-language services. Senior centers were the focus of efforts to recruit older individuals. To recruit individuals without high school diplomas, the firm relied on community-based organizations with a focus on those that assist adults in realizing educational milestones, such as General Educational Development (GED) preparatory classes, Adult Basic Education classes, and workforce development services.

Individuals who expressed an interest in participating in the study were screened by telephone to ensure they met the demographic targets discussed earlier. Those who did were invited to prearranged testing sites on specific dates.

EurekaFacts personnel trained by the MMPI-3 development team to administer the MMPI-2-RF-EX following standard procedures collected the data at these sites, typically hotel conference rooms or community facilities (e.g., senior centers). Nearly all participants (98%) completed the MMPI-2-RF-EX on computer tablets. Individuals who were reluctant to use the tablets or who had trouble doing so were tested with paper and pencil. The comparability of MMPI test results obtained by paper and pencil versus computer (cf., Finger & Ones, 1999) and computer laptop versus tablet (Menton et al., 2019) is well established. Collection of data by digital means provided the development team immediate access to the normative data as they were being collected. Prior to data collection and in accordance with procedures approved by Kent State University's Institutional Review Board, participants signed consent forms. All were paid $50 per session regardless of whether they completed the testing.

Assembling the Normative Samples

THE ENGLISH-LANGUAGE NORMATIVE SAMPLE

To achieve the recruitment targets, a total of 2,383 individuals were tested for possible inclusion in the English-language MMPI-3 normative sample. Of these, 2,008 produced valid protocols based on standard MMPI-2-RF exclusion criteria (CNS > 17, VRIN-r and/or TRIN-r > 79T, F-r = 120, or Fp-r > 99). Because a disproportionate number of individuals with lower education levels produced invalid protocols, it was necessary to remove from the final normative sample some individuals with higher education levels to achieve the demographic distribution targets for the sample. To create the final MMPI-3 English-language normative sample for derivation of nongendered norms (which requires an equal number of men and women), a total of 1,620 of the valid protocols (810 men and 810 women) were selected randomly from the larger pool of valid protocols to the approximate 2020 U.S. Census Bureau population proportion estimates for race/ethnicity, age, and education listed in Tables 2–5 through 2–7 of the *MMPI-3 Technical Manual*.

THE SPANISH-LANGUAGE NORMATIVE SAMPLE

Normative data for the Spanish-language MMPI-3 sample were collected at four sites: Dallas, Texas; Miami, Florida; San Diego, California; and Washington, DC. EurekaFacts staff used the same methods described earlier for collecting the English-language normative data to recruit participants for the Spanish-language data collection. A total of 655 Spanish-language MMPI-2-RF-EX protocols (307 men and 348 women) were collected for developing the Spanish-language norms. Individuals with 20 or more unscorable responses were excluded from further analyses. For the remaining 635 individuals, provisional T scores were created for the VRIN, TRIN, F, and Fp scales. Those with T scores

80 or greater on VRIN or TRIN, 90 or greater on F, or 80 or greater on Fp were excluded from further analyses. This left 275 men and 310 women with valid MMPI-3 protocols. To create the final MMPI-3 Spanish-language normative sample for derivation of nongendered norms (which requires an equal number of men and women), 275 of the 310 women with valid MMPI-3 protocols were selected randomly, resulting in a final normative sample 550 individuals.

Composition of the Normative Samples

THE ENGLISH-LANGUAGE NORMATIVE SAMPLE

Race, age, and education distributions of the 810 men and 810 women that make up the MMPI-3 English-language normative sample are reported in Tables 2–5 through 2–7 of the *MMPI-3 Technical Manual*. These tables also include the 2020 census estimates that served as the recruitment targets and the MMPI-2-RF normative sample distributions, which are the same as the MMPI-2 normative sample distributions. These data show that the English-language normative sample matches well the 2020 census projections for race/ethnicity. A slight underrepresentation of the adult Hispanic population in the MMPI-3 English-language normative sample reflects the fact that a sizable proportion of individuals of this origin in the United States are not sufficiently bilingual to be tested in English. Indeed, the proportion of individuals of Hispanic origin in the MMPI-3 normative sample overrepresents the portion of this population who could be tested in English at the time the norms were developed. The sample is likely to sufficiently represent English-speaking test takers of Hispanic origin as the relative proportion of this population in the United States continues to grow. Similarly, the slight underrepresentation of the White population is consistent with future trends. By contrast, the MMPI-2/MMPI-2-RF normative sample substantially overrepresented White people and substantially underrepresented individuals of Hispanic and Asian origins.

Data reported in Table 2–6 of the *MMPI-3 Technical Manual* indicate that the MMPI-3 English-language normative sample slightly underrepresents individuals ages 60–79 years old and particularly underrepresents those who are 80 years old and older. The latter proved challenging to recruit despite the significant efforts described earlier; however, individuals who are 80 years and older are less likely to be administered the MMPI-3.

Findings in Table 2–7 of the *MMPI-3 Technical Manual* show a slight underrepresentation in the MMPI-3 normative sample of those with less than a high school education and a slight overrepresentation of individuals with college or graduate education. These proportions, however, are substantial improvements over the MMPI-2/MMPI-2-RF normative sample, which underrepresented lower education levels and overrepresented higher ones to a much greater extent. Here as well, concerted outreach efforts were made to obtain data from individuals with less than a high school education, but those efforts were limited by the higher proportion of invalid protocols generated by this subgroup. Owing to literacy constraints, individuals with less than a high school education are also generally underrepresented among those tested with the MMPI instruments.

The MMPI-2-RF-EX material that was used to collect the MMPI-3 normative sample database included additional biographical questions. Information gleaned from these questions is reported and discussed in Appendix C of the *MMPI-3 Technical Manual*.

THE SPANISH-LANGUAGE NORMATIVE SAMPLE

Tables 2–1 through 2–4 of the *MMPI-3 Manual Supplement for the U.S. Spanish Translation* (henceforth the manual supplement) present demographic characteristics of the MMPI-3 Spanish-language normative sample. As reported in Table 2–1, 88.2% of the normative sample participants self-identified their primary ethnicity as Hispanic, with 9.1% self-identifying as being of mixed ethnicity and 2.7% responding "Other" to this item. Table 2–2 of the manual supplement reports participants' self-reported ancestral origins. Wording of this item in the biographical questionnaire proved to be confusing, leading nearly one-third of participants to leave it unanswered and resulting in 180 normative sample members whose ancestral origin is unknown. Although the question was not asked because all normative sample members were fluent Spanish speakers (as screened by EurekaFacts and indicated by their ability to produce a valid Spanish-language MMPI-3 protocol), it is likely that the handful of individuals who reported non-Hispanic ethnicity or ancestral origin are of Spanish-European origins.

Table 2–3 of the manual supplement reports age distributions for the MMPI-3 Spanish-language normative sample. As shown in this table, more sample members were in the range of 30–59 years old, with approximately a quarter of the sample falling in the range of 18–29 years old. Only 12.4% of the normative sample members were in the range of 60–79 years old and none were older. As reported earlier, EurekaFacts made considerable efforts to recruit older individuals, a historically hard-to-reach population, particularly so in the case of Spanish speakers in the United States. However, these efforts were unsuccessful. As reported earlier, efforts to recruit older adults for the English-language normative sample, although more successful than with older Spanish-speaking adults, also came up short of the developers' goals. However, older adults are also less likely to be tested with the MMPI. Consequently, underrepresentation of this subpopulation in the MMPI-3 normative samples likely reflects the age range of individuals assessed with the inventory. Nevertheless, particularly as the population continues to age, additional efforts will be needed to collect and study MMPI-3 data for older adults in both languages.

Table 2–4 of the manual supplement presents education levels for the Spanish-language sample. As shown in this table, efforts to recruit individuals with lower education levels were successful (22.7% of the sample), particularly in comparison with the English-language normative sample (only 8.6%, as reported in the MMPI-3 *Manual for Administration, Scoring, and Interpretation*).

Comparison of the MMPI-2-RF and MMPI-3 Norms

Figures 3.1 through 3.5 report a series of comparisons used to gauge the extent to which the MMPI-3 norms differ from the MMPI-2-RF norms. These figures depict the mean scores of the men and women of the MMPI-3 normative sample on the MMPI-2-RF scales, scored with the MMPI-2-RF norms. Had members of the MMPI-3 normative sample produced means and standard deviations similar to those of the MMPI-2-RF normative sample, the mean MMPI-3 T scores depicted in these figures would be 50 with standard deviations of 10. The extent to which the MMPI-3 means and standard deviations deviate from these values represents differences in score levels and variability between the two normative samples. These differences, in turn, are reflected in the T scores derived from the MMPI-3 norms and will be discussed next.

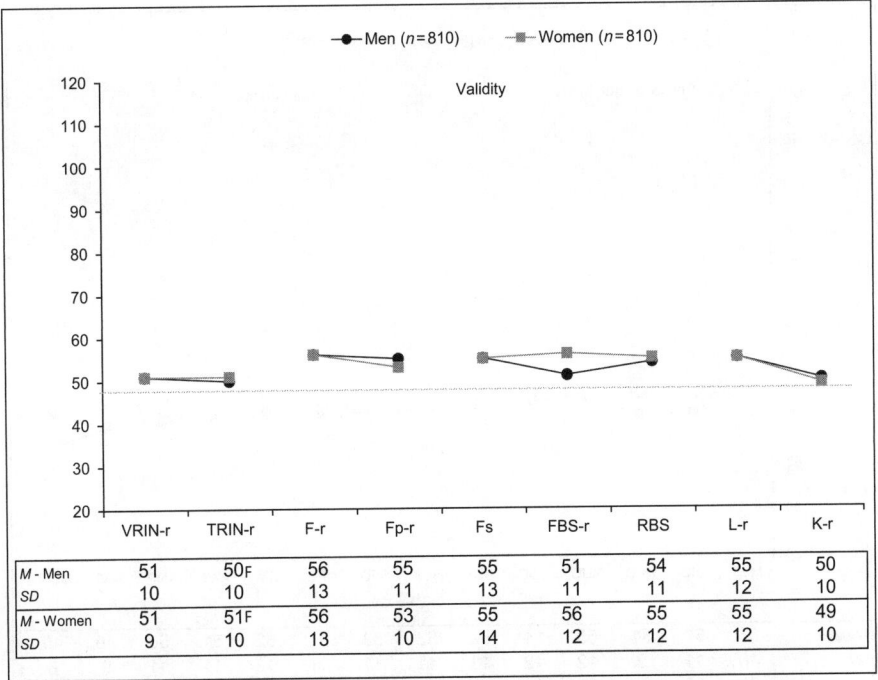

	VRIN-r	TRIN-r	F-r	Fp-r	Fs	FBS-r	RBS	L-r	K-r
M - Men	51	50F	56	55	55	51	54	55	50
SD	10	10	13	11	13	11	11	12	10
M - Women	51	51F	56	53	55	56	55	55	49
SD	9	10	13	10	14	12	12	12	10

FIGURE 3.1. MMPI-2-RF Scores of MMPI-3 Normative Sample Men and Women—Validity Scales

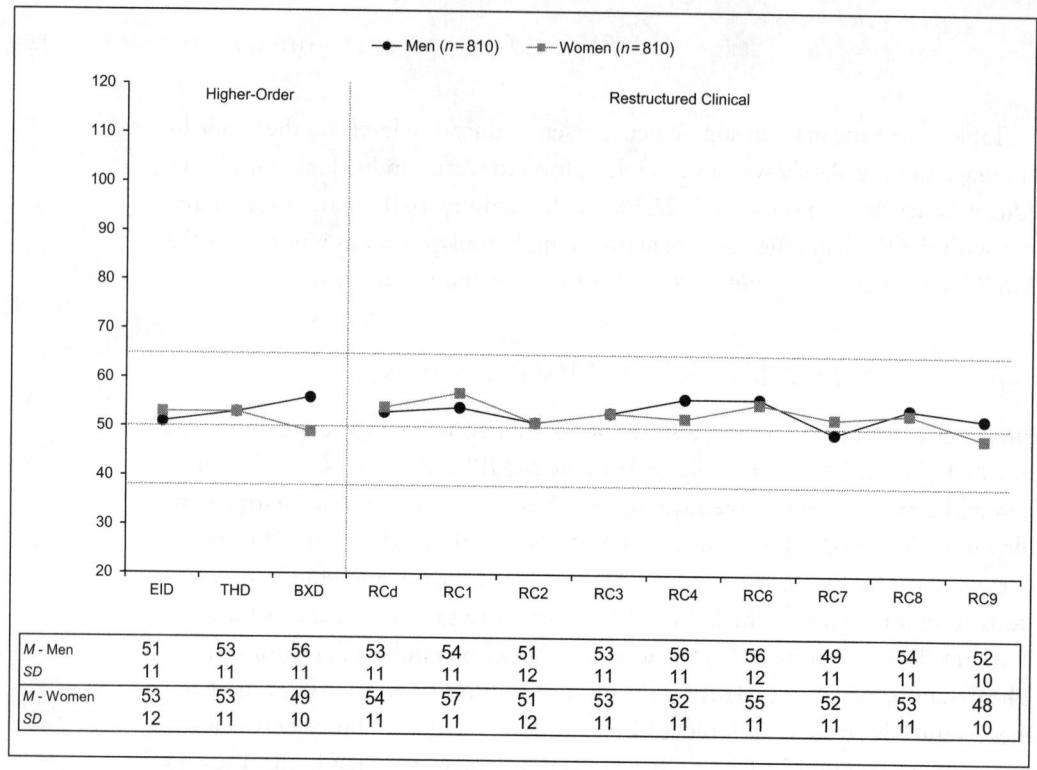

FIGURE 3.2. MMPI-2-RF Scores of MMPI-3 Normative Sample Men and Women—Higher-Order and Restructured Clinical Scales

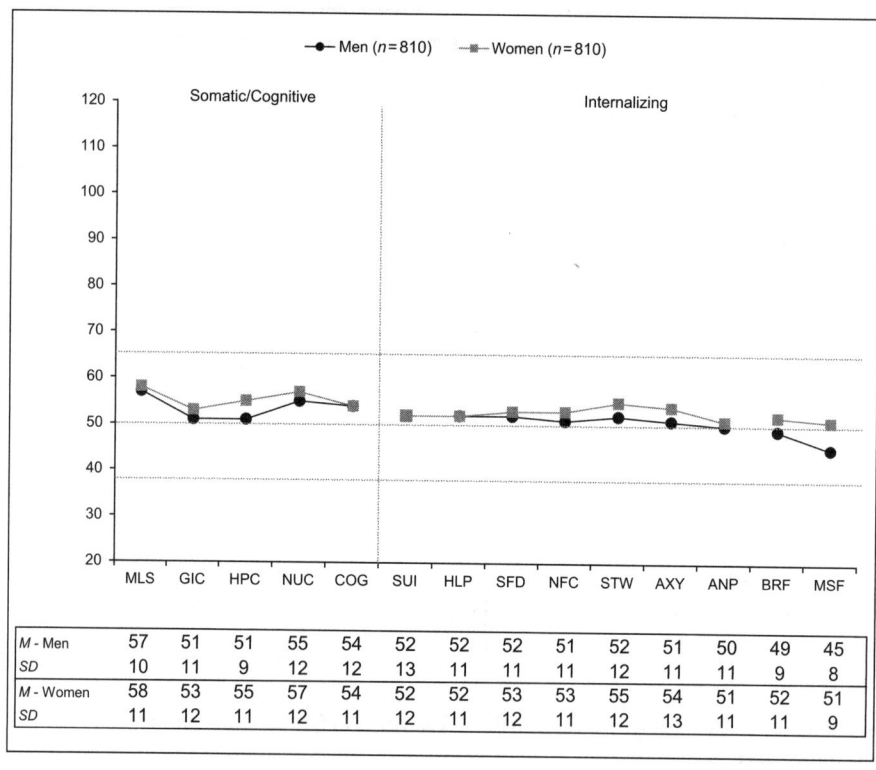

FIGURE 3.3. MMPI-2-RF Scores of MMPI-3 Normative Sample Men and Women—Somatic/Cognitive and Internalizing Scales

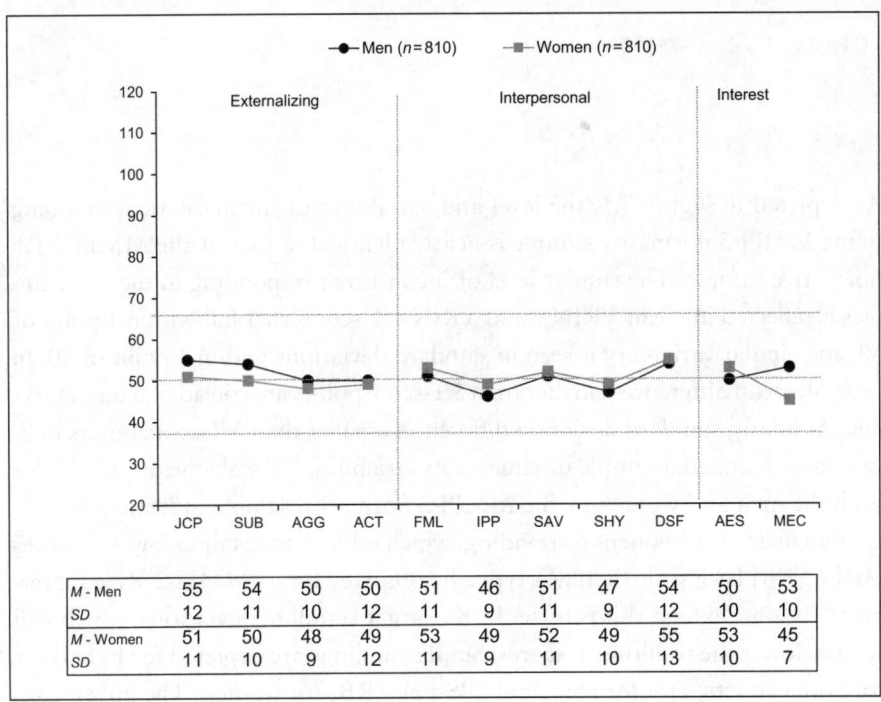

FIGURE 3.4. MMPI-2-RF Scores of MMPI-3 Normative Sample Men and Women—Externalizing, Interpersonal, and Interest Scales

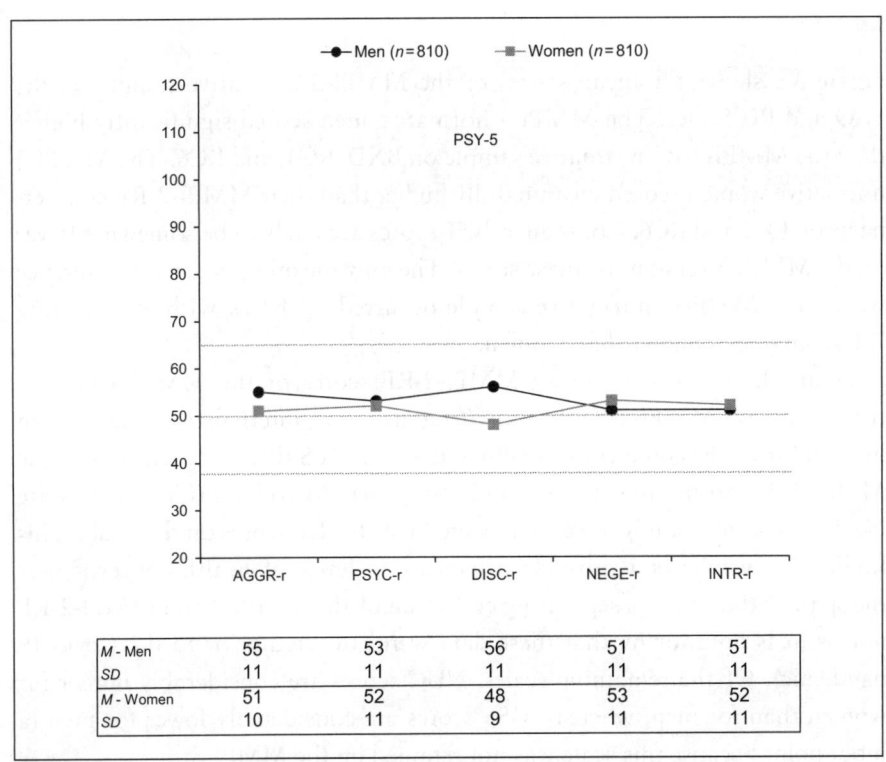

FIGURE 3.5. MMPI-2-RF Scores of MMPI-3 Normative Sample Men and Women—Personality Psychopathology Five Scales

Validity Scales

As depicted in Figure 3.1, the level and variability of inconsistent responding in the MMPI-3 normative sample is nearly identical to that of the MMPI-2-RF normative sample. The similar level of inconsistent responding in the two samples is reflected in mean VRIN-r and TRIN-r T scores that fall within 1 point of 50, and similar variability is seen in standard deviations within 1 point of 10. In general, mean differences smaller than 5 T-score points are considered unremarkable. Similarly, standard deviation differences smaller than 3 T-score points indicate inconsequential sample differences in variability. F-r scale means of 56T for both the men and women of the MMPI-3 normative sample indicate a significant increase in infrequent responding, which is likely to result in lower T scores on the MMPI-3 F scale than was typically observed for its MMPI-2-RF counterpart. To some extent, this is offset by the larger standard deviations, which will tend to lower the resulting T scores. Similar findings are depicted for Fs and L-r for both genders, Fp-r for men, and FBS-r and RBS for women. The only meaningful gender difference depicted in Figure 3.1 is on FBS-r at a level comparable to the difference between men and women in the MMPI-2-RF normative sample.

Substantive Scales

Figure 3.2 shows the mean scores of the MMPI-3 normative sample on the H-O and RC Scales. The MMPI-3 normative men scored significantly higher than the MMPI-2-RF normative sample on BXD, RC4, and RC6. The MMPI-3 normative women scored meaningfully higher than their MMPI-2-RF counterparts on RC1 and RC6. Consequently, T scores are likely to be somewhat lower on the MMPI-3 versions of these scales. The only meaningful gender difference within the MMPI-3 normative sample occurred on BXD, with men scoring 7 T-score points higher than women.

Figure 3.3 depicts the mean MMPI-2-RF scores of the MMPI-3 normative sample on MMPI-2-RF Somatic/Cognitive and Internalizing Scales. Both men and women scored considerably higher on MLS than did members of the MMPI-2-RF normative samples, indicating that MMPI-3 MLS T scores are likely to be considerably lower than were MMPI-2-RF scores on this scale. This finding likely reflects a substantial increase in levels of health concerns over the span of the 35 years separating collection of the MMPI-3 and MMPI-2-RF norms (it is noteworthy that these data were collected prior to the Covid-19 pandemic). Of the remaining scales, NUC scores are considerably higher for women than for men, whereas MSF scores are considerably lower for men (a moot point because this scale was not retained on the MMPI-3).

Shown in Figure 3.4, the MMPI-3 normative sample women scored considerably higher than their MMPI-2-RF counterparts on DSF, but otherwise there is considerable stability of scores on the Externalizing and Interpersonal Scales. Meaningful gender differences were observed only on one of the two Interest Scales, which were not carried over to the MMPI-3. Figure 3.5 depicts meaningfully higher scores for the MMPI-3 normative men on AGGR and DISC, with a substantial gender difference on the latter, a finding consistent with most other gender comparisons on this scale.

Overall, these findings point to relative stability in means and variability on most of the domains assessed by the MMPI-3. Nevertheless, meaningful normative shifts are reflected in the T scores of scales carried over from the MMPI-2-RF, reflecting a clear need to update the test norms.

Comparison of the MMPI-3 English- and Spanish-Language Norms

Figures 3.6 through 3.10 report mean MMPI-3 English-language T scores for the MMPI-3 Spanish-language normative sample. These data facilitate a direct comparison of the two sets of norms. Had the Spanish-language normative sample members produced scores identical to those of the English-language cohort, the resulting T score means would be 50, with standard deviations equaling 10. The extent to which the descriptive findings in Figures 3.6 through 3.10 deviate from these values represents central tendency and dispersion differences between the samples.

As seen in Figures 3.6 through 3.10, for both men and women the vast majority of Spanish-language sample means (46 of the 52) fall within 5 T-score points of the English-language means, a difference typically considered not interpretatively meaningful. However, scores on F, L, and BRF are about 10 T-score points higher for the Spanish-language sample for both men and women. To some extent, standard deviations larger than 10 associated with these means counter the impact of the mean score differences on the resulting T scores, leaving the resulting Spanish-language T-score conversions more in line with the English-language conversions. On MLS, both the Spanish-language men and women scored approximately 7 T-score points lower than their English-language counterparts, which results in higher Spanish-language T-score values on this scale. The Spanish-language women also scored considerably lower than their English-language counterparts on three externalizing scales—BXD, RC4, and DISC—but with smaller standard deviations, resulting in Spanish-language T-score values for these scales being considerably higher than those derived from the English-language normative sample.

	CRIN	VRIN	TRIN	F	Fp	Fs	FBS	RBS	L	K
M - Men	55	52	51[F]	51	57	51	50	54	61	53
SD	13	12	16	12	16	10	9	9	12	10
M - Women	53	52	52[F]	50	55	52	51	55	60	53
SD	12	12	14	12	15	10	9	10	12	10

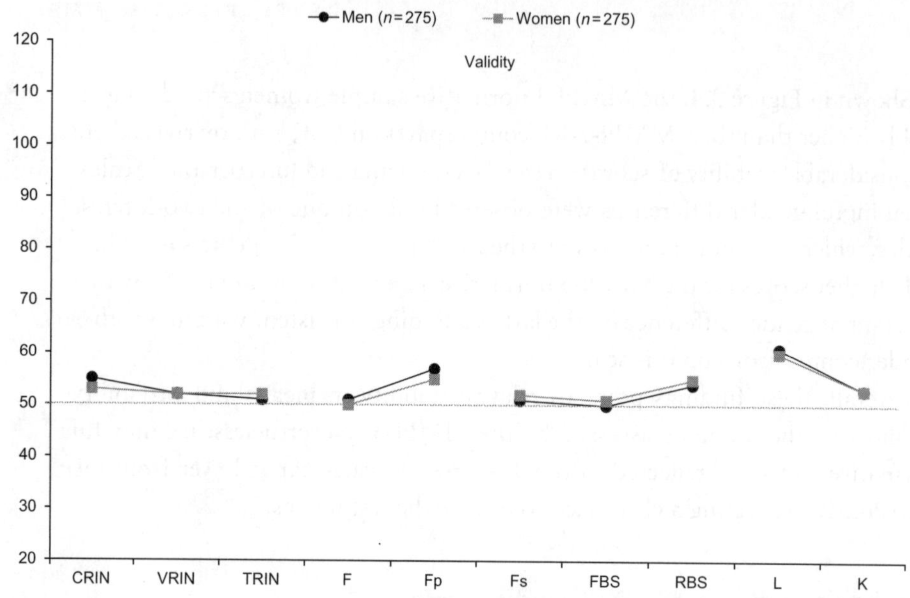

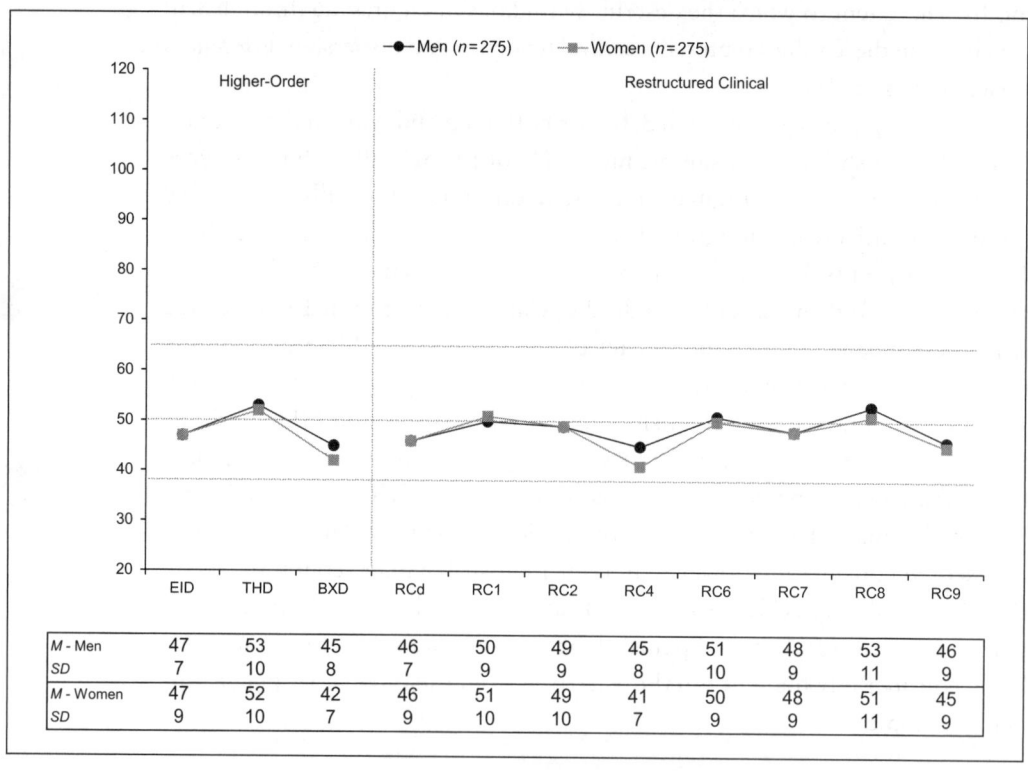

FIGURE 3.6. Spanish-Language MMPI-3 Normative Sample Scored Using English-Language MMPI-3 Norms—Validity Scales

	EID	THD	BXD	RCd	RC1	RC2	RC4	RC6	RC7	RC8	RC9
M - Men	47	53	45	46	50	49	45	51	48	53	46
SD	7	10	8	7	9	9	8	10	9	11	9
M - Women	47	52	42	46	51	49	41	50	48	51	45
SD	9	10	7	9	10	10	7	9	9	11	9

FIGURE 3.7. Spanish-Language MMPI-3 Normative Sample Scored Using English- Language MMPI-3 Norms—Higher-Order and Restructured Clinical Scales

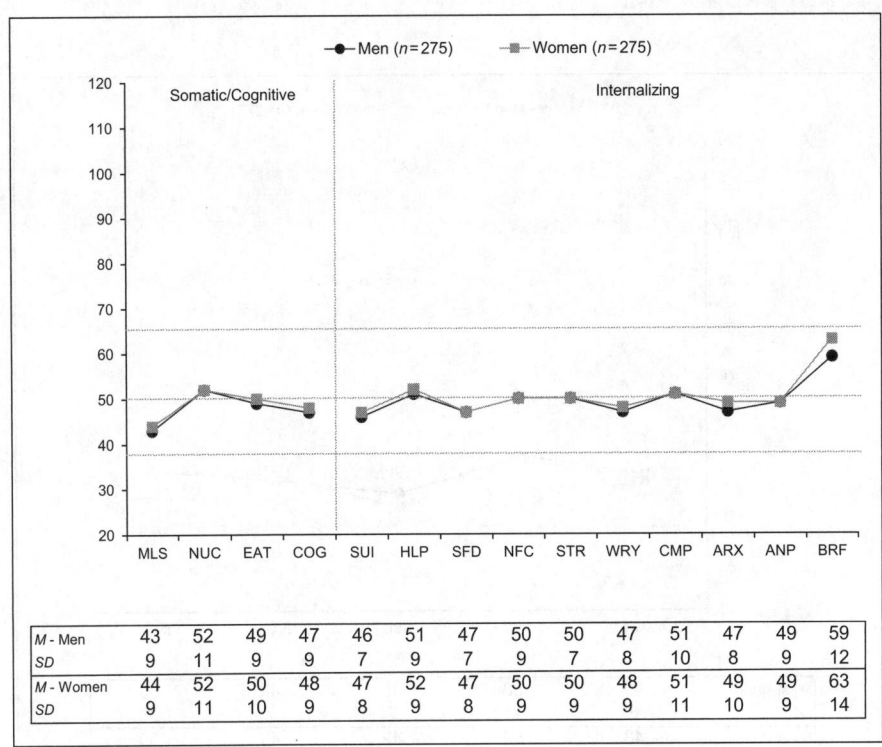

FIGURE 3.8. Spanish-Language MMPI-3 Normative Sample Scored Using English-Language MMPI-3 Norms—Somatic/Cognitive and Internalizing Scales

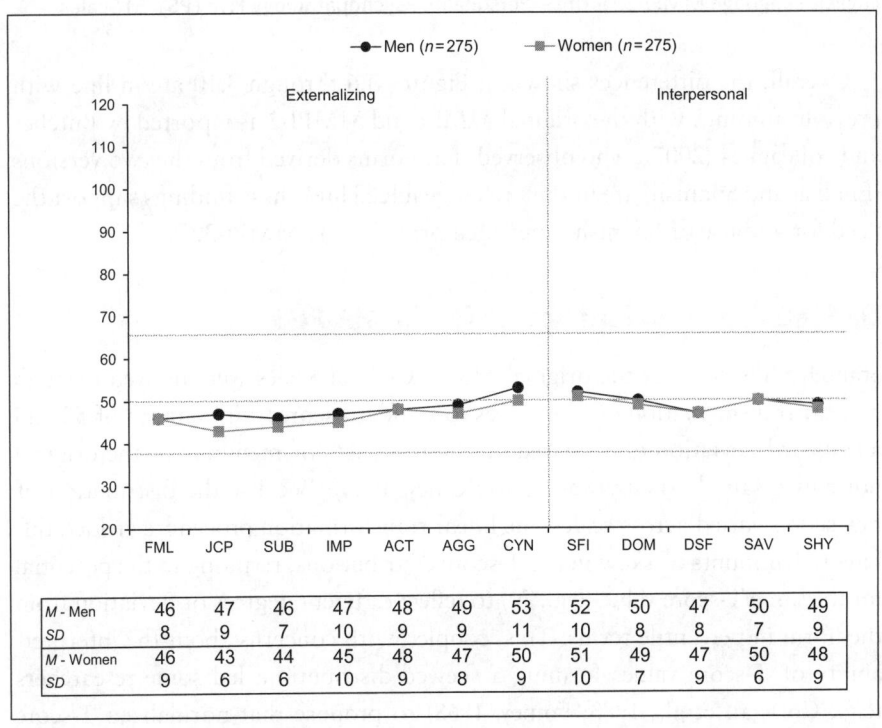

FIGURE 3.9. Spanish-Language MMPI-3 Normative Sample Scored Using English-Language MMPI-3 Norms—Externalizing and Interpersonal Scales

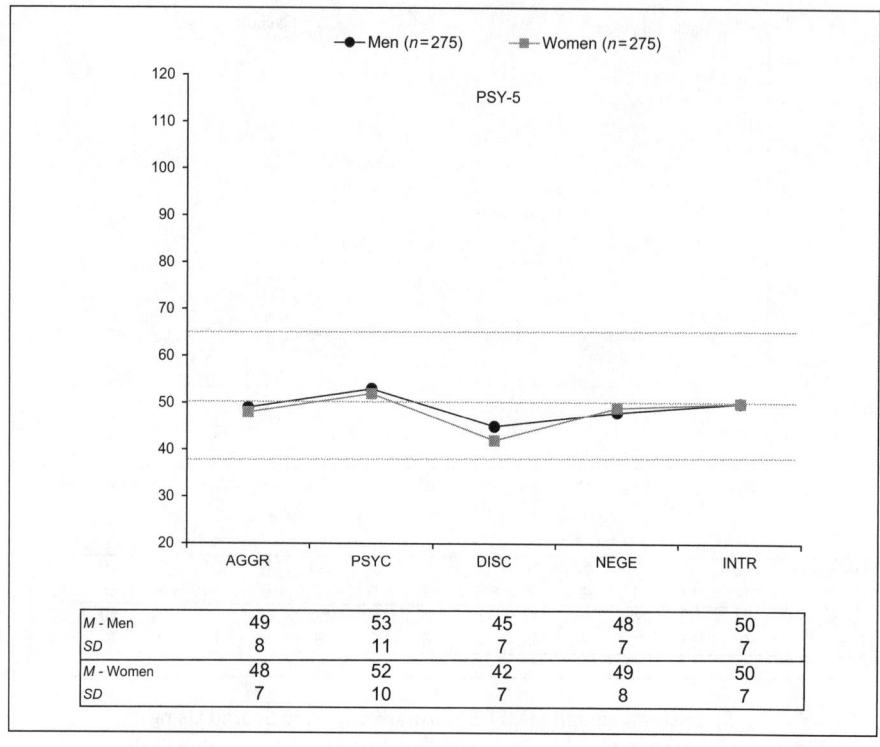

FIGURE 3.10. Spanish-Language MMPI-3 Normative Sample Scored Using English-Language MMPI-3 Norms—Personality Psychopathology Five (PSY-5) Scales

Overall, the differences shown in Figures 3.6 through 3.10 are in line with previous findings with the original MMPI and MMPI-2 as reported by Butcher and colleagues (2007), who observed that norms derived from the two versions (English and Spanish) are not interchangeable. Thus, these findings support the need for and use of Spanish-language norms for the MMPI-3.

Derivation of Standard Scores for the MMPI-3

Standard T scores for the original MMPI Clinical Scales were derived through a linear transformation of raw scores to standard scores with a mean of 50 and a standard deviation of 10 based on the responses of members of the original normative sample (Hathaway & McKinley, 1943). Because the distribution of raw scores varied across scales, the linear transformation procedure yielded differential amounts of skew in the T-score distributions, resulting in the potential for the same T-score value (e.g., 70) to reflect different degrees of deviation from the norm in percentile terms. This, coupled with concerns about the interpretability of T-score values forming a skewed distribution, led some researchers (e.g., Colligan et al., 1983; Finney, 1968) to propose that normalized T-score values be adopted instead.

Examination of the raw-score distributions of the MMPI-2 Clinical Scales revealed that the positive skew characterized the normative distributions of most of the scales in the 1940s and in the 1989 normative data. The positive skew is to be expected for measures of psychopathology and can be viewed as typical for such measures and as more appropriate than a normal distribution (Tellegen & Ben-Porath, 1992). However, for both sets of norms, the degree of skewness of the raw-score distributions and of the corresponding linear T-score distributions varied from scale to scale. Consequently, the same linear T-score value (e.g., a T score of 70) could have different percentile values for different scales.

For the MMPI-2, this undesirable feature of linear T scores was corrected with a minimum of change in the original linear T-score distributions, preserving the typical positive skewness of the MMPI Clinical Scales. This correction was accomplished by deriving uniform T scores (Tellegen & Ben-Porath, 1992), which were designed to have distributions approximating the "prototypical" linear T-score distribution of the MMPI-2 Clinical Scales. Such a distribution was derived empirically for that purpose and was adopted as a standard. This prototypical distribution is essentially a composite of 16 individual distributions, namely, the non-K-corrected linear T-score distributions of the eight original MMPI Clinical Scales in the normative samples for both men and women (omitting Scales 5 and 0 because of their distinctive distributions and methods of derivation).

To arrive at this composite target distribution, linear T scores were first derived for each of the 16 raw-score distributions using the formula $T = 50 + [10(X-M)]/SD$, where X is the raw score and M and SD are the mean and standard deviation of the raw score, respectively. Next, a series of linear T-score values was derived through interpolation, namely, the T-score values corresponding to percentiles 0.5, 1, 2, . . . 98, 99, 99.5 in each of the 16 distributions. In other words, for each percentile value, 16 linear T-score values were derived and then averaged. The resulting series of average or composite T-score values (one average T-score value for each percentile) was adopted as the composite target distribution. As expected, this distribution is positively skewed, as illustrated in Figure 3.11.

The composite standard is numerically illustrated in Table 3.2, which provides the percentile values for a subset of representative composite T-score values. Reflecting the same positive skew as Figure 3.11, Table 3.2 shows, for example, that a high composite T score of 70 (two standard deviations above 50) has a percentile value of 96, whereas the correspondingly low composite T score of 30 (two standard deviations below 50) has a more extreme percentile value of less than 1. Regression methods were then developed to transform the raw scores of each scale directly into uniform T scores that would conform as closely as possible to the composite standard. The uniform T-score transformation largely eliminated the original linear T-score distributional differences between the Clinical Scales because the obtained uniform T-score distributions do conform

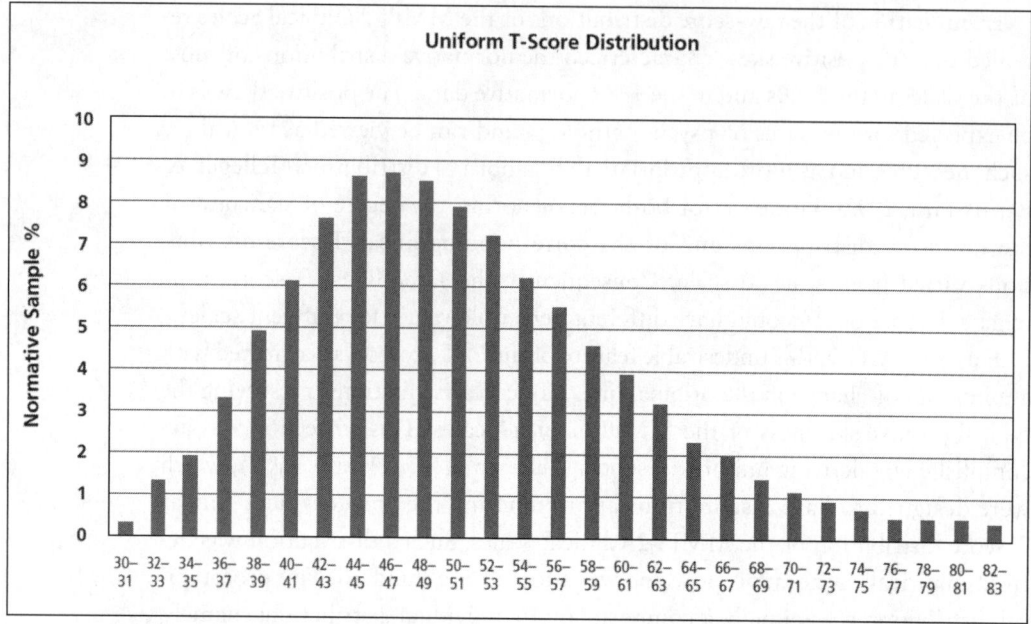

FIGURE 3.11. Prototype Distribution Serving as Target in the Derivation of the Uniform T Scores

TABLE 3.2. Percentile Equivalents of Uniform T Scores

Uniform T score	Equivalent percentile
30	< 1
35	4
40	15
45	34
50	55
55	73
60	85
65	92
70	96
75	98
80	> 99

well to the adopted standard and are consequently quite similar (Tellegen & Ben-Porath, 1992).

Uniform T scores were developed for the eight original MMPI-2 Clinical Scales as well as for the Content Scales (Butcher, Graham, Williams & Ben-Porath, 1990), the PSY-5 Scales (Harkness et al., 1995), the RC Scales (Tellegen et al., 2003), and other selected Supplementary Scales. Uniform T scores were adopted for the MMPI-2-RF, except for the Validity and Interest Scales; linear T scores were used for these scales because they have distinctive distributions dissimilar to the composite uniform distribution. Uniform T scores are similarly used with the MMPI-3 Substantive Scales but not the Validity Scales. The composite distribution that was targeted to derive uniform T scores for the MMPI-2 was also used in calculating uniform T scores for the MMPI-2-RF and MMPI-3 so that the standard scores are directly comparable across versions of the instrument. Raw-score to T-score conversions for all the MMPI-3 scales are reported in Appendix B of the *MMPI-3 Manual for Administration, Scoring, and Interpretation*.

The MMPI-3 Validity Scales 4

The historical developments of the MMPI Validity Scales and the new and revised versions for the MMPI-3 were described in chapters 2 and 3. The goal of this chapter is to consider the psychometric literature that supports the validity and utility of the MMPI-3 Validity Scales in making decisions about both protocol validity as well as the evaluee's general approach to a psychological evaluation.

For organizational purposes, we follow Ben-Porath's (2013) framework for considering response bias assessment through three broad domains: non-content-based responding, overreporting, and underreporting. Chapter 8 discusses these concepts in much greater detail in the context of interpretation. In brief, the measures of content-inconsistent responding (CNS, CRIN, VRIN, and TRIN) more specifically assess non-responding (CNS; percent scorable responding for individual scales), random or variable inconsistent responding (CRIN and VRIN), and fixed indiscriminant responding (TRIN). Five scales measure overreporting of psychopathology and emotional complaints (F, Fp), somatic complaints (Fs, FBS), and cognitive complaints (FBS, RBS). Finally, two scales measure underreporting, and specifically, target uncommon virtues and general positive impression management (L) and an exaggerated or unrealistic portrayal of good psychological adjustment (K).

APPLICABILITY OF THE MMPI-2-RF LITERATURE

As discussed in chapter 3, the MMPI-3 Validity Scales are revised versions of their MMPI-2-RF counterparts, except for CRIN, which is a new scale. Therefore, an important question is whether the previous MMPI-2-RF literature on the nine revised scales can be applied to their MMPI-3 counterparts. For two of these scales, FBS and RBS, the answer is unambiguously yes, because the MMPI-2-RF and MMPI-3 versions completely overlap in item content. In addition, the *MMPI-3 Technical Manual* presents information confirming that the MMPI-2-RF literature can be applied to the other seven scales.

Table 2–3 in the *MMPI-3 Technical Manual* provides information about item overlap across MMPI-2-RF and MMPI-3 scales. For VRIN and TRIN, these scales have 24 (45%) and 16 (62%) of their item pairs also appearing on their respective MMPI-2-RF counterparts, suggesting substantial, but far from complete, overlap. The three infrequency scales, which were revised to ensure that items remained infrequently answered in the keyed direction in contemporary samples, also show substantial overlap. The 26 MMPI-3 F items (81%) also appeared on the MMPI-2-RF F-r scale; 17 Fp items (81%) were scored on the MMPI-2-RF Fp-r scale; and 13 Fs items (81%) appeared on the MMPI-2-RF version of the Fs scale. With regard to the underreporting scales, 12 L items (86%) were scored on the MMPI-2-RF version of the scale, whereas the overlap was smaller (8 items; 57%) for K.

The *MMPI-3 Technical Manual* (Tables 3–7 to 3–16) reports correlations between the revised MMPI-3 scales and their MMPI-2-RF counterparts in relevant samples. More specifically, these intercorrelations are derived from the MMPI-3 normative sample with random response insertion, the normative sample with True indiscriminant response insertion, the normative sample with False indiscriminant response insertion, an overreporting simulation sample, an ADHD simulation sample, a forensic disability claimant sample, an underreporting simulation sample, and a public safety personnel screening sample. These samples, which would have incentives or prompts for different types of response styles, were deemed important to optimize the variability of the validity scale scores in the correlational analyses. VRIN and VRIN-r correlated at .88 in the normative sample with random response insertion; TRIN and TRIN-r correlated at .96 and .95 in the normative sample with True and False indiscriminant response insertion, respectively. As would be expected, CRIN correlated most strongly with VRIN-r (.89) in the normative sample with random response insertion, whereas the associations were stronger with TRIN-r in the samples with fixed indiscriminant response insertion (.91 to .72).

For the overreporting scales, the general overreporting, ADHD simulation, and the forensic disability samples were most relevant. The correlations between F and F-r ranged from .94 to .97 (median = .97) across these samples. The Fp and Fp-r correlations ranged from .84 to .99 and were unsurprisingly smaller in forensic disability men (.85) and women (.84) than the two simulation samples (.94 to .99), given that overreporting of severe psychopathology is less prevalent among disability claimants. The Fs correlations ranged from .93 to .99 (median = .96). Because they completely overlap, the FBS and RBS scales correlated 1.00 with their MMPI-2-RF counterparts across all samples.

The underreporting scales showed a similar pattern in the underreporting simulation sample and the public safety personnel screening samples (men and women separately). The correlations between L and L-r ranged from .93 to .98 (median = .95). For K and K-r, they ranged from .87 to .93 (median = .88).

Overall, these findings demonstrate that the revised MMPI-3 Validity Scales and their MMPI-2-RF counterparts assess the same underlying response styles, particularly in samples where sufficient variability of the response style in question is present. As a result, researchers and clinicians can be confident that research on the MMPI-2-RF versions of these scales can be applied to their MMPI-3 counterparts, albeit with different interpretive cutoffs in some cases. Because of differences between the responses of the MMPI-2-RF and MMPI-3 normative samples, the recommended cut scores associated with several of the MMPI-3 Validity Scales (most notably, F, FBS, and RBS) have changed. Ben-Porath and Tellegen (2020b) adjusted these cutoffs to maintain the selection ratio of invalid responding in the MMPI-3 normative sample at similar levels to those associated with their MMPI-2-RF counterparts in the MMPI-2/MMPI-2-RF normative sample. Given the magnitude of correlations between the MMPI-3 and MMPI-2-RF versions of these scales, and given that the selection ratios across versions were maintained, it is likely that classification accuracy statistics will apply similarly across versions. However, this latter issue requires empirical analyses using contemporary samples, which is discussed in later sections.

ARE VALIDITY SCALES NEEDED?

To some readers, this might appear as a question with an obvious answer. It makes logical sense that when individuals distort their responses to a self-report inventory, the results will not provide an accurate reflection of their psychological functioning. However, some scholars have questioned this premise. McGrath et al. (2010) claimed, based on a meta-analysis they conducted, that response bias measurement was of limited utility, as Validity Scales did not moderate substantive scale score associations with external criteria. However, as detailed by Morey (2012) and Rohling et al. (2011), this conclusion was ill-founded. Central to their utility is the question of whether Validity Scales can identify known response bias and differentiate it from genuine responding. Moreover, several studies using the MMPI-2-RF (and now MMPI-3) do illustrate the need for validity indicators in important ways.

Burchett and Ben-Porath (2010) examined 312 university students who completed a series of self-report questionnaires with standard instructions and were then randomly assigned to complete the MMPI-2-RF under the conditions of overreporting psychopathology, overreporting physical problems, or standard responding. The authors found that overreporters' mean MMPI-2-RF scores were substantially elevated relative to those of standard instruction participants, and that the psychometric validity of these scores was seriously compromised, as reflected by attenuated correlations with the criterion measures in the two overreporting conditions. Wiggins et al. (2012) replicated these findings using a naturalistic design in which they used the MMPI-2-RF Validity Scales to identify overreporters versus genuine responders in a large sample ($N = 2{,}275$) of disability claimants. Here, too, the authors found that scores on the MMPI-2-RF Substantive Scales exhibited substantially attenuated correlations with extratest measures in the overreporting condition relative to those deemed to be genuine responders. Forbey et al. (2013) replicated these latter findings in large university and prison samples, but unlike Wiggins et al., Forbey et al. also examined the effects of underreporting on MMPI-2-RF scale scores. In both samples, these scores were substantially lower for those who provided invalid profiles due to underreporting, and correlations between MMPI-2-RF scales with external criteria were also compromised as a consequence of underreporting.

Two recent MMPI-3 studies have shown very similar results. Whitman et al. (2021a) randomly assigned 753 undergraduate students, who had passed a posttest questionnaire that inquired about what instructions they followed, to complete the MMPI-2-RF-EX (from which MMPI-3 scores were derived) under one of three sets of instructions: standard instruction ($n = 288$), overreporting ($n = 250$), and underreporting ($n = 215$). Prior to completing the MMPI-2-RF-EX, participants had completed, under standard instructions, other measures of constructs conceptually relevant to MMPI-3 scale scores. Their findings replicated those of Burchett and Ben-Porath (2010) in that MMPI-3 substantive scale scores were much higher (at large effect size magnitudes) in the overreporting group compared to the other two groups, and significantly lower in the underreporting group compared to the other groups. In addition, the correlations between MMPI-3 scales and conceptually relevant criteria observed in the standard instruction group substantially attenuated at a minimum of a medium effect size in 84% of the comparisons in the overreporting group and 77% of comparisons in the underreporting groups. Reeves et al. (2022) replicated these findings in the overreporting context using New Zealand university and community mental health samples.

Overall, these results indicate that MMPI-2-RF and MMPI-3 scores are substantially altered, and their psychometric validities are attenuated, in the context of overreporting and underreporting response styles. They also unequivocally refute the contention by McGrath et al. (2010) that validity scales are unnecessary.

PSYCHOMETRIC FINDINGS WITH THE MMPI-2-RF/ MMPI-3 VALIDITY SCALES

In this next section, we review the psychometric findings concerning the MMPI-3 Validity Scales as presented both in the *MMPI-3 Technical Manual* and the published literature. Where applicable to validity and utility, we also rely on the MMPI-2-RF literature for reasons described earlier.

Reliability

Reliability estimates for the MMPI-3 Validity Scales are reported in Table 3–2 of the *Technical Manual*. Test-retest reliability estimates range from .47 for TRIN to .87 for FBS for men and .87 for K for women. Internal consistency coefficients in the normative sample range from .31 for women on Fp to .78 for women on F. Internal consistency findings in the outpatient mental health sample are generally higher, ranging from .23 on CRIN for women to .83 on F for both men and women. Standard errors of measurement (*SEMs*; expressed in T-score values) based on the normative test-retest data range from 3 on FBS to as high as 7 on TRIN. *SEMs* based on the internal consistency coefficients in the normative sample range from 5 for several scales to 8 for Fp in both men and women. For the clinical samples, *SEMs* range from 5 for TRIN in men and for L in women to 10 on Fp in both men and women.

These reliability findings need to be considered in light of the composition of the samples used in the analyses, which consisted largely of cooperative and test-competent individuals for whom one would not expect to encounter large, reliable variations in invalid responding. Relatively low reliability estimates stand out in particular for the inconsistent responding indicators, CRIN, VRIN, and TRIN. These results are not surprising because the inconsistency scales were designed to be content-free indicators and have an even greater restriction of range than do the other validity indicators. Thus, range restriction owing to sample characteristics and the nature of the Validity Scales attenuates the reliability estimates to some extent. This is borne out by the standard error of measurement findings, which incorporate variability in the analyses and generally reflect only marginally greater measurement error in the validity indicators than that found with the Substantive Scales.

Higher *SEM* values indicate a need to use higher cutoffs to identify significant deviations from the norm. Interpretive recommendations for most of the MMPI-3 Validity Scales do in fact require more substantial deviation from the norm (than that required for the Substantive Scales) to raise substantial concerns about the validity of a test protocol. Exceptions to the requirement for greater deviations from the mean are L and K, for which *SEM* findings are comparable to those reported for the Substantive Scales.

Validity

Validation data reported in the *MMPI-3 Technical Manual* are limited to internal correlates. As described earlier, correlations between the new validity indicators and the MMPI-3 Validity Scales and their MMPI-2-RF counterparts are reported for several samples. Extratest findings with the MMPI-3 and MMPI-2-RF Validity Scales have been reported in journal articles published over the past 13 years. We focus next on this peer-reviewed literature.

Non-Content-Based Invalid Responding

In two clinical examples, Dragon et al. (2012) examined the impact of unscorable item responses on the validity and interpretability of scores on the MMPI-2-RF Restructured (RC) Scales. Unscorable responses were inserted randomly in place of the participants' actual responses to the items of each of the RC Scales. Unscorable response insertion was increased in 10% increments ranging from 10% to 90% of the items of each scale. With only a 10% insertion of unscorable responses, a sizable proportion of individuals who scored at or above 65T on each RC scale no longer produced a clinically elevated score on that scale. Scores that remained elevated when 10% unscorable responses were inserted declined considerably. In contrast, examination of correlations between RC scale scores and extratest criteria indicated that the validity coefficients were remarkably robust when substantial levels of unscorable responses were inserted. Nevertheless, considering the significant reduction in the proportion of elevated scores resulting from unscorable responses, and the substantial lowering of scores that remained elevated, the authors recommended that scores on scales with 10% or more unscorable responses be interpreted with caution. Specifically, nonelevated scores should not be interpreted as indicating the absence of problems measured by the scale, and elevated scores should be interpreted noting the possibility that the resulting scale score may underestimate the problems assessed by that measure. Because the study by Dragon et al. (2012) focused on nonresponding, an issue not affected by normative data, these findings apply to the MMPI-3 as well. Assessment and interpretation of nonresponding is discussed further in chapter 8.

Handel et al. (2010) evaluated the effects of increasing degrees of simulated random and fixed responding on VRIN-r and TRIN-r scores and compared the performance of these scales with their MMPI-2 counterparts. Overall, the authors concluded that their findings supported the interpretive recommendations for VRIN-r and TRIN-r in the MMPI-2-RF manual (Ben-Porath & Tellegen, 2008/2011). These guidelines recommended that T scores at or above 80 on the inconsistency scales be interpreted as indicating that the protocol is invalid and uninterpretable owing to excessive variable or fixed responding. The authors noted that at lower T-score levels (70–79 on VRIN-r or TRIN-r in the True direction), caution should be exercised when interpreting scores on RC6 and RC8. TRIN-r T scores in the 70–79 range in the False direction indicate that caution should be exercised when interpreting scores on RC1 and RC2. These findings continue to apply to the MMPI-3 as the VRIN and TRIN scales correlate highly with their MMPI-2-RF counterparts in this same simulation context.

Mason et al. (2013) randomly assigned undergraduate students to respond honestly, feign posttraumatic stress disorder (PTSD), respond completely randomly, or respond partially randomly to the MMPI-2-RF. They also compared these scores to a genuine PTSD group derived from a Veterans Administration (VA) sample. In analyses comparing the fully and partially random groups to the honest group, VRIN-r was associated with very large effect size magnitudes. Classification accuracy statistics indicated perfect specificity even at T = 70 for VRIN in the honest sample, though this value was 0.93 in the genuine PTSD group. However, the study samples were very small, likely too small for stable classification parameters, but nevertheless these authors replicated the findings in Handel et al. (2010).

Shkalim et al. (2016) replicated the findings by Handel et al. (2010) by using the Hebrew-language normative sample and a clinical sample. The U.S. versions of VRIN-r and TRIN-r performed quite comparably to what Handel et al. (2010) observed. Interestingly, alternative Hebrew version scales optimized for correlations among item pairs in the Hebrew normative sample did not outperform the original U.S. scales; indeed, they performed worse. As such, the U.S. versions of VRIN-r and TRIN-r were deemed to be optimal indicators of random and fixed indiscriminant responding in a different cultural context.

Burchett et al. (2016) published an important study that added to the foundation for developing the CRIN scale for the MMPI-3. In a series of samples from a range of clinical and nonclinical contexts, they examined the rate of *false feigning*, which was defined as elevations on overreporting scales in the context of in consistent or fixed indiscriminant responding that VRIN-r and TRIN-r had failed to identify (i.e., scores on these scales were < 80T). Using the same methodology as Handel et al. (2010), they iteratively simulated increasing levels of random, fixed acquiescent, or fixed counteracquiescent responding. Although false feigning was rare (< 10%), especially at higher rates of simulated random or fixed indiscriminate responding, it did occur at nontrivial rates, particularly for scales with very infrequently endorsed items (Fp-r, Fs). Follow-up examinations indicated that scales were particularly susceptible to the effects of non-content-based invalid responding if they were brief, consisted of rarely endorsed items, included a relatively high percentage of True-keyed items, or required a low percentage of endorsed items to reach clinical significance. Consequently, a CRIN scale can provide important additional coverage, especially in cases where individuals change response styles (e.g., from random to fixed), to reduce the likelihood that an individual might be misidentified as having overreported.

Two additional studies have attempted to determine the reasons for non-content-based invalid responding (particularly based on VRIN-r and TRIN-r). Gu et al. (2017) examined this issue in criminal defendants undergoing competency restoration. They observed that 31% of the individuals in their sample had invalid protocols owing to non-content-based invalid responding. They found that low intelligence and low education were the best predictors of this outcome. They also observed that mood disturbance was associated specifically with fixed indiscriminant responding. Finally, feigning based on Structured Interview of Reported Symptoms (SIRS) scores was also related to non-content-based invalid responding, though the actual rate of feigning in these individuals was quite low. In a second study, Gervais et al. (2018) examined associations between VRIN-r and TRIN-r scores and extratest variables in a very large forensic disability sample. They replicated Gu and colleagues' findings with respect to intelligence and education, as well as reading limitations, but also found that scores on these scales (particularly TRIN-r) were associated with uncooperativeness.

In summary, the MMPI-2-RF literature on assessing non-content-based invalid responding indicates strong support for Cannot Say, VRIN-r, and TRIN-r in detecting such responding across contexts and cultures, albeit not perfectly (Burchett et al., 2016). Non-content-based invalid responding can be attributed to multiple factors, including lower intelligence, lower education, and low reading level, but also intentional factors such as uncooperativeness. These findings apply to the MMPI-3 versions of VRIN and TRIN—in future studies, it will also be useful to determine how the new CRIN scale further mitigates against false feigning by examining its incremental validity in the assessment of non-content-based invalid responding.

Overreporting

The MMPI-2-RF overreporting scales are the most widely studied set of scales on the instrument. It is therefore not surprising that two meta-analyses have already been published in this area. This literature shows that the overreporting scales have been evaluated in a variety of populations and settings, including military personnel (Armistead-Jehle et al., 2018; Ingram et al., 2020; Jones, 2016; Lange et al., 2015), VA patients (Goodwin et al., 2013; Jurick et al., 2019), forensic disability claimants (Chmielewski et al., 2017; Gervais et al., 2008, 2010, 2011; Nguyen et al., 2015; Sellbom, Wygant, et al., 2012), forensic neuropsychology (Donders et al., 2021; McBride et al., 2013; Rogers et al., 2011; Schroeder et al., 2012; Smart et al., 2008; Wygant et al., 2011), medical settings (Peck et al., 2013; Wygant et al., 2017), and criminal defendants (Sellbom et al., 2010). Coverage of every individual study on the MMPI-2-RF overreporting scales is unnecessary and beyond the scope of this chapter. Instead, we focus on two meta-analyses (Ingram & Ternes, 2016; Sharf et al., 2017), supplement them with the review of individual studies to make important points that could not be covered by those meta-analyses, and review the three studies on the MMPI-3 overreporting scales that have been published at the time of this writing.

Ingram and Ternes (2016) reviewed 25 studies of the MMPI-2-RF overreporting indicators, covering a wide range of samples and research designs. They applied a random effects model that allowed for consideration of moderating factors, including publication status, type of research design (simulation or known groups), specific diagnosis (e.g., combined, PTSD, traumatic brain injury [TBI], somatic), overreporting group (e.g., student, litigant, disability claimant, criminal defendant, veteran, psychiatric patient), comparison control group (e.g., student, litigant, disability claimant, criminal defendant, veteran, psychiatric patient), whether non-content-based invalid responding had been screened out, age of participants, and education (high school or more, no high school). These moderators, if statistically significant, allowed for the examination of variability of effects in differentiating overreporting and putatively honest groups with the MMPI-2-RF overreporting scales.

Ingram and Ternes (2016) reported that the average weighted effect size estimates (Hedges's g) were 1.04 (95% confidence interval [CI] = 0.87–1.22) for FBS-r; 1.18 (95% CI = 0.96–1.41) for RBS; 1.24 (95% CI = 1.06–1.42) for Fs; 1.32 (95% CI = 1.13–1.51) for F-r; and 1.43 (95% CI = 1.17–1.69) for Fp-r across all samples and designs. These effect sizes would all be considered large by conventional standards, including the lower bounds of each confidence interval reported. There were some significant moderator influences and, interestingly, the infrequency scales were far more moderated by the aforementioned variables than were FBS-r and RBS, which had more stable effects. An examination of the effect sizes across moderating variable conditions revealed a few general patterns. The infrequency scales (and RBS) tended to perform much better in analogue simulation designs (which are more internally controlled, but less generalizable to the real-world context) than known groups designs. The infrequency scales were also more susceptible, as would be expected, to effects of non-content-based invalid responding and therefore had larger effects in studies when such responding was not removed.

F-r tended to perform less effectively in contexts in which overreporters and control participants were either personal injury litigants or psychiatric patients, as well as when participants were diagnosed with TBIs or somatic complaints. However, this scale performed quite well for participants diagnosed with PTSD in veterans, disability, criminal, and nonclinical (student) contexts. The Fp-r scale consistently performed least effectively in studies using litigation or forensic disability contexts and in which TBI diagnosis was an issue, but it performed very well across all other contexts. This finding was not surprising as this Validity Scale should be more specific to overreporting of psychopathology and, in particular, severe psychopathology. The Fs scale performed somewhat less effectively in two studies in litigation contexts, when the overreporters were psychiatric patients and when TBI was the diagnosis in question. FBS-r and RBS both performed less effectively in the three studies in which psychiatric patients were both overreporters and the comparison group, but otherwise the effects were quite stable, as just stated. Overall, Ingram and Ternes's (2016) meta-analysis provided evidence of strong validity for the MMPI-2-RF overreporting scales across a range of contexts and participant conditions.

Sharf et al. (2017) examined 30 studies that met their stringent criteria for Validity Scale research. Although there was considerable overlap in the studies included in the two meta-analyses, Sharf et al. also calculated effect sizes for different types of comparisons. These authors calculated the overall weighted effect size estimates (Hedges's g) for overreporting versus all comparison groups, which were unsurprisingly almost identical to those reported by Ingram and Ternes. However, Sharf et al. focused primarily on the overreporting versus genuine patient comparison as such comparisons would have most direct relevance to clinical practice (in that the distinction the clinician is trying to make is whether the individual is overreporting or has genuine problems). In these overall comparisons, weighted effect sizes were 1.15 (F-r), 1.35 (Fp-r), 1.00 (Fs), 0.75 (FBS-r), and 0.85 (RBS). The Fp-r scale also performed the best when all feigners across studies were compared to those who had mixed diagnosis or specific mental health diagnosis, such as PTSD or major depressive disorder.

Sharf et al. (2017) also examined the three main forms of overreporting/malingering of psychopathology, cognitive impairment, and medical/somatic complaints. When assigning studies into these domains, Fp-r (and to a lesser extent F-r and Fs) performed the best in identifying feigned mental disorders; Fs, FBS-r, and RBS were the best at identifying feigned cognitive impairment; and Fs alone performed the best at identifying feigned medical complaints. Furthermore, the authors examined the classification accuracy for each of the scales across the three domains of overreporting. They concluded that "Fp-r performs exceptionally well in targeting feigned mental disorders" (p. 450); they also noted that very few patients with cognitive or medical symptoms would be misclassified by high Fp-r scores. F-r performed less well overall, and scores lower than 120T, which is the MMPI-2-RF administration manual's recommended cut score, would likely be associated with a high false positive rate. In terms of cognitive overreporting, both RBS > 100T and FBS-r > 90T appeared to be most effective, though RBS performed similarly regardless of type of overreporting. With respect to medical/somatic symptom overreporting, Fs performed the best, with 90T being a better cutoff considering low sensitivity rates at 100T.

Overall, Sharf et al.'s (2017) meta-analysis was very supportive of the MMPI-2-RF overreporting scales, and Fp-r in particular, for detecting feigned mental health problems. The authors also commented that the scales conceptually best suited for cognitive (FBS, RBS) and somatic (Fs) overreporting appeared to be the best scales for this purpose, but Fs and RBS in general were quite good at detecting overreporting regardless of type. Therefore, elevations on these scales would not automatically signal only cognitive or somatic overreporting. It is worth noting that, unlike Ingram and Ternes (2016), Sharf et al. did not rely on traditional methods for meta-analyses. They did not statistically test for moderation effects, and they did not compute confidence intervals associated with the effects observed.

Whitman et al. (2021a) published the first study examining overreporting on the MMPI-3. They randomly assigned 753 undergraduate students who had passed a posttest questionnaire that inquired about the instructions they received for completing the MMPI-2-RF-EX (from which MMPI-3 scores were derived). Participants were tested under one of three sets of instructions: standard instruction ($n = 288$), overreporting ($n = 250$), and underreporting ($n = 215$). The underreporting analyses will be covered in the next section. The overreporting instructions directed the participant to feign mental health problems in a hypothetical criminal court scenario. Whitman et al. observed that the overreporting group produced significantly higher mean overreporting scale T scores than the standard instruction group, with Fp being associated with the largest effect size (Cohen's $d = 5.56$), followed by F ($d = 4.53$), Fs ($d = 4.12$), RBS ($d = 3.61$), and FBS ($d = 2.35$). They also calculated classification accuracy statistics and observed very good support for the cut scores recommended in the *MMPI-3 Manual for Administration, Scoring, and Interpretation* and described later in chapter 8 of this book. As expected, the Fp and F scales performed better than the other three considering the mental health overreporting scenario.

Reeves et al. (2022) replicated the findings of Whitman et al. (2021a) in a New Zealand context. Their participants were 168 university students who completed the MMPI-3 for course credit under overreporting instructions. The authors selected a personal injury scenario in which the overreporting participants were seeking compensation for an emotional problem (such as PTSD). Unlike Whitman et al. (2021a), Reeves and colleagues contrasted the overreporting participants' responses to the MMPI-3 against those of a genuine patient group ($n = 223$) with predominately internalizing mental health problems. The overreporting group produced significantly higher mean T scores on the overreporting scales than did the genuine responding patient group, with Fp again being associated with the largest effect size (Cohen's $d = 1.29$), followed by RBS ($d = 1.11$), F ($d = 1.05$), Fs ($d = 0.90$), and FBS ($d = 0.83$). These effect sizes were quite similar to those reported in the meta-analysis by Sharf et al. (2017) for the comparison between overreporting participants and genuine patients. Finally, the classification accuracy results yielded strong support for the cut scores presented in the *MMPI-3 Manual for Administration, Scoring, and Interpretation*. They were not as strong as those reported by Whitman et al. (2021a), but this finding was likely a result of using a patient comparison group.

Tylicki, Gervais, and Ben-Porath (2020) evaluated the utility of the MMPI-3 overreporting scales in a forensic disability context using a known groups design. Participants were 550 individuals undergoing a non-head-injury disability-related evaluation. The five overreporting scales evinced small to medium correlations with conceptually relevant performance validity tests and moderate to large correlations with other symptom validity tests. These scales also significantly differentiated groups of individuals who passed versus failed performance validity tests across four such tests. Most notably, RBS was associated with the largest effect size (ds = 0.71 to 1.01; median d = 0.82) in each of the four comparisons, with FBS performing second best (ds = 0.58 to 0.86; median d = 0.72). As would be expected, Fp performed the worst in every comparison (ds = 0.12 to 1.39; median d = 0.37). Next, the participants were classified into one of four groups based on the criteria from Slick et al. (1999) for malingered neurocognitive dysfunction (MND) by using a range of both performance validity and other symptom validity tests. The groups were incentive only, possible MND, probable MND, and definite MND, though the latter two ultimately had to be combined. In the comparison of the incentive-only group to the combined probably/definite MND, RBS was associated with the largest effect size (Cohen's d = 1.34), followed by Fs (d = 1.30), F (d = 1.17), FBS (d = 1.07), and Fp (d = 0.76). Classification accuracies generally supported the highest cut scores in the *Manual for Administration, Scoring, and Interpretation* with respect to very high specificity rates and the highest positive predictive power values, but only RBS was found to have a marginally acceptable sensitivity at > 90T (.39). The lower bound cut scores per the manual were supported by sensitivity values, but at the expected and substantial expense of false positive prediction errors, especially at lower base rates of malingering.

There are two additional points we wish to make with respect to MMPI-2-RF/MMPI-3 and overreporting. First, none of the studies reviewed allowed us to make more nuanced points in the area of somatic overreporting assessment. Although several studies have demonstrated the utility of the MMPI-2-RF Validity Scales in differentiating groups based on malingered pain-related dysfunction criteria from Bianchini et al. (2005) (also see Bianchini et al., 2018; Wygant et al., 2011), these studies have focused on samples and criteria that mix both cognitive and somatic overreporting. There are two studies that provide the most specificity in understanding how the overreporting scales perform specifically with respect to overreporting physical health complaints. Sellbom, Wygant, and Bagby (2012) examined 114 university students who had been explicitly asked to overreport medical problems, 69 patients who had been diagnosed with a somatoform disorder (via structured interview), and 74 patients with genuine medical problems but no mental health diagnosis. FBS-r was the best at differentiating the overreporting group from the genuine medical patient group (d = 1.91), followed by Fs (d = 1.42); however, the latter was much better at differentiating the overreporting group from the somatoform patient group ($d = 0.73$). In fact, the somatoform patient group scored higher than the overreporting group on FBS-r ($d = -0.58$) at a medium effect size magnitude; this pattern was also seen for the RBS, though at a smaller effect size ($d = -0.37$). Moreover, the classification accuracy statistics revealed very good support for Fs in differentiating the somatic overreporting group from the medical patients, supporting the manual's cutoff of 100T, but even higher scores (115T) would be needed to separate somatic overreporting from somatoform disorder with greater certainty. In the second relevant study, Wygant et al. (2017) examined 230 outpatient chronic pain patients who completed the MMPI-2-RF and were rated on the nonorganic signs from the study by Waddell et al. (1980). Fs had the largest effect size ($d = 1.31$) in comparing patients with a Waddell score of 0 and those with scores above 2, which was substantially higher than that for FBS-r ($d = 0.87$). Overall, these studies show that Fs is the Validity Scale most specific to somatic/medical overreporting, whereas FBS and to some degree RBS scores are more sensitive to actual somatoform psychopathology. MMPI-3 users in clinical practice should therefore consider profiles in which FBS scores are very high as potential noncredible somatic responding, but scores on Fs can help indicate whether this responding is more likely a reflection of psychopathology as opposed to overreporting. Indeed, if Fs is relatively low, the former is more likely.

The second point we wish to make with respect to MMPI-2-RF/MMPI-3 and overreporting is that there has been recent interest in evaluating the MMPI-2-RF Validity Scales' utility in detecting overreported ADHD, which is an important task when individuals seek stimulant medication with abuse potential or are trying to gain study accommodations at the university level. Harp et al. (2011) examined a small sample of university students with and without ADHD. Individuals from each group were randomly assigned to overreporting ADHD versus honest responding groups. Fs performed the best at differentiating between nonpsychiatric students feigning ADHD ($n = 22$) from students with confirmed ADHD diagnoses ($n = 20$) ($d = 0.95$), followed by F-r ($d = 0.75$), Fp-r ($d = 0.73$), and FBS-r ($d = 0.40$). RBS was not available in this study as it was not part of the MMPI-2-RF scoring materials when it was conducted. The groups were too small to provide much confidence in the reported classification accuracies.

Robinson and Rogers (2018) used an analogue simulation design in which two groups overreported either ADHD ($n = 32$) or general psychiatric problems ($n = 35$) on the MMPI-2-RF; one group completed the MMPI-2-RF under standard instructions, and another group consisted of patients with confirmed ADHD diagnoses ($n = 51$). Both simulation groups had passed a posttest questionnaire. In addition to the standard five MMPI-2-RF overreporting scales, Robinson and Rogers also developed a specific Dissimulation scale for ADHD (Ds-ADHD). In general, the overreporting group scored substantially higher than the overreporting ADHD group on Fp-r and FBS-r, and Ds-ADHD. For reasons not explained in the article, the RBS scale did not show this pattern. As in the Harp et al. (2011) study, the Fs scale performed the best in differentiating between the ADHD overreporting and the ADHD patient groups (Cohen's $d = 1.14$), whereas Fp-r was the best in differentiating general overreporters from the ADHD diagnostic group ($d = 1.09$). In the classification accuracy analyses for differentiating the ADHD overreporting and the ADHD patient groups, specificity was perfect for Fs, but sensitivity was low (.26) at the reported cut score of 90T in the classification analysis. Ds-ADHD unsurprisingly performed the best, but it was developed in the study sample based on items that optimally differentiated the groups.

In an MMPI-2 study, Young and Gross (2011) included the RBS scale as scored on the MMPI-2-RF/MMPI-3. Specifically, they examined individuals instructed to feign ADHD and compared them to patients with an ADHD diagnosis. RBS scale scores were 77.9T ($SD = 16.5$) on average in the simulation groups and 63.9T ($SD = 9.7$) in the clinical ADHD group, which results in a Cohen's $d = 1.03$. For classification purposes, no one scored at the level required for 100T, with a raw score of 12 being optimal for RBS in differentiating the groups. Overall, Fs appears to be the best scale in differentiating overreported ADHD from patients with such a diagnosis, but in a different study that included RBS but not Fs, RBS seemingly performed comparably, at least with respect to effect size magnitude.

In summary, studies employing simulation and known group methodologies have established that the MMPI-2-RF and now the MMPI-3 overreporting indicators can effectively detect noncredible reporting of psychological, somatic, and cognitive symptoms. F-r/F is sensitive to the broadest range of overreported symptoms, and it performed well, but not the best, in the studies just reviewed. Fp-r/Fp is clearly most sensitive to overreported psychological symptoms and less effective than the other measures in detecting overreported somatic and cognitive complaints. These findings replicate across the MMPI-2-RF and MMPI-3. This scale is particularly effective in differentiating genuine, severe psychopathology from overreported psychological symptoms. Fs and FBS-r are the best MMPI-2-RF predictors of overreported somatic symptoms, but FBS-r does not differentiate well from somatoform psychopathology. FBS-r/FBS and RBS are the best measures of noncredible cognitive complaints. RBS is most specifically associated with overreported memory complaints. Specific to the emerging topic of malingered ADHD, Fs and possibly RBS appear to have the most promise, but more research is needed that includes all five standard MMPI-3 overreporting scales. Most of the studies just reviewed also included classification accuracy findings that support the interpretive cutoffs recommended in the MMPI-2-RF manual, and while these are different in the MMPI-3 manual, similar support has now been observed in three MMPI-3 studies as well.

Underreporting

As was the case with the previous MMPI versions, a smaller number of studies have examined the utility of the MMPI-2-RF and MMPI-3 underreporting indicators. Sellbom and Bagby (2008) reported the results of two studies designed to examine the validity of L-r and K-r. In their first investigation, both scales significantly differentiated a sample of patients diagnosed with schizophrenia who took the test under standard instructions from a randomly selected patient cohort instructed to "answer the questions as if you were applying for employment and wanted to keep your history of psychiatric problems or symptoms private" (Sellbom & Bagby, 2008, p. 372). The patients who took the test under the simulation instructions scored lower than did their counterparts tested under standard instructions on all the RC scales except RC3 and RC9. The simulators scored higher than the control group on both L-r and K-r. Hierarchical regression analyses showed that each scale added incrementally to the detection of underreporting beyond the other. Sellbom and Bagby (2008) replicated these findings with a sample of undergraduate students, with the exception that the underreporting students scored lower than did their counterparts tested under standard instructions on RC6 and RC9 and L-r did not add incrementally beyond K-r in differentiating the two subsamples from each other.

In their second study, Sellbom and Bagby (2008) sought to replicate and extend their findings across research designs and settings. This study included a sample of undergraduates tested with standard instructions or under instructions to "fake good" under scenarios that included gaining custody of or access to their child. A second sample used in this study consisted of 86 individuals tested in child custody evaluations in which it is assumed that individuals are motivated to present themselves in a favorable manner. The first sample was used to replicate the simulation findings from the first study, and the second sample was used to examine whether these results would extend to a differential prevalence design. RC, L-r, and K-r scale scores of the students simulating a custody evaluation and the custody litigants were compared with those of the students tested under standard instructions. The simulating students scored lower than did their standard instruction counterparts on all the RC Scales except for RC6. The custody litigants scored lower than the nonsimulating students on all but RC1, RC2, and RC6. Significant differences were found for both groups on L-r and K-r, with the custody litigants and custody litigation simulators scoring higher than the control group on both measures. In hierarchical regression analyses, each scale added incrementally to the other in predicting underreporting.

Crighton et al. (2017) examined the validity of the MMPI-2-RF L-r and K-r scales using an analogue simulation design (i.e., random assignment to underreporting versus standard instruction conditions) in a sample of university students. The authors specifically advocated for the use of a manipulation check to be administered after completion of the MMPI-2-RF to allow for better assessment of the number of participants who were complying with the underreporting instructions. Using this manipulation check (a posttest questionnaire) in conjunction with invalid MMPI-2-RF profiles due to content non-responsiveness, they determined that participants could be divided into three groups: Standard Compliant, Underreporting Noncompliant, and Underreporting Compliant. Furthermore, the authors observed that the scores of those who completed the MMPI-2-RF with underreporting instructions in a noncompliant manner were similar to those who had completed the MMPI-2-RF in a compliant manner under standard conditions. Therefore, this manipulation check made it possible to obtain clearer results for examining the utility of the L-r and K-r scales in that it isolated the data of those who had actually underreported from those who failed to adhere to such instructions. Crighton et al. also proposed that a lack of incentive to underreport might have diminished the strength of their results and therefore advocated for the use of incentives for simulation study participants. Crighton et al. found that the scores on the L-r and K-r scales for the Underreporting Compliant group were significantly higher than for the Standard Compliant group at large effect size magnitudes (Hedges's $g = 1.50$ [L-r] and 1.34 [K-r]). They also showed that L-r and K-r incremented one another in the prediction of Underreporting Compliant vs. Standard Complaint groups in a hierarchical logistic regression analysis. Finally, Crighton et al. reported classification accuracy statistics that indicated good support for the manual's recommended cut scores for underreporting (80T for L-r and 70T for K-r).

Brown and Sellbom (2020) further replicated the findings of Crighton et al. (2017) and Sellbom and Bagby (2008) in a New Zealand university sample. More specifically, they asked 173 participants to underreport on the MMPI-2-RF as if they were trying to secure their dream job. They used a posttest manipulation check per Crighton et al. and also promised $50 to the participants who could underreport and not be identified as such. Their responses were contrasted with those of 611 university student participants who completed the MMPI-2-RF under standard instructions. Brown and Sellbom observed that L-r and K-r both differentiated the underreporting group from the genuine responding group (Hedges's $g = 1.38$ and 1.65, respectively). They also found that both scales evinced incremental validity above and beyond one another in differentiating the groups. Classification accuracy statistics supported the recommended cut scores for probable invalid responding in clinical settings (80T for L-r and 70T for K-r) but indicated that scores representing possible underreporting (65T and 60T, respectively) were also associated with good sensitivity without considerable expense of specificity.

Roma et al. (2018) examined whether speed and response latency would have an impact on underreporting scales in an analogue simulation design. They asked 67 young adult volunteers to underreport as if they were applying for a job; half were assigned to a speed condition in which they had to respond faster as their performance would look more impressive to the prospective employer, whereas the other underreporting group did not receive such instructions. They were compared to two groups asked to respond honestly; half of these responders were also asked to respond faster. The authors found that underreporting groups scores significantly higher on L-r and K-r than either of the honest groups. Moreover, those who underreported in the speed condition scored significantly higher than those in the nonspeed condition. These findings suggested that individuals who take more time to respond while underreporting might have lower scores on L-r and K-r than those who try to respond quickly.

The most recent simulation study has been conducted using the MMPI-3. The previously reviewed Whitman et al. (2021a) study (see Overreporting section) also asked 215 university students to underreport on the MMPI-2-RF-EX from which the MMPI-3 was scored. They were contrasted with 288 students who completed the MMPI-2-RF-EX under standard instructions. Scores on the L and K scales were associated with very large effect size magnitudes (Cohen's ds = 2.19 and 2.03, respectively) in differentiating the two groups. Classification accuracy analysis results were quite consistent with, if not better than, those of both Brown and Sellbom (2020) and Crighton et al. (2017) with respect to supporting the cut scores reported both in the *MMPI-3 Manual for Administration, Scoring, and Interpretation* and chapter 8 of this book.

Detrick and Chibnall (2014) used a differential prevalence design in which they compared MMPI-2-RF scores of a preemployment sample (individuals who were motivated to be hired as police officers) with scores generated by the same individuals after they had successfully completed their training, with no stake in the results of the second assessment (and, thus, no incentive to underreport). The authors observed L-r and K-r differences between the two administrations with medium to large effect sizes, which was consistent with conceptual expectations. In a series of regression analyses, the authors also observed that prehire and posthire differences in L-r scores best predicted changes in scores on various externalizing MMPI-2-RF scales, whereas prehire and posthire differences in K-r scores predicted differences in internalizing MMPI-2-RF scale scores. In other words, in this context, higher L-r scores were better linked to underreporting of behavioral problems, whereas higher K-r scores were associated with underreporting of emotional problems.

Two MMPI-2-RF studies have also attempted to evaluate the degree to which traditional backgrounds have an impact on MMPI-2-RF L-r scores, which would also generalize to MMPI-3 L scores as they share 12 of 14 items. Bridges and Baum (2013) examined the L-r total scores and item responses in a sample of 166 university students enrolled at a Christian university. They found using a one-sample t-test that the Christian students scored significantly higher on

L-r (M = 53.8T; SD = 11.7) than the MMPI-2-RF normative sample. This difference translates into a small effect size magnitude (Cohen's d = 0.35). Moreover, female and male students, respectively, endorsed six and five individual L-r items in the keyed direction at a significantly greater rate than female and male members of the MMPI-2-RF normative sample.

In a subsequent study, Bagby et al. (2020) examined the L-r score in 232 university students who self-identified as being of Muslim faith. Their average L-r score was 56.41 (SD = 10.07), indicating approximately a medium effect size difference from the MMPI-2-RF normative sample. The L-r score also showed a medium-sized correlation with the Balanced Inventory for Desirable Responding Impression Management (IM) score (r = .45) and with the Multidimensional Measure of Islamic Spirituality (MMS) (r = .34). A regression model indicated that both IM and MMS scores contributed uniquely to the prediction of L-r scores, though the former was associated with a larger beta weight. However, when very high L-r scores (> 70T) were removed, IM and MMS scores' contribution to explaining L-r variance were approximately equal. In other words, endorsement of religious spirituality accounts for individual differences in L-r scores, particularly at moderate levels, which supports the MMPI-2-RF (and MMPI-3) administration manual's recommendation to consider the contribution of a traditional background when interpreting an L score in the 65–79T range.

In summary, research on the MMPI-2-RF and MMPI-3 underreporting scales has been quite supportive of their validity and clinical utility. The effect size magnitudes associated with differences between underreporters and those deemed to be genuine responders have been consistently large, especially in analogue simulation designs. Classification accuracy statistics in the studies that have reported them have been consistently supportive of the cut scores reported in the MMPI-2-RF/MMPI-3 administration manuals. Moreover, the effect size magnitudes are at least comparable and, on average, better than those reported for the MMPI-2 L and K scales in Baer and Miller's (2002) meta-analysis (L: d = 1.19; K: d = 1.13). In addition, although only one MMPI-3 study has been published to date, those effect sizes are among the largest observed for L and K across any version of the MMPI, which is very promising. Finally, research has clearly supported the traditional background hypothesis (particularly as religiosity is concerned), and MMPI-3 users should take note of such backgrounds when interpreting moderate elevations on L.

TWO FUNCTIONS OF THE SCALES

The MMPI-3 Validity Scales canvass the full range of threats to protocol validity. Their original and primary function is to assist the MMPI-3 user with determining whether the scores on the test are valid for interpretation. However, like their predecessors, they also serve a second function by providing information relevant to the assessment of malingering and its counterpart, intentional concealment of problems. We discuss next some important considerations for interpreting or using the Validity Scales within each of these domains.

Assessing Threats to Protocol Validity

As detailed in chapter 8, validity problems associated with nonresponding are assessed with CNS and the Response % statistic reported for each scale in the computerized reports. Random (or quasi random) responding is assessed with CRIN and VRIN scales, which are equally sensitive to intentional and unintentional random responding but do not distinguish between the two. Regardless of intentionality, excessive levels of random responding invalidate the test protocol. Fixed responding in either the True or False direction is assessed with TRIN, and excessive levels of either type of fixed responding also invalidate the resulting test protocol.

The MMPI-3 overreporting indicators identify noncredible reports of psychopathology, somatic symptoms, and cognitive difficulties, which can distort scores on various Substantive Scales. Because the primary focus of the MMPI-3 Substantive Scales is psychopathology or maladaptive personality traits, very substantial deviations from the general population mean on F or Fp indicate that a test protocol is invalid and uninterpretable owing to excessive overreporting. Scores on all five MMPI-3 overreporting indicators are affected by both intentional and unintentional overreporting. For example, individuals with a somatoform disorder or a psychotic disorder that includes somatic delusions may produce very high scores on Fs or FBS by reporting problems they genuinely but mistakenly believe they are experiencing. Extremely demoralized individuals with a highly negativistic perceptual style may perceive and present themselves as having more problems than they actually exhibit.

L and K alert the interpreter to the possible impact of underreporting on substantive scale scores. Elevated L scores indicate that a test taker presents an unlikely picture of moral virtues associated with underreporting. High K scores reflect an unlikely presentation of good psychological adjustment when observed in clinical contexts. A distinction between intentional and unintentional underreporting is often associated with Paulhus's (1984) conceptualization of the roles of self-deception and impression management in self-report. Paulhus cited Meehl and Hathaway's (1946) distinction between "conscious falsehood" and self-deception in this regard. However, identification of L as reflecting primarily impression management and K as a measure of self-deception is inconsistent both with how the developers conceptualized these scales and with subsequent empirical findings. Hathaway, McKinley, and Meehl viewed both scales as measures of intentional and unintentional underreporting. Simulation studies conducted with the original and revised versions of these scales indicate that scores on both L and K change significantly when subjects are instructed to appear better adjusted than they are. Thus, both scales are sensitive to impression management. Both may also be affected by (and reflect) distorted self-perceptions. However, if Detrick and Chibnall's (2014) findings are replicated, the form of psychopathology being minimized (intentionally or unintentionally) might be linked to which underreporting scale is elevated. Excessive endorsement of moral virtues has been linked to underreporting of externalizing and rule-breaking proclivities, which makes intuitive sense, whereas the portrayal of unrealistic psychological adjustment as indicated by elevated K scores is reflected in attenuated scores on internalizing scales. Detrick and Chibnall conducted their study in a relevant but nevertheless highly specific population of public safety personnel, and their sample sizes were relatively small.

Detecting Malingering and Concealment of Psychopathology

Although they were not developed for this purpose, a second function of MMPI validity indicators was identified shortly after the test was introduced. As has often been the case with psychological testing, this development occurred in the context of efforts to use the MMPI in screening military personnel. Meehl and Hathaway (1946) described what was likely the first MMPI "faking" study, in which military personnel simulated faking bad to "avoid being accepted into the draft" (p. 537) and faking good "to make certain that they would be acceptable to army induction." (p. 538). Follow-up studies explored the utility of the MMPI validity indicators in detecting externally motivated, intentional overreporting and underreporting (Cofer et al., 1949; Gough, 1947; Hunt, 1948).

After the conclusion of World War II, there was a lull in efforts to investigate the utility of the MMPI in detecting malingering. Dahlstrom and Welsh (1960) allocated just two pages to the topic in the first edition of their *MMPI Handbook* and even less space in the second edition (Dahlstrom et al., 1972). Graham (1977) devoted approximately two pages of text to the topic in the first edition of his MMPI textbook, and the term does not appear in the index of Greene's (1980) first MMPI interpretive manual.

Interest in using the MMPI to detect malingering was revived as psychologists became increasingly involved with the legal system in the 1980s. Discussions and investigations of use of the test to detect malingering focused on disability claimants and personal injury litigants (Butcher, 1985; Fairbank et al., 1985; Lees-Haley, 1984; Pollack & Grainey, 1984; Snibe et al., 1980), criminal defendants (Hawk & Cornell, 1989; Parwatiker et al., 1985; Wasyliw et al., 1988), and prison inmates (Schretlen & Arkowitz, 1990; Walters et al., 1988). With the transition to the MMPI-2, and with even greater involvement of psychologists with the civil and criminal justice systems during the 1990s, research on using the Validity Scales to detect malingering grew at an exponential pace. This pattern has carried over to the MMPI-2-RF. In fact, the overwhelming majority of empirical studies of the MMPI, MMPI-2, and MMPI-2-RF validity indicators have focused on their use in the detection of malingering and to a lesser extent on concealment of psychopathology. We expect this trend to continue with the MMPI-3.

Conclusion

Although the MMPI validity indicators were developed to assess threats to protocol validity, most of the published research on these scales has focused on their second function, detecting malingering or concealment of problems. A substantial body of empirical findings demonstrates the utility of the MMPI-2-RF/MMPI-3 Validity Scales in serving both functions. This chapter has focused on the conceptual and empirical foundations for using these measures to assess protocol validity. Interpretive guidelines for this use of the validity indicators are provided in chapter 8. Detection of malingering and concealment of psychopathology have been studied primarily in forensic settings. Interpretive guidelines for this application of the MMPI-3 validity indicators, emphasizing the need to consider extratest data, are provided in chapter 10.

The MMPI-3 Substantive Scales 5

The goal of this chapter is to discuss the psychometric findings and literature available to support interpretation of the MMPI-3 Substantive Scales. The main part of the chapter, which concerns construct validity, will be organized into two sections. First, we discuss each of the individual scales with respect to psychometric properties presented in the *MMPI-3 Technical Manual*, existing MMPI-2-RF literature (where applicable), and current MMPI-3 literature available at the time of this writing. The second section will focus on mapping the MMPI-3 scales onto contemporary models of psychopathology and personality. This latter section is important for MMPI-3 users to consider; one of the key aims with the MMPI-2-RF and MMPI-3 was better grounding in contemporary psychopathology science to situate the instrument within influential conceptual and empirical frameworks.

Of the 42 MMPI-3 Substantive Scales, 36 are sufficiently similar across the MMPI-2-RF and MMPI-3. Furthermore, Ben-Porath and Tellegen (2020b; see Appendix E) demonstrated that these scales have identical correlates across a range of settings and criterion modalities. For these two reasons, MMPI-2-RF literature can be relied upon when interpreting these MMPI-3 scales. This literature is therefore incorporated in the following review. Given that four of the Specific Problems (SP) Scales are completely new to the instrument (EAT, CMP, IMP, SFI), and the MMPI-2-RF Stress/Worry (STW) scale has been bifurcated into two separate scales—Stress (STR) and Worry (WRY)—consideration of these six scales will be based on the MMPI-3 literature.

Ben-Porath and Tellegen (2020b) report empirical correlate data for the MMPI-3 Scales based on samples of individuals receiving outpatient mental health services in a community mental health center or private practice; individuals undergoing presurgical, preemployment, and forensic disability evaluations; prison inmates; and university students. Various types of criteria were available for these analyses, including extensive ratings provided by therapists and intake workers at an outpatient community mental health center; systematic record reviews conducted at a private practice clinic; posthire performance ratings of police candidates; and various commonly used self-report measures for mental health and medical outpatients, disability claimants, and university students. Although *MMPI-3 Technical Manual* findings will be referenced, and readers are encouraged to review the data presented in that manual, the MMPI-2-RF literature on these scales as well as the emerging MMPI-3 literature will be emphasized when construct validity is discussed.

HIGHER-ORDER (H-O) SCALES

Psychometric Properties

In the *MMPI-3 Technical Manual,* Ben-Porath and Tellegen (2020b) report reliability estimates for the H-O Scales that range from .76 (THD) to .92 (EID) in the normative sample and .79 (THD) to .92 (EID) in the mental health sample. The associated *SEM*s (expressed in T-score values) range from 3 to 5 across settings, reflecting overall good reliability of H-O Scale scores in clinical and nonclinical samples. Ben-Porath and Tellegen also report intercorrelations between the H-O Scales in the normative and mental health sample. These range from .25 to .42, reflecting moderate covariation consistent with the goals and expectations for these scales. They also correlate substantially with their MMPI-2-RF counterparts in the normative and clinical samples, .99 to .99 (EID), .95 to .97 (THD), and .93 to .95 (BXD), indicating that the constructs assessed across the two versions of scales are virtually identical.

In chapter 2, we provided the conceptual underpinnings for the MMPI-2-RF H-O Scales, which apply to the MMPI-3 versions as well. Although we will discuss the entire MMPI-3 in the context of contemporary psychopathology literature later in this chapter, we want to emphasize the importance of these measures in the assessment of higher-order psychopathology spectra here as well. Contemporary psychopathology literature, especially within the last decade, has consistently shown that when a sufficient set of psychopathology markers is available for analysis, the structure at the three-factor level reflects internalizing, thought, and externalizing dysfunction (Bagby et al., 2014; Caspi et al., 2014; Forbes et al., 2017; Kotov et al., 2011; Sellbom, Carragher et al., 2020; Wright et al., 2013; see also Kotov et al., 2021). The MMPI-3 H-O Scales are measures of these broad psychopathology domains. The research base available to guide and support their use is unparalleled relative to alternative instruments. Next, we provide a summary of the *MMPI-3 Technical Manual* correlates of the H-O Scales and key findings from the MMPI-2-RF/MMPI-3 literature to date.

Emotional/Internalizing Dysfunction (EID)

In both men and women of the community mental health center outpatient sample, higher scores on EID were associated with being described by intake workers as sad and depressed, in despair, hopeless, and anhedonic. These patients were described by their therapists as sad, insecure, anhedonic, depressed, being restricted in affect, being anxious, worrying, having intrusive memories, being obsessive, and having difficulties concentrating. Additionally, men were described as feeling overwhelmed and being socially awkward, shy, and introverted, and women were described as engaging in self-injurious behavior, being agitated, and having nightmares. Empirical correlates of EID that replicated across gender and settings in the private practice outpatient sample included presenting with complaints of depression and anxiety, being prescribed antidepressant and anxiolytic medication, and being diagnosed with depression and anxiety disorders. In a spine surgery/spinal cord stimulator candidate sample, the EID scale correlated with measures of catastrophizing coping strategies, negative affect, and pain impairment in both men and women. In a forensic disability claimant sample, EID correlated with a range of emotional, internalizing, and somatic impairment variables across both men and women. In this sample, EID also correlated across both genders with most internalizing scales from the Detailed Assessment of PTSD (Briere, 2001), and with respect to the Personality Assessment Inventory (PAI; Morey, 1991), EID exhibited large correlations across both genders with scales measuring depression, anxiety and anxiety-related disorders, paranoia, schizophrenia, borderline features, suicidal ideation, nonsupport, stress, low warmth, and low treatment rejection. An examination of the subscales clarified associations with schizophrenia and paranoia as pertaining mostly to social detachment, thought difficulties, and resentment rather than overt psychotic experiences. Finally, in a university sample, the EID scale exhibited large correlations with a wide range of extratest scales measuring internalizing problems (i.e., depression, anxiety, fear, emotional regulation, posttraumatic distress, obsessive-compulsive symptoms) in both genders. Moreover, in both men and women, EID showed large correlations with personality trait scales reflective of the general negative affectivity domain (e.g., depressivity, affective lability, anhedonia, self-harm, relationship insecurity). The extant literature on the MMPI-3 includes one study of empirical correlates of the H-O Scales. Specifically, Whitman et al. (2021b) examined associations between a range of presenting problems, neurocognitive variables, and psychiatric diagnosis in 207 patients from a neuropsychology practice. The EID scale was meaningfully associated with presenting emotional problems, cognitive symptoms from neurocognitive assessments, suicidal ideation, history of psychiatric hospitalizations, and depressive disorders. Small correlations were also observed between EID and anxiety, adjustment, PTSD, and eating disorder diagnoses.

The MMPI-2-RF literature on EID has clearly established that this H-O Scale corresponds to broader psychological constructs and psychiatric syndromes representing internalizing or emotional dysfunction. For instance, Lanyon and Thomas (2013) showed that it correlated highly and loaded on the same latent dimension as the Psychological Screening Inventory Discomfort scale, which is also a broadband measure of emotional distress. Both Lee et al. (2018) and Sellbom, Bagby et al. (2012) have shown that the EID scale differentiates depression from schizophrenia and bipolar disorder in multiple psychiatric samples. Moreover, in various mental health, correctional, and university samples, this H-O Scale most strongly correlates with personality disorder symptoms and traits reflective of internalizing/negative affect problems (Anderson et al., 2015a, 2015b; van der Heijden et al., 2013a) as well as neuroticism and negative emotionality from major personality models (Anderson & Sellbom, 2021; Avdeyeva et al., 2011; Tarescavage & Menton, 2020; Tellegen & Ben-Porath, 2008/2011; Tylicki, Phillips et al., 2020; van der Heijden et al., 2013b, 2013c).

The MMPI-2-RF literature has also indicated significant applied utility of EID scale scores. For instance, elevated scores on this H-O Scale have been associated with significantly greater likelihood of suicidal behavior 12 months following testing in a forensic psychiatric sample (Tarescavage, Glassmire, & Burchett, 2018). Marek et al. (2015) have shown that EID scores are associated with increased postoperative disability, pain, and negative affect in those undergoing spine surgery. Marek et al. (2021a) also observed this scale to predict worsening of certain psychosocial outcomes 6 years after bariatric surgery. Tarescavage, Scheman, and Ben-Porath (2018) found that higher pretreatment EID scores were associated with poorer treatment outcomes in a chronic pain sample. Anestis et al. (2015) observed that higher scores on this scale were also associated with premature treatment termination in a mental health sample. Furthermore, Tarescavage, Corey, and Ben-Porath (2015) and Tarescavage, Corey, Gupton, and Ben-Porath (2015) reported positive correlations between EID scores and problematic posthire behavioral outcomes in prehire police candidates undergoing psychological screening.

Thought Dysfunction (THD)

Few empirical correlates were found for THD at the outpatient community mental health center because individuals with thought disorders were referred to a different agency. Only one intake variable—history of physical abuse—replicated across genders in that sample. In terms of therapists' ratings, THD was consistently associated with having many nightmares and intrusive memories, being angry, being hostile, being aggressive, acting out, having stormy relationships, and having delusional thinking. In the private practice sample, there were fewer directly relevant correlates to thought disorder, and THD was only associated with a history of antipsychotic medication and being diagnosed with bipolar disorder in women. THD scores were also associated with a history of being bullied and diagnoses of ADHD and cannabis use in men. In the spine surgery/spinal cord stimulator candidate sample, THD was moderately correlated with self-reported tendency to catastrophize in both genders. This H-O Scale also showed a range of moderate correlations in men and women with self-reported somatic complaints, anxiety, depression, borderline tendencies, and family dysfunction. Moreover, the THD scale showed moderate correlations with various self-reported PTSD symptoms, especially reexperiencing, avoidance, and dissociative symptoms, in men (but not in women). With respect to PAI correlates, in both men and women, THD exhibited a large correlation with paranoia and moderate sized correlations with schizophrenia, mania, anxiety and anxiety-related disorders, and borderline features. Unlike other H-O Scales, prominent PAI subscale correlates included the two scales that explicitly focus on psychotic experiences (i.e., Paranoia-Persecution and Schizophrenia-Psychotic Experiences). With regard to the university sample correlates, the most prominent correlates that replicated across gender were moderate to large correlations with a range of thought dysfunction measures that included paranoid ideation, various forms of dissociation, and magical ideation, as well as fantasy proneness, peculiarity, unusual beliefs, and unusual experiences.

In the current MMPI-3 literature, the THD scale has been prominently associated with mania and hallucinations/paranoia in a neuropsychology sample, but not other variables—indicating good discriminant validity (Whitman et al., 2021b). The MMPI-2-RF literature on the THD scale has clearly established it as a major marker for the thought disorder spectrum. Research has shown that this scale differentiates patients with schizophrenia from those with depression (Lee et al., 2018; Sellbom, Babgy, et al., 2012). In several samples, this H-O Scale has shown moderate to large correlations with Cluster A personality disorders, particularly schizotypal (Anderson et al., 2015b; Sellbom & Smith, 2017; Zahn et al., 2017). In terms of dimensional adaptive and maladaptive personality traits, THD correlates with measures of absorption, self-transcendence, fantasy proneness, unusual thinking, unusual experiences, and magical ideation in various mental health and university samples (Avdeyeva et al., 2011; Anderson et al., 2015a; Tarescavage & Menton, 2020; van der Heijden et al., 2013b, 2013c).

Regarding applied utility, THD scale scores have been found to predict aggression and violent behavior in both general forensic psychiatric hospital patients and those confined under sexual violent predator laws (Grossi et al., 2015; Tarescavage, Azizian, et al., 2019). THD scores also moderately predicted increased likelihood of probation failure in a criminal court sample (Tarescavage et al.,

2014). Tarescavage, Scheman, and Ben-Porath (2018) observed that higher pretreatment THD scores were associated with poorer treatment outcomes in a chronic pain sample. Finally, Tarescavage, Corey, and Ben-Porath (2016) reported positive correlations between THD scores and problematic posthire behavioral outcomes in prehire police candidates undergoing psychological screening.

Behavioral/Externalizing Dysfunction (BXD)

In both men and women assessed at the outpatient community mental health center, higher BXD scores were associated with intake workers' descriptions of patients being impulsive and being diagnosed with alcohol and drug use disorders, as well as with being less likely to have a generalized anxiety disorder diagnosis. Moreover, the BXD scale was associated across both genders with therapists' ratings of being angry, being hostile, being aggressive, having intrusive memories, engaging in antisocial behavior, acting out, drinking alcohol excessively, using illicit substances, being impulsive and excitable, and having stormy relationships. In the outpatient private practice sample, BXD scale scores were associated across genders with a history of having engaged in bullying, having current alcohol and drug use, and being diagnosed with alcohol use disorder and bipolar disorder. In a forensic disability sample, BXD scores were moderately correlated across men and women with borderline features, self-ratings of hostility, substance use problems, chronic maladjustment, and being a survivor of violence. In terms of correlations with the PAI, large correlations were observed with antisocial features, drug problems, and aggression in both genders. In a university sample, the BXD scale was moderately correlated with several measures of externalizing dysfunction, including impulsivity and drug and alcohol use. Regarding personality traits, BXD scores were moderately associated in both genders with norm violation, risk-taking, hostile aggression, affective lability, anger, cognitive problems, and exhibitionism. Distinct from the other two H-O Scales, BXD scores were also moderately to largely associated with psychopathic personality traits and antisocial behavior in a male prison sample.

In the current MMPI-3 literature, in a neuropsychology sample, BXD scale scores were weakly associated with behavioral problems and cognitive symptoms on neuropsychological testing, as hypothesized (Whitman et al., 2021b). They were also associated with mania, violence, and history of being incarcerated as well as substance use disorder diagnoses. The MMPI-2-RF literature has established BXD as a well-validated measure of externalizing dysfunction. BXD scores correlate with a range of externalizing disorders, including antisocial personality disorder and borderline personality disorder—such scores also correlate with alcohol use and other substance-related problems, and general antisocial and aggressive behavior (Anderson et al., 2015b; Laurinaitytė et al., 2017; Sellbom & Smith, 2017; Tellegen & Ben-Porath, 2008/2011; Zahn et al.,

2017). Moreover, research linking the MMPI-2-RF to dimensional personality traits has shown direct associations with both the antagonism-agreeableness domain and the disinhibition-conscientiousness domain as well as their subfacets (e.g., callousness, manipulativeness, grandiosity, impulsivity, irresponsibility, risk-taking; Anderson & Sellbom, 2021; Anderson et al., 2015a; Avdeyeva et al., 2011; Tarescavage & Menton, 2020; Tellegen & Ben-Porath, 2008/2011; Tylicki, Phillips et al., 2020).

The BXD scale also demonstrates good, applied utility in several contexts, generally consistent with conceptual expectations. In the area of risk assessment, BXD scores are associated with histories of violence and aggression, and they are predictive of various forms of future violence and aggression in several correctional and forensic psychiatric contexts (Laurinaitytė et al., 2017; Tarescavage, Azizian, Broderick, & English, 2019; Tarescavage, Cappo, & Ben-Porath, 2018; Tarescavage, Glassmire, & Burchett, 2016; Tarescavage, Luna-Jones, & Ben-Porath, 2014; Whitman et al., 2021b). Moreover, BXD scores have been predictive of negative outcomes 6 years after surgery in a bariatric presurgery candidate sample (Marek et al., 2021a). Scores on this H-O Scale have also been linked to poor treatment adherence and premature treatment termination in a range of mental health and chronic pain samples (Anestis et al., 2015; Patel & Suhr, 2019; Tarescavage, Scheman, & Ben-Porath, 2018; Tylicki et al., 2019). Finally, elevated BXD scores have predicted posthire negative outcomes in police candidates undergoing preemployment evaluation; however, extremely low scores on this scale have also evidenced posthire difficulties related to excessive rigidity and difficulties adapting to changing circumstances (Corey, Sellbom, & Ben-Porath, 2018).

Summary

The empirical correlates just reviewed illustrate that scores on each of the H-O Scales are associated with a broad range of construct-relevant criteria, as would be expected of broadband measures of psychopathology and personality. The distinctive nature of these correlates, reflecting limited cross-scale overlap, illustrates the discriminant validity of the scales. The psychopathology symptoms, personality characteristics, and behavioral proclivities represented by these correlates are consistent with features of the targeted constructs that have been identified in the literature. These findings indicate good construct validity of the H-O Scales, providing a link between the MMPI-3 and current perspectives on psychopathology, which includes recognition of the association between psychopathology and personality and the hierarchical nature of psychopathology (Conway et al., 2019; Kotov et al., 2017, 2021; Ruggero et al., 2019), with broad dimensional constructs accounting for phenotypic comorbidity and genotypic commonalities.

RESTRUCTURED CLINICAL (RC) SCALES

As discussed in chapter 2, Tellegen's exploratory scale construction approach produced a set of nine RC Scales; one designed to assess the long-recognized MMPI common factor and eight measures of distinctive core components of the original Clinical Scales. This approach to scale development produced measures of open constructs, the delineation of which can be accomplished by considering the theoretical formulations that guided their development, the content of the resulting scales, and empirical findings on their convergent and discriminant associations with constructs that were already known. This section provides a detailed description of the eight RC Scale constructs and scales based on these three recognized indicators of construct validity (Loevinger, 1957). As a reminder, on the MMPI-3, the MMPI-2-RF RC3 (Cynicism) scale is placed among the SP Scales and abbreviated CYN. Also note that the RC Scale literature dates to studies from 2003 when the scales became available for the MMPI-2. The overwhelming psychometric literature reviewed for these scales is therefore based on the MMPI-2/MMPI-2-RF versions, but as stated at the beginning of this chapter, this literature applies to the MMPI-3 versions as well.

Psychometric Properties

The psychometric properties of the MMPI-3 RC Scales are reported in the *MMPI-3 Technical Manual*. Ben-Porath and Tellegen (2020b) report that test-retest reliabilities range from .81 (RC6) to .94 (RC4) and internal consistency reliability estimates range from .69 (RC8) to .89 (RCd) in the normative sample and .76 (RC4) to .93 (RCd) in the mental health sample. The associated *SEM*s (expressed in T-score values) range from 3 to 6 across settings, reflecting overall good reliability of RC scale scores in clinical and nonclinical samples. Ben-Porath and Tellegen also report intercorrelations between the RC Scales in the normative and a composite clinical sample. These range from −.13 to .70, with most in the small to moderate range, reflecting moderate covariation consistent with the goals and expectations for these scales. They also correlate substantially with their MMPI-2-RF counterparts in the normative and mental health samples, .77 to .83 (RC9) to .97 to .98 (RCd, RC8), with RC9 being the only scale consistently below .90, indicating that the constructs across the two versions of these scales are virtually identical (with the possible exception of RC9). Data in Appendix E of the *MMPI-3 Technical Manual* show similar correlates for the MMPI-2-RF and MMPI-3 versions, including for RC9; however, the magnitudes of RC9 correlates related to bipolar disorder and impulsivity are substantially higher for the MMPI-3 version of the scale, reflecting success in efforts to enhance this measure.

Demoralization (RCd)

CONCEPTUALIZING DEMORALIZATION

The demoralization construct was introduced in chapter 2. As noted there, Tellegen concluded that this affect-laden phenomenon was the source of problematic excessive intercorrelations between the Clinical Scales and conceptualized it as the equivalent of the Pleasantness/Unpleasantness or Happiness/Unhappiness dimension of self-reported mood. Frank (1974, 1985) identified amelioration of demoralization as the mechanism underlying the nonspecific effects of psychotherapy. Dohrenwend et al. (1980) linked Frank's demoralization construct to their finding of substantial intercorrelations between scores on psychiatric rating scales and equated its role in the assessment of psychopathology with that of taking a patient's temperature in medicine. Consistent with these views of demoralization, the RCd items reflect the presence of dysphoric affect, distress, self-attributed inefficacy, low self-esteem, and a sense of having given up.

Other than Tellegen's work linking mood, personality, and psychopathology, prior to the introduction of the RC Scales, the demoralization construct did not figure prominently in the assessment literature. As just noted, an exception was the work of Dohrenwend et al. (1980), who observed that there was considerable phenotypic overlap between demoralization and depression. They also noted that there were important differences between the constructs, and that demoralization appeared closer to "Minor Depressive Disorder" as described by Spitzer et al. (1978) in the research diagnostic criteria that preceded the *DSM-III*.

Following Dohrenwend et al. (1980), other authors have commented on and investigated similarities and differences between demoralization and depression. De Figuiredo (1993), a former student of Frank's who continued to develop the demoralization construct, noted that whereas both conditions may manifest in subjective distress and dysphoric affect, vegetative symptoms of depression such as poor sleep and appetite are less likely to accompany demoralization. De Figuiredo also observed that the dysphoric affect often found in individuals with medical disorders is more likely a product of demoralization than of depression, and Clarke and Kissane (2002) noted that depression is characterized uniquely by anhedonia.

Recognition of the role demoralization plays in the psychological problems experienced by individuals with physical illness led to its inclusion as a distinct diagnostic category in the Diagnostic Criteria for Psychosomatic Research (DCPR, Fava et al., 1995). Using these criteria, researchers have found significant rates of demoralization in breast cancer patients (Grassi et al., 2004), patients with coronary artery disease (Rafanelli et al., 2005), and general medical outpatients (Mangelli et al., 2005). Investigators have also found that demoralization plays a significant role in the psychological reactions of individuals exposed to trauma, including military veterans (Frank & Frank, 1996), holocaust survivors (Fenig & Levav, 1991), Southeast Asian refugees (Kroll, 2003; Kroll & McDonald, 2003; Ying & Akutsu, 1997), and immigrants (Gutkovich et al., 1999). Demoralization has also been linked to depression (Mangelli et al., 2005; Strada, 2009) and suicidality in individuals with schizophrenia (Restifo et al., 2009; Tandon & Jibson, 2003), individuals with severe disabilities (Tweed et al., 1988), and elderly individuals in Japan struggling with modernization (Watanabe et al., 1995).

Others have also recently been investigating the role of demoralization in self-report questionnaires. Noordhof et al. (2015) examined the influence of demoralization on the NEO Personality Inventory–Revised (NEO PI-R; Costa & McCrae, 1992), a measure of the influential five-factor model of personality, in a Dutch clinical sample. Through sophisticated latent modeling approaches, these researchers identified items that measured demoralization rather than their primary trait domain (mostly, but not exclusively, neuroticism). Revised scales from which demoralization was removed had substantially improved discriminant validities against external criteria. A follow-up study by Noordhof et al. (2018) showed that personality trait changes following treatment via antidepressant medication or psychotherapy were mostly attributable to changes in demoralization (as measured with the NEO PI-R) rather than specific trait changes.

EMPIRICAL FINDINGS WITH RCD

Several studies have examined the conceptualized link between RCd and Positive and Negative Activation. Tellegen et al. (2003, 2006) found demoralization to be the MMPI-2 equivalent of the Pleasant-Unpleasant (or Happy-Unhappy) mood dimension in Watson and Tellegen's (1985) widely studied model of affect. Consistent with this model, RCd is strongly associated with both low positive and high negative temperament as measured in three different personality inventories: Tellegen's (1982) Multidimensional Personality Questionnaire (MPQ; Avdeyeva et al., 2011 and Sellbom & Ben-Porath, 2005, in university students), NEO PI-R (Forbey & Ben-Porath, 2008, in university students; Noordhof et al., 2015, and Sellbom, Ben-Porath, & Bagby, 2008b, in mental health patients), and Clark's (1993) Schedule for Nonadaptive and Adaptive Personality (SNAP; Simms et al., 2005, in a clinical sample and sample of community-dwelling veterans; see also Kotelnikova et al., 2019).

Consistent with the broadly unhappy content endorsed by individuals scoring high on the Demoralization scale, external correlates of RCd include generalized emotional distress and unhappiness, depressed mood, and anxiety (Arbisi, Sellbom, & Ben-Porath, 2008, in psychiatric inpatients; Burchett & Ben-Porath, 2010, in university students; Binford & Liljequist, 2008, in mental health outpatients; Forbey & Ben-Porath, 2008, in university students; Forbey, Ben-Porath & Gartland, 2009, in prison inmates; Handel & Archer, 2008, in psychiatric inpatients; Ingram et al., 2021, in a very large sample of military veterans; McCord and Drerup, 2011, in chronic pain patients; McDevitt-Murphy, Weathers, Flood, Eakin, & Benson, 2007 and Moultrie and Engel, 2017, in psychiatric inpatients; Monnot, Quirck, Hoerger, & Brewer, 2009, in substance abuse treatment patients; Osberg, Haseley, & Kamas, 2008, in university students; Sellbom, Ben-Porath, & Bagby, 2008a, in university students and mental health outpatients; Sellbom, Ben-Porath & Graham, 2006, in a college counseling setting; Sellbom, Graham, & Schenk, 2006, in an independent mental health practice; Shkalim, 2015, in an Israeli psychiatric patient sample; Shkalim et al., 2017, in a sample of Israeli psychiatric outpatients; Simms et al., 2005, in a clinical sample and sample of community-dwelling veterans; van der Heijden et al., 2013a, 2013b, in Dutch mental health patient samples; Wolf et al., 2008, in veterans assessed for PTSD; Wygant, Boutacoff et al., 2007, in bariatric surgery candidates). Congruent with these findings, RCd is also associated with symptoms of nonspecific distress such as decreased sleep, decreased appetite, guilt, feelings of worthlessness, decreased energy, and poor concentration (Arbisi et al., 2008, psychiatric inpatients; Handel & Archer, 2008, in a different sample of psychiatric inpatients). In terms of the MMPI-3 version of this scale, Whitman et al. (2021b) showed that it was correlated with depression diagnosis in a clinical neuropsychology sample.

With respect to explicit differential diagnosis, Sellbom, Bagby et al. (2012) and Lee et al. (2018) have both shown that RCd scores differentiate between patients with major depressive disorder from those with schizophrenia at medium to large effect size estimates in independent psychiatric samples. As a measure of nonspecific emotional distress and dysphoria, RCd has also emerged as one of the best predictors of PTSD symptoms on the MMPI-2-RF and MMPI-3 (Ben-Porath & Tellegen, 2020b). Ingram et al. (2021) found that RCd scores exhibited large to very large correlations with a range of self-report PTSD measures, and this scale was the best predictor of Cluster D symptoms (which essentially measure dysphoria). Sellbom, Lee et al. (2012) found that RCd was the only RC Scale to significantly predict PTSD symptoms in the context of a latent regression model in a sample of forensic disability claimants. The *MMPI-3 Technical Manual* replicates these findings against a range of PTSD measures in forensic disability and other samples.

Consistent with Frank's (1974) conceptualization of demoralization as a condition characterized by helplessness and hopelessness, low self-esteem, and insecurity, RCd correlates include all of these features (Arbisi, Sellbom, & Ben-Porath, 2008, in psychiatric inpatients; Burchett & Ben-Porath, 2010, in university students; Forbey & Ben-Porath, 2007, in individuals receiving substance abuse treatment; Sellbom, Ben-Porath, & Graham, 2006, in a college counseling settings; Osberg, Haseley, & Kamas, 2008, in university students; Tellegen et al., 2003, in psychiatric inpatients). And congruent with research linking demoralization with increased risk for suicidal ideation, findings from various settings and samples indicate an association between scores on RCd and current suicidal ideation and/or recent suicide attempts (Arbisi, Sellbom, & Ben-Porath, 2008, in psychiatric inpatients; Binford & Liljequist, 2008, in mental health outpatients; Handel & Archer, 2008, in psychiatric inpatients; Tellegen & Ben-Porath, 2008/2011, in criminal defendants undergoing court-ordered evaluations). Whitman et al. (2021b) extended this evidence base to a clinical neuropsychology sample for the MMPI-3 version of the scale. Glassmire et al. (2016) and Tarescavage, Glassmire, and Burchett (2018) also found that RCd correlated with suicidal ideation and future suicide attempts in two forensic psychiatric hospital samples drawn from the same population. Additionally, one study found RCd scores to be associated with clinician-rated suicide risk in a university psychology clinic (Anestis et al., 2018). Finally, Stanley et al. (2018) found that RCd interacted with RC9, a measure of behavioral hyperactivation, in the prediction of suicide attempts in a university psychology clinic.

SUMMARY

Empirical findings support the construct validity of RCd as a measure of a general, affectively colored distress factor linked with symptomatic anxiety and depression, helplessness and hopelessness, low self-esteem, and a sense of inefficacy, as conceptualized by Frank (1974), and with low positive activation and high negative activation, as conceptualized by Tellegen (1985). Scores on this scale are associated with an increased risk for current suicidal ideation and recent suicide attempts. Consistent with findings from behavioral medicine research, where demoralization has been identified as an incrementally informative construct separate from depression, Sellbom, Ben-Porath, and Bagby (2008a) and Shkalim et al. (2017) found that demoralization, as assessed by RCd, represents a distinctive primary marker of distress disorders including major depression, dysthymia, generalized anxiety, and PTSD.

Somatic Complaints (RC1)

CONCEPTUALIZING SOMATIC COMPLAINTS

Psychological disorders involving unexplained somatic complaints have been described and diagnosed since at least the civilization of ancient Egypt (Trimble, 2004). Lamberty (2008) recounts that a "wandering uterus" was first implicated as causing unexplained physical symptoms in women in ancient Egypt, a theory later formalized in the label *hysteria,* coined by the Greek physician Hippocrates. During the Renaissance, British physician Thomas Sydenham observed that symptoms of hysteria could also be found in men and coined the term *hypochondriasis* to designate hysteria's male counterpart. Sydenham is also credited with advancing the view that these conditions were a product of the nervous system, a notion reiterated by the 19th century French psychiatrist Paul Briquet (Lamberty,

2008). Two other 19th century French physicians, Jean-Martin Charcot and Pierre Janet, began their influential work in this area adhering to Briquet's conceptualization that excessive somatic complaining was a neurologically based disease. However, after collaborating with Sigmund Freud, they shifted to a view that it was a disorder of the mind that could afflict both women and men (Lamberty, 2008). Freud's notion of *conversion,* a psychological process that transformed traumatic experiences into symbolic physical symptoms, became the dominant viewpoint in the first part of the 20th century and remains embedded in the label *conversion disorder,* still used in the *DSM-5* (APA, 2013).

Although previous iterations of the *DSM* included multiple categories of somatoform disorders (e.g., hypochondriasis, pain disorder, somatization disorder), the inclusion of etiologically distinct phenomena under one broad heading, Somatoform Disorders, garnered substantial criticism and calls for reform (e.g., Lamberty, 2008). In response, the *DSM-5* included these disorders in one main disorder category, somatic symptom disorder, whereas conversion disorder would be retained as a separate disorder in the *DSM-5*, rebranded functional neurological/conversion disorder. This approach is generally consistent with the broader literature (albeit imperfectly). Watson et al. (2022) provide a comprehensive review of studies conducted across a diverse range of countries incorporating a broad array of populations and measurement modalities that have yielded support for a somatoform higher order factor in structural research. The various indicators have mostly represented an array of bodily distress symptoms (e.g., pain, gastrointestinal, cardiopulmonary, chronic fatigue, functional neurological) akin to the bodily distress syndrome (BDS) proposed by Fink and colleagues (e.g., Fink, 2017; Petersen et al., 2020). Thus, structural models clearly point to a shared underlying cause of bodily distress.

The revamping of the somatic symptom disorders nicely illustrates one of the advantages of delinking the RC Scales from any given nosological system or version. Multiple lines of research have supported a dimensional higher order somatic symptom or bodily distress construct (Watson et al., 2022). More importantly, the developments in this general field have been consistent with the intended use of RC1, which concerns the identification of individuals who present with an unrealistically large number and range of somatic symptom complaints. Moreover, the items of RC1 include a combination of gastrointestinal, pain, and neurological symptoms, thus tapping all but the sexual symptoms required for a *DSM-5* somatic symptom disorder or Fink and colleagues' bodily distress syndrome—a testament to the richness of the original MMPI item pool.

EMPIRICAL FINDINGS WITH RC1

Identified empirical correlates for RC1 include various forms, indices, and manifestations of somatoform psychopathology. Substantial correlations between RC1 scores and a screener for somatoform disorders (Janca et al., 1995) have been reported by Forbey and Ben-Porath (2008) in university students, Forbey et al. (2009) in prison inmates, and Tellegen and Ben-Porath (2008/2011) in mental health and medical outpatient samples. Burchett and Ben-Porath (2010) reported comparable findings with the Somatization scale of the SCL-90-R (Derogatis, 1994) with university students.

In mental health outpatient samples, Sellbom, Ben-Porath, and Graham (2006) reported significant correlations of RC1 scores with therapist ratings of somatization and excessive somatic concern in individuals receiving treatment at a college counseling clinic. Sellbom, Graham, and Schenk (2006) reported a sizable correlation for RC1 scores with self-reported somatization symptoms in a sample of individuals seen for outpatient treatment by independent practitioners. Shkalim (2015) found a moderate correlation between RC1 and clinician-rated somatic symptoms in an Israeli psychiatric sample.

Simms et al. (2005) found significant correlations for RC1 scores with diagnoses of current and lifetime somatoform disorders based on a structured clinical interview in a sample of community-dwelling veterans. In a different sample of veterans, Wolf et al. (2008) reported particularly high correlations for RC1 with hyperarousal symptoms in a sample of individuals diagnosed with PTSD. Tarescavage, Scheman et al. (2015) reported correlations between RC1 and somatoform disorder diagnosis in a chronic pain sample. Van der Heijden et al. (2012) and van der Heijden et al. (2013a) reported moderate to large correlations between RC1 and somatoform disorders in separate Dutch psychiatric samples. Whitman et al. (2021b) found that MMPI-3 RC1 moderately correlated with somatic symptom disorder diagnosis in a clinical neuropsychology sample.

Locke et al. (2010) evaluated the ability of the MMPI-2-RF to differentiate between patients diagnosed with epileptic versus psychogenic nonepileptic seizures in an epilepsy monitoring unit. These authors found RC1 to perform best in this task, with a sensitivity of .76 and specificity of .60. They also reported that RC1 was able to account for unique variance in this differential diagnosis, beyond that explained by demographic variables and medical history risk factors. Thomas and Locke (2010) conducted a series of taxometric and item response theory (IRT) analyses of the RC1 items and scores with the same sample and concluded that the scale accurately assesses the latent structure of somatization for individuals who produce clinically elevated scores.

Aguerrevere et al. (2018) reported that in a large, incentivized sample undergoing evaluations for chronic pain, individuals who were identified via cluster analysis to be valid responders on the MMPI-2-RF, and less likely to be malingering than those belonging to a different cluster, were clearly defined by elevated RC1 scores more so than by any other RC scale. Baez et al. (2018) found that RC1 scores were correlated with pain-related dysfunction at both intake and discharge from a Veterans Administration (VA) facility. Tarescavage, Scheman et al. (2015) reported correlations between RC1 and pain disability in a chronic pain treatment sample. Block et al. (2014) reported that RC1 was associated with pain ratings and with overall disability in a worker's compensation sample seeking spine surgery. Marek et al. (2020) also observed correlations between RC1 and general health complaints as well as with various bodily complaints in spine surgery and spinal cord stimulator surgery samples. RC1 scores were associated with decreased quality of life as well as various eating and weight concerns in a sample who had undergone bariatric surgery 6 years earlier (Marek et al., 2021a). RC1 scores have also been linked to outcomes in various presurgical evaluations. For example, Marek et al. (2014) found that RC1 scores predicted postoperative somatic complaints 1 and 3 months after bariatric surgery.

In studies related to symptom overreporting, Wygant, Sellbom et al. (2007) found that criminal defendants and civil litigants who fail symptom validity or effort tests are likely to produce higher RC1 scores than are their counterparts who show no signs of reduced effort on these measures. Henry et al. (2008) reported that RC1 scores were less highly correlated with effort test failure than were relevant MMPI-2 overreporting measures. Together, these findings indicate, as expected, that individuals suspected of symptom overreporting produce elevated scores on RC1. However, the scale is not intended nor ideally suited to serve as a validity indicator.

SUMMARY

Medically unexplained somatic complaints have garnered the attention of physicians and mental health professionals for as long as written historical records have been available. Specific types of complaints have varied, depending in part on cultural factors and advances in medical knowledge and technology. As chronicled by Lamberty (2008), unexplained paralyses, a hallmark of these conditions in the late 19th and early 20th centuries, have largely given way to other, more vaguely manifested conditions (e.g., multiple chemical sensitivities [MCSs]). Epidemiological data indicate a relatively high prevalence rate for medically unexplained somatic complaints, with most individuals experiencing these conditions seen initially in primary care and neurology clinics rather than by mental health professionals.

The empirical findings just summarized indicate that the Somatic Complaints scale (RC1), including the MMPI-3 version, is sensitive to somatoform symptomatology, but it is not specific to one type of condition within this family of disorders. Moreover, because somatic complaints are primary or secondary features of several nonsomatoform conditions, elevations in RC1 are not specific to that class of disorders and can be observed for individuals with somatic delusions, anxiety disorders, and numerous other psychological conditions with physiological symptoms.

Low Positive Emotions (RC2)

CONCEPTUALIZING LOW POSITIVE EMOTIONS

As discussed earlier, Tellegen (1985) posited that a lack of positive emotional responsiveness is a core personological risk factor for depression, related to but distinguishable from demoralization (see "Capturing Demoralization" in Step 1 of deriving the RC Scales in chapter 2). Analyses designed to identify the distinctive core component of Clinical Scale 2 corroborated this hypothesis when a subset of Scale 2 items with content reflecting low positive emotions emerged as markers of the major distinctive core component of this scale.

Tellegen's conceptualization was consistent with a model proposed by Klein (1974) who distinguished between "acute dysphoria," an acute depressive reaction to situational factors; "neurotic depression," characterized as a chronic emotional or personality disorder related to low self-esteem, overly severe disappointment reactions, and feelings of helplessness; and "endogenomorphic depression," which Klein postulated was associated with "a sharp, unreactive, pervasive impairment of the capacity to experience pleasure or to respond affectively to the anticipation of pleasure" (p. 449). Klein went on to posit that only the endogenomorphic group would be characterized by "an inhibited pleasure mechanism leading to a decreased ability to respond affectively to pleasurable sensations" (p. 450), whereas "all [three] groups would show symptomatology associated with . . . two intervening variables . . . demoralization associated with low self-esteem and anticipation of decreased pleasure and relatively increased pain" (p. 450). Klein's (1974) characterization of neurotic depression is clearly consistent with Frank's concept, though he did not refer to Frank's work when using the term "demoralization."

A lack or loss of positive emotional responsiveness characterizes other medical and mental health conditions, and therefore, cannot be considered pathognomonic of depression. Kring and Germans (2000) noted that the French physician T. H. Ribot coined the term *anhedonia* when describing a patient who experienced loss of pleasure secondary to liver damage, and following Rado (1956), Meehl (1962) characterized anhedonia as "a marked, widespread and refractory deficit in pleasure capacity" (p. 829).

Meehl (2001) advocated that the term anhedonia be replaced with *hypohedonia,* which he thought was preferable because the former suggests a complete absence of pleasure, whereas he conceptualized the construct as "an individual differences variable of hedonic capacity, not requiring anything pathological in the usual sense, analogous to traits like Spearman's g, social introversion, or dominance, that show wide dispersion in the general population" (p. 189). He characterized hypohedonia as "an impaired disposition to experience pleasure" (p. 189). Although Meehl's alternative term did not take hold, the label of RC2, Low Positive Emotions, captures Meehl's descriptively more accurate terminology.

Klein's (1974) model of depression, distinguishing between a more chronic "neurotic" depression akin to demoralization, and an endogenous, and more clearly biologically linked depression marked by anhedonia, has received considerable empirical support. Santor and Coyne (2001) studied individuals with and without a clinical diagnosis of depression who reported equal levels of depressed mood (i.e., demoralization) and found that those who met diagnostic criteria for a depressive disorder had considerably higher levels of anhedonia than those who did not. They concluded that this finding refutes a view of depression as falling on a single continuum ranging from depressed mood to major depression. Brown, Chiporta, and Barlow (1998) similarly found that low positive affect contributed uniquely to depressive disorder, whereas a variable they labeled "negative affect" was associated with a broad range of disorders including depression but also generalized anxiety disorder, panic disorder/agoraphobia, obsessive-compulsive disorder, and social phobia. (In contrast, Sellbom, Ben-Porath, and Bagby [2008a] showed that negative affect is better represented by demoralization as measured by RCd.) Lewinsohn, Petit, Joiner, and Seeley (2003) examined the concordance of depressed mood and anhedonia in a sample of individuals with a diagnosis of major depression and found that 64% of their sample concurrently experienced both symptoms, 28% experienced depressed mood without anhedonia, and 5% were found to have anhedonia but not depressed mood.

More recently, Sellbom, Carragher et al. (2020) examined the influence of personality domains on psychopathology constructs at different levels of hierarchical structure in a large community-representative Australian sample. They showed that detachment (i.e., low positive emotionality) and negative affectivity both uniquely predicted variance in latent depression and latent social anxiety constructs, consistent with the broader literature that anhedonia/low positive emotionality plays a distinct role in these, but not other forms of internalizing psychopathology (Brown, 2007; Naragon-Gainey et al., 2009).

In their review of this literature, Joiner, Walker, Pettit, Perez, and Cukrowicz (2005) highlighted the importance of distinguishing between demoralization and anhedonia when assessing for depressive disorder. They concluded, "depression is clearly more than just distress, demoralization, or depressed mood . . . depressed mood, although very common among those experiencing major depression, is not very specific to the syndrome; anhedonia, by contrast, is more unique to major depression" (p. 270). Similar findings continue to accumulate in the literature. For example, in a study of a measure of postnatal depression, Tuohy and McVey (2008) found distinctive factors assessing "nonspecific depression" (i.e., demoralization, anhedonia, and anxiety).

The findings just cited demonstrate the importance of separate assessment of demoralization and anhedonia for psychodiagnostic purposes. Klein (1974) also identified potential implications for treatment stemming from their supposition that anhedonia-linked depression has a clearer biological origin than demoralization, making it potentially more amenable to treatment with antidepressant medication. Several studies have provided support for the biological link hypothesis and its treatment implications. Using an animal model research design, Sammut et al. (2002) demonstrated an ability of antidepressant medication to alleviate signs of chemically induced anhedonia. Stones et al. (2006) found in a sample of older adults that individuals displaying prominent symptoms of anhedonia were more likely to be prescribed antidepressant medication than those who were not anhedonic. Schlaepfer et al. (2008) found that deep brain stimulation to reward circuitry alleviated anhedonia in patients with refractory major depression. Interestingly, patients in that study did not report feeling differently with the onset of stimulation, but they spontaneously expressed a desire to engage in pleasurable activity (e.g., take up bowling again).

The research just cited established a clear and distinctive link between anhedonia and depressive disorders. However, as noted earlier, low positive emotions are not specific to depression. Meehl's (1962, 1975, 1987, 2001) writings on anhedonia's role in schizophrenia have stimulated a sizable empirical literature on this topic as well as the development of several measures of this construct. Chapman et al. (1976) constructed measures of physical and social anhedonia and found that patients with schizophrenia scored higher than normal participants on both. Using a revised version of the Social Anhedonia scale described by Chapman et al., Blanchard et al. (2001) found that patients with schizophrenia demonstrated stable, trait-like high levels of social anhedonia whereas individuals diagnosed with depression showed reduced social anhedonia upon recovery from a depressive episode. Horan et al. (2006) reviewed the subsequent literature on this topic and concluded that there is good evidence that anhedonia reflects an enduring trait in schizophrenia and is episodic in depressed patients.

Low positive emotions are also possibly relevant to the assessment and diagnosis of social anxiety disorder and posttraumatic stress disorder (PTSD). For instance, Naragon-Gainey et al. (2009) examined the differential association for positive affectivity with depression and social anxiety. Low positive affect was comparably related to social anxiety and to depression, even when controlling for their overlap. As such, low positive affect is associated with social anxiety disorder—this association is distinct from its association with depression and occurs beyond shared variance with the interpersonal components of extraversion. With respect to PTSD, particular emotional numbing symptoms, such as markedly diminished interest or participation in significant activities, detachment or estrangement from others, and a restricted range of affect, directly link to anhedonia. Supporting this specific link between anhedonia and PTSD, Kashdan, Elhai, and Frueh (2006) found anhedonia to be associated with emotional numbing but not with the other types of symptoms required for the diagnosis of PTSD, though the degree to which this association is distinct from depression comorbidity is unclear (Gros et al., 2010). Indeed, Sellbom, Lee et al. (2012) did not show support for RC2 as a predictor of PTSD symptoms in a large forensic disability sample.

In summary, empirical findings have established a clear link for anhedonia with depression, schizophrenia, social anxiety, and possibly PTSD. Assessing for low positive emotions provides information relevant to diagnostic consideration for every one of these disorders, although for each, different additional symptoms also need to be present.

EMPIRICAL FINDINGS WITH RC2

The external correlates of RC2 are consistent with a lack of positive emotional responsiveness and corroborate its construct validity. RC2 is strongly correlated with various measures of low positive temperament or extraversion in broad-spectrum personality inventories—the MPQ (Sellbom & Ben-Porath, 2005, in university students), the NEO PI-R (Sellbom, Ben-Porath, & Bagby, 2008b, and Noordhof et al., 2015, in mental health settings), and the SNAP (Simms et al., 2005, in a clinical sample and a sample of community-dwelling veterans; see also Kotelnikova et al., 2019). It is the strongest RC Scale marker of the low positive emotionality (PEM) construct on all three measures.

RC2 is correlated with depressive mood symptoms in a broad range of settings and populations (Arbisi et al., 2008, in psychiatric inpatients; Binford & Liljequist, 2008, in mental health outpatients; Forbey & Ben-Porath, 2007, in individuals in substance abuse treatment; Forbey & Ben-Porath, 2008, in university students; Forbey et al., 2009, in prison inmates; Handel & Archer, 2008, in psychiatric inpatients; McCord & Drerup, 2011, in chronic pain patients; Monnot, et al., 2009, in individuals in treatment for substance abuse; Moultrie & Engel, 2017, in psychiatric inpatients; Osberg et al., 2008, in university students; Sellbom, Ben-Porath & Bagby, 2008a, in university students and mental health outpatients; Sellbom, Ben-Porath, & Graham, 2006, in a college counseling clinic; Sellbom, Graham, & Schenk, 2006, in individuals in treatment at a private practice; Shkalim et al., 2017, in psychiatric outpatients; Tellegen et al., 2003, in mental health inpatients and outpatients; Tellegen et al., 2006, in university students; Wygant, Boutacoff et al., 2007, in candidates for bariatric surgery). This includes the MMPI-3 version of RC2, which was associated with depressive disorder diagnosis in a clinical neuropsychology sample (Whitman et al., 2021b). Lee et al. (2018) and Sellbom, Bagby et al. (2012) both found that RC2 scores differentiated patients diagnosed with major depressive disorder from those with schizophrenia; Sellbom, Bagby et al. further found that RC2 scores also differentiated patients with major depressive order from those with bipolar disorder.

Specific depression markers, such as anhedonia and loss of interest, as well as nonspecific markers such as decreased appetite, sleep problems, concentration problems, low energy, suicidal thoughts, worthlessness, and hopelessness (but not specific anxiety markers) are also associated with RC2 on the MMPI-2-RF and the MMPI-3 (MMPI-2-RF: Arbisi et al., 2008, in psychiatric inpatients; Forbey & Ben-Porath, 2007, in university students; Handel & Archer, 2008, in psychiatric inpatients; Moultrie and Engel, 2017, in German psychiatric inpatients; Shkalim, 2015, in Israeli psychiatric patients; MMPI-3: Whitman et al., 2021b, in a clinical neuropsychology sample). Glassmire et al. (2016) also found that RC2 correlated with suicidal ideation and future suicide attempts in a forensic psychiatric hospital.

Consistent with the broader empirical literature on anhedonia, scores on RC2 are correlated with an increased likelihood of being prescribed antidepressant medication (Arbisi et al., 2008, in inpatients) and with PTSD symptoms, most prominently those associated with emotional numbing (Miller et al., 2010; Wolf et al., 2008, in veterans diagnosed with PTSD). Hall, Lee et al. (2021) observed that RC2 had significant negative associations with positive affect, self-esteem, optimism, and life satisfaction. On the other hand, in contrast with the well-established association between anhedonia and schizophrenia, Tellegen and Ben-Porath (2008/2011) reported negligible to modest negative correlations between RC2 and this diagnosis in psychiatric inpatients. Lee et al. (2018) found that RC2 scores differentiated patients with depression from those with schizophrenia at a large effect size magnitude. Examination of the RC2 items reveals a possible reason for this finding. Gard et al. (2007) found that deficits in anticipatory, but not consummatory pleasure, were associated with impairment in patients with schizophrenia. Only a few of the RC2 items have anticipatory pleasure content, whereas a sizable number of items on this scale have consummatory content.

SUMMARY

A lack of positive emotional experiences has long been recognized as an important (though neither defining nor exclusive) feature of depression, social anxiety disorder, schizophrenia, and, more recently, PTSD. Research reviewed in this section indicates that an elevation on RC2, particularly if accompanied by a high score on RCd (indicating the presence of both dysphoric mood and anhedonia) is associated with an increased likelihood that the test taker would meet diagnostic criteria for a major depressive episode and may benefit from antidepressant medication. Elevations on RC2 coupled with high scores on other scales may reflect the presence of anhedonia associated with other disorders (e.g., schizophrenia if RC8 is also elevated; social anxiety disorder or avoidant personality disorder if Social Avoidance (SAV) and Shyness (SHY) SP Scales are also elevated; PTSD, if RCd, RC7, and Anxiety-Related Experiences (AXR) SP Scales are elevated). As discussed in chapter 9, a "positive" finding on the MMPI-3 provides direction for further diagnostic consideration, rather than the final word on a diagnosis.

Antisocial Behavior—RC4

CONCEPTUALIZING ANTISOCIAL BEHAVIOR

Antisocial behavior is a heterogeneous construct that is almost completely analogous to externalizing problems. Research studies using factor analysis of common mental disorders have revealed that externalizing psychopathology is distinctive from an internalizing psychopathology factor (i.e., unipolar mood and anxiety disorders) in studies using both youth (i.e., child and adolescent) and adult samples (see Krueger & Markon, 2006, for a meta-analysis). More nuanced research has indicated that externalizing psychopathology is a higher-order construct (which is measured via the H-O Scale BXD on the MMPI-3) that bifurcates into two more specific domains: antagonistic-externalizing and disinhibited-externalizing (see Kotov et al., 2017, for a review). Numerous studies have supported that these two externalizing domains downstream directly from a broader externalizing factor in both personality (Markon et al., 2005) and psychopathology (Wright et al., 2012) models (see Krueger et al., 2021, for a review). Moreover, several studies have clearly demonstrated that these correlated domains are meaningfully distinct in various structural studies across multiple samples (McNulty & Overstreet, 2014; Røysamb et al., 2011; Wright & Simms, 2015). As articulated by Kotov et al. (2017) and Krueger et al. (2007, 2021), disinhibited-externalizing emphasizes psychopathology constructs with problematic impulse control, irresponsibility, sensation seeking, and risk-taking at its core, as manifested in antisocial personality disorder, conduct disorder, ADHD, and alcohol and other substance use disorders. Antagonistic-externalizing, on the other hand, is typically manifest in disorders characterized by maladaptive antagonism, including callousness, manipulativeness, deceitfulness, grandiosity, suspiciousness, and interpersonal aggression and hostility. This type of externalizing psychopathology is observed in various personality disorders (in particular, psychopathy/antisocial, narcissistic, and paranoid).

Antisocial behavior can be caused by both disinhibition and antagonism (Vize et al., 2020), and it is important to note that RC4 covers aspects of both. Indeed, an examination of the RC4 items indicates that they canvas a broad spectrum of conduct, including adult and juvenile criminal behavior, various other manifestations of juvenile misconduct, substance abuse, aggressive behavior, familial conflict, impulsive behavior, and deceit. However, it is clear from various structural models that most of these symptoms tend to be particularly linked to disinhibited-externalizing (Wright & Simms, 2015), and we would therefore view the construct underlying RC4 as more aligned with disinhibition than antagonism.

The core *DSM-5* diagnoses most central to externalizing are antisocial personality disorder (ASPD) and alcohol and other substance use disorders (SUD). ASPD is primarily albeit not exclusively linked to disinhibition (Sellbom, 2019a).

Although RC4, like all MMPI-3 scales, is not designed or recommended for use as a direct diagnostic indicator, it is noteworthy that of the seven *DSM-5* ASPD criteria for "disregard for and violation of the rights of others," the first four (failure to conform to social norms, deceitfulness, impulsivity, and aggression) are represented by the RC4 item pool, and the ASPD diagnostic requirement of evidence of a juvenile conduct disorder is represented as well. However, the last three (reckless disregard for the safety of self or others, consistent irresponsibility, and lack of remorse) are not. On the other hand, the RC4 pool includes several items describing substance abuse and familial discord that are not related directly to any of the ASPD criteria. Thus, although there is substantial overlap between the antisocial behaviors covered by RC4 and ASPD, the two constructs are by no means isomorphic. Again, the added emphasis on SUD coverage in RC4 makes it better linked to the broader spectrum of disinhibited-externalizing.

Furthermore, epidemiological investigations have established a high comorbidity rate for substance use disorders and ASPD. For example, Moran (1999) reported that in a community sample, up to 80% of individuals diagnosed with ASPD met lifetime criteria of at least one substance use disorder, and 70% of individuals who met diagnostic criteria for a substance use disorder were also diagnosed with ASPD. Moreover, behavioral genetic studies have demonstrated a common genetic liability for ASPD and substance use disorders (Waldman & Slutske, 2000), leading Krueger et al. (2007) to assert that "DSM-defined substance use disorders and antisocial behavior disorders can be understood as elements within a genetically coherent, continuously varying liability spectrum" (p. 647).

A final note deserves mention. The original Clinical Scale 4, Psychopathic Deviate, was meant to reflect the traditional construct of psychopathic personality disorder. However, though some authors (e.g., Caldwell, 2006) have asserted that this clinical scale indeed measures a psychopathy syndrome, most research has found that Clinical Scale 4 fails to capture the core affective-interpersonal component of the psychopathic personality trait constellation (Hare, 1985; Sellbom, Ben-Porath, and Stafford, 2007). Sellbom, Ben-Porath, and Stafford (2007) also demonstrated that neither Clinical Scale 4 nor RC4 capture these core psychopathy traits, but RC4 was clearly a better marker of behavioral psychopathy traits and general externalizing than its clinical scale counterpart. In other words, RC4's emphasis on disinhibited rather than antagonistic externalizing makes it an incomplete measure of psychopathy, as the latter construct requires a far greater emphasis on both antagonism and low negative emotionality (i.e., low scores on internalizing scales; see Sellbom, Ben-Porath et al., 2012).

EMPIRICAL FINDINGS WITH RC4

Scores on RC4 are correlated with a variety of antisocial behaviors. Correlations with a history of juvenile delinquency and adult criminal conduct—recorded by others and self-reported—have been found in a variety of settings (Arbisi et al., 2008, in psychiatric inpatients; Binford and Liljequist, 2008, in mental health outpatients; Burchett & Ben-Porath, 2010, with university students; Handel & Archer, 2008, in psychiatric inpatients; Laurinaitytė et al., 2017, in a sample of Lithuanian prison inmates; Sellbom, Ben-Porath, Baum, Erez, & Gregory, 2008, in a sample of men tested at intake to a batterers intervention program; Sellbom, Ben-Porath, & Graham, 2006, in a college counseling sample; Sellbom, Ben-Porath, & Stafford, 2007, in a sample of pretrial criminal defendants).

Correlations with alcohol and substance abuse, both current and lifetime, have also been reported in various settings and populations (Arbisi et al., 2008, in psychiatric inpatients; Binford and Liljequist, 2008, in mental health outpatients; Forbey & Ben-Porath, 2008, in a college student sample; Forbey, Ben-Porath, & Gartland, 2009, in a correctional setting; Handel & Archer, 2008, in psychiatric inpatients; Laurinaitytė et al., 2017, in a sample of Lithuanian prison inmates; Sellbom, Ben-Porath, Baum, Erez, & Gregory, 2008, in a sample of male batterers; Sellbom, Ben-Porath, & Graham, 2006, in a college counseling sample; Sellbom, Ben-Porath, & Stafford, 2007, in a sample of pretrial criminal defendants; Tellegen et al., 2003, in mental health outpatients). Whitman et al. (2021b) reported that the MMPI-3 version of the scale was associated with substance use disorder diagnoses in a clinical neuropsychology sample.

Scores on RC4 are also correlated with aggressive and violent behavior (Forbey & Ben-Porath, 2007, in a sample of men receiving substance abuse treatment; Laurinaitytė et al., 2017, in a sample of Lithuanian prison inmates) and family dysfunction (Sellbom, Ben-Porath, Baum, Erez, & Gregory, 2008, in a sample of men enrolled in a batterers intervention program; Wygant, Boutacoff et al., 2007, in a sample of bariatric surgery candidates). Furthermore, RC4 scores are also correlated with risk assessment tools in sex offender samples in both the United States and in Germany (Anderson et al., 2020; Tarescavage, Cappo, & Ben-Porath, 2018).

In the personality domain, high RC4 scores are associated with low constraint, particularly with low behavioral control, low agreeableness and conscientiousness, impulsiveness and anger (Sellbom & Ben-Porath, 2005; Forbey & Ben-Porath, 2007, in a substance abuse treatment sample; Forbey & Ben-Porath, 2008, in nonclinical samples; Forbey et al., 2009, in a male prison inmate sample; Sellbom, Ben-Porath, & Bagby, 2008b, in a mental health setting; Sellbom, Ben-Porath, Baum, Erez, & Gregory, 2008, in a sample of male batterers; Simms et al. 2005, in a clinical setting and sample of community-dwelling veterans; Wygant, Boutacoff et al., 2007, in a sample of bariatric surgery candidates).

Several studies have reported correlations between RC4 scores and measures of psychopathy. Using Lilienfeld and Andrews's (1996) Psychopathic Personality Inventory (PPI), Sellbom et al. (2005) reported a correlation of .52 with the total score, .56 with a Social Deviance factor score, and correlations in the .40s with related measures of Machiavellian Egocentricity, Carefree Nonplanfulness, Blame Externalization, and Impulsive Nonconformity. In a sample of pretrial criminal defendants, Sellbom, Ben-Porath, and Stafford (2007) reported a correlation of .50 with the total score on the Screening Version of the Psychopathy Checklist (PCL-SV; Hart, Cox, & Hare, 1995) and correlations of .29 and .62 respectively with Factors 1 and 2 of the PCL-SV. Klein Haneveld et al. (2017) replicated these findings against the Psychopathy Checklist–Revised (PCL-R; Hare, 1991) in a Dutch male offender sample, as did Anderson, Brockhaus et al. (2020) against the PCL-SV in a sample of German prison inmates. Furthermore, Sellbom (2011) reported substantial correlations between RC4 scores and psychopathy as measured by the Levenson Self-Report Psychopathy scale (Levenson, Kiehl, & Fitzpatrick, 1995) in a correctional sample. Sellbom, Ben-Porath, Patrick, Wygant, Gartland, and Stafford (2012) found similar correlations between RC4 and Psychopathic Personality Inventory (PPI)-assessed psychopathy in the same sample, and these findings were replicated by Phillips et al. (2014) in a female correctional sample. Sellbom, Laurinavičius et al. (2018) showed correlations between RC4 and scores on the Triarchic Psychopathy Measure (Patrick, 2010) in a Lithuanian male offender sample. Bolinsky, Trumbetta, Hanson, and Gottesman (2010) found, in a prospective study, that scores on an abridged version of RC4 (made up of original MMPI items) predicted risk for adult psychopathy 30 years later in a cohort of adolescents tested in the 1950s. Overall, these findings show, as expected, that scores on RC4 are associated primarily with the behavioral/disinhibition domain of psychopathy, but they are also weakly to moderately associated with the affective-interpersonal (mostly reflecting antagonism) domain across these studies.

Related to psychopathy, several studies have reported correlations between scores on RC4 and antisocial personality disorder (Anderson, Burchett et al., 2021, in a sample of forensic psychiatric patients; Anderson et al., 2015b, in samples of Dutch mental health patients and forensic psychiatric patients; Monnot et al., 2009, in a sample of veterans receiving treatment for substance abuse; Sellbom & Smith, 2017, in a sample of university students; Simms et al., 2005, in a sample of community-dwelling veterans; van der Heijden et al., 2013a, in a sample of Dutch outpatients; Wolf et al, 2008, in veterans receiving PTSD treatment; Zahn et al., 2017, in a sample of private practice outpatients).

In various prospective studies, RC4 scores were associated with an increased risk for negative outcomes. In a study of police candidates tested for a prehire evaluation, Sellbom, Fischler, and Ben-Porath (2007) found scores on RC4 to be associated with being uncooperative toward peers and supervisors, using their position for personal advantage, abusing sick leave, and conduct unbecoming a police officer; Tarescavage, Corey, and Ben-Porath (2016) replicated these findings in a separate sample of individuals undergoing preemployment evaluations. Wygant, Boutacoff et al. (2007) and Tarescavage, Wygant et al.

(2013) found scores on RC4 to be associated with failing to adhere to the aftercare program in a sample of bariatric surgery candidates. Mattson et al. (2012) found that RC4 scores were correlated with failure to complete drug court requirements. Tarescavage, Glassmire, and Burchett (2016) found that RC4 scores were correlated with future incidents of aggression in a sample of patients in a forensic psychiatric hospital. Tarescavage, Luna-Jones, and Ben-Porath (2014) found that RC4 differentiated between offenders who completed community probation requirements from those who violated such requirements 12 months after sentencing at a large effect size magnitude.

SUMMARY

The RC4 correlates just reviewed provide evidence that supports the construct validity of the scale as a measure of antisocial behavior. Across a wide range of settings, scores on RC4 are associated with rule breaking and irresponsible conduct linked empirically and conceptually to antisocial personality disorder and psychopathy. Regarding the former, RC4 correlates include behaviors indicative of failure to conform to social norms, deceitfulness, impulsivity, aggressiveness, and consistent irresponsibility, as well as a history of juvenile misconduct. Strong associations between RC4 and substance misuse are consistent with the high comorbidity rates for antisocial personality and substance use disorder; the associations also reflect the generally higher base rate of substance misuse compared with that of criminal conduct. Elevations on RC4 have robust associations with the behavioral facets of psychopathy as well as the total psychopathy score on several measures of this construct. As is the case with all MMPI-3 scales, these correlates do not allow for the direct diagnosis of either disorder, but rather indicate that both should be given consideration in differential diagnosis. Moreover, elevations on RC4 indicate a strong likelihood of acting-out behaviors, across various contexts, that are likely to occur regardless of whether an individual meets diagnostic criteria for antisocial personality disorder or psychopathy.

Ideas of Persecution (RC6)

CONCEPTUALIZING IDEAS OF PERSECUTION

The RC6 items describe self-referential beliefs that one is being singled out for mistreatment ranging from being called names to being poisoned. Data reported later in this section show, as expected, that scores on this scale are associated with paranoid delusional thought dysfunction; however, as implied by its label, the scale most directly assesses the extent to which a test taker reports experiencing persecutory thoughts (see also chapter 6 for a discussion of how "cultural mistrust" can potentially influence RC6 scores). In a review of the concept of paranoid thinking and its assessment, Manschreck (1979) noted that the term *paranoia* was coined by the ancient Greeks and that Hippocrates used it to describe delirium associated with high fever. It subsequently fell into disuse until the 19th century, when Karl Kahlbaum classified paranoia as a separate mental illness, "a form of partial insanity, which, throughout the course of the disease, principally affected the sphere of the intellect" (as cited in Lewis, 1970, p. 3). Manschreck (1979) also noted that in addition to thought disorder, paranoid features are associated with a wide range of conditions, including neurological conditions, metabolic conditions, other psychiatric conditions, sex chromosome anomalies, infections, substance misuse, and use of various pharmacologic agents. However, most efforts to conceptualize paranoid thinking and identify its origins have focused on the domain of thought dysfunction.

Maher (1974) noted that efforts to study paranoia had been, to the point of their review, either descriptive, yielding systematic descriptions of delusional thought processes, or explanatory, involving an inner state that disrupts the process of logical reasoning. He offered and studied an alternative explanation whereby "a delusion is a hypothesis designed to explain unusual perceptual phenomena and developed through operation of normal cognitive processes" (p. 103). He postulated that "the explanations (i.e., the delusions) of the patient are derived by cognitive activity that is essentially indistinguishable from that employed by nonpatients, by scientists, by people generally. The structural coherence and internal consistency of the explanation will be a reflection of the intelligence of the individual patient" (p. 103).

More recently, Freeman (2007) postulated that in addition to the factors described by Maher, "there is a large direct affective contribution to the experience [of persecutory delusions]" (p. 425). In particular, Freeman proposed and cited empirical findings to support the notion that anxiety affects the content, distress, and persistence of paranoia, although affect alone is not sufficient to induce paranoid experiences. He proposed a threat anticipation cognitive model of persecutory delusions, which were hypothesized to arise from an interaction of emotional processes, anomalous experiences (as did Maher, 1974), and reasoning biases. Freeman (2007) also noted that owing to their self-referential nature, persecutory delusions were disruptive of the individual's social functioning.

Freeman and Garety (2000) had previously proposed that to be classified as persecutory delusions, the individual's beliefs must include both the anticipation that harm (not necessarily physical) is occurring or going to occur to themselves and that the persecutor has the intent to cause harm. Freeman (2007) elaborated that paranoia is a hierarchical phenomenon, characterized by five levels of perceived threat, which, in increasing order of severity, are as follows:

1. Social evaluative concerns (e.g., fear of rejection and feelings of vulnerability)
2. Ideas of reference (e.g., being talked about or watched by others)
3. Mild threat (e.g., people trying to cause minor distress such as irritation)

4. Moderate threat (e.g., people going out of their way to get at the individual)
5. Severe threat (e.g., people trying to cause significant physical, psychological, or social harm to the individual)

Examination of the RC6 items indicates that most of them range from descriptions of mild to severe threat, with roughly equal numbers of each type.

Investigators following Freeman's (2007) conceptualization of persecutory delusions have sought to elaborate their nature and correlates. Green et al. (2006) conducted semistructured interviews with individuals identified as having current persecutory delusions. Green et al. found that their beliefs frequently involved multiple human persecutors known to the individual, and for the majority, the perceived threat was severe, ongoing, and coupled with feelings of vulnerability. Specific aspects of these individuals' beliefs were associated with emotional distress (or, in MMPI-3 terms, demoralization). For example, those who believed they had more power in the face of persecution were less demoralized.

Freeman et al. (2007) described the development and validation of a measure of "state paranoia" that can be used in experimental investigations of the phenomenon. The State Social Paranoia scale is composed of 10 items designed to assess the two elements of Freeman and Garety's (2000) criteria for paranoia: feared harm and perpetrator intent. Using this scale along with measures of social anxiety, Freeman et al. (2008) exposed a nonclinical sample to a sophisticated socially neutral virtual reality situation, simulating a train ride on the London underground. In support of Freeman's (2007) model, the authors found that social anxiety and persecutory ideation shared many predictive factors, but perceptual anomalies coupled with social anxiety were distinct predictors of paranoia.

Also following Freemen and Garety's (2000) definition, McKay et al. (2006) constructed the 10-item Persecutory Ideation Questionnaire (PIQ), which includes content that very closely resembles that of RC6. The authors found that PIQ scores predicted the severity of persecutory delusions in a sample of individuals already identified as experiencing persecutory delusions.

Noting that an erroneous clinical decision can lead to unnecessary treatment or lack of appropriate treatment, Brown (2008) reviewed the available literature on the prevalence of actual persecutory experiences to assist in differentiating them from persecutory delusional beliefs. He found events such as criminal victimization, stalking, and discrimination based on race, gender, or mental illness to be quite common, occurring in more than 10% of certain population subgroups, whereas government surveillance and intentional poisoning were very uncommon (less than 0.1%) across all population segments.

Finally, epidemiological and neurobiological findings not only indicate dimensionality in paranoia but suggest potential liabilities for paranoid delusions and related symptoms that might be separate from other forms of psychosis

(Bentall et al., 2001; Blackwood et al., 2001). Specific attentional (Blackwood et al., 2001) and attributional (Bentall, 1994) processes likely contribute to paranoid thinking and maintenance beyond that of general psychosis (Bentall et al., 2001; Shayegan & Stahl, 2005; Williams et al., 2004). Distinct neurobiological abnormalities related to these processes have been observed in patients with paranoid psychosis versus healthy controls (Haut & McDonald, 2010; Williams et al., 2004) and those with nonparanoid schizophrenia or psychosis. Taken together, these data suggest distinct liabilities for paranoid psychotic cognitive processes (Bentall et al., 2001; Blackwood et al., 2001; Shayegan and Stahl, 2005), further supporting the necessity in separating the constructs assessed by RC6 and RC8.

EMPIRICAL FINDINGS WITH RC6
The empirical correlates of RC6 show it to be a valid indicator of persecutory ideation and paranoid thinking across research on both the MMPI-3 and MMPI-2-RF. They include delusions, particularly of a persecutory nature, and ideas of reference (Arbisi et al., 2008, in a sample of psychiatric inpatients; Handel & Archer, 2008, in a different sample of psychiatric inpatients), paranoia and interpersonal mistrust (Sellbom, Graham, & Schenk, 2006, in a sample of outpatients treated in independent practice settings; Simms et al., 2005, in a clinical setting and sample of community-dwelling veterans), alienation and blame externalization (Handel & Archer, 2008, in psychiatric inpatients; Sellbom & Ben-Porath, 2005, in a nonclinical sample; Sellbom, Ben-Porath, Baum, Erez, & Gregory, 2008, in a sample of men referred to a batterers intervention program), and various self-report and clinician-rated measures of paranoid personality disorder (Simms et al., 2005; Anderson et al., 2015b; Sellbom & Smith, 2017; Zahn et al., 2017). Whitman et al. (2021b) found that MMPI-3 RC6 scores were moderately associated with ratings of hallucinations and paranoia in a clinical neuropsychology sample.

As would be expected, RC6 is also correlated with a broader range of psychotic symptoms, including hallucinations and nonparanoid delusions in psychiatric inpatients (Arbisi et al., 2008; Handel & Archer, 2008) and with a schizophrenia diagnosis in a sample of individuals entering substance abuse treatment (Monnot, Quirck, & Brewer, 2009). Lee et al. (2018) and Sellbom, Bagby et al. (2012) showed in separate samples that RC6 scores differentiated patients diagnosed with schizophrenia from those with major depressive disorder. Furthermore, RC6 scores are also correlated with both the Magical Ideation and Perceptual Aberration scales (Chapman , Chapman, & Raulin, 1978; Eckblad & Chapman, 1983), but, as expected, more so with Magical Ideation in nonclinical samples (Forbey & Ben-Porath, 2008), correctional samples (Forbey et al., 2009), mental health outpatient samples (Tellegen & Ben-Porath, 2008), and medical outpatient samples (Tellegen & Ben-Porath, 2008/2011). Finally, Sellbom

(2017b) used a large sample of individuals undergoing pretrial forensic evaluations and found that individuals opined by their forensic examiner to be incompetent to stand trial scored significantly higher on RC6 than those opined to be competent to proceed.

Studies of at least four independent samples in which one would not expect to find thought dysfunction that rises to the level of a formal thought disorder have identified additional, informative correlates of RC6. In a sample of bariatric surgery candidates, Wygant, Boutacoff et al. (2007) found RC6 scores to be associated with a history of weight-related teasing in childhood, offering a possible window onto the development of persecutory thoughts in this population. In a study of risk factors for negative outcomes in police candidates, Sellbom, Fischler, and Ben-Porath (2007) found moderate deviations from the norm on RC6 scores (i.e., T scores in the 55–60 range) to be associated with a number of undesirable outcomes, including involuntary departure, citizen complaints, use of excessive force, rude behavior, having a negative attitude toward the public, being uncooperative with supervisors, being a defendant in civil litigation, deceptiveness, abuse of authority, failing to take responsibility for mistakes, using their position for internal gain, showing biased attitudes toward others, and poor responding to previous constructive feedback; Tarescavage, Fischler et al. (2015) replicated many of these findings with a larger sample including police candidates from a different jurisdiction. Tarescavage, Corey, Gupton, and Ben-Porath (2015) found that those with moderate scores in a preemployment sample were rated posthire as having learning, navigational, and radio problems, as well as difficulties with multitasking during stress. Tarescavage, Corey, and Ben-Porath (2016) found in a fourth preemployment sample that those with moderate RC6 scores had posthire problems with excessive force and failure to attend court.

SUMMARY

Persecutory ideation, in some cases rising to the level of persistent paranoid delusional beliefs, has been recognized as a form of psychological dysfunction for several millennia. Current conceptualizations of persecutory delusional beliefs postulate that they are the product of unusual experiences that are anxiety-inducing and misinterpreted as signs of malevolent intent by others. Efforts to develop measures of persecutory beliefs have produced scales that are very similar in content to RC6. Studies of its empirical correlates support the construct validity of the scale and have identified paranoid delusions, less extreme persecutory beliefs, interpersonal suspiciousness and alienation, and mistrust as the strongest correlates of RC6. The possibility that the test taker is in fact experiencing some persecution always needs to be considered when interpreting scores on this scale.

Dysfunctional Negative Emotions (RC7)

CONCEPTUALIZING DYSFUNCTIONAL NEGATIVE EMOTIONS

Tellegen (1985) described Negative Emotionality (NEM) as a higher-order personality trait characterized by a tendency to worry, be anxious, feel victimized and resentful, and appraise situations generally in ways that foster negative emotions. He linked the construct to two well-known models: Gray's (1970) emotion-based psychobiological model (see e.g., Gray & McNaughton, 2000, for an update), relating temperament to psychiatric disorder, and Freud's anxiety-signal system. Tellegen (1985) linked Negative Emotionality to Gray's (1970) Behavioral Inhibition System, presumed to regulate extinction and passive avoidance in response to signals of punishment. In Freud's model, Tellegen (1985) associated Negative Emotionality with the two-process anxiety theory that postulates an anxiety-signal system, activated by external and internal drive-related stimuli, which controls avoidance of distress. Tellegen (1985) noted that both models included a second system (Behavior Activation in Gray's and a hope-signal system in Freud's) that closely resembled a construct he labeled Positive Emotionality (assessed on the MMPI-3 with RC2).

Tellegen (1985) linked these two broad personality trait dimensions to two psychological domains, mood and psychopathology. In the mood domain, Tellegen (1985) associated Negative Emotionality and Positive Emotionality with two broad dimensions labeled *Negative Affect* and *Positive Affect*, which had emerged from a review of the literature on self-reported mood conducted by Watson and Tellegen (1985). Tellegen (1985) conceptualized Negative Emotionality (NEM) and Positive Emotionality (PEM) as the trait counterparts to these mood states. In the psychopathology domain, in keeping with the models of Gray and Freud, Tellegen (1985) postulated that high NEM is associated with anxiety-related psychopathology whereas low PEM is related to depression. In support of these conceptually grounded hypotheses about associations between personality traits, mood states, and psychopathology, Tellegen (1985) reported findings from analyses of five scales, each of which measured one of the following: negative and positive affect, unpleasant mood, anxiety, and depression. Whereas scores on the depression and anxiety scales were highly correlated with each other and with unpleasant mood (i.e., demoralization), the measures of negative and positive affect were relatively independent of each other and distinctively correlated with scores on the anxiety and depression scales, respectively. The finding that after controlling for demoralization, NEM and PEM emerge as the major distinctive components of the primary MMPI measures of anxiety and depression (Clinical Scales 7 and 2), described earlier in chapter 2, provides further corroboration of Tellegen's (1985) model.

Green, Goldman, and Salovey (1993) questioned Watson and Tellgen's (1985) two-factor mood model and suggested instead that mood variance could more parsimoniously be attributed to a single, largely bipolar factor marked by positive and negative affect at its opposing ends. In response, Tellegen, Watson, and Clark (1999) clarified that the single factor emphasized by Green, Goldman, and Salovey (1993) corresponded to the *Pleasant versus Unpleasant* mood dimension in Watson and Tellegen's (1985) mood model (now relabeled *Happiness versus Unhappiness*). They demonstrated that the three mood dimensions conform to a hierarchical structure, with a general Happiness–Unhappiness dimension and relatively independent Positive Affect and Negative Affect dimensions at a lower level. In RC scale terms, Happiness–Unhappiness corresponds to Demoralization and is assessed with RCd, Positive Affect inversely corresponds to Low Positive Emotions and is assessed by RC2, and Negative Affect corresponds to Dysfunctional Negative Emotions and is assessed with RC7.

A Terminological Confound

Some authors have used the terms Negative Affectivity in a manner that is not consistent with the framework just discussed, resulting in conceptual confusion and inconsistent empirical findings. For instance, the influential Personality Inventory for *DSM-5* (PID-5; Krueger et al., 2012) includes a personality domain with this label. This regrettable mix-up can be traced back to a comprehensive review of personality measures conducted by Watson and Clark (1984), who concluded that various scales, labeled alternatively trait anxiety, neuroticism, ego strength, general maladjustment (and more), were in fact all measures of a general mood dispositional dimension they labeled Negative Affectivity. Examination of the data reported in Watson and Clark's (1984) review shows that the single best MMPI marker of this dimension was Welsh's (1956) Anxiety (A) scale, now recognized as a measure of demoralization (Tellegen et al., 2006). By labeling this factor Negative Affectivity and associating it with Tellegen's concept of Negative Affect, Watson and Clark (1984) confounded two related but distinctive dimensions. This misconstrual was subsequently carried over to Clark and Watson's (1991) influential tripartite model of anxiety and depression, in which they posited that a general affective dimension labeled Negative Affectivity (but in fact corresponding to Demoralization, Pleasantness–Unpleasantness, or Happiness–Unhappiness) was responsible for high rates of comorbidity of these disorders. This was further carried over to subsequent elaborations and revisions of the tripartite model (e.g., Mineka et al., 1998) and remains a source of confusion and ambiguity in the personality, psychopathology, and mood literature.

Several contemporary measures of negative affectivity (e.g., PID-5) aim to target the neuroticism domain that is common across numerous trait models, which is technically a 45-degree rotated version of Tellegen's NEM domain (Tellegen & Waller, 2008) and thus includes the commonality of Tellegen's negative emotionality and demoralization. Although this blend of measurement is commonplace, we believe the separation of measurement of demoralization and negative affectivity/emotionality to be important. Indeed, Sellbom, Ben-Porath, and Bagby (2008a) tested a model in which MMPI-2-RF Demoralization was a primary marker of distress disorders, Dysfunctional Negative Emotions was a primary marker of fear disorders, and Low Positive Emotions was specifically associated with major depression and social phobia (see earlier discussion of RC2). In two separate studies, this elaborated three-domain model produced a better fit to observed data than a model that focused exclusively on negative emotionality as a marker of both distress and fear with low positive emotionality as a marker of major depression and social phobia. These findings indicate that Demoralization, rather than Negative Emotionality, corresponds better to the general distress factor Watson and Clark (1984) labeled *Negative Affectivity*, and that separating the measurement of negative affectivity and demoralization is a helpful bifurcation in the assessment of mood and anxiety-related psychopathology. A good example of how demoralization is subsumed within various trait models is the measurement of "depressivity." On the PID-5, for instance, it is viewed as an interstitial trait, which loads on both negative affectivity (.43) and detachment (.50; a broader domain that includes anhedonia) in Watters and Bagby's (2018) meta-analysis. Based on Tellegen's (1985) framework, this finding occurs because demoralization is associated with the high pole of negative affect and low pole of positive affect (i.e., detachment) with depressivity being a good marker for demoralization. From our perspective, rather than measuring demoralization repeatedly in both negative affectivity and detachment, assessing this construct separately provides a more nuanced and discriminantly valid characterization of an individual's emotional proclivities.

EMPIRICAL FINDINGS WITH RC7

Empirical findings with RC7 indicate that it is strongly correlated with other, non-MMPI measures of dysfunctional negative emotions (Sellbom & Ben-Porath, 2005, with the NEM score on Tellegen's MPQ in university students, and Simms et al., 2005, with the Negative Temperament score on Clark's [1993] SNAP in a clinical sample and sample of community-dwelling veterans; see also Kotelnikova et al., 2019). Sellbom, Ben-Porath, and Bagby (2008b) and Noordhof et al. (2015) have also shown that RC7 has large correlations with the Neuroticism domain on the NEO PI-R. Consistent with Tellegen's (1985) conceptualization of NEM, scores on RC7 are correlated substantially with a measure of Gray's Behavioral Inhibition System (BIS) in mental health and medical outpatients (Tellegen & Ben-Porath, 2008/2011).

RC7 scores are associated with various measures and indicators of anxiety in psychiatric inpatients (Arbisi et al., 2008; Handel & Archer, 2008; Moultrie & Engel, 2017; Shkalim, 2015), individuals in treatment at a community mental health setting (Ben-Porath & Tellegen, 2020b; Shkalim, 2015), a college counseling setting (Sellbom, Ben-Porath, & Graham, 2006), individuals receiving mental health outpatient treatment in an independent practice setting (Sellbom, Graham, & Schenk, 2006), a sample of disability claimants (Ben-Porath & Tellegen, 2020b), a nonclinical sample (Forbey & Ben-Porath, 2008), a clinical sample and sample of community-dwelling veterans (Simms et al., 2005), and a clinical neuropsychology sample (Whitman et al., 2021b). RC7 scores have also been found to be associated with dysfunctional negative emotions other than anxiety, such as anger, in prison inmates (Forbey et al., 2009), individuals receiving treatment for substance abuse (Forbey & Ben-Porath, 2007), psychiatric inpatients (Handel & Archer, 2008), and a nonclinical sample (Forbey & Ben-Porath, 2008). Sellbom, Ben-Porath, and Bagby (2008a) and Shkalim et al. (2017) also reported associations with various measures of fear disorder (e.g., panic, social anxiety, phobias) in university and clinical samples.

Empirical findings with RC7 are also consistent with associations (described earlier) between dysfunctional negative emotions and PTSD. Wolf et al. (2008) reported substantial correlations between RC7 scores and PTSD symptoms and diagnoses in samples of male and female combat veterans, and Ben-Porath and Tellegen (2020b) reported mostly moderate-sized correlations between RC7 scores and self-report PTSD measures in both forensic disability and university samples. Arbisi et al. (2008) reported significant associations between RC7 scores and flashbacks and sleep difficulties in psychiatric inpatients. Miller et al. (2010) found substantial correlations between RC7 and PTSD symptoms related to reexperiencing, avoidance, numbing, and hyperarousal in a veterans sample. Forbes et al. (2010) reported higher RC7 scores in a sample of Australian combat veterans diagnosed with PTSD. McDevitt-Murphy, Weathers, Flood, Eakin, and Benson (2007) found significant elevations on RC7 in a sample of trauma-exposed university students. Monnot et al. (2009) reported a significant correlation between RC7 scores and a diagnosis of PTSD in a sample of veterans receiving treatment for substance abuse. However, Sellbom, Lee et al. (2012) found that RC7 did not increment RCd in the prediction of PTSD symptoms in a forensic disability sample, and Whitman et al. (2021b) also did not find a significant correlation between MMPI-3 RC7 scores and PTSD diagnosis in a clinical neuropsychology sample.

SUMMARY

Tellegen (1985) conceptualized NEM as an affectively linked personality trait associated with increased risk for anxiety-related psychopathology. The finding that the major component of MMPI Clinical Scale 7 (a measure of anxiety-related psychopathology) is in fact marked by a set of items describing dysfunctional negative emotions, which are distinct from demoralization, corroborated Tellegen's model. Scores on the resulting scale, RC7, are indeed associated with a variety of dysfunctional negative emotions, most notably anxiety, fear, and anger. The scale also converges in expected ways with features of PTSD, though whether it increments RCd, a better measure of distress disorders (of which PTSD is one), needs to be further investigated with the MMPI-3. RC7 scores are also associated with measures of Gray's (1970) original BIS, consistent with Tellegen's (1985) conceptualization of NEM. The findings just summarized thus provide good evidence of the construct validity of RC7.

Some terminological confusion has been introduced by use of the label *Negative Affectivity* to describe a general mood-related disposition associated with a variety of personality variables related to psychological dysfunction (Watson & Clark, 1984) and as responsible for phenotypic comorbidity reflected on measures of anxiety and depression. Used in this manner, the term Negative Affectivity is also directly linked to Demoralization, rather than specifically Negative Emotionality or Dysfunctional Negative Emotions.

Aberrant Experiences (RC8)

CONCEPTUALIZING ABERRANT EXPERIENCES

RC8 items describe a variety of sensory, perceptual, cognitive, and motor experiences that fall well outside the range of normal experiences. These phenomena have long been associated with thought disturbance, although they are neither unique to this form of psychopathology nor an exhaustive list of its manifestations. Two distinct, discipline-linked lines of clinical research have converged upon these experiences as core components of disordered thinking: the medical/psychiatric tradition and the psychometric/psychological approach.

In the medical/psychiatric tradition, thought dysfunction has been linked primarily with schizophrenia, which has been conceptualized, like all psychiatric disorders, as a categorical phenomenon, following the structure proposed by Kraepelin and Bleuler. In their description of the clinical picture associated with schizophrenia, Combs and Mueser (2007) identify three groups of characteristic symptoms, including positive symptoms (hallucinations, delusions, and bizarre, disorganized behavior); negative symptoms (blunted or flat affect, poverty of speech, anhedonia, apathy, psychomotor retardation, and physical inertia); and cognitive impairments (difficulties in visual and verbal learning, memory problems, attentional deficits, and impaired capacities for abstract reasoning and executive functions). The aberrant experiences assessed by RC8 fall in the first group. Combs and Mueser (2007) note that among the positive symptoms, persecutory delusions are the most common. However, these are assessed by RC6, leaving the domain of RC8 focused on experiences associated with hallucinations and nonpersecutory delusions. Research discussed in relation to RC6 also indicates the appropriateness of separating RC6 and RC8 construct measurement.

Walker, Bollini, Hochman, Kestler, and Mittal (2007) note that current approaches to the diagnosis of schizophrenia rely heavily on Schneider's (1959) description of the features of this disorder, involving primarily those he characterized as first rank symptoms. The first-rank symptoms, all of which would be classified as positive symptoms in the typology just reviewed, include thought broadcasting (a belief that others can hear one's thoughts being broadcast out loud), thought intrusion (a belief that some of one's thoughts are being planted by others), thought withdrawal (a belief that others are removing one's thoughts), somatic hallucinations (unusual, unexplained bodily sensations), passivity experiences (a belief that one's thoughts, feelings, or actions are controlled by others), and delusional perception (a fixed false belief about everyday occurrences). Most of the RC8 items describe one of these Schneiderian first-rank symptoms, with some related to one specific type of symptom and others, worded more broadly, conceivably encompassing more than one type of symptom.

The psychometric/psychological approach is often linked to Meehl's (1962) theory of schizotypy, a personality dimension thought at high levels to place an individual at risk for developing schizophrenia, and at lower levels to manifest in various peculiarities of affect, thinking, and behavior. This theoretical framework led Loren and Jean Chapman and their colleagues to develop measures of five features associated with Meehl's schizotypic personality construct, labeled Physical Anhedonia, Social Anhedonia, Impulsive Nonconformity, Perceptual Aberration, and Magical Ideation. The first two scales were discussed earlier in the context of RC2. The last two overlap conceptually and in some of their content with RC8. The Perceptual Aberration Scale (PAS) includes items described by Chapman et al. (1978) as designed to tap grossly schizophrenic-like distortions in the perceptions of one's body as well as other perceptual distortions. The Magical Ideation Scale (MIS) is comprised of items described by Eckblad and Chapman (1983) as involving beliefs in forms of causation that by conventional standards would be deemed invalid or magical. These scales were conceptualized as measures of psychosis proneness.

To investigate links between psychosis proneness, as measured by the schizotypy scales, and the development of psychotic symptoms, Chapman and Chapman (1980) also developed an interview-based rating system for identifying psychotic and psychotic like deviancy. The system yielded ratings of six categories of deviancy, including transmission of one's own thoughts (the individual believes that others can read their mind or that thoughts leave their head); passivity experiences (such as possession by demonic spirits); auditory experiences (hearing voices); thought withdrawal (the belief that others are able to steal one's thoughts); aberrant beliefs (such as being able to control objects with one's thoughts); and visual experiences (seeing things that others cannot see). A seventh category, olfactory experiences (including olfactory hallucinations), was added later. Nearly all of the RC8 items can be linked to one of these rating categories, perceptual aberration, or magical ideation.

More recent work on the construct of schizotypy has focused on its multidimensional nature. Chapman and Chapman's (1980) work focused mostly on positive schizotypy features such as magical beliefs, referential thinking, mind reading, thought transmission, supernatural experiences, and unusual perceptual and somatic experiences. Kwapil et al. (2018) noted that disorganized (e.g., confusion, racing thoughts, loose associations, disrupted speech, difficulty following conversations, and slowness of thought) and negative features (e.g., social disinterest, flat affect, anhedonia) of schizotypy need to be considered and assessed as well for a full profile of psychosis proneness. Kwapil and colleagues developed the Multidimensional Schizotypy Scales for this purpose. From this perspective, RC8 does indeed target nearly all the positive features, and to a lesser degree, some of the disorganized features. Other disorganized features are assessed by RC9 and Activation (both described later), and the negative features are assessed predominantly by RC2 (Low Positive Emotions) as discussed earlier.

EMPIRICAL FINDINGS WITH RC8

In clinical samples, Arbisi et al. (2008) found elevations on RC8 in psychiatric inpatients to be associated with various types of hallucinations, nonparanoid delusions, and being prescribed antipsychotic medication upon discharge. Also in inpatients, Handel and Archer (2008) reported significant correlations between RC8 and Brief Psychiatric Rating Scale (BPRS; Overall & Gorham, 1988) ratings on conceptual disorganization, hallucinatory behavior, and unusual thought content. Monnot et al. (2009) reported a significant correlation between RC8 scores and a diagnosis of schizophrenia in a sample of veterans undergoing substance abuse treatment. Sellbom, Graham, and Schenk (2006) found a substantial correlation between RC8 and a measure of bizarre experiences in a sample of individuals receiving outpatient therapy in private practice settings. Whitman et al. (2021b) found that MMPI-3 RC8 was associated with symptoms of paranoia and hallucinations as well as the presence of neurological symptoms in individuals undergoing neuropsychological evaluations. Although Lee et al. (2018) found that RC8 scores differentiated patients with schizophrenia from those with major depressive disorder, Sellbom, Bagby et al. (2012) failed to find the same result; one hypothesis is that many of those in the latter study were in the residual phase of schizophrenic illness and therefore less likely to be exhibiting overt positive psychosis, whereas participants in the study by Lee et al. were inpatients.

At the personality level, Avdeyeva et al. (2011) and Sellbom and Ben-Porath (2005) reported substantial correlations in university students between RC8 scores and the Absorption scale on Tellegen's MPQ (Tellegen et al., 2023). Of the two MPQ Absorption subscales, scores on RC8 were most strongly associated with the one measuring proneness to imaginative and altered states. Simms et al. (2005) reported very high correlations between RC8 scores and the Eccentric Perceptions scale on Clark's (1993) SNAP in a clinical setting and sample of community-dwelling veterans. The SNAP also includes personality disorder measures, and on those scales, Simms et al. found that RC8 scores were associated most strongly with a measure of schizotypal personality disorder. Studies that examine the alternative model of personality disorders (AMPD) of the *DSM-5* have consistently found associations between RC8 scores and the Psychoticism domain, as well as its three specific facets of Eccentricity, Unusual Beliefs and Experiences, and Cognitive and Perceptual Dysregulation (Anderson et al., 2015a; Sellbom, Anderson, & Bagby, 2013).

Reports from several investigations include sizable correlations between RC8 and the PAS and MIS psychosis-proneness measures (Forbey & Ben-Porath, 2008, in a nonclinical setting; Forbey et al., 2009, in a sample of prison inmates; Tellegen & Ben-Porath, 2008/2011, in mental health and medical outpatients). RC8 correlations with MIS generally run higher than those with PAS (although both fall primarily in the .50 to .70 range) in all settings. Research on personality disorders have also linked RC8 to various measures of schizotypal personality disorder in a range of community, mental health, and forensic samples (Anderson et al., 2015b; Brown & Sellbom, 2021; Sellbom & Smith, 2017; Zahn et al., 2017).

Studies have also linked RC8 to trauma-related symptoms, most prominently reexperiencing and dissociation. Choi (2017) reported correlations between RC8 and various forms of traumatic experiences and a Korean version of a PTSD measure in a psychiatric sample. Moreover, Guetta et al. (2019) specifically found that high RC8 scores were linked to dissociation symptoms in the context of PTSD in an epidemiological military veteran sample. Ingram et al. (2021) reported weak to moderate correlations between RC8 scores and various self-reported PTSD measures in a large VA sample; these were generally smaller than those reported for the various Internalizing Scales. Wolf et al. (2008) reported correlations between RC8 and PTSD in male, but not female, VA patients. However, it should be noted that Sellbom, Lee et al. (2012) failed to find evidence supporting the incremental validity of RC8 scale scores above and beyond RCd scores in the prediction of PTSD symptoms in a forensic disability sample. Thus, RC8 is most likely to be helpful in specifically identifying dissociative experiences in those with PTSD symptoms rather than being as a robust predictor of the overall construct (see also findings reported in the *MMPI-3 Technical Manual*).

Finally, in assessments of candidates for positions in law enforcement, RC8 scores have been found to be correlated with difficulties performing under stressful conditions (Ben-Porath & Tellegen, 2020b), difficulties carrying out tasks under nonstressful conditions (Tarescavage, Brewster et al., 2015; Tarescavage, Corey, & Ben-Porath, 2015), cognitive adaptation problems (Ben-Porath & Tellegen, 2020b), report writing problems (Ben-Porath & Tellegen, 2020b), and difficulties with decision-making (Ben-Porath & Tellegen, 2020b).

SUMMARY

The aberrant experiences assessed by RC8 have been linked with various mental disorders and, more broadly, with characteristics of individuals at increased risk for developing thought disorders. The empirical correlates of the scale include expected associations with personality characteristics related to unusual thinking and perceptual processes, well-established measures of psychosis proneness, and a host of clinical phenomena related to nonpersecutory symptoms of thought disorder. It is important to consider, however, that none of the studies just reviewed included measures of psychotic symptoms unrelated to primary thought disorder (e.g., substance-induced psychosis), and there is no reason to assume that the aberrant experiences reported by an individual who scores high on this scale are associated specifically or exclusively with a primary thought disorder. Nevertheless, the findings just reported provide evidence of the construct validity of RC8 as a measure of psychosis proneness and nonpersecutory psychotic symptoms.

Hypomanic Activation (RC9)

CONCEPTUALIZING HYPOMANIC ACTIVATION

Conceptual and descriptive models of hypomania and mania often trace their origins to Kraepelin's (1921) treatise on manic-depressive insanity and paranoia. Kraepelin (1921) differentiated between "*manic states* with the essential morbid symptoms of flight of ideas, exalted mood, and pressure of activity, and *melancholia or depressive states* with sad or anxious moodiness and also sluggishness of thought or action. These two opposed phases of the clinical state have given the disease its name" (pp. 3–4), but went on to note, "but besides them we observe also clinical *mixed forms,* in which the phenomena of mania and melancholia are combined with each other, so that states arise, which indeed are composed of the same morbid symptoms as these, but cannot without coercion be classified either with the one or with the other" (p. 4). These descriptions have by and large been retained in the *DSM-IV* criteria for diagnosing various types of bipolar disorder.

Kraepelin (1921) differentiated between transient manic states (just described) and what he called "fundamental states," which currently might be called traits. Regarding manic states, he singled out one of the three essential features of mania just cited, noting that "in manic states the morbid picture is dominated by pressure of activity; here we have to do with general volitional excitement" (p. 26). He associated two fundamental states (i.e., traits) with mania—the manic and irritable temperaments. Kraepelin (1921) described the manic temperament as consisting of "constitutional excitement" (p. 125), characterized by carelessness, very marked self-confidence and a related sense of superiority, restlessness, and irresponsible conduct. He described the irritable temperament as "a mixture of the fundamental states" (p. 130), and noted that

> The patients display from youth up extraordinarily great fluctuations in emotional equilibrium and are greatly moved by all experiences, frequently in an unpleasant way. While on the one hand they appear sensitive and inclined to sentimentality and exuberance, they display on the other hand great irritability and sensitiveness. They are easily offended and hot tempered; they flare up, and on the most trivial occasions fall into outbursts of boundless fury. . . . It then comes to violent scenes with abuse, screaming, and a tendency to rough behaviour. (p. 130)

Kraepelin (1921) also noted that the mood of individuals with an irritable temperament ". . . is subject to frequent change. In general, the patients are perhaps cheerful, self-conscious, unrestrained; but periods are interpolated in which they are irritable and ill-humoured, also perhaps sad, spiritless, anxious; they shed tears without cause, give expression to thoughts of suicide, bring forward hypochondriacal complaints, go to bed" (p. 131).

Kraepelin's (1921) state-temperament distinction has important implications for the assessment of mania and hypomania. Two features associated with manic states, their transient nature and the existence of a mixed state consisting of seemingly incongruent symptoms, create substantial difficulties in the assessment of acute manic or even less extreme, hypomanic episodes. In contrast, the more stable manic and irritable temperaments are more amenable to reliable assessment. Examination of the RC9 item indicates that the vast majority of them describe features associated with manic or irritable temperament. A smaller proportion can be linked to Kraepelin's notion of "pressure of activity," the cardinal feature of a manic or hypomanic state.

Several lines of research have sought to provide empirically based elaborations on Kraepelin's insights regarding manic-depressive illness. One involves efforts to identify salient features of mania and hypomania in patients diagnosed with bipolar disorder. Wittenborn (1951) conducted an early factor analysis of symptom ratings of 140 psychiatric patients and linked one of the symptom clusters he identified to Kraepelin's (1921) description of manic patients. The symptom ratings associated with this factor included temper tantrums, loudness, attention-demanding behavior, assaultive behavior, fantastic thinking, exaggerated sense of well-being, feelings of persecution, and abrupt mood changes. Ruggero et al. (2014) reviewed 23 studies that have examined the factor structure of manic symptoms, and all but one found mania to be multifactorial, with a range of 2 to 6 factors (modal number was 3). The general nature of these subdimensions were psychomotor activation/increased energy, excessive euphoria, and irritability-aggression. Ruggero et al. noted that these studies were inconsistent about how these dimensions were formed, which was likely owing at least in part to various methodological and statistical differences. These authors therefore conducted their own investigation of a series of 24 distinct mania symptoms derived from the Interview for Mood and Anxiety Disorders (IMAS; Watson et al., 2012) in one student (in mental health treatment) sample and one patient sample. They observed a four-factor structure that was replicated across samples: euphoric activation, hyperactive cognition, reckless overconfidence, and irritability. An examination of the RC9 item content also shows that items tap into each of these four domains.

Of the features associated with manic and hypomanic activation, aggression has been singled out for attention because of its potentially destructive consequences to the aggressor as well as to others. For example, McNeil, Binder, and Greenfield (1988) reported that patients with mania who had displayed violent behavior in the community during the 2 weeks preceding their hospitalization had higher rates of violence during their first 3 days of inpatient treatment. Binder and McNeil (1988) reported that during the first 24 hours of hospitalization, patients with mania had higher rates of violence than those diagnosed with schizophrenia and other disorders. Barlow, Grenyer, and Ilkiw-Lavalle (2000) found similarly that among hospitalized patients, those diagnosed with bipolar disorder were the most likely to act out aggressively. Based on a review of the literature in this area, Najt et al. (2007) concluded that poor impulse control was a likely mediator between aggressive impulses and behavior during manic episodes. Michaelis et al. (2004) found that aggression and impulsivity were associated with increased risk for suicide attempts in patients with bipolar disorder, and Grunebaum et al. (2006) reported findings indicating that an earlier age of onset of aggression in patients with bipolar disorder was associated with later development of comorbid substance abuse. For these reasons, RC9 and the Specific Problems Scales Activation and Aggression (both described later) are placed within the behavioral dysfunction interpretative domain.

EMPIRICAL FINDINGS WITH RC9

The external correlates of RC9 in clinical settings include symptoms of manic episodes and bipolar disorder. Whitman et al. (2021b) reported moderate associations between MMPI-3 RC9 and symptoms of both mania and bipolar disorder diagnoses in a clinical neuropsychology context. In inpatient settings, Arbisi et al. (2008) found RC9 scores to be correlated with experiencing racing thoughts and increased likelihood of being prescribed mood stabilizers at discharge, and Handel and Archer (2008) identified grandiosity and overexcitement as RC9 correlates. In an outpatient private practice sample, Sellbom, Graham, and Schenk (2006) found that RC9 scores were substantially correlated with a measure of manic symptoms. Burchett and Ben-Porath (2010) found that RC9 scores correlated with manic symptoms in a college student sample. Sellbom, Bagby et al. (2012) and Watson, Quilty, and Bagby (2011) compared the MMPI-2-RF scores of individuals diagnosed with bipolar disorder or major depression and found RC9 to be the best differential diagnostic indicator among the RC Scales.

Construct-relevant correlates have also been reported for RC9, including hostility, aggression, and antisocial features in a college counseling setting (Sellbom, Ben-Porath, & Graham, 2006), and aggression in a sample of individuals in treatment for substance abuse (Forbey & Ben-Porath, 2007), in an outpatient community mental health sample (Tellegen et al., 2003), and in mental health and medical outpatients at a VA medical center (Tellegen & Ben-Porath, 2008/2011). Substantial correlations between RC9 and indices of aggression have also been reported in a correctional setting (Forbey et al., 2009), in a clinical sample and sample of community-dwelling veterans (Simms et al., 2005), and in college student samples (Forbey & Ben-Porath, 2008; Sellbom & Ben-Porath, 2005). Anderson et al. (2020) reported positive correlations between RC9 scores and a history of nonsexual violent offending in German sexual offenders. In a sample of domestic violence offenders, higher scores on RC9 were associated with lower confidence in offenders' ability to stop acting violently (Sellbom, Ben-Porath, Baum, Erez, & Gregory, 2008). Other correlates in this population included poorer treatment outcome and increased risk for recidivism (Sellbom, Ben-Porath, Baum, Erez, & Gregory, 2008; Whitman et al., 2020). Tarescavage, Glassmire, and Burchett (2016) found that RC9 was a predictor of future violence in patients admitted to a forensic psychiatric hospital. In a sample of law enforcement candidates, scores on RC9 were associated with subsequent use of excessive force (Sellbom, Fischler, & Ben-Porath, 2007).

Correlates of RC9 in the personality and personality disorder domains include narcissism, manipulativeness, and dominance/social potency (Handel & Archer, 2008, in psychiatric inpatients; Sellbom & Ben-Porath, 2005, in a college student sample; Simms et al., 2005, in a clinical setting and sample of community-dwelling veterans); this includes correlations with antisocial personality disorder, narcissistic personality disorder, and psychopathy (Anderson et al., 2020; Anderson et al., 2015b; Phillips et al., 2014; Sellbom, Ben-Porath et al., 2012; Sellbom et al., 2005, 2018; Sellbom & Smith, 2017; Zahn et al., 2017). Some of the strongest personality correlates of RC9 are a low level on the Agreeableness domain of the five-factor model of personality (Sellbom, Ben-Porath, & Bagby, 2008b) and high levels on the Antagonism/Dissociality domain of the personality models of the International Classification of Diseases 11th Revision (ICD-11) or the AMPD (Anderson & Sellbom, 2021; Anderson et al., 2015a; Sellbom, Anderson, & Bagby, 2013; Tarescavage & Menton, 2020). Other personality correlates of RC9 include sensation seeking/behavioral fearlessness (Sellbom, Ben-Porath, Lilienfeld, Patrick, & Graham, 2005, in university students; Sellbom, Ben-Porath, & Bagby, 2008b, in psychiatric patients; Simms et al., 2005, in a clinical setting and sample of community-dwelling veterans) and disinhibition and impulsivity (Forbey & Ben-Porath, 2007, in individuals receiving treatment for substance abuse; Forbey & Ben-Porath, 2008, in university students; Forbey et al., 2009, in prison inmates; and Simms et al., 2005, in a clinical setting and sample of community-dwelling veterans).

In assessments of police officer candidates, higher RC9 scores have been reported to be associated with a having greater likelihood of being self-centered (Ben-Porath & Tellegen, 2020b), having a history of difficulty getting along with others, being more likely to be opinionated, being demanding, behaving impulsively, and having anger management difficulties (Detrick et al., 2016; Tarescavage, Fischler et al., 2015).

SUMMARY

The construct targeted by RC9, hypomanic activation, represents a challenge for assessment devices such as the MMPI-3 because of the inherently transient nature of some of its core manifestations. Nevertheless, the correlates just summarized include many of the features of manic and hypomanic states catalogued in Kraepelin's (1921) nosology and captured in subsequent empirical studies; these features include the two core temperamental traits identified by Kraepelin (1921), aggression and overexcitation (i.e., activation), as well as the domains of more contemporary structural models (Ruggero et al., 2014). RC9 scores are not associated substantially with the expansive mood component of hypomania, which would instead be reflected in low scores on RC2, indicating the need to consider scores on multiple MMPI-3 scales in the process of differential diagnosis (discussed further in chapter 9).

Most individuals with hypomanic personality traits do not go on to develop a full-fledged bipolar disorder, though it is associated with an increased risk for this diagnosis (Kwapil et al., 2000). Thus, as is the case with all the RC Scales, an elevated score on RC9 indicates a need to consider a *possible* diagnosis of a bipolar disorder (by referencing the actual diagnostic criteria). However, the behavioral and personological correlates just listed are likely to apply. Indeed, in most cases, as consistent with various personality correlates, elevated RC9 scores are likely to be reflective of a mixture of antagonistic and disinhibited personality traits.

SPECIFIC PROBLEMS (SP) SCALES

The 26 Specific Problems (SP) Scales are organized into four domains—Somatic/Cognitive, Internalizing, Externalizing, and Interpersonal—which are identified through both conceptual considerations and correlation analyses with the Higher Order (H-O) and RC Scales (Ben-Porath & Tellegen, 2020a, 2020b).

Somatic/Cognitive SP Scales

Constructs

There are four Somatic/Cognitive SP Scales: Malaise (MLS), Neurological Complaints (NUC), Eating Concerns (EAT), and Cognitive Complaints (COG). Three of these scales (MLS, NUC, COG) represent specific manifestations of the somatoform spectrum (Sellbom, Forbush, Gould, Markon, Watson, & Witthöft, 2022; Watson et al., 2022) and specifically, the bodily distress syndrome (assessed via RC1), whereas the fourth scale (EAT) also maps onto internalizing psychopathology at a structural level (Forbush et al., 2010). Because EAT does directly reflect physical symptom reporting (as opposed to internal affective experiences), it was placed in this domain. It is also noteworthy that, while acknowledging that eating pathology structurally belongs to the internalizing spectrum (Kotov et al., 2017, 2021), the Hierarchical Taxonomy of Psychopathology (HiTOP) consortium's measurement workgroup nevertheless decided to include eating disorder measurement with the somatoform spectrum.

The first scale in this set, Malaise (MLS), targets one of the multiple constructs embedded within the item pool of original MMPI Clinical Scale 3 (Hysteria [Hy]). The MLS items, all of which were scored on the Harris-Lingoes Lassitude-Malaise (Hy3) scale, describe an overall sense of physical debilitation and poor health. Bigos et al. (1991) reported that in a large sample of employees of the Boeing company, those who scored higher on Scale 3 were more likely to report a back injury at some point later in their careers, and Fordyce et al. (1992) later clarified that the items scored on Hy3 were the strongest predictors of this outcome. Gatchel et al. (1995) found higher scores on Scale 3 to be associated with a reduced likelihood of return to work following back injury, a finding replicated later by Vendrig (1999). Vendrig et al. (1999) later clarified that Hy3 was the best predictor of this negative outcome, a result that had also been reported in Bigos et al. (1991).

Malaise has also been hypothesized and found to play a role in various unexplained medical conditions associated with somatoform psychopathology. For example, Aragona et al. (2008) found that a combination of MMPI-2 items scored on RC1 and MLS on the MMPI-2-RF best differentiated individuals diagnosed with pain disorder from individuals experiencing pain with an identified somatic origin. Along the same lines, Fordyce (1998) emphasized the need to distinguish between pain, suffering, and disability in chronic pain patients. Priebe et al. (2008) found that perceived functional incapacity (a construct similar to Malaise as assessed by the MLS scale) was the primary characteristic of chronic fatigue syndrome, another somatic condition that frequently manifests in medically unexplained symptoms. Taken together, MLS can be conceptually and to some degree empirically linked to the distress component of Fink and colleagues' body distress syndrome (BDS; Budtz-Lilly et al., 2015; Fink & Schröder, 2010; Petersen et al., 2020; see Fink, 2017 for a review).

The Neurological Complaints (NUC) scale measures a specific type of somatic symptom reports, functional neurological symptoms. As discussed in chapter 1, the MMPI was designed to be used in a medical setting with general medical patients as well as individuals with psychiatric disorders. Moreover, two of the original Clinical Scales targeted somatoform disorders marked by unexplainable physical symptoms. As a result, the MMPI and MMPI-2 include a relatively large number of items that describe specific somatic symptoms associated with somatoform conditions. Although most of these are now efficiently harnessed within RC1 and conceptualized under a general somatic symptom disorder (*DSM-5*) or BDS, functional neurological symptoms have a rich tradition of separate consideration and diagnosis (which is retained in *DSM-5*), and therefore merit distinct assessment (see also Sellbom, Forbush et al., 2022, for a similar discussion). Indeed, Sellbom, Forbush et al. (2022) recently demonstrated that although symptoms of both bodily distress and health anxiety are not infrequently endorsed in nonclinical samples, the endorsement of functional neurological complaints is quite rare, suggesting the potential of distinct mechanisms in development.

The Eating Concerns (EAT) scale was developed specifically to measure behaviors that place the individual at risk for an eating disorder. This scale is new to the MMPI-3, and previous iterations of the MMPI have failed to directly assess for these important symptom domains. More specifically, the scale consists of five items: two of which assess binge-eating symptoms, two items assess purging behaviors (specifically vomiting), and one item assesses restrictive eating. Although the item content of the scale does not capture every important eating disorder symptom or phenomenon, it does assess for the most critical symptoms in the three primary *DSM-5* eating disorders, specifically, anorexia nervosa (AN), bulimia nervosa (BN), and binge-eating disorder (BED). Ben-Porath and Tellegen (2020a) recommend that elevations on EAT scale scores should signal to clinicians a need to evaluate for diagnoses related to disordered eating as well as consideration of disordered eating as a focus for intervention.

A final scale in this set, Cognitive Complaints (COG), was developed by analyzing items scored on two of the Harris-Lingoes subscales for Clinical Scale 8: (1) Lack of Ego Mastery and (2) Cognitive and Lack of Ego Mastery, Conative. These items (including some scored on both subscales) describe various cognitive complaints related to memory, attention, and concentration. COG was added to the set of somatic scales based on correlational analyses revealing considerable covariation with these measures as well as a literature reflecting significant co-occurrence of somatic and cognitive complaints (e.g., following mild traumatic brain injury [Stulemeijer, Vos, Bleijenberg, & van der Werf, 2007], stroke [Duits, Munnecom, van Heugten, & Oostenbrugge, 2008], and seizure [Velissaris, Wilson, Newton, Berkovic, & Saling, 2009]). Cognitive complaints can also occur without a clear somatic or other origin and without concomitant evidence of impaired cognitive functioning. Indeed, Budtz-Lilly et al. (2015) and Petersen et al. (2020) showed factor analytical evidence that memory, concentration, and attention difficulties load on a general (or nonspecific) factor within the broader BDS construct. However, readers should be aware that subjective cognitive complaints are common across a wide range of internalizing, thought, and externalizing disorders as well, and COG elevations are thus unlikely to be specific to somatic symptom manifestations.

Psychometric Findings

Reliability data reported in the *MMPI-3 Technical Manual* indicate that scores on the Somatic/Cognitive Scales are adequately reliable, with test-retest correlations ranging from .68 (EAT) to .90 (COG) and internal consistency estimates ranging from .49 (EAT) to .86 (COG) in the normative sample and .54 (EAT) to .88 (COG) in the mental health sample. The somewhat lower reliability estimates in the normative sample are a function of the restricted range of scores on these scales in nonclinical settings. This is reflected in comparable standard errors of measurements (*SEMs*) (ranging from 3 to 8 T-score units) in the normative and mental health samples. Intercorrelations within the Somatic/Cognitive Scales range from .17 to .49 in the normative sample and .10 to .51 in the mental health sample. For the two scales that appear on both the MMPI-2-RF and MMPI-3, the cross-version correlations were .92–.94 (MLS) and .87–.89 (COG) across samples. NUC was unchanged across versions and EAT is new to the MMPI-3.

In terms of published MMPI-3 research, Whitman et al. (2021b) reported that MLS and NUC were associated with diagnoses of somatoform disorder in a sample of individuals undergoing neuropsychological evaluations. In this sample, MLS and NUC were also associated with neurological symptoms, with NUC unsurprisingly demonstrating a larger correlation with this variable. COG evinced a medium correlation with presenting problems being cognitive; the scale also showed as a large correlation with the evaluation in revealing cognitive symptoms.

In terms of research using the MMPI-2-RF, MLS, NUC, and COG were also associated with pain ratings and overall disability in a workers' compensation sample (Block et al., 2014). Tarescavage, Scheman et al. (2015) reported correlations between MLS and NUC and pain disability in a chronic pain treatment sample. All three scales were also associated with poor health complaints and various bodily complaints in a larger spine surgery and spinal cord stimulator surgery sample (Marek et al., 2020). These scales were further associated with decreased quality of life as well as with various eating and weight concerns in a sample who had undergone bariatric surgery 6 years earlier (Marek et al., 2021a).

The Somatic/Cognitive Scales have also been linked to outcomes in various presurgical evaluations. MLS in particular has been linked to low postoperative quality of life across various domains in individuals undergoing presurgery evaluations for bariatric surgery (Tarescavage, Wygant et al. 2013). High scores on MLS (80T) and COG (75T) predicted postimplant disability ratings in individuals who had undergone spinal cord stimulator surgery (Block, Marek, Ben-Porath, & Kukal, 2017). Marek et al. (2014) found that NUC scores predicted postoperative somatic complaints 1 and 3 months after bariatric surgery. Locke et al. (2010) found that scores on NUC were best able to differentiate between individuals experiencing epileptic and nonepileptic seizures on an epilepsy monitoring unit. Gervais, Ben-Porath, and Wygant (2009) found that scores on COG were strongly associated with subjective cognitive and emotional complaints; however, they were not associated with actual cognitive deficits as intended. Forbey, Lee, and Handel (2010) found COG scores to be correlated with scores on the Cognitive Failures Questionnaire (Broadbent et al., 1982) in a college student sample.

The EAT scale is new to the MMPI-3 and has therefore not undergone the same degree of empirical evaluation as the other Somatic/Cognitive scales. The *MMPI-3 Technical Manual* presented preliminary data on correlations for scores on this scale with scores on the Eating Attitudes Test-26 (EAT-26; Garner et al., 1982) and the Eating Disorder Examination Questionnaire (EDE-Q; Fairburn & Beglin, 1994) in a university sample (Ben-Porath & Tellegen, 2020b). More specifically, these correlations were generally weak (EAT-26 scales) to moderate (EDE-Q scales) in a male subsample and generally large (EAT-26 and EDE-Q scales) in a female subsample. The *MMPI-3 Technical Manual* also indicates that EAT scale scores were associated with therapists' ratings of both excessive eating and concerns about body image in a community mental health sample.

Whitman et al. (2021b) found that EAT scale scores were moderately correlated with eating disorder diagnoses in a clinical neuropsychology sample. Marek et al. (2021b) studied 38 patients who underwent bariatric surgery 5 years prior to completing the MMPI-3. They showed that EAT scale scores have large correlations with scores on Eating Concerns, Shape Concerns, and the total score of the EDE-Q. Furthermore, there were smaller correlations between the MMPI-3 EAT scale scores and scores on the EDE-Q Restraint and Weight Concerns scales. EAT scale scores were also moderately correlated with higher proportion of weight loss. Vaňousová et al. (2021) found that EAT scale scores were associated with a range of eating disorder symptoms as assessed via the EDE-Q, Eating Pathology Symptom Inventory (EPSI; Forbush et al., 2013), Eating Disorder Diagnostic Scale for *DSM-5* (EDDS; Stice et al., 2000), and specific measures of binge eating and body dissatisfaction. Most of these correlations were of large magnitude. Moreover, the EAT scale also incremented scores from the other 25 SP Scales in the assessment of core eating disorder symptoms. Most recently, Marek and Anderson (2022) replicated several of these findings in a U.S. university sample.

Internalizing SP Scales

Constructs

The 10 Internalizing SP Scales can be divided into two clusters: four measures of constructs associated (both conceptually and statistically) with demoralization and six associated with various manifestations of negative emotionality. As noted earlier, RCd shows the strongest association with current suicidal ideation and recent suicide attempts among the eight RC Scales. It is therefore not surprising that all the demoralization-related SP Scales are associated with suicide risk factors. The first of these, Suicidal/Death Ideation (SUI), consists of items directly related to suicide and preoccupation with death. The importance of inquiring about suicide-related thoughts is highlighted by Wingate et al. (2004), who concluded, based on a review of the empirical literature, that "patients' own self-report of suicidal symptoms deserves considerable attention within the suicide assessment framework. Unless there are clear reasons to the contrary, self-report regarding suicide potential should be a major source of data" (p. 663). Glassmire et al. (2001) found that some individuals willing to endorse suicide-related MMPI-2 items did not acknowledge these experiences in face-to-face interviews, consistent with findings from Glassmire et al. (2016) that the MMPI-2-RF SUI scale outperformed suicidal ideation expressed in clinical interview in the prediction of suicide attempts 12 months later. These findings underscore the importance of incorporating self-report measures when obtaining information about possible suicidal thoughts.

The second demoralization-related SP scale, Helplessness/Hopelessness (HLP), includes items keyed to convey pessimism about one's future prospects and the ability to improve them through self-change. The constructs of helplessness and hopelessness have figured prominently in the suicide risk assessment literature. Based on a meta-analysis of the literature on the Beck Hopelessness Scale (BHS; Beck et al., 1974), McMillan et al. (2007) concluded that the test is useful in identifying individuals at high risk for suicide and nonfatal self-harm. More broadly, hopelessness, and specifically negative expectations for the future, has been implicated as a risk factor for depressive and possibly also anxiety disorders (Miranda et al., 2008; Williams et al., 2008). Consistent with the notion that demoralization-related depression may be less responsive to antidepressant medication than is anhedonic depression (discussed in chapter 2), Papakostas et al. (2007) found that higher levels of hopelessness were associated with nonresponsiveness to fluoxetine in patients diagnosed with a major depressive disorder. Also, within the mood disorder domain, hopelessness has been implicated in bipolar disorder in general, and in different phases of the disorder (Valtonen et al., 2009). Finally, hopelessness and helplessness have also been identified as playing a role in various medical conditions including hypertension (Stern et al., 2009), other forms of cardiovascular disease (Pedersen et al., 2009), and metabolic syndrome (Valtonen et al., 2008).

The next measure of internalizing dysfunction within the subset of demoralization-linked scales, Self-Doubt (SFD), is made up of items that describe low self-esteem, worthlessness, and a sense of being inferior to others. The construct assessed by this scale is closely linked to the one measured by the final scale in this subset, Inefficacy (NFC), which consists of items keyed to convey a sense of feeling overwhelmed, having trouble coping with and an inability to make important decisions when facing crises or difficulties. Conceptual and empirical links between the self-doubt and inefficacy constructs have been demonstrated. Judge et al. (2002) found that a single trait (analogous to demoralization) could account for variance in both these constructs (as well as locus of control). However, each construct was also found to predict relevant criteria in a discriminantly valid manner. Lightsey et al. (2006) similarly found substantial covariation between self-esteem and self-efficacy, and concluded that the two constructs are also distinct, though self-efficacy may play a role in the development of self-esteem.

Focusing specifically on self-doubt or low self-esteem, Neiss et al. (2009) reported data showing that self-esteem, depression, and negative emotionality covary as a function of genetic influences, and Orth et al. (2009) reported that strong cross-sectional correlations between low self-esteem and depression reflect a vulnerability to depression associated with premorbid self-doubt. Underscoring the importance of assessing self-doubt as part of a comprehensive psychological evaluation, Bhar et al. (2008) found that low self-esteem was a risk factor for suicidal ideation when controlling for depressed mood (i.e., demoralization) and hopelessness. Self-doubt has also been implicated as a risk factor for borderline and avoidant personality disorders (Lynum et al., 2008), eating disorders (Dunkley & Grilo, 2007), and posttraumatic stress disorder (Kashdan, Uswatte, Steger, & Julian, 2006).

Bandura (1994) defines general self-efficacy as "people's beliefs about their capabilities to produce designated levels of performance that exercise influence over events that affect their lives" (p. 71), which, according to Bandura (2001), is the foundation of human agency. In research, a distinction is made between general self-efficacy and self-efficacy with respect to more narrowly defined areas of functioning. Wu (2009) evaluated the factorial stability of general self-efficacy in 25 countries and found that a single latent factor best accounted for the data in all. The NFC scale is a measure of general rather than domain-specific efficacy.

The next six internalizing scales are all linked conceptually and empirically to the negative emotionality domain, assessed by RC7. Stress (STR) includes items that describe experiencing stress reactivity, nervousness, and inability to control anxiety. Worry (WRY) measures excessive worry (also termed apprehensive anxiety) and rumination, which is an essential feature of *DSM-5* generalized anxiety disorder (GAD), though the WRY scale is not specific to GAD. Although stress reactivity and worry/rumination are highly related constructs, the STR and WRY scales do have distinct correlates (Ben-Porath & Tellegen, 2020b). The former scale is better linked to poor stress management and ability to manage and control nervousness, anxiety, or tension, whereas the WRY scale is more directly focused on cognitive aspects of anxiety, including future-oriented apprehensive worry and rumination about negative events. Both scales measure transdiagnostic constructs; worry and rumination, for instance have been linked to both depression and anxiety disorders (Hughes et al., 2008). From the perspective of psychopathology structure, internalizing psychopathology bifurcates into *distress* (e.g., depression, generalized anxiety) and *fear* disorders (panic, phobias, obsessive-compulsive disorder, social anxiety; see e.g., Watson et al., 2022). Although STR and WRY are both markers of negative emotionality, they would be more closely linked to distress than fear and hence have been placed in the middle of the internalizing profile.

The next internalizing measure in the negative emotionality domain is Compulsivity (CMP), which is a new scale on the MMPI-3. This SP scale was developed to capture a construct that was generally absent from previous versions of the MMPI instruments (Sellbom, 2019b). The CMP scale measures obsessional thinking and rigid compulsive and ritualistic behavior (e.g., counting, checking). It is also associated with rigid perfectionism. The *MMPI-3 Technical Manual* clearly links it to other symptom measures of obsessive-compulsive disorder (OCD) and disorders related to it. Interestingly, OCD is an interstitial construct from a psychopathology structure perspective (as it loads on both internalizing/fear and thought disorder; Sellbom, Carragher et al., 2020), and CMP is also associated with a range of thought disorder measures (Ben-Porath & Tellegen, 2020b).

Anxiety-Related Experiences (AXR) is a substantially revised scale from its MMPI-2-RF counterpart (Anxiety [AXY]). In addition to items that describe pervasive anxiety marked by near-daily experiences of fright and nightmares, which have been linked to posttraumatic distress, newly written and added items assess additional anxiety-related experiences pertaining to panic attacks and cognitive components of anxiety such as catastrophizing. The continued inclusion of items reflecting reexperiencing and intrusive ideation symptoms make this scale a good measure of posttraumatic distress, as such symptoms differentiate PTSD from other distress disorders (Keane et al. 1997). However, this scale now reflects an even broader array of anxiety and especially fear disorder-related experiences that involve heightened arousal.

The next internalizing measure on the negative emotionality cluster, Anger Proneness (ANP), consists of items that describe becoming easily angered, irritable, and impatient when interacting with others and being overwhelmed with anger. Drawing from the work of Spielberger and colleagues (Spielberger, Jacobs, Russle, and Crane, 1983) and Novaco (1994), Eckhardt et al. (2004) drew distinctions between hostility, an interpersonal attitude (measured partly by the MMPI-3 CYN scale); anger, an affective experience; and aggression, a behavioral construct assessed on the MMPI-3 by an identically named externalizing scale. Scarpa and Raine (1997), for instance, noted that the affective experience of anger does not always lead to aggressive behavior, and that aggression and violence do not always occur within the context of angry affect. However, underscoring the importance of assessing anger, Novaco and Taylor (2004) found that patient-reported anger was a significant predictor of postadmission (to an inpatient forensic unit) assaults in a sample of male offenders with various mental and neurological disabilities. Although anger proneness has not featured prominently in the hierarchical structure of psychopathology because it is not directly linked to a specific mental disorder, it frequently does load on negative affectivity domains (Wright & Simms, 2015).

The final negative emotionality-related internalizing scale, Behavior Restrictive Fears (BRF), is made up of items that describe various fears that inhibit and significantly restrict the individual's normal range of behaviors. The *DSM-5* similarly distinguishes between anxiety and fears that result in avoidant behavior that impairs the individual's ability to work or carry out other responsibilities (i.e., agoraphobia) and specific phobias involving persistent fear of circumscribed objects or situations (simple phobia). The latter tend to co-occur and are classified into animal, natural environment, blood-injection-injury, situational, and other subtypes; these latter specific phobias are not directly assessed on the MMPI-3. The BRF scale directly assesses fear-related pathology as part of the fear subdomain of internalizing. The *DSM-5* also includes a fear-related disorder, social anxiety disorder, which belongs to multiple psychopathology spectra (including detachment/introversion) and is assessed with the interpersonal scale Shyness (SHY; described later) on the MMPI-3.

Psychometric Findings

Data reported by Ben-Porath & Tellegen (2020b) reflect adequate reliability for the Internalizing Scales. Test-retest reliability estimates based on a subset of the normative sample range from .76 (HLP) to .90 (ANP). Internal consistencies range from .40 (BRF) to .86 (ANP) in the normative sample, and from .43 (BRF) to .89 (ANP) in the mental health sample. *SEM*s (expressed in T-score units) range from 3 (NFC, ANP) to 5 (multiple) based on the normative test-retest reliability estimates and from 4 (ANP) to 10 (BRF) based on internal consistency estimates in the mental health sample. Ben-Porath and Tellegen (2020b) note that for scales with larger *SEM*s, more extreme T scores are needed to justify clinically significant inferences. Intercorrelations between the Internalizing Scales fall mainly in the .20 to .60 range across all samples. In terms of the scales that overlap across the MMPI-2-RF and MMPI-3, these ranged from .75 (AXR) to .96 (ANP, BRF) across normative and mental health samples; most were greater than .90. We did not include CMP since it is new, or STR and WRY since they only have the combined STW counterpart on the MMPI-2-RF.

The MMPI-3 SUI scale has been linked to reports of suicidal ideation, suicide attempts, psychiatric hospitalization, and more surprisingly, violence in a sample of individuals undergoing neuropsychological evaluations (Whitman et al., 2021b). It was also strongly correlated with scores on the Self-Harm Inventory (SHI; Sansone et al., 1998) in a university sample (Whitman et al., 2021a). These findings are consistent with large correlations with both clinician ratings as well as self-report measures of suicidality and attempts reported across samples in the *MMPI-3 Technical Manual*. The MMPI-2-RF version of this scale has correlated with clinician-rated risk for suicide, as well as the thwarted belongingness and perceived burdensomeness constructs from the interpersonal theory of suicide in a university psychology clinic sample (Anestis et al., 2018). Both Gottfried et al. (2014) and Rogers et al. (2017) found very large associations between SUI scores and multiple measures of suicide in subsamples from the same university psychology clinic, with SUI scores also differentiating across ascending levels of clinician-rated suicide risk. Tarescavage, Glassmire, and Burchett (2018) examined SUI scores in a sample of 1,110 forensic psychiatric inpatients and found that the scale predicted future suicide attempts 12 months later (as did HLP, SFD, NFC, AXY, and ANP among the Internalizing Scales); Glassmire et al. (2016) showed that SUI was the best predictor of future suicide attempts in a smaller subsample of forensic outpatients and that, as a predictor, the scale outperformed expression of suicidal ideation and a past history of suicide attempts. Khazem et al. (2021) observed a large correlation between SUI scores and suicidal ideation frequency in 293 patients enrolled in a VA partial psychiatric hospitalization program; Miller et al. (2018) found SUI to be the best predictor of both suicidal ideation and moving from ideation to attempt in a large VA inpatient sample. Moultrie and Engel (2016) found that SUI was the best predictor of suicidal ideation and historical suicide attempts in a large German inpatient sample.

HLP was associated with ratings of hopelessness and pessimism in a German inpatient sample (Moultrie & Engel, 2017). It was also a robust predictor of the dependency observed in dependent personality disorder in both university and outpatient samples (Sellbom & Smith, 2017; Zahn et al., 2017). SFD was associated with feelings of inadequacy, low self-esteem, and rumination in a German inpatient sample (Moultrie & Engel, 2017). SFD scores have also been a particularly potent predictor of the unstable self-concept, low self-esteem, and feelings of ineptitude that pervade the borderline, avoidant, and dependent personality disorders across samples of university and psychiatric patient samples (Anderson et al., 2015b; Brown & Sellbom, 2021; Sellbom & Smith, 2017; Zahn et al., 2017). Whitman and Ben-Porath (2021) also demonstrated that, in multiple university samples, high SFD scores were associated with distinct correlates and that the scale was a better predictor of low self-esteem than were low SFI scale scores.

The MMPI-3 NFC scale was moderately associated with scores on the Subjective Incompetence Scale (Cockram et al., 2009) in a university sample (Whitman et al., 2021a). This scale was also associated with cognitive symptoms in a sample of individuals undergoing neuropsychological evaluations (Whitman et al., 2021b). Both MMPI-3 SFD and NFC were correlated with presenting with emotional problems in this sample (Whitman et al., 2021b).

Collectively, MMPI-3 HLP, SFD, and NFC have been associated with suicidal ideation and psychiatric hospitalization in a clinical neuropsychology sample (Whitman et al., 2021b). Their MMPI-2-RF counterparts have been associated with poor quality of life in various domains in individuals 6 years after bariatric surgery (Marek et al., 2021a), as well as pain severity and quality of life disability ratings in a postspine surgery sample (Block et al., 2014). These scales have been associated with thwarted belongingness and perceived burdensomeness constructs from the interpersonal theory of suicide in a university psychology clinic sample (Anestis et al., 2018; Rogers et al., 2017). Both the MMPI-3 and MMPI-2-RF versions have been linked to depressive disorders and related symptoms in a range of clinical samples (Moultrie & Engel, 2017; Haber & Baum, 2014; Lee et al., 2018; Sellbom, Bagby et al., 2012; Whitman et al., 2021b). The MMPI-2-RF versions of these scales were also prominently elevated, on average, in a well-defined sample of patients with Cluster C personality disorders (De Saeger et al., 2020), which makes conceptual sense, as helplessness, inefficacy, inability to cope, and low self-esteem are germane to these disorders.

The Stress (STR) and Worry (WRY) scales are technically new to the MMPI-3, as discussed earlier. The MMPI-3 literature on these scales has shown that both are associated with physical, cognitive, and social aspects of anxiety sensitivity in a university sample, though in a regression model, only WRY emerged as a unique predictor (Kremyar & Lee, 2021). These scales were also associated with the Comprehensive Assessment of Traits relevant to Personality Disorders (CAT-PD; Simms et al., 2011) Anxiousness trait scale in a university sample (Whitman et al., 2021a). The STR scale (but not WRY) was associated with the presentation of emotional problems in a sample undergoing neuropsychological evaluations; however, both were associated with diagnosis of depressive and anxiety disorders, suicidal ideation, manic symptoms, and psychiatric hospitalizations (Whitman et al., 2021b).

The CMP scale is new to the MMPI-3 and has therefore not featured as much in the literature as other internalizing scales. In a university sample, Whitman et al. (2021a) reported large correlations between CMP and the Schedule of Compulsions, Obsessions, and Pathological Impulses (SCOPI; Watson & Wu, 2005) and three subscales of the Inventory for Depression and Anxiety Symptoms–II (IDAS-II; Watson et al., 2012): Checking, Ordering, and Cleaning. Brown and Sellbom (2021) reported large associations between CMP and symptoms of obsessive-compulsive personality disorder in a university sample. In a subsequent study, Brown and Sellbom (2022) also reported moderate to large correlations between CMP scores and measures of anankastia, perfectionism, workaholism, and rigidity. Furthermore, the *MMPI-3 Technical Manual* also report a range of meaningful and expected correlates of the CMP scale. For instance, CMP correlates with therapists' ratings of being compulsive and obsessive in a community mental health sample, diagnoses of generalized anxiety in an outpatient private practice sample, and obsessive-compulsive and thought disorder symptoms in a forensic disability sample. CMP scores were also negatively associated with self-reported cognitive flexibility and positively correlated with hostility in a preemployment police candidate sample. In a university sample, CMP scores were correlated with a wide range of self-reported obsessive-compulsive disorder symptoms (e.g., obsessions, compulsive behavior, hoarding) across various scales as well as CAT-PD Perfectionism and Rigidity trait scales.

The MMPI-3 ARX scale has been associated with the CAT-PD Anxiousness trait scale (Brown & Sellbom, 2022; Whitman et al., 2021a), the IDAS-II Traumatic Intrusions and Panic subscales, and the Severity Measure for Panic Disorder–Adult (Craske et al., 2013) in a university sample (Whitman et al., 2021a). This scale was also associated with diagnosis of PTSD, depression, and anxiety disorder, as well as suicidal ideation and psychiatric hospitalization in a sample of individuals undergoing neuropsychological evaluations (Whitman et al., 2021b). These are generally consistent with reported associations between ARX and symptoms of PTSD, panic, catastrophizing, and general anxiousness reported in several samples in the *MMPI-3 Technical Manual* (Ben-Porath & Tellegen, 2020b). Furthermore, research on the AXY scale, which is the MMPI-2-RF precursor to ARX, has linked the scale to various symptoms of anxiety in several studies (Moultrie & Engel, 2017). This scale has also proven to be the most robust predictor of PTSD symptoms on the MMPI-2-RF. In a sample of National Guard soldiers who had returned from deployment in Iraq, Arbisi et al. (2011) found AXY scores to be substantially correlated with screening positive for PTSD symptoms. Sellbom, Lee et al. (2012) found that the AXY scale outperformed all other MMPI-2-RF scales in the prediction of a range of individual PTSD symptom clusters in a large forensic disability sample. Ingram et al. (2021) reported that AXY scores in a large VA sample had the strongest correlations with a range of self-report PTSD measures among the SP Scales, as well as the largest correlations for some of the PTSD measures among all MMPI-2-RF scales. This scale also outperformed all other MMPI-2-RF scales in terms of associations with generalized anxiety disorder symptoms and scores on the Beck Anxiety Inventory (BAI; Beck et al., 1988). Tarescavage, Forner, and Ben-Porath (2021) found similar results with respect to the Anxiety scale of the Patient-Reported Outcomes Measurement Information System (PROMIS; Pilkonis et al., 2011) in a university sample.

The MMPI-3 ANP scale has been found to correlate with the CAT-PD trait anger scale and the IDAS-II Ill Temper subscale in a university sample (Whitman et al., 2021a). This scale also correlated with violence history and mania symptoms in a clinical neuropsychology sample (Whitman et al., 2021b). Its MMPI-2-RF counterpart had a large correlation with self-reported anger symptoms in a large university psychology clinic sample (Rogers et al., 2017). Tarescavage, Forner, and Ben-Porath (2021) found that ANP was the best MMPI-2-RF predictor of PROMIS Anger scale scores in a university sample. Furthermore, Sellbom, Laurinavičius et al. (2018) reported large positive correlations between ANP scores and disinhibitory psychopathy traits in a Lithuanian prison sample. Such scores also evinced a weak but significant correlation with scores on the Levels of Service Inventory–Revised (LSI-R; Andrews & Bonta, 2010) in a child sex offender sample (Tarescavage, Cappo, & Ben-Porath, 2018). Finally, Tarescavage, Azizian et al. (2019) found that ANP scores were the best individual predictor of future violence in a forensic psychiatric hospital, and that such scores exponentiated the predictions of other scales (most notably THD and BXD) in the assessment of future violence.

Whitman et al. (2021a) found a moderate correlation between MMPI-3 BRF scores and the IDAS-II Claustrophobia scale in a university sample. This scale was also positively correlated with diagnosis of PTSD and anxiety disorders, as well as presence of hallucinations and paranoia, in a sample of individuals undergoing neuropsychological evaluations (Whitman et al., 2021b). Moreover, the MMPI-2-RF BRF version was associated with anxiety in a German inpatient sample (Moultrie & Engel, 2017) as well as in a university sample (Tarescavage, Forner, & Ben-Porath, 2021). The BRF scale has also become an important predictor of postoperative outcomes for those having undergone spine and spinal cord stimulator surgeries. Specifically, BRF was associated with postsurgery outcome measures of pain severity and a range of disability ratings in a spine surgery sample (Block et al., 2014); concurrently associated with poor health orientation, bodily complaints, and pain treatment orientation problems in a larger spine surgery sample (Marek et al., 2020); and associated with worsening postoperative negative affect in those undergoing spinal cord stimulator surgery (Marek et al., 2015).

Externalizing SP Scales

Constructs

There are seven Externalizing SP Scales, and with the possible exceptions of Family Problems (FML) and Activation (ACT), they are clear markers of the externalizing psychopathology spectrum (Sellbom, 2016, 2017a). Although ACT is listed fourth (of six) in the externalizing profile on the MMPI-3 Score Report, we discuss it last in this section as the underlying construct is conceptually different from the other externalizing scales.

Family Problems (FML) is the first MMPI-3 externalizing scale. On the MMPI-2-RF, it was included among the Interpersonal Scales, but upon review of the MMPI-2-RF literature as well as the fact that several FML items appear on RC4, an externalizing scale, it was moved to the externalizing section. Moreover, it is the scale listed first because it borders the internalizing profile, as such symptoms are also correlated with family discord and alienation. The items do not differentiate between current family and family of origin; thus, FML elevations may indicate dysfunction in either set of relationships or both. The importance of assessing familial dysfunction is underscored by research linking this experience with a broad range of negative outcomes in adults. In a comprehensive longitudinal investigation, Pardis et al. (2009) found increased incidences of depression, low self-esteem, antisocial behavior, substance abuse, unemployment, and physical health problems among individuals exposed to a dysfunctional family environment while growing up. Pilowsky et al. (2006) found family discord to be associated with increased risk for major depression and substance abuse in offspring of depressed and nondepressed parents. Klonsky et al. (2000) found familial dysfunction to be associated with increased risk for personality disorder in general, but they did not identify associations with specific disorders, though on the MMPI-2-RF (Anderson et al., 2015b; Sellbom & Smith, 2017; Zahn et al., 2017) and MMPI-3 (Brown & Sellbom, 2021), this scale has been particularly linked to borderline personality psychopathology. Kaslow et al. (2000) reported an association between family problems and risk for suicide attempts in a sample of African American women.

Familial dysfunction has also been found to play a detrimental role in psychological interventions. For example, Evans et al. (2009) found that problematic familial relationships can have a negative impact on PTSD treatment efforts. Thus, elevations on FML may be associated with a broad range of psychological dysfunction and have negative implications for treatment efforts, indicating the advisability of addressing these issues in treatment planning.

Structural research has indicated that externalizing psychopathology is a higher order construct that bifurcates into two more specific domains: disinhibited-externalizing and antagonistic-externalizing (see Kotov et al., 2017, for a review). The next five scales (Juvenile Conduct Problems [JCP], Substance Abuse [SUB], Impulsivity [IMP], Aggression [AGG], and Cynicism [CYN]) are considered in the context of being explicit markers of externalizing psychopathology, and in particular, these two subdomains of disinhibited-externalizing and antagonistic-externalizing. Numerous studies have supported that these domains are directly downstream from a broader externalizing factor in both personality (Markon et al., 2005) and psychopathology (Wright et al., 2012) models. Moreover, several studies have observed these correlated domains as sufficiently distinct in various structural studies across multiple samples (McNulty & Overstreet, 2014; Røysamb et al., 2011; Wright & Simms, 2015).

Disinhibited-externalizing emphasizes psychopathology constructs with problematic impulse control, irresponsibility, sensation seeking, and risk-taking at its core, such as antisocial personality disorder, conduct disorder, ADHD, and alcohol and other substance use disorders. From this perspective, JCP, SUB, and IMP provide for more specific measurement of this domain. JCP specifically is made up of items that describe a history of juvenile misconduct involving stealing, negative peer-group influence, and problematic behavior in school. Diagnostic criteria for adult antisocial personality disorder require a history of juvenile conduct disorder, and numerous studies have demonstrated that such a history is predictive of various negative outcomes in adults. Conduct problems are also associated with a range of risk factors for adult psychopathology. For instance, Knop et al. (2009) similarly found that juvenile conduct problems comorbid with ADHD were predictive of alcohol dependence in adults. Burke, Loeber, and Lahey (2007) reported finding that conduct disorder and teacher-rated interpersonal callousness in adolescence were predictive of psychopathy in young adults. The MMPI-3 SUB scale consists of items that describe problematic alcohol use, drug use, and misuse of prescription medication, and directly assesses this component of disinhibited-externalizing. Substance misuse also serves as a risk factor for a range of problems; for instance, increased risk for interpersonal violence is associated with this behavior in a variety of patients and circumstances (e.g., individuals diagnosed with schizophrenia, Fazel et al., 2009; perpetrators of intimate partner violence, Hirschel et al., 2010; violent offenders, Sacks et al., 2009). Finally, the MMPI-3 IMP scale is new to the test and consists of items that refer to nonplanful behavior and acting without considering consequences. Impulsivity measures the very core of disinhibition and is prominent in all forms of disinhibited psychopathology (Beauchaine et al., 2017).

Antagonistic-externalizing, on the other hand, is typically characterized by psychopathology emphasizing maladaptive antagonism, including callousness, manipulativeness, deceitfulness, grandiosity, suspiciousness, and interpersonal aggression and hostility; this domain is implicated in various personality disorders, particularly psychopathy/antisocial, narcissistic, and paranoid personality disorders (Sellbom, 2019a). On the MMPI-3, AGG and CYN capture components of callousness, deceitfulness, suspiciousness, and interpersonal aggression and hostility—and more specifically, AGG includes items that describe engaging in physically violent behavior toward others, acting violently in response to angry affect, and enjoying thoughts about, or actual infliction of, physical aggression toward others. Although aggressive ideation and behavior saturate the scale, there are elements of callous aggression contained within this item pool, and the empirical literature on psychopathy have identified AGG items as reflective of core psychopathic traits (e.g., Sellbom, 2016).

Cynicism (CYN), which was formerly RC3 on the MMPI-2 and MMPI-2-RF, consists of items that reflect non-self-referential beliefs and attitudes about the world and other people. More specifically, items clearly reflect antagonistic (or "Machiavellian") attitudes that others cannot be trusted and that most people lie, manipulate, exploit, cheat, and engage in various forms of antisocial conduct, with implicit approval. Monaghan et al. (2016), for instance, have linked cynicism to Machiavellianism, a trait construct that represents several aspects of interpersonal antagonism (Vize et al., 2019). Several studies have also revealed that CYN (or RC3) scores have been linked to psychopathy (Ben-Porath & Tellegen, 2020b; Glenn & Sellbom, 2015; Sellbom, Ben-Porath et al., 2012), paranoid personality (Anderson et al., 2015b; Brown & Sellbom, 2021), and future police officer misconduct (Sellbom, Fischler et al., 2007), further supporting its linkage to antagonistic-externalizing behavior.

The final externalizing scale discussed in this section, Activation (ACT), is made up of items that reflect racing thoughts, elated mood, a state of overexcitation, and cycling moods. This content resembles many of the items included in Eckblad and Chapman's (1986) Hypomanic Personality scale (HYP), although the latter covers a somewhat broader domain than the ACT items. Studies with HYP show that higher scores on this scale are associated with an increased likelihood for bipolar disorder symptoms. Kwapil et al. (2000) found at a 13-year follow up that former university students who scored high on this scale were more likely than were control participants to have developed a bipolar disorder, have psychotic-like experiences, manifest symptoms of borderline personality disorder, and have higher rates of substance abuse. As documented later, the ACT scale has shown similar aptitude in the prediction of bipolar disorder (Sellbom, Bagby et al., 2012; Watson et al., 2011).

In the externalizing section of the MMPI-3 Externalizing and Interpersonal Scales profile, ACT is strategically placed between the disinhibition scales (JCP, SUB, IMP) and antagonism scales (AGG, CYN), as the latter also link up with interpersonal features of antagonism that are measured by MMPI-3 Interpersonal Scales appearing next in that profile (SFI, DOM; discussed later). The ACT scale is not necessarily a measure of externalizing per se. Indeed, Sellbom (2016) demonstrated convincingly across three large samples–one correctional sample, one forensic sample, and one community sample–that the ACT items better reflect an independent latent construct that is correlated with, but outside of, the externalizing spectrum, rather than being part of its structure. McNulty and Overstreet (2014), Sellbom (2017a), and Sellbom, Kremyar, and Wygant (2021) have also shown that this scale loads most strongly with the thought dysfunction scales when the full range of MMPI-2-RF/MMPI-3 scales are considered in a factor analysis. This finding is generally consistent with literature on mania, as such symptoms tend to load consistently on the thought disorder spectrum, and is consistent with the finding that bipolar I disorder and schizophrenia share many common genetic risk factors (Kotov et al., 2020). However, the MMPI-3 does not have SP Scales that assess thought dysfunction, and considering the overt behavioral sequelae associated with manic symptoms as well as many ACT items appearing on RC9 (which has a range of externalizing correlates), ACT is placed among the Externalizing Scales.

Psychometric Findings

Data reported by Ben-Porath and Tellegen (2020b) indicate that test-retest reliability estimates for the Externalizing Scales in the normative sample range from .75 (ACT) to .92 (SUB). Internal consistencies in the normative sample range from .54 (AGG) to .79 (CYN). In the mental health sample, these same coefficients range from .63 (AGG) to .82 (CYN). The *SEM*s (expressed in T-score values) range from 3 to 6 based on the test-retest reliability estimates and from 5 to 9 based on internal consistencies. Intercorrelations between the Externalizing Scales fall in the .11 to .50 range in the normative sample and .14 to .51 in the mental health sample. In terms of associations with their MMPI-2-RF counterparts, these ranged .93 (SUB) to .99 (JCP) in the normative and mental health samples. CYN was compared to RC3, whereas IMP was not included because it was a new scale, and ACT was unchanged across versions.

Research on FML has linked the scale to a host of externalizing difficulties, which would be conceptually relevant to those with both historical and ongoing familial discord and alienation. Whitman et al. (2021b) showed that, in a sample of individuals undergoing neuropsychological evaluations, MMPI-3 FML scores were correlated with a range of psychological and behavioral problems, including reports of suicidal ideation, violence, being to jail, mania, hallucinations, paranoia, and a psychiatric hospitalization history. FML scores were also correlated with various internalizing disorders. This scale, however, has also been found to assess the specific problems it was designed to measure. For instance, the *MMPI-3 Technical Manual* indicates that in a community mental health sample, higher scorers on FML report blaming their family members for causing their difficulties and generally experiencing familial discord. In terms of MMPI-2-RF research, Lee, Taylor et al. (2019) found that FML was associated with both self-rated and partner-rated dyadic distress in the MMPI-2/MMPI-2-RF normative couples sample. Gregory et al. (2021) found support for the FML scale in characterizing interpersonal conflict between missionary husbands and wives.

Similar to our earlier conceptual discussion, we separate JCP, SUB, IMP, AGG, and CYN as markers of externalizing from ACT, which we will discuss last. The *MMPI-3 Technical Manual* provides evidence that JCP, SUB, and IMP tend to have larger correlations with clinician-rated externalizing disorders that reflect disinhibition (antisocial, conduct disorder, ADHD, and substance use disorders) than AGG and CYN, which reflect antagonistic-externalizing. The latter two scales were more strongly correlated with egocentric and callous psychopathic personality traits. Furthermore, in a clinical neuropsychology evaluation sample, Whitman et al. (2021b) showed that JCP and SUB were most strongly correlated with a history of being in jail, whereas AGG was the best predictor of a history of violent behavior. SUB was also unsurprisingly most strongly correlated with being diagnosed with a substance use disorder.

The MMPI-2-RF versions of the Externalizing Scales, JCP, SUB, and AGG, have undergone substantial validation in a range of forensic contexts. All three correlate with diagnoses of antisocial personality disorder (Anderson, Burchett et al., 2021; Anderson et al., 2015b) and psychopathic personality traits, particularly those that reflect disinhibition/behavioral traits in correctional samples (Anderson et al., 2020; Klein Haneveld et al., 2017; Sellbom, Laurinavičius et al., 2018)—though in some studies, AGG correlated with the core affective-interpersonal traits as well (Anderson et al., 2020; Sellbom, Laurinavičius et al., 2018). Research on the MMPI-2-RF precursor to CYN, RC3, also showed evidence for correlation with both the affective and lifestyle facets of the PCL-SV (Anderson et al., 2020).

JCP has also been consistently associated with a history of violent and nonviolent offenses in correctional samples (Anderson et al., 2020; Laurinaitytė et al., 2017). SUB has been a good predictor of substance use problems, including in the context of other criminal activities (Anderson et al., 2020; Laurinaitytė et al., 2017; Lincourt et al., 2020; Sellbom, 2016). This scale has also been found to correlate with stimulant abuse in university samples (Thornton et al., 2020). AGG has been consistently correlated with aggression and violence across samples of forensic examinees and prison inmates (Anderson et al., 2020; Laurinaitytė et al., 2017; Lincourt et al., 2020; Sellbom, 2016).

These scales have been observed to correlate concurrently with various risk assessment tools as well. Laurinaitytė et al. (2017) found that JCP, SUB, AGG correlated moderately with the Offender Assessment System (Home Office, 2002) in a Lithuanian prison sample. Anderson et al. (2020) found that all three scales correlated with total scores from the Sexual Violence Risk (SVR)-20 in a German incarcerated sex offender sample. Tarescavage, Cappo, and Ben-Porath (2018) reported significant correlations between the Static-99 and both JCP and AGG in a U.S. child sex offender sample; these authors also showed significant correlations between the LSI-R and both these scales. Furthermore, in terms of the prediction of future violence and aggression, Tarescavage, Glassmire, and Burchett (2016) found that JCP and AGG predicted future aggression in a forensic psychiatric hospital; however, Tarescavage, Azazian et al. (2019) replicated this finding only for AGG in a different forensic psychiatric hospital for sexual offenders. Tarescavage, Luna-Jones, and Ben-Porath (2014) found that all three scales, JCP, SUB, and AGG, predicted community probation requirement violations.

The IMP scale is new to the MMPI-3 and has therefore not been featured in the MMPI-2-RF literature just reviewed. In addition to the *MMPI-3 Technical Manual* findings and those of Whitman et al. (2021b) discussed earlier, research reported in the *MMPI-3 Technical Manual* has shown specific evidence for criterion and convergent validity across samples. For instance, IMP scores are associated with clinicians' ratings of impulsivity in a community mental health sample; Antisocial and Borderline Features scales on the PAI in a forensic disability sample; and poor self-control in a police candidate sample. Whitman et al. (2021a) reported moderate to large correlations between scores on the Barratt Impulsivity Scale and with CAT-PD Non-Planfulness, Non-Perseverance, and Irresponsibility trait scales in a university sample. Research with a university sample in New Zealand has linked IMP scale scores to antisocial, borderline, and histrionic personality disorder (Brown & Sellbom, 2021) as well as personality traits reflective of irresponsibility, nonperseverance, nonplanfulness, and normviolation (Brown & Sellbom, 2022). Furthermore, in a community sample recruited for externalizing proclivities, Neo, McNaughton, and Sellbom (2021) found that IMP scores were associated with increased reward sensitivity as measured via evoked electroencephalography (EEG) responses to unexpected reward in a monetary gain/loss task.

As explained earlier, the MMPI-2-RF RC3 (Cynicism) scale was moved to the SP scale level (as CYN) on the MMPI-3. Because of its consistent correlates with a range of externalizing attitudes and behaviors, and particularly with respect to measurement of antagonistic-externalizing behavior (as reviewed earlier), it was best situated as an externalizing scale. The *MMPI-3 Technical Manual* has indeed reported positive correlations with various aspects of interpersonal mistrust and psychopathic personality traits, and Brown and Sellbom (2022) found correlations with personality traits indicating mistrust, callousness, rudeness, manipulativeness, and normviolation in a university sample. Research published on MMPI-2-RF RC3 has also supported CYN as an externalizing scale. For instance, high RC3 scores are associated with hostility, anger, and low trust (Burchett & Ben-Porath, 2010, in a college sample; Sellbom, Ben-Porath, & Bagby, 2008b, in a clinical sample; Tellegen & Ben-Porath, 2008/2011, in various settings), negative beliefs about others (Forbey & Ben-Porath, 2007, in a sample of individuals being treated for substance abuse; Forbey & Ben-Porath, 2008, in a nonclinical sample; Handel & Archer, 2008, in psychiatric inpatients), and alienation and blame externalization (Sellbom & Ben-Porath, 2005, in a nonclinical sample; Sellbom, Ben-Porath, Baum, Erez, & Gregory, 2008, in a sample of male batterers). Ingram, Kelso, and McCord (2011) found RC3 scores to be associated with Machiavellianism and alienation in a university student sample. In a police officer sample, higher RC3 scores at the time of prehire psychological evaluation predicted a variety of posthire problems, including citizen complaints, rude behaviors, abuse of authority, externalizing blame, and uncooperativeness (Sellbom, Fischler, & Ben-Porath, 2007). Additionally, Anderson et al. (2020) found RC3 scores to be associated with a range of risk factors on the SVR-20, including psychopathy, relationship problems, and blame externalizing. Tarescavage, Cappo, and Ben-Porath (2018) observed associations of RC3 scores with the LSI-R in a child sex offender sample, and Tarescavage, Azazian et al. (2019) observed a weak but significant correlation between RC3 and future aggression in a forensic psychiatric sample.

The *MMPI-3 Technical Manual* has reported correlations between the ACT scale and a variety of externalizing variables, which highlights the externalizing behavior sequelae of hypomanic and manic symptomatology. Most prominently, the ACT scale has shown to be particularly relevant in the assessment of manic symptoms. The MMPI-3 version was the most strongly correlated scale with both manic episodes and diagnosis of bipolar disorder in a sample of individuals undergoing neuropsychological evaluations (Whitman et al., 2021b). Furthermore, two MMPI-2-RF studies have revealed similar findings. Watson, Quilty, and Bagby (2011) examined the utility of MMPI-2-RF scales in differentiating patients diagnosed with bipolar disorder and major depressive disorder. ACT scores were the best MMPI-2-RF predictors of this differential diagnosis, including for a subsample in which the patients with bipolar disorder with "depressed" as their most recent episode. Moreover, using a sample drawn from the same population, Sellbom, Bagby et al. (2012) similarly observed that the ACT scale performed the best among the MMPI-2-RF scales in differentiating patients with bipolar disorder from those with major depressive disorder and schizophrenia.

Interpersonal SP Scales

Constructs

Scores on many of the MMPI-3 scales already discussed in this chapter and chapter 3 are associated conceptually and empirically with interpersonal difficulties. What distinguishes the scales included in this next set from others is an exclusive focus on interpersonal functioning. There are five Interpersonal SP Scales on the MMPI-3: Self-Importance (SFI), Dominance (DOM), Disaffiliativeness (DSF),

Social Avoidance (SAV), and Shyness (SHY). These scales relate, by varying degrees, to the antagonistic-externalizing and detachment psychopathology spectra (Kotov et al., 2017, 2021; Sellbom, 2019b) and can also be considered with respect to varying positions on the interpersonal circumplex (Ayearst et al., 2013). The scales are ordered in the interpersonal profile by their degree of association with antagonism versus detachment.

The first scale, Self-Importance (SFI), is new to the MMPI-3. It was developed to improve upon the coverage of narcissism measurement in general and grandiosity in particular, which had been deemed deficient in previous MMPI versions (Sellbom, 2019b). However, in keeping with the aim for scale labels that do not automatically infer psychopathology (e.g., well-adjusted and appropriately self-confident individuals might score high on this scale), a more neutral label (as opposed to "grandiosity") was selected. The SFI items, seven of which are new to the MMPI-3, reflecting an avowal of self-importance, self-confidence, being extraordinary, having special talents, being brilliant, and being superior to others, can also be linked to Tellegen's self-evaluative positive valence construct from the "big seven" model (Tellegen, 1993). In most individuals, high scores will be reflective of dispositional grandiosity (Sellbom, 2021; Whitman & Ben-Porath, 2021), which is linked to various forms of psychopathology, most prominently narcissistic personality disorder and psychopathy; also, in the context of psychosis or mania, high scores will reflect grandiose delusions. Grandiosity is a core trait component of antagonism (or low agreeableness) as demonstrated in numerous studies on the structure of personality and psychopathology (Sleep et al., 2021).

The second scale in this subset, Dominance (DOM), consists of items that describe an assertive and domineering interpersonal style as keyed. This scale was labeled Interpersonal Passivity (IPP) on the MMPI-2-RF, but the keying has been reversed for the MMPI-3 to reflect the more common dysfunctional correlates associated with maladaptive dominance. Low scores remain reflective of interpersonal submissiveness and unassertiveness. High dominance and assertiveness, especially in the context of dysfunction, are related to narcissistic personality disorder, histrionic personality disorder, and psychopathy (see Johnson et al., 2012, for a review), whereas low assertiveness is linked to dependent personality disorder. Bornstein (2005), for instance, reviewed the theoretical and empirical literature related to this association and concluded that an interaction between passive-submissive tendencies and situational factors best accounts for the long-observed link between this interpersonal style and the development of dependency. In terms of the structure of psychopathology and personality, maladaptive dominance is linked to the broader structure of antagonism (Sleep et al., 2021) but is also viewed as a reflection of dysfunctional extraversion (or low detachment; Widiger, 2020).

The last three MMPI-3 measures of interpersonal functioning, Disaffiliativeness (DSF), Social Avoidance (SAV), and Shyness (SHY), assess various causes and effects of social withdrawal. DSF is made up of items that indicate a lack of interest in being around others, lack of interest in connecting with others, misanthropy, and a preference for being on one's own. Although primarily reflecting detachment (Kotov et al., 2017, 2021), there is also an element of interpersonal antagonism in that this scale has been linked to callous, unempathic, and remorseless aspects of psychopathy (Ben-Porath & Tellegen, 2020b). Indeed, while Ayearst et al. (2013) showed its MMPI-2-RF counterpart being mostly linked to the social-avoidant quadrant of the interpersonal circumplex, there was evidence of association with interpersonal coldness as well. The other two scales were clearly associated with social avoidance, though SHY was also linked to unassertiveness.

The SAV items describe a lack of interest in and efforts to avoid social situations, particularly those in which the individual is likely to be the center of attention. Items scored on SHY describe experiences of anxiety and discomfort associated with interacting with others. The three scales assess features of three *DSM-5* disorders marked by social withdrawal, schizoid personality disorder, avoidant personality disorder, and social anxiety disorder (Anderson et al., 2015b; Brown & Sellbom, 2021; Sellbom & Smith, 2017; Zahn et al., 2017). However, the disaffiliativeness, social avoidance, and shyness constructs are not synonymous with these disorders, and likely interact to form particular dysfunctional interpersonal profiles that in some individuals might be indicative of such personality pathology.

Taylor et al. (2004) note that socially avoidant behavior is part of a broader pattern that includes efforts to avoid emotional experiences and novel situations. Diagnostically, it is a core feature of avoidant personality disorder, which is characterized by social isolation resulting from apprehensiveness about being viewed negatively by others, rather than a lack of interest in social contact. Hofmann et al. (2009) characterize shyness as one of the most heritable temperament characteristics and a core component of social anxiety disorder. However, Heiser et al. (2009) found that shyness and social anxiety disorder are not interchangeable constructs, that it is possible for individuals to be very shy without meeting diagnostic criteria for social anxiety disorder. Social anxiety is characterized by more symptomatology and impairment and a lower quality of life. Furthermore, Bernstein et al. (2009) observed that a central distinction between the avoidant and schizoid personality disorders is that individuals diagnosed with the latter lack the desire or ability to form social relationships (assessed on the MMPI-3 with the DSF scale), whereas those with avoidant personality disorder desire interpersonal contact but avoid it out of feelings of inferiority and an intense fear of rejection and humiliation. Millon (1981) was among the first to note this distinction and characterized the difference between the two disorders as one of passive (schizoid) versus active (avoidant) detachment. Based on these conceptualizations, avoidant personality/social anxiety disorder would be particularly marked by high scores on both SHY and SAV, whereas schizoid personality disorder would be primarily linked to DSF and SAV, but not SHY.

Psychometric Findings

Ben-Porath and Tellegen (2020b) reported normative test-retest coefficients ranging from .72 (DSF) to .91 (SHY) and internal consistency coefficients ranging from .65 (DOM) to .81 (DSF). Internal consistency coefficients for the Interpersonal Scales in the mental health sample tend to be higher because of larger variances, ranging from .69 (DOM) to .85 (SAV). Intercorrelations between the Interpersonal Scales range from −.34 to .50 in the normative sample and from −.38 to .59 in the mental health sample. The correlations between SAV and SHY and between SAV and DSF in both the normative and clinical samples are consistently the largest. This pattern is consistent with the perspective that the three scales have a common theme of social isolation, but they can assist in differentiating the factors leading to and resulting from this experience. In terms of associations with their MMPI-2-RF counterparts, these correlations were −.96 to −.97 (DOM/IPP), .74 to .82 (DSF), and .99 to .99 (SAV) across the samples. SFI is new to the MMPI-3 and SHY is unchanged across versions, so they are not included in these comparisons.

The literature on the new SFI scale is not extensive. However, two separate studies featuring research on this scale have already been published. Sellbom (2021) showed large correlations between SFI scores and various measures of grandiose, but not vulnerable, narcissism in a large university sample from New Zealand. He also showed that SFI scores were moderately correlated with measures of narcissistic personality disorder. SFI scores also incremented the other 25 SP Scales, as well as the five PSY-5 Scales, in the prediction of grandiose narcissism and narcissistic personality disorder. Whitman and Ben-Porath (2021) replicated these general findings in a series of university samples. These researchers also showed that, though the two scales are negatively correlated, SFI has distinct correlates from the SFD scale, and these scales do not merely represent respective ends of the same bipolar dimension. Furthermore, Whitman et al. (2021b) showed that SFI scores were negatively correlated with depression and suicidal ideation in a clinical neuropsychology sample.

The MMPI-3 DOM scale remains quite similar to its MMPI-2-RF counterpart, Interpersonal Passivity (IPP), except for the reversal of item keying. Consequently, the MMPI-2-RF IPP research continues to apply. Ayearst et al. (2013) observed a large negative correlation between the dominance domain and IPP scores in the context of the interpersonal circumplex in a Canadian university sample. IPP was also negatively correlated with CAT-PD Domineering, Exhibitionism, Rudeness, and Hostile Aggression trait scales and positively correlated with Submissiveness in a university sample (Franz et al., 2017). Research has demonstrated positive correlations between IPP scores and avoidant personality disorder (Anderson et al., 2015b; van der Heijden et al., 2013a; Zahn et al., 2017) and dependent personality disorder symptoms (Zahn et al., 2017), and negative correlations with narcissistic personality disorder symptoms (Anderson et al., 2015b; Sellbom & Smith, 2017; van der Heijden et al., 2013a). Furthermore, recent MMPI-3 research has shown that DOM correlates negatively with dependent personality disorder symptoms and submissiveness, and positively with domineering and exhibitionism, in a university sample (Brown & Sellbom, 2021, 2022).

Both the MMPI-3 and MMPI-2-RF versions of the DSF scale have been found to be correlated with CAT-PD Emotional Detachment in university samples (Brown & Sellbom, 2022; Franz et al., 2017; Whitman et al., 2021a). Franz et al. (2017) also reported correlations with the CAT-PD Anhedonia, Callousness, Mistrust, and Social Withdrawal scales. These findings are replicated in the *MMPI-3 Technical Manual,* which also shows significant correlations between MMPI-3 DSF scores and callous/affective aspects of psychopathic personality in a community-externalizing sample. Moreover, Ayearst et al. (2013) observed meaningful correlation between DSF scores and both the coldhearted and aloof-introverted octants of the interpersonal circumplex. DSF scores have also been linked to schizoid personality disorder (van der Heijden et al., 2013a; Zahn et al., 2017) and avoidant personality disorder (Anderson et al., 2015b; van der Heijden et al., 2013a) across university and clinical samples.

The MMPI-3 and MMPI-2-RF SAV scale has been found to be positively correlated with CAT-PD Anhedonia and Social Withdrawal and negatively correlated with Exhibitionism (Ben-Porath & Tellegen, 2020b; Brown & Sellbom, 2022; Franz et al., 2017; Whitman et al., 2021a). Ayearst et al. (2013) observed a large correlation with the socially avoidant octant of the interpersonal circumplex. De Saeger et al. (2020) reported that this scale was prominently elevated in a sample of individuals with well-defined Cluster C personality disorders. And more specifically, SAV scores have been positively correlated with schizoid personality disorder (Anderson et al., 2015b; Brown & Sellbom, 2021; Sellbom & Smith, 2017; Zahn et al., 2017), avoidant personality disorder (Anderson et al., 2015b; Brown & Sellbom, 2021; Sellbom & Smith, 2017; van der Heijden et al., 2013a; Zahn et al., 2017), obsessive-compulsive personality disorder (Anderson et al., 2015b; Zahn et al., 2017), and negatively correlated with histrionic personality disorder (Anderson et al., 2015b; Sellbom & Smith, 2017).

Finally, the MMPI-3 SHY scale reflects both detachment and internalizing dysfunction at the interpersonal level; consequently, this scale is associated with a range of emotional and social avoidance problems. Whitman et al. (2021b) found that SHY was correlated with both depressive and anxiety disorder diagnoses in a clinical neuropsychology sample. Whitman et al. (2021a) further showed that such scale scores were correlated with IDAS-II Social Anxiety in a university sample. Both MMPI-3 and MMPI-2-RF versions have been correlated with the CAT-PD trait scales Anxiousness, Social Withdrawal, and low Exhibitionism (Ben-Porath & Tellegen, 2020b; Brown & Sellbom, 2022; Franz et al., 2017; Whitman et al., 2021a). De Saeger et al. (2020) reported that this scale was prominently elevated in a sample of individuals with well-defined Cluster C personality disorders. In terms of specific personality disorders, SHY has been positively correlated with avoidant personality disorder (Anderson et al., 2015b; Brown & Sellbom, 2021; Sellbom & Smith, 2017; van der Heijden et al., 2013a; Zahn et al., 2017) and schizotypal personality disorder (van der Heijden et al., 2013a; Zahn et al., 2017) in multiple studies and across various university and clinical samples.

Summary

The SP Scales reviewed in this section are reliable sources of information related to somatic and cognitive complaints, internalizing difficulties, externalizing behavioral proclivities, and interpersonal functioning. The empirical correlates reported for each of the 26 scales are generally consistent with expectations for measures of constructs that the scales target, documenting their convergent validities. Although not summarized here, the extensive data reported in the *MMPI-3 Technical Manual* and the available MMPI-2-RF literature have also provided support for the discriminant validity of the MMPI-3 SP Scales. Together, these findings provide evidence supporting the construct validity of the scales.

PERSONALITY PSYCHOPATHOLOGY FIVE (PSY-5) SCALES

The Personality Psychopathology-Five (PSY-5) Scales are designed to assess a dimensional model of personality disorder. Such models have become the focus of contemporary personality disorder science and have been incorporated into current diagnostic manuals. The *DSM-5,* for instance, includes the AMPD in Section III (APA, 2013). More recently, the World Health Organization (WHO) has included a fully dimensional classification system for personality disorders in the ICD-11, which must be used for coding purposes by WHO member states beginning in 2022 (Bach & First, 2018; Reed et al., 2019; WHO, 2022). The AMPD and ICD-11 approaches to personality disorders are overall quite similar as both require impairments in self- and interpersonal functioning (Bender et al., 2011; Crawford et al., 2011) along with specification of pathological personality traits. ICD-11 personality disorder is offered on one-dimensional severity rating scale (no personality disorder, difficulty, mild, moderate, and severe), whereas the AMPD takes a more complex approach that includes mapping impairment and traits onto 6 of the original 10 disorders. Moreover, each model shares four personality trait domains—negative affectivity, detachment, antagonism (or dissociality), and disinhibition—but differs on the fifth domain. The AMPD model includes psychoticism, in large part due to schizotypal personality disorder, which is not considered a personality disorder in the ICD-11, but rather part of the psychosis spectrum. The ICD-11 trait model includes anankastia (compulsivity) instead. The PSY-5 Scales measure dysfunctional trait domains that align conceptually and empirically with the AMPD (Anderson et al., 2013; Harkness et al., 2012; Sellbom, Smid et al., 2014).

It should be noted, however, that the conceptual PSY-5 model (which was subsequently operationalized by the MMPI-2; Harkness et al., 1995) was developed and validated long before the AMPD and ICD-11 models were first introduced (see Harkness et al., 2012, for a review). In this respect, the AMPD effort (see Krueger et al., 2012, in particular) is a replication of the PSY-5 model. Harkness (1992) described his initial work in this area as intended to develop a dimensional measurement model of personality disorders. In assembling the item pool that he used for this purpose, Harkness (1992) augmented a list of *DSM-III-R* personality disorder criteria with items reflecting psychopathy and normal personality constructs. Thus, in contrast with other five-factor models, which have been explored ex-post-facto as dimensional models of personality disorders (e.g., Widiger & Costa, 2002), the PSY-5 constructs originated directly from the clinical criteria for diagnosing these conditions. Abandoning the categorical measurement model embodied in the *DSM-III-R* in favor of a dimensional model of personality disorders was quite novel at the time Harkness began work on this project in the 1980s. The development of the PSY-5 model, including its conceptual underpinnings and subsequent scales for the MMPI-2, is described in chapter 2.

Harkness et al. (2014) provided a foundational review of systems theory for clinical psychology and psychiatry. They argued for an evolutionary-based model that gives rise to underlying adaptive systems to the environment, which are in part biologically based. These systems—reality modeling for action, short-term danger detection, long-term cost–benefit projection, resource acquisition, and agenda protection—were respectively linked to the PSY-5 constructs of psychoticism, negative emotionality/neuroticism, disconstraint, introversion/low positive emotionality, and aggressiveness. These authors also discussed how the PSY-5 Scales mapped onto the AMPD, historical theories in psychology, and other neurobiological dimensional models of psychopathology (e.g., the Research Domain Criteria proposed by the National Institute of Mental Health; Insel et al., 2010).

Harkness et al. (2012) reviewed the literature on the PSY-5 Scales, most of which was based on the MMPI-2 versions, along with the scales' conceptual foundations and links to emerging models of personality psychopathology. For instance, Bagby, Ryder, Ben-Dat, Bacchiochi, and Parker (2002) have validated the dimensional structure of the PSY-5 Scales with confirmatory factor analyses conducted with both a clinical and nonclinical sample. Rouse et al. (1999) conducted an IRT analysis of the scales and concluded that they assess unidimensional constructs that conform to IRT assumptions. Rouse (2007) examined the reliability generalization of the PSY-5 Scales with a broad range of clinical and nonclinical samples and found evidence of adequate reliability overall of PSY-5 scale scores across settings.

There is also research linking the PSY-5 Scales to dimensional models of personality. Harkness et al. (1995) reported correlations between scores on the PSY-5 Scales and Tellegen's MPQ in a college student sample. The findings provided evidence of a convergent and discriminant validity of PSY-5 scale scores when evaluated in the context of a measure of normal personality traits. Harkness et al. (2002) similarly found evidence of the convergent and discriminant validity of the PSY-5 scale scores using a different normal personality measure, the Sixteen Personality Factor Questionnaire (16PF; Cattell, Eber, & Tatsuoka, 1970), completed by a sample of community-dwelling veterans. Moreover, given the similarities between the PSY-5 model and the five-factor model of personality, several investigators have examined correlations between scores on the PSY-5 Scales and five-factor model measures. Trull et al. (1995) found expected patterns of associations between truncated PSY-5 Scales (based on the original MMPI item pool) and the NEO-PI (Costa & McCrae, 1985) in a community sample, and between the full PSY-5 Scales and the NEO PI-R in a clinical sample. Egger et al. (2003) replicated these findings in a sample of Dutch psychiatric inpatients.

A substantial number of studies have focused on correlations between PSY-5 scale scores and criteria related to personality disorders. Sharpe and Desai (2001), Trull et al. (1995), and Bagby et al. (2008) compared the predictive power of the scales of the PSY-5 and NEO-PI-R in a variety of clinical samples, and concluded that although there is substantial overlap between the two sets of scales, each provides incrementally valid information in predicting personality-disorder-related extratest criteria. Wygant et al. (2006) found expected patterns of correlations between the PSY-5 Scales and self-reported personality disorder symptoms in a mental health outpatient sample.

Miller et al. (2004) used the PSY-5 Scales to replicate and extend prior findings of internalizing and externalizing subtypes of posttraumatic response. These authors conducted cluster analyses of PSY-5 scale scores with a large sample of combat veterans diagnosed with PTSD and classified these individuals into low pathology, externalizing, and internalizing subgroups; the authors found expected correlations between group membership and extratest criterion variables. Miller, Vogt, Mozley, Kaloupek, and Keane (2006) reported that scores on the PSY-5 DISC scale mediated between PTSD diagnoses and substance abuse. Ferrier-Auerbach et al. (2009) found scores on truncated measures of DISC and NEGE to be associated with alcohol use in a predeployment sample of National Guard soldiers. Sellbom, Ben-Porath, and Stafford (2007) reported correlations between DISC scores and a psychopathy measure in a sample of criminal defendants. Egger et al. (2003) found scores on this scale to differentiate between patients diagnosed with psychotic and bipolar disorders. Petroskey et al. (2003) reported correlations between PSY-5 scale scores and a wide range of extratest criteria in a forensic sample and concluded that the empirical correlates they found for the scales were consistent with those reported previously for general mental health settings. Vendrig, Derksen, and de Mey (2000) presented evidence that the PSY-5 Scales predict treatment outcome for chronic pain patients.

Finally, consistent with expectations for measures of relatively enduring personality pathology, Langwerden et al. (2021) reported 20-year stability coefficients ranging from .30 for Psychoticism (PSYC) to .73 for Aggressiveness (AGGR), with a median of .63, in 66 community adults who were administered the MMPI-2 in 1992 and MMPI-2-RF in 2012. They also showed impressive mean-level stability of the sample over the 20 years (all Cohen's d values < .05).

Psychometric Findings with the MMPI-3 PSY-5 Scales

Data reported in the *MMPI-3 Technical Manual* indicate that scores on the revised PSY-5 Scales are reliable, with test-retest reliability estimates ranging from .72 for PSYC to .93 for DISC. Internal consistency estimates in the normative sample range from .67 for men on PSYC to .88 for women on NEGE. In the mental health sample, alpha coefficients range from .72 for men on AGGR to .90 for men on NEGE. *SEM*s estimated based on these reliability data range from 3 to 6 T-score points and are consistent with those found with the H-O and RC Scales. Intercorrelations between the PSY-5 Scales reported in the *MMPI-3 Technical Manual* range from −.03 to .35 in the normative sample and .00 to .37 in the mental health sample. The patterns are consistent with intercorrelations among the MMPI-2 versions of the PSY-5 Scales reported by Harkness et al. (2002) and the MMPI-2-RF versions (Tellegen & Ben-Porath, 2008/2011). However, the magnitudes of these correlations are generally lower for the MMPI-3 PSY-5 Scales, especially in relation to those on the MMPI-2. Correlations between the MMPI-2-RF and MMPI-3 PSY-5 Scale counterparts were quite large, ranging from .83 (DISC) to .94 (AGGR) in the normative sample and .84 (DISC) to .94 (AGGR) in the mental health sample, with medians of .91 in the normative sample and .93 in the mental health sample.

The key criteria for evaluating the PSY-5 Scales pertain to the assessment of personality pathology both from dimensional model perspectives and the traditional DSM personality disorder model. The *MMPI-3 Technical Manual* and subsequently Brown and Sellbom (2022) provide findings related to dimensional maladaptive personality traits in university samples from the United States and New Zealand, respectively. Specifically, AGGR was consistently most strongly associated with CAT-PD traits from the general antagonism domain, such as Exhibitionism, Hostile Aggression, Manipulativeness, Domineering, Grandiosity, and Rudeness. These correlations only reached a medium effect size threshold in the male sample. PSYC was consistently associated with CAT-PD Cognitive Problems, Fantasy Proneness, Peculiarity, Unusual Beliefs, and Unusual Experiences from the psychoticism domain, but also Hostile Aggression, Grandiosity, and Relationship Insecurity. As would be expected, DISC was correlated with Norm Violation and Risk-Taking in both genders, but also with Affective Lability and Anger in men, and with Irresponsibility, Non-Perseverance, and Non-Planning in women. Furthermore, NEGE was consistently correlated across genders with various traits that are commonly associated with the CAT-PD negative emotionality domain, such as Depressivity, Affective Lability, Anxiousness, Anger, Relationship Insecurity—and in women, NEGE was also associated with Self-Harm, Health Anxiety, and Mistrust. Finally, INTR was consistently associated with various traits from the detachment domain, including Anhedonia, Emotional Detachment, Romantic Disinterest, and Social Withdrawal, but also several other traits that were mostly conceptually relevant, including Depressivity, Self-Harm, low Exhibitionism, Mistrust, Relationship Insecurity, and Peculiarity. Overall, this pattern of correlations is generally promising for the PSY-5 Scales as reflecting the broad domains of maladaptive personality included in prominent contemporary models.

Further research on the overlap between the PSY-5 Scales and personality pathology comes from the MMPI-2-RF literature (Finn et al., 2014; Sellbom, Smid et al., 2014; Sellbom & Smith, 2017; Zahn et al., 2017) and one recent MMPI-3 study (Brown & Sellbom, 2021). Sellbom, Smid et al. (2014) examined the associations between the MMPI-2-RF PSY-5 Scales and 6 of the 10 personality disorders (assessed via structured clinical interviews) in two Dutch clinical and forensic samples. They specifically evaluated the personality trait profiles proposed for the AMPD, as the PSY-5 traits are conceptual and empirical cognates of the AMPD personality trait dimensions (Anderson et al., 2013; Harkness et al., 2012). Sellbom, Smid et al. (2014) found that the PSY-5 Scales generally predicted Section II personality disorders in accordance with the AMPD. More specifically, DISC was the best predictor of antisocial personality disorder; NEGE, DISC, and PSYC were unique predictors of borderline personality disorder; INTR, NEGE, and low AGGR were unique predictors of avoidant personality disorder; AGGR was the primary predictor of narcissistic personality disorder; and PSYC was the sole predictor of schizotypal personality disorder.

Finn et al. (2014) examined the association between MMPI-2-RF PSY-5 Scales and the 10 Section II personality disorders in non-treatment-seeking samples of both National Guard soldiers and university students. Their findings were quite similar to those of Sellbom, Smid et al. (2014) with some notable exceptions. Narcissistic personality disorder was more strongly correlated with NEGE and PSYC in these samples; obsessive-compulsive personality disorder was primarily associated with NEGE, and schizotypal personality disorder also evinced a sizable correlation with NEGE. Moreover, paranoid and dependent personality disorders were primarily associated with NEGE and PSYC, histrionic personality disorder was associated with low INTR. However, schizoid personality disorder evinced its largest (albeit of small effect size) correlation with INTR. Two subsequent studies (Sellbom & Smith, 2017; Zahn et al., 2017) sought to replicate the findings in the three previous studies. Sellbom and Smith (2017) examined the associations between MMPI-2-RF scales and self-reported personality disorder criteria in a university sample. Their PSY-5 Scale findings were similar to the aforementioned studies, with the exception of PSYC having a larger correlation than INTR with schizoid personality disorder. Finally, Zahn et al. (2017) further replicated these findings in a large sample of private practice clients. The main divergent findings from previous studies were that AGGR was not correlated at the authors' a priori threshold with any self-reported personality disorder symptom counts and that DISC did not meaningfully associate with borderline personality disorder symptoms. These findings likely reflect the very low base rate of externalizing in this sample.

Sellbom and Brown (2021) examined the MMPI-3 PSY-5 Scales in their associations with two measures of personality disorders in a large New Zealand university sample. Many of the MMPI-2-RF findings just described were replicated with the MMPI-3 versions of these scales, except that AGGR was not meaningfully associated with paranoid, antisocial, or narcissistic personality disorder.

Several MMPI-2-RF studies and one MMPI-3 study have also examined associations between the PSY-5 Scales and dimensional trait models that are featured in current dimensional models of personality disorders. The PSY-5 Scales were evaluated against the AMPD in two studies (Anderson et al., 2015a; Anderson et al., 2013) and against the ICD-11 trait model in more recent studies (Anderson & Sellbom, 2021; Brown & Sellbom, 2022; Sellbom, Solomon-Krakus et al., 2020; Tarescavage & Menton, 2020). In a university sample, Anderson and colleagues (2013) initially examined the MMPI-2-RF PSY-5 Scales and their associations with the AMPD trait model as operationalized by the PID-5. They found substantial one-on-one convergence between PSY-5 and PID-5 domain scales, specifically AGGR with Antagonism, PSYC with Psychoticism, DISC with Disinhibition, NEGE with Negative Affectivity, and INTR with Detachment. The main qualification to this pattern was that some aspects of the PID-5 Antagonism domain (e.g., deceitfulness, manipulativeness) were better aligned with DISC than AGGR; thus, these findings suggested that AGGR is narrower than DISC in capturing more externalizing traits of personality disorder. Anderson et al. (2015a) replicated these PSY-5 and PID-5 associations in a psychiatric patient sample, and via latent variable modeling they revealed a higher-order externalizing domain broader than the two individual domains (AGGR, DISC, Antagonism, and Disinhibition) in these patients with traditionally more psychotic and emotional disorders.

Anderson and Sellbom (2021) examined the MMPI-2-RF PSY-5 Scales in relation to the five ICD-11 trait qualifier domains (Negative Affectivity, Detachment, Dissociality, Disinhibition, and Anankastia) in a community sample weighted toward externalizing proclivities. The ICD-11 trait domains were scored using algorithms for the PID-5 (Bach et al., 2017; Sellbom, Solomon-Krakus et al., 2020). As with previous research, AGGR was primarily associated with Dissociality, DISC with Disinhibition, NEGE with Negative Affectivity, and INTR with Detachment. PSYC was not included as it was not hypothesized to be associated with any ICD-11 domain. As expected, NEGE also predicted scores on Anankastia (though to a smaller degree than with Negative Affectivity), but DISC did not correlate (negatively) with this ICD-11 domain, which was contrary to hypotheses. Sellbom, Solomon-Krakus et al., 2020 reported similar results in a Canadian psychiatric sample. Carnovale et al. (2020) and Tarescavage and Menton (2020) examined associations between the MMPI-2-RF PSY-5 Scales and the Personality Inventory for ICD-11 (Oltmanns & Widiger, 2018) in separate university samples; most of Anderson and Sellbom's (2021) findings were replicated across these two studies, except Tarescavage and Menton (2020) did observe a moderate negative association between DISC and Anankastia. Overall, the findings indicate good replication for the PSY-5 Scales in mapping onto other maladaptive trait domains in a manner conceptually indicated.

Most recently, in the only MMPI-3 study to date, Brown and Sellbom (2022) examined associations between PSY-5 Scales and the personality trait domains across the AMPD and ICD-11, which were operationalized using the CAT-PD, in a university sample. The same general pattern of findings emerged as for the MMPI-2-RF studies, except none of the PSY-5 Scales were meaningfully associated with the Anankastia domain.

In summary, the MMPI-2-RF/MMPI-3 PSY-5 Scales show replicable associations with measures of personality psychopathology, both from the perspective of the traditional categorical DSM model as well as models that align with contemporary personality disorder science. Although beyond the scope of this review, the *MMPI-3 Technical Manual* also shows correlations between the PSY-5 Scales and a host of other external criterion variables, which converge on a pattern that would be generally expected by measures of these personality trait domains. For instance, a body of research on the empirical correlates of

MMPI-3 scales in assessments of candidates for police and public safety positions (see Corey and Ben-Porath, 2024, for a detailed review) complements the findings discussed in this chapter, illustrating that the constructs assessed by the MMPI-3 Substantive Scales generalize to, and are relevant to, a broad range of assessments contexts.

Conclusion

The 42 scales discussed in this chapter constitute the Substantive Scales of the MMPI-3. Each of these measures can be linked to familiar psychological constructs, and all have been empirically validated. The empirically grounded interpretive recommendations for these scales provided in chapter 9 are founded on the empirical correlates listed in chapters 4 and 5.

MAPPING THE MMPI-3 ONTO CONTEMPORARY PSYCHOPATHOLOGY MODELS

The second section of this chapter reviews how the MMPI-3 Substantive Scales map more broadly onto contemporary models of psychopathology and personality. This latter section is important to MMPI-3 users, as better grounding in contemporary psychopathology science was a primary goal of the MMPI-2-RF and MMPI-3 development, and because such grounding positions the instrument and its scales within frameworks that are rapidly becoming influential. The original MMPI/MMPI-2 Clinical Scales were designed to assess psychiatric syndromes but, for reasons discussed in previous chapters, they did so with inadequate utility. The MMPI-3 Substantive Scales measure psychological constructs, and more specifically, symptom and maladaptive personality trait dimensions that are transdiagnostic in nature, reflecting current advances in psychopathology science (Insel et al., 2010; Kotov et al., 2017, 2021). Although multiple frameworks are available, we will consider in particular two emerging models for psychopathology, the Hierarchical Taxonomy of Psychopathology (HiTOP; Kotov et al., 2017, 2021) and dimensional models of personality disorders (AMPD and ICD-11).

Hierarchical Taxonomy of Psychopathology

The HiTOP (http://medicine.stonybrookmedicine.edu/HITOP) consortium consists of a group of researchers and clinicians (including the second author of this book) who are developing an empirically driven classification system of psychopathology, mostly based on scientific evidence from independent structural modeling and validation studies of multiple research groups (Kotov et al., 2017, 2021; for reviews of psychopathology superspectra, see Kotov et al., 2020; Krueger et al., 2021; Watson et al., 2022).

Like the MMPI-3, the HiTOP model endeavors to be more clinically informative than traditional categorical diagnostic systems (i.e., the DSM and ICD) and overcomes many of the empirical and conceptual limitations associated with these systems (Ruggero et al., 2019). For example, by conceptualizing psychopathology by using dimensions instead of categories, the nosological system avoids problems of arbitrary thresholds between disorders. Relatedly, the hierarchical classification (see below) avoids subthreshold, diagnostic "orphans" and "not otherwise specified" cases, as everyone can be placed along a set of dimensions, even those with low levels of psychopathology. Additionally, the quantitative classification approach resolves the problem of heterogeneity within categorical disorders by constructing dimensions based on the observed covariation of particular symptoms, thereby identifying coherent constructs and reducing diagnostic heterogeneity (Kotov et al., 2017).

The HiTOP model (see Kotov et al., 2021, for most recent iteration) consists of three psychopathology superspectra (emotional/internalizing, externalizing, and psychosis) and six broad underlying spectra (somatoform, internalizing, thought disorder, disinhibited-externalizing, antagonistic-externalizing, and detachment). Similar syndromes are combined into subfactors (e.g., the distress subfactor includes major depression, dysthymia, generalized anxiety, posttraumatic stress, and some borderline personality traits; a fear subfactor includes panic disorder, agoraphobia, social phobia, and specific phobias). Finally, it combines symptoms, signs, and maladaptive behaviors into closely grouped symptom components (e.g., insomnia) and maladaptive traits (these are specific pathological personality characteristics, such as submissiveness or emotional lability).

Research with both the MMPI-3 and MMPI-2-RF has shown promising evidence for mapping the MMPI-3 Substantive Scales onto the HiTOP structure. The three H-O Scales clearly map onto the three HiTOP superpectra, though it is noteworthy that this was not necessarily intentional, as these scales were originally developed for the MMPI-2-RF based on factor analyses of the nine RC Scales (Tellegen & Ben-Porath, 2008/2011; Sellbom et al., 2008b) rather than being rationally targeted and designed. Indeed, Hoelzle and Meyer (2008) and Sellbom et al. (2008b) factor analyzed the RC Scales in independent psychiatric samples from the United States and Canada, respectively, and reported virtually identical results. All studies found robust evidence for a three-factor structure that clearly represents internalizing, externalizing, and thought dysfunction.

Subsequent studies examining additional MMPI-2-RF Scales have revealed a more nuanced structure. McNulty and Overstreet (2014) conducted arguably the most informative study to date. These researchers carried out factor analyses of the MMPI-2-RF scales, corrected for item overlap, in two large clinical outpatient and inpatient samples (separated into men and women subgroups). An identical six-factor structured emerged across all four groups: somatoform, aggressiveness (akin to antagonism), psychoticism, disconstraint, negative emotionality, and introversion. These six factors are virtually identical to the six HiTOP spectra.

Sellbom (2017a) conducted factor analyses of the 23 MMPI-2-RF SP Scales and two Interest Scales in large outpatient mental health and correctional samples. He found consistent support for somatization, internalizing (negative affect), externalizing, and detachment factors. Noteworthy is that the MMPI-2-RF SP Scales do not have thought disorder markers; as such, Sellbom (2017a) conducted a subsequent analysis in which he included RC6 and RC8 in the model, and a five-factor structure with a thought dysfunction factor emerged. The ACT scale joined RC6 and RC8 as a primary marker for this fifth factor.

Marek et al. (2020) examined the structure of 18 MMPI-2-RF SP Scales in bariatric presurgery and spine surgery/spinal cord stimulator presurgery samples, as well as in a sample seeking chronic pain treatment. They tested a particular hypothesis that a somatoform factor would be revealed because there would be sufficient variability on this domain in these medical samples. Using a confirmatory factor analysis, Marek et al. (2020) found support for somatization, internalizing, externalizing, and detachment factors in all three samples. Correlations between these higher order factors and conceptually relevant external criterion variables revealed a pattern of findings that were consistent with their conceptual expectations.

The MMPI-2-RF literature has also revealed more specific support for scales that map onto structural components within spectra. Watson (2005) originally proposed that internalizing disorders could be divided into distress (depression, generalized anxiety, PTSD) and fear (panic, agoraphobia, social phobia, specific phobia) disorders. This structure has been empirically supported (see, for instance, Krueger & Markon's, 2006 meta-analysis). Sellbom, Ben-Porath, and Bagby (2008a) and later Shkalim et al. (2017) found in university and psychiatric samples that RCd appeared to be a specific marker for distress disorders, whereas RC7 was the better marker of fear disorders, especially in a latent regression model controlling for their commonality. RC2, on the other hand, as a specific measure of anhedonia, specifically predicted depression and social anxiety disorders.

Furthermore, MMPI-2-RF research has also examined how the Externalizing SP Scales map onto a contemporary model of externalizing psychopathology. Sellbom (2016) used the items from JCP, SUB, AGG, and ACT to model Krueger and colleagues' (2007) elaborated externalizing spectrum in large correctional, forensic, and community samples. He reported two key sets of findings. First, the ACT scale was not part of the structure of externalizing; rather, the ACT items were better modelled as a correlated but distinct construct (these findings were mentioned previously). Second, the items for JCP, SUB, and AGG conformed to a structure of externalizing that mapped onto a model by Krueger et al. (2007). The structure was also invariant across setting, gender, and race.

Latent factor representations of the scales also correlated with external criteria in the forensic sample in a manner consistent with conceptual expectations.

Most recently, Sellbom, Kremyar, and Wygant (2021) sought to examine the structure of the MMPI-3 scales with respect to mapping onto the HiTOP model. They examined the 26 SP Scales as well as RC6 and RC8; the two RC Scales were included because thought dysfunction is not represented at the SP scale level. They specified and tested a hierarchical confirmatory factor analysis model in a mental health sample and in a prison sample. The models marginally fit the observed data, but they provided support for the six HiTOP spectra (somatoform, internalizing, thought dysfunction, disinhibited-externalizing, antagonistic-externalizing, and detachment) as well as for the three superspectra (internalizing, externalizing, and thought dysfunction). The HiTOP structure is slightly different from the MMPI-3 interpretive organization (see chapter 10) because MMPI-3 domains were not designed to cover HiTOP. For instance, the Interpersonal Scales loaded on antagonism (SFI, DOM, DSF) or detachment (SAV, SHY, DSF), a finding generally consistent with the interpersonal circumplex findings reviewed earlier (Ayearst et al., 2013). As hypothesized, CYN and AGG loaded on antagonism, whereas JCP, SUB, and IMP loaded on disinhibition. RC6, RC8, ACT, and CMP loaded primarily on a thought dysfunction factor, which is not surprising as other researchers (e.g., Caspi et al., 2014) have also demonstrated that obsessive-compulsive disorder structurally loads prominently with other markers of thought disorder.

Sellbom and colleagues (2021) also examined how the structure of MMPI-3 scales would emerge at descending levels of a hierarchy using a sequential hierarchical factoring approach (labeled in a somewhat sophomoric manner "bass-ackwards" by Goldberg [2006]), which involved using exploratory factor analysis to estimate one-, two-, three-, etc. factor models all the way to a final level. Sellbom et al. chose six factor levels and correlated the factors at the levels above with those below to see which factors remained stable and which bifurcated into more specific factors. This exploratory approach generally replicated most, but not all, of the HiTOP spectra. In the mental health sample, the three-factor level was internalizing, detachment, and thought dysfunction/externalizing, likely owing to the range restriction of the indicators representing the latter factor in this sample; the prison sample, however, revealed the typical internalizing, thought dysfunction, and externalizing model. At the six-factor level in the mental health sample, distress, negative affect/fear, detachment, thought dysfunction, disinhibited-externalizing, and antagonistic-externalizing emerged. The main difference from HiTOP was that the two internalizing subfactors (distress and fear) emerged rather than the somatoform spectrum, which was likely owing to relatively few "pure" somatoform indicators (MLS, NUC, COG). In the prison sample, Sellbom et al. had to stop at a five-factor level, which was similar, except antagonism and disinhibition remained combined into externalizing. Overall, the authors concluded that the general structure of these MMPI-3 scales mapped onto contemporary psychopathology models, including HiTOP, in a conceptually expected manner. Most recently, Brown et al. (2023) replicated these sequential hierarchical factoring analyses in a sample of primary care patients, though at the sixth level, these authors' antagonism factor was substantially more narrow (resembling narcissism more specifically).

Summary

The MMPI-2-RF literature and the more recent MMPI-3 literature clearly show that the scales comprising this inventory capture psychopathology and maladaptive personality in a manner similar to the extant psychopathology literature. Figure 5.1 provides a graphic representation of a HiTOP and MMPI-3 scale mapping based on the literature just reviewed. These findings represent strong support for both construct validity as well as the general hierarchical structure of the instrument. Clinicians who use the MMPI-3 can use a general hierarchical approach to interpretation that is consistent with contemporary findings in psychopathology.

Dimensional Models of Personality Disorder

Although it will likely take time for the official diagnostic manuals to adhere to models like HiTOP, dimensional approaches to diagnosis have begun to slowly take hold in the area of personality disorders. As described earlier in the PSY-5 Scale section, both the *DSM-5* and the ICD-11 incorporate dimensional personality disorder models. The AMPD is not currently used in practice, or at least not formally per the *DSM-5*, but the ICD-11, which became effective in all WHO member states on January 1, 2022, has switched from categorical personality disorders to a fully dimensional system. Given the plethora of research studies on these systems, especially the AMPD, the *DSM* will likely follow suit.

As discussed earlier, the AMPD and ICD-11 personality disorder models are quite similar. Both nosologies consider impairment in personality functioning as a requirement for diagnosis and use a personality trait model to characterize the psychopathology. The AMPD is more complicated in that it requires an impairment consideration across self-functioning and interpersonal functioning domains, whereas the ICD-11 has just one severity dimension directly linked to diagnosis (no personality disorder, difficulty, mild, moderate, and severe). The AMPD requires consideration of 25 personality trait facets (which underlie five broad domains) that in different constellations map onto six legacy personality disorder types as well as one "trait-specified" disorder type that does not match any of the six standard disorders. The ICD-11 does not try to recreate previous categories and instead allows simply for the characterization of the personality

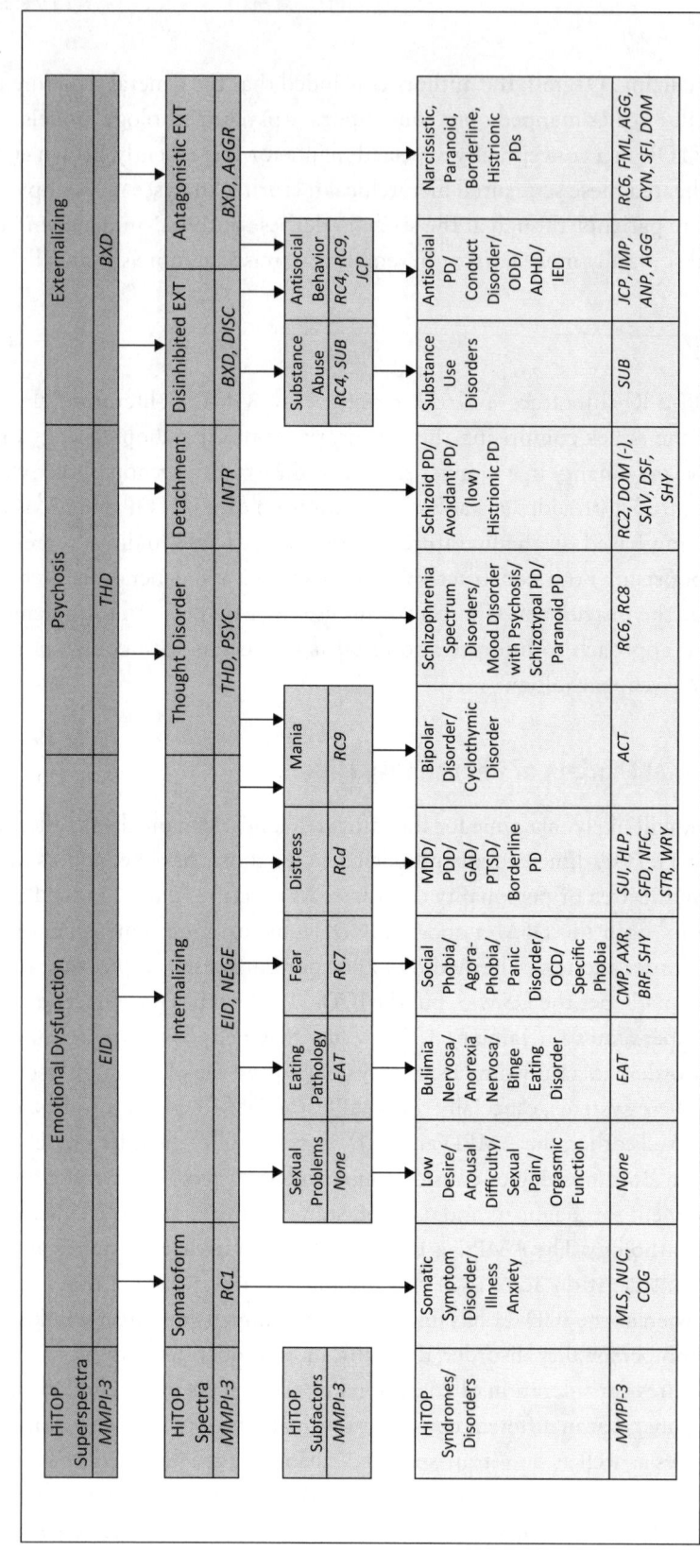

FIGURE 5.1. HiTOP and MMPI-3 Scale Mapping

TABLE 5.1. Corresponding PSY-5 Scales, AMPD Trait Domains, and ICD-11 Trait Qualifier Domains

PSY-5 Scales	AMPD	ICD-11
Aggressiveness	Antagonism	Dissociality
Psychoticism	Psychoticism	None [a]
Disconstraint	Disinhibition	Disinhibition
Negative Emotionality/Neuroticism	Negative Affectivity	Negative Affectivity
Introversion/Low Positive Emotionality	Detachment	Detachment
None [b]	None [b]	Anankastia

Note. PSY-5 = Personality Psychopathology Five; AMPD = Alternative Model of Personality Disorders; ICD-11 = International Classification of Diseases 11 Revision.
[a] Psychoticism is not necessary in the ICD-11 model because the primary form of personality pathology, schizotypal disorder, has never been considered a personality disorder in the ICD; it has always been part of the schizophrenia spectrum.
[b] Anankastia (compulsivity) is typically considered the theoretical low pole of the Disconstraint/Disinhibition trait domain.

disorder from the perspective of five trait qualifier domains (e.g., moderate personality disorder, with negative affectivity and detachment). The one exception is a *borderline features* qualifier, which retains the nine borderline personality disorder (BPD) criteria. This latter adjustment was not linked to any scientific findings when the ICD-11 personality disorder model was unveiled, and the BPD qualifier was first explained at the International Society for the Study of Personality Disorders in Heidelberg, Germany in 2017.

To date, MMPI-2-RF and MMPI-3 research has focused on the assessment of the personality trait dimensions but not impairment. We reviewed important aspects of this research earlier in the PSY-5 section (Anderson & Sellbom, 2021; Anderson et al., 2015a; Brown & Sellbom, 2022; Carnovale et al., 2020; Finn et al., 2014; Sellbom, Solomon-Krakus et al., 2020; Tarescavage & Menton, 2020). The PSY-5 Scales map onto their AMPD counterparts as expected and onto four of the five ICD-11 trait qualifiers (see Table 5.1). The research is somewhat inconsistent with how the PSY-5 captures Anankastia, with one study finding support for low DISC (Tarescavage & Menton, 2020) but others finding that NEGE has larger correlations with this domain (e.g., Sellbom, Solomon-Krakus et al., 2020). Although no published data are currently available, the second author of this book showed in a conference presentation that clinician ratings of the ICD-11 Anankastia domain and the MMPI-3 Compulsivity (CMP) scale had a moderate correlation (.36) in a sample of community mental health patients (current $N = 173$) in Dunedin, New Zealand—and this correlation was larger than for any other MMPI-3 scale (Sellbom, Brown, & Vaňousová, 2021).

The PSY-5 Scales might not be sufficient, however, in representing an individual's trait profiles from the perspective of the AMPD or ICD-11. As just mentioned, the five AMPD domains break down into 25 trait facets, which are primarily used instead of the domains for deriving personality disorder diagnoses. Although the ICD-11 trait qualifier domains are indeed the ones used for diagnosis in that model, trait facets have been articulated (WHO, 2022). For instance, Negative Affectivity facets are emotional lability/poor emotional regulation, negativistic attitudes, low self-esteem/poor self-confidence, mistrustfulness; Detachment facets are social detachment and emotional detachment. Interestingly, without labeling it as demoralization, the WHO considers internalized emotions such as depression, sadness, and anxiety to be a product of Negative Affectivity and Detachment (whereas externalizing emotions, anger and hostility, would be a product of Negative Affectivity and Dissociality). The primary implication of personality trait facets in these models is that the PSY-5 Scales are too broad for this level of articulation, and other MMPI-3 scales would be necessary to supplement measurement at this level.

Surprisingly, there are only two studies available on the MMPI-2-RF that have examined overlap between these scales and the AMPD trait facets (note, there is not currently a measure available for the ICD-11 trait facets). Anderson et al. (2015a) and Sellbom et al. (2013) demonstrated substantial overlap between the MMPI-2-RF scales and PID-5 trait facet scales in a manner that was consistent with conceptual expectations in both psychiatric inpatient and university student samples. Sellbom et al. (2013) also observed that a substantial proportion of variance (47% to 60%) could be explained in trait aggregate scores representing antisocial, avoidant, borderline, and schizotypal personality disorders, with smaller (albeit still large) proportions being accounted for in narcissistic and obsessive-compulsive personality disorders.

The *MMPI-3 Technical Manual* and Brown and Sellbom (2022) present correlations between the MMPI-3 scales and CAT-PD in a university sample (see also Whitman et al., 2021a). The CAT-PD was developed through a large National Institute of Mental Health grant (Simms et al., 2011) in parallel with the AMPD, with the primary aim to achieve the same goal: articulating a comprehensive personality trait model for the diagnosis of personality disorder. The resulting 33 CAT-PD traits cover all 25 AMPD traits as well as all ICD-11 trait facets. The findings reported in the *MMPI-3 Technical Manual* and Brown and Sellbom (2022) are quite promising. Although there is not a perfect one-to-one correspondence between the MMPI-3 scales and CAT-PD trait scales, most of the latter are captured within the MMPI-3. For instance, RCd correlates with Depressiveness, RC2 with Anhedonia, WRY and ARX with Anxiousness, ANP with Anger, COG with Cognitive Problems, RC8 with Fantasy Proneness, IMP with Non-Planfulness, and SAV with Social Withdrawal.

Summary

There is a substantial literature available now to support the convergence between MMPI-3 scales and AMPD and ICD-11 traits in a theoretically expected manner. Though there is no one-to-one correspondence at the trait facet level, MMPI-3 scores capture most of the relevant variance in the AMPD traits and are therefore well-positioned to indicate the presence of personality psychopathology from dimensional perspectives. Additional research is required to further articulate how the MMPI-3 scales other than the PSY-5 Scales map onto individual trait facets across samples and when using additional measures of AMPD traits and personality impairment (i.e., Levels of Personality Functioning or ICD-11 severity ratings). Readers can be assured, however, that as these new dimensional models are adopted into practice, the MMPI-3 is well-positioned to assess the constructs that form these emerging nosologies.

Diversity-Sensitive Assessment With the MMPI-3

6

The original MMPI was developed and normed in the late 1930s and early 1940s using samples composed almost exclusively of White individuals living in the state of Minnesota. When the MMPI was revised during the 1980s, diversity considerations focused primarily on race, to the exclusion of other important variables such as gender identity and socioeconomic status (to name just a few). Among psychologists focused on diversity-sensitive assessment, these historical factors created concern about using the test. However, as the test has evolved, the MMPI instruments have been used successfully with diverse groups within the United States and internationally across a wide range of cultures and languages.

Throughout the process of developing the MMPI-3, including writing of the test manuals and interpretive guidelines, the authors were guided by the *Standards for Educational and Psychological Testing* (American Educational Research Association [AERA] et al., 2014). The standards include a chapter on fairness in testing with guidance on ways to achieve fairness through test design, development, administration, scoring, and interpretation procedures. The recommended procedures were implemented to mitigate any threats to fair use of the MMPI-3.

We begin this chapter with a discussion of the terminology used throughout the text. Next, we review the broad empirical literature examining associations of MMPI scores with diversity-related factors and multicultural experiences. Based on this review, we then recommend best practices for diversity-sensitive assessment with the MMPI-3.

The evolution of diversity-related nomenclature during the 8 decades since the MMPI was first published poses a challenge when reviewing and discussing this literature. As reflected in the *Inclusive Language Guidelines* published by the American Psychological Association in 2021, the recommended terminology of inclusive language is constantly evolving, such that terms recommended in past APA style guidelines are no longer recommended when writing about individuals of diverse identity groups. This process will certainly continue after the publication of this book. We therefore wish to acknowledge that some terms used in this chapter may seem anachronistic to future readers. Moreover, as highlighted in the *Inclusive Language Guidelines,* there may be differences in preferred terminology even within diverse groups. As a result, some terms used in this chapter may inadequately center the voices of individuals within marginalized or stereotyped groups. We regret any discomfort that the terms used or ideas expressed in this chapter may cause.

A second challenge when writing on this topic relates to the scope of groups and individuals covered by the term diversity. In their edited volume *Diversity-Sensitive Personality Assessment,* Smith and Krishnamurthy (2018) note that the term is not limited to race and ethnicity. Differences related to gender, sexuality and gender identity, class, immigration status, age, nationality, disability, and religion, and the intersections among them, must also be considered when conducting diversity-sensitive assessments. Although, as reviewed next, there is extensive literature on use of the MMPI with some groups (e.g., race, language), the empirical literature guiding use of the test with other groups is limited or entirely lacking. Moreover, even for those variables for which an extensive research literature has accumulated, for example the Black–White comparisons discussed throughout the chapter, within-group diversity has largely been ignored. Samples of Black individuals in the United States include individuals whose ancestors were brought here as slaves as well as later immigrants from African and some Caribbean and Latin American countries. The diversity-sensitive practices described in the final part of this chapter emphasize the importance intersectionality and within-group diversity and are recommended for use with all groups pending accumulation of additional research.

LITERATURE REVIEW

The literature exploring use of the MMPI instruments with diverse groups in the United States and internationally spans a range of studies beyond the scope of a single chapter. Here we highlight the main themes and findings of this research. Readers are encouraged to consult the comprehensive sources cited for additional details. Two primary branches of the MMPI literature are reviewed: studies related to use of English-language versions of the test with diverse populations (primarily within the United States) and research pertaining to international adaptations of the instrument.

English-Language Studies

The Original MMPI

As discussed in chapter 1, the original MMPI was developed and normed using a sample of visitors to the University of Minnesota Hospital that was exclusively White and consisted primarily of unskilled laborers and farmers with an average of 8 years of education. Though representative of the initial target population for the test (their friends and relatives whom they were visiting), as time progressed and use of the inventory spread beyond Minnesota, the MMPI came to be used with a considerably more diverse population, raising questions, and motivating research about its appropriateness for use with non-White individuals.

Most of the original MMPI literature examining possible diversity-related factors and test scores focused on comparisons of Black and White individuals. We begin this review with a discussion of these comparison. We then turn to research focused on other race and ethnicity samples, followed by studies examining MMPI scores of other demographic groups.

BLACK AND WHITE COMPARISONS

W. G. Dahlstrom and Gynther (1986) conducted a comprehensive review of the literature comparing MMPI validity and clinical scale scores of samples of Black and White individuals. These authors noted that early studies focused on comparing mean scores across these groups (Ball, 1960; Butcher, Ball & Ray, 1964; Hokanson & Calden, 1960; McDonald & Gynther, 1962, 1963) reported finding some differences, with Black participants scoring higher than White participants on Validity Scales L and F and Clinical Scales 8 and 9. Based on this literature, Gynther (1972) advocated the development of separate MMPI norms for Black individuals. However, subsequent research in which Black and White participants were matched on several potential confounding variables such as age and education, and in which data were aggregated across studies, indicated that differences between the two groups were small, inconsistent, or not present (Dahlstrom et al., 1986; Penk et al., 1986). Greene (1987) subsequently reviewed this literature and concluded that there was no consistent pattern across studies of differences between Black and White individuals on the original MMPI. Some investigators nevertheless continued to report finding relatively minor mean group differences.

Prichard and Rosenblatt (1980) observed that the meaning and interpretation of any mean group differences between Black and White samples were ambiguous insofar as the possibility of test bias was concerned,[1] noting that "even if large racial differences on the MMPI scales are eventually documented for certain subgroups, their relevance to the question of test bias is questionable" (p. 265). They went on to explain that "unless the black and white subgroups in a sample are matched for psychopathology (or lack of psychopathology) . . . [i]t is always possible that such mean differences in unmatched subgroups are due to actual subgroup differences in psychopathology that the MMPI accurately detects" (p. 265). They added an important corollary of this view, that the absence of differences cannot be viewed as evidence of the absence of test bias. Instead, they advocated for research that compared across Black and White subsamples the accuracy of predictions made based on their MMPI scores. In other words, Prichard and Rosenblatt (1980) emphasized that examination of the potential for test bias requires predictive validity comparisons across groups and noted that a limited literature on this topic had not identified differential predictive validity of MMPI results across Black and White groups.

OTHER RACIAL AND ETHNIC GROUPS

Research comparing original MMPI findings of individuals of Hispanic origin with White individuals, though not as extensive as the literature comparing Black and White individuals, focused exclusively on mean score differences.[2] A unique challenge encountered by investigators of this topic required consideration of English-language fluency and the related potential impact of acculturation on MMPI scores and psychological functioning more generally. Campos (1989) reviewed the results of 16 studies comparing mean MMPI validity and clinical scale scores of White and Hispanic individuals and concluded that when language and acculturation factors were considered, the only consistent difference between the groups was that individuals of Hispanic origin tended to score about half a standard deviation higher than White individuals on the L scale. However, as noted earlier, Prichard and Rosenblatt (1980) had pointed out that the absence of differences was not evidence of the absence of bias. Studies comparing the predictive validity of MMPI scores of White and Hispanic participants were needed to address this question; however, at that time, there were no published MMPI investigations available to make such comparisons.

Studies comparing original MMPI findings of American Indian and White samples also focused exclusively on mean groups differences, yielding inconsistent results. Based on their literature review, Kline, Rozynko, Flint, and Roberts (1973) concluded that American Indian males with alcoholism scored higher than White males with alcoholism on several MMPI scales. However, subsequent investigators found considerably greater similarity among American Indian and White individuals with alcohol use disorders (Page and Bozlee, 1982; Uecker, Boutilier, & Richardson, 1980). Pollack and Shore (1980) reported similar findings with other diagnostic groups, whereas Butcher, Braswell, and Raney (1983) concluded that MMPI scores of American Indian psychiatric inpatients were less elevated than those of White and Black inpatients. Literature on the original MMPI scores of American Indian people lacked studies comparing predictive validity with scores of White individuals.

Research examining the original MMPI scores of individuals of Asian origin in the United States was limited. Marsella et al. (1975) compared MMPI scores of White individuals and those of Asian origin on MMPI Clinical Scale 2 and the Beck Depression Inventory, finding that the latter group scored higher on both measures. Tsushima and Onorato (1982) found no substantial differences between MMPI scale scores of White individuals and those of Asian origin when diagnosis was held constant. On the other hand, Sue and Sue (1974) reported finding considerably greater differences in scores of college students seeking mental health services, with students of Asian origins scoring higher than White students on several MMPI scales, which was consistent with their hypothesis that the former would be more reluctant to seek mental health services for cultural reasons, and as a consequence, those seeking services would evidence more severe psychopathology. As with the other groups discussed in this section, no published studies compared the predictive validity of MMPI scores across individuals of Asian origin and White individuals.

GENDER DIVERSITY

Early studies with gender diverse individuals and the MMPI reported finding moderate psychopathology levels (Finney et al., 1975; Roback et al., 1976; Rosen, 1974). Most of the differences reported between gender diverse and cisgender samples were found on Clinical Scale 5, which was later understood to be a measure of interests rather than psychopathology (Ben-Porath & Tellegen, 2008/2011). In some studies, other than on Scale 5, gender diverse samples tended to score in the same range as or lower than cisgender samples on the remaining Clinical Scales (e.g., Tsushima & Wedding, 1979). As noted by Bryant (2020), most of the original MMPI studies of gender diverse individuals were underpowered. Moreover, none of these investigations compared the predictive validity of MMPI scores for cisgender and gender diverse samples.

OLDER ADULTS

Most original MMPI investigations reported finding that older individuals tended to score higher than younger individuals on Clinical Scales 1, 2, 3, and 0 and lower on 4 and 9 (Gynther, 1979; Leon et al., 1979; Lezak, 1987). However, most of the studies conducted in this area relied on cross-sectional designs, raising the possibility that any differences observed were at least partly the product of generational dissimilarities, rather than aging per se, or cohort effects. Moreover, Graham (2012) noted the moderate differences observed in these and similar investigations could have reflected age-related differences to some extent in health and energy rather than psychopathology. Here too, without studies that examined predictive validity across age cohorts, interpretation of the origin and meaning of these differences was ambiguous.

OTHER DIVERSE GROUPS

L. E. Dahlstrom (1986) examined the literature on MMPI scores generated by various groups in different regions of the United States, including clinical scale profile patterns of psychiatric patients, college students, and prison inmates. She concluded that code-type patterns did not differ as a function of geographic regions. Dahlstrom also reviewed the literature on MMPI differences among various religious groups in the United States and concluded that "there may well be systematic differences but that they are likely to be small and must be considered in the larger view of the individual being tested" (p. 56)—an important point we return to later in this chapter.

SUMMARY OF ORIGINAL MMPI FINDINGS

As noted earlier, the research literature pertaining to original MMPI scores generated by diverse groups of individuals is vast, far exceeding the scope of this brief review. But one common finding across diversity domains was relatively small mean differences between groups, often within of 5 T score points.[3] Moreover, both the nondiverse controls and members of diverse groups tended to score above average on several of the Clinical Scales. This last observation likely reflected some shortcomings of the original MMPI normative sample (discussed in chapter 1), which led to development of the MMPI-2. A frequent limitation of early MMPI literature stemmed from the near exclusive focus on mean group differences in scale scores or code-type patterns. The absence of data comparing the predictive validity of MMPI scores across groups left important questions about the implications for MMPI interpretation of any observed differences (or lack thereof) unaddressed.

The MMPI-2

As detailed in chapter 1, a primary objective of the MMPI-2 development was to replace the original normative sample, which had become increasingly inadequate, with a new, nationally representative sample of the adult population of the United States. The availability of new norms and introduction of new scales sparked renewed interest in examination of associations between MMPI-2 scale scores and diverse group membership. Efforts to examine the implications of any observed differences (or lack thereof) began to focus on investigations of the comparative validity of MMPI-2 scores across diverse groups. In the following, where comparative validity research is available, we focus our review on this literature.

BLACK AND WHITE COMPARISONS

In a landmark study, Timbrook and Graham (1994) compared the clinical scale scores of Black and White members of the MMPI-2 normative sample. After matching these groups for age, education, and family income, they found no differences that exceeded 5 T-score points, the standard for identifying clinically meaningful group mean differences. These authors were among the first to incorporate a predictive validity component in their investigation. A subset of members of the MMPI-2 normative sample included married or cohabitating couples who, in addition to taking the test, provided ratings of each other's personality and psychological functioning. These ratings were used to create criterion rating scales for variables labeled Depression, Antisocial Characteristics, Anxiety, Mania, and Social Discomfort. Using all available rating data, the authors conducted regression analyses to create equations that could be used to predict for each individual their partner's rating on the five criterion variables and then compare this prediction with the actual rating the partner provided, yielding a mean error score. Timbrook and Graham (1994) then compared mean error scores for their matched samples of Black and White individuals, finding that prediction accuracy did not differ significantly on any of the variables for men. For women, the only significant difference found was on Scale 7, which slightly underpredicted anxiety ratings for Black women.

A general absence of differential predictive validity was found in several subsequent studies. McNulty et al. (1997) compared the predictive validity of MMPI-2 scale scores in Black and White individuals receiving therapy at an outpatient community mental health center, with therapist ratings serving as the criteria. No significant differences were found in correlations between MMPI-2 scale scores and therapist ratings. Castro et al. (2008) reached similar conclusions using a different mental health outpatient sample and information provided in the client application form as the criterion.

Arbisi et al. (2002) used data extracted via systematic record reviews of Black and White psychiatric inpatients' medical charts as the criteria for one of the first investigations of possible predictive bias that relied on moderated regression analyses to test for slope and intercept bias. Significant slope bias would indicate differential associations between scale scores and criteria, whereas significant intercept bias would indicate underprediction or overprediction of the criteria based on MMPI-2 scores. Arbisi and colleagues found minimal evidence of slope bias, but some evidence of intercept bias, though the effect sizes were quite small. In all instances of significant intercept bias, psychopathology was underpredicted for Black inpatients. That is, MMPI-2 scores reflected less psychological dysfunction in Black participants than was indicated by their therapists' ratings. Using a similar methodology applied to a sample of individuals receiving substance misuse treatment, Monnot et al. (2009) found some evidence of intercept bias indicating for some scales overprediction and underprediction of comorbid psychiatric diagnoses for both Black and White groups, with small effect sizes.

OTHER RACIAL AND ETHNIC GROUPS

Limited research was conducted examining differences between individuals of Hispanic origin and White individuals on the MMPI-2, and none of these studies tested for evidence of predictive bias. Whitworth and McBlaine (1993) reported that Hispanic college students scored higher on L and lower on K and Clinical Scales 3 and 4 than did a sample of White students, but all the differences were within the 5 T-score-point range. Whitworth and Unterbrink (1994) reported similar findings for a different college sample; however, in that study, Hispanic students scored higher than Whites students on two of the MMPI-2 Content Scales—Family Problems and Cynicism. Hall et al. (1999) reviewed findings from 13 original MMPI and MMPI-2 studies and found no consistent differences between individuals of Hispanic origin and White individuals that reached or exceeded 5 T-score points. Several studies focused on acculturation as a variable hypothesized to account for scores of Hispanic individuals on the MMPI-2. Canul and Cross (1994) found higher L scores among Hispanic individuals who were lower on acculturation, whereas Lessenger (1997) reported no significant association between acculturation and MMPI-2 scores in a Hispanic sample.

Robin et al. (2003) compared scores on most of the MMPI-2 scales generated by two large samples of Southwestern and Plains American Indian people. Scores of the two Indigenous samples were compared with each other and with scores generated by the MMPI-2 normative sample. The authors reported finding no clinically meaningful differences between members of the Indigenous groups; however, both samples scored meaningfully higher than the normative sample on several MMPI-2 Clinical and Content Scales. These differences were somewhat reduced but nevertheless remained clinically significant (i.e., at least 5 T-score points) when the Indigenous and normative samples were matched for age, gender, and education. In an accompanying study, Greene et al. (2003) explored the validity of MMPI-2 scores for the same two Indigenous samples using diagnoses generated via structured interviews. Similar analyses could not be performed with members of the MMPI-2 normative sample, making it impossible to test for predictive bias. Nevertheless, Greene and colleagues reported significant associations between MMPI-2 scores and expected diagnoses for most of the scales they examined.

Pace et al. (2006) examined MMPI-2 scores from two other American Indian samples and similarly found that their scores were significantly different from the MMPI-2 normative sample on several scales. Acculturation level did not account for these differences. The authors concluded that although elevated MMPI-2 scores of American Indian individuals may to some extent reflect psychological difficulties stemming from historical oppression and past adversity, they may also be a product of a divergent worldview that is not associated with psychological difficulties.

Hill et al. (2010) followed up on Pace et al. (2006) to identify items to which the American Indian samples' responses were substantially different from those of the MMPI-2 normative sample and explore potential cultural/experiential factors that accounted for these differences. The authors identified 30 MMPI-2 items scored on scales F, 1, 6, 8, and 9, that contributed to substantial group mean differences on these scales. Follow-up semistructured interviews were conducted to identify themes using a qualitative coding analysis. Nine themes were identified and labeled core belief system, experiences of racism and discrimination, conflicting epistemologies, living in two worlds, community connectedness, responsibility and accountability to the community, traditional knowledge, stories as traditional knowledge, and language and historic loss. Hill and colleagues concluded that these cultural factors were sufficient to skew scores and pathologize the American Indian participants who produced elevated scores on these scales. The authors called for the use of local norms and acculturation status norms when assessing Indigenous groups with the MMPI-2. We discuss this issue as it relates to the MMPI-3 in the final section of this chapter.

Limited research on MMPI-2 scores of individuals of Asian origin in the United States relied primarily on college students. Stevens et al. (1993) compared the MMPI-2 scores of a small sample of foreign-born Chinese students studying in the United States with those of a matched sample of White students. The Chinese men scored significantly higher than the White men on Clinical Scale 0, whereas the Chinese women scored significantly higher than the White women on scale L. Sue et al. (1996) compared MMPI-2 scores of Asian American college students with those of White students. Acculturation level was also assessed for the Asian American sample. The authors reported finding that Asian American students with low levels of acculturation scored higher than the White students on several MMPI-2 scales, most notably Validity Scale F and Clinical Scales 7 and 8. However, scores of Asian American students high on acculturation did not differ meaningfully from those generated by their White counterparts. Tsai and Pike (2000) replicated these findings with different samples. No studies in the literature compared the predictive validity of MMPI-2 scores generated by individuals of Asian origins and White individuals in the United States.

GENDER DIVERSITY

Caron and Archer (1997) compared the MMPI-2 scores of 56 individuals seeking gender affirming surgery from male to female (MtF) and 56 individuals seeking gender affirming surgery from female to male (FtM) with those generated by 112 psychiatric inpatients and the MMPI-2 normative sample. Members of the gender affirming surgery sample were administered the test as part of the presurgical evaluation process that adhered to standards for conducting such evaluations during that time period. All had met the initial screening criteria, including having lived and worked in the gender with which they identified for at least 2 years and having received hormone treatment for at least 1 year. They were also required to have participated in therapy, with their therapist endorsing the requested gender affirming surgery. Finally, a screening committee determined that these individuals had strong and persistent gender identification that was opposite the sex they had been assigned at birth and that all candidates were deemed to be free of substance misuse at the time of their evaluation. The combined gender affirming surgery sample was found to score substantially higher than the normative sample on scales F and 5, essentially the same as the normative sample on the remaining Clinical Scales, and substantially lower than the psychiatric sample on most of the Clinical Scales. Caron and Archer observed that contrary to their expectations, the gender affirming surgery sample produced scores that were very similar to those of the MMPI-2 normative sample. In contrast with prior MMPI studies that reported finding evidence of psychological dysfunction in samples of transgender individuals, the sample they studied consisted of a highly selected group of individuals who had met stringent criteria for approval for gender affirming surgery, and therefore this sample was not representative of the transgender community in general.

In a study of 82 individuals assigned male at birth seeking gender affirming surgery to female, Miach et al. (2000) divided the sample into 48 with a *DSM-III-R* diagnosis of transsexualism and 34 with a *DSM-III-R* diagnosis of gender identity disorder of adolescence and adulthood, nontranssexual type (GIDAANT). The authors reported finding that the transsexual diagnosis subsample scored very similarly to the men in the MMPI-2 normative sample, whereas the subsample diagnosed with GIDAANT scored substantially and meaningfully higher than the other transsexual sample on several MMPI-2 scales, reflecting dysphoric affect.

Keo-Meier et al. (2015) compared baseline and 3-month posttreatment follow-up MMPI-2 scores in a sample of 48 transgender men to assess the potential impact of testosterone treatment on mental health. The authors reported finding substantial reductions in mean MMPI-2 scores on several Clinical Scales, most notably in Scales 1, 3, 4, and 7. These findings were consistent with those reported by Caron and Archer (1997), who found that following 1 year of hormone treatment, individuals in their gender affirming surgery sample scored similarly to those in the MMPI-2 normative sample.

OLDER ADULTS

Butcher et al. (1991) examined age-related changes in MMPI-2 scores for two samples: a group of healthy men taking part in the longitudinal Boston Normative Aging Study and the men of the MMPI-2 normative sample. Age-related differences within both samples were modest. The authors attributed the changes they did find to cohort effects (the data for both samples were analyzed cross-sectionally) as well as possible age-related changes in health, social status, and energy, and they concluded that separate norms were not needed when using the MMPI-2 with older individuals. Similar findings were reported by Priest and Meunier (1993) for a sample of older women and Strassberg et al. (1991) for a sample of older men and women living in Australia.

SUMMARY OF MMPI-2 FINDINGS

Findings reported in the MMPI-2 diversity-related literature were largely similar to those of the original MMPI literature reviewed earlier. The most widely studied group was Black Americans. Mean score differences between Black and White individuals were comparable to those reported with the original MMPI. However, a significant advancement with the MMPI-2 literature involved the addition of predictive validity comparisons, which by and large pointed to considerable similarity across Black and White individuals, although some studies reported evidence of intercept bias, indicating that MMPI-2 scores of Black individuals underpredict some extratest indications of psychological dysfunction. Unfortunately, predictive validity comparisons were not conducted with other race and ethnicity groups. The possibility that cultural bias may impact MMPI-2 assessments of American Indian people was raised based on qualitative research related to item-level response differences, leading the authors of that study to suggest it may be advisable to use separate norms for Indigenous groups. A study that included a subsample of individuals experiencing dysphoria related to their gender identity showed evidence of dysphoric affect in their MMPI-2 scores, whereas those approved for gender affirming surgery and receiving hormone treatment did not produce substantially different MMPI-2 scores when compared with members of the normative sample. Age-related MMPI-2 differences were small and consistent with age-related changes in health, social activity, and energy.

The MMPI-2-RF

Owing to the shorter length of time it has been in use, fewer MMPI-2-RF studies focused on diversity-related matters have been published in comparison with the MMPI and MMPI-2. However, there is reason to assume that general findings with the previous versions apply to the MMPI-2-RF. This assumption is supported by common items across the three versions, common norms of the MMPI-2 and MMPI-2-RF, and literature reviewed next that replicated and extended findings with the previous MMPI versions.

RACE AND ETHNICITY

In an early study that included analyses of the RC Scales, Castro et al. (2008) examined the possibility of differential predictive validity in a sample of Black and White outpatient mental health clients. The sample included 452 individuals who identified as White and 46 who identified as Black. Nearly half the White subsample but only a quarter of the Black subsample identified as male. The annual income for the White subsample was nearly double that of the Black subsample. The Black subsample had a higher proportion of participants with no postsecondary education (30%) than the White subsample (18%). Black participants scored statistically and clinically significantly (defined as at least 5 T-score points) higher than White participants on RC1, RC3, RC6, and RC8. Follow-up regression analyses using extratest criteria that were available for RC1, RC4, and RC8 found, no evidence of prediction bias was found, as indicated by a nonsignificant incremental contribution of a variable that consisted of the cross product between the RC Scale score and race beyond the contribution of the score and race alone. Castro and colleagues concluded that their findings were consistent with prior MMPI-2 investigations that yielded no evidence of predictive bias in MMPI-2 scores of Black test takers.

Monnot et al. (2009) compared the predictive validity of the RC Scales using a large sample of male psychiatric inpatients (735 Black and 449 White individuals) assessed for substance abuse in a large Veterans Administration (VA) hospital. Demographic comparisons indicated that members of the Black subsample were more likely than members of the White subsample to be employed in semiskilled and unskilled jobs; however, the two subsamples were otherwise similar in their demographic makeup. A comparison of mean RC Scale scores identified two scales on which the group difference in mean score exceeded 5 T-score points. White individuals scored meaningfully higher than Black individuals on RC2, whereas Black individuals scored significantly higher than White individuals on RC6. Predictive validity analyses were conducted using diagnoses derived from a self-administered version of the Structured Clinical Interview for the *DSM-III* (SCID). Monnot and colleagues conducted step-down regression analyses to test for evidence of slope bias (differential association between scale score and diagnosis) or intercept bias (underprediction or overprediction of diagnosis by a given scale score). They also reported zero-order correlations between scale scores and diagnoses. Statistically significant slope bias was found for several RC Scales when predicting diagnoses; however, the effect sizes associated with these findings were minimal, accounting in most instances for less than 2% of the variance in predicting diagnoses. The largest effect size accounted for 2.7% of variance in a bipolar disorder diagnosis predicted by RC9. Examination of the zero-order correlations across race indicated that this finding reflected adequate predictive validity for the Black subsample and an absence of predictive validity for the White subsample. Levels of intercept bias identified in Monnot and colleagues' analyses were slightly larger in magnitude (statistically significant in 6 out of the 39 analyses that were conducted), though none accounted for more than 4.7% of the variance in diagnoses—whereas most accounted for less than 4% of the variance.

Marek et al. (2015) examined the validity of MMPI-2-RF substantive scale scores as a function of race and ethnicity using a large sample of patients (872 men and 2,337 women) who were tested as part of a presurgical evaluation of candidates for bariatric surgery. Of these individuals, 2,204 identified as White, 744 as Black, and 96 as Hispanic. Overall, men and women in the three race/ethnicity groups produced highly similar mean T scores across the 51 MMPI-2-RF scales. Black men scored more than 5 T-score points higher than White men on L-r, whereas White men scored higher than Black men on the PSY-5 scale Introversion/Low Positive Emotions-Revised (INTR-r). Black women scored higher than White women on Multiple Specific Fears (MSF) and PSY-5 Aggressiveness-Revised (AGGR-r). The only clinically meaningful difference found for the Hispanic women was that they scored higher than White women on L-r.

Logistic regression analyses were performed to test for predictive bias using as criteria the results of a semistructured interview conducted at the time of the assessment. Of the 40 analyses for ethnicity, 10 indicated statistical significance but produced a small effect size at most. There was evidence of slope bias for RCd predicting past psychotropic medication use, indicating better prediction for White individuals; however, the effect size was small and clinically insignificant. Statistical significance for intercept bias was found in 10 analyses, with evidence of small magnitude underprediction of criteria in Black individuals. That is, MMPI-2-RF scale scores underpredicted psychological dysfunction as reflected in interview findings in Black individuals but with mainly negligible effect sizes. Overall, these analyses indicated comparable scores and generally equivalent predictive validity in Black and Hispanic bariatric surgery candidates when compared with White candidates.

Glassmire et al. (2017) examined endorsement frequencies (percent of the sample or subsample responding to an item in the keyed direction) for the 21 items of the Fp-r scale in a sample of 438 forensic psychiatric inpatients (58.7% White, 20.6% Black, 15.4% Hispanic) who were hospitalized following acquittal by reason of insanity. As discussed in chapter 2, items had to be answered in the keyed direction by less than 20% of several inpatient samples to be included on the Fp-r scale. Glassmire et al. reported endorsement frequencies exceeding 20% for only one of the 21 Fp-r items (an item related to avoidance of stepping on sidewalk cracks), with more than 20% of the members from all three groups (White, Black, and Hispanic) responding in the keyed direction. For the remining 20 Fp-r items, no member of any group responded in the keyed direction in more than 20% of cases.

Whitman et al. (2019) compared the validity of MMPI-2-RF scores in prospective prediction of suicidal behavior (e.g., documented attempts) in a sample of 751 forensic inpatients self-identified as White, Black, or Hispanic who were committed to a state hospital following acquittal by reason of insanity and in the prospective prediction of documented institutional violence in a subsample of 303 patients at the same facility. Regression analyses were conducted to test for slope and intercept bias using 40 of the MMPI-2-RF Substantive Scales (the two Interest scales were excluded from the analyses). Of the 40 tests for slope bias in prediction of future suicidal behavior, only three yielded statistically significant findings with negligible-to-small effect sizes, reflecting slightly higher predictive validity for the White subsample than the Hispanic subsample on the Activation (ACT) and Negative Emotionality/Neuroticism-Revised (NEGE-r) scales and slightly higher predictive validity for the Black subsample compared to the Hispanic subsample on Anger Proneness (ANP). Of the 40 tests of intercept bias, only one was statistically significant with a small effect size, indicating underprediction of risk for future suicidal behavior in the Black subsample based on Multiple Specific Fears (MSF) scale scores. Of the 40 tests for slope bias in predicting future institutional violence, eight indicated statistically significant findings, all with small effect sizes. Scores on the Aggression (AGG) and Anger Proneness (ANP) scales were more strongly associated with future violence among Black individuals than among Hispanic individuals. Scores on RC7, Gastrointestinal Complaints (GIC), Cognitive Complaints (COG), Suicidal/Death Ideation (SUI), and Anxiety (AXY) evidenced stronger associations with future violent behavior among Black individuals than among Hispanic and White individuals in this sample. None of the 40 tests of intercept bias were statistically significant.

GENDER DIVERSITY

Bryant et al. (2021) reported descriptive findings on the 42 MMPI-2-RF Substantive Scales for a sample of 85 transgender and gender diverse (TGD) individuals. Of these individuals, 37 were not receiving mental health services at the time of their participation, whereas 48 members were receiving mental health outpatient services. Three sets of comparisons were conducted. The MMPI-2-RF scores of TGD individuals not in treatment were compared with scores of the MMPI-2-RF normative sample and with those of TGD individuals receiving mental health services, and scores of TGD individuals in treatment were compared with those of a large sample of individuals receiving outpatient services at a community mental health center.

Based on research documenting mental health challenges associated with sexual and gender diversity, the authors hypothesized that the nontreatment TGD sample would score higher than the normative sample on measures of emotional difficulties and substance use. Findings were consistent with these hypotheses for the MMPI-2-RF internalizing scales but not the Substance Abuse (SUB) scale. The nontreatment TGD sample scored at least 5 T-score points higher than the normative sample on additional MMPI-2-RF scales related to persecutory beliefs, somaticizing, and interpersonal difficulties, which the authors interpreted as being consistent with the lived experiences of TGD individuals.

Mean scores of the subsample of TGD individuals receiving treatment were substantially higher than those of the TGD individuals not in treatment, particularly on measures of internalizing dysfunction where the treatment subsample mean score was clinically elevated above 65T on several MMPI-2-RF scales, reflecting the higher level of psychological difficulties that likely led these individuals to seek mental health services. Scores of the TGD subsample receiving treatment were largely similar to those of the outpatient community mental health center sample, except for the COG, Stress/Worry (STW), and AXY scales on which the TGD treatment-receiving subsample scored substantially higher.

Bryant et al. (2021) did not conduct tests of predictive bias, and the sample sizes available for their investigation were relatively small, indicating a need to replicate and extend the findings with larger samples. Nevertheless, Bryant and colleagues' results revealed that MMPI-2-RF scores were able to reflect and characterize mental health difficulties experienced by TGD individuals.

OLDER ADULTS

Marek et al. (2015) compared the mean scores and predictive validity of MMPI-2-RF scales as a function of age in a sample of bariatric surgery candidates. Candidates were divided into subsamples of age ranges: 18–35 years (n = 454), 36–49 years (n = 1,154), 50–64 years (n = 1,246), and 65 years or older (n = 355). As would be expected, older individuals scored higher than younger individuals on measures related to somatic complaints, whereas younger individuals scored higher than the older individuals on measures of externalizing behaviors.

Regression analyses were conducted by Marek and colleagues (2015) to test for slope and intercept bias, with clinical interview findings serving as the criteria. Mean score comparisons identified few differences that reached clinical significance (5 T-score points or higher). Of the 40 analyses conducted (one for each MMPI-2-RF Substantive Scale except the Interest scales), three reached statistical significance (with small effect sizes), indicating prediction bias on those three scales. There was evidence of slope bias for NEGE-r predicting a history of outpatient therapy with better prediction for younger individuals. Evidence of intercept bias was found in three analyses. Specifically, NEGE-r overpredicted a history of outpatient therapy for older adults and Malaise (MLS) overpredicted a history of not exercising and having a higher presenting body mass index for older adults. All the effect sizes in these analyses were small. Overall, these findings showed substantial consistency in the predictive validity of MMPI-2-RF scores as a function of age.

SUMMARY OF MMPI-2-RF FINDINGS

The MMPI-2-RF studies reviewed in this section produced results largely consistent with those obtained in research with previous versions of the test. Mean group differences generally did not reach clinical significance, except in cases where it might be expected, such as the comparison of TGD individuals receiving mental health services with those not in treatment, or in the case of somatic complaints among older bariatric surgery candidates. Predictive validity analyses mostly documented comparable validity across race and ethnicity, gender diversity, and age groups. In the small proportion of analyses that did detect statistically significant differences, effect sizes were negligible to small and the predictive validity findings did not consistently indicate that test scores were more valid for any one group. Most importantly, in these analyses, MMPI-2-RF scales accounted for much larger proportions of variance in the criteria than did variables reflecting predictive bias. Overall, these findings indicate that there are substantially larger differences in psychological functioning within the groups studied than between them and that MMPI-2-RF scale scores reflect these differences as indicated by meaningful associations with extratest criteria.

The MMPI-3

Studies comparing MMPI-3 scale scores and their predictive validity across diverse groups are limited given the relatively short amount of time that has passed since the MMPI-3 was released. However, as noted in previous chapters, Appendix E of the *MMPI-3 Technical Manual* provides extensive empirical evidence indicating that MMPI-3 versions of MMPI-2-RF Substantive Scales have essentially the same empirical correlates as their MMPI-2-RF counterparts across a range of settings. Data reported in chapter 3 of the *Technical Manual* indicate that MMPI-3 versions of MMPI-2-RF Validity Scales, particularly the overreporting and underreporting indicators, are correlated (.93 and higher) with the MMPI-2-RF versions. The empirical correlates presented in the *Technical Manual* and the MMPI-2-RF literature just reviewed indicate that MMPI-2-RF findings can be applied to MMPI-3 interpretation. Therefore, it is reasonable to assume that future MMPI-3 studies related to diversity will yield comparable results. This does not apply to the five scales that have been added to the MMPI-3, for which new research is needed.

In the first MMPI-3 study comparing the predictive validity of test scores among Whites and People of Color (POC), Anestis et al. (2022) examined the ability of the MMPI-3 scales to predict reactions to an experimental behavioral task designed to induce feelings of rejection and ostracism. Their sample included 180 undergraduate students (80.6% female, 17.2% male; 59.5% White, 40.5% POC), and analyses were conducted using the full sample as well as race-based subsamples. In most instances, MMPI-3 scales demonstrated consistent associations with post-ostracism outcome variables across the race-based subsamples. However, a small number of notable correlation differences were observed. As with validity comparisons conducted with previous MMPI versions, there was no consistent pattern of stronger correlations for the White subsample compared with the POC subsample.

Although not directly comparing predictive validity, a study by Dixon et al (2023) provides important information about the possible impact of cultural mistrust on MMPI-3 scores. The authors sought to identify MMPI-2-RF or MMPI-3 items that might be endorsed by People of Color because of cultural mistrust. They were particularly interested in whether items scored on the Restructured Clinical Scale Ideas of Persecution (RC6) were disproportionately reflective of cultural mistrust and how this might impact the scores of racialized groups on this scale. Expert raters (three Black men and three Black women, all psychologists) were asked to review the tests' item pool and identify MMPI-2-RF or MMPI-3 items reflective of cultural mistrust. The experts identified a total of ten such items (nine scored on the MMPI-2-RF and nine scored on the MMPI-3). They hypothesized that when responding to items that may reflect cultural mistrust, Black college students would endorse the highest level of cultural mistrust items, followed by Latina/o students, and then White students. They hypothesized that the same pattern of findings would occur in forensic inpatients, but that the differences would be attenuated because of the high base rate of psychiatric symptomatology and the nature of the forensic assessment setting. Consistent with Dixon et al.'s expectations, Black college students endorsed the highest number of cultural mistrust items, followed by Latina/o students, and then White students, resulting in small-to-medium effect sizes. Although they observed some item-level differences in forensic patients, the overall pattern of item endorsement did not significantly differ in this group. Black college students scored higher on the MMPI-3 version of RC6 than both Latina/o and White students, whereas the difference between Latina/o and White participants was not significant. The forensic sample differences on the MMPI-2-RF version of RC6 were negligible. Overall, Dixon et al.'s (2023) findings indicate that roughly 3% of the MMPI-3 items were found by experts to be potentially confounded with cultural mistrust and that these items disproportionately appear on RC6, indicating the importance of considering the potential impact of cultural mistrust when interpreting scores on this scale.

The sample used for the MMPI-2-RF study of TGD individuals described earlier was tested using the expanded version of the MMPI-2-RF (MMPI-2-RF-EX), which made it possible to score both the MMPI-2-RF and the MMPI-3 with the study data. Bryant et al. (2023) replicated the analyses by Bryant et al. (2021) using the MMPI-3. An important difference between the two investigations is that the later study eliminated a critical confound inherent in the earlier one. As previously described, Bryant et al. (2021) compared the MMPI-2-RF scores of TGD individuals not in treatment with scores of the MMPI-2-RF normative sample and with those of TGD individuals receiving mental health services, and scores of TGD individuals in treatment were compared with those of a large sample of individuals receiving outpatient services at a community mental health center. The confound involved comparison of the nontreatment-receiving TGD sample collected in the late 2010s with the MMPI-2-RF normative sample collected in the mid-1980s and a comparison of the treatment-receiving TGD sample collected in the late 2010s with a community mental health outpatient sample collected in the early 1990s. In the Bryant et al. (2023) study, the TGD samples, normative sample, and community mental health sample were all tested in the late 2010s, eliminating potentially confounding cohort effects. The authors also added analyses of the validity of MMPI-3 scale scores of TGD individuals based on correlations with relevant collateral measures.

Bryant et al. (2023) reported finding evidence of adequate reliability (as estimated by internal consistency) and convergent and discriminant validity for a combined sample of TGD individuals receiving treatment and those not receiving treatment. Because the criterion measures used in these analyses were only administered to the TGD samples, it was not possible to conduct predictive validity comparisons with the non-TGD samples.

Comparisons of MMPI-3 scores of the TGD sample not in treatment with those of the current normative sample indicated that most of the mean score differences found were less than 5 T score points, which, as described earlier, is the standard used to identify clinically significant differences. Scores on several MMPI-3 measures of internalizing and somatic/cognitive difficulties reached or approached this level, whereas scores on the externalizing, thought dysfunction, and interpersonal scales did not. However, the TGD sample not in treatment had higher standard deviations on most MMPI-3 scales compared with those of the normative sample, indicating greater variability among the former. A noteworthy exception was a mean T score of 59.24 ($SD = 12.82$) on the SUI scale for the TGD sample not in treatment. Of note in this context, the recommended cutoff for clinically significant elevation on this scale is 58T (see chapter 9). This finding is consistent with literature documenting increased risk for suicide among TGD individuals, including those not receiving mental health services.

Comparisons of the scores of the TGD sample receiving treatment with those of the outpatient community mental health sample found nearly identical means on all but a handful of MMPI-3 scales. Here too, the most prominent difference was on the SUI scale, on which the TGD treatment-receiving sample ($M = 68.40$, $SD = 15.20$) scored 10 points higher than the outpatient community mental health sample ($M = 58.32$, $SD = 15.41$), highlighting the increased suicide risk among TGD individuals receiving mental health services. Finally, in comparisons of the MMPI-3 scores of the two TGD samples, the one receiving mental health services scored clinically significantly higher than the nontreatment sample on most but not all the MMPI-3 Substantive Scales, indicating that the test was sensitive to a range of psychological difficulties that led TGD individuals to receive mental health services.

Summary of English-Language Studies

A large body of empirical research has explored associations between MMPI scores and diversity-relevant variables including race and ethnicity, gender diversity, and age. Original MMPI studies focused on differences among Black and White individuals, with subsequent research examining scores of additional groups including individuals of Hispanic and Asian origins as well as American Indian samples. These studies identified relatively few replicable mean group differences, with mainly negligible, nonclinically significant effect sizes. A significant limitation of these studies was the lack of cross-group comparisons of scale score validity. Beginning with the MMPI-2 and continuing with the MMPI-2-RF, investigators incorporated research designs that allowed for such comparisons, which are needed to rule in or out the possibility of test score bias. The studies reviewed in this section identified very few meaningful cross-group predictive differences. In the small number of analyses in which such differences were found, there was no evidence of systematic bias that favored one group or another. There is a need to conduct similar studies with the MMPI-3. Given the comparability of MMPI-2-RF and MMPI-3 empirical correlates, and considering the improved representation of diverse groups in the MMPI-3 normative sample, it is very likely that similar findings will be obtained with the MMPI-3.

We turn next to the second branch of MMPI research literature related to diversity considerations involving translations and international adaptations of the test.

MMPI TRANSLATIONS AND INTERNATIONAL ADAPTATIONS

Soon after the original MMPI was introduced, efforts began to translate the inventory and adapt it for use outside the United States. As recounted in the *MMPI-3 Manual Supplement for the U.S. Spanish Translation,* one of the first efforts involved MMPI developer Starke Hathaway, who, in collaboration with Cuban psychologist Idelfonso Bernal del Riesgo, introduced a Spanish-language version of the test in 1951 for use in Cuba. By the end of that decade, Dahlstrom and Welsh (1960) described in the first edition of the *MMPI Handbook* three available translations, including the Spanish-language translation just mentioned, along with translations of the inventory into French and Italian. They also provided information about ongoing efforts to translate and adapt the

MMPI for use in Austria, China, Czechoslovakia, Germany, Iraq, Japan, Korea, the Netherlands, Norway, Poland, and Portugal. In the second edition of the *MMPI Handbook,* Dahlstrom, Welsh, and Dahlstrom (1975) noted that there were then 30 MMPI translation projects underway, though they did not describe the projects in detail. In the first comprehensive publication on international adaptations of the MMPI, Butcher and Pancheri (1976) provided information about additional translation and adaptation projects underway in Australia, Costa Rica, Denmark, Belgium, Finland, India, Lithuania, Mexico, the Philippines, Puerto Rico, Russia, Scotland, Spain, Sweden, Thailand, Turkey, and Wales.

Original MMPI translations were developed in a somewhat haphazard manner, without coordination. When, as described in chapter 1, the MMPI publisher, the University of Minnesota Press, resumed editorial management of the test and with the subsequent publication of the MMPI-2 in 1989, a standard procedure for developing and approving translations was instituted. The most up-to-date MMPI translation guidelines can be found on the publisher's website (https://www.upress.umn.edu/test-division/translations-permissions/GUIDELINES). Key aspects of these guidelines include:

Identification of a project director from the country or culture for which the translation is being developed. The project director must be fluent in the target language, and they must also be a credible authority in personality assessment, diagnosis, and psychopathology.

The translation should be developed by a team of no less than two individuals fluent in the target language and the English-language. The translators will independently translate the items and then compare the results, negotiating differences until a consensus is reached on the translation of all items.

The translated items should then be back-translated into the English-language by someone other than the translators to determine whether they are equivalent in meaning to the original English-language items. Any substantive differences between an original and back-translated item should be considered by the translation team and revised as appropriate.

A language service employed by the University of Minnesota Press reviews the translation to determine whether each translated item is equivalent in meaning to the English-language original. A report is then sent to the translation team who must respond to any identified concerns with appropriate revisions or explanations.

The revised translation is then administered to a sample of at least 35 individuals fluent in both the target language and the English-language, once in each language in a counterbalanced manner. The results are then compared to examine scale score differences (using the English-language norms) and to identify substantial differences in item responses. Cross-language scale score correlations are compared with test-retest correlations for the English-language normative sample reported in the English-language test manual.

Normative and clinical data are then collected. At a minimum, a valid normative sample that includes 250 men and 250 women demographically representative of the country the target language is primarily spoken is required, as well as a clinical sample of 100 men and 100 women representative of the same country with valid MMPI protocols.

Using the target language normative sample, linear T scores are developed for the Validity Scales and uniform T scores (Tellegen & Ben-Porath, 1992) are developed for the Substantive Scales. Uniform T scores are developed using software provided by the University of Minnesota Press.

A final report on data collection and standardization of the translation is submitted to the University of Minnesota Press before approval for publication is granted. Once approved, the translation may be distributed by the licensed publisher.

A total of 20 MMPI-2 projects went through this rigorous process, producing Bulgarian, Chinese, Croatian, Czech/Slovak, Danish, Dutch/Flemish, German, Greek, Hebrew, Hungarian, Italian, Korean, Norwegian, Polish, Romanian, Russian, Spanish (for Mexico and Spain), Swedish, and Ukrainian translations.

These same guidelines were followed to produce 13 translations of the MMPI-2-RF in Croatian, Danish, Dutch/Flemish, French, German, Hebrew, Italian, Korean, Norwegian, Portuguese (for Brazil), Spanish (separate versions for Mexico and Spain), and Swedish. Development of MMPI-2-RF translations was facilitated by use of existing MMPI-2 translations as the starting point, which allowed for MMPI-2-RF translations to be developed without the need for additional translation work and normative and clinical data collection.

Unlike the MMPI-2-RF, development of MMPI-3 translations requires translation of the 24 MMPI-2 items revised for the MMPI-3 and 72 new items written for the test. At this time, the University of Minnesota Press has signed translation agreements for the MMPI-3 in Chinese, Danish, Dutch/Flemish, French, German, Greek, Hebrew, Hindi, Italian, Korean, Norwegian, Portuguese, Spanish for Mexico, Spanish for Spain, and Swedish. A Japanese translation has been released. The remaining projects are in various stages of planning and completion. A current list of approved translations and contact information for their international publishers/distributors can be found on the University of Minnesota Press website (https://www.upress.umn.edu/test-division/translations-permissions/available-translations).

The peer reviewed literature includes dozens of empirical studies that have used MMPI translations to establish and expand upon their reliability and validity and to study general assessment related topics within various countries and cultures. An exhaustive review of this literature is beyond the scope of this chapter. To date, investigations most relevant to use of the MMPI-3 have been conducted with the MMPI-2-RF. They include but are not limited to use of the Dutch translation in studies of the psychometric properties of the RC Scales (van der Heijden et al., 2008), the robustness of personality patterns over a 20-year period (Lanwerden et al., 2021), associations between personality and wellbeing in younger and older adults (Steenhaut et al., 2019), and self-awareness of cognitive dysfunction in patients with alcohol-induced mild or major neurocognitive dysfunction (Walvoort et al., 2016). Studies using the Korean translation have included identification of depression-related features (Choi et al., 2020), psychological characteristics of suicide attempters with depression (Choi et al., 2021), and the measurement invariance of RC4 scores in Korean- and English-speaking samples (Wang et al., 2021). Research with the Hebrew translation has included studies of the psychometric functioning of the RC Scales (Shkalim, 2015), mapping the RC Scales on mood markers (Shkalim et al., 2016), and examining current conceptualizations of psychopathology with the RC Scales (Shkalim et al., 2017). Work using the Italian translation has focused on assessment of quality of life in cancer patients (Granieri et al., 2013), personality assessment using machine learning (Mazza et al., 2019), and detection of underreporting based on reaction time (Roma et al., 2018). Research with the Spanish for Spain translation has explored symptom exaggeration in patients diagnosed with anxiety and depression (Blaso Saiz et al., 2013), assessment of fibromyalgia (Capilla Ramirez et al., 2013), assessment of social desirability (Jimenez-Gomez et al., 2013), smoking cessation related personality factors (Martínez et al., 2017, 2018), and assessment of overreporting (Sanchez et al., 2017).

Discussion of MMPI Translations and International Adaptations

The work described in this section illustrates the robustness of the MMPI to translation and cross-national and cross-cultural adaptation, which undoubtedly is facilitated by the rigorous guidelines adopted by the test publisher. A limitation of this literature is that most of the translation projects have been conducted in European countries and western cultures—noteworthy exceptions include work done in Israel, Korea, Japan, and Mexico. Ongoing work on a Hindi translation of the MMPI-3 for use in India, as well as an adaptation of the English-language version for use in that country, will further broaden the cultural scope of the test, as will adaptation of the MMPI-3 for use in China. Efforts to develop an Arabic translation of the inventory are underway and will add another important language and culture with which the MMPI-3 can be used. Almost entirely absent to date are efforts to adopt the MMPI for use in African countries—a critical gap we hope to see addressed in future translation work with the instrument.

MMPI-3 FEATURES THAT ENHANCE DIVERSITY-SENSITIVE ASSESSMENT

In addition to the extensive literature reviewed thus far examining MMPI assessment of diverse groups and cross-cultural adaptations of the test, several features introduced with the MMPI-3 enhance test users' ability to conduct diversity-sensitive assessment.

The MMPI-3 Norms

As detailed in chapter 3, a primary objective of the MMPI-3 development was updating the test norms to reflect substantial demographic shifts in the adult population of the United States since the MMPI-2/MMPI-2-RF normative sample was collected in the mid-1980s. This effort included the development of separate norms for the U.S. Spanish-language translation—a first in the test's history. Data reported in Tables 2–5 through 2–7 of the *MMPI-3 Technical Manual* indicate that the demographic makeup of the MMPI-3 English-language normative sample aligns well with current demographics of the U.S. population.

Table 2–5 of the *MMPI-3 Technical Manual* compares the demographic makeup of the MMPI-3 and MMPI-2/MMPI-2-RF normative samples, showing that the MMPI-3 normative sample closely matches projections of the 2020 U.S. Census Bureau. Whereas only 2.9% of the MMPI-2/MMPI-2-RF normative sample identified as being of Hispanic origin, 14% of the MMPI-3 normative sample identify as Hispanic. The U.S. Census Bureau projections for 2020 indicated that 16.8% of the adult population would identify as being of Hispanic origin; however, this proportion includes individuals who would not be sufficiently proficient in the English-language to be tested with the English-language version of the MMPI-3. As described in chapter 3, the MMPI-3 Spanish-language normative sample consists of an additional 550 individuals (275 men and 275 women) whose native language is Spanish. The market research firm used to collect data for the MMPI-3 English- and Spanish-language norms was selected for its expertise in data collection with difficult to reach populations. At their advice, data were collected in a manner that did not require disclosure of immigration status; however, a concerted effort was made to include undocumented immigrants among those tested for both normative samples.

The other major shift reflected in Table 2–5 of the *Technical Manual* is that 60.3% of the MMPI-3 normative sample identifies as White, consistent with the 2020 U.S. census projection, whereas 81.8% of the MMPI-2/MMPI-2-RF normative sample identified as White, consistent with the 1980 U.S. census. Table 2–5 also shows that the MMPI-3 normative sample more closely matches the 2020 census projection for individuals of Asian origin.

As seen in Table 2–6 of the *Technical Manual,* the MMPI-3 closely matches 2020 census projections for age, except for an underrepresentation of individuals 80 years old and above. Data reported in the *MMPI-3 Manual Supplement for the U.S. Spanish Translation* indicate that older adults are underrepresented in the MMPI-3 Spanish-language normative sample as well. As discussed in chapter 3 of this book, to some extent underrepresentation of older adults reflects that a smaller proportion of individuals in this age range can be tested with the MMPI-3 because of cognitive and physical health limitations more prevalent among individuals in this age group. Nevertheless, as the adult population in the United States continues to age and includes a greater number of older individuals, additional work will be needed to examine the validity of MMPI-3 scores with this population and identify means to optimally use the test with older individuals.

MMPI-3 Technical Manual Table 2–7 shows that the English-language normative sample represents the targeted 2020 census projections for education well, except for the lowest range of individuals with less than a high school education. Although a significant improvement over the MMPI-2/MMPI-2-RF normative sample, the proportion of individuals with no high school degree or GED in the MMPI-3 sample falls short of the 2020 projections for the adult population of the United States. To some extent, this likely reflects that a certain proportion of individuals with less than a high school education may not be testable with the MMPI-3 because of reading and language comprehension limitations. Data reported in the *MMPI-3 Manual Supplement for the U.S. Spanish Translation* reflect approximately even distributions of education levels in that sample.

Appendix C of the *MMPI-3 Technical Manual* provides extensive additional data about members of the MMPI-3 English-language normative sample. This includes information regarding employment status and occupation, parental education levels and occupations, family income, ancestral origins, dwelling, disability status, and physical, mental health, and substance use history. These data provide MMPI-3 users additional details needed to consider similarities and differences between the individuals they assess and members of the normative sample.

The simultaneous publication of newly normed English- and Spanish-language versions of the test for use in the United States represents a critical advance that facilitates diversity-sensitive use of the MMPI-3. Details about the development and norming of the Spanish-language version are provided in chapter 3. This represents the first time that norms are available for using a Spanish-language version of the MMPI in the United States.

A final and important advantage of having contemporary English- and Spanish-language normative samples for the MMPI-3 is that the test norms reflect current societal experiences. The adult U.S. population changed experientially in many ways since the test norms were last updated in the 1980s. The MMPI-3 normative samples represent a population living in a more diverse society in which technology, particularly the internet and social media, plays a major role.

Gender Diversity and the MMPI-3

Several MMPI-3 features enhance the utility of the inventory when used with gender diverse individuals. As discussed in chapters 3 and 7, the MMPI-3 norms are nongendered. Consequently, and contrary to previous versions of the test, it is not necessary for a binary gender to be specified for the purpose of converting raw scores to T scores, nor is it necessary (as it was in the past) for a binary gender to be entered into the software used to score the test. In addition, as described in chapter 7, the MMPI-3 software-based interpretive reports provide an option to generate reports that use gender-neutral language if a binary gender is not specified for the test taker.

Diversity-Sensitive Assessment With the MMPI-3

As reviewed in detail in the first part of this chapter, studies comparing the predictive validity of MMPI scores across diverse groups in the United States have mainly documented a general absence of psychometric bias, with a small number of exceptions identifying negligible-to-small effect sizes that do not systematically favor any group when statistically significant slope or intercept bias were found. Successful translation and adaptation of the test for use in a broad range of languages and cultures reflects the cross-culture robustness of inventory.

Three factors that replicate across the broad range of empirical work reviewed in this chapter have implications for diversity-sensitive assessment with the MMPI-3. First, MMPI scores generally show greater differences within groups than they do across the various groups studied. Second, associations between MMPI scores and extratest criteria are substantially larger than the effect sizes for bias in studies where it has been reported. Third, the test has been translated and successfully adapted for use in a diverse range of cultures and languages. Together, these features of the test indicate that important individual differences relevant to the assessment of personality and psychopathology are reflected in the MMPI scores produced by diverse groups of individuals.

Next, we consider implications of these test features for diversity-sensitive assessment with the MMPI-3.

Uniqueness of the Individual

Our emphasis on the robustness of MMPI scores does not mean that diversity-related factors can be ignored when using the MMPI-3. On the contrary, a plausible explanation for the findings reviewed in this chapter is that the entirety of the individual's background and lived experiences contributes to individual differences in the variables assessed with the MMPI-3. These factors include but are not limited to the demographic variables of race/ethnicity, gender, gender identity and sexual orientation, age, religion, and socioeconomic status, as well as the individual's unique family, developmental, social, environmental (including homelessness, institutional residence, incarceration, urban versus rural dwelling, living alone or with others, environmental stressors), educational, occupational, substance use, medical, and mental health history. That some of these factors in isolation are not associated consistently, or to a substantial degree, with MMPI scores or their predictive validity is consistent with the view that intersections among these and other relevant variables that are unique to the test taker account for individual differences on variables assessed with the inventory. Consequently, *all these factors should be considered in the context of the individual's lived experiences when interpreting the MMPI-3.* Diversity-sensitive assessment with the MMPI-3 requires that the evaluator be knowledgeable about both the test and factors that contribute uniquely to the individual's psychological functioning.

Group-Specific Norms

Earlier in this chapter, we discussed the publisher's requirement that nationally representative norms be collected in the target country for translated versions of the MMPI. Language-specific norms are needed to account for any nuances introduced when a test is translated. A unique and heretofore neglected challenge arises when an English-language version of the MMPI is used outside the United States. Early MMPI research that compared United States and Australian convenience samples revealed relatively few mean score differences on the Clinical Scales (e.g., Taft, 1957). Nevertheless, there are substantial demographic, especially racial and ethnic, group differences across English-speaking countries. New Zealand, for instance, has a local Indigenous group (Māori) that accounts for 17% of the population (and are overrepresented in both mental health and correctional settings). This cultural group is not represented in the U.S. English-language normative sample. To address this and other cultural differences, Sellbom (2022) developed formal population-representative MMPI-3 comparison groups for the New Zealand and Australian communities. Sellbom (2022) reported that whereas members of both community samples score similar to the U.S. English-language normative sample, there are meaningful differences. Going forward, it will be important to establish similar MMPI-3 community comparison groups for use in other English-speaking countries.

Earlier in this chapter, we noted that some authors (e.g., Gynther, 1972; Hill et al., 2010) have proposed that separate MMPI norms be developed for use with subgroups of the U.S. population, such as Black and Indigenous groups. We respectfully disagree with these suggestions for the following reasons. First, as Pace et al. (2006) noted in the context of findings with American Indian people, elevated MMPI scores may to some extent reflect psychological challenges that stem from historical oppression and past adversity, but such scores may also be a product of a divergent worldview that is not associated with psychological difficulties. Use of group-specific norms would mask the impact of adversity on MMPI-3 scores much the same way that gender-based norms on the original MMPI and MMPI-2 masked actual gender-related differences in psychological functioning. Use of a common metric, derived from normative samples, makes it possible for test scores to reflect actual group differences.

Impact of Potential Confounds

The potential for confounds to impact test results, such as a divergent worldview stemming from the individual's lived experiences, should be considered when conducting diversity-sensitive assessments with the MMPI-3. Culturally competent use of the test requires the interpreter to be familiar with potential confounds and consider them when interpreting test scores. For example, as highlighted by the findings of Dixon et al. (2023) that were discussed earlier, an individual's scores on scales reflecting mistrust of others' motives or holding of persecutory beliefs need to be considered in the context of potential lived experiences of discrimination, just as scores on measures of somatic complaints should be considered in the context of an individual's medical history and condition. In both examples, moderate elevations may reflect experiences unrelated to psychological dysfunction. However, as the score increases within the clinically elevated range, the likelihood of psychological dysfunction increases.

FUTURE DIRECTIONS

The MMPI instruments have been the subject of unparalleled research with diverse groups within the United States and extensive adaptation for use in other languages and cultures. Nevertheless, considerable work remains to be done. Findings of minimal differences between test scores across diverse groups, which generalized across previous versions of the test, have yet to be replicated with the MMPI-3. It will be important to empirically establish the extent to which MMPI-3 scale scores evidence predictive bias. MMPI-3 studies focused on the diverse groups discussed in this chapter are needed. Given the continuity of MMPI-2-RF and MMPI-3 research findings, it is very likely that previous results indicating comparable validity across diversity groups will replicate with the MMPI-3.

Nearly all the test bias research reviewed thus far has focused on differential predictive validity. In many respects, this is the ultimate test for psychometric bias. However, such analyses assume that the scales assess the underlying constructs in an equivalent manner across the groups. Recently, Han et al. (2019) provided detailed recommendations for multicultural assessment in which they emphasized the need to test for measurement invariance to examine whether an underlying construct is measured equivalently across groups. In brief, such analyses are conducted with unidimensional scales in the context of confirmatory factor analysis. Specifically, there are two forms of measurement invariance: metric and scalar. Metric measurement invariance examines equivalence in factor structure (i.e., determining whether factor loadings are the same across groups), whereas scalar measurement invariance examines underlying mean structure (i.e., determining whether items are associated with the same construct level). If metric invariance is not tenable, the underlying construct being measured is not associated with the items in the same manner across groups. In the absence of scalar invariance, mean scale scores cannot be compared across groups. MMPI researchers might have deemphasized measurement invariance in the past because invariance testing assumes that scale scores are unidimensional, which was not the case until more recently with the MMPI-2-RF and MMPI-3. We recommend that future MMPI-3 studies evaluate measurement invariance in addition to differential predictive validity.

No work to date, using any version of the MMPI, has focused on how intersections among the unique factors that contribute to the individual's lived experiences are reflected in test results. At this time, MMPI-3 users are encouraged to exercise clinical judgement informed by culturally competent knowledge of how various factors that contribute uniquely to the individual's psychological makeup may be reflected in their MMPI-3 scale scores.

Finally, international translation and adaption projects will be instructive regarding the cross-national and cross-cultural robustness of the MMPI-3. As noted earlier, additional work is needed to establish community comparison groups in English-speaking countries outside the United States. Several decades of experience indicates that the MMPI-3 will function effectively across the diverse cultures and languages in which previous versions have been successfully adopted.

Part II
Applications

Administering and Scoring the MMPI-3

7

This chapter describes and illustrates standard administration and scoring procedures for the MMPI-3. Standard procedures enhance the reliability of psychological test scores and facilitate comparison of a test taker's results with relevant reference groups, including the MMPI-3 normative samples. Adherence to the procedures presented in this chapter increases the likelihood that MMPI-3 findings will reflect characteristics of the test taker rather than idiosyncrasies introduced in the administration or scoring of the test. Deviations from standard procedures should be mentioned, and their impact considered, when reporting MMPI-3 results.

The chapter begins with a delineation of standard administration procedures for the MMPI-3. Standard scoring procedures are reviewed next. Software-based reports available for the MMPI-3 are described in detail in the third and final part of the chapter.

ADMINISTERING THE MMPI-3

The MMPI-3 can be administered by a qualified test user or a trained assistant working under a qualified user's supervision (see chapters 2 and 4 of the *MMPI-3 Manual for Administration, Scoring, and Interpretation*). Proper administration of the test requires consideration of whether the potential test taker is an appropriate candidate for assessment with the inventory, use of standard administration and response-recording modalities, and adherence to standard administration procedures.

Before Testing

Consider the Test Taker's Age

The MMPI-3 is normed for use with individuals ages 18 years and older. The top of the age range for the adolescent versions of the inventory is also 18, creating a one-year overlap in the test norms. Comparing the MMPI-2 and MMPI-A, Shaevel and Archer (1996) noted that the norms for the two tests produced substantially different T scores for 18-year-olds, with MMPI-2 norms generally producing lower validity scale scores and higher clinical scale values than did the MMPI-A norms. Osberg and Poland (2002) compared the MMPI-2 and MMPI-A scores of a sample of 18-year-olds who completed both versions and found incongruent scores in about half the sample. We recommend that 18-year-olds who are still living at home and attending high school be administered the MMPI-A-RF and that the MMPI-3 be used with those who are pursuing tertiary education, working, or otherwise living on their own.

Inquire About Prior Testing

Individuals involved previously with mental health or behavioral medicine systems, and those who have already been evaluated in a forensic or preemployment screening context, may have had prior experience with the MMPI. Inquiring about prior testing and, if the individual has previously completed the test, asking about their experiences, impressions, and expectations for the current evaluation can help identify and correct misconceptions. However, to avoid undue influence on current test results, asking about previous experiences is best conducted in the early stages of an assessment rather than immediately before the MMPI-3 is administered.

Assess the Testability of the Test Taker

The MMPI-3 is typically administered via a visual medium: a test booklet or a computer screen. For a test taker to provide meaningful results, they must be able to see, read, and comprehend the test items. The test administrator should conduct a preliminary assessment of the testability of the test taker by determining whether the individual has any limitations or conditions that might impair their ability to respond meaningfully to the test items and, if so, whether proper corrective steps can be taken. Individuals experiencing acute psychotic episodes or delirium and some potential test takers with severe cognitive impairments may be unable to complete a valid and interpretable MMPI-3.

Physical disabilities may require that accommodations be made to ensure valid testing. The test taker should be asked whether they have any visual impairment.

If they require reading glasses, these should be available. If the test taker's visual impairment is not correctable with reading glasses, a standard audio administration of the MMPI-3 should be done (see description below) and arrangements made for the test taker to record their responses privately. It is strongly recommended that the test taker not be asked to respond to the test items orally and that the items not be read to the test taker. Private recording of the test taker's responses can be implemented by providing an appropriate means for recording the responses (e.g., a notepad or a computer), which can later be transcribed onto an answer sheet or entered into the computerized scoring and reporting systems. An alternative is standard computerized administration of the MMPI-3 with Pearson scoring and reporting systems (described later in this chapter and in greater detail in the *MMPI-3 User's Guide for Score and Clinical Interpretive Reports;* Ben-Porath & Tellegen, 2020c), which includes audio as well as visual administration of the test items and ensures response privacy.

READING LEVEL

After confirming that the test taker can see the test items (or after providing appropriate accommodations), their reading ability should be considered. The reading level required for test takers to respond meaningfully to the MMPI has been the subject of some discussion and confusion. In the last edition of the original MMPI manual, Hathaway and McKinley (1967) indicated that an individual "with at least six years of successful schooling can be expected to complete the MMPI without difficulty" (p. 9). By contrast, the authors of the initial edition of the MMPI-2 manual indicated that "based on contemporary proficiency levels, the test would now require an eighth-grade reading level to comprehend the content of all the test items and to respond to them appropriately" (Butcher et al., 1989, p. 14). The apparent increase in reading level required to complete the MMPI-2 was unexpected considering the historical trend for generational improvement in reading proficiencies, simplification of wording for some of the original MMPI items in the MMPI-2 booklet, and attention paid to wording of the items that were added to the MMPI-2.

Prompted by these unexpected findings, Dahlstrom and colleagues (1994) conducted a comprehensive analysis of the readability of the MMPI, MMPI-2, and MMPI-A item pools and concluded that the average reading difficulty of all three MMPI instruments was about the sixth-grade level. Schinka and Borum (1993) had previously conducted an item-by-item examination of standard reading difficulty indicators and concluded that most MMPI-2 items were written at a fourth- or fifth-grade level, although some required a greater reading ability. These findings indicated that establishing a reading level requirement does not guarantee that a test taker will be able to read every item of an instrument, unless the level is set considerably higher than what is required to read most of the test items. Because the data reported by Dahlstrom et al. (1994) indicated that most of the MMPI-2 items require less than a seventh-grade reading ability, the recommended reading level for the MMPI-2 was changed from eighth to sixth grade in the revised edition of the test manual (Butcher et al., 2001).

A second source of confusion regarding the reading difficulty of MMPI items stems from comparisons with other tests. Morey (2007) reported that the Personality Assessment Inventory (PAI) requires the ability to read at the fourth-grade level. Some authors inferred that this makes the PAI a more appropriate instrument in settings where test takers may have lower reading levels. For example, Morey and colleagues (2007) commented that the lower reading level required for the PAI is "an important issue in forensic settings where reading ability is commonly lower than average" (p. 108). However, comparisons of the MMPI-2 and PAI reading levels, estimated at the sixth- and fourth-grade levels, respectively, were incomplete because the two estimates were derived with different methodologies. Butcher et al. (2001) relied on analyses using Lexile values (Stenner et al., 1988), whereas Morey (2007) derived the PAI estimate based on analysis of the test's entire item pool using the Flesch–Kincaid reading level index available in Microsoft Word, which yields a score of 4.0. Applying the same procedure to the MMPI-3 item pool produces a Flesch–Kincaid index of 4.5, consistent with the results reported by Dahlstrom et al. (1994) and Schinka and Borum (1993).

Establishing and comparing reading levels for self-report inventories is complicated further when different response formats are used. The True/False response format of the MMPI-3 is less complex than Likert-scale response formats and, all things being equal, should be less challenging for test takers with limited cognitive abilities. This is particularly true of items that include quantifiers (e.g., "I sometimes . . ." or "I frequently . . .") or are worded negatively (e.g., "I don't . . ." or "I rarely . . ."), which gives rise to ambiguities when used with a Likert response format that also includes quantifiers (such as "somewhat true"). Therefore, evaluations of the difficulties involved in administering tests based solely on item content and ignoring response format differences do not offer a complete comparison of the cognitive resources needed to meaningfully respond to self-report measures such as the MMPI-3.

If a test taker's ability to read the MMPI-3 items is in doubt (e.g., because of possible reading limitations or because the test taker is not a native English speaker), administration of a standard test of reading ability is recommended. If the test taker's reading level is less than sixth grade, or if it is not feasible to administer a reading test when reading comprehension is in doubt, administration of the MMPI-3 using the standard audio recording with paper and pencil or the audio within the computer scoring and reporting system is recommended. Forbey and colleagues (2009) reported empirical correlates of an audio administration of the MMPI-2 that were comparable to those obtained with paper and pencil and computer administration of the test.

Reading the items to the test taker represents a deviation from standard administration procedures and introduces an uncontrolled interpersonal element to the testing. This method compromises the test user's ability to rely on test norms and comparison group data for interpreting the MMPI-3 results and is not recommended.

Test takers who have the visual ability and requisite reading skills to respond to a standard administration of the MMPI-3 may still be unable to respond meaningfully to the test items due to lack of comprehension. Himsl et al. (2017) examined the association between measures of reading ability and language comprehension and MMPI-2-RF VRIN-r (Variable Response Inconsistency–Revised) and TRIN-r (True Response Inconsistency–Revised) scale scores among 136 forensic inpatients (90 men, 46 women). The authors found a meaningful negative correlation between VRIN-r scores and language comprehension, indicating that those with lower comprehension levels are more likely to provide variably inconsistent responses to the test items. Language comprehension deficits may occur with nonnative English speakers as well as test takers whose cognitive functioning is compromised by dementia, delirium, intoxication, or acute primary psychopathology. The test taker's English-language proficiency and mental status should be examined prior to administration of the MMPI-3.

If an individual lacking the requisite reading ability or language facility is administered the MMPI-3 without aid of an audio presentation of the items, the Validity Scales, particularly CRIN and VRIN, should detect it (following the interpretive recommendations described in chapter 8). A T score of 60 or below on these scales is very unlikely when the test taker lacks the ability to read and respond meaningfully to the items.

To summarize, setting a specific reading level for a self-report instrument can be misleading because individual items vary in difficulty. However, for comparison purposes, estimating MMPI-3 reading difficulty by calculating the Flesch–Kincaid index produces a recommended reading level of 4.5 grades. For individuals with limited cognitive abilities, the True/False response format may be less challenging than responding on a Likert scale. Audio administration can facilitate testing if the individual lacks the requisite reading ability to complete the MMPI-3; however, this does not address language comprehension deficits.

Standard Administration and Response-Recording Modalities

Standard MMPI-3 administration modalities include a booklet, computerized administration using Pearson's scoring and reporting systems, and audio recordings of the test items. Each of these includes standard instructions for completing the test, which should not be altered or augmented. If a test taker requests clarification or interpretation of an item, refrain from providing guidance other than supportively restating the standard instructions. When the booklet or audio recording is used to administer the test, an answer sheet is the recording modality. In addition to the Spanish-language MMPI-3 (Ben-Porath et al., 2020), several other approved translations of the test are in development. Up-to-date information on approved translations of the MMPI-3 can be obtained at www.upress.umn.edu/test-division.

Remote administration of the MMPI-3 is possible using Pearson's scoring and reporting systems. Corey and Ben-Porath (2020) provide guidance for this procedure. A key requirement is that remote visual and audio supervision be incorporated in a remote administration of the test by means of a telehealth service that complies with jurisdictional mandates. Remote supervision is necessary to maintain test security and the integrity of test scores under Standard 9.21 of the Standard for Educational and Psychological Testing (American Educational Research Association [AERA], 2014).

Booklet or Computer Administration

Several studies have established that booklet and computer (also known as on-screen) administrations of the MMPI yield comparable results (e.g., Forbey et al., 2009). On-screen administration offers two primary advantages. First, it is appreciably faster than using a booklet and answer sheet. Test takers with normal-range cognitive functioning and reading skills can typically complete a computer administration of the MMPI-3 in 25–35 minutes. Booklet and answer sheet administration typically requires 35–50 minutes. Computerized administration is faster because the test taker does not need to go back and forth between the booklet and answer sheet and fill in 335 bubbles. In addition, in an on-screen administration, the test taker inputs their responses directly into the scoring and reporting system, allowing for an immediate scoring of the test, saving the time needed to input the responses and avoiding potential error associated with manual entry (discussed later). The primary disadvantage of on-screen administration is that it requires that a test taker have access to a computer and for some platforms the internet, which is not feasible or practical in some settings.

The challenge of computer access has been ameliorated with the proliferation of handheld devices (tablets, smartphones) that can also be used to administer the MMPI-3. Menton et al. (2019) investigated the comparability of laptop-computer and tablet-based administration modes for the MMPI-2-RF. Employing a counterbalanced within-subjects design, the MMPI-2-RF was administered via both modes to a sample of college undergraduates. Administration modes were compared in terms of mean scale scores, internal consistency, test–retest consistency, external validity, and administration time. Mean scores were generally similar, and scores produced via both methods appeared approximately equal in internal and test–retest consistency. Scores from the two modalities also evidenced highly similar patterns of validity, as reflected in associations with external criteria.

Supervise Testing and Maintain Test Security

The *Standards for Educational and Psychological Testing* (AERA, 2014; Standard 9.21) require that test users make reasonable efforts to protect the integrity of test scores by eliminating opportunities for test takers to obtain scores fraudulently. Although the MMPI-3 is a self-administered test, a qualified user or a technician working under the supervision of a qualified user must supervise completion of the inventory. Adequate supervision ensures that the test taker completes the inventory on their own, that any unusual events that may occur during testing are recorded and can be considered in the interpretation of the results, and that conditions conducive to obtaining optimally valid information are maintained. In addition, to protect test security, test takers should not be allowed to take photographs of MMPI-3 test materials.

Supervision does not require that the individual administering the test be in the same room as the test taker throughout the session. However, the test taker should be within the supervisor's line of sight. For the same reasons, MMPI-3 materials should not be sent home with test takers nor should test takers in institutional settings be allowed to complete the instrument in their rooms or anywhere else where supervision is not possible. As just discussed, remote MMPI-3 administration should be conducted with supervision.

Maintain a Quiet, Comfortable Environment

MMPI-3 administration should occur in a quiet, comfortable environment in which the test taker is free of distraction. Testing can be conducted individually or in groups, but when more than one individual is tested, the supervisor must remain in the room (or in visual line of sight) to ensure that test takers do not bother or distract each other.

SCORING THE MMPI-3

MMPI-3 protocols can be scored by computer or by hand. Computerized scoring offers several advantages (discussed in detail later). It may also be cost-effective if the clerical expenditures associated with hand scoring are considered. The most efficient way to implement computerized scoring is to administer the MMPI-3 by computer (including tablet) using Pearson's scoring and reporting systems. As noted, this eliminates the need to enter the test taker's responses into the system and shortens administration time considerably. If administering the MMPI-3 by booklet and answer sheet, users can use a scanner to enter the item responses into the Pearson scoring and reporting systems or users can enter the test taker's responses by keyboard and score the test by using the scoring and reporting systems. If keying in the responses, the scoring and reporting systems provide the option of reentering a protocol (double entry or "verification"), which is strongly recommended to reduce the likelihood of entry error. Users can also mail answer sheets to Pearson for computerized scoring.

Hand scoring requires the use of answer keys (plastic templates) available from Pearson. Given the number of scales on the MMPI-3 (52) and the complexity of scoring some of these scales (particularly VRIN and TRIN), hand scorers may be tempted not to score all the scales. Because scores on all the MMPI-3 scales need to be considered for a comprehensive and complete interpretation of a protocol, users should not omit scoring any scales. Even the most time-consuming mode of response entry for computer scoring (double-entry by keyboard) requires considerably less time than does hand scoring the 52 MMPI-3 scales. An experienced user or clerical assistant can typically double enter an MMPI-3 protocol in 10–12 minutes. Hand scoring by an experienced user or clerical assistant typically requires 25–30 minutes. Moreover, research has shown that hand scoring is error-prone (Allard & Faust, 2000; Simon et al., 2002). By contrast, as just noted, the only error possible when using automated scoring is inaccurate keyboard entry of item responses, which can be greatly reduced by using the double-entry option.

The accuracy advantage afforded by automated scoring is, of course, contingent on the accuracy of the scoring program. Allard and Faust (2000) found substantial scoring errors in several nonstandard software systems used in the clinical settings in which they collected their data. Furthermore, the creation and use of unauthorized computer scoring programs is illegal. The MMPI-3 scoring algorithm included in the Pearson scoring system is rigorously checked for errors, and it is the only authorized, commercially available system for computer scoring the MMPI-3.

A final and noteworthy advantage of computer scoring involves the additional information provided in the MMPI-3 computer-generated reports discussed next.

COMPUTER-GENERATED MMPI-3 REPORTS

Several reports can be generated using Pearson scoring and reporting systems. The MMPI-3 Score Report (referred to as "Score Report" throughout this chapter) provides a test taker's scores on the 52 scales of the inventory along with information about the individual's responses to test items. The MMPI-3 Interpretive Report for Clinical Settings includes all elements of the Score Report and an automated interpretation of the results. The Pearson scoring and reporting systems provide opportunities to customize these reports by including a variety of optional data (described in the following sections). Additional information about the reports and how to interface with the scoring and reporting systems to generate them is provided in the *MMPI-3 User's Guide for the Score and Clinical Interpretive Reports* (Ben-Porath & Tellegen, 2020b).

The MMPI-3 Score Report

The MMPI-3 Score Report provides raw scores and standard T scores for the 52 scales of the instrument. Item-level information about unscorable, critical, and user-designated responses is also presented. To generate a score report with this system, the test taker's identification number, date of birth, and test administration date must be recorded. No report will be printed if any of this information is omitted, if the calculated age shows the test taker to be younger than 18, or if no item responses are recorded. The test taker's gender, years of education, and marital status can also be recorded, but this information is not required and will be listed on the cover page as "Not indicated" for gender and "Not reported" for years of education or marital status if omitted. The test taker's name can be recorded as well and, if provided, can be printed on the cover page. Finally, it is possible to record the test taker's race or ethnicity for record-keeping purposes, but this information will not be printed on the cover page.

A sample MMPI-3 Score Report is reproduced in Figure 7.1. The scores are those of a 44-year-old man, Mr. J, tested at intake to an outpatient community mental health clinic. The cover page for the report provides identifying information as recorded on the MMPI-3 answer sheet or during on-screen administration. Scores on the 52 scales of the MMPI-3 are reported on five profiles that appear on pages 2–6 of the Score Report. They are followed by a one-page summary of the scale scores under the heading MMPI-3 T Scores (by Domain) on page 7. Item-level information is provided in the remaining pages of the report.

Profiles

The second page of the report provides a profile of the scores on the MMPI-3 Validity Scales. Standard linear T scores are plotted in four groups: (a) inconsistent responding (Combined Response Inconsistency [CRIN], Variable Response Inconsistency [VRIN], and True Response Inconsistency [TRIN]); (b) overreporting psychopathology (Infrequent Responses [F] and Infrequent Psychopathology Responses [Fp]); (c) overreporting somatic and cognitive complaints (Infrequent Somatic Responses [Fs], Symptom Validity Scale [FBS], and Response Bias Scale [RBS]); and (d) underreporting (Uncommon Virtues [L] and Adjustment Validity [K]). The Validity Scales profile has a horizontal line drawn at a T score of 50, representing the mean score for the MMPI-3 normative sample. Unlike the remaining profiles, this is the only demarcation line on the Validity Scales profile

Minnesota Multiphasic Personality Inventory®-3

Score Report

MMPI®-3
Minnesota Multiphasic Personality Inventory®-3
Yossef S. Ben-Porath, PhD, & Auke Tellegen, PhD

ID Number:	Mr. J
Age:	44
Gender:	Male
Marital Status:	Not reported
Years of Education:	Not reported
Date Assessed:	08/01/2020

Copyright © 2020 by the Regents of the University of Minnesota. All rights reserved. Distributed exclusively under license from the University of Minnesota by NCS Pearson, Inc. Portions reproduced from the MMPI-3 test booklet. Copyright © 2020 by the Regents of the University of Minnesota. All rights reserved. Portions excerpted from the *MMPI-3 Manual for Administration, Scoring, and Interpretation*. Copyright © 2020 by the Regents of the University of Minnesota. All rights reserved. Portions excerpted from the *MMPI-3 Technical Manual*. Copyright © 2020 by the Regents of the University of Minnesota. All rights reserved. Used by permission of the University of Minnesota Press.

Minnesota Multiphasic Personality Inventory and **MMPI** are registered trademarks of the University of Minnesota. **Pearson** is a trademark in the U.S. and/or other countries of Pearson Education, Inc., or its affiliate(s).

This report contains copyrighted material and trade secrets. Qualified licensees may excerpt portions of this output report, limited to the minimum text necessary to accurately describe their significant core conclusions, for incorporation into a written evaluation of the examinee, in accordance with their profession's citation standards, if any. No adaptations, translations, modifications, or special versions may be made of this report without prior written permission from the University of Minnesota Press.

[1.0 / RE1 / QG1]

ALWAYS LEARNING   PEARSON

FIGURE 7.1. Mr. J's MMPI-3 Score Report

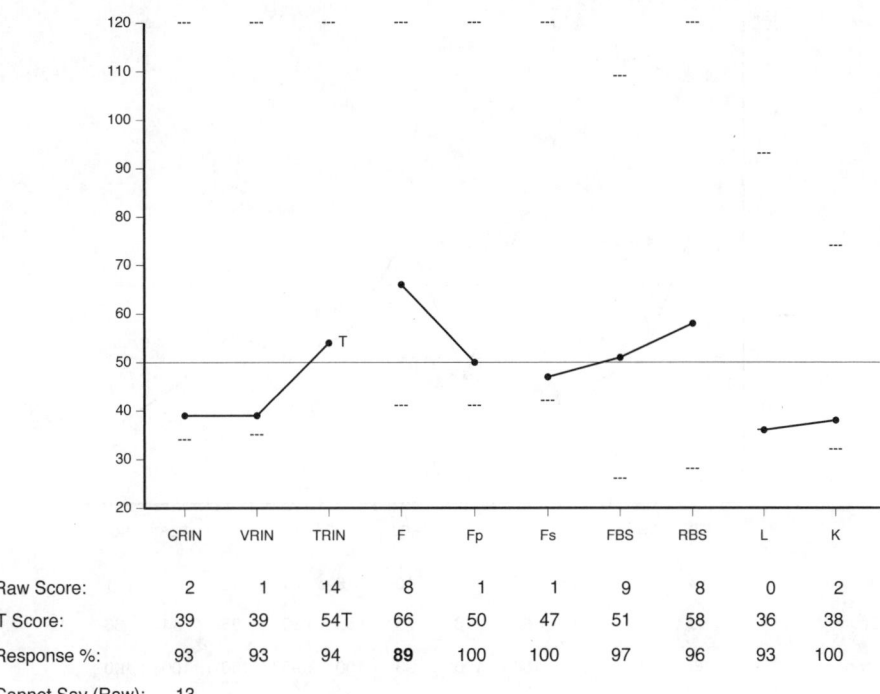

FIGURE 7.1. Mr. J's MMPI-3 Score Report, continued

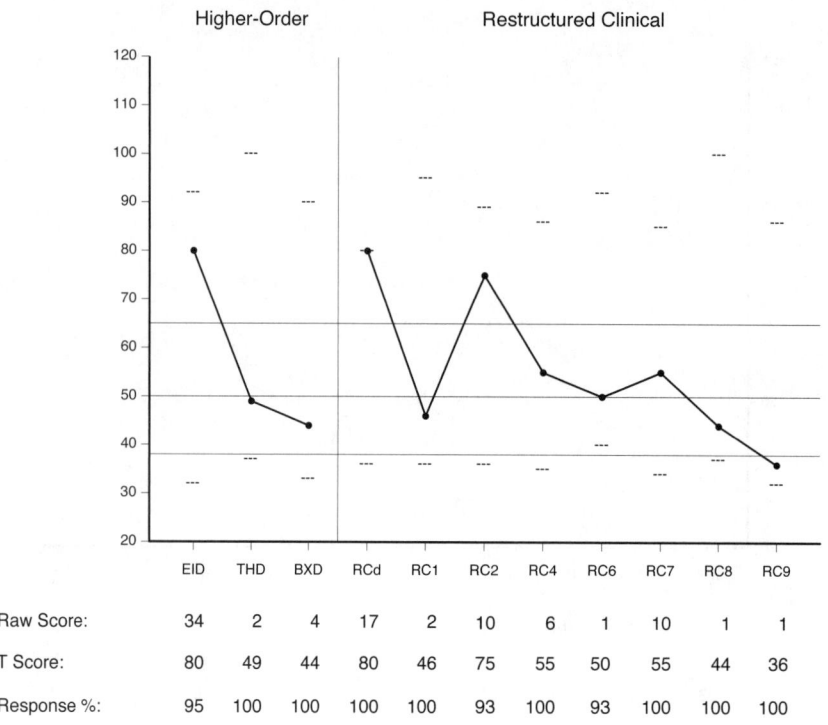

FIGURE 7.1. Mr. J's MMPI-3 Score Report, continued

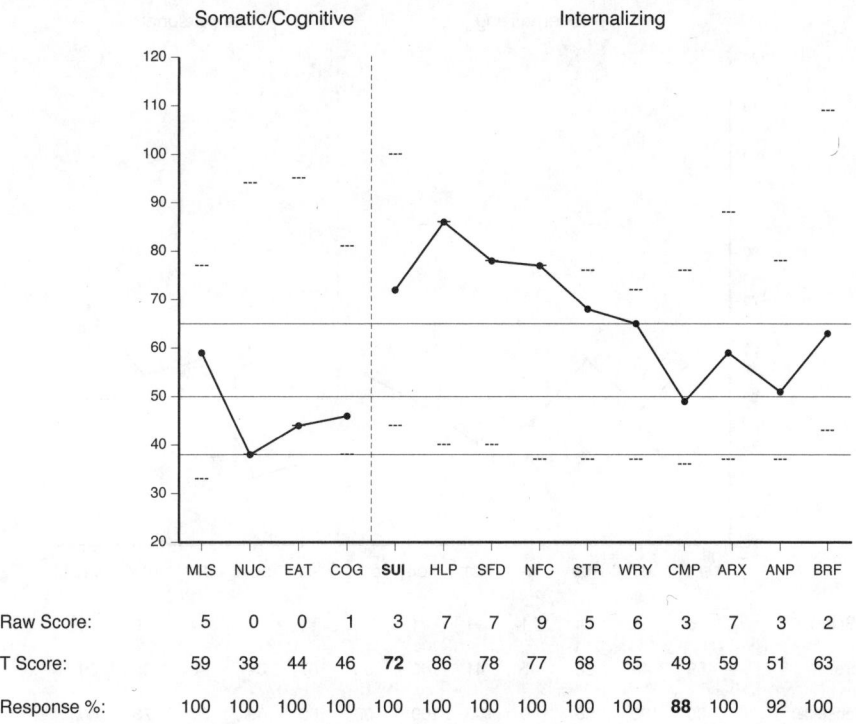

FIGURE 7.1. Mr. J's MMPI-3 Score Report, continued

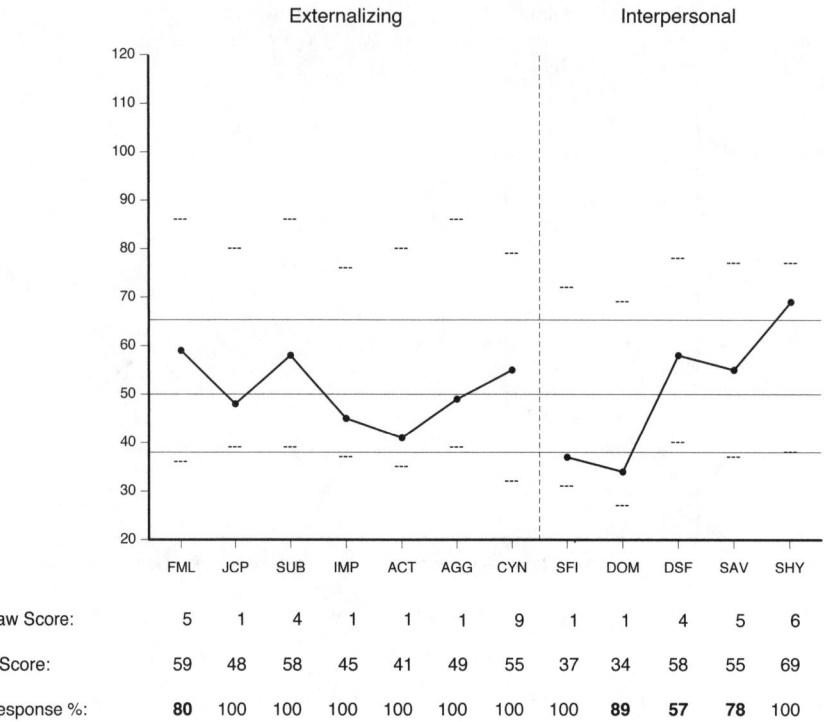

FIGURE 7.1. Mr. J's MMPI-3 Score Report, continued

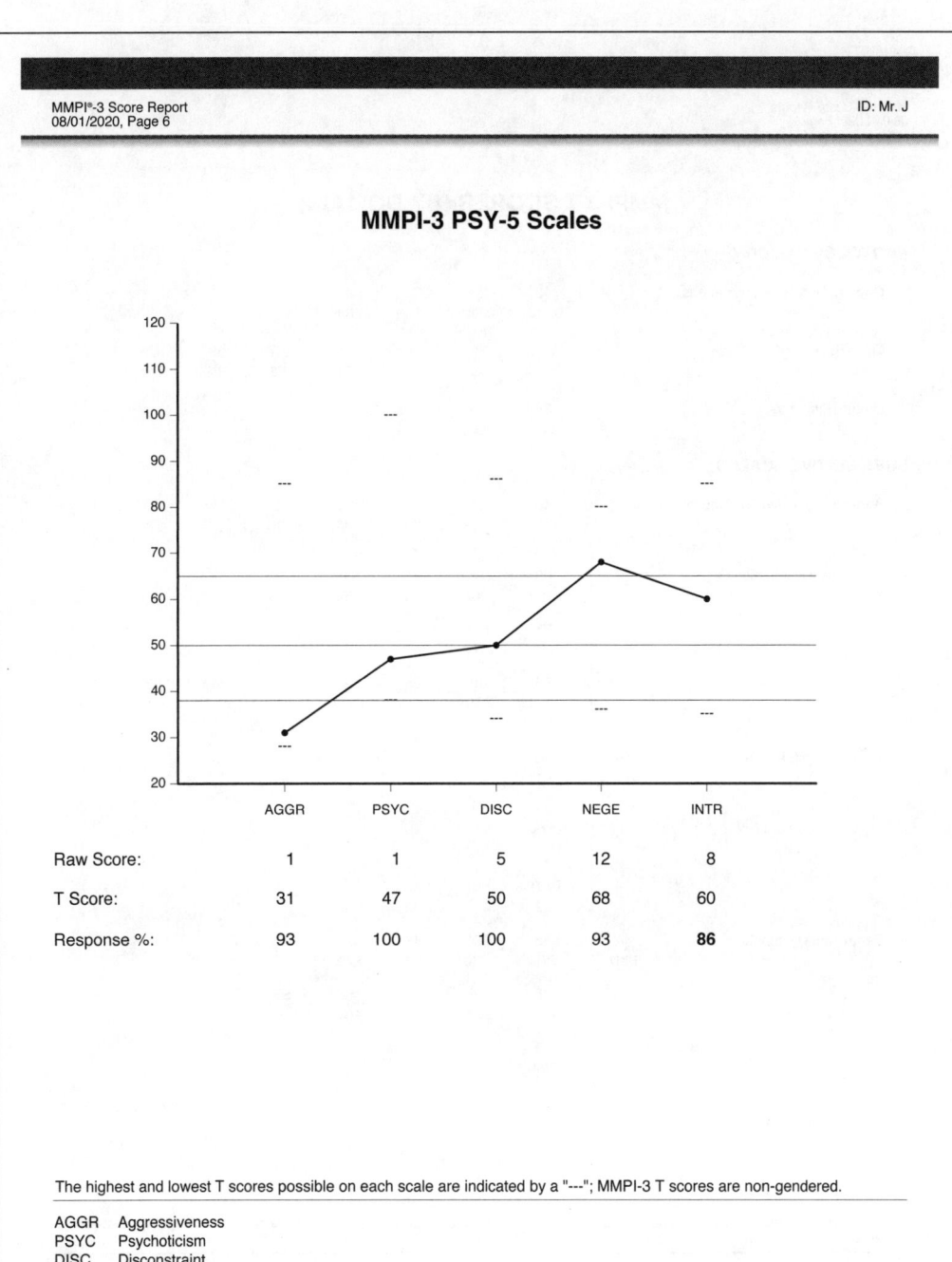

FIGURE 7.1. Mr. J's MMPI-3 Score Report, continued

MMPI-3 T SCORES (BY DOMAIN)

PROTOCOL VALIDITY

Content Non-Responsiveness

CNS	CRIN	VRIN	TRIN
13	39	39	54 T

Over-Reporting

F	Fp	Fs	FBS	RBS
66*	50	47	51	58

Under-Reporting

L	K
36	38

SUBSTANTIVE SCALES

Somatic/Cognitive Dysfunction

RC1	MLS	NUC	EAT	COG
46	59	38	44	46

Emotional Dysfunction

EID: 80

RCd	SUI	HLP	SFD	NFC		
80	72	86	78	77		

RC2	INTR					
75	60*					

RC7	STR	WRY	CMP	ARX	ANP	BRF	NEGE
55	68	65	49*	59	51	63	68

Thought Dysfunction

THD: 49

RC6
50

RC8
44

PSYC
47

Behavioral Dysfunction

BXD: 44

RC4	FML	JCP	SUB
55	59*	48	58

RC9	IMP	ACT	AGG	CYN
36	45	41	49	55

DISC
50

Interpersonal Functioning

SFI	DOM	AGGR	DSF	SAV	SHY
37	34*	31	58*	55*	69

*The test taker provided scorable responses to less than 90% of the items scored on this scale. See the relevant profile page for the specific percentage.

Note. This information is provided to facilitate interpretation following the recommended structure for MMPI-3 interpretation in Chapter 5 of the *MMPI-3 Manual for Administration, Scoring, and Interpretation*, which provides details in the text and an outline in Table 5-1.

FIGURE 7.1. Mr. J's MMPI-3 Score Report, continued

ITEM-LEVEL INFORMATION

Unscorable Responses

Following is a list of items to which the test taker did not provide scorable responses. Unanswered or double answered (both True and False) items are unscorable. The scale(s) on which the items appear are in parentheses following the item content.

    Item number and content omitted. (CRIN, VRIN, SAV, INTR)
    Item number and content omitted. (CMP)
    Item number and content omitted. (CRIN, TRIN, F, DSF)
    Item number and content omitted. (CRIN, TRIN, F, FML)
    Item number and content omitted. (CRIN, VRIN, DSF)
    Item number and content omitted. (FBS)
    Item number and content omitted. (DOM, AGGR)
    Item number and content omitted. (EID, RC2, SAV, INTR)
    Item number and content omitted. (RBS, L)
    Item number and content omitted. (F, FML)
    Item number and content omitted. (CRIN, VRIN, DSF)
    Item number and content omitted. (CRIN, VRIN, EID, ANP, NEGE)
    Item number and content omitted. (F, RC6)

Critical Responses

Seven MMPI-3 scales—Suicidal/Death Ideation (SUI), Helplessness/Hopelessness (HLP), Anxiety-Related Experiences (ARX), Ideas of Persecution (RC6), Aberrant Experiences (RC8), Substance Abuse (SUB), and Aggression (AGG)—have been designated by the test authors as having critical item content that may require immediate attention and follow-up. Items answered by the individual in the keyed direction (True or False) on a critical scale are listed below if his T score on that scale is 65 or higher. However, any item answered in the keyed direction on SUI is listed. The percentage of the MMPI-3 normative sample that answered each item in the keyed direction is provided in parentheses following the item content.

Suicidal/Death Ideation (SUI, T Score = 72)

    Item number and content omitted. (True, 22.2%)
    Item number and content omitted. (True, 8.1%)
    Item number and content omitted. (True, 2.5%)

Helplessness/Hopelessness (HLP, T Score = 86)

    Item number and content omitted. (True, 10.9%)
    Item number and content omitted. (True, 8.7%)
    Item number and content omitted. (True, 12.3%)
    Item number and content omitted. (True, 4.6%)
    Item number and content omitted. (True, 45.4%)
    Item number and content omitted. (False, 22.0%)
    Item number and content omitted. (True, 8.4%)

FIGURE 7.1. Mr. J's MMPI-3 Score Report, continued

User-Designated Item-Level Information

The following item-level information is based on the report user's selection of additional scales, and/or of lower cutoffs for the critical scales from the previous section. Items answered by the test taker in the keyed direction (True or False) on a selected scale are listed below if his T score on that scale is at the user-designated cutoff score or higher. The percentage of the MMPI-3 normative sample that answered each item in the keyed direction is provided in parentheses following the item content.

Demoralization (RCd, T Score = 80)

    Item number and content omitted. (True, 11.3%)
    Item number and content omitted. (True, 44.5%)
    Item number and content omitted. (True, 14.9%)
    Item number and content omitted. (True, 29.4%)
    Item number and content omitted. (True, 41.0%)
    Item number and content omitted. (False, 15.7%)
    Item number and content omitted. (True, 35.3%)
    Item number and content omitted. (True, 23.9%)
    Item number and content omitted. (True, 21.9%)
    Item number and content omitted. (True, 21.5%)
    Item number and content omitted. (True, 58.0%)
    Item number and content omitted. (True, 27.8%)
    Item number and content omitted. (False, 46.0%)
    Item number and content omitted. (True, 28.7%)
    Item number and content omitted. (True, 25.7%)
    Item number and content omitted. (True, 32.0%)
    Item number and content omitted. (True, 22.0%)

Low Positive Emotions (RC2, T Score = 75)

    Item number and content omitted. (False, 17.9%)
    Item number and content omitted. (False, 27.2%)
    Item number and content omitted. (False, 41.2%)
    Item number and content omitted. (False, 29.7%)
    Item number and content omitted. (True, 13.2%)
    Item number and content omitted. (False, 7.3%)
    Item number and content omitted. (False, 9.1%)
    Item number and content omitted. (False, 22.0%)
    Item number and content omitted. (False, 33.5%)
    Item number and content omitted. (False, 27.0%)

Self-Doubt (SFD, T Score = 78)

    Item number and content omitted. (True, 11.3%)
    Item number and content omitted. (True, 29.4%)
    Item number and content omitted. (True, 41.0%)
    Item number and content omitted. (True, 11.8%)
    Item number and content omitted. (True, 28.7%)
    Item number and content omitted. (True, 14.6%)
    Item number and content omitted. (True, 32.0%)

Inefficacy (NFC, T Score = 77)

    Item number and content omitted. (True, 37.7%)
    Item number and content omitted. (True, 45.2%)
    Item number and content omitted. (True, 42.3%)
    Item number and content omitted. (True, 35.3%)

FIGURE 7.1. Mr. J's MMPI-3 Score Report, continued

Item number and content omitted. (True, 23.9%)
Item number and content omitted. (True, 25.2%)
Item number and content omitted. (True, 29.0%)
Item number and content omitted. (True, 20.9%)
Item number and content omitted. (True, 40.2%)

Stress (STR, T Score = 68)

Item number and content omitted. (False, 31.7%)
Item number and content omitted. (False, 26.7%)
Item number and content omitted. (True, 30.9%)
Item number and content omitted. (True, 31.6%)
Item number and content omitted. (False, 58.8%)

Worry (WRY, T Score = 65)

Item number and content omitted. (True, 42.5%)
Item number and content omitted. (True, 26.3%)
Item number and content omitted. (True, 40.6%)
Item number and content omitted. (True, 54.0%)
Item number and content omitted. (True, 57.8%)
Item number and content omitted. (True, 50.9%)

Shyness (SHY, T Score = 69)

Item number and content omitted. (True, 27.8%)
Item number and content omitted. (True, 29.1%)
Item number and content omitted. (True, 38.0%)
Item number and content omitted. (True, 38.6%)
Item number and content omitted. (True, 52.2%)
Item number and content omitted. (False, 32.3%)

Negative Emotionality/Neuroticism (NEGE, T Score = 68)

Item number and content omitted. (True, 31.2%)
Item number and content omitted. (False, 26.7%)
Item number and content omitted. (True, 16.9%)
Item number and content omitted. (True, 26.3%)
Item number and content omitted. (True, 38.4%)
Item number and content omitted. (True, 40.6%)
Item number and content omitted. (True, 46.0%)
Item number and content omitted. (True, 26.0%)
Item number and content omitted. (True, 35.8%)
Item number and content omitted. (True, 59.1%)
Item number and content omitted. (True, 54.0%)
Item number and content omitted. (True, 50.9%)

End of Report

FIGURE 7.1. Mr. J's MMPI-3 Score Report, continued

because different cutoffs are used in the interpretation of scores on these scales (see chapter 8 for details). Three hyphens (---) denote the highest and lowest possible T scores on each scale.

The first three rows of numbers below the profile show the raw score, T score, and percentage of scorable responses to the items on each of the 10 scales. Responses are unscorable when the test taker fails to mark an answer or responds both True and False to an item. The fourth row includes the count of the number of unscorable responses (Cannot Say) in the protocol, which, in the case of Mr. J, is 13.

As described in chapter 8, consideration of scores on the MMPI-3 begins with an examination of the Cannot Say score. The interpretive guidelines indicate that for scales on which less than 90% of the item responses are scorable, the absence of elevation is uninterpretable. Moreover, elevated scores on such scales may underestimate the significance or severity of associated problems. To facilitate identification of scales potentially compromised by an excessive number of unscorable responses, if the percentage of scorable items on a scale falls below 90, it is highlighted in bold in the third row of numbers under the profile. In Mr. J's case, less than 90% of the items on F are scorable. A list of the 13 unscorable items is provided on page 8 of the report.

The third page of the report provides scores on the three Higher-Order (H-O) Scales and the eight Restructured Clinical (RC) Scales. In addition to the features just described for the Validity Scales, the profiles for these and the remaining Substantive Scales include two more lines of demarcation, drawn at T scores of 65 and 38. The higher line, drawn at the 92nd percentile for uniform T scores, indicates the minimal level of elevation required for the interpretive recommendations made in chapter 9 for most of the Substantive Scales. The lower line, indicating the 8th percentile for uniform T scores, is designed to assist in identifying interpretable low scores.

The fourth page of the report provides scores on two sets of MMPI-3 measures, the Somatic/Cognitive and Internalizing Scales. A unique feature on this page of the report appears in cases (such as Mr. J) when the score on the Suicidal/Death Ideation (SUI) scale is elevated. The abbreviated scale name and the T score appear in boldface below the profile to draw the user's attention to that score. The fifth page of the report provides scores for the Externalizing and Interpersonal Scales. Scores for the Personality Psychopathology Five (PSY-5) Scales are provided on page 6 of the report.

MMPI-3 T Scores (by Domain)

The seventh page of the report provides a summary of scores on the 52 MMPI-3 scales organized by domains. This summary page is intended to facilitate the interpretation process by arranging the individual's scores according to the recommended structure for MMPI-3 interpretation with the aid of the MMPI-3 Interpretation Worksheet as described and illustrated in chapter 10. This interpretive approach indicates, for example, that interpretation of the substantive scale scores begins with the most elevated H-O Scale, followed by the RC Scales associated with it in order of elevation. RC scale interpretation incorporates the affiliated SP Scales. On page 7, Mr. J has an elevated score on EID, which would be interpreted first, followed by RCd, SUI, HLP, SFD, and NFC. An asterisk identifies scales for which Mr. J provided less than 90% scorable item responses (F, INTR, CMP, FML, DOM, DSF, and SAV), which, as noted, limits their interpretability.

Item-Level Information

Easily accessible item-level information is another important advantage of automated scoring over hand scoring of the MMPI-3. Although this information can be obtained by detailed examination of the answer sheet, doing so would add considerably to the already time-consuming process of hand scoring the protocol. In the sections below, the three types of item-level information available in the Score Report are described.

UNSCORABLE RESPONSES

A list of items to which the test taker did not provide scorable answers appears under the heading *Unscorable Responses* (see page 8 of the report).[1] As defined earlier, unscorable responses occur when the test taker either fails to mark an answer or responds both True and False to an item. Unscorable items are listed in the order in which they appear in the MMPI-3 protocol. The scale or scales on which each item is scored appear in parentheses following the item number and content. This makes it possible to examine the content of the unscorable items to detect possible themes. If the test taker is available for a follow-up interview, they can be asked why no responses or a double responses were given to these items.

In the example provided on page 8, three of the 13 unscorable items appear on the Disaffiliativeness scale, DSF. Examination of page 5, containing scores on the Interpersonal Scales, indicates that Mr. J provided scorable responses to only 57% of the DSF items. This finding should not be interpreted as an indication that he lacks an interest in affiliating with others, but it does indicate that he avoided responding to test items relating to such attitudes. This could be an area for follow-up as part of the assessment, which could begin with a discussion of why Mr. J did not respond to these specific items.

CRITICAL RESPONSES

A second type of item-level information appears under the heading *Critical Responses*. The critical responses approach relies on scale-level data to identify a test taker who may be experiencing critical difficulties that warrant immediate attention. If they generate an elevated score on one or more of the scales designated as having critical content, then item-level data can be used to identify the specific difficulties being reported by the test taker. The MMPI-3 authors designated seven Substantive Scales as having critical item content that might require immediate attention and follow-up: Suicidal/Death Ideation (SUI), Helplessness/Hopelessness (HLP), Anxiety-Related Experiences (ARX), Ideas of Persecution (RC6), Aberrant Experiences (RC8), Substance Abuse (SUB), and Aggression (AGG). Items answered by the individual in the keyed direction on a critical scale are listed if the test taker's T score on that scale is 65 or higher (except for the SUI scale, discussed next). The percentage of the MMPI-3 normative sample who answered each item listed in the keyed direction is provided in parentheses following the item content. Because of the particularly critical nature of the items scored on the SUI scale, any item answered in the keyed direction on this scale will be listed in this section and printed in bold.

The Critical Responses list informs the interpreter of the specific responses a test taker gave to obtain an elevated score on the seven scales identified as having critical item content. This information can be used to guide a follow-up interview that might include asking the test taker to elaborate on certain responses they provided. To protect test security and avoid inadvertently coaching test takers, we recommend test users refrain from reading specific item content when following up on critical responses. Instead, inquire about content themes rather than specific item content. Test takers sometimes attribute their responses to misunderstanding the item content or incorrectly recording their answers. However, if a test taker cites multiple such misunderstandings or mistakes to "explain away" a pattern of unusual or otherwise worrisome responses, this may raise questions about their explanations.

In the example provided on page 8, Mr. J has elevated scores on two of the seven scales: SUI and HLP. The unredacted item-level responses for SUI show that he wishes that he were dead and that he has thought about attempting to kill himself and how he might do so. This information should trigger an immediate assessment of suicide risk. Responses to critical items on HLP raise concerns about despair and an elevated risk for self-harm.

USER-DESIGNATED ITEM-LEVEL INFORMATION

The Pearson scoring and reporting systems provide an option for the user to designate additional scales and/or alternative cutoff levels for generating a third type of item-level information. Users can select any MMPI-3 scale for inclusion in this part of the report. By default, item-level information will be printed if a test taker's score reaches a level for which interpretive recommendations are provided in chapter 9 (excluding interpretive recommendations for low scores). For the Substantive Scales, the default T-score cutoff is 65. The default values for the validity indicators vary depending upon the interpretive recommendations provided in chapter 8.

The ability to customize cutoffs can be particularly helpful in settings in which interpretable deviations from reference group means occur at lower levels. For example, cutoffs of 60 and 55 can be used to identify potentially problematic characteristics of candidates for public safety positions. In such cases, users may wish to select alternative cutoffs for generating supplementary item-level information.

The option to select additional scales can be helpful when an initial review of the results identifies areas requiring further attention in addition to those incorporated in the Critical Responses section. For example, an elevated score on RCd is a central finding in Mr. J's case. Although RCd, RC2, SFD, NFC, STR, WRY, SHY, and NEGE are not among the scales in the Critical Responses section, selecting them for inclusion in the User-Designated Item-Level Information section in this case provides additional information about Mr. J's problems (see pages 9–10 of Figure 7.1).

An MMPI-3 Score Report can be reprinted with different options selected (e.g., adding scales to the User-Designated Item-Level Information list) without incurring additional cost. One approach to using this option is to begin with a preliminary examination of the report with no scales selected for this section. If the user then identifies additional scales or alternative cutoffs that might provide useful information, these options can be selected and the report reprinted. Chapter 5 of the *MMPI-3 User's Guide for the Score and Clinical Interpretive Reports* (Ben-Porath & Tellegen, 2020c) includes a detailed description of how to interface with the Pearson scoring and reporting systems to select additional scales and alternative cutoffs.

Comparison Groups

The Pearson scoring and reporting systems used to generate the Score Report and Interpretive Report for Clinical Settings provide an option to plot the test taker's MMPI-3 standard scores along with descriptive data for various comparison groups. The descriptive data include means and standard deviations on all 52 scales, the percentage of individuals in the comparison group who scored at or below the test taker on each scale, and the percentage of individuals in the comparison group who responded the same as the test taker to the items listed under Critical Responses and User-Designated Item-Level Information. These data make it possible to compare a test taker's scores and item-level responses with those of individuals tested in a similar setting, usually under similar circumstances, or with just the men or just the women of the MMPI-3 normative sample. This additional, setting-specific information complements what can be learned from the standard T scores and item-level information included in the reports, which characterize the test taker's scores and responses in reference to the general population norms. Two options are available for selecting comparison groups, as discussed next.

STANDARD COMPARISON GROUPS

A set of standard comparison groups, representing a range of settings in which the MMPI-3 is used, is available for selection in the Pearson scoring and reporting systems. This optional feature is illustrated in Figure 7.2 for the same case that was just used to illustrate the Score Report. As a reminder, the scores are those of Mr. J, a 44-year-old man tested at intake to an outpatient community mental health center. Therefore, the outpatient community mental health sample of men was selected as the comparison group for this protocol. All the standard information included in the MMPI-3 reports (i.e., raw scores, T scores, percentage of items answered on each scale, and item-level information) is printed when the comparison group option is chosen. As shown on pages 2–6 of Figure 7.2, the comparison group data are plotted with dashed lines connecting the sample's mean scores (marked by open diamonds) and grey bars reflecting the associated standard deviation for each mean. (By contrast, the standard scores are represented by a solid line.) These descriptive data are also reported numerically under the test taker's scores below the profile. A third row, below the comparison group means and standard deviations, reports, for each scale, the percentage of comparison group members who scored at or below the test taker's score for that scale. Although calculated in a somewhat different manner, these values are similar to and can be interpreted the same as percentiles.

Page 2 shows that the mean T score on CRIN for the 233 men in the comparison group of community mental health outpatients is 54, with a standard deviation of 8. The bar for CRIN on the profile represents a range of one standard deviation above and below the group's mean score on this scale (i.e., 46–62). Mr. J's score (39) is 15 points lower than the comparison group mean, indicating that overall, his MMPI-3 responses were considerably more consistent than those of the comparison group members. The final row of data below the CRIN score shows that only 4% of the individuals in the comparison group scored at or below Mr. J's T score of 39 on the CRIN scale. His VRIN T score of 39 is also quite low for a mental health outpatient. Only 7% of the male outpatient community mental health comparison group members scored at or below this level on VRIN. Mr. J's scores fall within one standard deviation of the mean on TRIN, F, Fp, Fs, FBS, and RBS. His T score of 36 on L falls considerably below the comparison group mean (50). Only 5% of the men in this group score this low on L. The added perspective afforded by comparison group findings can be seen by consideration of Mr. J's T score of 38 on K, which, though similar in

Score Report

MMPI®-3
Minnesota Multiphasic Personality Inventory®-3
Yossef S. Ben-Porath, PhD, & Auke Tellegen, PhD

ID Number:	Mr. J
Age:	44
Gender:	Male
Marital Status:	Not reported
Years of Education:	Not reported
Date Assessed:	08/01/2020

Copyright © 2020 by the Regents of the University of Minnesota. All rights reserved. Distributed exclusively under license from the University of Minnesota by NCS Pearson, Inc. Portions reproduced from the MMPI-3 test booklet. Copyright © 2020 by the Regents of the University of Minnesota. All rights reserved. Portions excerpted from the *MMPI-3 Manual for Administration, Scoring, and Interpretation*. Copyright © 2020 by the Regents of the University of Minnesota. All rights reserved. Portions excerpted from the *MMPI-3 Technical Manual*. Copyright © 2020 by the Regents of the University of Minnesota. All rights reserved. Used by permission of the University of Minnesota Press.

Minnesota Multiphasic Personality Inventory and **MMPI** are registered trademarks of the University of Minnesota. **Pearson** is a trademark in the U.S. and/or other countries of Pearson Education, Inc., or its affiliate(s).

This report contains copyrighted material and trade secrets. Qualified licensees may excerpt portions of this output report, limited to the minimum text necessary to accurately describe their significant core conclusions, for incorporation into a written evaluation of the examinee, in accordance with their profession's citation standards, if any. No adaptations, translations, modifications, or special versions may be made of this report without prior written permission from the University of Minnesota Press.

[1.0 / RE1 / QG1]

ALWAYS LEARNING   PEARSON

FIGURE 7.2. Mr. J's MMPI-3 Score Report With Comparison Group Data

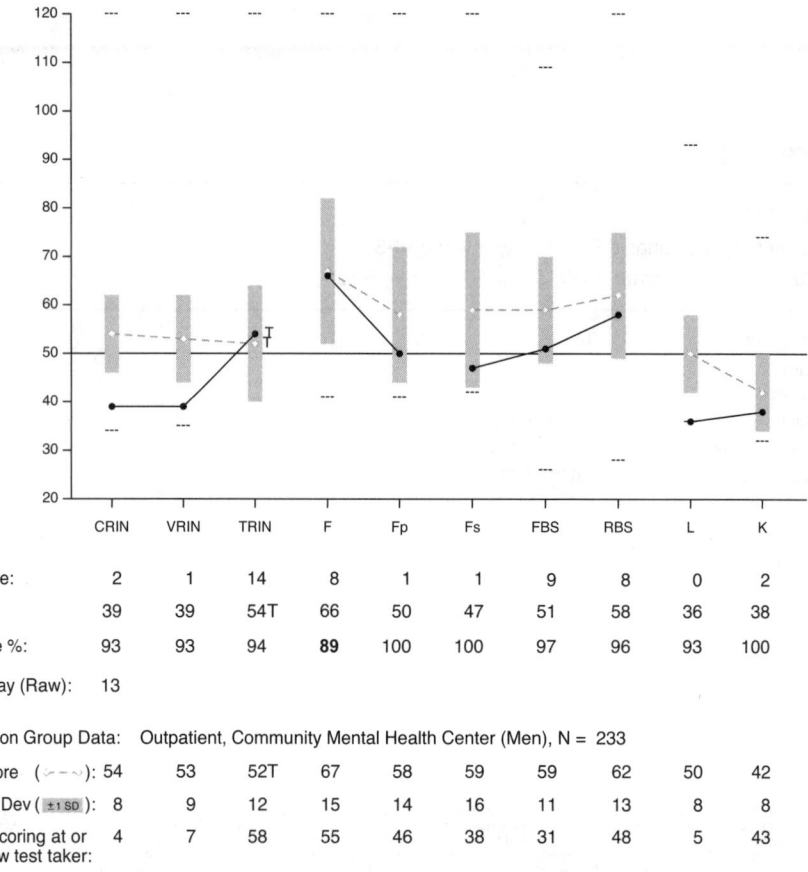

FIGURE 7.2. Mr. J's MMPI-3 Score Report With Comparison Group Data, continued

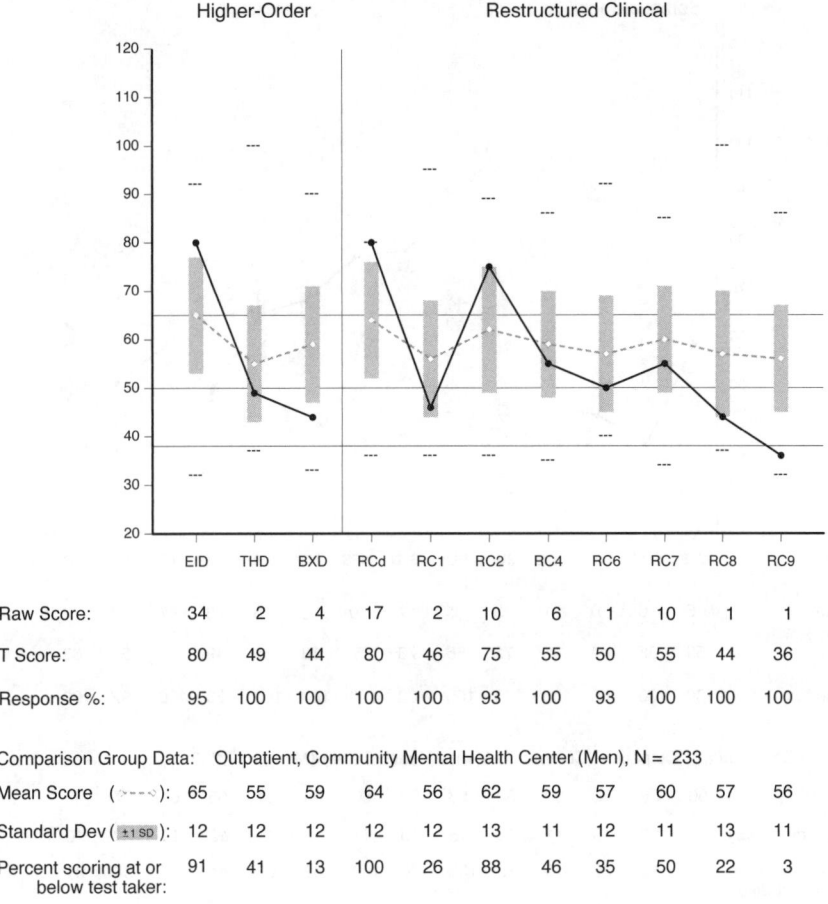

FIGURE 7.2. Mr. J's MMPI-3 Score Report With Comparison Group Data, continued

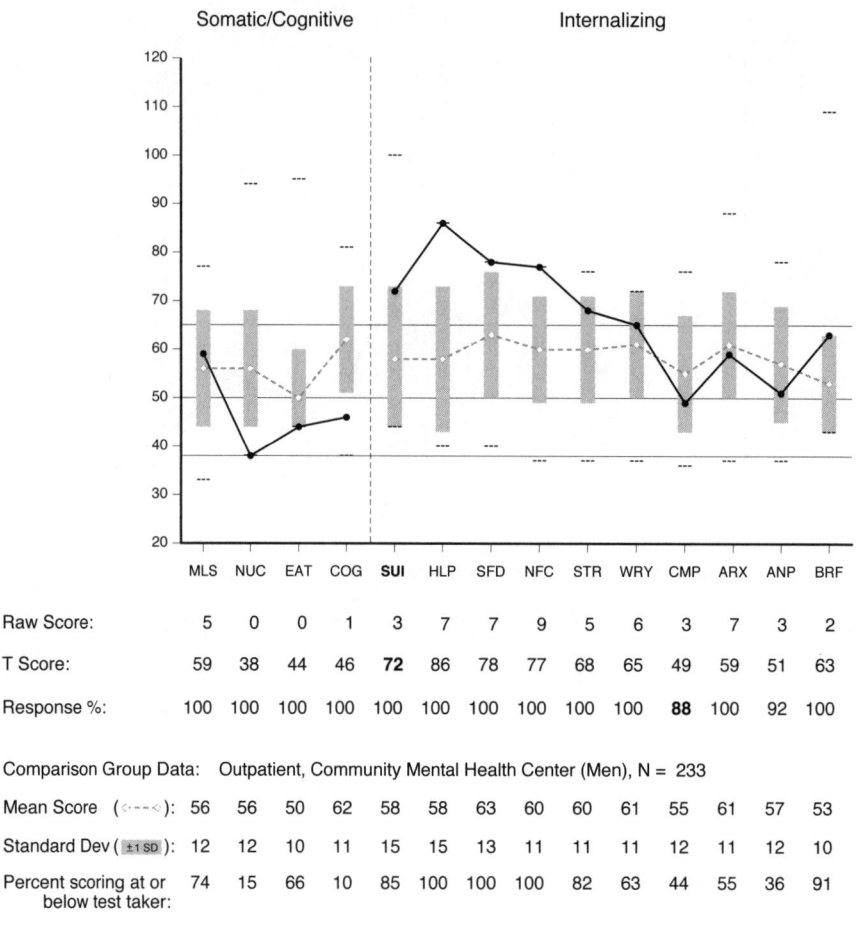

FIGURE 7.2. Mr. J's MMPI-3 Score Report With Comparison Group Data, continued

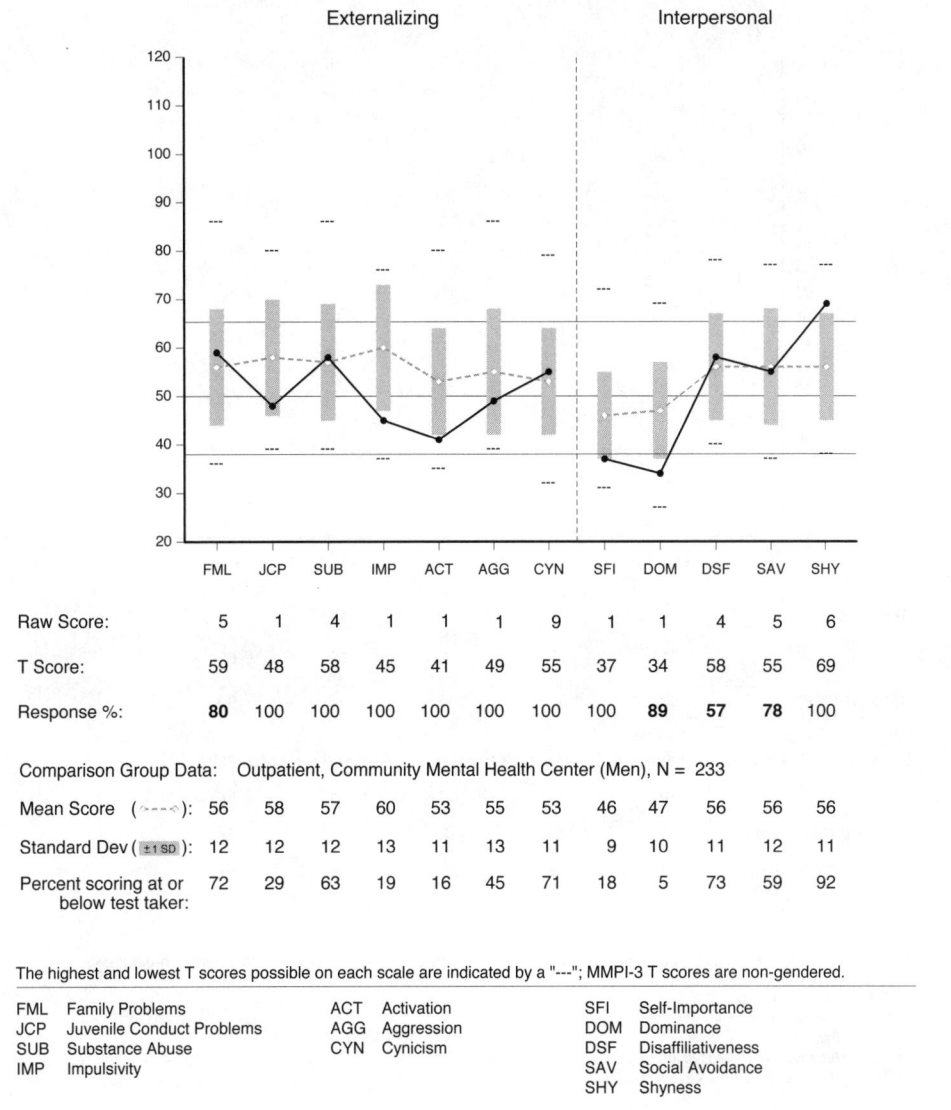

FIGURE 7.2. Mr. J's MMPI-3 Score Report With Comparison Group Data, continued

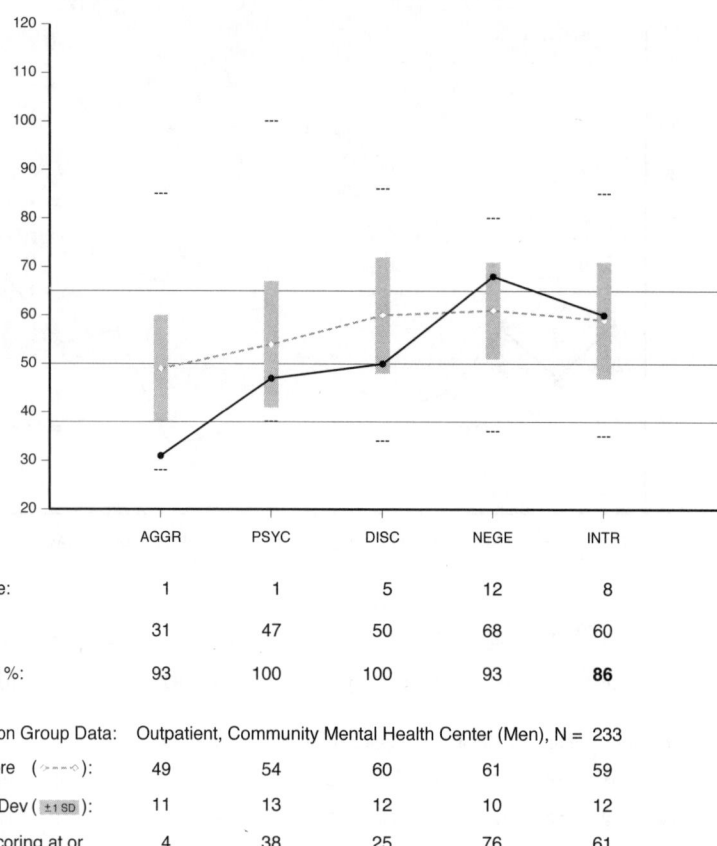

FIGURE 7.2. Mr. J's MMPI-3 Score Report With Comparison Group Data, continued

MMPI-3 T SCORES (BY DOMAIN)

PROTOCOL VALIDITY

Content Non-Responsiveness

13	39	39	54 T
CNS	CRIN	VRIN	TRIN

Over-Reporting

66*	50		47	51	58
F	Fp		Fs	FBS	RBS

Under-Reporting

36	38
L	K

SUBSTANTIVE SCALES

Somatic/Cognitive Dysfunction

	46	59	38	44	46
	RC1	MLS	NUC	EAT	COG

Emotional Dysfunction

80							
EID							

80	72	86	78	77
RCd	SUI	HLP	SFD	NFC

75	60*
RC2	INTR

55	68	65	49*	59	51	63	68
RC7	STR	WRY	CMP	ARX	ANP	BRF	NEGE

Thought Dysfunction

49
THD

50
RC6

44
RC8

47
PSYC

Behavioral Dysfunction

44
BXD

55	59*	48	58
RC4	FML	JCP	SUB

36	45	41	49	55
RC9	IMP	ACT	AGG	CYN

50
DISC

Interpersonal Functioning

37	34*	31	58*	55*	69
SFI	DOM	AGGR	DSF	SAV	SHY

*The test taker provided scorable responses to less than 90% of the items scored on this scale. See the relevant profile page for the specific percentage.

Note. This information is provided to facilitate interpretation following the recommended structure for MMPI-3 interpretation in Chapter 5 of the *MMPI-3 Manual for Administration, Scoring, and Interpretation*, which provides details in the text and an outline in Table 5-1.

FIGURE 7.2. Mr. J's MMPI-3 Score Report With Comparison Group Data, continued

ITEM-LEVEL INFORMATION

Unscorable Responses

Following is a list of items to which the test taker did not provide scorable responses. Unanswered or double answered (both True and False) items are unscorable. The scale(s) on which the items appear are in parentheses following the item content.

    Item number and content omitted. (CRIN, VRIN, SAV, INTR)
    Item number and content omitted. (CMP)
    Item number and content omitted. (CRIN, TRIN, F, DSF)
    Item number and content omitted. (CRIN, TRIN, F, FML)
    Item number and content omitted. (CRIN, VRIN, DSF)
    Item number and content omitted. (FBS)
    Item number and content omitted. (DOM, AGGR)
    Item number and content omitted. (EID, RC2, SAV, INTR)
    Item number and content omitted. (RBS, L)
    Item number and content omitted. (F, FML)
    Item number and content omitted. (CRIN, VRIN, DSF)
    Item number and content omitted. (CRIN, VRIN, EID, ANP, NEGE)
    Item number and content omitted. (F, RC6)

Critical Responses

Seven MMPI-3 scales—Suicidal/Death Ideation (SUI), Helplessness/Hopelessness (HLP), Anxiety-Related Experiences (ARX), Ideas of Persecution (RC6), Aberrant Experiences (RC8), Substance Abuse (SUB), and Aggression (AGG)—have been designated by the test authors as having critical item content that may require immediate attention and follow-up. Items answered by the individual in the keyed direction (True or False) on a critical scale are listed below if his T score on that scale is 65 or higher. However, any item answered in the keyed direction on SUI is listed. The percentage of the MMPI-3 normative sample (NS) and of the Outpatient, Community Mental Health Center (Men) Comparison Group (CG) that answered each item in the keyed direction are provided in parentheses following the item content.

Suicidal/Death Ideation (SUI, T Score = 72)
    Item number and content omitted. (True; NS 22.2%, CG 43.3%)
    Item number and content omitted. (True; NS 8.1%, CG 25.8%)
    Item number and content omitted. (True; NS 2.5%, CG 20.2%)

Helplessness/Hopelessness (HLP, T Score = 86)
    Item number and content omitted. (True; NS 10.9%, CG 21.9%)
    Item number and content omitted. (True; NS 8.7%, CG 37.3%)
    Item number and content omitted. (True; NS 12.3%, CG 23.6%)
    Item number and content omitted. (True; NS 4.6%, CG 28.3%)
    Item number and content omitted. (True; NS 45.4%, CG 50.6%)
    Item number and content omitted. (False; NS 22.0%, CG 40.8%)
    Item number and content omitted. (True; NS 8.4%, CG 27.9%)

FIGURE 7.2. Mr. J's MMPI-3 Score Report With Comparison Group Data, continued

User-Designated Item-Level Information

The following item-level information is based on the report user's selection of additional scales, and/or of lower cutoffs for the critical scales from the previous section. Items answered by the test taker in the keyed direction (True or False) on a selected scale are listed below if his T score on that scale is at the user-designated cutoff score or higher. The percentage of the MMPI-3 normative sample (NS) and of the Outpatient, Community Mental Health Center (Men) Comparison Group (CG) that answered each item in the keyed direction are provided in parentheses following the item content.

Demoralization (RCd, T Score = 80)

    Item number and content omitted. (True; NS 11.3%, CG 50.6%)
    Item number and content omitted. (True; NS 44.5%, CG 82.8%)
    Item number and content omitted. (True; NS 14.9%, CG 55.8%)
    Item number and content omitted. (True; NS 29.4%, CG 66.1%)
    Item number and content omitted. (True; NS 41.0%, CG 74.7%)
    Item number and content omitted. (False; NS 15.7%, CG 60.9%)
    Item number and content omitted. (True; NS 35.3%, CG 68.2%)
    Item number and content omitted. (True; NS 23.9%, CG 51.5%)
    Item number and content omitted. (True; NS 21.9%, CG 58.4%)
    Item number and content omitted. (True; NS 21.5%, CG 59.7%)
    Item number and content omitted. (True; NS 58.0%, CG 86.7%)
    Item number and content omitted. (True; NS 27.8%, CG 67.8%)
    Item number and content omitted. (False; NS 46.0%, CG 75.1%)
    Item number and content omitted. (True; NS 28.7%, CG 70.8%)
    Item number and content omitted. (True; NS 25.7%, CG 61.8%)
    Item number and content omitted. (True; NS 32.0%, CG 69.5%)
    Item number and content omitted. (True; NS 22.0%, CG 60.5%)

Low Positive Emotions (RC2, T Score = 75)

    Item number and content omitted. (False; NS 17.9%, CG 57.1%)
    Item number and content omitted. (False; NS 27.2%, CG 51.1%)
    Item number and content omitted. (False; NS 41.2%, CG 59.7%)
    Item number and content omitted. (False; NS 29.7%, CG 50.6%)
    Item number and content omitted. (True; NS 13.2%, CG 49.8%)
    Item number and content omitted. (False; NS 7.3%, CG 36.1%)
    Item number and content omitted. (False; NS 9.1%, CG 27.9%)
    Item number and content omitted. (False; NS 22.0%, CG 40.8%)
    Item number and content omitted. (False; NS 33.5%, CG 51.9%)
    Item number and content omitted. (False; NS 27.0%, CG 48.9%)

Self-Doubt (SFD, T Score = 78)

    Item number and content omitted. (True; NS 11.3%, CG 50.6%)
    Item number and content omitted. (True; NS 29.4%, CG 66.1%)
    Item number and content omitted. (True; NS 41.0%, CG 74.7%)
    Item number and content omitted. (True; NS 11.8%, CG 52.4%)
    Item number and content omitted. (True; NS 28.7%, CG 70.8%)
    Item number and content omitted. (True; NS 14.6%, CG 42.9%)
    Item number and content omitted. (True; NS 32.0%, CG 69.5%)

Inefficacy (NFC, T Score = 77)

    Item number and content omitted. (True; NS 37.7%, CG 67.0%)

FIGURE 7.2. Mr. J's MMPI-3 Score Report With Comparison Group Data, continued

Item number and content omitted. (True; NS 45.2%, CG 63.1%)
Item number and content omitted. (True; NS 42.3%, CG 62.2%)
Item number and content omitted. (True; NS 35.3%, CG 68.2%)
Item number and content omitted. (True; NS 23.9%, CG 51.5%)
Item number and content omitted. (True; NS 25.2%, CG 47.2%)
Item number and content omitted. (True; NS 29.0%, CG 66.5%)
Item number and content omitted. (True; NS 20.9%, CG 48.5%)
Item number and content omitted. (True; NS 40.2%, CG 62.7%)

Stress (STR, T Score = 68)

Item number and content omitted. (False; NS 31.7%, CG 54.9%)
Item number and content omitted. (False; NS 26.7%, CG 53.6%)
Item number and content omitted. (True; NS 30.9%, CG 57.9%)
Item number and content omitted. (True; NS 31.6%, CG 66.1%)
Item number and content omitted. (False; NS 58.8%, CG 89.3%)

Worry (WRY, T Score = 65)

Item number and content omitted. (True; NS 42.5%, CG 79.0%)
Item number and content omitted. (True; NS 26.3%, CG 60.9%)
Item number and content omitted. (True; NS 40.6%, CG 71.7%)
Item number and content omitted. (True; NS 54.0%, CG 84.1%)
Item number and content omitted. (True; NS 57.8%, CG 76.8%)
Item number and content omitted. (True; NS 50.9%, CG 83.3%)

Shyness (SHY, T Score = 69)

Item number and content omitted. (True; NS 27.8%, CG 56.7%)
Item number and content omitted. (True; NS 29.1%, CG 46.8%)
Item number and content omitted. (True; NS 38.0%, CG 56.7%)
Item number and content omitted. (True; NS 38.6%, CG 63.9%)
Item number and content omitted. (True; NS 52.2%, CG 66.5%)
Item number and content omitted. (False; NS 32.3%, CG 52.4%)

Negative Emotionality/Neuroticism (NEGE, T Score = 68)

Item number and content omitted. (True; NS 31.2%, CG 77.3%)
Item number and content omitted. (False; NS 26.7%, CG 53.6%)
Item number and content omitted. (True; NS 16.9%, CG 44.2%)
Item number and content omitted. (True; NS 26.3%, CG 60.9%)
Item number and content omitted. (True; NS 38.4%, CG 67.4%)
Item number and content omitted. (True; NS 40.6%, CG 71.7%)
Item number and content omitted. (True; NS 46.0%, CG 66.5%)
Item number and content omitted. (True; NS 26.0%, CG 73.0%)
Item number and content omitted. (True; NS 35.8%, CG 75.1%)
Item number and content omitted. (True; NS 59.1%, CG 83.7%)
Item number and content omitted. (True; NS 54.0%, CG 84.1%)
Item number and content omitted. (True; NS 50.9%, CG 83.3%)

End of Report

FIGURE 7.2. Mr. J's MMPI-3 Score Report With Comparison Group Data, continued

T score terms to his score on L, falls well within the range of scores obtained by comparison group members on the K scale.

Page 4 of Figure 7.2 illustrates an important caveat regarding interpretation of comparison group data. Although Mr. J's T score (72) on the Suicidal/Death Ideation (SUI) scale falls within one standard deviation from the mean for male community mental health outpatients, this in no way mitigates the significance of the finding that he produced a substantially elevated score on this scale, which indicates that he is preoccupied with suicide and may be at risk for death by suicide. Significant deviations from the comparison group mean on a scale may provide additional information about the test taker, but any scores that reach the cutoffs for interpretation recommended in chapter 9 remain interpretable.

Page 5 illustrates another important caveat. Mr. J's T score (34) on the DOM scale falls considerably below the community mental health outpatient mean (47) on this scale. However, as highlighted in the Response % row under this scale, Mr. J provided scorable responses to less than 90% of the DOM items, which renders his low score uninterpretable in this case. In contrast, Mr. J's low score (31) on AGGR (page 6) is interpretable and indicates that he is likely interpersonally passive and unassertive.

Comparison group data are also provided for item-level information (redacted for test security purposes on pages 8–10 of Figure 7.2). Specifically, if the test taker produces an elevated score on one or more of the seven scales identified as having critical item content or on a scale selected for the User-Designated Item-Level Information section, the percentage of the members of the normative sample (NS) and the comparison group (CG) who answered the items on these scales in the keyed direction is presented. For example, on page 8, we see that 22.2% of the normative sample responded True to the first item listed under Suicidal/Death Ideation, compared to 43.3% of the men in the community mental health outpatient sample.

CUSTOM COMPARISON GROUPS

Pearson's scoring systems for the MMPI-3 include a feature for generating custom comparison groups from cases previously scored. Chapter 5 of the *MMPI-3 User's Guide for the Score and Clinical Interpretive Reports* describes the procedures for doing so in detail. Following is a brief description of the process. After activating this module, the user is prompted to assign a name to the custom comparison group and identify cases to be included. A minimum of 200 valid cases is required to form a comparison group. The same exclusionary criteria used when forming the standard comparison groups are employed with user-designated comparison groups. Protocols with excessive item omissions (Cannot Say ≥ 18), inconsistent responding (CRIN, VRIN, or TRIN ≥ 80), or infrequent responding (F or Fp ≥ 100) are considered invalid for this purpose.

After a sample of at least 200 valid cases is selected, the scoring and reporting system calculates raw score means and standard deviations for the 52 MMPI-3 scales and converts them to T-score values. The custom comparison group is then added to a drop-down menu under the user-supplied name for this group. Users can export these files should they choose to share their custom comparison groups with other users.

An MMPI-3 protocol can be printed along with the means and standard deviations for any of the standard or custom comparison groups. It is possible to reprint the report with different comparison groups at no additional cost. However, it is not possible to include more than one comparison group in the same printing of the report.

The MMPI-3 Interpretive Report for Clinical Settings

The *MMPI-3 Interpretive Report for Clinical Settings* (referred to as the "Interpretive Report" throughout this chapter) consists of all the information provided in the Score Report, including the optional comparison group data just described, as well as an automated interpretation of the test results. The interpretation is based on the interpretive guidelines provided in chapters 8 and 9. The demographic information needed to produce a Score Report (described earlier) is also required to generate an Interpretive Report.

Figure 7.3 provides the standard output of the Interpretive Report for the MMPI-3 results of Mr. J, whose test results were also used to illustrate features of the Score Report and the optional comparison groups. Pages 1–6 include the same cover page and scale score profiles that appear in the Score Report for this case. Page 7, which provides the MMPI-3 T Scores (by Domain) information, differs from the Score Report summary page in that any score interpreted in the report (e.g., EID 80) is printed in bold.

The computer-generated interpretation begins on page 8 of the report. The opening paragraphs in every report state:

> *This interpretive report is intended for use by a professional qualified to interpret the MMPI-3. The information it contains should be considered in the context of the test taker's background, the circumstances of the assessment, and other available information.*
>
> *The report includes extensive annotation, which appears as superscripts following each statement in the narrative, keyed to Endnotes with accompanying Research References, which appear in the final two sections of the report. Additional information about the annotation features is provided in the headnotes to these sections and in the* MMPI-3 User's Guide for the Score and Clinical Interpretive Reports.

Minnesota Multiphasic Personality Inventory®-3

Interpretive Report: Clinical Settings

MMPI®-3
Minnesota Multiphasic Personality Inventory®-3
Yossef S. Ben-Porath, PhD, & Auke Tellegen, PhD

ID Number:	Mr. J
Age:	44
Gender:	Male
Marital Status:	Not reported
Years of Education:	Not reported
Date Assessed:	08/01/2020

Copyright © 2020 by the Regents of the University of Minnesota. All rights reserved. Distributed exclusively under license from the University of Minnesota by NCS Pearson, Inc. Portions reproduced from the MMPI-3 test booklet. Copyright © 2020 by the Regents of the University of Minnesota. All rights reserved. Portions excerpted from the *MMPI-3 Manual for Administration, Scoring, and Interpretation.* Copyright © 2020 by the Regents of the University of Minnesota. All rights reserved. Portions excerpted from the *MMPI-3 Technical Manual.* Copyright © 2020 by the Regents of the University of Minnesota. All rights reserved. Used by permission of the University of Minnesota Press.

Minnesota Multiphasic Personality Inventory and **MMPI** are registered trademarks of the University of Minnesota. **Pearson** is a trademark in the U.S. and/or other countries of Pearson Education, Inc., or its affiliate(s).

This report contains copyrighted material and trade secrets. Qualified licensees may excerpt portions of this output report, limited to the minimum text necessary to accurately describe their significant core conclusions, for incorporation into a written evaluation of the examinee, in accordance with their profession's citation standards, if any. No adaptations, translations, modifications, or special versions may be made of this report without prior written permission from the University of Minnesota Press.

[1.0 / RE1 / QG1]

ALWAYS LEARNING   **PEARSON**

FIGURE 7.3. Mr. J's MMPI-3 Interpretive Report for Clinical Settings

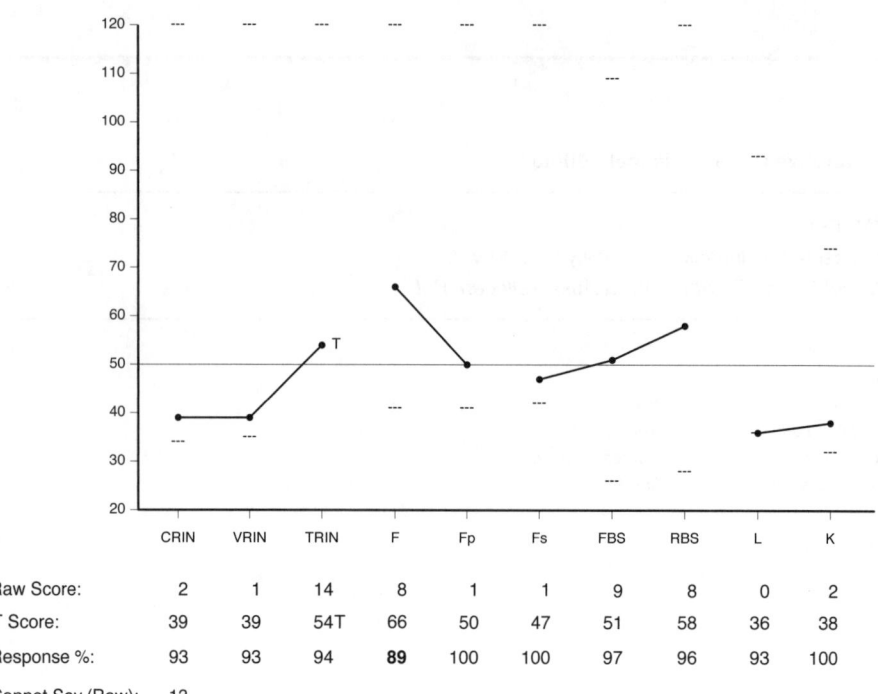

FIGURE 7.3. Mr. J's MMPI-3 Interpretive Report for Clinical Settings, continued

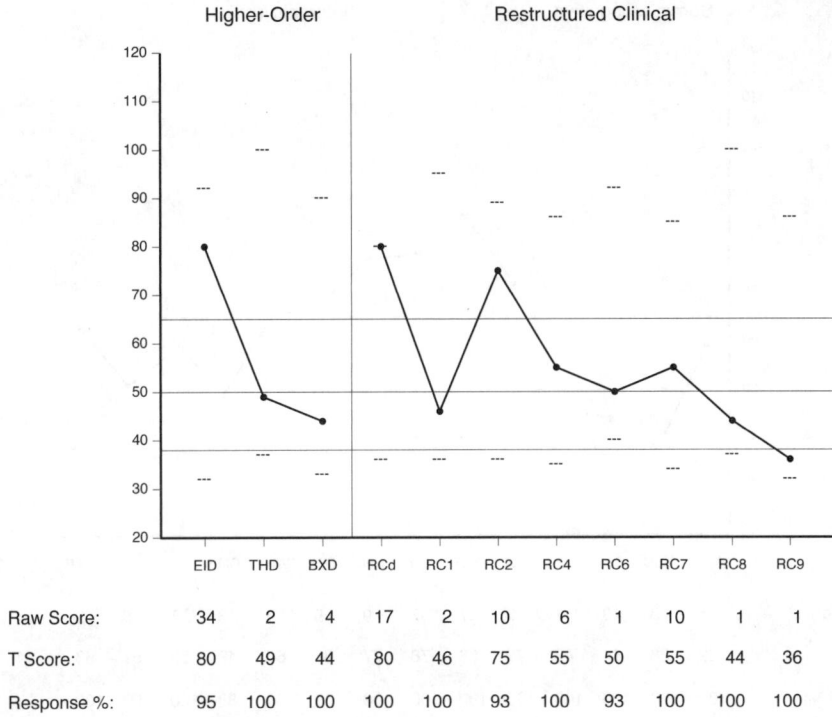

FIGURE 7.3. Mr. J's MMPI-3 Interpretive Report for Clinical Settings, continued

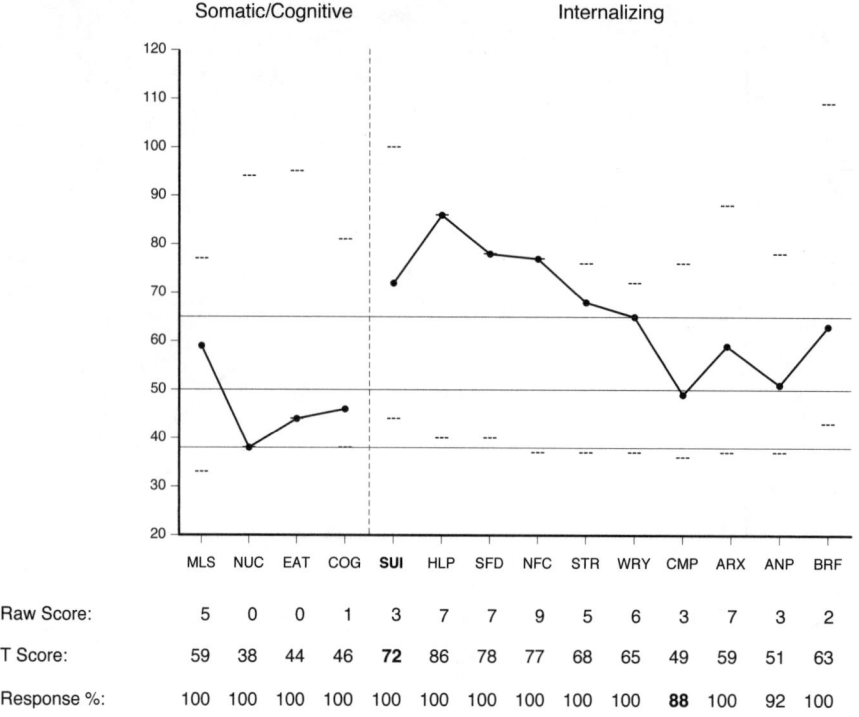

FIGURE 7.3. Mr. J's MMPI-3 Interpretive Report for Clinical Settings, continued

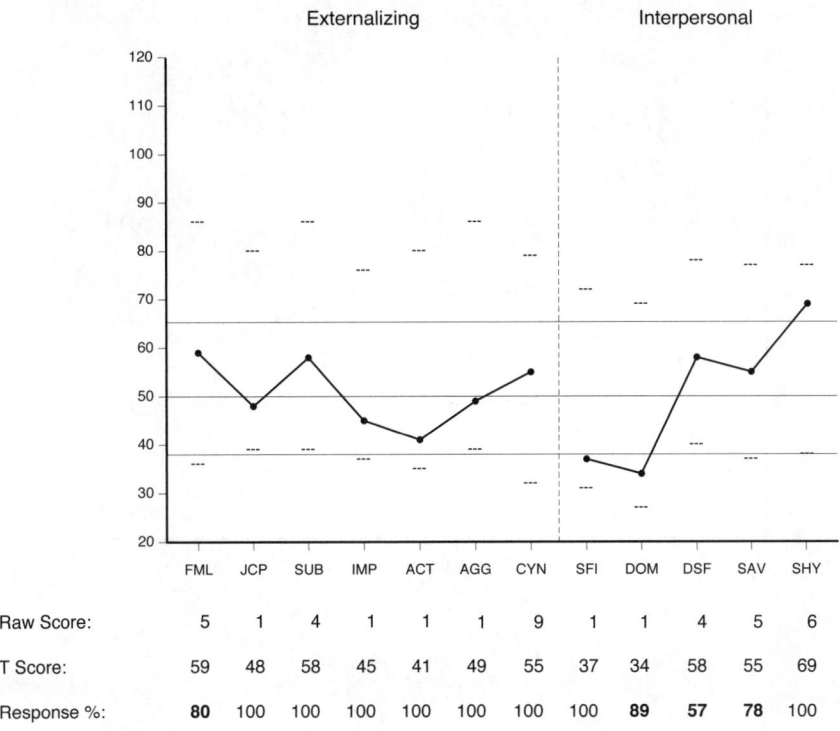

FIGURE 7.3. Mr. J's MMPI-3 Interpretive Report for Clinical Settings, continued

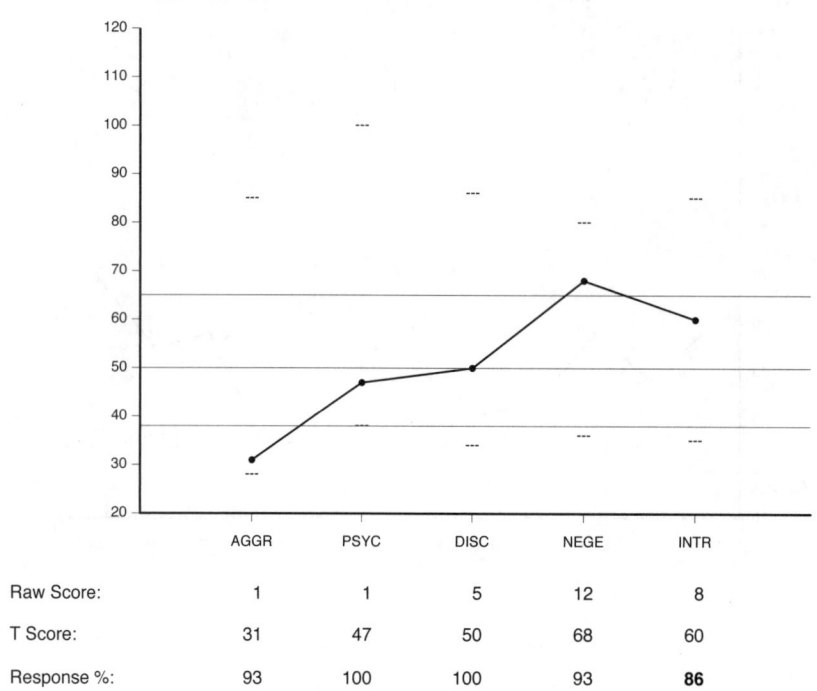

FIGURE 7.3. Mr. J's MMPI-3 Interpretive Report for Clinical Settings, continued

MMPI-3 T SCORES (BY DOMAIN)

PROTOCOL VALIDITY

Content Non-Responsiveness

13	39	39	54 T
CNS	CRIN	VRIN	TRIN

Over-Reporting

66*	50		47	51	58
F	Fp		Fs	FBS	RBS

Under-Reporting

36	38
L	K

SUBSTANTIVE SCALES

Somatic/Cognitive Dysfunction

46	59	38	44	46
RC1	MLS	NUC	EAT	COG

Emotional Dysfunction

80	**80**	72	**86**	78	77
EID	**RCd**	SUI	**HLP**	SFD	NFC

	75	60*			
	RC2	INTR			

	55	**68**	65	49*	59	51	63	**68**
	RC7	**STR**	WRY	CMP	ARX	ANP	BRF	**NEGE**

Thought Dysfunction

49	50
THD	RC6

	44
	RC8

	47
	PSYC

Behavioral Dysfunction

44	55	59*	48	58
BXD	RC4	FML	JCP	SUB

	36	45	41	49	55
	RC9	IMP	ACT	AGG	CYN

	50
	DISC

Interpersonal Functioning

37	34*	31	58*	55*	**69**
SFI	DOM	AGGR	DSF	SAV	**SHY**

*The test taker provided scorable responses to less than 90% of the items scored on this scale. See the relevant profile page for the specific percentage.
Scale scores shown in bold font are interpreted in the report.

Note. This information is provided to facilitate interpretation following the recommended structure for MMPI-3 interpretation in Chapter 5 of the *MMPI-3 Manual for Administration, Scoring, and Interpretation*, which provides details in the text and an outline in Table 5-1.

FIGURE 7.3. Mr. J's MMPI-3 Interpretive Report for Clinical Settings, continued

MMPI®-3 Interpretive Report: Clinical Settings
08/01/2020, Page 8

ID: Mr. J

This interpretive report is intended for use by a professional qualified to interpret the MMPI-3. The information it contains should be considered in the context of the test taker's background, the circumstances of the assessment, and other available information.

The report includes extensive annotation, which appears as superscripts following each statement in the narrative, keyed to Endnotes with accompanying Research References, which appear in the final two sections of the report. Additional information about the annotation features is provided in the headnotes to these sections and in the MMPI-3 User's Guide for the Score and Clinical Interpretive Reports.

SYNOPSIS

Scores on the MMPI-3 Validity Scales raise concerns about the possible impact of unscorable responses on the validity of this protocol. With that caution noted, scores on the Substantive Scales indicate emotional, behavioral, and interpersonal dysfunction. Emotional-internalizing findings include **suicidal ideation**, demoralization, lack of positive emotions, helplessness and hopelessness, self-doubt, perceived inefficacy, negative emotionality, stress, and worry. Behavioral-externalizing problems relate to lack of energy and engagement. Interpersonal difficulties include lack of self-esteem and social anxiety.

PROTOCOL VALIDITY

Content Non-Responsiveness

Unscorable Responses

The test taker answered less than 90% of the items on the following scales. The resulting scores may therefore be artificially lowered. In particular, the absence of elevation on these scales is not interpretable[1]. A list of all items for which the test taker provided unscorable responses appears under the heading "Item-Level Information."

  Infrequent Responses (F): 89%
  Compulsivity (CMP): 88%
  Family Problems (FML): 80%
  Dominance (DOM): 89%
  Disaffiliativeness (DSF): 57%
  Social Avoidance (SAV): 78%
  Introversion/Low Positive Emotionality (INTR): 86%

Inconsistent Responding

The test taker responded to the items in a consistent manner, indicating that he responded relevantly.

Over-Reporting

The test taker may have over-reported general psychological dysfunction. The extent of possible over-reporting cannot be precisely determined because of 4 unscorable responses on the 35-item Infrequent Responses (F) scale. The following table shows what the T scores for F would be if the unscorable items had been answered in the keyed direction.

FIGURE 7.3. Mr. J's MMPI-3 Interpretive Report for Clinical Settings, continued

Scale: F	
T score based on scorable responses:	66
Cutoff for over-reporting concern:	75

If answered in the keyed direction	The T score would be
1	69
2	72
3	75
4	78

See Chapter 5 of the *MMPI-3 Manual for Administration, Scoring, and Interpretation* for guidance on interpreting elevated scores on F.

Under-Reporting

There are no indications of under-reporting in this protocol.

SUBSTANTIVE SCALE INTERPRETATION

Clinical symptoms, personality characteristics, and behavioral tendencies of the test taker are described in this section and organized according to an empirically guided framework. (Please see Chapter 5 of the MMPI-3 Manual for Administration, Scoring, and Interpretation *for details.) Statements containing the word "reports" are based on the item content of MMPI-3 scales, whereas statements that include the word "likely" are based on empirical correlates of scale scores. Specific sources for each statement can be viewed with the annotation features of this report.*

The following interpretation needs to be considered in light of cautions noted about the possible impact of unscorable responses on the validity of this protocol.

Somatic/Cognitive Dysfunction

There are no indications of somatic or cognitive dysfunction in this protocol.

Emotional Dysfunction

The test taker reports a history of suicidal/death ideation and/or past suicide attempts[2]. He likely is at risk for self-harm[3], is preoccupied with suicide and death[4], and is at risk for current suicidal ideation and attempts[5].

His responses indicate considerable emotional distress that is likely to be perceived as a crisis[6]. More specifically, he reports experiencing significant demoralization, feeling overwhelmed, and being extremely unhappy, sad, and dissatisfied with his life[7]. He very likely complains about significant depression[8] and experiences sadness and despair[9]. In particular, he reports having lost hope and believing he cannot change and overcome his problems and is incapable of reaching his life goals[10]. He very likely feels hopeless, overwhelmed, and that life is a strain[11], believes he cannot be helped[11] and gets a raw deal from life[12], and lacks motivation for change[13]. He also reports lacking confidence, feeling worthless, and believing he is a burden to others[14]. He very likely experiences self-doubt, feels insecure and inferior, and is self-disparaging and intropunitive[15]. In addition, he reports being very indecisive and inefficacious, believing he is incapable of making decisions and dealing effectively with crisis situations, and even having difficulties dealing with small, inconsequential matters[16]. He very likely experiences subjective incompetence and shame[17] and lacks perseverance and self-reliance[18].

The test taker reports a lack of positive emotional experiences and a lack of interest[19]. He likely is pessimistic[20] and presents with anhedonia[21].

He reports experiencing an elevated level of negative emotionality[22] and indeed likely experiences various negative emotions[23]. More specifically, he reports an above average level of stress[24]. He likely complains about

FIGURE 7.3. Mr. J's MMPI-3 Interpretive Report for Clinical Settings, continued

stress[25] and feels incapable of controlling his anxiety level[25]. He also reports excessive worry, including worries about misfortune and finances, as well as preoccupation with disappointments[26]. He indeed likely worries excessively[27] and ruminates[28].

Thought Dysfunction
There are no indications of disordered thinking in this protocol.

Behavioral Dysfunction
There are no indications of maladaptive externalizing behavior in this protocol. The test taker reports a low energy level[29] and indeed likely has a low energy level[30] and is disengaged from his normal activities[30].

Interpersonal Functioning Scales
The test taker describes himself as lacking in positive qualities[31].

He reports being shy, easily embarrassed, and uncomfortable around others[32]. He is likely to be socially introverted[33] and inhibited[34], anxious and nervous in social situations[35], and viewed by others as socially awkward[36].

DIAGNOSTIC CONSIDERATIONS

This section provides recommendations for psychodiagnostic assessment based on the test taker's MMPI-3 results. It is recommended that he be evaluated for the following, **bearing in mind possible threats to protocol validity noted earlier in this report:**

Emotional-Internalizing Disorders
- Major depression and other anhedonia-related disorders[37]
- Features of personality disorders involving negative emotionality such as Dependent[38]
- Generalized anxiety disorder[25]
- Disorders involving excessive worry[39]

Interpersonal Disorders
- Social anxiety disorder (social phobia)[40]

TREATMENT CONSIDERATIONS

This section provides inferential treatment-related recommendations based on the test taker's MMPI-3 scores. **The following recommendations need to be considered in light of cautions noted earlier about possible threats to protocol validity.**

Areas for Further Evaluation
- <u>**Risk for suicide**</u> **should be assessed immediately**[41].
- Need for antidepressant medication[42].

Psychotherapy Process Issues
- Serious emotional difficulties may motivate him for treatment[43].
- Indecisiveness may interfere with establishing treatment goals and progress in treatment[44].

FIGURE 7.3. Mr. J's MMPI-3 Interpretive Report for Clinical Settings, continued

Possible Targets for Treatment
- Demoralization as an initial target[45]
- Loss of hope and feelings of despair as early targets for intervention[46]
- Low self-esteem and other manifestations of self-doubt[47]
- Anhedonia[48]
- Developing stress management skills[49]
- Excessive worry and rumination[39]
- Anxiety in social situations[40]

ITEM-LEVEL INFORMATION

Unscorable Responses

Following is a list of items to which the test taker did not provide scorable responses. Unanswered or double answered (both True and False) items are unscorable. The scale(s) on which the items appear are in parentheses following the item content.

    Item number and content omitted. (CRIN, VRIN, SAV, INTR)
    Item number and content omitted. (CMP)
    Item number and content omitted. (CRIN, TRIN, F, DSF)
    Item number and content omitted. (CRIN, TRIN, F, FML)
    Item number and content omitted. (CRIN, VRIN, DSF)
    Item number and content omitted. (FBS)
    Item number and content omitted. (DOM, AGGR)
    Item number and content omitted. (EID, RC2, SAV, INTR)
    Item number and content omitted. (RBS, L)
    Item number and content omitted. (F, FML)
    Item number and content omitted. (CRIN, VRIN, DSF)
    Item number and content omitted. (CRIN, VRIN, EID, ANP, NEGE)
    Item number and content omitted. (F, RC6)

Critical Responses

Seven MMPI-3 scales—Suicidal/Death Ideation (SUI), Helplessness/Hopelessness (HLP), Anxiety-Related Experiences (ARX), Ideas of Persecution (RC6), Aberrant Experiences (RC8), Substance Abuse (SUB), and Aggression (AGG)—have been designated by the test authors as having critical item content that may require immediate attention and follow-up. Items answered by the individual in the keyed direction (True or False) on a critical scale are listed below if his T score on that scale is 65 or higher. However, any item answered in the keyed direction on SUI is listed. The percentage of the MMPI-3 normative sample that answered each item in the keyed direction is provided in parentheses following the item content.

Suicidal/Death Ideation (SUI, T Score = 72)
    Item number and content omitted. (True, 22.2%)
    Item number and content omitted. (True, 8.1%)
    Item number and content omitted. (True, 2.5%)

Helplessness/Hopelessness (HLP, T Score = 86)
    Item number and content omitted. (True, 10.9%)
    Item number and content omitted. (True, 8.7%)
    Item number and content omitted. (True, 12.3%)
    Item number and content omitted. (True, 4.6%)
    Item number and content omitted. (True, 45.4%)

FIGURE 7.3. Mr. J's MMPI-3 Interpretive Report for Clinical Settings, continued

Item number and content omitted. (False, 22.0%)
Item number and content omitted. (True, 8.4%)

User-Designated Item-Level Information

The following item-level information is based on the report user's selection of additional scales, and/or of lower cutoffs for the critical scales from the previous section. Items answered by the test taker in the keyed direction (True or False) on a selected scale are listed below if his T score on that scale is at the user-designated cutoff score or higher. The percentage of the MMPI-3 normative sample that answered each item in the keyed direction is provided in parentheses following the item content.

Demoralization (RCd, T Score = 80)

    Item number and content omitted. (True, 11.3%)
    Item number and content omitted. (True, 44.5%)
    Item number and content omitted. (True, 14.9%)
    Item number and content omitted. (True, 29.4%)
    Item number and content omitted. (True, 41.0%)
    Item number and content omitted. (False, 15.7%)
    Item number and content omitted. (True, 35.3%)
    Item number and content omitted. (True, 23.9%)
    Item number and content omitted. (True, 21.9%)
    Item number and content omitted. (True, 21.5%)
    Item number and content omitted. (True, 58.0%)
    Item number and content omitted. (True, 27.8%)
    Item number and content omitted. (False, 46.0%)
    Item number and content omitted. (True, 28.7%)
    Item number and content omitted. (True, 25.7%)
    Item number and content omitted. (True, 32.0%)
    Item number and content omitted. (True, 22.0%)

Low Positive Emotions (RC2, T Score = 75)

    Item number and content omitted. (False, 17.9%)
    Item number and content omitted. (False, 27.2%)
    Item number and content omitted. (False, 41.2%)
    Item number and content omitted. (False, 29.7%)
    Item number and content omitted. (True, 13.2%)
    Item number and content omitted. (False, 7.3%)
    Item number and content omitted. (False, 9.1%)
    Item number and content omitted. (False, 22.0%)
    Item number and content omitted. (False, 33.5%)
    Item number and content omitted. (False, 27.0%)

Self-Doubt (SFD, T Score = 78)

    Item number and content omitted. (True, 11.3%)
    Item number and content omitted. (True, 29.4%)
    Item number and content omitted. (True, 41.0%)
    Item number and content omitted. (True, 11.8%)
    Item number and content omitted. (True, 28.7%)
    Item number and content omitted. (True, 14.6%)
    Item number and content omitted. (True, 32.0%)

FIGURE 7.3. Mr. J's MMPI-3 Interpretive Report for Clinical Settings, continued

Inefficacy (NFC, T Score = 77)

    Item number and content omitted. (True, 37.7%)
    Item number and content omitted. (True, 45.2%)
    Item number and content omitted. (True, 42.3%)
    Item number and content omitted. (True, 35.3%)
    Item number and content omitted. (True, 23.9%)
    Item number and content omitted. (True, 25.2%)
    Item number and content omitted. (True, 29.0%)
    Item number and content omitted. (True, 20.9%)
    Item number and content omitted. (True, 40.2%)

Stress (STR, T Score = 68)

    Item number and content omitted. (False, 31.7%)
    Item number and content omitted. (False, 26.7%)
    Item number and content omitted. (True, 30.9%)
    Item number and content omitted. (True, 31.6%)
    Item number and content omitted. (False, 58.8%)

Worry (WRY, T Score = 65)

    Item number and content omitted. (True, 42.5%)
    Item number and content omitted. (True, 26.3%)
    Item number and content omitted. (True, 40.6%)
    Item number and content omitted. (True, 54.0%)
    Item number and content omitted. (True, 57.8%)
    Item number and content omitted. (True, 50.9%)

Shyness (SHY, T Score = 69)

    Item number and content omitted. (True, 27.8%)
    Item number and content omitted. (True, 29.1%)
    Item number and content omitted. (True, 38.0%)
    Item number and content omitted. (True, 38.6%)
    Item number and content omitted. (True, 52.2%)
    Item number and content omitted. (False, 32.3%)

Negative Emotionality/Neuroticism (NEGE, T Score = 68)

    Item number and content omitted. (True, 31.2%)
    Item number and content omitted. (False, 26.7%)
    Item number and content omitted. (True, 16.9%)
    Item number and content omitted. (True, 26.3%)
    Item number and content omitted. (True, 38.4%)
    Item number and content omitted. (True, 40.6%)
    Item number and content omitted. (True, 46.0%)
    Item number and content omitted. (True, 26.0%)
    Item number and content omitted. (True, 35.8%)
    Item number and content omitted. (True, 59.1%)
    Item number and content omitted. (True, 54.0%)
    Item number and content omitted. (True, 50.9%)

FIGURE 7.3. Mr. J's MMPI-3 Interpretive Report for Clinical Settings, continued

ENDNOTES

This section lists for each statement in the report the MMPI-3 score(s) that triggered it. In addition, each statement is identified as a <u>Test Response</u>, if based on item content, a <u>Correlate</u>, if based on empirical correlates, or an <u>Inference</u>, if based on the report authors' judgment. (This information can also be accessed on-screen by placing the cursor on a given statement.) For correlate-based statements, research references (Ref. No.) are provided, keyed to the consecutively numbered reference list following the endnotes.

[1] Correlate: Response % < 90, Ref. 12
[2] Test Response: SUI=72
[3] Correlate: SUI=72, Ref. 7, 26, 31
[4] Correlate: SUI=72, Ref. 4, 7, 20, 21, 30, 31, 32, 42, 45
[5] Correlate: SUI=72, Ref. 4, 7, 20, 21, 31, 42, 43, 45
[6] Correlate: EID=80, Ref. 7, 25, 33, 45
[7] Test Response: RCd=80
[8] Correlate: RCd=80, Ref. 1, 5, 7, 8, 9, 10, 13, 14, 16, 17, 18, 23, 24, 29, 30, 34, 36, 37, 38, 40, 41, 44, 45, 46, 47, 49, 50; RC2=75, Ref. 1, 5, 7, 8, 9, 10, 16, 17, 18, 23, 24, 34, 36, 37, 38, 40, 41, 45, 46, 47, 49, 50
[9] Correlate: RCd=80, Ref. 7
[10] Test Response: HLP=86
[11] Correlate: HLP=86, Ref. 45
[12] Correlate: RCd=80, Ref. 45; HLP=86, Ref. 45
[13] Correlate: HLP=86, Ref. 7
[14] Test Response: SFD=78
[15] Correlate: SFD=78, Ref. 7, 45
[16] Test Response: NFC=77
[17] Correlate: NFC=77, Ref. 7
[18] Correlate: NFC=77, Ref. 10
[19] Test Response: RC2=75
[20] Correlate: RC2=75, Ref. 15, 40, 45; HLP=86, Ref. 45
[21] Correlate: RC2=75, Ref. 7, 45
[22] Test Response: NEGE=68
[23] Correlate: NEGE=68, Ref. 7
[24] Test Response: STR=68
[25] Correlate: STR=68, Ref. 7
[26] Test Response: WRY=65
[27] Correlate: WRY=65, Ref. 7
[28] Correlate: WRY=65, Ref. 7; SFD=78, Ref. 7, 45
[29] Test Response: RC9=36
[30] Correlate: RC9=36, Ref. 7, 45
[31] Test Response: SFI=37
[32] Test Response: SHY=69
[33] Correlate: SHY=69, Ref. 1, 2, 6, 7, 11
[34] Correlate: SHY=69, Ref. 1, 6, 7, 45
[35] Correlate: SHY=69, Ref. 6, 7, 10, 19, 30
[36] Correlate: SHY=69, Ref. 7, 45
[37] Correlate: RCd=80, Ref. 7, 22, 27, 28, 35, 41, 45, 48; RC2=75, Ref. 7, 22, 27, 28, 35, 41, 45, 48
[38] Correlate: NEGE=68, Ref. 3, 7, 39
[39] Inference: WRY=65
[40] Inference: SHY=69
[41] Inference: SUI=72
[42] Correlate: RC2=75, Ref. 7
[43] Inference: EID=80; RCd=80; NEGE=68
[44] Inference: NFC=77
[45] Inference: RCd=80

FIGURE 7.3. Mr. J's MMPI-3 Interpretive Report for Clinical Settings, continued

⁴⁶ Inference: HLP=86
⁴⁷ Inference: SFD=78
⁴⁸ Inference: RC2=75
⁴⁹ Inference: STR=68

FIGURE 7.3. Mr. J's MMPI-3 Interpretive Report for Clinical Settings, continued

RESEARCH REFERENCE LIST

The following studies are sources for empirical correlates identified in the Endnotes section of this report.

1. Anderson, J. L., Sellbom, M., Ayearst, L., Quilty, L. C., Chmielewski, M., & Bagby, R. M. (2015). Associations between DSM-5 Section III personality traits and the Minnesota Multiphasic Personality Inventory 2-Restructured Form (MMPI-2-RF) scales in a psychiatric patient sample. *Psychological Assessment, 27*(3), 801–815. https://doi.org/10.1037/pas0000096

2. Anderson, J. L., Sellbom, M., Pymont, C., Smid, W., De Saeger, H., & Kamphuis, J. H. (2015). Measurement of DSM-5 Section II personality disorder constructs using the MMPI-2-RF in clinical and forensic samples. *Psychological Assessment, 27*(3), 786–800. https://doi.org/10.1037/pas0000103

3. Anderson, J. L., Wood, M. E., Tarescavage, A. M., Burchett, D., & Glassmire, D. M. (2018). The role of dimensional personality psychopathology in a forensic inpatient psychiatric setting. *Journal of Personality Disorders, 32*(4), 447–464. https://doi.org/10.1521/pedi_2017_31_301

4. Anestis, J. C., Finn, J. A., Gottfried, E. D., Hames, J. L., Bodell, L. P., Hagan, C. R., Arnau, R. C., Anestis, M. D., Arbisi, P. A., & Joiner, T. E. (2018). Burdensomeness, belongingness, and capability: Assessing the interpersonal-psychological theory of suicide with MMPI-2-RF scales. *Assessment, 25*(4), 415–431. https://doi.org/10.1177/1073191116652227

5. Arbisi, P. A., Sellbom, M., & Ben-Porath, Y. S. (2008). Empirical correlates of the MMPI-2 Restructured Clinical (RC) Scales in psychiatric inpatients. *Journal of Personality Assessment, 90*(2), 122–128. https://doi.org/10.1080/00223890701845146

6. Ayearst, L. E., Sellbom, M., Trobst, K. K., & Bagby, R. M. (2013). Evaluating the interpersonal content of the MMPI-2-RF Interpersonal Scales. *Journal of Personality Assessment, 95*(2), 187–196. https://doi.org/10.1080/00223891.2012.730085

7. Ben-Porath, Y. S., & Tellegen, A. (2020). *The Minnesota Multiphasic Personality Inventory-3 (MMPI-3): Technical manual.* University of Minnesota Press.

8. Binford, A., & Liljequist, L. (2008). Behavioral correlates of selected MMPI-2 Clinical, Content, and Restructured Clinical scales. *Journal of Personality Assessment, 90*(6), 608–614. https://doi.org/10.1080/00223890802388657

9. Block, A. R., Ben-Porath, Y. S., & Marek, R. J. (2013). Psychological risk factors for poor outcome of spine surgery and spinal cord stimulator implant: A review of the literature and their assessment with the MMPI-2-RF. *The Clinical Neuropsychologist, 27*(1), 81–107. https://doi.org/10.1080/13854046.2012.721007

10. Burchett, D. L., & Ben-Porath, Y. S. (2010). The impact of over-reporting on MMPI-2-RF substantive scale score validity. *Assessment, 17*(4), 497–516. https://doi.org/10.1177/1073191110378972

11. Crighton, A. H., Tarescavage, A. M., Gervais, R. O., & Ben-Porath, Y. S. (2017). The generalizability of over-reporting across self-report measures: An investigation with the Minnesota Multiphasic Personality Inventory-2-Restructured Form and the Personality Assessment Inventory in a civil disability sample. *Assessment, 24*(5), 555–574. https://doi.org/10.1177/1073191115621791

12. Dragon, W. R., Ben-Porath, Y. S., & Handel, R. W. (2012). Examining the impact of unscorable item responses on the validity and interpretability of MMPI-2/MMPI-2-RF Restructured Clinical (RC) Scale scores. *Assessment, 19*(1), 101–113. https://doi.org/10.1177/1073191111415362

13. Erbes, C. R., Polusny, M. A., Arbisi, P. A., & Koffel, E. (2012). PTSD symptoms in a cohort of National Guard Soldiers deployed to Iraq: Evidence for nonspecific and specific components. *Journal of Affective Disorders, 142*(1–3), 269–274. https://doi.org/10.1016/j.jad.2012.05.013

FIGURE 7.3. Mr. J's MMPI-3 Interpretive Report for Clinical Settings, continued

14. Finn, J. A., Ben-Porath, Y. S., & Tellegen, A. (2015). Dichotomous versus polytomous response options in psychopathology assessment: Method or meaningful variance? *Psychological Assessment, 27*(1), 184–193. https://doi.org/10.1037/pas0000044

15. Forbey, J. D., & Ben-Porath, Y. S. (2007). A comparison of the MMPI-2 Restructured Clinical (RC) and Clinical Scales in a substance abuse treatment sample. *Psychological Services, 4*(1), 46–58. https://doi.org/10.1037/1541-1559.4.1.46

16. Forbey, J. D., & Ben-Porath, Y. S. (2008). Empirical correlates of the MMPI-2 Restructured Clinical (RC) Scales in a non-clinical setting. *Journal of Personality Assessment, 90*(2), 136–141. https://doi.org/10.1080/00223890701845161

17. Forbey, J. D., Ben-Porath, Y. S., & Arbisi, P. A. (2012). The MMPI-2 computer adaptive version (MMPI-2-CA) in a Veterans Administration medical outpatient facility. *Psychological Assessment, 24*(3), 628–639. https://doi.org/10.1037/a0026509

18. Forbey, J. D., Ben-Porath, Y. S., & Gartland, D. (2009). Validation of the MMPI-2 Computerized Adaptive version (MMPI-2-CA) in a correctional intake facility. *Psychological Services, 6*(4), 279–292. https://doi.org/10.1037/a0016195

19. Forbey, J. D., Lee, T. T. C., & Handel, R. W. (2010). Correlates of the MMPI-2-RF in a college setting. *Psychological Assessment, 22*(4), 737–744. https://doi.org/10.1037/a0020645

20. Glassmire, D. M, Tarescavage, A. M., Burchett, D., Martinez, J., & Gomez, A. (2016). Clinical utility of the MMPI-2-RF SUI items and scale in a forensic inpatient setting: Association with interview self-reports and future suicidal behavior. *Psychological Assessment, 28*(11), 1502–1509. https://doi.org/10.1037/pas0000220

21. Gottfried, E., Bodell, L., Carbonell, J., & Joiner, T. (2014). The clinical utility of the MMPI-2-RF Suicidal/Death Ideation Scale. *Psychological Assessment, 26*(4), 1205–1211. https://doi.org/10.1037/pas0000017

22. Haber, J. C., & Baum, L. J. (2014). Minnesota Multiphasic Personality Inventory-2 Restructured Form (MMPI-2-RF) Scales as predictors of psychiatric diagnoses. *South African Journal of Psychology, 44*(4), 439–453. https://doi.org/10.1177/0081246314532788

23. Handel, R. W., & Archer, R. P. (2008). An investigation of the psychometric properties of the MMPI-2 Restructured Clinical (RC) Scales with mental health inpatients. *Journal of Personality Assessment, 90*(3), 239–249. https://doi.org/10.1080/00223890701884954

24. Kamphuis, J. H., Arbisi, P. A., Ben-Porath, Y. S., & McNulty, J. L. (2008). Detecting comorbid Axis-II status among inpatients using the MMPI-2 Restructured Clinical Scales. *European Journal of Psychological Assessment, 24,* 157–164. https://doi.org/10.1027/1015-5759.24.3.157

25. Lanyon, R. I., & Thomas, M. L. (2013). Assessment of global psychiatric categories: The PSI/PSI-2 and the MMPI-2-RF. *Psychological Assessment, 25*(1), 227–232. https://doi.org/10.1037/a0030313

26. Laurinaityte, I., Laurinavicius, A., Ustinaviciute, L., Wygant, D. B., Sellbom, M. (2017). Utility of the MMPI-2 Restructured Form (MMPI-2-RF) in a sample of Lithuanian male offenders. *Law and Human Behavior, 41*(5), 494–505. https://doi.org/10.1037/lhb0000254

27. Lee, T. T. C., Graham, J. R., & Arbisi, P. A. (2018). The utility of MMPI-2-RF scale scores in the differential diagnosis of schizophrenia and major depressive disorder. *Journal of Personality Assessment, 100*(3), 305–312. https://doi.org/10.1080/00223891.2017.1300906

FIGURE 7.3. Mr. J's MMPI-3 Interpretive Report for Clinical Settings, continued

28. McCord, D. M., & Drerup, L. C. (2011). Relative practical utility of the Minnesota Multiphasic Personality Inventory-2 Restructured Clinical Scales versus the Clinical Scales in a chronic pain patient sample. *Journal of Clinical and Experimental Neuropsychology, 33*(1), 140–146. https://doi.org/10.1080/13803395.2010.495056

29. McDevitt-Murphy, M. E., Weathers, F. W., Flood, A. M., Eakin, D. E., & Benson, T. A. (2007). The utility of the PAI and the MMPI-2 for discriminating PTSD, depression, and social phobia in trauma-exposed college students. *Assessment, 14*(2), 181–195. https://doi.org/10.1177/1073191106295914

30. Menton, W. H., Crighton, A. H., Tarescavage, A. M., Marek, R. J., Hicks, A. D., & Ben-Porath, Y. S. (2019). Equivalence of laptop and tablet administrations of the Minnesota Multiphasic Personality Inventory-2 Restructured Form. *Assessment, 26*(4), 661–669. https://doi.org/10.1177/1073191117714558

31. Miller, S. N., Bozzay, M. L., Ben-Porath, Y. S., & Arbisi, P. A. (2019). Distinguishing levels of suicide risk in depressed male veterans: The role of internalizing and externalizing psychopathology as measured by the MMPI-2-RF. *Assessment, 26*(1), 85–98. https://doi.org/10.1177/1073191117743787

32. Rogers, M. L., Anestis, J. C., Harrop, T. M., Schneider, M., Bender, T. W., Ringer, F. B., & Joiner, T. E. (2017). Examination of MMPI-2-RF substantive scales as indicators of acute suicidal affective disturbance components. *Journal of Personality Assessment, 99*(4), 424–434. https://doi.org/10.1080/00223891.2016.1222393

33. Romero, I. E., Toorabally, N., Burchett, D., Tarescavage, A. M., & Glassmire, D. M. (2017). Mapping the MMPI-2-RF substantive scales onto, internalizing, externalizing, and thought dysfunction dimensions in a forensic inpatient setting. *Journal of Personality Assessment, 99*(4), 351–362. https://doi.org/10.1080/00223891.2016.1223681

34. Sellbom, M., Anderson, J. L., & Bagby, R. M. (2013). Assessing DSM-5 Section III personality traits and disorders with the MMPI-2-RF. *Assessment, 20*(6), 709–722. https://doi.org/10.1177/1073191113508808

35. Sellbom, M., Bagby, R. M., Kushner, S., Quilty, L. C., & Ayearst, L. E. (2011). Diagnostic construct validity of the MMPI-2 Restructured Form (MMPI-2-RF) scale scores. *Assessment, 19*(2), 176–186. https://doi.org/10.1177/1073191111428763

36. Sellbom, M., Ben-Porath, Y. S., & Bagby, R. M. (2008). On the hierarchical structure of mood and anxiety disorders: Confirmatory evidence and elaboration of a model of temperament markers. *Journal of Abnormal Psychology, 117*(3), 576–590. https://doi.org/10.1037/a0012536

37. Sellbom, M., Ben-Porath, Y. S., & Graham, J. R. (2006). Correlates of the MMPI-2 Restructured Clinical (RC) Scales in a college counseling setting. *Journal of Personality Assessment, 86*(1), 89–99. https://doi.org/10.1207/s15327752jpa8601_10

38. Sellbom, M., Graham, J. R., & Schenk, P. W. (2006). Incremental validity of the MMPI-2 Restructured Clinical (RC) Scales in a private practice sample. *Journal of Personality Assessment, 86*(2), 196–205. https://doi.org/10.1207/s15327752jpa8602_09

39. Sellbom, M., & Smith, A. (2017). Assessment of DSM-5 Section II personality disorders with the MMPI-2-RF in a nonclinical sample. *Journal of Personality Assessment, 99*(4), 384–397. https://doi.org/10.1080/00223891.2016.1242074

40. Shkalim, E. (2015). Psychometric evaluation of the MMPI-2/MMPI-2-RF Restructured Clinical Scales in an Israeli sample. *Assessment, 22*(4), 607–618. https://doi.org/10.1177/1073191114555884

41. Simms, L. J., Casillas, A., Clark, L. A., Watson, D., & Doebbeling, B. N. (2005). Psychometric evaluation of the Restructured Clinical Scales of the MMPI-2. *Psychological Assessment, 17*(3), 345–358. https://doi.org/10.1037/1040-3590.17.3.345

FIGURE 7.3. Mr. J's MMPI-3 Interpretive Report for Clinical Settings, continued

42. Stanley, I. H., Yancey, J. R., Patrick, C. J., & Joiner, T. E. (2018). A distinct configuration of MMPI-2-RF scales RCd and RC9/ACT is associated with suicide attempt risk among suicide ideators in a psychiatric outpatient sample. *Psychological Assessment, 30*(9), 1249–1254. https://doi.org/10.1037/pas0000588

43. Tarescavage, A. M., Glassmire, D. M., & Burchett, D. (2018). Minnesota Multiphasic Personality Inventory-2-Restructured Form markers of future suicidal behavior in a forensic psychiatric hospital. *Psychological Assessment, 30*(2), 170–178. https://doi.org/10.1037/pas0000463

44. Tarescavage, A. M., Scheman, J., & Ben-Porath, Y. S. (2015). Reliability and validity of the Minnesota Multiphasic Personality Inventory-2-Restructured Form (MMPI-2-RF) in evaluations of chronic low back pain patients. *Psychological Assessment, 27*(2), 433–446. https://doi.org/10.1037/pas0000056

45. Tellegen, A., & Ben-Porath, Y. S. (2008/2011). *Minnesota Multiphasic Personality Inventory-2-Restructured Form (MMPI-2-RF): Technical manual*. University of Minnesota Press.

46. Tellegen, A., Ben-Porath, Y. S., Sellbom, M., Arbisi, P. A., McNulty, J. L., & Graham, J. R. (2006). Further evidence on the validity of the MMPI-2 Restructured Clinical (RC) Scales: Addressing questions raised by Rogers, Sewell, Harrison, and Jordan and Nichols. *Journal of Personality Assessment, 87*,(2), 148–171. https://doi.org/10.1207/s15327752jpa8702_04

47. Vachon, D. D., Sellbom, M., Ryder, A. G., Miller, J. D., & Bagby, R. M. (2009). A five-factor model description of depressive personality disorder. *Journal of Personality Disorders, 23*(5), 447–465. https://doi.org/10.1521/pedi.2009.23.5.447

48. Van der Heijden, P. T., Egger, J. I. M., Rossi, G. M. P., Grundel, G., & Derksen, J. J. L. (2013). The MMPI-2-Restructured Form and the standard MMPI-2 Clinical Scales in relation to DSM-IV. *European Journal of Psychological Assessment, 29*(3), 182–188. https://doi.org/10.1027/1015-5759/a000140

49. Wolf, E. J., Miller, M. W., Orazem, R. J., Weierich, M. R., Castillo, D. T., Milford, J., Kaloupek, D. G., & Keane, T. M. (2008). The MMPI-2 Restructured Clinical Scales in the assessment of posttraumatic stress disorder and comorbid disorders. *Psychological Assessment, 20*(4), 327–340. https://doi.org/10.1037/a0012948

50. Wygant, D. B., Boutacoff, L. I., Arbisi, P. A., Ben-Porath, Y. S., Kelly, P. H., & Rupp, W. M. (2007). Examination of the MMPI-2 Restructured Clinical (RC) Scales in a sample of bariatric surgery candidates. *Journal of Clinical Psychology in Medical Settings, 14*(3), 197–205. https://doi.org/10.1007/s10880-007-9073-8

End of Report

FIGURE 7.3. Mr. J's MMPI-3 Interpretive Report for Clinical Settings, continued

The automated interpretation appears next, under six major headings: Synopsis, Protocol Validity, Substantive Scale Interpretation, Diagnostic Considerations, Treatment Considerations, and Item-Level Information.

Synopsis

The Synopsis section provides a brief overview of the major findings pertaining to the interpretability of the results and the major conclusions indicated by the test taker's scores on the Substantive Scales of the test.

Protocol Validity

The Protocol Validity section provides information about three types of threats to the validity of the test results: content nonresponsiveness (i.e., unscorable and/or inconsistent responses), overreporting, and underreporting. A detailed discussion of these issues appears in chapter 8. In cases for which no protocol validity concerns are indicated by scores on the Validity Scales, a brief statement to that effect will appear in this section.

In cases in which one or more possible concerns about protocol validity are indicated, the three types of threats (content nonresponsiveness, overreporting, and underreporting) are addressed under separate subheadings (as in the case of Mr. J on pages 8–9 of Figure 7.3). If the test taker answered less than 90% of the items on one or more scales, the affected scales and the percentage of scorable items on each are listed in this section. A complete list of the test taker's unscorable responses appears later, in the Item-Level Information section of the report (see page 11 of the report in Figure 7.3). In cases in which one or more Validity Scales may be impacted by unscorable responses, the report includes an analysis of the potential impact of nonresponding on the ability to assess the relevant protocol validity threats. In Mr. J's case, the F scale had 89% scorable responses. Beginning at the bottom of page 8, the report indicates:

> *The test taker may have over-reported general psychological dysfunction. The extent of possible over-reporting cannot be precisely determined because of 4 unscorable responses on the 35-item Infrequent Responses (F) scale. The following table shows what the T scores for F would be if the unscorable items had been answered in the keyed direction.*

The table just mentioned (top of page 9) shows that if Mr. J had responded to three of the four unscorable items in the keyed direction, his F T score would have reached 75, which is the cutoff for identifying possible overreporting based on the F scale. As shown in this case, any score that reaches an interpretable level is printed in bold. It is also noteworthy that in this case, even if all the unscorable F items had been answered in the keyed direction, Mr. J's T score would not have reached 100, the cutoff for invalidating an MMPI-3 protocol.

Substantive Scale Interpretation

The Substantive Scale Interpretation section begins on page 9 (Figure 7.3) and concludes at the top of page 11 of the sample output. The standard introductory paragraph reads:

> *Clinical symptoms, personality characteristics, and behavioral tendencies of the test taker are described in this section and organized according to an empirically guided framework. (Please see Chapter 5 of the* MMPI-3 Manual for Administration, Scoring, and Interpretation *for details.) Statements containing the word "reports" are based on the item content of MMPI-3 scales, whereas statements that include the word "likely" are based on empirical correlates of scale scores. Specific sources for each statement can be viewed with the annotation features of this report.*

As indicated in this introduction, nearly all statements that appear in this section of the report are based either on scale item content, in which case they contain the word reports, or on empirical correlates of the scales, in which case they include the word likely. The annotation feature mentioned in the introductory paragraph is described later in this chapter.

If scores on the Validity Scales indicate the need for caution in interpreting the results of the Substantive Scales, a cautionary statement is printed in boldface immediately following the introductory paragraph. In the case of Mr. J, cautions related to unscorable responses are reiterated in the middle of page 9 (Figure 7.3).

Following a structure outlined in chapter 5 of the *MMPI-3 Manual for Administration, Scoring, and Interpretation* (see also chapter 10 in this book), the Substantive Scale Interpretation section of the report is divided into five subsections: Somatic/Cognitive Dysfunction, Emotional Dysfunction, Thought Dysfunction, Behavioral Dysfunction, and Interpersonal Functioning Scales. Findings on the 42 Substantive Scales are interpreted (if certain scale score cutoffs are reached) in these subsections.

Interpretive guidelines in chapter 9 include low scores (T score 38 and below) for some Substantive Scales. An example of an interpreted low score can be seen on page 10 of Figure 7.3, where Mr. J's low RC9 T score (36) is interpreted under Behavioral Dysfunction.

Diagnostic Considerations

The Diagnostic Considerations section appears on page 10 of Mr. J's report. If no diagnostic possibilities are indicated by a test taker's scores, this statement appears: "No specific psychodiagnostic recommendations are indicated by this MMPI-3 protocol." If diagnostic possibilities are indicated by scores on the Substantive Scales, this section begins with a standard introduction. If scores on the Validity Scales raise possible concerns, as in Mr. J's case, the introduction will include a caution to that effect printed in bold:

> This section provides recommendations for psychodiagnostic assessment based on the test taker's MMPI-3 results. It is recommended that he be evaluated for the following, bearing in mind possible threats to protocol validity noted earlier in this report.

Diagnostic possibilities are listed next under four possible subheadings: Emotional-Internalizing Disorders, Thought Disorders, Behavioral-Externalizing Disorders, and Interpersonal Disorders. If none of the diagnostic possibilities related to one of these domains is indicated by the test taker's scores, that subheading is not printed in the report. For example, in Mr. J's case, none of the possible diagnostic considerations related to Thought Disorders or Behavioral-Externalizing Disorders are indicated by his test results; therefore, these subheadings do not appear in his Interpretive Report.

Treatment Considerations

The Treatment Considerations section appears on pages 10–11 of Mr. J's report. If none of the possible treatment-related recommendations are indicated by the test results, then this statement appears under the Treatment Considerations section heading: "No specific recommendations for treatment are indicated by this MMPI-3 protocol." If any of the possible treatment considerations are indicated, the first sentence under this heading will state:

> This section provides inferential treatment-related recommendations based on the test taker's MMPI-3 scores.

In cases such as Mr. J's, in which protocol validity concerns are indicated by the validity scale findings, the following caution is added in bold: "The following recommendations need to be considered in light of cautions noted earlier about possible threats to protocol validity."

The recommendations are characterized as inferential because they are based on the MMPI-3 authors' judgments of the treatment implications of certain test results. These judgments were guided by the construct validity (i.e., empirical correlates and content and the resulting links to theoretical constructs) of the Substantive Scales of the test.

Three types of treatment-related recommendations may appear under separate subheadings in this section of the report: Areas for Further Evaluation, Psychotherapy Process Issues, and Possible Targets for Treatment. If no recommendations are indicated for one of these areas by the test taker's scores, the corresponding subheading is not printed in the report.

Areas for further evaluation may include assessment of risk for suicide (which, if indicated, as in Mr. J's case, will be listed first and printed in bold), evaluation of need for medication and/or hospitalization, and evaluation of the origin of various somatic and cognitive complaints. Psychotherapy process issues that may be identified include readiness and motivation for treatment, possible hindrances to the formation of a therapeutic relationship, and factors that may increase the risk for treatment noncompliance. Possible targets for treatment include a broad range of somatic, cognitive, emotional, thought, behavioral, and interpersonal difficulties assessed by the Substantive Scales.

Item-Level Information

The Item-Level Information section appears on pages 11–13 of Mr. J's Interpretive Report. The content of this section is identical to the similarly labeled section of the Score Report. Three types of item-level information are provided: a list of unscorable responses, a list of critical responses, and a list of user-designated item-level responses. A detailed description of the information contained in these sections was described earlier for the Score Report. Briefly, a list of items to which the test taker did not provide scorable answers is provided under the heading Unscorable Responses (see page 11 of the report in Figure 7.3). The items are listed in the order in which they appear in the MMPI-3 protocol. A list of the scale or scales on which each item is scored appears in parentheses following the item number and its content.

The MMPI-3 authors designated seven MMPI-3 Substantive Scales—Suicidal/Death Ideation (SUI), Helplessness/Hopelessness (HLP), Anxiety-Related Experiences (ARX), Ideas of Persecution (RC6), Aberrant Experiences (RC8), Substance Abuse (SUB), and Aggression (AGG)—as having critical item content that may require immediate attention and follow-up. If a test taker's T score is 65 or higher on one or more of these scales, the items he or she answered in the keyed direction (True or False) on those scales are listed under the heading Critical Responses. For each item listed, the percentage of the MMPI-3 normative sample that also answered in the keyed direction is provided in parentheses following the item content. This information appears on pages 11 and 12 of Mr. J's report. Finally, user-designated item-level information is provided if this option is selected prior to printing the report. An example appears on pages 12 and 13 of Figure 7.3. This option was described in detail earlier for the Score Report.

Annotation

Standard 6.11 of the *Standards for Educational and Psychological Testing* (American Educational Research Association et al., 2014) states: "When automatically generated interpretations of test response protocols or test performance are reported, the sources, rationale, and empirical basis for these interpretations should be available . . . ." To meet this standard, the annotation feature of the Interpretive Report identifies the origin of the interpretive statements (i.e., attributes the statements to the individual's score[s] on a specific scale or scales); indicates whether the statements are based on the test taker's responses, direct empirical correlates, or construct-based inferences; and provides citations to empirical studies that support the correlate-based statements.

Figure 7.3 shows the annotation feature as it appears in a report. Each statement is followed by a superscripted number linked to endnotes that appear on pages 14 and 15 of the report. The endnotes are explained in a standard opening paragraph (page 14) that reads:

> *This section lists for each statement in the report the MMPI-3 score(s) that triggered it. In addition, each statement is identified as a Test Response, if based on item content, a Correlate, if based on empirical correlates, or an Inference, if based on the report authors' judgment. (This information can also be accessed on-screen by placing the cursor on a given statement.) For correlate-based statements, research references (Ref. No.) are provided, keyed to the consecutively numbered reference list following the endnotes.*

For example, the first statement in the Emotional Dysfunction section (page 9 of the report in Figure 7.3) reads: "The test taker reports a history of suicidal/death ideation and/or past suicide attempts[2]." In the Endnotes section of the report (page 14), endnote 2 identifies this statement as being test-response-based, meaning that it is an item-content-based statement reflecting a content theme of the scale, and indicates that the source for the statement is a T score of 72 on the SUI scale. The next statement, "He likely is at risk for self-harm[3]," is linked to the same scale score. However, endnote 3 on page 14 indicates that it is identified as a correlate, meaning that it is based on the empirical correlates of the SUI scale. The last entry for this endnote, "Ref. 7, 26, 31," indicates that the empirical findings that support this statement are reported in references 7, 26, and 31 in the Research Reference List that appears on pages 16–19 of the report in Figure 7.3. The list of references that support empirical correlate-based statements in the report is generated individually for each report, and the master list of supporting literature is updated regularly.

As indicated in the standard opening paragraph for the Endnotes section of the report, users who choose to read the Interpretive Report on-screen while interfacing with the Pearson scoring and reporting system can find information on the sources for an interpretive statement by pointing the cursor at that statement. This will produce hover text, which identifies the score(s) on a scale or scales that triggered the statement and whether it is based on test responses, correlates, or inferences made by the report authors.

If a user prefers not to have the annotation included in the output, this part of the report can be suppressed at the time of printing, as described in chapter 5 of the *MMPI-3 User's Guide for the Score and Clinical Interpretive Reports*.

Additional Features of the Interpretive Report

COMPARISON GROUPS

The Comparison Groups option for the Interpretive Report provides the same information as it does in the Score Report. This option aligns the profiles of the test taker's MMPI-3 scores with descriptive data (means and standard deviations for the 52 scales and frequencies of critical responses to items) for a selected comparison group. These data make it possible to contrast a test taker's scores with those of individuals tested in a similar setting, usually under similar circumstances. This additional, setting-specific information complements what can be learned from the standard T scores that characterize the test taker's scores in reference to the general population norms. Choosing to include comparison group data for a case does not alter the resulting narrative interpretation, which is based on the test taker's scores and the interpretive guidelines detailed in chapters 8 and 9.

INVALID PROTOCOLS

The full text of the Interpretive Report will not be generated if scores on the Validity Scales raise significant concerns about the interpretability of the results. In such cases, the profiles will be plotted but will be marked by a statement indicating that the protocol is invalid. The automated interpretation in these cases will be limited to addressing concerns about the validity of the protocol. Three types of validity problems invalidate the protocol: excessive unscorable responses to items on the Validity Scales, excessive inconsistent responding, and indications of excessive infrequent responding that raise serious concerns about overreporting.

Unscorable Responses

If a test taker does not provide scorable responses to at least 70% of items on all the Validity Scales, the protocol will be identified as invalid. An excessive number of unscorable responses to the items limits the user's ability to rely on the Validity Scales to provide an accurate assessment of the interpretability of the test taker's results. If this occurs, the report provides all the standard information about unscorable responses (i.e., which scales are affected by unscorable items and which items were not answered) and any Validity Scale interpretations that are not compromised by unscorable responses. Scores on the overreporting and underreporting Validity Scales that have less than 70% scorable responses are not interpreted, nor are any scores on the Substantive Scales. Item-level information (including both unscorable and critical responses) is provided.

Inconsistent Responding

If a test taker scores 80T or higher on CRIN, VRIN, or TRIN, the protocol is identified as invalid. In such cases, the report provides the standard information about unscorable responses and an interpretation of scores on CRIN, VRIN, and TRIN. However, scores on the overreporting and underreporting indicators and the Substantive Scales are not interpreted because evidence of excessive inconsistent responding indicates that the test taker probably did not respond to the content of the test items. Item-level information is provided about unscorable responses but not critical responses.

Overreporting

If a test taker's T score is 100 or higher on F or Fp, the protocol is identified as invalid. In such cases, the report provides a full interpretation of the results of all the Validity Scales but no interpretation of the substantive scale scores. Item-level information is provided about both unscorable and critical responses. However, the Critical Responses section includes the following cautionary statement: *"These responses need to be considered with caution in light of the finding, discussed earlier, that this protocol is invalid because of indications of over-reporting."*

GENDER-NEUTRAL REPORT LANGUAGE

If the gender demographic is defined as anything other than Male or Female, the report will automatically use gender-neutral language as recommended by the *Publication Manual of the American Psychological Association* (7th ed.; APA, 2020). For reports generated using Q Local, gender-neutral language is triggered if gender is omitted. For reports generated using Q-global, gender-neutral language is triggered if gender is omitted or is set to Unspecified or Other.

The MMPI-3 Public Safety Candidate Interpretive Reports

A suite of MMPI-3 reports is also available for use in preemployment evaluations of public safety candidates. The MMPI-3 Police Candidate Interpretive Report (PCIR), Correctional Candidate Interpretive Report (CCIR), Dispatcher

Candidate Interpretive Report (DCIR), and Firefighter Candidate Interpretive Report (FCIR) are described in detail in the *MMPI-3 User's Guide for the Public Safety Candidate Interpretive Reports* (Corey & Ben-Porath, 2022). The MMPI-3 Public Safety Candidate Interpretive Reports (PSCIRs) include all the elements of the Interpretive Report for Clinical Settings that were just described, augmented by information designed to assist the interpreter in understanding validity scale findings, descriptions of the candidate's functioning in reference to the appropriate candidate comparison group, and job-relevant empirical correlates from the peer-reviewed literature. The correlates are linked to potential problems in ten job-relevant domains. The annotation, research references, and gender-neutral report language option described earlier are also available for the PSCIRs. Use of the MMPI-3 in assessments of public safety personnel is covered in detail by Corey and Ben-Porath (2024).

Interpreting the MMPI-3 Validity Scales

This chapter provides interpretive guidelines for the MMPI-3 Validity Scales. Development of the scales is described in chapter 3. The literature available to help guide and support their interpretation is reviewed in chapter 4. We begin by discussing a conceptual framework for understanding and using Validity Scales as measures of threats to protocol validity. Next, we map the MMPI-3 Validity Scales onto this framework and identify potential confounds that complicate their interpretation. In the subsequent section we provide interpretive guidelines for each of the MMPI-3 validity indicators, which include consideration of the confounds just mentioned. The chapter concludes with a review of cases that illustrate MMPI-3 Validity Scale interpretation.

THREATS TO PROTOCOL VALIDITY

To provide useful information in response to the statements that make up a self-report inventory, a test taker must read, comprehend, and respond accurately to the test items. Failure to do so, intentionally or unintentionally, compromises the utility of the resulting test scores, and, in extreme cases, renders them uninterpretable. Therefore, prior to drawing any substantive inferences from self-report measures, careful consideration must be given to the quality of information provided by the test taker, that is, to the validity of the individual test protocol.

Ben-Porath (2013) described a conceptual framework for understanding and using Validity Scales as measures of protocol validity. This approach distinguishes between *instrument validity*, which refers to the extent that scale scores predict relevant criteria, canvas a relevant content domain, or reflect an underlying construct (i.e., criterion, content, or construct validity), and *protocol validity*, which refers to the interpretability of a test taker's scores. The premise underlying this approach is that even if a hypothetically 100% valid self-report measure were available, any given administration of the instrument could nonetheless yield invalid results if the test taker was unable or chose not to respond accurately to the test items. Threats to protocol validity fall broadly into two categories that reflect the role of item content in invalid responding: non-content-based and content-based. Important distinctions can be made within each of these categories as well.

Non-Content-Based Invalid Responding

Non-content-based invalid responding occurs when the test taker's responses are not based on an accurate reading and comprehension of the test items. Its deleterious effects on protocol validity are obvious: to the extent that a test taker's responses do not reflect their reactions to the actual items, the responses cannot gauge the individual's standing on the constructs of interest. This invalid test-taking approach can be divided further into three subtypes: nonresponding, random responding, and fixed responding.

Nonresponding

Nonresponding occurs when the test taker fails to provide a scorable response to an item. Typically, this is the absence of a response, but if the test taker answers both True and False to an item (which is only possible with paper and pencil administration), that is also considered a nonresponse. Nonresponding may occur for a variety of reasons. Test takers who are uncooperative or defensive may fail to respond to items, but excessive nonresponding may also reflect a test taker's lack of reading and language comprehension, cognitive functioning deficits leading to confusion or obsessing over responses, or limited introspection and insight.

The effect of nonresponding on protocol validity depends partly on the response format of the instrument. In tests that use a True/False response format, a nonresponse is typically considered a response in the nonkeyed direction because raw scores are derived by counting the number of responses given in the keyed direction. However, it cannot be assumed that these de facto responses approximate how the test taker would have actually responded. Therefore, to the extent that nonresponding occurs in a protocol, it will distort the resulting test scores by lowering them artificially. If not identified and considered, nonresponding can lead to underestimation of the individual's standing on the constructs measured by the affected scales.

Random Responding

Random responding is characterized by an unsystematic response pattern that is not based on an accurate reading and comprehension of test items. It is not a dichotomous phenomenon, meaning that random responding may be present to varying degrees in a test protocol. Two types of random responding can be distinguished. *Intentional random responding* occurs when the individual has the capacity to respond relevantly to test items but chooses to respond irrelevantly in an unsystematic manner. An uncooperative test taker may engage in intentional random responding instead of becoming involved in a confrontation with the examiner over their refusal to participate. In this example, the test taker provides answers to items without reading or considering their content. They may do this intermittently or consistently throughout the test protocol. This form of responding is also most common among uncooperative research participants.

Unintentional random responding occurs when the individual is unable to respond relevantly to test items but responds anyway without understanding their content. Test takers are often not aware that they are responding in this way. Several factors may contribute to unintentional random responding. Reading difficulties could compromise the test taker's ability to respond relevantly. Most current self-report measures require a fourth- to sixth-grade reading level for the test taker to be able to read, comprehend, and respond relevantly to test items. This is not synonymous with having completed 4 to 6 years of education. Comprehension deficits can also lead to random responding. The individual may be able to read the test items but does not have the necessary language comprehension skills to process and understand them. This could be a product of low verbal ability or, for nonnative speakers, a lack of facility with the language in which the test is administered. Reading and comprehension difficulties tend to be relatively stable test taker characteristics that will likely compromise protocol validity regardless of when a test is administered. Other factors, such as confusion and thought disorganization, may be transitory. Finally, unintentional random responding may result from response recording errors. If the test taker mismarks responses on the answer sheet, they are essentially providing random responses. This could occur if an individual accidentally skips an item on the answer sheet or generally has a careless approach to response recording.

Fixed Responding

Fixed responding is an invalidating test-taking approach characterized by a systematic response pattern that is not based on an accurate reading and comprehension of test items. In contrast to random responding, the test taker provides the same non-content-based responses (e.g., True) to various items without considering their content. If the test taker provides both True and False responses indiscriminately, then they are engaging in random responding. In fixed responding, the indiscriminate responses are stereotypic, either True or False, or in the case of a Likert scale response format, the test taker marks items indiscriminately at the same level without considering content.

Like nonresponding and random responding, fixed responding is a matter of degree rather than a dichotomous all-or-none phenomenon. Unlike nonresponding and random responding, fixed responding has received a great deal of attention in the assessment literature. Jackson and Messick (1962) sparked this discussion when they proposed that much (if not all) of the variance in MMPI scale scores was attributable to two response styles, termed acquiescence and social desirability. Acquiescence was defined as a tendency to respond True to MMPI items without consideration of their content (i.e., fixed True responding). These authors factor analyzed MMPI scale scores in a broad range of samples and recurrently found that two factors accounted for much of the variance in scores. They attributed variance on these factors to two response styles, acquiescence and social desirability, and cautioned that MMPI scale scores appeared primarily to reflect individual differences on these nonsubstantive dimensions. Furthermore, they suggested that MMPI scales were particularly vulnerable to the effects of acquiescence and its counterpart, counteracquiescence (defined as a tendency to respond False to MMPI items without consideration of their content), because the scoring keys were unbalanced; that is, for some MMPI scales, many, if not most, of the items were keyed True, whereas on other scales, most of the items were keyed False. Contrasting with Jackson and Messick's findings, Block (1965) demonstrated in an extensive and sophisticated series of analyses that the two primary MMPI factors reflected substantive personality dimensions rather than stylistic response tendencies.

Although fixed responding does not pose as broad a threat to protocol validity as Jackson and Messick argued, in the infrequent cases when a test taker uses this response style excessively, the resulting scale scores will be invalid and uninterpretable. Contrary to Jackson and Messick's assertion, constructing scales with balanced keys or Likert scale response formats does not make self-report measures less susceptible to this threat to protocol validity. An indiscriminate set of True responses is invalid regardless of whether the scoring key is balanced, and Likert scales provide even more opportunity for stereotypic responses.

Content-Based Invalid Responding

Content-based invalid responding occurs when the test taker skews their responses to items and creates a misleading impression as a result. This test-taking approach falls broadly into two classes discussed under various labels in the literature. The first class has been termed overreporting, feigning, faking bad, negative response bias, and malingering; the second has been termed underreporting, faking good, positive response bias, denial, defensiveness, and positive malingering. Because both types of content-based invalid responding can be generated intentionally and unintentionally, the more neutral descriptive terms overreporting and underreporting are preferred.

Overreporting

Overreporting occurs when a test taker reports problems they do not actually have or exaggerates the significance of difficulties they do have. In a hypothetical situation, if a completely objective assessment of the individual's functioning were available, the overreporter's subjective self-report would indicate greater dysfunction than the objective assessment.

Intentional overreporting occurs when the individual knowingly slants their self-report to appear dysfunctional. Such a test taker may be motivated by some external gain and thus fit the *DSM-5* definition of malingering (American Psychiatric Association [APA], 2013). However, intentional overreporting is not synonymous with malingering because, for example, in the absence of an external incentive, it may correspond to the *DSM-5* definition of factitious disorder, or merely uncooperativeness. Moreover, intentional overreporting is not in itself an indication that psychopathology is absent. An individual with genuine psychological difficulties may amplify their extent or significance or may fabricate others but may nonetheless be experiencing significant dysfunction. In such a scenario it is important for the interpreter to be aware of the likelihood that the test taker's substantive scale scores reflect a level of dysfunction greater than they are experiencing.

Unintentional overreporting occurs when a test taker is unaware that they are describing themself in an unrealistically negative manner. It is the test taker's self-concept rather than the self-report that is skewed. Individuals who engage in this test-taking approach mistakenly believe that their responses are accurate when in fact they are overreporting. Individuals with somatic symptom disorders, for example, report significant somatic problems that cannot be explained by objective medical findings (Lamberty, 2008). They believe their symptoms to be the result of some heretofore undiagnosed condition. Test takers who tend to catastrophize and see things as worse than they actually are may also unintentionally overreport in response to self-report measures.

Underreporting

Underreporting occurs when a test taker describes themself as having less serious or a smaller number of difficulties (or both) than they have. Referring back to the hypothetical objective benchmark just mentioned, an underreporting test taker would paint a picture of better functioning than would be indicated by an objective assessment. Here, too, a distinction may be drawn between intentional and unintentional underreporting.

In *intentional underreporting*, the individual knowingly denies or minimizes the extent of the psychological difficulties or negative characteristics they know they have. As a result, the test scores underestimate their level of dysfunction. Differentiating denial from minimization is important but complex. In the former, an individual blatantly denies problems that they know exist; in the latter, the individual acknowledges some difficulties or negative characteristics but minimizes their extent or impact. *Unintentional underreporting* occurs when the individual unknowingly denies or minimizes difficulties or negative characteristics. Here, too, objective and subjective indicators of psychological functioning would be at odds; however, in unintentional underreporting, this discrepancy results from the individual's distorted self-concept rather than from an intentional effort to produce misleading test results.

Assessing Protocol Validity Threats With the MMPI-3 and Consideration of Confounds

Table 8.1 lists the possible threats to protocol validity assessed by the MMPI-3 Validity Scales as well as other potential influences that can confound Validity Scale interpretation if not considered. The "Non-Content-Based Threats" listed in the first column of Table 8.1 reflect the approach used to detect inconsistent responding with the MMPI-3. As described in chapter 3, the Combined Response Inconsistency (CRIN), Variable Response Inconsistency (VRIN), and True Response Inconsistency (TRIN) scales assess for inconsistent responding by considering a test taker's response to item pairs. The item pairs (called composites) scored on VRIN are keyed such that a True response to one and a False response to the other, or vice versa, adds a point to the scale's raw score. The scale label reflects that these are *variable* (one True and the other False) inconsistent responses. The composites scored on TRIN are keyed such that a combination of inconsistent True responses or a combination of inconsistent False responses contributes to the scale's raw score. The inconsistent True responses and inconsistent False responses are counted separately, with the latter then subtracted from the former followed by the addition of a constant to avoid negative raw score values. The resulting raw score indicates whether a test taker has engaged in a predominant pattern of *fixed True responding* or *fixed False responding* (reflected by a letter T or F following the TRIN T score). CRIN is scored by adding the count of variable inconsistent responses, the count of fixed True responses, and the count of fixed False responses to provide an overall indication of the level of *combined inconsistent responding* in a protocol.

INTERPRETING THE MMPI-3 VALIDITY SCALES | 339

TABLE 8.1. MMPI-3 Validity Scales: Threats to Protocol Validity and Confounds

	CNS	CRIN	VRIN	TRIN	F	Fp	Fs	FBS	RBS	L	K
Threats											
NON-CONTENT-BASED											
Nonresponding	X	−	−	−	−	−	−	−	−	−	−
Random responding		X	X		+	+	+	+	+	+	+
Variable inconsistent responding			X		+	+	+	+	+	+	+
Fixed True responding				X	+	+	+	+	+	−	−
Fixed False responding				X	+	+	+	+	+	+	+
CONTENT-BASED											
Overreporting					X	X	X	X	X		
Underreporting										X	X
Extratest Confounds											
Reading/comprehension problems	+	+	+	+							
Psychopathology/ psychological distress					+	+	+	+	+		
Medical conditions								+	+		
Traditional upbringing										+	
Good adjustment											+

Note. x = Scale designed to assess this threat; + = Confound artifactually increases score; − = Confound artifactually lowers score; CNS = Cannot Say; CRIN = Combined Response Inconsistency; VRIN = Variable Response Inconsistency; TRIN = True Response Inconsistency; F = Infrequent Responses; Fp = Infrequent Psychopathology Responses; Fs = Infrequent Somatic Responses; FBS = Symptom Validity Scale; RBS = Response Bias Scale; L = Uncommon Virtues; K = Adjustment Validity
 Shaded area identifies confounds that can invalidate scores on the corresponding validity scales.

An X in the grid of Table 8.1 identifies the primary MMPI-3 scale(s) for assessing each threat. Interpretation of scores on the validity indicators marked with an X can be confounded by invalid responding other than the type assessed by a scale as well as by the *extratest confounds* listed in Table 8.1. A plus sign (+) in the grid indicates a confound that can artifactually increase scores on a validity indicator; a minus sign (−) indicates a confound that can artifactually lower scores. For example, nonresponding can confound interpretation of scores on all the MMPI-3 validity indicators (except CNS) by lowering the resulting score (as indicated by the minus sign [−] in the *Nonresponding* row under each of these scales). Confounds listed in the shaded cells can reach levels that invalidate scores on a validity indicator, rendering them uninterpretable. For example, under CRIN, nonresponding is identified as a confound that can artifactually lower scores on this scale. In an extreme example, if a test taker does not provide scorable responses to any of the CRIN items, the resulting raw score of zero is uninterpretable insofar as assessment of random responding is concerned. Although extratest confounds do not render validity scale scores uninterpretable, they must be considered carefully to avoid misinterpreting their effects as indications of intentional invalid responding.

INTERPRETIVE GUIDELINES

Tables 8.2 through 8.12 provide interpretive guidelines for the MMPI-3 Validity Scales. For each Validity Scale, these tables list the protocol validity concerns, possible reasons why a test taker may score in a designated range, and the interpretive implications of scores within those ranges. The lists of possible reasons for a score and interpretive implications include guidance for identifying the protocol validity threats and possible confounds just discussed. For example, the tables describing scales that assess for content-based invalid responding indicate the need to rule out inconsistent responding before reaching inferences about overreporting or underreporting. Three subsets of the MMPI-3 Validity Scales address the threats to protocol validity—content nonresponsiveness, overreporting, and underreporting.

Content Nonresponsiveness Scales

Cannot Say (CNS)

The Cannot Say (CNS) score is a count of unscorable responses to the 335 MMPI-3 items and is a raw score. The most common type of unscorable response is no response; however, if the test taker marked both True and False for an item, that response would also be unscorable. As discussed earlier, unscorable responses artifactually lower scores on the MMPI-3 because the scoring method used (counting the number of items on a scale answered in the keyed direction) treats these responses as though the test taker answered in the nonkeyed direction. Scores on scales with at least 90% of the items answered are not likely to be affected by unscorable responses to a degree that would compromise interpretability (Dragon et al., 2012). However, the absence of elevation (including a low score) on a given scale becomes increasingly uninterpretable as the proportion of unscorable item responses on that scale goes beyond 10%. Elevated scores on a scale are still interpretable as such when the test taker has responded to less than 90% of the items, but the scores may underestimate the problems assessed by that scale.

Table 8.2 provides interpretive recommendations for the CNS score. A score of 15 or greater raises concerns about the possibility of compromised validity owing to unscorable responses. Which scales are affected can be deter-

TABLE 8.2. Cannot Say (CNS) Score Interpretation

Raw score	Protocol validity concerns	Possible reasons for score	Interpretive implications
≥ 15	Scores on some scales may be invalid.	Reading or language limitations Severe psychopathology Obsessiveness Lack of insight Lack of cooperation	Examine the content of unscorable items to detect possible themes. The impact is scale dependent. For scales on which less than 90% of the items were scorable, the absence of elevation is uninterpretable. Elevated scores on such scales may underestimate the significance or severity of associated problems.
1–14	Scores on some of the shorter scales may be invalid.	Selective nonresponsiveness	Examine the content of unscorable items to detect possible themes. The impact is scale dependent. For scales on which less than 90% of the items were scorable, the absence of elevation is uninterpretable. Elevated scores on such scales may underestimate the significance or severity of associated problems.

mined only by calculating the percentage of items answered on each scale—a process greatly facilitated by computerized scoring (see chapter 7). As indicated in Table 8.2, an excessive number of unscorable responses may reflect lack of cooperation by the test taker but may also occur if the test taker lacks adequate reading or language comprehension skills, is seriously disturbed, is overly obsessive, or lacks the necessary insight or self-awareness to respond to some test items. The interpreter will need to consider which of these factors may be involved based on extratest information (e.g., background, interview, results of other testing).

Combined Response Inconsistency (CRIN)

The Combined Response Inconsistency (CRIN) scale is a global measure of response inconsistency. CRIN scores indicate the overall level of inconsistent responding in an MMPI-3 protocol, combining information about both variable and fixed inconsistent responding. It includes the 86 item pairs of both the Variable Response Inconsistency (VRIN) and True Response Inconsistency (TRIN) scales (described in the next sections). The CRIN scale can be particularly helpful in identifying test takers who intermittently engage in invalid quasi-random and fixed responding and/or alternating patterns of fixed True and fixed False responding; such test takers may not have elevated scores on VRIN or TRIN. Table 8.3 provides interpretive recommendations for CRIN. A score of 80T or higher indicates that the protocol is invalid because of excessive response inconsistency. This score does not necessarily mean that the test taker was intentionally uncooperative. Other possible reasons for elevation need to be considered based on extratest information. However, this score does indicate that scores on the remaining content-based Validity Scales (the

TABLE 8.3. CRIN (Combined Response Inconsistency) Interpretation

T score	Protocol validity concerns	Possible reasons for score	Interpretive implications
≥ 80	This protocol is invalid because of excessive response inconsistency.	Reading or language limitations Cognitive impairment Errors in recording responses Intentional random responding An uncooperative test-taking approach	The protocol is uninterpretable.
70–79	There is some evidence of response inconsistency.	Reading or language limitations Cognitive impairment Errors in recording responses Carelessness An uncooperative test-taking approach	Scores on the content-based invalid responding indicators and the Substantive Scales should be interpreted with some caution.
39–69	None	The test taker was able to comprehend and respond relevantly to the test items.	No concerns
30–38	There is evidence of remarkably consistent responding.	The test taker was deliberate in their approach to the assessment.	No concerns

overreporting and underreporting indicators) and the Substantive Scales cannot be interpreted.

Variable Response Inconsistency (VRIN)

The Variable Response Inconsistency (VRIN) score is based on the test taker's responses to 53 item pairs selected so that members of each pair are similar in content. The raw VRIN score equals the number of pairs answered inconsistently (i.e., True-False or False-True). The T score derived from the raw score is used to identify protocols marked by excessive variable inconsistent responding. Table 8.4 provides interpretive recommendations for VRIN. A score of 80T or higher indicates that the protocol is invalid because of excessive variable response inconsistency. As noted, this score does not necessarily mean that the test taker was intentionally uncooperative. Other possible reasons for elevation need to be considered based on extratest information. However, this score does indicate that scores on the remaining content-based Validity Scales (the overreporting and underreporting indicators) and on the Substantive Scales cannot be interpreted.

True Response Inconsistency (TRIN)

The True Response Inconsistency (TRIN) score is based on the test taker's responses to 33 item pairs. The members of each pair are quasi reversals in content and keyed so that the raw TRIN score equals the number of pairs (inconsistently) answered True-True minus the number of pairs (inconsistently) answered False-False. Thus, high raw TRIN scores indicate fixed (semantically inconsistent, indiscriminate) True responding, whereas low scores indicate

TABLE 8.4. VRIN (Variable Response Inconsistency) Interpretation

T score	Protocol validity concerns	Possible reasons for score	Interpretive implications
≥ 80	The protocol is invalid because of excessive variable response inconsistency.	Reading or language limitations Cognitive impairment Errors in recording responses Intentional random responding An uncooperative test-taking approach	The protocol is uninterpretable.
70–79	There is some evidence of variable response inconsistency.	Reading or language limitations Cognitive impairment Errors in recording responses Carelessness	Scores on the content-based invalid responding indicators and the Substantive Scales should be interpreted with some caution.
39–69	There is evidence of consistent responding.	The test taker was able to comprehend and respond relevantly to the test items.	No concerns

TABLE 8.5. TRIN (True Response Inconsistency) Interpretation

T score	Protocol validity concerns	Possible reasons for score	Interpretive implications
≥ 80T	The protocol is invalid because of excessive fixed, content-inconsistent True responding.	An uncooperative test-taking approach Difficulties with double negatives	The protocol is uninterpretable.
70T–79T	There is some evidence of fixed, content-inconsistent True responding.	An uncooperative test-taking approach Difficulties with double negatives	Scores on the content-based invalid responding indicators and the Substantive Scales should be interpreted with some caution.
50–69	There is no evidence of fixed, content-inconsistent responding.		No concerns
70F–79F	There is some evidence of fixed, content-inconsistent False responding.	An uncooperative test-taking approach Difficulties with double negatives	Scores on the content-based invalid responding indicators and the Substantive Scales should be interpreted with some caution.
≥ 80F	The protocol is invalid because of excessive fixed, content-inconsistent False responding.	An uncooperative test-taking approach Difficulties with double negatives	The protocol is uninterpretable.

fixed False responding. The TRIN T scores were derived by first transforming the raw scores into linear T scores and then *reflecting* all T-score values below 50 (those deviating from the mean in the counteracquiescent direction). For example, an initial T score of 80, indicative of acquiescence, is left unchanged, but a T score of 20, indicating an equally large deviation in the counteracquiescent direction, is reflected and consequently also becomes 80. To distinguish acquiescent from counteracquiescent scores, the former are displayed with the letter T (e.g., 80T) and the latter with the letter F (80F). Table 8.5

provides interpretive recommendations for TRIN. A T score of 80 or higher on TRIN (in either direction, True or False) indicates that the protocol is invalid because of excessive inconsistent fixed responding and that scores on the remaining content-based Validity Scales (the overreporting and underreporting indicators) and on the Substantive Scales cannot be interpreted.

Overreporting Scales

Overreporting is defined as occurring when the test taker's self-presentation portrays a degree of dysfunction that is "noncredible" (i.e., more extreme than would be indicated by a hypothetical objective assessment of the individual). The general term *overreporting* is preferred over expressions that imply intentionality, which typically require consideration of extratest data. "Faking bad" is an example of such an expression. A diagnosis of *malingering* is another example because it requires evidence of an incentive to exaggerate or fabricate symptoms. In other words, neither faking bad nor malingering can be inferred from the test data alone; however, elevations on the MMPI-3 overreporting scales raise and support the possibility that the test taker is faking bad or malingering.

Particularly in regard to intentionality, it is necessary to consider the possible impact of various psychological disorders characterized by unintentional overreporting of symptoms (e.g., somatic symptom disorders) or misperception of reality (e.g., thought disorders). Moreover, even when there is extratest evidence of intentionality, the current diagnostic system calls for a differential diagnosis of malingering, requiring an external motive (e.g., avoidance of legal responsibility), rather than a factitious disorder that would be inferred to have an internal motive (i.e., a psychogenic need to assume the "sick role"). Scores on the MMPI-3 Validity Scales do not provide specific indications of intentionality or motivation when there is evidence of overreporting. However, test results indicative of overreporting (or lack thereof) can be used to support (or refute) inferences about feigning or malingering, just as scores on the Substantive Scales can suggest diagnostic possibilities to be considered and evaluated with the aid of extratest data (e.g., historical records, other test results, behavioral observations, interviews). In addition, as outlined next, indications of overreporting on the MMPI-3 Validity Scales have implications for the interpretability of scores on the Substantive Scales.

As reflected in Table 8.1 and discussed earlier, scores on the MMPI-3 overreporting indicators are artifactually elevated by random and fixed responding. Therefore, as indicated in the following interpretive guidelines, overreporting can be inferred only if excessive inconsistent responding has been ruled out. As defined here, overreporting is the inaccurate reporting of dysfunction. Broadly speaking, test takers may overreport psychopathology symptoms (e.g., depression, psychosis), cognitive symptoms (e.g., attention difficulties, memory impairment), or somatic symptoms (e.g., pain, poor health). The MMPI-3 Validity Scales are differentially associated with these various areas of noncredible responding. These differences are highlighted in the interpretive recommendations that follow.

As discussed earlier, it is important to note that a finding of overreporting or malingering is not evidence that a test taker is free of dysfunction. Psychopathology and overreporting are not mutually exclusive. Individuals with genuine disorders may overreport their symptoms or fabricate others for a variety of reasons. Therefore, positive findings on the MMPI-3 overreporting indicators do not, in themselves, rule out the possibility that the test taker is psychologically disordered.

Infrequent Responses (F)

The Infrequent Responses (F) scale consists of 35 items rarely answered in the keyed direction by members of the MMPI-3 normative sample. Elevated scores on F are associated with overreporting a broad range of psychological, cognitive, and somatic symptoms. However, as indicated in Table 8.1, elevated scores up to a certain level can also be generated by individuals experiencing genuine difficulties manifesting in psychopathology or psychological distress. Therefore, extratest considerations (e.g., whether the individual has a documented history of significant dysfunction) are critical to proper interpretation of scores on this scale.

Table 8.6 provides interpretive recommendations for F. As outlined, scores in the 75T–99T range raise concerns about possible overreporting of psychological dysfunction that need to be considered in the context of a history or current extratest findings of dysfunction. Significant psychopathology and/or pronounced emotional distress can also result in deviant scores on this scale. As the score on F rises, evidence of a greater degree of genuine dysfunction is needed to rule out overreporting. A T score of 100 or greater on F is uncommon even in individuals with genuine, severe dysfunction and indicates that the protocol is invalid and uninterpretable.

Infrequent Psychopathology Responses (Fp)

The Infrequent Psychopathology Responses (Fp) scale consists of 21 items rarely answered in the keyed direction by individuals with genuine, severe psychopathology. As a result, in contrast with F, scores on Fp are less likely to be confounded with severe disorder or distress. Therefore, this scale is particularly helpful in assessing overreporting in settings and with populations characterized

TABLE 8.6. F (Infrequent Responses) Interpretation

T score	Protocol validity concerns	Possible reasons for score	Interpretive implications
≥ 100	The protocol is invalid. Overreporting is indicated by an excessive number of infrequent responses.	Inconsistent responding Overreporting	Inconsistent responding should be considered by examining the CRIN, VRIN, and TRIN scores. If it is ruled out, note that this level of infrequent responding is uncommon even in individuals with genuine, severe psychological difficulties who report credible symptoms. Scores on the Substantive Scales should not be interpreted.
90-99	The protocol may be invalid. Overreporting of psychological dysfunction is indicated by a considerably larger than average number of infrequent responses.	Inconsistent responding Severe psychopathology Severe emotional distress Overreporting	Inconsistent responding should be considered by examining the CRIN, VRIN, and TRIN scores. If it is ruled out, note that this level of infrequent responding may occur in individuals with genuine, severe psychological difficulties who report credible symptoms. However, for individuals with no history or current corroborating evidence of dysfunction, it most likely indicates overreporting.
80-89	Possible overreporting of psychological dysfunction is indicated by a much larger than average number of infrequent responses.	Inconsistent responding Significant psychopathology Significant emotional distress Overreporting	Inconsistent responding should be considered by examining the CRIN, VRIN, and TRIN scores. If it is ruled out, note that this level of infrequent responding may occur in individuals with genuine, substantial psychological difficulties who report credible symptoms. However, for individuals with no history or current corroborating evidence of dysfunction, it very likely indicates overreporting.
75-79	Possible overreporting of psychological dysfunction is indicated by a larger than average number of infrequent responses.	Inconsistent responding Significant psychopathology Significant emotional distress Overreporting	Inconsistent responding should be considered by examining the CRIN, VRIN, and TRIN scores. If it is ruled out, note that this level of infrequent responding may occur in individuals with genuine psychological difficulties who report credible symptoms. However, for individuals with no history or current corroborating evidence of dysfunction, it likely indicates overreporting.
< 75	There is no evidence of overreporting.		No concerns

by high base rates of significant psychological disorders, most notably those marked by psychotic symptoms or severe emotional dysfunction.

Table 8.7 provides interpretive recommendations for Fp. As indicated, scores in the 80T–99T range raise substantial concerns about the possibility of symptom exaggeration, even for test takers with a significant history of mental health problems. Scores that reach or exceed 100T indicate that the protocol is invalid owing to the strong likelihood of substantial overreporting.

TABLE 8.7. Fp (Infrequent Psychopathology Responses) Interpretation

T score	Protocol validity concerns	Possible reasons for score	Interpretive implications
≥ 100	The protocol is invalid. Overreporting is indicated by assertion of a considerably larger than average number of symptoms rarely described by individuals with genuine, severe psychopathology.	Inconsistent responding Overreporting	Inconsistent responding should be considered by examining the CRIN, VRIN, and TRIN scores. If it is ruled out, note that this level of infrequent responding is very uncommon even in individuals with genuine, severe psychopathology who report credible symptoms. Scores on the Substantive Scales should not be interpreted.
80-99	Possible overreporting is indicated by assertion of a much larger than average number of symptoms rarely described by individuals with genuine, severe psychopathology.	Inconsistent responding Severe psychopathology Overreporting	Inconsistent responding should be considered by examining the CRIN, VRIN, and TRIN scores. If it is ruled out, note that this level of infrequent responding may occur in individuals with genuine, severe psychopathology who report credible symptoms, but it could also reflect exaggeration. For individuals with no history or current corroborating evidence of psychopathology, scores in this range very likely indicate overreporting.
70-79	Possible overreporting is indicated by assertion of a larger than average number of symptoms rarely described by individuals with genuine, severe psychopathology.	Inconsistent responding Severe psychopathology Overreporting	Inconsistent responding should be considered by examining the CRIN, VRIN, and TRIN scores. If it is ruled out, note that this level of infrequent responding may occur in individuals with genuine, severe psychopathology who report credible symptoms. However, for individuals with no history or current corroborating evidence of psychopathology, scores in this range likely indicate overreporting.

Scores on Fp can be particularly helpful when a test taker produces a markedly elevated score on F and the interpreter needs to determine whether this reflects overreporting or genuine dysfunction. The lower the score on Fp, the less likely it is that an elevation on F reflects overreporting and the more likely it is that an F elevation reflects accurate reporting of experiences that are uncommon in the general population but not in individuals with significant psychological difficulties. This is particularly true if the individual presents with symptoms of thought dysfunction. However, test takers who overreport problems associated with emotional (e.g., depression, anxiety) rather than thought dysfunction may also produce substantially higher scores on F than on Fp. F scores may also be higher than Fp scores when test takers report noncredible somatic or cognitive symptoms. These individuals would also be expected to generate elevated scores on Fs, FBS, and/or RBS as described next.

TABLE 8.8. Fs (Infrequent Somatic Responses) Interpretation

T score	Protocol validity concerns	Possible reasons for score	Interpretive implications
≥ 100	Scores on the somatic scales may be invalid. Overreporting of somatic symptoms is reflected in the assertion of a considerably larger than average number of somatic symptoms rarely described by individuals with genuine medical problems.	Inconsistent responding Overreporting of somatic complaints	Inconsistent responding should be considered by examining the CRIN, VRIN, and TRIN scores. If it is ruled out, note that this level of infrequent responding is very uncommon even in individuals with substantial medical problems who report credible symptoms. Scores on the somatic scales should be interpreted cautiously.
80–99	Possible overreporting of somatic symptoms is reflected in the assertion of a much larger than average number of somatic symptoms rarely described by individuals with genuine medical problems.	Inconsistent responding Significant and/or multiple medical conditions Overreporting of somatic complaints	Inconsistent responding should be considered by examining the CRIN, VRIN, and TRIN scores. If it is ruled out, note that this level and type of infrequent responding may occur in individuals with substantial medical conditions who report credible symptoms, but it could also reflect exaggeration. In individuals with no history or corroborating evidence of physical health problems, this probably indicates noncredible reporting of somatic symptoms. Scores on the somatic scales should be interpreted cautiously.
< 80	There is no evidence of overreporting.		No concerns

Infrequent Somatic Responses (Fs)

The Infrequent Somatic Responses (Fs) scale consists of 16 items with somatic content uncommonly endorsed by medical patients receiving treatment for various physical diseases. Based on the same rare-symptoms rationale as the other two MMPI-3 infrequent response indicators (F and Fp), Fs is designed to identify test takers who overreport somatic symptoms by endorsing many somatic complaints rarely reported by medical patients. Table 8.8 provides interpretive recommendations for scores on Fs. As shown, scores in the 80T–99T range raise concerns about possible overreporting of somatic symptoms. Scores of 100T or higher indicate that overreporting of somatic complaints has likely occurred, limiting the interpretability of scores on Somatic Complaints (RC1), Malaise (MLS), and Neurological Complaints (NUC) scales.

To reiterate an important point made earlier, overreporting is not synonymous with faking or malingering. Noncredible somatic complaints may stem from a variety of sources, including an external incentive but also the internal psychological factors underlying a somatic symptom disorder or somatic delusions. Extratest data (in this case, a detailed medical and psychological history) are needed to make these distinctions.

TABLE 8.9. FBS (Symptom Validity Scale) Interpretation

T score	Protocol validity concerns	Possible reasons for score	Interpretive implications
≥ 90	Scores on the Somatic/Cognitive Scales may be invalid. Overreporting is indicated by a very unusual combination of responses that is associated with noncredible reporting of somatic and/or cognitive symptoms.	Inconsistent responding Overreporting of somatic and/or cognitive symptoms	Inconsistent responding should be considered by examining the CRIN, VRIN, and TRIN scores. If it is ruled out, note that this combination of responses is very uncommon even in individuals with substantial medical problems who report credible symptoms. Scores on the Somatic/Cognitive Scales should be interpreted cautiously.
78–89	Possible overreporting is indicated by an unusual combination of responses that is associated with noncredible reporting of somatic and/or cognitive symptoms.	Inconsistent responding Significant and/or multiple medical conditions Overreporting of somatic and/or cognitive complaints	Inconsistent responding should be considered by examining the CRIN, VRIN, and TRIN scores. If it is ruled out, note that this combination of responses may occur in individuals with substantial medical problems who report credible symptoms, but it could also reflect exaggeration. Scores on the Somatic/Cognitive Scales should be interpreted cautiously.
< 78	There is no evidence of overreporting.		No concerns

Symptom Validity Scale (FBS)

The Symptom Validity Scale (FBS) consists of 30 items. A longer version of the scale was originally developed to complement the MMPI-2's F scale by identifying individuals presenting with noncredible symptoms in the context of civil litigation. Table 8.9 provides interpretive recommendations for FBS. As indicated, scores in the 78T–89T range identify possible overreporting as reflected in an unusual combination of responses that is associated with noncredible presentation of somatic and/or cognitive symptoms. Scores of 90T or higher indicate likely overreporting of such symptoms, limiting the interpretability of the scales RC1, MLS, NUC, and COG. The extratest data needed to make inferences about possible motives for noncredible symptom reporting for Fs should be considered in the interpretation of scores on FBS as well.

As reflected in the respective interpretive recommendations, both Fs and FBS provide information about possible noncredible somatic symptom reporting. Scores on the two scales are only moderately correlated, indicating relatedness but by no means redundancy. Therefore, scores on both scales need to be considered with appropriate attention to the setting.

TABLE 8.10. RBS (Response Bias Scale) Interpretation

T score	Protocol validity concerns	Possible reasons for score	Interpretive implications
≥ 90	Scores on the Cognitive Complaints scale may be invalid. Overreporting is indicated by a very unusual combination of responses that is strongly associated with noncredible memory complaints.	Inconsistent responding Overreporting of memory complaints	Inconsistent responding should be considered by examining the CRIN, VRIN, and TRIN scores. If it is ruled out, note that this combination of responses is very uncommon even in individuals with substantial emotional dysfunction who report credible symptoms. Scores on the Cognitive Complaints scale should be interpreted cautiously.
75–89	Possible overreporting is indicated by an unusual combination of responses that is associated with noncredible memory complaints.	Inconsistent responding Significant emotional dysfunction Overreporting of memory complaints	Inconsistent responding should be considered by examining the CRIN, VRIN, and TRIN scores. If it is ruled out, note that this combination of responses may occur in individuals with substantial emotional dysfunction who report credible symptoms, but it could also reflect exaggeration. Scores on the Cognitive Complaints scale should be interpreted cautiously.
< 75	There is no evidence of overreporting.		No concerns

Response Bias Scale (RBS)

The Response Bias Scale (RBS) is composed of 28 items associated empirically with scoring below established cutoffs on psychological tests designed to detect inadequate effort on cognitive testing, known as performance validity tests (PVTs). Table 8.10 provides interpretive recommendations for RBS. As indicated, scores in the 75T–89T range indicate possible overreporting reflected as an unusual combination of responses associated with noncredible memory complaints. However, scores in this range may also indicate that individuals are experiencing substantial emotional dysfunction. Scores of 90T or higher indicate likely overreporting of memory problems, limiting the interpretability of scores on the COG scale. Although PVTs were used in the development of RBS, the scale is not intended or recommended for use as a measure of effort on cognitive tests.

Underreporting Scales

Underreporting is defined as occurring when the test taker's self-presentation suggests a level of functioning that is better than would be indicated by a hypothetical objective assessment of the individual. As with the term *overreporting*, the term *underreporting* is preferred over terms such as "faking good" or "positive malingering," which connote an intentionality that cannot be inferred from test data alone. Self-report measures of personality and psychopathology are inherently susceptible to intentional underreporting, which is most likely to occur when, given the assessment context, good adjustment is a highly desirable quality and the individual has a great deal at stake (e.g., child custody evaluations, preemployment assessments, or release from involuntary commitment). However, underreporting can also result from lack of awareness of or insight into psychological dysfunction.

As with overreporting, differentiating intentional from unintentional underreporting requires consideration of extratest data. For example, if a test taker presents as extraordinarily well adjusted but is experiencing considerable psychosocial difficulties, this increases the likelihood that the individual is knowingly underreporting. At the same time, as will be explained shortly and is reflected in Table 8.1, elevated scores on the two MMPI-3 underreporting indicators can to some extent reflect factors (confounds) other than underreporting (e.g., being raised in a very traditional environment or being considerably better adjusted than average).

Regardless of whether the underreporting is intentional, unintentional, or can be explained by other factors, elevated scores on the MMPI-3 underreporting scales indicate a need for caution in the interpretation of scores on the Substantive Scales. Specifically, nonelevated and, in particular, low scores (i.e., 38T or lower) on the Substantive Scales are uninterpretable and cannot be relied upon to rule out problems when there are indications of possible underreporting. Elevated scores on one or more of these scales are interpretable but may underestimate the problems associated with the elevation(s).

As is the case with the overreporting indicators, scores on the underreporting scales can be significantly distorted if a protocol is marked by considerable inconsistent responding. This is particularly true of fixed False responding, which artifactually elevates scores on both underreporting indicators because most of the items on these measures are keyed in that direction.

Uncommon Virtues (L)

The Uncommon Virtues (L) scale consists of 14 items. Elevated L scores indicate that the test taker presented themselves in a favorable light by denying minor faults and shortcomings that most individuals acknowledge. An important consideration in understanding the significance of an elevated L score in each case is whether the test taker was raised in an environment stressing traditional values, an important cultural factor discussed in chapter 4. If so, inferences about underreporting need to be tempered, particularly for moderate levels of elevation on this scale.

TABLE 8.11. L (Uncommon Virtues) Interpretation

T score	Protocol validity concerns	Possible reasons for score	Interpretive implications
≥ 80	The protocol may be invalid. Underreporting is indicated by the test taker presenting themself in an extremely positive light by denying many minor faults and shortcomings that most people acknowledge.	Inconsistent responding Underreporting	Inconsistent responding should be considered by examining the CRIN, VRIN, and TRIN scores. If it is ruled out, note that this level of virtuous self-presentation is very uncommon even in individuals with a background stressing traditional values. Any absence of elevation on the Substantive Scales is uninterpretable. Elevated scores on the Substantive Scales may underestimate the problems assessed by those scales.
70–79	Possible underreporting is indicated by the test taker presenting themself in a very positive light by denying several minor faults and shortcomings that most people acknowledge.	Inconsistent responding Traditional upbringing Underreporting	Inconsistent responding should be considered by examining the CRIN, VRIN, and TRIN scores. If it is ruled out, note that this level of virtuous self-presentation is uncommon but may, to some extent, reflect a background stressing traditional values. Any absence of elevation on the Substantive Scales should be interpreted with caution. Elevated scores on the Substantive Scales may underestimate the problems assessed by those scales.
65–69	Possible underreporting is indicated by the test taker presenting themself in a very positive light by denying some minor faults and shortcomings that most people acknowledge.	Inconsistent responding Traditional upbringing Underreporting	Inconsistent responding should be considered by examining the CRIN, VRIN, and TRIN scores. If it is ruled out, note that this level of virtuous self-presentation may reflect a background stressing traditional values. Any absence of elevation on the Substantive Scales should be interpreted with caution. Elevated scores on the Substantive Scales may underestimate the problems assessed by those scales.

Table 8.11 provides interpretive recommendations for L. Scores in the 65T–69T and 70T–79T ranges reflect possible underreporting, with higher scores indicating an increased likelihood of this being the case (and a reduced possibility that a traditional upbringing can account fully for the elevation). Scores of 80T or higher indicate that substantial underreporting very likely occurred and raise the possibility that the protocol is consequently of limited utility or invalid.[1] When L scores reach this level, elevated scores on the Substantive Scales are interpretable but may underestimate the problems associated with these elevations. Absence of elevation on the Substantive Scales is uninterpretable when L scores are this high.

TABLE 8.12. K (Adjustment Validity) Interpretation

T score	Protocol validity concerns	Possible reasons for score	Interpretive implications
≥ 70	Underreporting is indicated by the test taker presenting themselves as remarkably well adjusted.	Inconsistent responding Underreporting	Inconsistent responding should be considered by examining the CRIN, VRIN, and TRIN scores. If it is ruled out, note that this level of psychological adjustment is rare in the general population. Any absence of elevation on the Substantive Scales should be interpreted with caution. Elevated scores on the Substantive Scales may underestimate the problems assessed by those scales.
66–69	Possible underreporting is indicated by the test taker presenting themselves as very well adjusted.	Inconsistent responding Very good psychological adjustment Underreporting	Inconsistent responding should be considered by examining the CRIN, VRIN, and TRIN scores. If it is ruled out, note that this level of psychological adjustment is rare in the general population. For individuals who are not especially well adjusted, any absence of elevation on the Substantive Scales should be interpreted with caution. Elevated scores on the Substantive Scales may underestimate the problems assessed by those scales.
60–65	Possible underreporting is indicated by the test taker presenting themselves as very well adjusted.	Inconsistent responding Good psychological adjustment Underreporting	Inconsistent responding should be considered by examining the CRIN, VRIN, and TRIN scores. If it is ruled out, for individuals who are not well adjusted, any absence of elevation on the Substantive Scales should be interpreted with caution. Elevated scores on the Substantive Scales may underestimate the problems assessed by those scales.
< 60	There is no evidence of underreporting.		No concerns

Adjustment Validity (K)

The Adjustment Validity (K) scale consists of 14 of items. Elevated K scores indicate that the test taker presented themselves as well adjusted, with higher scores representing a higher level of adjustment. This type of self-presentation is associated with underreporting. However, the possibility that the test taker is in fact better adjusted than average also needs to be considered in the interpretation of an elevated K score. Extratest indications that the individual is not well adjusted would support a conclusion that an elevated K score indicates underreporting, whereas evidence that they are well adjusted would temper this interpretation.

Table 8.12 provides interpretive recommendations for K. Scores in the 60T–65T and 66T–69T ranges indicate possible underreporting, with higher scores suggesting a greater likelihood of underreporting and requiring evidence of better adjustment to rule out this interpretation. T scores above 70 indicate that the test taker presented themselves as remarkably well adjusted. Without extratest indications to the contrary, this level of elevation on K indicates in most settings that nonelevated scores on the Substantive Scales represent favorable self-portrayal reflecting an underreporting tendency and cannot be interpreted as indicating the absence of the problems they are intended to assess. Elevated substantive scale scores may not fully reflect the magnitude or severity of associated problems when the K score reaches this level.

CASE ILLUSTRATIONS

We turn next to a series of cases selected to illustrate MMPI-3 Validity Scale interpretation. Figure 8.1 presents the validity scale scores for a test taker who provided 32 unscorable responses (the Cannot Say raw score appears in the fourth row under the profile). The third row provides the percent scorable responses (Response %) for each of the MMPI-3 Validity Scales. As noted earlier, the score on any scale for which this percentage falls below 90 cannot be interpreted following the standard guidelines in Tables 8.2 through 8.12. Specifically, the absence of elevation on these scales cannot be interpreted as indicating the absence of the protocol validity threat assessed by that scale. In Figure 8.1, this applies to the scores on CRIN, VRIN, TRIN, FBS, and K, for which the percent scorable responses are all lower than 90% and hence are printed in bold. In the case of the CRIN scale, which has 83% scorable responses, this translates into 15 unscorable item pairs. Had the test taker responded to at least 10 of those item pairs inconsistently, their CRIN T score would reach 80, invalidating the protocol. Therefore, it is not possible to rule out that this is an invalid MMPI-3 protocol. As seen in Figure 8.2, this individual's scores on the MMPI-3 Higher-Order (H-O) and Restructured Clinical (RC) Scales are all well within normal limits. However, the percent scorable responses on more than half of these scales falls below 90. The absence of elevation on these scales cannot be interpreted as indicating the absence of the problems they assess.

The Validity Scales profile depicted in Figure 8.3 illustrates a case in which neither the VRIN nor the TRIN score reaches a level that would invalidate this MMPI-3 protocol. A T score of 83 on CRIN indicates nonetheless that this is an invalid protocol. This case illustrates one way in which the CRIN scale provides incremental information beyond VRIN and TRIN. As described earlier, the CRIN raw score equals the sum of the inconsistent variable (one True the other False), inconsistent True, and inconsistent False responses, which is 17 in this case. This random pattern, reflected in intermittent variable and fixed responding, invalidates the protocol. As indicated under the *Possible reasons for score* heading in Table 8.3, this level of inconsistent responding can

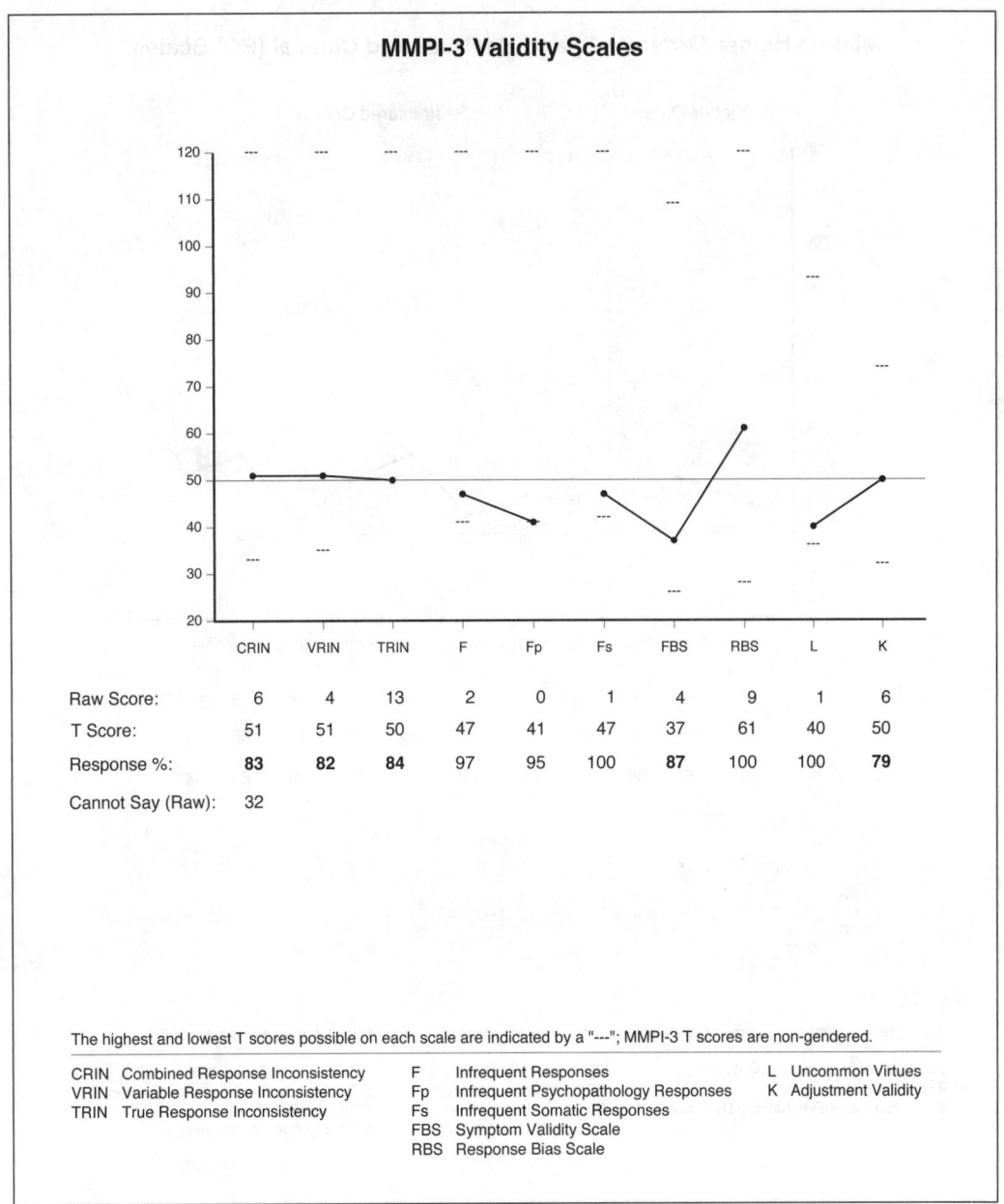

FIGURE 8.1. MMPI-3 Score Report Validity Scales Profile Showing Nonresponding

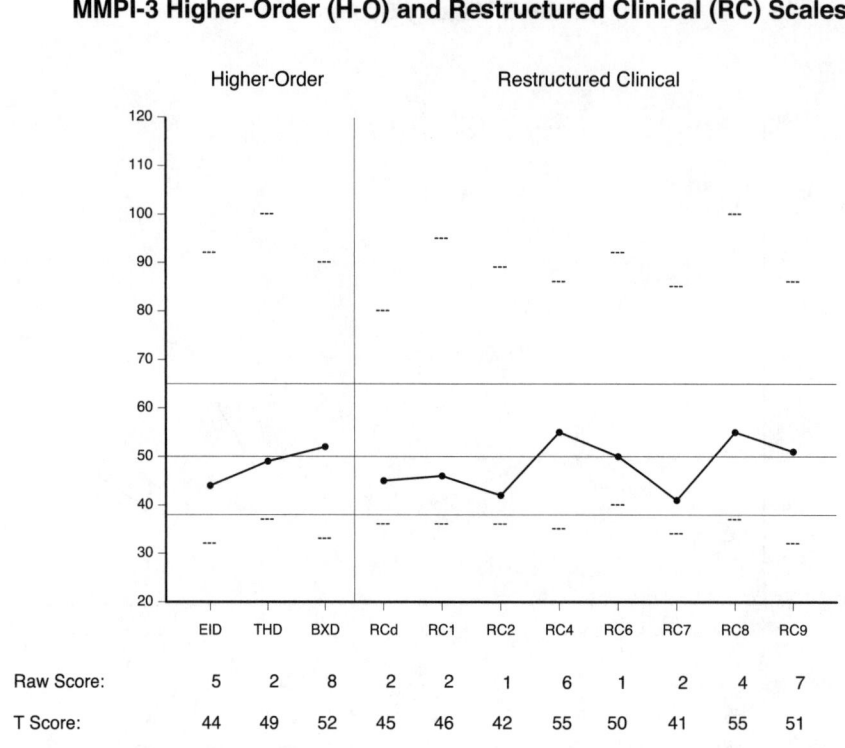

FIGURE 8.2. MMPI-3 Score Report Validity Scales Profile Showing Nonresponding

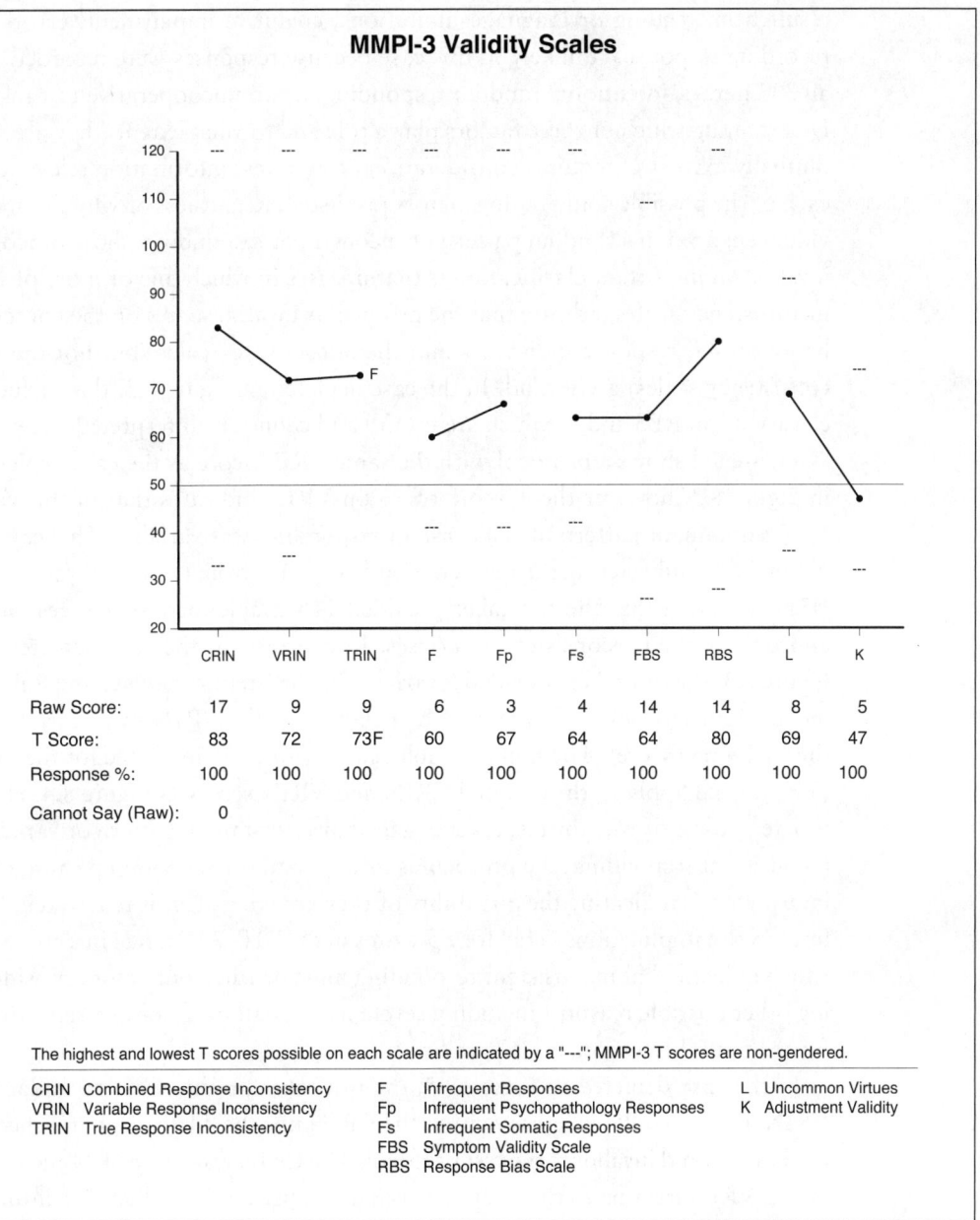

FIGURE 8.3. MMPI-3 Score Report Validity Scales Profile Showing Combined Inconsistent Responding

result from reading or language limitations, cognitive impairment, errors in recording responses (unlikely in this case because responses were recorded for all 335 items), intentional random responding, or an uncooperative test taker. Determining which of these factors play a role and to what extent (they are not mutually exclusive) requires consideration of extratest information relevant to each of the possible contributing factors just listed. Regardless of why this individual engaged in a random pattern of inconsistent responding, the protocol is invalid. An important clarification is that in cases in which one or more of the inconsistency scales indicate that the protocol is invalid, scores on the content-based invalid response indicators and the Substantive Scales (but not the inconsistency scales) are invalid. In the case depicted in Figure 8.3, this includes elevations on RBS and L, which are invalid and cannot be interpreted.

Figure 8.4 shows a protocol with the same CRIN score as the case depicted in Figure 8.3; however the T score of 93 on VRIN indicates that in this case the predominant pattern of inconsistent responding was variable. This can be discerned by subtracting the raw score on VRIN (14) from the CRIN raw score (17), indicating that the test taker provided 14 variable inconsistent response and only 3 fixed inconsistent responses. In contrast, in the case depicted in Figure 8.3, the test taker provided 9 variable inconsistent responses and 8 fixed inconsistent responses (determined by subtracting the VRIN raw score from the CRIN raw score). The same possible reasons for elevation listed for the case in Figure 8.3 apply to the elevated CRIN and VRIN scores in Figure 8.4. Here too, regardless of why the test taker engaged in a substantial pattern of variable inconsistent responding, the protocol is invalid, and the score on Fp cannot be interpreted as indicating the possibility of overreporting. This is reflected in the interpretive implications listed for Fp scores in the 70T–79T range in Table 8.7, which indicate that inconsistent responding must be ruled out before considering other possible reasons (including severe psychopathology or overreporting) for the test taker's score of 76T on Fp.

In the case depicted in Figure 8.5, the test taker produced an invalidating VRIN T score of 85, whereas neither the CRIN nor the TRIN score reached a level that would invalidate the test protocol. The CRIN raw score of 14 includes the 12 VRIN item pairs that were answered inconsistently and two additional TRIN item pairs answered inconsistently. A TRIN T score of 50 indicates that the two inconsistent pairs of responses offset each other, with one pair keyed True and the other False. Thus, nearly all the inconsistent responding in this protocol was variable (one item keyed True the other False). The resulting scores on the content-based invalid response indicators and the Substantive Scales are invalid and uninterpretable.

Figure 8.6 shows a Validity Scales profile marked by a very high level of fixed, content-inconsistent True responding that invalidates the test protocol. Examination of the interpretive guidelines for TRIN in Table 8.5, indicates that this

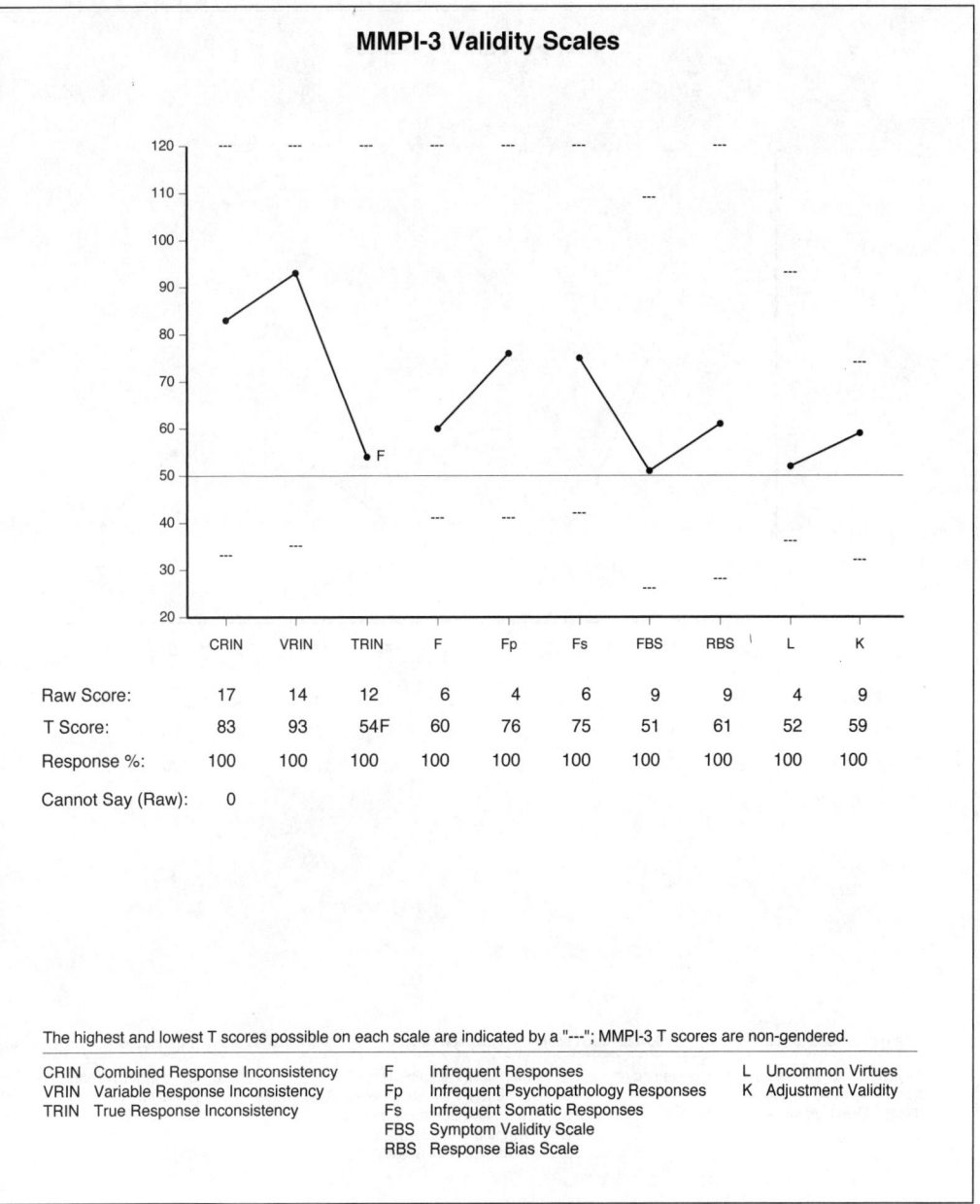

FIGURE 8.4. MMPI-3 Score Report Validity Scales Profile Showing Variable Inconsistent Responding

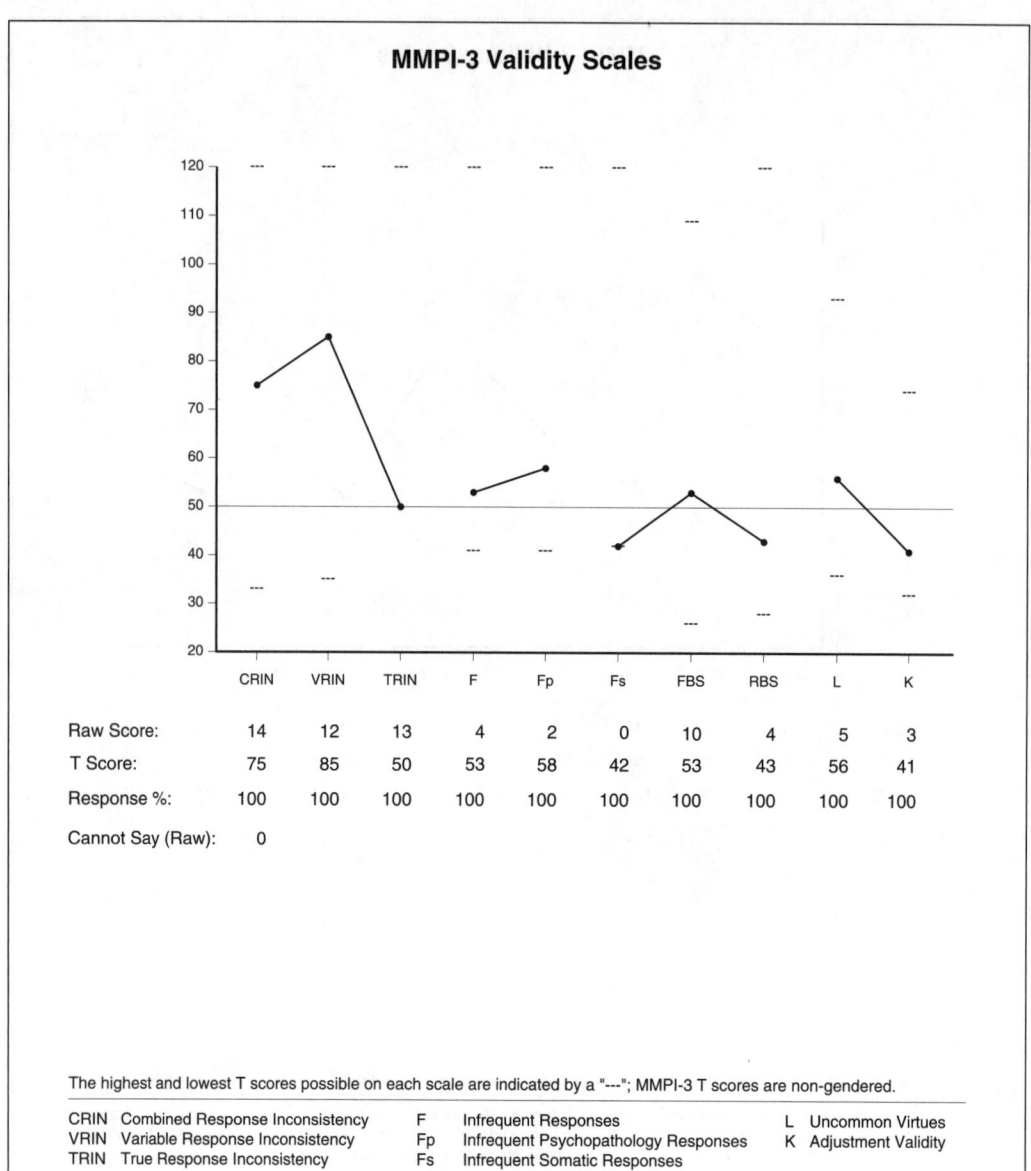

FIGURE 8.5. MMPI-3 Score Report Validity Scales Profile Showing Variable Inconsistent Responding

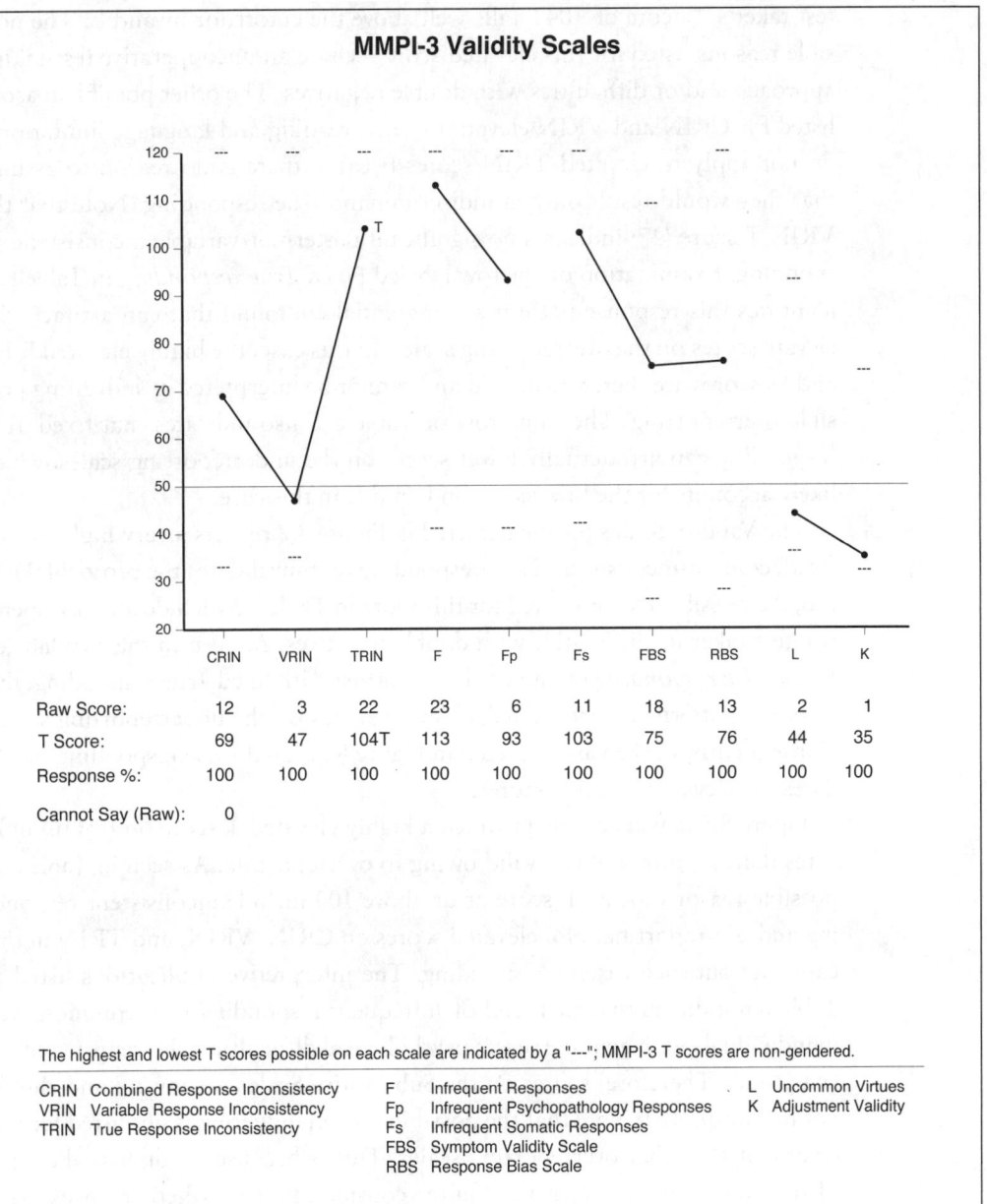

FIGURE 8.6. MMPI-3 Score Report Validity Scales Profile Showing Fixed, Content-Inconsistent True Responding

test taker's T score of 104T falls well above the cutoff for invalidity. The possible reasons listed for this elevated score include an uncooperative test-taking approach and/or difficulties with double negatives. The other possible reasons listed for CRIN and VRIN elevations (e.g., reading and language limitations) do not apply to elevated TRIN scores because there is no reason to assume that they would result only in indiscriminant True responding. Note that the VRIN T score (47) indicates no significant pattern of variable inconsistent responding. Examination of the row labeled *Fixed True responding* in Table 8.1, identifies this response pattern as a potential confound that can artifactually elevate scores on the overreporting scales. In this case, the highly elevated F, Fp, and Fs scores are therefore invalid and cannot be interpreted as indicating possible overreporting. The same row of Table 8.1 also indicates that fixed True responding can artifactually lower scores on the underreporting scales, which likely accounts for the low scores on L and K in this case.

The Validity Scales profile depicted in Figure 8.7 reflects a very high level of fixed, content-inconsistent False responding that invalidates the protocol. Here too, the possible reasons listed for this score in Table 8.5 include an uncooperative test taker or difficulties with double negatives. As seen in the row labeled *Fixed false responding* in Table 8.1, in contrast with fixed True responding, this response pattern can artifactually elevate scores on the underreporting scales. Consequently, in the case depicted in Figure 8.7, fixed False responding invalidates the elevated L and K scores.

Figure 8.8 depicts a case in which a highly elevated T score on F (116) indicates that the protocol is invalid owing to overreporting. As seen in Table 8.6, possible reasons for an F score at or above 100 include inconsistent responding and overreporting. Nonelevated scores on CRIN, VRIN, and TRIN in this case rule out inconsistent responding. The interpretive implications listed in Table 8.6 indicate that this level of infrequent responding is uncommon even in individuals with genuine severe psychological difficulties who report credible symptoms. Therefore, scores on the Substantive Scales are invalid and should not be interpreted. Note that the possibility of malingering is not listed for this or any of the other overreporting scales. This is because, as discussed earlier, identification of malingering requires consideration of whether an external incentive is present and integration of other information sources. Nevertheless, evidence of overreporting (such as in this case), properly integrated with other information, can support an inference that the test taker is malingering. It is worth noting in this context that much of the empirical research supporting and guiding interpretation of MMPI overreporting indicators has relied on simulation and known group research designs in which malingering was the criterion (see chapter 4).

In the case depicted in Figure 8.9, a T score of 101 on Fp indicates that the protocol is invalid owing to an assertion of a considerably larger than aver-

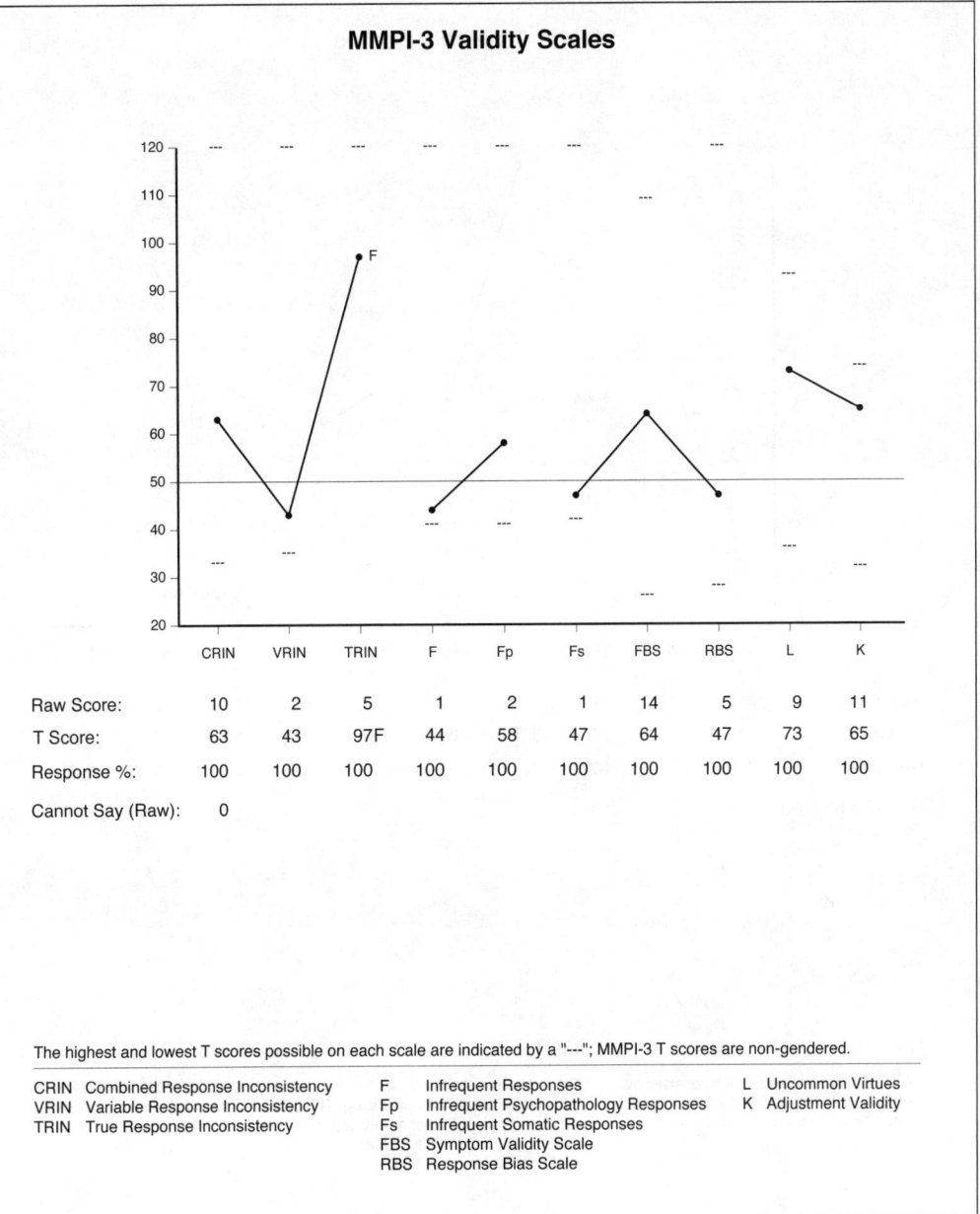

FIGURE 8.7. MMPI-3 Score Report Validity Scales Profile Showing Fixed, Content-Inconsistent False Responding

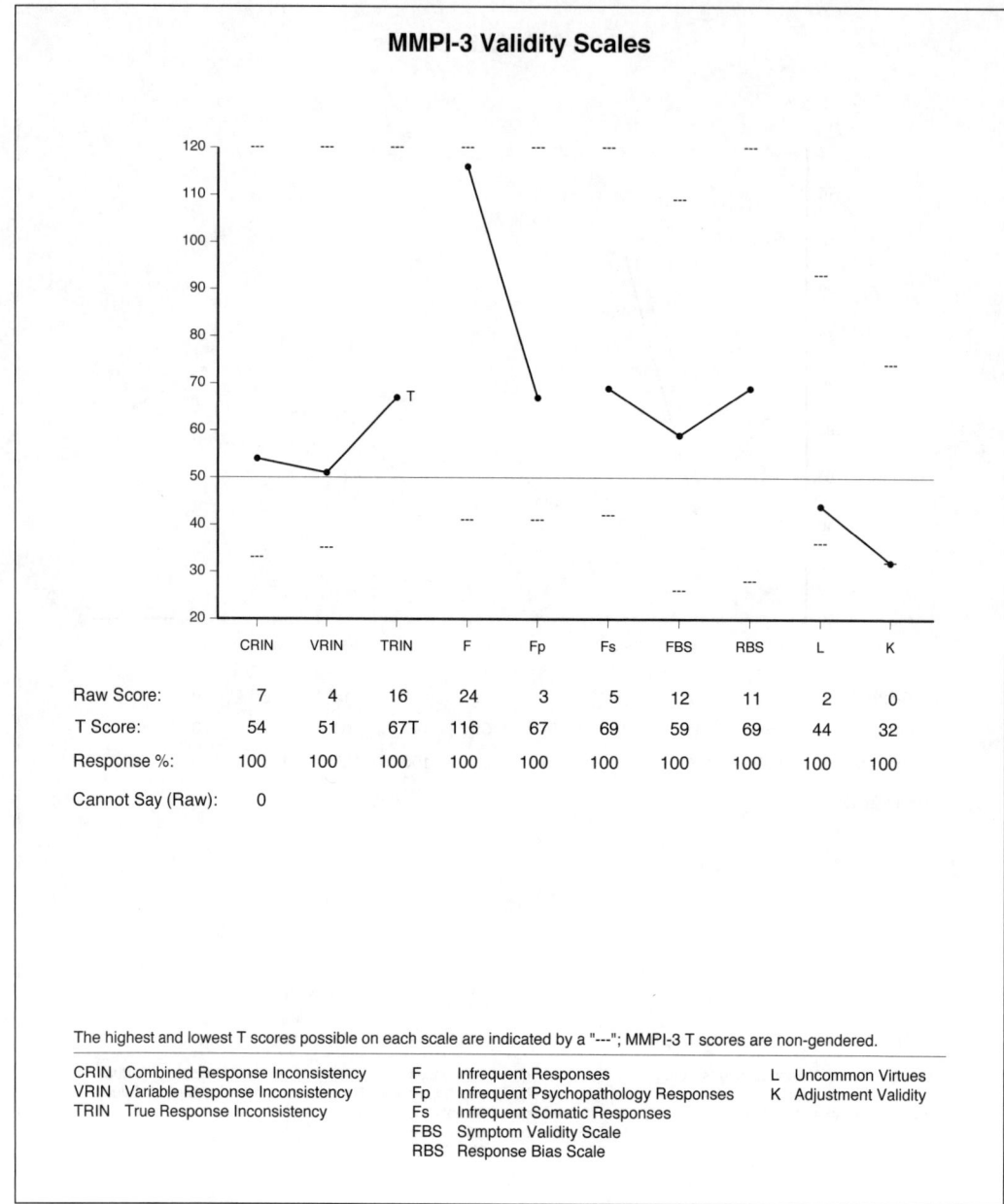

FIGURE 8.8. MMPI-3 Score Report Validity Scales Profile Showing a Highly Elevated F Score Reflecting Overreporting

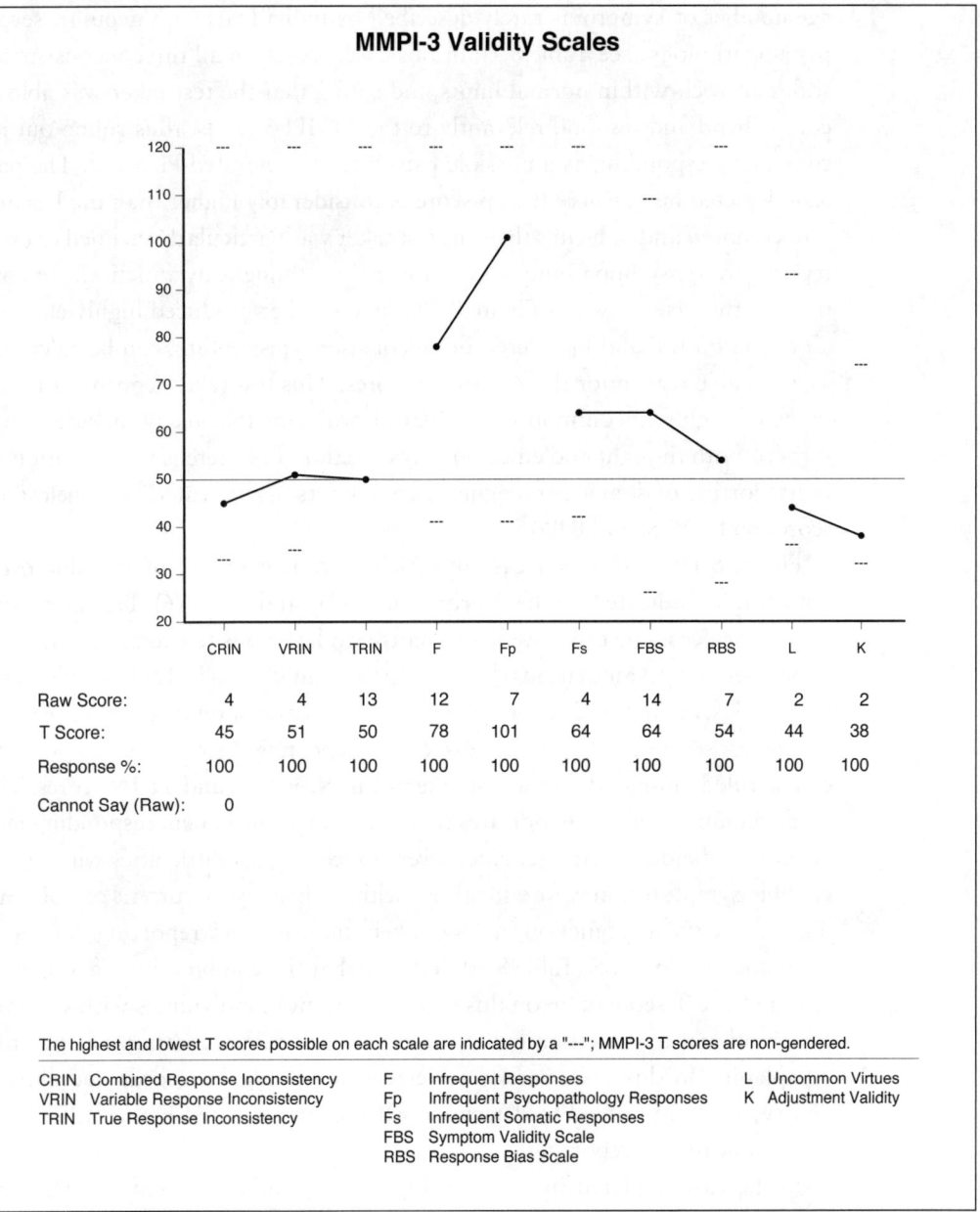

FIGURE 8.9. MMPI-3 Score Report Validity Scales Profile Showing an Elevated Fp Score Reflecting Overreporting of Severe Psychopathology

age number of symptoms rarely described by individuals with genuine, severe psychopathology (see Table 8.7). In this case, scores on all three inconsistency scales are well within normal limits, indicating that the test taker was able to comprehend and respond relevantly to the MMPI-3 items, thus ruling out inconsistent responding as a possible reason for the elevated Fp score. The pattern depicted here, where the Fp score is considerably higher than the F score, is uncommon and indicates that this test taker was particularly inclined to overreport severe psychopathology symptoms (e.g., thought dysfunction). In contrast, in the case shown in Figure 8.10, the test taker produced highly elevated scores on both F and Fp. Here, too, inconsistent responding can be ruled out as a possible reason for these extreme scores. This test taker reported a broad range of highly uncommon psychological problems that likely include symptoms of both thought and emotional dysfunction, but there is no indication of overreporting of somatic or cognitive complaints (as indicated by nonelevated scores on Fs, FBS, and RBS).

Figure 8.11 illustrates a case in which there is evidence of possible overreporting as indicated by the T scores on F (91) and RBS (76). However, contrary to the cases just reviewed, alternative explanations to overreporting need to be ruled out. Examination of the interpretive guidelines in Table 8.6 indicates that the F score in this case may reflect inconsistent responding, severe psychopathology, severe emotional distress, or overreporting. Inconsistent responding can be ruled out based on the test taker's CRIN, VRIN, and TRIN scores. The final column of Table 8.6 indicates that this level of infrequent responding may occur in individuals with genuine, severe psychological difficulties who report credible symptoms; however, for those with no history or current corroborating evidence of dysfunction, it most likely indicates overreporting. Similarly, the guidelines for RBS (Table 8.10) indicate that the combination of responses reflected in a T score of 76 on this scale may occur in individuals with substantial emotional dysfunction, but it could also reflect exaggeration of cognitive complaints. In this case, careful review of any available records and clinical observations are needed to determine whether the elevated F and RBS scores likely indicate overreporting.

In the case depicted in Figure 8.12, the very high Fs T score (103) indicates that overreporting of somatic symptoms is reflected in the assertion of a considerably larger than average number of somatic symptoms rarely described by individuals with genuine medical problems. The guidance provided in Table 8.8 indicates that this level of infrequent responding is very uncommon even in individuals who report credible medical symptoms. Note that, in itself, this finding does not indicate that the test taker is free of genuine somatic symptoms. Rather, it indicates that their self-reported symptoms are unreliable and scores on the MMPI-3 somatic scales should be interpreted with particular caution.

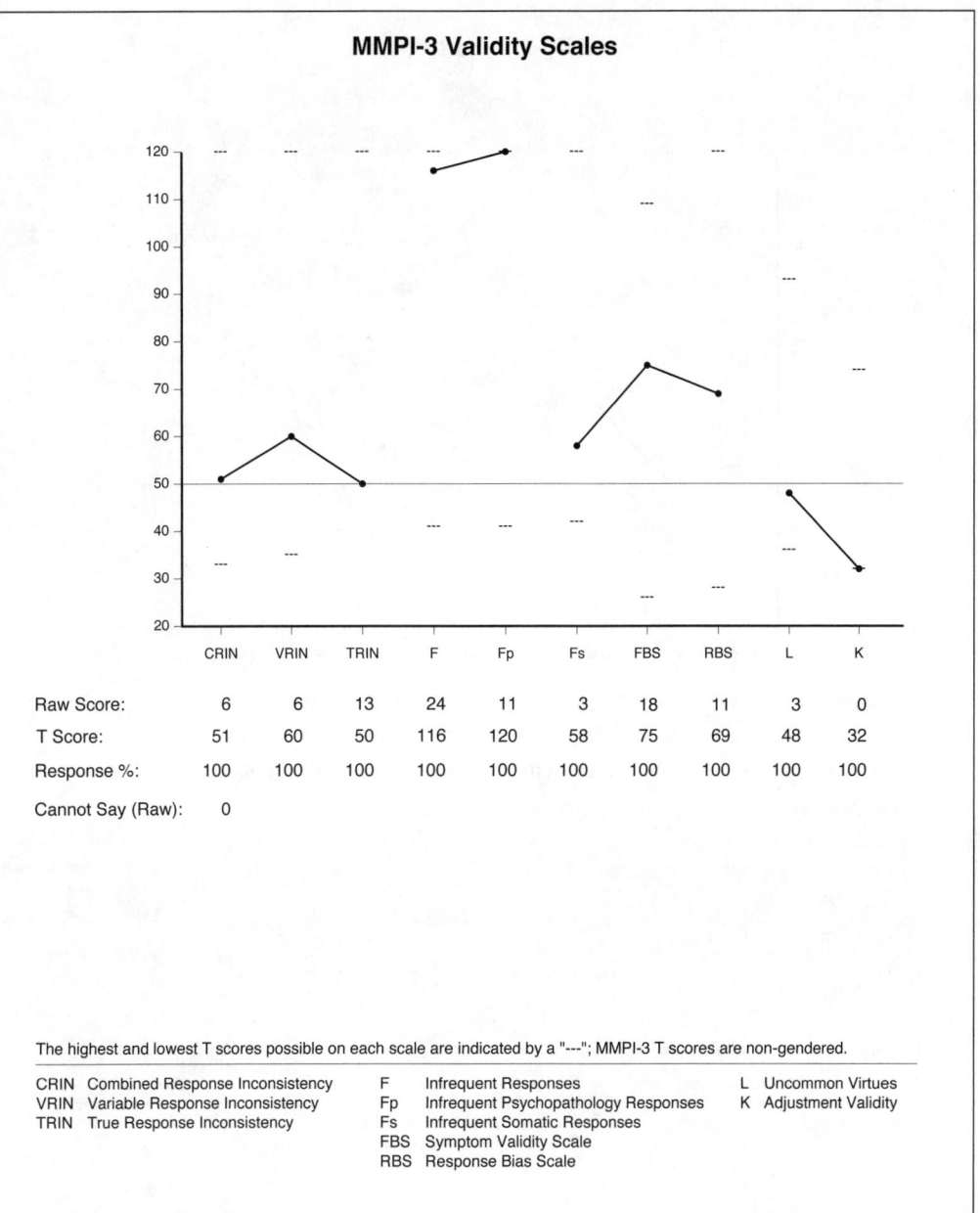

FIGURE 8.10. MMPI-3 Score Report Validity Scales Profile Showing Highly Elevated F and Fp Scores

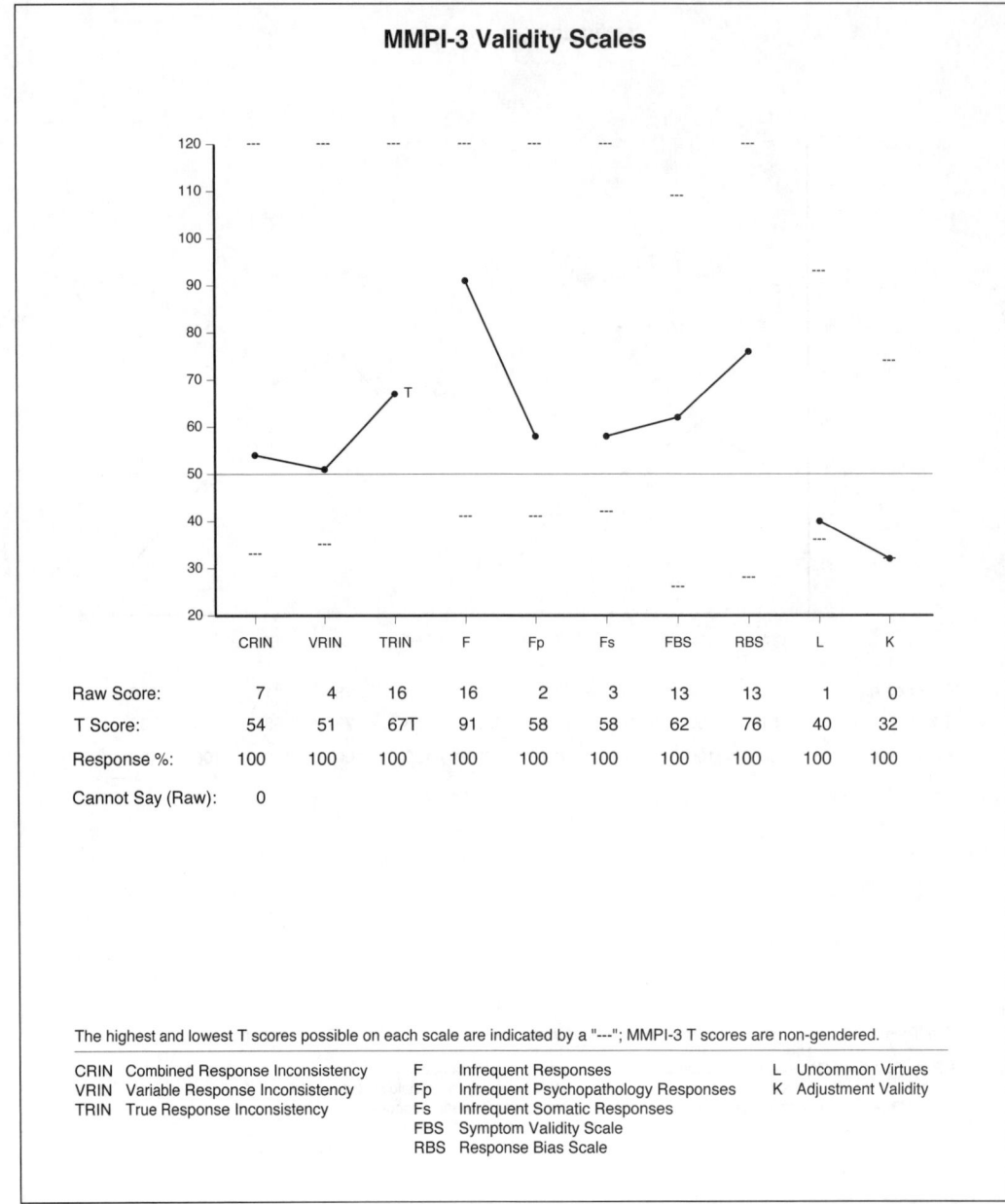

FIGURE 8.11. MMPI-3 Score Report Validity Scales Profile Showing a Moderately Elevated F Score

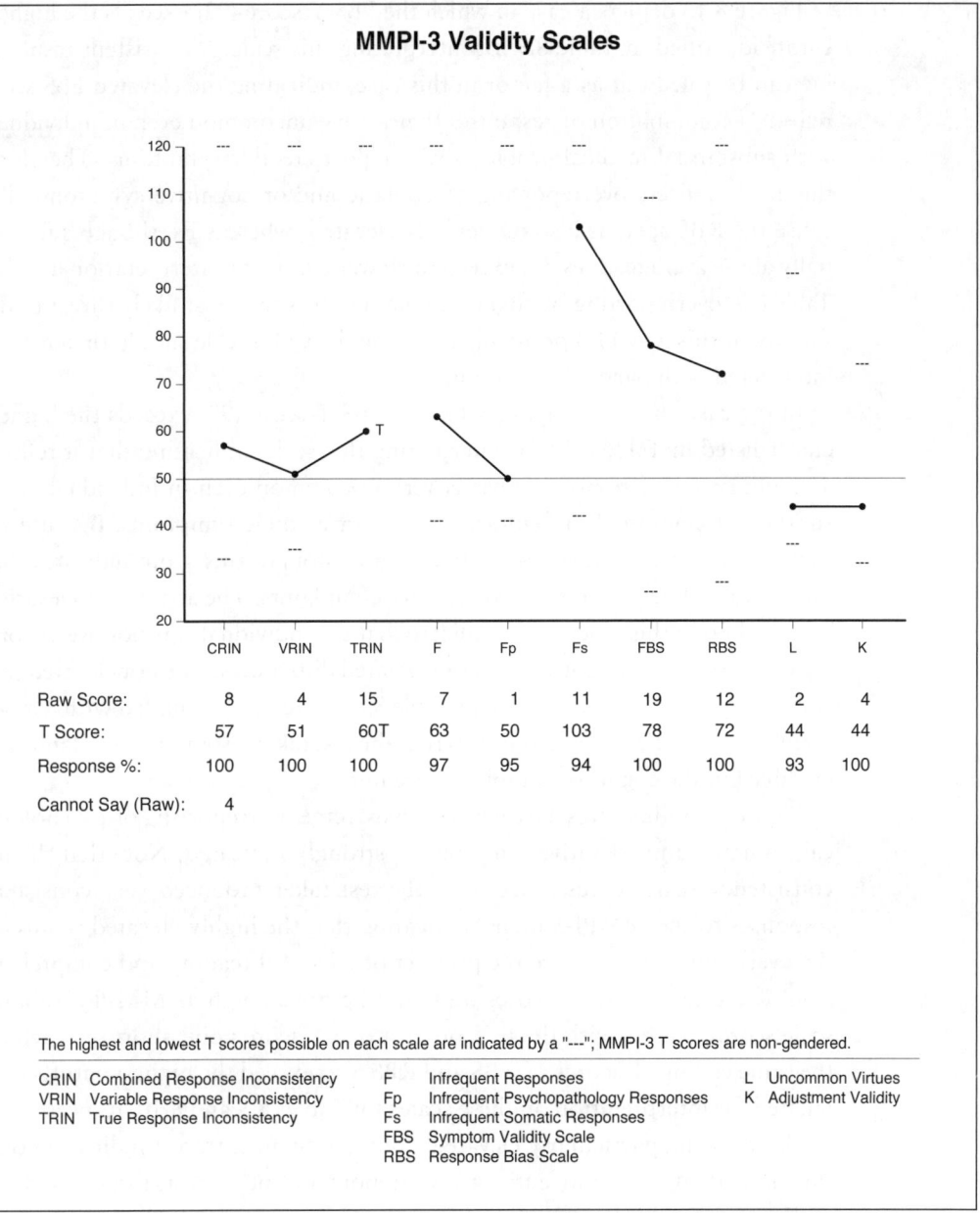

FIGURE 8.12. MMPI-3 Score Report Validity Scales Profile Showing an Elevated Fs Score Reflecting Overreporting of Somatic Symptoms

Figure 8.13 depicts a case in which the FBS T score (92) exceeds the highest cutoff identified in Table 8.9 for interpreting this scale. Inconsistent responding can be ruled out as a factor in this case, indicating the elevated FBS score reflects a combination of responses that is very uncommon even in individuals with substantial medical problems who report credible symptoms. Therefore, this likely reflects overreporting of somatic and/or cognitive symptoms. Because the RBS score is also moderately elevated, whereas Fs, though substantially above average, does not exceed the lower cutoff for interpretation listed in Table 8.8, overreporting of cognitive complaints is the most likely threat to the validity of this MMPI-3 protocol. Scores on the COG scale should therefore be interpreted with particular caution.

In the case shown in Figure 8.14, the RBS T score (98) exceeds the highest cutoff listed in Table 8.10 for interpreting this scale, indicating that it reflects a combination of responses that is very uncommon even in individuals with substantial emotional difficulties who report credible symptoms. Because we can rule out inconsistent responding as a confound, this score indicates that the test taker likely overreported memory complaints. The absence of elevation on F and Fp in this case would indicate that the individual was not overreporting emotional or thought-dysfunction-related difficulties. The nonelevated (beyond the lowest cutoff indicated in Table 8.8) score on Fs, coupled with a moderately elevated FBS score, indicates that the test taker's somatic complaints are credible but the cognitive complaints are not.

Figure 8.15 illustrates a case in which extreme overreporting of psychological, somatic, and cognitive symptoms is strongly indicated. Note that the inconsistency scale scores reflect that the test taker produced very consistent responses to the MMPI-3 items, indicating that the highly elevated scores on the overreporting scales are the product of a careful reading and comprehension of the test items. T scores on F and Fp are as high as MMPI-3 validity scale scores can be, with the Fs score just one T score point short of reaching the same ceiling. T scores on FBS and RBS also exceed the highest cutoffs designated for interpretation on these scales (in Tables 8.9 and 8.10, respectively), the latter being particularly elevated. Along with an extratest indication that this individual has an incentive to overreport and other test, interview data, and/or collateral information consistent with overreporting, the MMPI-3 validity scale scores in this case would provide strong support for an inference that this test taker is malingering. As emphasized earlier, in themselves, such findings do not indicate that this individual is free of psychological dysfunction, but they do clearly indicate that the MMPI-3 substantive scale scores are invalid and uninterpretable.

We turn next to a series of cases with elevated scores on the MMPI-3 underreporting scales.[2] In the case depicted in Figure 8.16, the elevated L score (81) indicates (after ruling out inconsistent responding) that the test taker engaged

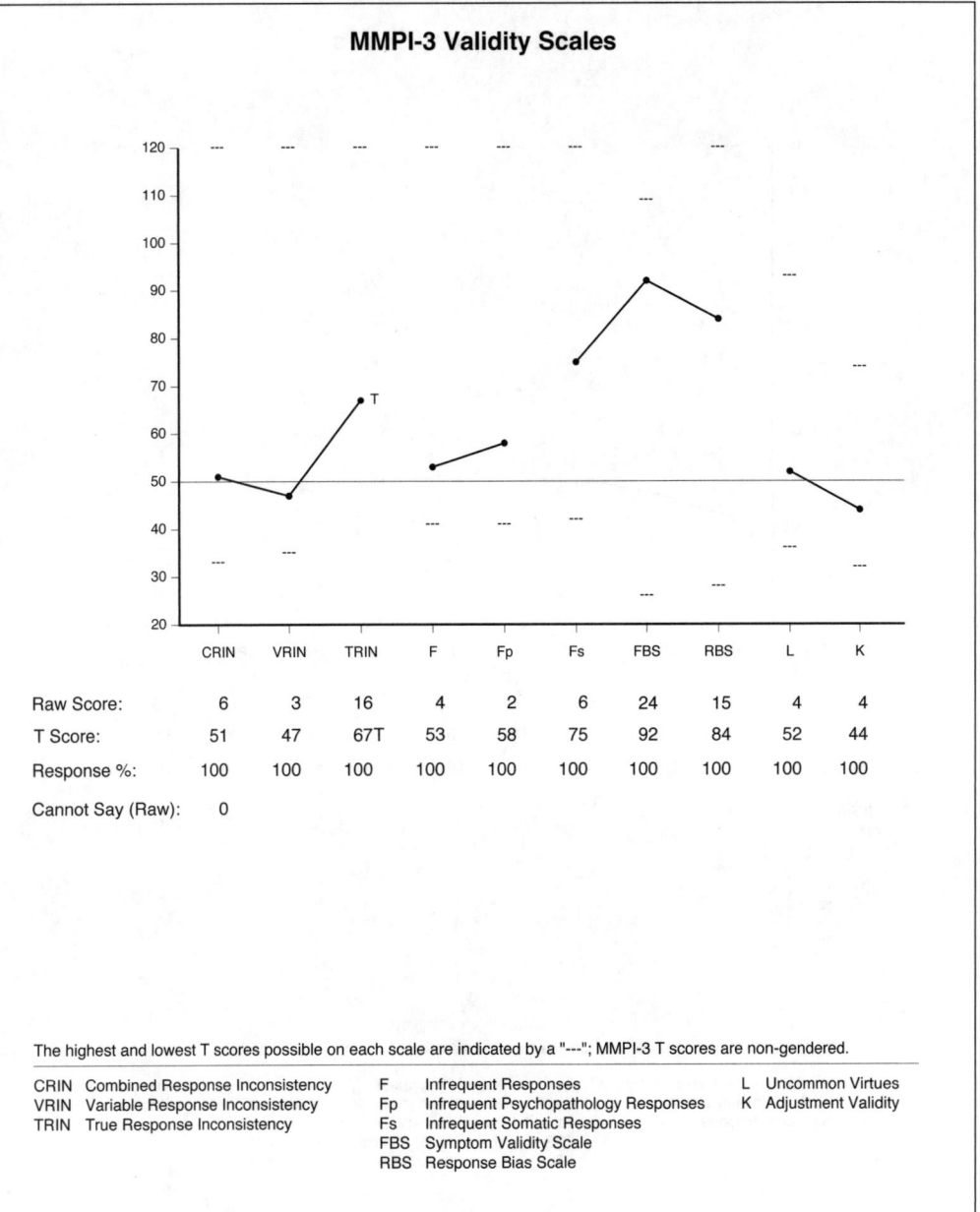

FIGURE 8.13. MMPI-3 Score Report Validity Scales Profile Showing an Elevated FBS Score and a Moderately Elevated RBS Score

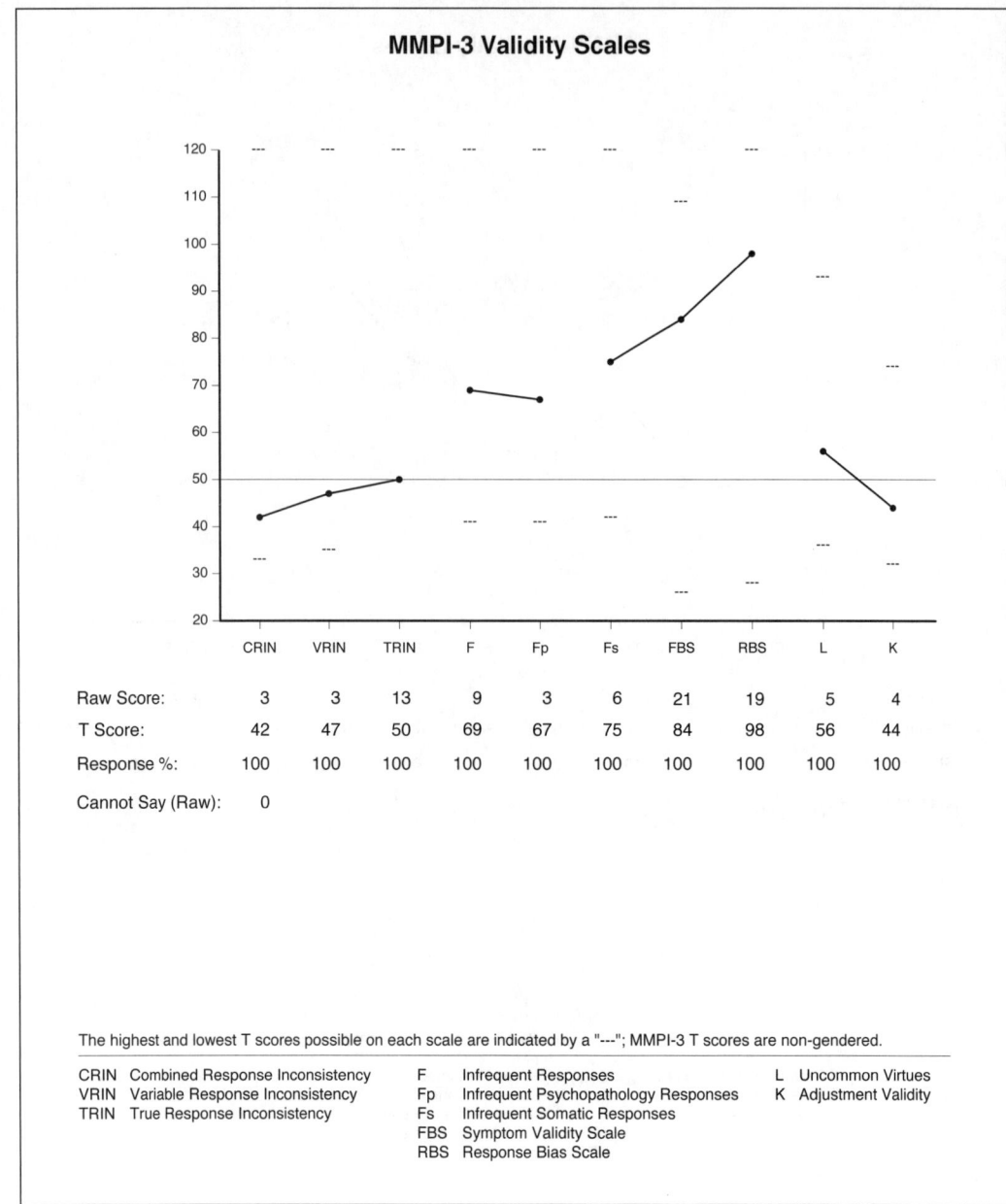

FIGURE 8.14. MMPI-3 Score Report Validity Scales Profile Showing an Elevated RBS Score and a Moderately Elevated FBS Score

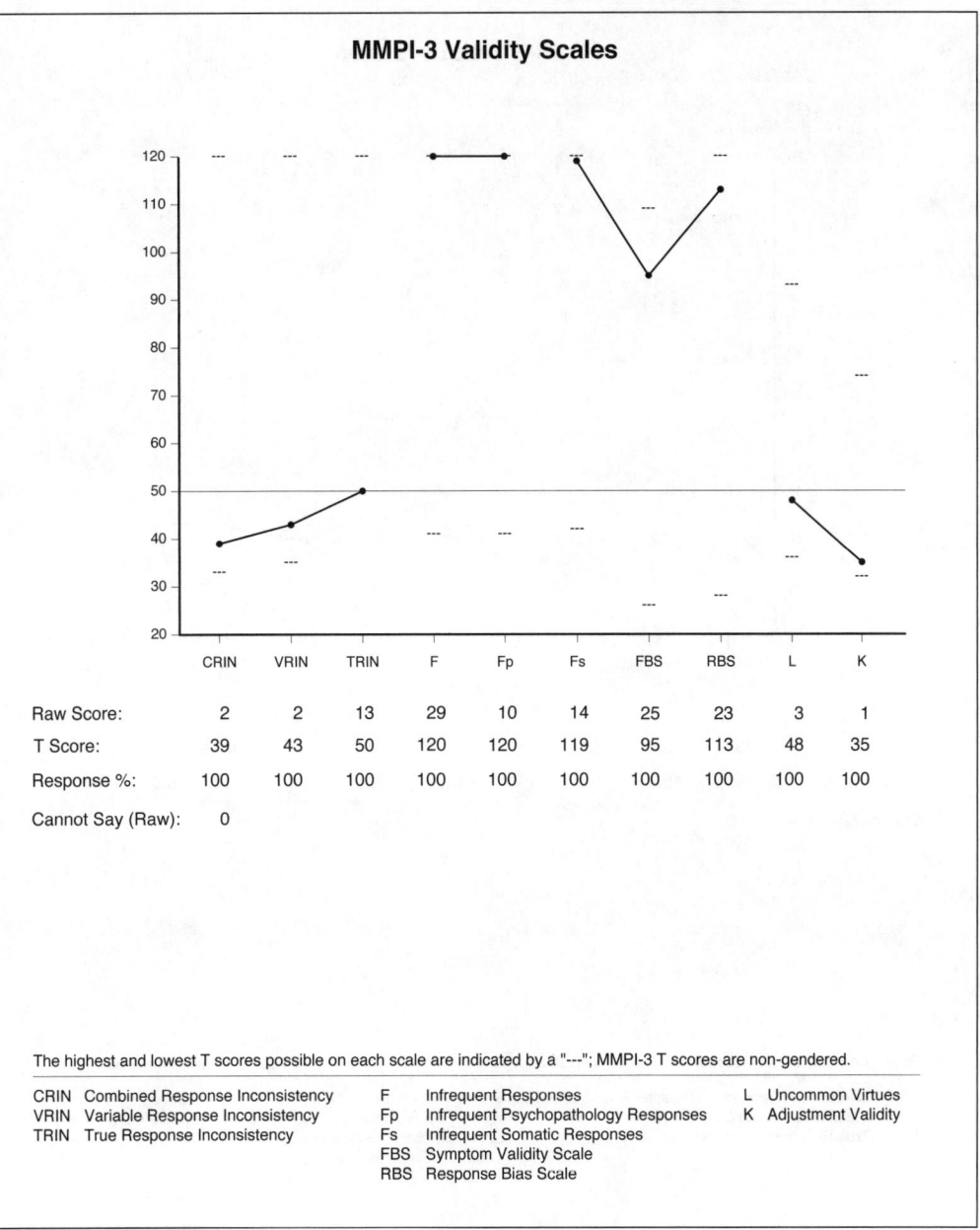

FIGURE 8.15. MMPI-3 Score Report Validity Scales Profile Showing Highly Elevated Scores on All Overreporting Scales

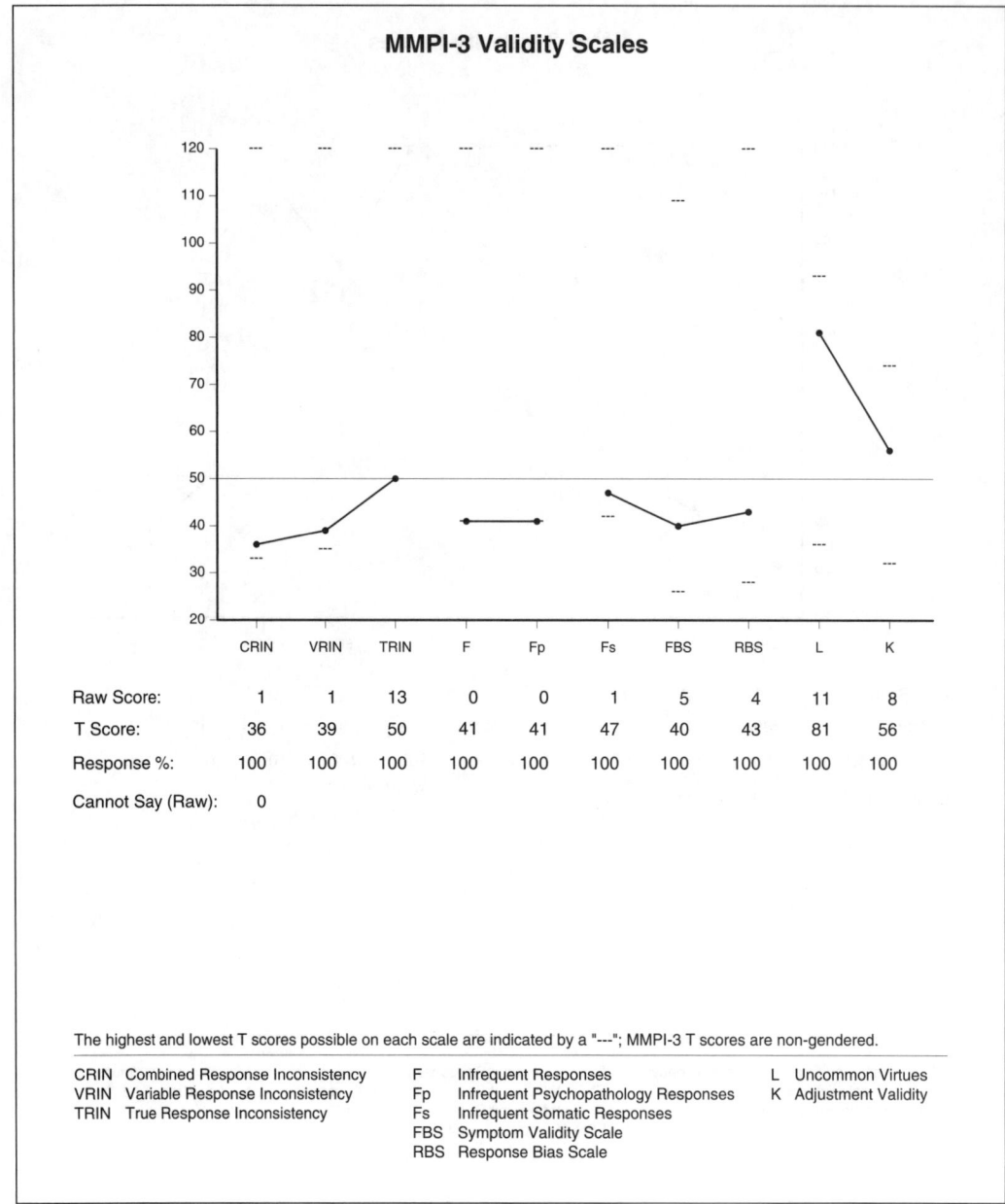

FIGURE 8.16. MMPI-3 Score Report Validity Scales Profile Showing an Elevated L Score

in a level of virtuous self-presentation that is uncommon even in individuals with a background stressing traditional values (a potential extratest confound for L scores listed in Table 8.1). The nonelevated K score indicates that underreporting in this case was limited to an effort to present in an extremely positive light by denying minor faults and shortcomings that most people acknowledge, but there was no effort by the test taker to appear better adjusted than average. This pattern of underreporting is most likely to impact scores on the Substantive Scales that assess for behavioral and interpersonal problems. On those measures in particular, the absence of elevation cannot be interpreted as indicating the absence of the difficulties they assess.

Figure 8.17 shows a case where the test taker produced the highest possible T score on K and the lowest possible T score on L. This test taker very likely underreported by presenting as remarkably well adjusted. As indicated in Table 8.12, the level of psychological adjustment reflected by the high K score is rare even in the general population, and it would be particularly unrealistic in individuals seen in clinical settings or about whom collateral data indicate a significant psychological dysfunction. With a score this high on K, it is very unlikely that any of the substantive scale scores would be elevated, indeed most would likely be considerably below average. Considering the high K score, the absence of elevation and low scores on the Substantive Scales would be uninterpretable. The low L score in this case indicates that though this test taker presented with a very unlikely level of good psychological adjustment, they made no effort to claim moral virtues.

The validity scale scores in Figure 8.18, depict a case where the test taker responded to 27 of the 28 L and K items in the keyed direction. This individual presented in an extremely positive light by denying many minor faults and shortcomings that most people acknowledge. This level of virtuous self-presentation is uncommon even in individuals with a background stressing traditional values. The test taker also presented as remarkably well adjusted, at a level that is rare even in the general population. Together, these scores indicate a concerted effort to underreport (as reflected by low CRIN and VRIN scores) and that any absence of elevation on the substantive scale scores is uninterpretable.

Figure 8.19 shows a protocol in which both overreporting and underreporting are indicated. The very high F T score (119) falls just one raw score point shy of the highest level possible on this scale. Overreporting is indicated by an excessive amount of infrequent responding, which reaches a level that invalidates the test protocol. As indicated in Table 8.6, this level of infrequent responding is uncommon even in individuals with genuine, severe psychological difficulties who report credible symptoms. In a seeming contradiction, as reflected in Table 8.11, the elevated L score in this case shows that possible underreporting is indicated by the test taker presenting in a very positive light by denying some minor faults and shortcomings that most people acknowledge. Note, however,

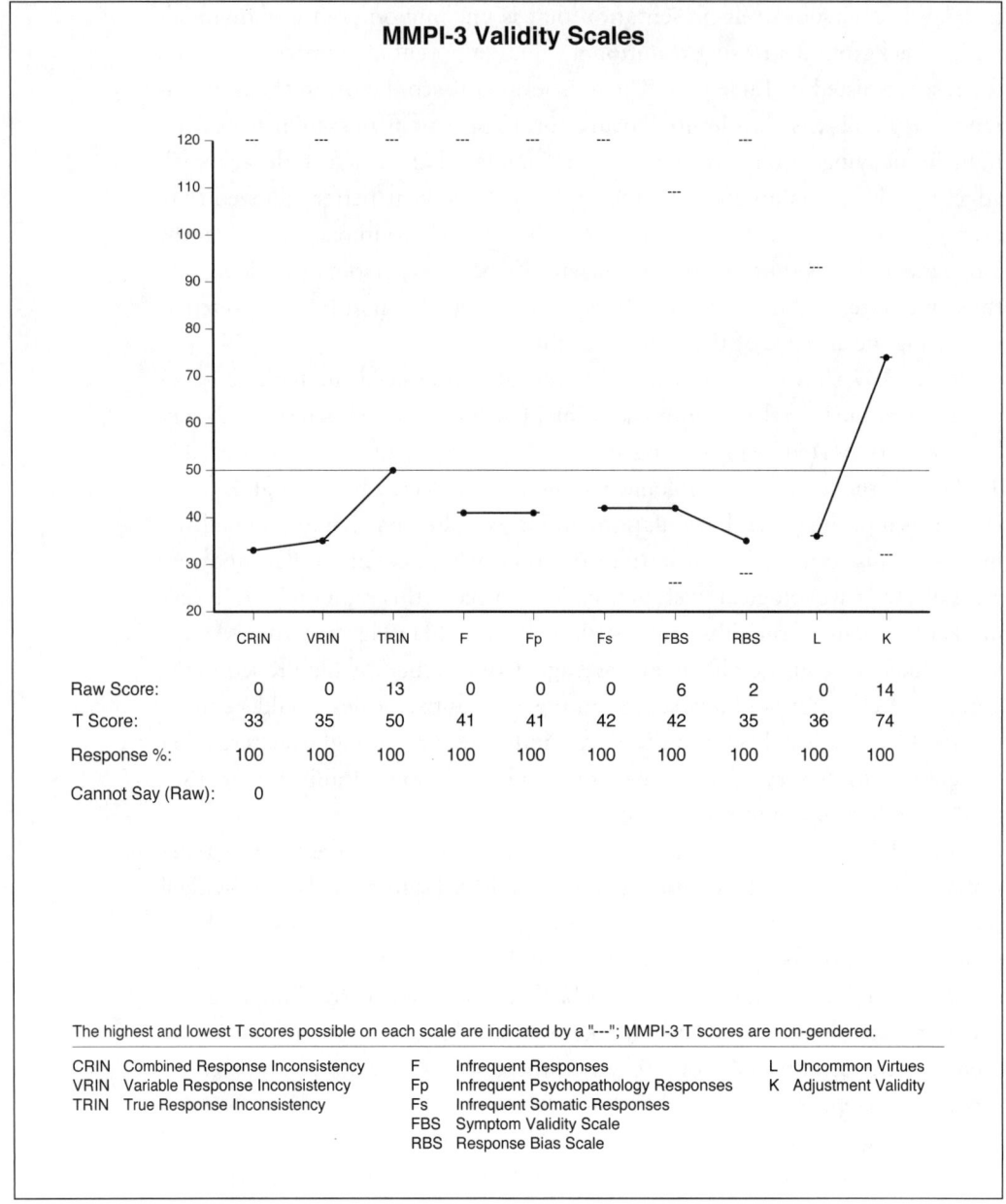

FIGURE 8.17. MMPI-3 Score Report Validity Scales Profile Showing an Elevated K Score With a Low L Score

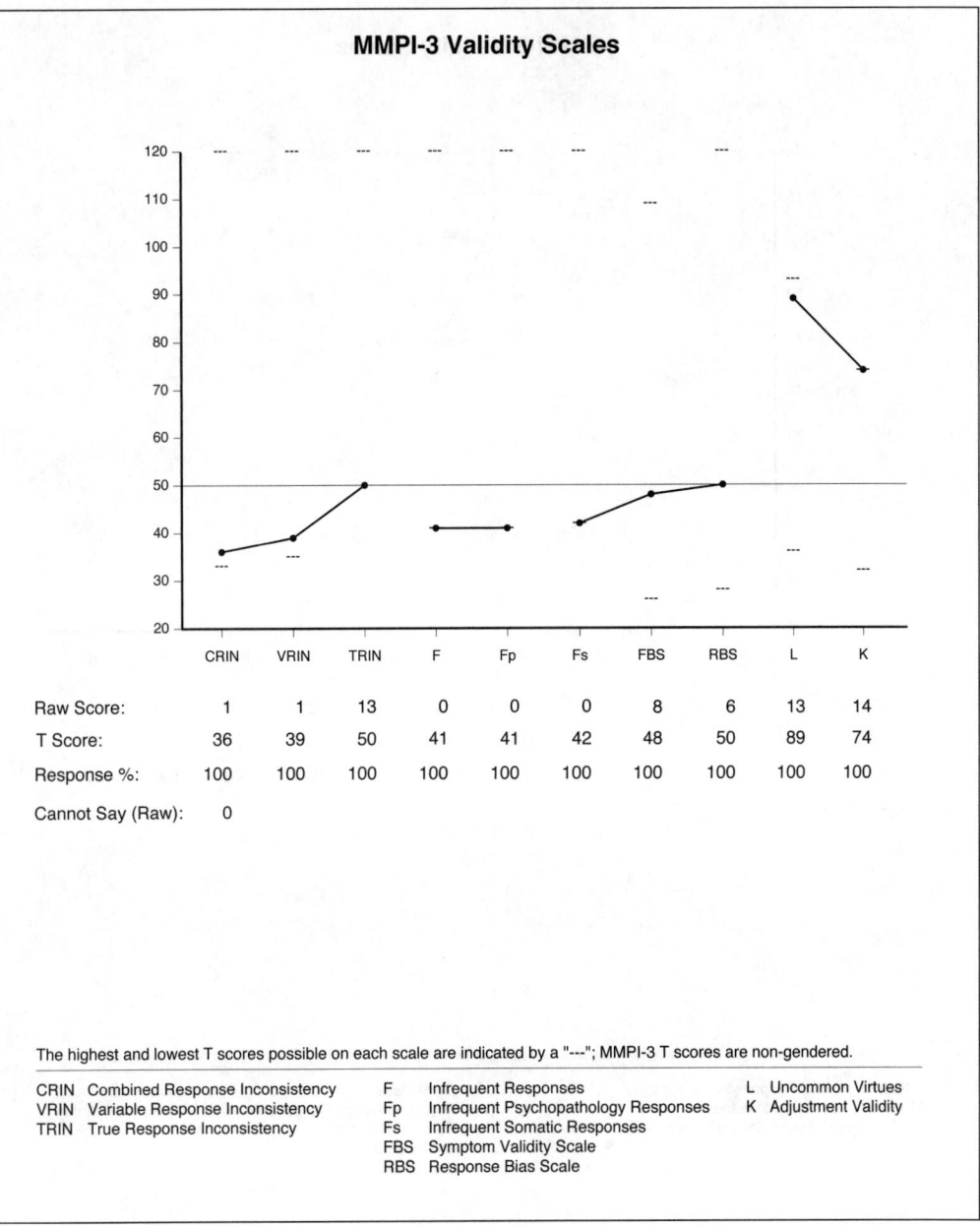

FIGURE 8.18. MMPI-3 Score Report Validity Scales Profile Showing Elevated L and K Scores

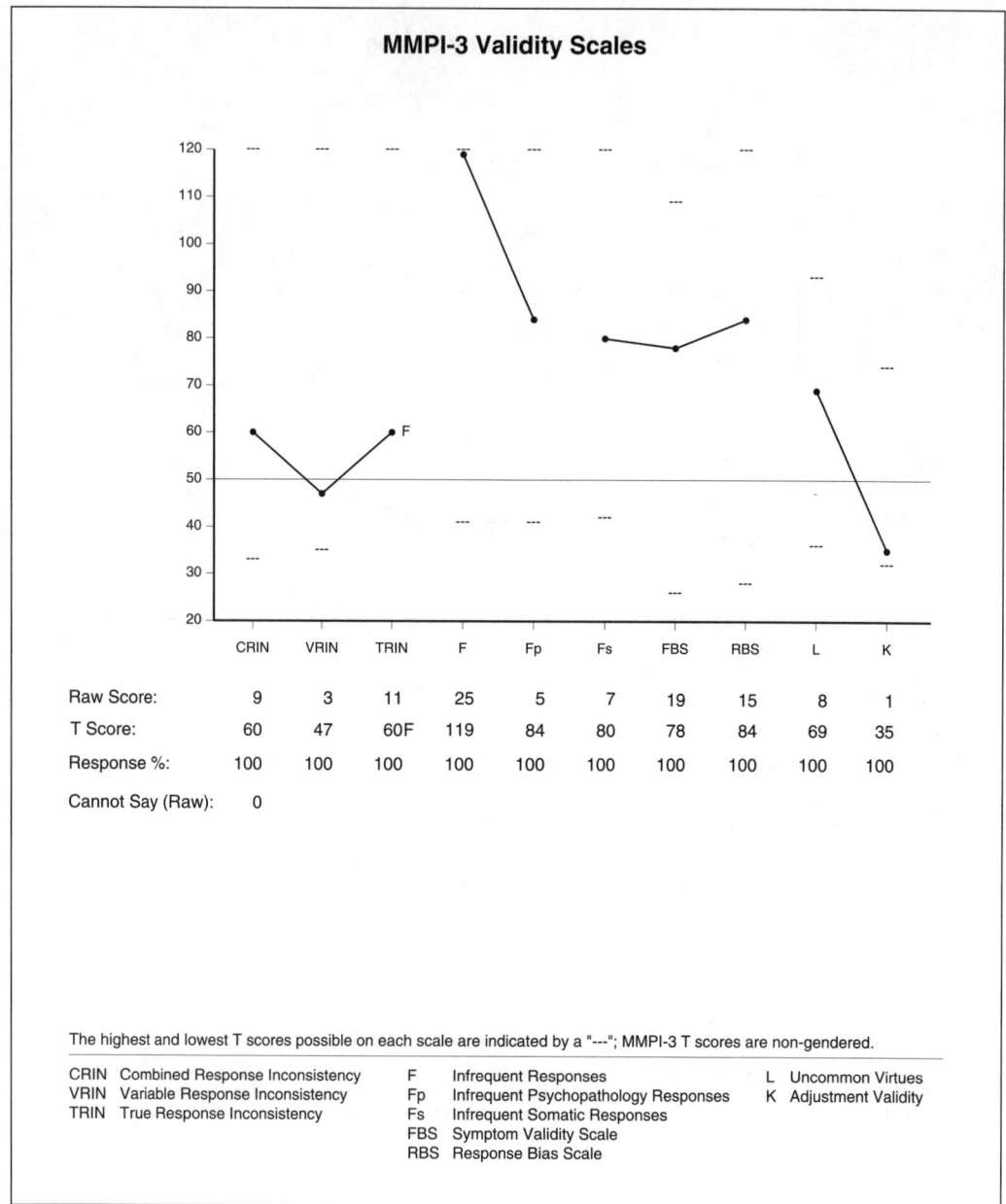

FIGURE 8.19. MMPI-3 Score Report Validity Scales Profile Showing Elevated F and L Scores Reflecting Overreporting While Claiming Uncommon Virtues

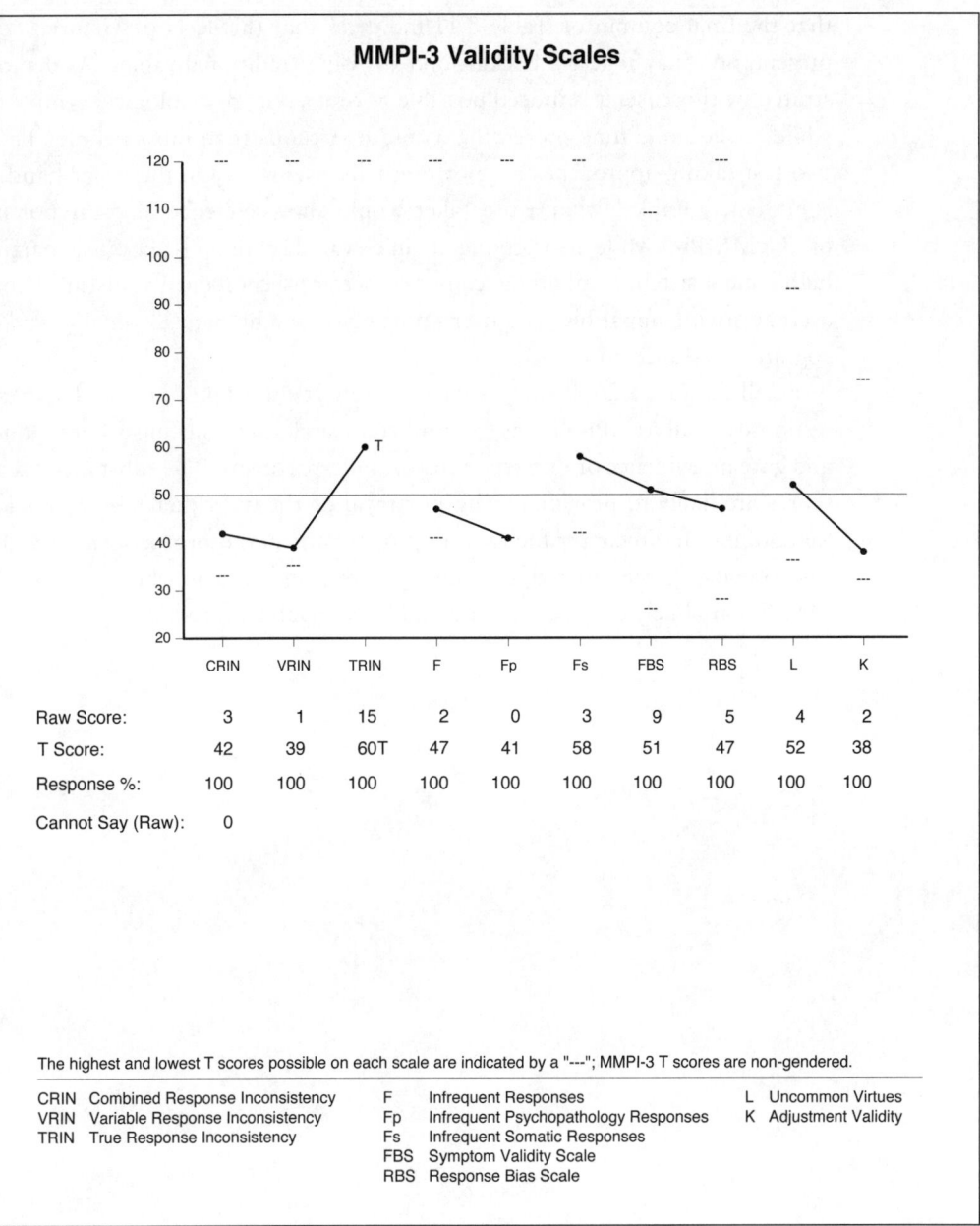

FIGURE 8.20. MMPI-3 Score Report Validity Scales Profile Showing a Valid Protocol

that the final column of Table 8.11 indicates that this level of virtuous self-presentation may reflect a background stressing traditional values. As demonstrated by this case, it is indeed possible to overreport psychological symptoms while at the same time presenting as more virtuous than most people. These two test-taking approaches are not mutually exclusive. On the other hand, it is extremely unlikely that a test taker would show evidence of overreporting on the MMPI-3 while also producing an elevated score on K, because, barring highly inconsistent responding, claims of better psychological adjustment than average are incompatible with overreporting of psychological, somatic, and/or cognitive dysfunction.

Finally, Figure 8.20 illustrates a case where the test taker provided scorable responses to all MMPI-3 items, responded in a relevant and consistent manner, and gave no evidence of overreporting or underreporting. The substantive scale scores are likely to provide a valid portrayal of the individual's psychological functioning. In a chapter focused on possible threats to protocol validity, this case provides a reminder that in most settings individuals who complete the MMPI-3 are likely to produce valid and interpretable protocols.

Interpreting the MMPI-3 Substantive Scales

9

This chapter provides interpretive statements recommended for various levels of scores on the MMPI-3 Substantive Scales. Interpretation of scores on these scales should proceed only after careful consideration of the potential threats to the validity of the test protocol and with whatever caveats are indicated based on a review of the validity scale scores. For example, as discussed in chapter 8, low scores on the Substantive Scales should not be interpreted at face value if there are indications of underreporting on the L or K scales. As also discussed in chapter 8, the protocol is invalid and uninterpretable if there are indications of excessive inconsistent responding or marked overreporting. A second important caveat is that the interpretive guidelines provided in this chapter are general and need to be considered in the context of unique cultural factors, as discussed in chapters 6 and 10 and illustrated in chapter 11.

The cutoffs provided in the interpretive tables included in this chapter are intended to function as heuristic guidelines rather than as rigid demarcation rules. They are designed to apply broadly to test results in mental health settings. Population differences, reflected in dissimilar MMPI-3 scale score means and standard deviations, may suggest the need to alter these interpretive ranges in specific settings. For example, Corey and Ben-Porath (2024) provide empirically grounded interpretive guidelines for assessing public safety candidates with the MMPI-3. Comparison group data provided in the *MMPI-3 Technical Manual* and embedded in the Pearson scoring software can assist in making these judgments. Use of comparison group data in MMPI-3 interpretation was discussed in chapter 7 and is illustrated with case studies in chapter 11.

In the descriptive accounts in this chapter, the content of the items in each MMPI-3 scale is defined from a measurement perspective as the content of the responses to these items as keyed for that scale. For example, Somatic Complaints (RC1) contains 11 True-keyed items regarding a variety of somatic concerns and 10 False-keyed items indicating a sense of physical well-being or the absence of physical difficulties. However, the statement that the RC1 items describe "a range of somatic complaints" is a general characterization of responses to all 21 items as keyed for that scale.

Interpretive guidelines for each of the 42 MMPI-3 Substantive Scales are provided in Tables 9.1 through 9.42, which are reproduced from the *MMPI-3 Manual for Administration, Scoring, and Interpretation*. The recommended interpretive statements in each table are organized into three sections labeled "Clinical Symptoms, Behavioral Tendencies, and Personality Characteristics"; "Diagnostic Considerations"; and "Treatment Considerations." The first section is divided into statements based on content (generated based on item content for that scale) that appear under the heading "Test Responses" and statements based on extratest correlates of the scales that appear under the heading "Empirical Correlates." The latter are based on findings reported in Appendix A of the *MMPI-2-RF Technical Manual*, Appendixes D and E of the *MMPI-3 Technical Manual*, and the published literature reviewed in chapters 4 and 5 of this book.

Rather than provide an exhaustive list of the empirical correlates, which would include many redundant entries given the hierarchical structure of the test, the interpretive statements emphasize the distinctive correlates of each scale. Redundant correlates are usually attributed to the scale with which they are most highly correlated. Some statements under "Diagnostic Considerations" are based on empirical data, whereas others are the test authors' inferences. Most statements under "Treatment Considerations" are inferential, meaning that they reflect the MMPI-3 authors' conclusions about the implications of test findings for treatment planning.

Most of the Substantive Scales include both low scores and high scores that are interpretable as distinctive from average scores. Interpretation of low scores reflects the quasi-continuous nature of the MMPI-3 scales and the constructs they assess. Unless indicated otherwise, interpretive statements about distinctive low scores refer to T scores of 38 or lower.

Unless otherwise specified, the interpretive statements about elevated scores listed in Tables 9.1 through 9.42 are intended to apply to T scores of 65 and higher, which corresponds to the 92nd percentile and higher. For most scales, guidelines for the content-based statements are linked to at least two specified levels of elevated scores. For the first level, these statements reflect the general theme of the item content as keyed on a scale. At higher levels of elevation, interpretive statements reflect the specific content of items the test taker must answer in the keyed direction to obtain a score in the specified range. Similarly, if a T-score level above 65 is specified for a statement in the "Empirical Correlates," "Diagnostic Considerations," or "Treatment Considerations" sections, it is indicated in parentheses following the statement (i.e., >75). In general, the higher the score on a scale, the more likely it is that the statements listed for it will apply, and the more severe will be the impairment reflected in those statements. Severity may be inferred in this manner owing to the continuous nature of the MMPI-3 scales.

The following interpretive recommendations for the Substantive Scales are organized into four sets of scales—Higher-Order (H-O), Restructured Clinical (RC), Specific Problems (SP), and Personality Psychopathology Five (PSY-5). A detailed description of the development, conceptualization, and psychometric properties of these scales can be found in chapter 2 for scales first developed for the MMPI-2-RF and chapter 3 for scales newly developed or substantially revised for the MMPI-3. To summarize, the H-O Scales represent the broadest constructs; the RC Scales represent the more circumscribed, though generally multifaceted, mid-level constructs; and the SP Scales represent narrower-band constructs designed either to highlight facets of (but not necessarily represented by items from) the RC Scales or to measure features not directly targeted by the higher-level scales. The SP Scales are in turn subdivided into subsets on the basis of empirical (correlational) analyses and conceptual considerations. The PSY-5 Scales embody Harkness and McNulty's (1994) model of personality pathology and link the clinically oriented content of the MMPI-3 to the alternative *DSM-5* model of personality disorders as discussed in chapter 5. The PSY-5 dimensions are clearly related to but also distinct from the hierarchical structure that was developed based on the RC Scales (see chapter 2 for details).

HIGHER-ORDER (H-O) SCALES

From factor analyses (described in chapter 2), three H-O dimensions have clearly emerged: Emotional/Internalizing Dysfunction (EID), Thought Dysfunction (THD), and Behavioral/Externalizing Dysfunction (BXD), demarcating clinically important individual variations in the basic domains of affect, thought, and action. It may be helpful to view the role of these broad measures as analogous to the function of broadband intelligence measures in cognitive assessments, such as the Verbal Comprehension, Perceptual Reasoning, Working Memory, and Processing Speed scales of the Wechsler Adult Intelligence Scale–Fourth Edition (WAIS-IV; Wechsler, 2008). On one hand, an individual's MMPI-3 EID, THD, and BXD scores will often provide meaningful indications of overall dysfunction in the three respective domains; on the other hand, as in the aptitude area, score levels within the average range on the H-O Scales may be the result of contrasting within-domain strengths and weaknesses, which may be revealed by narrower-band subdomain measures. In other words, the absence of elevation on an H-O Scale does not rule out all problems within that domain. For example, a test taker may produce an average score on the EID scale, while showing evidence of risk for a depressive disorder, as indicated by an elevated score on Low Positive

Emotions (RC2). Finally, the relative order of elevation on the H-O Scales can provide an indication of the prominence of the difficulties they assess when more than one exceeds an interpretable threshold.

Emotional/Internalizing Dysfunction (EID)

EID is a 42-item scale designed to assess a broad range of emotional and internalizing problems. The test taker's EID score provides an overall gauge of their emotional functioning. Low EID scores reflect a below-average level of emotional difficulties, whereas elevated scores indicate that the test taker reported a broad range of emotional and internalizing difficulties. Table 9.1 provides interpretive statements for different levels of EID. Specific additional information can be obtained from the interpretive tables for any of the EID-associated RC, SP, and PSY-5 Scales also listed in Table 9.1.

Thought Dysfunction (THD)

THD is a 27-item scale designed to assess a broad range of difficulties associated with thought dysfunction. The test taker's THD score provides an overall estimate of their level of reported thought dysfunction. Elevated scores indicate substantial difficulties associated with thought disturbance. Table 9.2 pro-

TABLE 9.1. Emotional/Internalizing Dysfunction (EID) Interpretation

Clinical symptoms, behavioral tendencies, and personality characteristics

Test responses

T score < 39
  Test taker's responses indicate a better-than-average level of emotional adjustment.
T score 65–79
  Test taker's responses indicate significant emotional distress.
T score ≥ 80
  Test taker's responses indicate considerable emotional distress that is likely to be perceived as a crisis.

Empirical correlates

  Broad range of symptoms and difficulties associated with demoralization, low positive emotions, and negative emotional experiences (e.g., low morale, depression, anxiety, or feeling overwhelmed, helpless, or pessimistic)

  Specific manifestations of emotional/internalizing dysfunction characterized by elevated scores on RCd, RC2, RC7, SUI, HLP, SFD, NFC, STR, WRY, CMP, ARX, ANP, BRF, NEGE, and INTR

Diagnostic considerations

Evaluate for internalizing disorders.

Treatment considerations

Emotional difficulties may motivate test takers to receive treatment.

TABLE 9.2. Thought Dysfunction (THD) Interpretation

Clinical symptoms, behavioral tendencies, and personality characteristics

Test responses

T score 65–79
   Test taker's responses indicate significant thought dysfunction.

T score ≥ 80
   Test taker's responses indicate serious thought dysfunction.

Empirical correlates

   Broad range of symptoms and difficulties associated with disordered thinking (e.g., paranoid and nonparanoid delusions, auditory and visual hallucinations, unrealistic thinking)

   Specific manifestations of thought dysfunction characterized by scores on RC6, RC8, and PSY-5

Diagnostic considerations

Evaluate for disorders associated with thought dysfunction.

Treatment considerations

May require inpatient treatment for thought dysfunction.

Need for antipsychotic medication should be evaluated.

---

vides interpretive statements for different elevation levels. Specific additional information can be obtained from the interpretive tables for any of the THD-related RC and PSY-5 Scales also listed in Table 9.2.

Behavioral/Externalizing Dysfunction (BXD)

BXD is a 24-item scale designed to assess a broad range of behavioral problems. The test taker's BXD score provides an overall gauge of their behavioral acting-out proclivities. Low scores indicate that the test taker reported a higher-than-average level of behavioral constraint, whereas elevated scores indicate a broad range of externalizing, acting-out behaviors. Table 9.3 provides interpretive statements for this scale. Specific additional information can be found in the interpretive tables for any of the BXD-linked RC, SP, and PSY-5 Scales also listed in Table 9.3.

RESTRUCTURED CLINICAL (RC) SCALES

Interpretive recommendations for the RC Scales are based on the empirical correlates reported in a substantial body of findings published since the introduction of the scales in 2003. For several of the RC Scales (RCd, RC1, RC4, RC7, and RC9), interpretation is facilitated by also examining the test taker's scores on the SP Scales that represent a facet of an RC scale or are empirically and conceptually linked to it. For each RC scale (e.g., RC4), findings on its affiliated SP Scales (in the case of RC4: FML, JCP, and SUB) can help the interpreter

TABLE 9.3. Behavioral/Externalizing Dysfunction (BXD) Interpretation

Clinical symptoms, behavioral tendencies, and personality characteristics

Test responses

T score < 39

    Test taker's responses indicate a higher-than-average level of behavioral constraint; they are unlikely to engage in externalizing, acting-out behavior.

T score 65–79

    Test taker's responses indicate significant externalizing, acting-out behavior that is likely to have gotten them into difficulties.

T score ≥ 80

    Test taker's responses indicate considerable externalizing, acting-out behavior that is very likely to result in marked dysfunction and to have gotten them into difficulties.

Empirical correlates

Broad range of behaviors and difficulties associated with undercontrolled behavior (e.g., substance abuse, a history of criminal behavior, violent and abusive behavior, poor impulse control)

Specific manifestations of behavioral/externalizing dysfunction reflected in elevated scores on RC4, RC9, FML, JCP, SUB, IMP, ACT, AGG, CYN, AGGR, and DISC

Diagnostic considerations

Evaluate for externalizing disorders.

Treatment considerations

Unlikely to be internally motivated for treatment.

At significant risk for treatment noncompliance.

Inadequate self-control as a target for intervention.

---

recognize those attributes that are linked to the RC scale and that should be emphasized or deemphasized in the interpretation. Table 10–1 lists the SP Scales associated with each RC scale. Most of the RC Scales (RCd, RC1, RC2, RC4, RC7, and RC9) include both low scores and high scores that are interpretable as distinctive from average scores. However, as noted earlier, whenever the Validity Scales indicate underreporting, interpretations of low scores should be qualified or avoided altogether, depending on the degree of underreporting.

Demoralization (RCd)

RCd is a 17-item scale representing a pervasive and affect-laden dimension of unhappiness and life dissatisfaction, referred to in the MMPI-3 as Demoralization. A low RCd score reflects avowal of a relatively high level of morale and life satisfaction. High Demoralization scores describe individuals who encounter problems of living that they experience as overwhelming and in the face of which they feel helpless and ineffective. Elevated scores on the other RC Scales and on the SP and PSY-5 Scales can help identify the types of problems that contribute to Demoralization. The SP Scales associated specifically with RCd—

Suicidal/Death Ideation (SUI), Helplessness/Hopelessness (HLP), Self-Doubt (SFD), and Inefficacy (NFC)—highlight its salient manifestations.

Suicidal ideation is one of the empirical RCd correlates to be considered in any assessment in which the test taker generates an elevated score on this scale. Two SP Scales, SUI and HLP, provide particularly relevant additional information. An elevated SUI score provides the most direct evidence of suicidal ideation and requires immediate attention. However, when RCd is elevated but SUI is not, a high HLP score still raises concerns about possible risk for self-harm that need to be addressed with a follow-up assessment. Table 9.4 lists these and other interpretive statements for RCd.

TABLE 9.4. Demoralization (RCd) Interpretation

Clinical symptoms, behavioral tendencies, and personality characteristics

Test responses

T score < 39
  Test taker reports a higher-than-average level of morale and life satisfaction.
T score 65–73
  Test taker reports:
    Feeling sad and unhappy
    Being dissatisfied with their current life circumstances.
T score ≥ 74
  Test taker reports:
    Experiencing significant demoralization
    Feeling overwhelmed
    Being extremely unhappy, sad, and dissatisfied with their life.

Empirical correlates

  Is at risk for suicidal ideation (if SUI or HLP ≥ 65)
  Complains about feeling depressed
  Experiences sadness and despair
  Feels hopeless and pessimistic about the future
  Does not cope well with stress
  Has low self-esteem
  Feels incapable of dealing with current life circumstances
  Has difficulty concentrating
  Is worry prone and ruminative
  Feels sad
  Is pessimistic
  Is insecure

Diagnostic considerations

Evaluate for depression-related disorder.

Treatment considerations

Evaluate risk for self-harm (if SUI or HLP ≥ 65).

Emotional difficulties may motivate test taker to receive treatment.

Focus on relief of demoralization as an initial target for intervention.

Somatic Complaints (RC1)

RC1 consists of 21 items that describe a range of somatic complaints associated with somatic symptom disorders. Low RC1 scores indicate a sense of relative physical well-being. As is true for any self-report measures of somatoform problems, a high RC1 score may, to some extent, reflect contributions of genuine physical health problems. Interpretations of the test taker's score need to take these contributions into careful consideration. Nevertheless, as the RC1 score increases in the clinical range so does the likelihood that psychological factors play a significant role in the somatic symptoms reported by the individual.

Four SP Scales—Malaise (MLS), Neurological Complaints (NUC), Eating Concerns (EAT), and Cognitive Complaints (COG)—provide more detailed information about the kinds of somatic or cognitive complaints or eating concerns reported by the test taker. Table 9.5 lists interpretive recommendations for RC1.

Low Positive Emotions (RC2)

RC2 is a 14-item scale designed to measure a lack of positive emotional experiences, or anhedonia, which has been identified as a distinctive feature of major

TABLE 9.5. Somatic Complaints (RC1) Interpretation

Clinical symptoms, behavioral tendencies, and personality characteristics
Test responses

T score < 39
    Test taker reports a sense of physical well-being.

T score 65–76
    Test taker reports multiple somatic complaints that may include head pain and neurological and gastrointestinal symptoms.

T score ≥ 77
    Test taker reports a diffuse pattern of somatic complaints involving different bodily systems that probably include head pain and neurological and gastrointestinal symptoms.

Empirical correlates
- Is preoccupied with physical health concerns
- Is prone to developing physical symptoms in response to stress
- Perceives their physical problems as interfering with life
- Has a psychological component to their somatic complaints
- Complains of fatigue
- Presents with multiple somatic complaints

Diagnostic considerations
Evaluate for somatic symptom disorder.

Treatment considerations
Test taker is likely to reject psychological interpretations of somatic complaints.

depression. Although Demoralization, or dysphoric affect, is also commonly found in individuals with a depressive disorder, it is not a distinctive characteristic of depression and co-occurs with many other conditions. Nevertheless, test takers with clinically elevated scores on both RCd and RC2 should be carefully evaluated for major depression. Although a distinctive feature of major depression, anhedonia is not unique to this condition. For example, it is also a negative symptom of schizophrenia and prominent in avoidant and schizoid personality disorders.

Because all but one of the items on RC2 are keyed False, in the case of a high score, care should be taken to ensure that fixed False responding (measured by TRIN) did not inflate the score. Low scores on RC2 indicate that the test taker reported a high level of psychological well-being and a wide range of emotionally positive experiences, provided that fixed True responding (again, as measured by TRIN) did not spuriously lower the score. None of the SP Scales are associated directly with this scale. Table 9.6 lists interpretive statements for RC2.

Antisocial Behavior (RC4)

RC4 consists of 14 items that describe various antisocial behaviors and related family conflict. Low scores on RC4 indicate that the test taker reported a below-average level of past antisocial behavior, indicating a reduced risk for the various acting-out behaviors associated empirically with this scale. Because many of the items on the scale are worded in the past tense, individuals who produce elevated scores are most accurately described as reporting a history of antisocial behavior. Specific interpretations of elevated RC4 scores are facilitated by considering scores on three SP Scales: Family Problems (FML), Juvenile Conduct Problems (JCP), and Substance Abuse (SUB). Table 9.7 provides interpretive statements for RC4.

Ideas of Persecution (RC6)

RC6 consists of 14 items designed to assess the extent to which the test taker holds persecutory beliefs. No SP Scales are linked directly to the interpretation of scores on RC6. Because significant persecutory thinking may require immediate intervention, RC6 has been designated as one of seven MMPI-3 scales with critical content. This means that when RC6 is elevated, the MMPI-3 Score Report and Interpretive Report for Clinical Settings will list the RC6 items the test taker answered in the keyed direction. This information can help the interpreter evaluate the extent and seriousness of the test taker's reported persecutory ideation. Table 9.8 outlines interpretive statements for RC6.

TABLE 9.6. Low Positive Emotions (RC2) Interpretation

Clinical symptoms, behavioral tendencies, and personality characteristics

Test responses

T score < 39
    Test taker reports the following:
        A high level of psychological well-being
        A wide range of emotionally positive experiences
        Feeling confident and energetic.

T score ≥ 65
    Test taker reports the following:
        A lack of positive emotional experiences
        Significant anhedonia
        Lack of interest.

Empirical correlates

T score < 39
    Is optimistic
    Is extroverted
    Is socially engaged

T score ≥ 65
    Presents with anhedonia
    Is pessimistic
    Is socially introverted
    Is socially disengaged
    Lacks energy
    Displays vegetative symptoms of depression (if T score > 79)

Diagnostic considerations

Evaluate for anhedonia-related disorder.

Evaluate for anhedonia-related disorder, possibly major depression (if T score ≥ 79).

Treatment considerations

Evaluate need for antidepressant medication.

May require inpatient treatment for significant depression (if RC2 ≥ 79).

Significant lack of positive emotions may interfere with engagement in treatment.

Focus on anhedonia as a target for intervention.

Dysfunctional Negative Emotions (RC7)

RC7 is a 19-item scale designed to assess the extent to which the test taker reported various negative emotional experiences (e.g., anxiety, anger, and fear). Low RC7 scores indicate a below-average level of reported dysfunctional negative emotional experiences and a lower risk for such experiences and the difficulties empirically associated with elevated scores on this scale. High scores have been linked in the literature to an increased risk for anxiety-related psychopathology. Although scores on RCd and RC7 are substantially correlated (consistent with theoretical expectations), the content and empirical correlates

TABLE 9.7. Antisocial Behavior (RC4) Interpretation

Clinical symptoms, behavioral tendencies, and personality characteristics

Test responses

T score < 39
  Test taker reports below-average level of past antisocial behavior.
T score 65–77
  Test taker reports a significant history of antisocial behavior.
T score ≥ 78
  Test taker reports serious past and current antisocial behavior.

Empirical correlates

- Has been involved with the criminal justice system
- Fails to conform to societal norms and expectations
- Has difficulty with individuals in positions of authority
- Experiences conflictual interpersonal relationships
- Is impulsive
- Acts out when bored
- Has antisocial characteristics
- Has a history of juvenile delinquency
- Engages in substance abuse
- Has family problems
- Is interpersonally aggressive

Diagnostic considerations

Evaluate for antisocial personality disorder, substance use disorders, and other externalizing disorders.

Treatment considerations

Acting-out tendencies can result in treatment noncompliance and interfere with the development of a therapeutic relationship.

Focus on inadequate self-control as a target for intervention.

---

of the two scales and the interpretive statements for each (see Tables 9.4 and 9.9, respectively) are distinctive.

Specific interpretations of RC7 scores are facilitated by considering the test taker's results on the following SP Scales: Stress (STR), Worry (WRY), Compulsivity (CMP), Anxiety-Related Experiences (ARX), Anger Proneness (ANP), and Behavior-Restricting Fears (BRF). Table 9.9 lists interpretive statements for RC7.

Aberrant Experiences (RC8)

RC8 consists of 18 items that describe various unusual thoughts and perceptual experiences characteristic of disordered thinking. Elevated scores are associated empirically with symptoms of psychotic disorders, and highly elevated scores indicate the possibility of significantly disorganized thinking. No SP Scales contribute directly to the interpretation of scores on RC8. Because the symptoms

TABLE 9.8. Ideas of Persecution (RC6) Interpretation

Clinical symptoms, behavioral tendencies, and personality characteristics

Test responses

T score 65–78
  Test taker reports significant persecutory ideation such as believing that others seek to harm them.

T score ≥ 79
  Test taker reports prominent persecutory ideation that may rise to the level of paranoid delusions.

Empirical correlates
  Has persecutory beliefs
  Is suspicious and distrustful
  Experiences interpersonal difficulties as a result of suspiciousness
  Lacks insight
  Blames others for their difficulties

Diagnostic considerations

Evaluate for disorders involving persecutory ideation.

Evaluate for disorders involving paranoid delusional thinking (if RC6 ≥ 79).

Treatment considerations

Persecutory ideation may interfere with forming a therapeutic relationship and treatment compliance.

Focus on persecutory ideation as a target for intervention.

May require inpatient treatment for paranoid delusional thinking (if RC6 ≥ 79).

Evaluate need for antipsychotic medication (if RC6 ≥ 79).

---

associated with elevated scores may require immediate intervention, RC8 has been included among the scales designated as having critical content. Accordingly, if the RC8 score is elevated, the MMPI-3 Score Report and Interpretive Report for Clinical Settings will list all items the test taker answered in the keyed direction.

As is the case with all self-report measures of thought and sensory-perceptual processes, certain neurological disorders (e.g., temporal lobe epilepsy) can account for at least some of the experiences described by the RC8 items. Substance-induced psychotic symptoms will also result in some elevation on this scale. As discussed in chapter 6, individuals from cultures that embrace spiritual beliefs may also respond to some of the RC8 items in the keyed direction. These possibilities underscore the need to use as much extratest information as possible in the interpretation of RC8 results. Table 9.10 presents interpretive statements for RC8.

Hypomanic Activation (RC9)

RC9 consists of 15 items describing a variety of emotions, cognitions, attitudes, and behaviors consistent with hypomanic activation. The specific item content

TABLE 9.9. Dysfunctional Negative Emotions (RC7) Interpretation

Clinical symptoms, behavioral tendencies, and personality characteristics

Test responses

T score < 39
  Test taker reports a below-average level of negative emotional experiences.
T score ≥ 65
  Test taker reports various negative emotional experiences including anxiety, anger, and fear.

Empirical correlates

  Is inhibited behaviorally because of negative emotions
  Experiences intrusive ideation
  Is anger prone
  Is stress reactive
  Experiences problems with sleep, including nightmares
  Worries excessively
  Engages in obsessive rumination
  Perceives others as overly critical
  Is self-critical and guilt prone

Diagnostic considerations

Evaluate for anxiety-related disorders.

Treatment considerations

Emotional difficulties may motivate them for treatment.

Focus on dysfunctional negative emotions as targets for intervention.

Evaluate need for anxiolytic medication (if RC7 ≥ 78).

---

includes racing thoughts, high energy, heightened mood, impulsivity, excitement seeking, and aggression.

Low RC9 scores indicate that the test taker reported a below-average level of activation and engagement with the environment. The co-occurrence of a low RC9 score and an elevated RC2 score reflects a combination of pronounced anhedonia and behavioral disengagement that may signal a vegetative depressive state.

Interpretation of elevated RC9 scores can be facilitated by considering the test taker's results on four SP Scales linked to RC9: Impulsivity (IMP), Activation (ACT), Aggression (AGG), and Cynicism (CYN). The interpersonal scales Self-Importance (SFI) and Dominance (DOM) may also be relevant. Table 9.11 provides interpretive statements for RC9.

SPECIFIC PROBLEMS (SP) SCALES

Most of the MMPI-3 Specific Problems (SP) Scales are intended to highlight important characteristics that are subsumed by or associated with one of the

TABLE 9.10. Aberrant Experiences (RC8) Interpretation

Clinical symptoms, behavioral tendencies, and personality characteristics

Test responses

T score 65–74
  Test taker reports unusual thoughts and perceptual processes.
T score ≥ 75
  Test taker reports many unusual thoughts and perceptions.

Empirical correlates

  Experiences thought disorganization
  Engages in unrealistic thinking
  Believes they have unusual sensory-perceptual abilities
  Aberrant experiences may include dissociation
  Aberrant experiences may include somatic delusions (if RC1 or NUC ≥ 65)
  Aberrant experiences may be substance induced (if SUB ≥ 65)
  Aberrant experiences may include auditory and/or visual hallucinations and nonpersecutory delusions such as thought broadcasting and mind reading (if T score ≥ 75)
  Reality testing may be significantly impaired (if RC8 ≥ 75)
  Experiences significant impairment in occupational and interpersonal functioning (if RC8 ≥ 75)

Diagnostic considerations

Evaluate for disorders manifesting psychotic symptoms.

Evaluate for disorders manifesting psychotic symptoms, including schizophrenia with paranoid features (if RC6 ≥ 79).

Evaluate for personality disorders manifesting unusual thoughts and perceptions.

Treatment considerations

Impaired thinking may disrupt treatment.

Assist them in gaining insight about their thought dysfunction.

Consider inpatient treatment for disorganized thinking (if RC8 ≥ 75).

Evaluate need for antipsychotic medication (if RC8 ≥ 75).

Significantly impaired thinking may disrupt treatment (if RC8 ≥ 75).

May need to be stabilized if treatment is to be successfully implemented (if RC8 ≥ 75).

Focus on psychotic symptoms as targets for intervention (if RC8 ≥ 75).

RC Scales but are not exclusively or directly targeted by that scale. However, it is important to note that the SP Scales are not limited to this auxiliary role and that their interpretation does not require a particular score on an associated RC scale. Data reported in the empirical literature and the *MMPI-3 Technical Manual* indicate that the SP Scales are sufficiently valid to be interpreted as substantive measures in their own right.

Based on empirical analyses and conceptual considerations, the SP Scales have been organized into four subsets: Somatic/Cognitive, Internalizing, Externalizing, and Interpersonal.

TABLE 9.11. Hypomanic Activation (RC9) Interpretation

Clinical symptoms, behavioral tendencies, and personality characteristics

Test responses

T score < 39
  Test taker reports a low energy level.

T score 65–74
  Test taker reports behaviors and experiences associated with hypomanic activation, such as excitability, impulsivity, and elevated mood.

T score ≥ 75
  Test taker reports many behaviors and experiences associated with hypomanic activation, such as excitability, impulsivity, and elevated mood.

Empirical correlates

T score < 39
  Has a low energy level
  Is disengaged from their normal activities

T score ≥ 65
  Is restless and easily bored
  Is overactivated as manifested in:
    Poor impulse control
    Sensation-seeking, risk-taking, and other forms of undercontrolled behavior
    Aggression
    Mood instability
    Euphoria
    Excitability
  May have a history of symptoms associated with manic or hypomanic episodes

Diagnostic considerations

T score ≥ 75
  Evaluate for:
    Manic or hypomanic episode
    Cycling mood disorder
    Schizoaffective disorder (if RC6 ≥ 79 or RC8 ≥ 75).

Treatment considerations

T score ≥ 75
  Excessive behavioral activation may interfere with treatment.
  Focus on mood stabilization in initial stages of treatment as a target for intervention.
  Consider inpatient treatment for hypomania.
  Evaluate need for mood-stabilizing medication.

Somatic/Cognitive Scales

Scores on the Somatic/Cognitive Scales should be interpreted considering the test taker's results on three Validity Scales in particular: Fs, FBS, and RBS. Elevated scores on these measures indicate the possibility that the test taker over-reported somatic (Fs, FBS) and cognitive (FBS, RBS) symptoms (see Tables 8.8, 8.9, and 8.10). Elevated scores on these three scales do not indicate that the individual is knowingly overreporting. Such an inference requires extratest data indicative of intentionality and, in the case of malingering, an external incentive. By contrast, in somatic symptom disorders, the patient genuinely experiences the distress and impairment associated with their complaints, even though the somatic symptoms they report cannot be explained by a medical condition. Therefore, when the Fs, FBS, or RBS scores reach or exceed the highest designated cutoff, the content-based statements for the Somatic/Cognitive Scales can be used to characterize the test taker's self-reported symptoms, but the (always probabilistic) empirical correlates of these scales, particularly the ones reflecting actual physical and cognitive symptoms, should not be included in the interpretation.

Malaise (MLS)

MLS consists of seven items describing a generalized sense of poor health and physical debilitation. As is true for all the Somatic Scales, accurate interpretation of the MLS score is dependent upon being adequately informed about the test taker's medical condition. It is particularly important to note that malaise, as defined and measured here, is a nonspecific manifestation of a broad range of acute and chronic medical conditions. A low MLS score indicates that the test taker reported a generalized sense of physical well-being. Table 9.12 lists interpretive statements for scores on MLS.

Neurological Complaints (NUC)

NUC consists of 10 items describing various problems that may have a neurological origin, such as dizziness, numbness, weakness, and involuntary movement. Elevated scores need to be considered in light of the test taker's medical condition. This may require a neuropsychological and/or neurological evaluation. If an underlying medical condition is ruled out, an elevated score on NUC, particularly if coupled with low scores on CYN and SHY, may suggest the inference of a somatoform condition such as a conversion disorder. Table 9.13 lists interpretive recommendations for NUC.

Eating Concerns (EAT)

EAT consists of five items that describe problematic eating behaviors such as binging, purging, and restricting. Empirical correlates of EAT scores include concerns about weight and body shape, restricted eating, and loss of control over eating. Table 9.14 lists interpretive recommendations for EAT.

TABLE 9.12. Malaise (MLS) Interpretation

Clinical symptoms, behavioral tendencies, and personality characteristics

Test responses

T score < 39
    Test taker reports a generalized sense of physical well-being.

T score 65–74
    Test taker reports experiencing poor health and feeling weak or tired.

T score ≥ 75
    Test taker reports a general sense of malaise manifested in poor health and feeling tired, weak, and incapacitated.

Empirical correlates

   Is preoccupied with poor health
   Likely to complain of:
       Sleep disturbance
       Fatigue
       Low energy
       Sexual dysfunction

Diagnostic considerations

If physical origin for malaise has been ruled out, evaluate for somatic symptom disorder.

Treatment considerations

Malaise may impede test taker's willingness or ability to engage in treatment.

TABLE 9.13. Neurological Complaints (NUC) Interpretation

Clinical symptoms, behavioral tendencies, and personality characteristics

Test responses

T score 65–87
    Test taker reports vague neurological complaints.

T score ≥ 88
    Test taker reports many vague neurological complaints (e.g., dizziness, loss of balance, numbness, weakness and paralysis, and loss of control over movement).

Empirical correlates

   Presents with multiple somatic complaints
   Is preoccupied with physical health concerns
   Is prone to developing physical symptoms in response to stress
   Is likely to present with:
       Dizziness
       Coordination difficulties
       Sensory problems

Diagnostic considerations

If physical origin for neurological complaints has been ruled out, evaluate for somatic symptom disorder (consider a conversion disorder if CYN ≤ 38 and SHY ≤ 38).

Treatment considerations

Test taker is likely to reject psychological interpretation of neurological complaints.

TABLE 9.14. Eating Concerns (EAT) Interpretation

Clinical symptoms, behavioral tendencies, and personality characteristics

Test responses

T score 75–84
    Test taker reports problematic eating behaviors.

T score ≥ 85
    Test taker reports problematic eating behaviors, including binging and purging.

Empirical correlates

    Likely experiences some combination of:
        Concerns about weight and body shape
        Restricted eating
        Loss of control over eating

Diagnostic considerations

Eating disorder (if EAT ≥ 75).

Treatment considerations

Focus on problematic eating behaviors as a target for intervention (if EAT ≥ 75).

Cognitive Complaints (COG)

COG consists of 11 items describing an assortment of cognitive difficulties including memory problems, intellectual limitations, difficulties concentrating, and confusion. Elevated scores are empirically associated with concentration problems, complaints about memory, not coping well with stress, and low tolerance for frustration. Because elevated scores on FBS and RBS (see recommended levels and interpretive implications in Tables 8.9 and 8.10) are associated with an increased likelihood of noncredible reporting of cognitive difficulties, a test taker's COG score should be interpreted only after careful consideration of their scores on these scales. Table 9.15 provides interpretive recommendations for COG.

Internalizing Scales

The 10 Internalizing Scales measure aspects or inherent correlates of two RC Scales: Demoralization (RCd) and Dysfunctional Negative Emotions (RC7). Suicidal/Death Ideation (SUI), Helplessness/Hopelessness (HLP), Self-Doubt (SFD), and Inefficacy (NFC) assess various manifestations or correlates of RCd. Stress (STR), Worry (WRY), Compulsivity (CMP), Anxiety-Related Experiences (ARX), Anger Proneness (ANP), and Behavior-Restricting Fears (BRF) measure facets of RC7. As expected, the correlations between the scales within each subset are rather high. However, Appendixes D and E of the *MMPI-3*

TABLE 9.15. Cognitive Complaints (COG) Interpretation

Clinical symptoms, behavioral tendencies, and personality characteristics

Test responses

T score 65–75
    Test taker reports a diffuse pattern of cognitive difficulties.

T score ≥ 76
    Test taker reports a diffuse pattern of cognitive difficulties including memory problems, difficulties with attention and concentration, and possible confusion.

Empirical correlates

    Complains about memory problems
    Has low tolerance for frustration
    Does not cope well with stress
    Experiences difficulties in attention and/or concentration

Diagnostic considerations

Attention-related disorders.

Treatment considerations

Origin of cognitive complaints should be explored. This may require a neuropsychological evaluation.

Technical Manual present for each of these scales unique empirical correlates that are reflected in the interpretive recommendations below. As noted earlier, SP Scales are not merely aids in the interpretation of findings on other scales but can also be used as substantive measures apart from this auxiliary role. Low scores are interpretable for four of the Internalizing scales: NFC, STR, WRY, and ARX.

Suicidal/Death Ideation (SUI)

SUI consists of seven items that describe recent or earlier suicidal ideation or acts, or preoccupation with death. Because of its critical content, interpretive guidelines for SUI begin at a T score of 58, which corresponds to a raw score of 1. Correlate data reported in the literature for the MMPI-2-RF version of this scale and in Appendixes D and E of the *MMPI-3 Technical Manual* indicate that SUI scores are strongly associated with recent suicidal ideation or attempts, and in some studies these scores prospectively predicted suicide attempts. Thus, an elevated SUI score indicates the need for an immediate suicide risk assessment. SUI is one of the seven MMPI-3 scales identified as having critical content. Therefore, if the test taker's SUI score is even minimally elevated (T score 58 or higher), the MMPI-3 Score Report and Interpretive Report for Clinical Settings list all SUI items answered in the keyed direction. Table 9.16 presents interpretive statements for SUI.

TABLE 9.16. Suicidal/Death Ideation (SUI) Interpretation

Clinical symptoms, behavioral tendencies, and personality characteristics

Test responses

T score 58–79
    Test taker reports a history of suicidal ideation and/or past suicide attempts.
T score ≥ 80
    Test taker reports current suicidal ideation and a history of suicidal ideation and attempts.

Empirical correlates
    Is preoccupied with suicide and death
    Is at risk for self-harm
    Is at risk for suicide attempt (this risk is exacerbated by poor impulse control if BXD, RC4, RC9, IMP, or DISC ≥ 65 and/or by substance abuse if SUB ≥ 65)
    May have recently attempted suicide

Diagnostic considerations
None.

Treatment considerations
Immediately assess risk for suicide (if SUI ≥ 58).

Helplessness/Hopelessness (HLP)

HLP is made up of seven items describing the belief that the individual is incapable of overcoming problems and of making changes needed to reach their life goals. Elevated scores are associated with feeling that life is a strain; feeling hopeless, helpless, and overwhelmed; believing that one gets a raw deal from life; and lacking motivation for change. Since HLP is one of the scales designated as having critical content, items answered in the keyed direction are printed in the MMPI-3 Score Report and Interpretive Report for Clinical Settings whenever the test taker's HLP score is elevated. Table 9.17 presents interpretive statements for HLP.

Self-Doubt (SFD)

SFD consists of seven items that describe lack of confidence and feeling useless. Elevated scores are associated with feelings of inferiority, insecurity, and self-disparagement. These self-esteem problems can be important targets for intervention. Table 9.18 provides interpretive statements for SFD.

Inefficacy (NFC)

NFC consists of nine items describing beliefs that one is incapable of making decisions and dealing effectively with major and minor crises. Low NFC scores

TABLE 9.17. Helplessness/Hopelessness (HLP) Interpretation

Clinical symptoms, behavioral tendencies, and personality characteristics

Test responses

T score 65–79
    Test taker reports feeling helpless and/or hopeless and pessimistic.

T score ≥ 80
    Test taker reports having lost hope and believing that they cannot change, cannot overcome their problems, and are incapable of reaching their life goals.

Empirical correlates
    Feels overwhelmed and that life is a strain
    Believes they cannot be helped
    Believes they get a raw deal from life
    Lacks motivation for change

Diagnostic considerations
None.

Treatment considerations
Focus on loss of hope and feelings of despair as early targets for intervention.

TABLE 9.18. Self-Doubt (SFD) Interpretation

Clinical symptoms, behavioral tendencies, and personality characteristics

Test responses

T score 65–77
    Test taker reports self-doubt and futility.

T score = 78
    Test taker reports lacking confidence, feeling worthless, and believing they are a burden to others.

Empirical correlates
    Feels inferior and insecure
    Is self-disparaging
    Is prone to rumination
    Is intropunitive
    Presents with lack of confidence and feelings of uselessness

Diagnostic considerations
None.

Treatment considerations
Focus on low self-esteem and other manifestations of self-doubt as targets for intervention.

---

indicate that the test taker described themself as someone who wants to be in control and is self-reliant. Elevated scores indicate that, faced with difficulties, the test taker is likely to be passive and lack self-reliance. Table 9.19 presents interpretive statements for NFC.

TABLE 9.19. Inefficacy (NFC) Interpretation

Clinical symptoms, behavioral tendencies, and personality characteristics

Test responses

T score < 39
  Test taker reports being decisive and efficacious.

T score 65–76
  Test taker reports being passive, indecisive, and inefficacious.

T score = 77
  Test taker reports:
    Being very indecisive and inefficacious
    Believing they are incapable of making decisions and dealing effectively with crisis situations
    Having difficulties when dealing with small, inconsequential matters.

Empirical correlates

T score < 39
  Likely to be self-reliant and power oriented

T score ≥ 65
  Experiences:
    Subjective incompetence
    Shame
    Lack of perseverance and self-reliance

Diagnostic considerations
None.

Treatment considerations
Indecisiveness may interfere with establishing treatment goals and progress in treatment.

Stress (STR)

STR is made up of six items that describe various problems involving experiences of stress and feeling nervous. Low scores indicate that the test taker reported a below-average stress level. Elevated scores can help identify the need for stress management as a target for intervention. Table 9.20 provides interpretive statements for STR.

Worry (WRY)

WRY consists of seven items that convey excessive worry, including worries about misfortune and finances, as well as preoccupation with disappointments. Empirical correlates of elevated WRY scores include rumination, which can be identified in such cases as a target for intervention. Table 9.21 presents interpretive statements for WRY.

TABLE 9.20. Stress (STR) Interpretation

Clinical symptoms, behavioral tendencies, and personality characteristics

Test responses

T score < 39
  Test taker reports a below-average level of stress.
T score 65–75
  Test taker reports an above-average level of stress.
T score = 76
  Test taker reports multiple problems involving stress and feeling nervous.

Empirical correlates
  Complains about stress
  Feels incapable of controlling their anxiety level

Diagnostic considerations

Evaluate for generalized anxiety disorder.

Treatment considerations

Focus on developing stress management skills as a target for intervention.

TABLE 9.21. Worry (WRY) Interpretation

Clinical symptoms, behavioral tendencies, and personality characteristics

Test responses

T score < 39
  Test taker reports a below-average level of worry.
T score ≥ 65
  Test taker reports excessive worry, including worries about misfortune and finances, as well as preoccupation with disappointments.

Empirical correlates
  Worries excessively
  Ruminates

Diagnostic considerations

Disorders involving excessive worry and rumination.

Treatment considerations

Focus on excessive worry and rumination as targets for intervention.

Compulsivity (CMP)

CMP includes eight items describing various compulsive behaviors such as repetitive checking and counting. Elevated scores (beginning at T score 62) are associated with engaging in compulsive behavior, experiencing obsessions, and being rigid and perfectionistic. Table 9.22 provides interpretive statements for CMP.

TABLE 9.22. Compulsivity (CMP) Interpretation

Clinical symptoms, behavioral tendencies, and personality characteristics

Test responses

T score 62–75
  Test taker reports engaging in compulsive behavior.
T score = 76
  Test taker reports engaging in compulsive behavior, including repetitive checking and counting.

Empirical correlates

  Engages in compulsive behavior such as repetitive checking
  Experiences obsessions
  Is rigid and perfectionistic

Diagnostic considerations

Evaluate for obsessive-compulsive disorder.

Treatment considerations

Focus on obsessive-compulsive behaviors as targets for intervention.

Anxiety-Related Experiences (ARX)

ARX consists of 15 items describing a range of anxiety-related experiences, including generalized anxiety, reexperiencing traumatic events, intrusive ideation, startle responses, and panic. ARX is the MMPI-3 scale most highly correlated with features of posttraumatic stress disorder (PTSD). However, it is not a specific measure of this condition. Highly elevated T scores (80 or greater) indicate the test taker may benefit from anxiolytic medication. Table 9.23 presents interpretive statements for ARX.

Anger Proneness (ANP)

ANP consists of 12 items that describe anger and anger-related tendencies including getting upset easily, being impatient with others, and becoming angered easily. Elevations on ANP are associated with anger problems, such as temper tantrums and holding grudges. ANP content and correlates center on the negative emotional experience and expression of anger rather than on aggressive acting out. The latter is more directly assessed by the Aggression (AGG) scale described later. Table 9.24 lists interpretive statements for ANP.

Behavior-Restricting Fears (BRF)

BRF consists of seven items describing fears that significantly restrict normal activities in and outside the home. BRF is associated empirically with agoraphobia and more generally with fearfulness. An elevated BRF score indicates

TABLE 9.23. Anxiety-Related Experiences (ARX) Interpretation

Clinical symptoms, behavioral tendencies, and personality characteristics

Test responses

T score < 39
 Test taker reports a below-average level of anxiety-related experiences.

T score 65–79
 Test taker reports multiple anxiety-related experiences, including generalized anxiety, reexperiencing, and/or panic.

T score 80–85
 Test taker reports multiple anxiety-related experiences, including generalized anxiety, reexperiencing, and panic.

T score = 88
 Test reports multiple anxiety-related experiences, including generalized anxiety, reexperiencing, intrusive ideation, startle responses, and panic.

Empirical correlates

Experiences:
 Significant anxiety and anxiety-related problems
 Intrusive ideation
 Sleep difficulties, including nightmares
 Possible posttraumatic distress
 Dissociative experiences (if RC8 ≥ 65)

Diagnostic considerations

Evaluate for anxiety-related disorders, including PTSD.

Treatment considerations

Evaluate need for anxiolytic medication (if ARX ≥ 80). Focus on anxiety as a target for intervention.

TABLE 9.24. Anger Proneness (ANP) Interpretation

Clinical symptoms, behavioral tendencies, and personality characteristics

Test responses

T score 65–77
 Test taker reports being anger prone.

T score = 78
 Test taker reports getting upset easily, being impatient with others, becoming easily angered, and sometimes even being overcome by anger.

Empirical correlates

Has problems with:
 Anger
 Irritability
 Low tolerance for frustration
 Holds grudges
 Has temper tantrums
 Is hostile and argumentative

Diagnostic considerations

Evaluate for anger-related disorders.

Treatment considerations

Focus on anger management as a target for intervention.

TABLE 9.25. Behavior-Restricting Fears (BRF) Interpretation

Clinical symptoms, behavioral tendencies, and personality characteristics

Test responses

T score 65–99
  Test taker reports multiple fears that significantly restrict normal activity in and outside the home.

T score = 100
  Test taker reports multiple fears that significantly restrict normal activity in and outside the home, including fears of leaving home, open spaces, small spaces, the dark, dirt, sharp objects, and handling money.

Empirical correlates
  Is fearful

Diagnostic considerations
Evaluate for anxiety disorders, particularly agoraphobia.

Treatment considerations
Focus on behavior-restricting fears as targets for intervention.

---

that behavior-restricting fears can be considered intervention targets. Table 9.25 provides interpretive statements for BRF.

Externalizing Scales

The seven Externalizing Scales measure facets of two RC Scales: Antisocial Behavior (RC4) and Hypomanic Activation (RC9). The Family Problems (FML), Juvenile Conduct Problems (JCP), and Substance Abuse (SUB) scales measure facets of RC4, while Impulsivity (IMP), Activation (ACT), Aggression (AGG), and Cynicism (CYN) assess facets of RC9. As is true of any SP scale, the Externalizing measures can help highlight the primary problems underlying elevated scores on the associated RC Scales but are also fully interpretable when the RC Scales in question are not elevated. For example, if a test taker produces a moderate elevation on RC4, an elevated score on JCP, but no elevation on FML or SUB, interpretation of the elevated RC4 score would emphasize the features associated with a history of juvenile misconduct and deemphasize features related to family problems and substance abuse. In cases where the RC4 score falls within the normal range, elevated scores on FML, JCP, and SUB remain interpretable. For four of the Externalizing scales—FML, IMP, ACT, and CYN—low scores are also interpretable.

Family Problems (FML)

FML consists of 10 items describing negative family experiences, including quarrels, dislike of family members, feeling unappreciated, and feeling that family

TABLE 9.26. Family Problems (FML) Interpretation

Clinical symptoms, behavioral tendencies, and personality characteristics

Test responses

T score < 39
    Test taker reports a predominantly conflict-free past and current family environment.

T score 65–79
    Test taker reports conflictual family relationships and lack of support from family members.

T score ≥ 80
    Test taker reports conflictual family relationships and lack of support from family members. Negative family attitudes and experiences include frequent quarrels, dislike of family members, feeling unappreciated by family members, and feeling that family members cannot be counted on in time of need.

Empirical correlates
    Has family conflicts
    Experiences poor family functioning
    Has strong negative feelings about family members
    Blames family members for their difficulties

Diagnostic considerations
None.

Treatment considerations
Focus on family problems as targets for intervention.

---

members cannot be counted on in times of need. A low FML score indicates that the test taker reported a comparatively conflict-free family environment. Elevated FML scores are associated with conflictual family relations: negative feelings about one's family members and blaming them for one's difficulties. Most of the FML items are worded in a way that could apply to the test taker's current family and/or their family of origin. A smaller number of items refer specifically (directly or indirectly) to the family of origin. Table 9.26 provides interpretive statements for FML.

Juvenile Conduct Problems (JCP)

JCP consists of seven items describing an early history of undesirable school conduct, stealing, and being negatively influenced by peers. Elevated JCP scores are associated with both juvenile delinquency and current acting out. If JCP is the only elevated behavioral dysfunction indicator (i.e., BXD, RC4, RC9, FML, SUB, IMP, ACT, AGG, CYN, and DISC are all within normal limits relative to the normative sample), the overall configuration may characterize a test taker who acknowledges a history of juvenile misconduct but no longer engages in acting-out behaviors. In addition, MMPI-3 scales BXD, RC4, and DISC include non-JCP items describing past antisocial conduct, which makes it possible for a

TABLE 9.27. Juvenile Conduct Problems (JCP) Interpretation

Clinical symptoms, behavioral tendencies, and personality characteristics

Test responses

T score 65–79
  Test taker reports a history of juvenile conduct problems.

T score = 80
  Test taker reports a history of juvenile conduct problems, such as problematic behavior at school, stealing, and being arrested.

Empirical correlates

  Has a history of juvenile delinquency and criminal or antisocial behavior
  Experiences conflictual interpersonal relationships
  Engages in acting-out behavior
  Has difficulties with individuals in positions of authority

Diagnostic considerations

Evaluate for externalizing disorders, particularly antisocial personality disorder.

Treatment considerations

None.

---

test taker to obtain elevated scores on these scales on the exclusive basis of past behaviors. Table 9.27 presents interpretive statements for JCP.

Substance Abuse (SUB)

SUB is made up of nine items that describe significant past or current substance abuse, with most of the item content focusing on alcohol misuse. Elevated scores are associated with a substantially increased risk for substance abuse, including both alcohol and drugs, impaired functioning resulting from substance abuse, and a general sensation-seeking tendency. Because the problems associated with an elevated SUB score may require immediate attention, the scale has been identified as having critical content. Therefore, if the test taker's SUB score is elevated, the items answered in the keyed direction are printed in the MMPI-3 Score Report and Interpretive Report for Clinical Settings. Table 9.28 presents interpretive statements for SUB.

Impulsivity (IMP)

IMP comprises six items describing various impulsive behaviors that are likely to be problematic for the test taker. IMP scores are associated with engaging in nonplanful conduct and with a history of poor impulse control, including possible features of hyperactive behavior. Table 9.29 presents interpretive statements for IMP.

TABLE 9.28. Substance Abuse (SUB) Interpretation

Clinical symptoms, behavioral tendencies, and personality characteristics

Test responses

T score 65–79
    Test taker reports significant past and current substance abuse.

T score ≥ 80
    Test taker reports:
        A significant history of substance abuse
        Current substance abuse
        Frequent use of alcohol and drugs
        Using alcohol to "relax and open up"
        Inappropriate use of prescription medication.

Empirical correlates
    Has a history of problematic use of alcohol or drugs, including misuse of prescription medication
    Has had legal problems as a result of substance abuse

Diagnostic considerations
Evaluate for substance-use-related disorders.

Treatment considerations
Focus on reduction or cessation of substance abuse as a target for intervention.

TABLE 9.29. Impulsivity (IMP) Interpretation

Clinical symptoms, behavioral tendencies, and personality characteristics

Test responses

T score < 39
    Test taker reports a below-average level of impulsive behavior.

T score ≥ 65
    Test taker reports engaging in problematic impulsive behavior.

Empirical correlates
    Engages in nonplanful behavior
    Has poor impulse control and a possible history of hyperactive behavior

Diagnostic considerations
Evaluate for impulse-control disorders.

Treatment considerations
Focus on improved impulse control as a possible target for intervention.
Impulsive behavior may interfere with treatment.

Activation (ACT)

ACT consists of eight items describing experiences of heightened excitation and energy level, uncontrollable mood swings, and lack of sleep. A low ACT score indicates that the test taker reported a below-average level of energy and

TABLE 9.30. Activation (ACT) Interpretation

Clinical symptoms, behavioral tendencies, and personality characteristics

Test responses

T score < 39
    Test taker reports a below-average level of energy and activation.

T score 65–79
    Test taker reports episodes of heightened excitation and energy level.

T score = 80
    Test taker reports episodes of heightened excitation and energy level, uncontrollable mood swings, and lack of sleep.

Empirical correlates

    Experiences excessive activation
    Has a history of symptoms associated with manic or hypomanic episodes

Diagnostic considerations

Evaluate for manic or hypomanic episodes or other conditions associated with excessive energy and activation.

Evaluate for cycling mood disorders.

Treatment considerations

Evaluate need for mood-stabilizing medication (T score ≥ 70).

Excessive behavioral activation may interfere with treatment.

---

activation. Elevated ACT scores are associated with a history of manic or hypomanic episodes and a current high level of activation. The possibility that some of the experiences described by the ACT items are substance-induced should be considered in weighing the diagnostic and treatment implications of an elevated score. Table 9.30 presents interpretive statements for ACT.

Aggression (AGG)

AGG consists of six items describing physically aggressive behavior and having a callous attitude about engaging in such conduct. Individuals with elevated AGG scores are likely to have a history of violence and interpersonal abusiveness. Because problems associated with elevated AGG scores may require immediate attention, the scale has been identified as having critical content. Accordingly, if the test taker's AGG score is elevated, the MMPI-3 Score Report and Interpretive Report for Clinical Settings lists all AGG items that were answered in the keyed direction. Table 9.31 presents interpretive statements for AGG.

Cynicism (CYN)

CYN consists of 13 items stating (as keyed) opinions that convey a highly negative view of human nature. Empirical findings with this scale indicate that

TABLE 9.31. Aggression (AGG) Interpretation

Clinical symptoms, behavioral tendencies, and personality characteristics

Test responses

T score 65–85
　Test taker reports engaging in physically aggressive, violent behavior and losing control.

T score = 86
　Test taker reports engaging in physically aggressive, violent behavior, including explosive behavior and physical altercations, and enjoying intimidating others.

Empirical correlates
　Has a history of violent behavior toward others
　Is abusive
　Experiences anger-related problems

Diagnostic considerations

Evaluate for disorders associated with interpersonal aggression.

Treatment considerations

Focus on reduction in interpersonally aggressive behavior as a target for intervention.

---

these attitudes are associated with antagonistic interpersonal interactions and behaviors. Low CYN scores indicate that the test taker describes others as well-intentioned and trustworthy and may reflect naivete. Individuals who produce elevated scores on this scale report a variety of cynical beliefs about other people's motivations. The content is "non-self-referential" in that the CYN items, as keyed, do not claim that one is personally being singled out for mistreatment, which would be indicated by an elevated score on RC6 (discussed earlier). Rather, the items assert that others look out only for their own interests and are not to be trusted. Table 9.32 lists interpretive statements for CYN.

Interpersonal Scales

The content and correlates of most, possibly all, MMPI-3 Substantive Scales include aspects that describe or have implications for interpersonal functioning. For example, individuals with elevated scores on RC2 are likely to be socially disengaged, those with elevations on RC6 are likely to experience interpersonal difficulties because of their persecutory beliefs, and those with high SUB scores are likely to experience impairment in social functioning resulting from substance abuse. However, for the five SP Scales included under this heading—Self-Importance (SFI), Dominance (DOM), Disaffiliativeness (DSF), Social Avoidance (SAV), and Shyness (SHY)—interpersonal functioning is the primary focus. Four of these scales (SFI, DOM, SAV, and SHY) include not only high scores but also interpretable low scores.

TABLE 9.32. Cynicism (CYN) Interpretation

Clinical symptoms, behavioral tendencies, and personality characteristics

Test responses

T score < 39
    Test taker describes others as well-intentioned and trustworthy, and disavows cynical beliefs about them.
    Test taker is possibly overly trusting.

T score 65–78
    Test taker reports:
        Having cynical beliefs
        Being distrustful of others
        Believing others look out only for their own interests.

T score = 79
    Test taker reports:
        Having cynical beliefs and a hostile view of others
        Being distrustful of others
        Believing others lie to get ahead and look out only for their own interests.

Empirical correlates
    Is hostile toward and feels alienated from others
    Is distrustful of others
    Is self-centered and lacking in empathy
    Has negative interpersonal experiences

Diagnostic considerations

Evaluate for personality disorders involving mistrust of and/or hostility toward others and acting-out behaviors.

Treatment considerations

Cynicism may interfere with forming a therapeutic relationship.

Cynical beliefs may result in treatment noncompliance.

Focus on lack of interpersonal trust as a target for intervention.

Self-Importance (SFI)

SFI consists of 10 items describing the test taker's belief that they have special talents and abilities that most others do not have, and that they are an extraordinary person. Low SFI scores are produced by test takers who describe themselves as lacking in positive qualities. Elevated scores are associated with acclaim-seeking and having a sense of superiority. Table 9.33 lists interpretive statements for SFI.

Dominance (DOM)

DOM is made up of nine items that describe having strong opinions, being assertive and direct with others, and having confidence in taking on leadership roles. Low DOM scores are found in test takers who portray themselves as being passive and submissive when interacting with others and being ready to

TABLE 9.33. Self-Importance (SFI) Interpretation

Clinical symptoms, behavioral tendencies, and personality characteristics

Test responses

T score < 39
    Test taker describes themself as lacking in positive qualities.

T score ≥ 65
    Test taker reports having special talents and abilities and many brilliant ideas, and describes themself as being an extraordinary person.

Empirical correlates
    Seeks acclaim
    Has a sense of superiority

Diagnostic considerations

Disorders involving excessive sense of self-importance such as narcissistic personality disorder.

Disorders involving delusions of grandeur (if RC9 ≥ 75).

Treatment considerations

Excessive sense of self-importance may interfere with forming a therapeutic relationship.

---

give in to others. Elevated scores are associated with being viewed as overly assertive and domineering. Table 9.34 presents interpretive statements for DOM.

Disaffiliativeness (DSF)

DSF consists of seven items that describe a dislike of people and being around them, never having had a close relationship, and preferring to be alone. Elevated DSF scores are associated with being asocial. If the DSF T score reaches 78, this may be one indication of a schizoid personality disorder. Table 9.35 presents interpretive statements for DSF.

Social Avoidance (SAV)

SAV consists of nine items keyed to indicate that the respondent avoids social situations and does not enjoy social events. A low SAV score indicates that the test taker is gregarious and enjoys social situations. Elevated SAV scores are associated with social introversion, being emotionally restricted, and having difficulties forming close relationships. Table 9.36 provides interpretive statements for SAV.

Shyness (SHY)

SHY consists of seven items describing various manifestations of social anxiety including being easily embarrassed and feeling uncomfortable around others. A

TABLE 9.34. Dominance (DOM) Interpretation

Clinical symptoms, behavioral tendencies, and personality characteristics
Test responses

T score < 39
    Test taker reports:
        Being passive and submissive
        Not liking to be in charge
        Being ready to give in to others.

T score ≥ 65
    Test taker describes themselves as:
        Having strong opinions
        Standing up for themself
        Being assertive and direct
        Being able to lead others.

Empirical correlates

T score < 39
    Is passive and submissive in interpersonal relationships

T score ≥ 65
    Believes they have leadership capabilities but are likely to be viewed by others as overly assertive and domineering

Diagnostic considerations

T score < 39
    Evaluate for disorders characterized by passive, submissive behavior, such as dependent personality disorder.

T score ≥ 65
    Evaluate for disorders involving excessively assertive, domineering behavior.

Treatment considerations

T score < 39
    Focus on reducing passive, submissive behavior as a target for intervention.

T score ≥ 65
    Domineering behavior may interfere with therapy.

TABLE 9.35. Disaffiliativeness (DSF) Interpretation

Clinical symptoms, behavioral tendencies, and personality characteristics
Test responses

T score 65–77
    Test taker reports disliking people and being around them.

T score = 78
    Test taker reports disliking people and being around them, preferring to be alone.

Empirical correlates
    Is:
        Asocial
        Socially introverted
        Emotionally disconnected

Diagnostic considerations
Evaluate for disorders involving lack of interest in close relationships.

Treatment considerations
Test taker's aversive response to close relationships may make it difficult to form a therapeutic alliance and achieve progress in treatment.

TABLE 9.36. Social Avoidance (SAV) Interpretation

Clinical symptoms, behavioral tendencies, and personality characteristics

Test responses

T score < 39
  Test taker reports enjoying social situations and events.
T score 65–76
  Test taker reports not enjoying social events and avoiding social situations.
T score = 77
  Test taker reports not enjoying social events and avoiding social situations, including parties and other events where crowds are likely to gather.

Empirical correlates

T score < 39
  Likely to be perceived as outgoing and gregarious
T score ≥ 65
  Is introverted
  Has difficulty forming close relationships
  Is emotionally restricted

Diagnostic considerations

T score ≥ 65
  Evaluate for disorders associated with social avoidance such as avoidant personality disorder.

Treatment considerations

Focus on difficulties associated with social avoidance as a target for intervention.

---

low SHY score indicates the relative absence of social anxiety, which is generally a normal-range personality characteristic but is also associated with psychopathy and conversion disorder when combined with certain other qualities (e.g., externalizing for psychopathy and somaticizing for conversion disorder). Elevated SHY scores are associated with social introversion and inhibition, feeling anxious in social situations, and the possibility that the test taker may meet diagnostic criteria for disorders associated with significant social anxiety. Table 9.37 presents interpretive statements for SHY.

PERSONALITY PSYCHOPATHOLOGY FIVE (PSY-5) SCALES

The MMPI-3 PSY-5 Scales are updated versions of five MMPI-2-RF scales that embody Harkness and McNulty's (1994) dimensional model of personality pathology. The analyses that yielded these revised scales are described in chapter 3, and the literature that supports their interpretation is reviewed in chapter 5. The PSY-5 Scales provide a temperament-oriented perspective on major dimensions of personality pathology linking the MMPI-3 to a psychopathology-focused five-factor model of personality very similar to the alternative *DSM-5* model for personality disorders (AMPD).

TABLE 9.37. Shyness (SHY) Interpretation

Clinical symptoms, behavioral tendencies, and personality characteristics

Test responses

T score < 39
  Test taker reports little or no social anxiety.
T score ≥ 65
  Test taker reports being shy, easily embarrassed, and uncomfortable around others.

Empirical correlates

  Is socially introverted and inhibited
  Is anxious and nervous in social situations
  Is viewed by others as socially awkward

Diagnostic considerations

Evaluate for disorders associated with social anxiety.

Treatment considerations

Focus on anxiety in social situations as a target for intervention.

Aggressiveness (AGGR)

AGGR consists of 15 items describing aggressively assertive behavior. Low AGGR scores indicate that the test taker is likely to be passive and submissive. Elevated scores are associated with instrumental aggressiveness (i.e., behavior designed to accomplish a desired goal as opposed to being reactive). AGGR is negatively correlated with the Agreeableness dimension of the five-factor model of personality and focuses more strongly on dysfunctional manifestations reflected in the Antagonism domain of AMPD. With respect to personality pathology, elevated AGGR scores are associated with features of narcissistic and antisocial personality disorders. Table 9.38 provides interpretive statements for AGGR.

Psychoticism (PSYC)

PSYC consists of 20 items that describe various experiences associated with thought disturbance. Elevated scores are associated with unusual perceptual experiences and thoughts and with being alienated from others. PSYC does not have a clear counterpart in the five-factor model of personality, although it has been linked by default to certain conceptions of the Openness dimension. It parallels the Psychoticism domain of the AMPD. In terms of personality pathology, elevated PSYC scores are associated with features of paranoid, schizotypal, and borderline personality disorders. Table 9.39 presents interpretive statements for PSYC.

TABLE 9.38. Aggressiveness (AGGR) Interpretation

Clinical symptoms, behavioral tendencies, and personality characteristics

Test responses

T score < 39
  Test taker reports being unassertive.
T score 65-79
  Test taker reports engaging in instrumentally aggressive behavior.
T score ≥ 80
  Test taker reports engaging in instrumentally aggressive behavior, including strongly standing up for themselves and their beliefs.

Empirical correlates

T score < 39
  Is passive and submissive in interpersonal relationships
T score ≥ 65
  Is overly assertive and socially dominant
  Engages in instrumentally aggressive behavior
  Is viewed by others as domineering

Diagnostic considerations

Evaluate for features of personality disorders involving antagonistic behavior, such as narcissistic and antisocial.

Treatment considerations

Focus on reduction of antagonistic behavior as a target for intervention.

Disconstraint (DISC)

DISC consists of 18 items describing a variety of manifestations of disconstrained behavior. Low DISC scores indicate a moderately high overall level of behavioral constraint. Elevated scores are associated with poor impulse control, acting out, and sensation- and excitement-seeking. DISC is (negatively) correlated with the Conscientiousness dimension of the five-factor model of personality but with a stronger focus on dysfunctional behavior represented by the Disinhibition domain of the AMPD. Among the personality disorders, elevated DISC scores are primarily associated with features of antisocial and borderline personality disorders. Table 9.40 presents interpretive statements for DISC.

Negative Emotionality/Neuroticism (NEGE)

NEGE includes 15 items describing a wide range of negative emotional experiences. Low NEGE scores indicate that the test taker reported not being prone to experience negative emotions. Elevated scores are associated with such negative emotions as anxiety, insecurity, and worry, as well as with a general tendency to catastrophize and expect the worst to happen. NEGE is associated with the Neuroticism dimension

TABLE 9.39. Psychoticism (PSYC) Interpretation

Clinical symptoms, behavioral tendencies, and personality characteristics

Test responses

T score 65–79
   Test taker reports unusual beliefs and perceptions.
T score ≥ 80
   Test taker reports a broad range of unusual beliefs and perceptions.

Empirical correlates

T score ≥ 65
   Experiences unusual thought processes and perceptual phenomena
   Is alienated from others
   Engages in unrealistic thinking
   Presents with impaired reality testing

Diagnostic considerations

Evaluate for features of personality disorders manifesting as unusual thoughts and perceptions such as schizotypal and paranoid disorders.

Treatment considerations

None.

TABLE 9.40. Disconstraint (DISC) Interpretation

Clinical symptoms, behavioral tendencies, and personality characteristics

Test responses

T score < 39
   Test taker reports overly constrained behavior.
T score ≥ 65
   Test taker reports a pattern of disconstrained behavior.

Empirical correlates

   Is behaviorally disconstrained
   Engages in acting-out behaviors
   Acts out impulsively
   Seeks sensation and excitement

Diagnostic considerations

Evaluate for features of personality disorders involving disinhibited behavior such as antisocial and borderline disorders.

Treatment considerations

Disinhibited behavior may interfere with treatment.

---

of the five-factor model of personality and the Negative Affectivity domain of the AMPD. Among the personality disorders, elevated NEGE scores are associated with features of paranoid, borderline, avoidant, dependent, and obsessive-compulsive personality disorders. Table 9.41 provides interpretive statements for NEGE.

TABLE 9.41. Negative Emotionality/Neuroticism (NEGE) Interpretation

Clinical symptoms, behavioral tendencies, and personality characteristics
Test responses

T score < 39
  Test taker reports not being prone to experiencing negative emotions.

T score ≥ 65
  Test taker reports experiencing an elevated level of negative emotionality.

Empirical correlates

  Experiences various negative emotions including:
    Anxiety
    Insecurity
    Worry
  Is inhibited behaviorally because of negative emotions
  Is self-critical and guilt prone
  Experiences intrusive ideation

Diagnostic considerations

Evaluate for features of personality disorders involving negative emotionality such as dependent and obsessive-compulsive disorders.

Treatment considerations

Emotional difficulties may motivate test takers to receive treatment.

Target intervention toward test taker's tendency to focus exclusively on negative information.

TABLE 9.42. Introversion/Low Positive Emotionality (INTR) Interpretation

Clinical symptoms, behavioral tendencies, and personality characteristics
Test responses

T score < 39
  Test taker reports being disposed to be socially engaged and to experience a wide range of positive emotions.

T score ≥ 65
  Test taker reports:
    A lack of positive emotional experiences
    Avoiding social situations.

Empirical correlates

  Lacks positive emotional experiences
  Experiences significant problems with anhedonia
  Lacks interests
  Is pessimistic
  Is socially introverted

Diagnostic considerations

Evaluate for features of personality disorders involving detachment, such as avoidant and schizoid disorders.

Treatment considerations

Lack of positive emotions may interfere with engagement in therapy.

Introversion/Low Positive Emotionality (INTR)

INTR consists of 14 items that describe a lack of positive emotional experiences and avoidance of social situations and interactions. Low INTR scores indicate that the test taker is disposed to be socially engaged and to experience a wide range of positive emotions. Elevated scores are associated with social introversion, anhedonia, restricted interests, and a pessimistic outlook. INTR is associated negatively with the Extraversion dimension of the five-factor model of personality. The parallel domain is called Detachment in the AMPD. Among the personality disorders, elevated INTR scores are associated with features of schizoid and avoidant personality disorders; low scores may be associated with histrionic personality disorder. Table 9.42 lists interpretive statements for INTR.

Interpreting the MMPI-3

Recommended Framework and Process

This chapter describes and illustrates a recommended framework and process for MMPI-3 interpretation. Note that for some specific contexts, such as evaluation of public safety personnel, other recommendations apply (e.g., Corey & Ben-Porath, 2024). Test users who follow the procedures spelled out in this chapter should produce reasonably similar interpretations of the same set of scores. This outcome is desirable in any evaluation, and necessary in some settings (e.g., forensic) in which discordant interpretations of the same protocol can raise significant questions about the credibility of the interpreter and the test. The chapter begins with a description of a recommended framework for organizing MMPI-3 findings and then describes a process for integrating the scale-by-scale interpretive statements provided in chapters 8 and 9. Case examples are used to illustrate how this information can serve as a starting point for generating a narrative interpretation of the test results.

USING THE MMPI-3 INTERPRETATION WORKSHEET

Table 10.1 provides a recommended framework for organizing MMPI-3 findings and identifies the sources of information (the MMPI-3 scale scores) relevant to each of the domains assessed with the test. This framework is incorporated in the MMPI-3 Interpretation Worksheet, which is reproduced in Figure 10.1.[1] By following the process described in this chapter, an MMPI-3 user can generate a worksheet that provides the same interpretive statements that would be found for a given protocol in an MMPI-3 Interpretive Report for Clinical Settings. Whether relying on the worksheet or the interpretive report,

TABLE 10.1. Recommended Framework and Sources of Information for MMPI-3 Interpretation

Domains	MMPI-3 sources
I. Protocol validity	
a. Content nonresponsiveness	CNS, CRIN, VRIN, TRIN
b. Overreporting	F, Fp, Fs, FBS, RBS
c. Underreporting	L, K
II. Substantive Scale interpretation	
a. Somatic/cognitive dysfunction	RC1, MLS, EAT, NUC, COG
b. Emotional dysfunction	EID, RCd, SUI, HLP, SFD, NFC, RC2, INTR, RC7, STR, WRY, CMP, ARX, ANP, BRF, NEGE
c. Thought dysfunction	THD, RC6, RC8, PSYC
d. Behavioral dysfunction	BXD, RC4, FML, JCP, SUB, RC9, IMP, ACT, AGG, CYN, DISC
e. Interpersonal functioning	SFI, DOM, DSF, SAV, SHY, AGGR
f. Diagnostic considerations	Most Substantive Scales
g. Treatment recommendations	All Substantive Scales

the process recommended in this chapter calls for the MMPI-3 user to generate their own interpretation of the test results by integrating test findings with extratest information in the context of the referral issues.

Because of the inherent limitations of self-report-based assessment, the first step in any interpretation is to appraise the validity of the test protocol. Therefore, the first part of the recommended framework for MMPI-3 interpretation presented in Table 10.1 is intended to facilitate consideration of scores on the Validity Scales. If the analysis of protocol validity indicates that interpretation of scores on the Substantive Scales is warranted, the Substantive Scale Findings section of the framework presents the seven domains addressed: Somatic/Cognitive Dysfunction, Emotional Dysfunction, Thought Dysfunction, Behavioral Dysfunction, Interpersonal Functioning, Diagnostic Considerations, and Treatment Recommendations.

As illustrated later, when writing a narrative report of MMPI-3 findings, the first four domains can be addressed according to their relative prominence in the protocol based on the Higher-Order (H-O) Scales. For example, when findings indicate that symptoms related to Emotional Dysfunction are likely to be the most prominent in a particular case, this topic would be addressed first, and scores on all the scales listed under this domain in Table 10.1 would be interpreted at this point. Typically, interpersonal functioning will be discussed in a report after the first four domains have been addressed. As explained by Ben-Porath and Tellegen (2020a), because the Somatic/Cognitive Dysfunction

MMPI®-3 Interpretation Worksheet

Protocol Validity

Content Nonresponsiveness   CNS ____   CRIN ____   VRIN ____   TRIN ____

Over-Reporting   F ____   Fp ____   Fs ____   FBS ____   RBS ____

Under-Reporting   L ____   K ____

FIGURE 10.1. MMPI-3 Interpretation Worksheet

Substantive Scale Interpretation

Somatic/Cognitive Dysfunction   RC1 _____   MLS _____   NUC _____   EAT _____   COG _____

_____
_____
_____
_____
_____
_____

Emotional Dysfunction   EID _____   RCd _____   RC2 _____   RC7 _____   NEGE _____

                                              SUI _____   STR _____   INTR _____

                                              HLP _____   WRY _____

                                              SFD _____   CMP _____

                                              NFC _____   ARX _____

                                                                      ANP _____

                                                                      BRF _____

_____
_____
_____
_____
_____
_____
_____
_____
_____
_____
_____
_____
_____
_____
_____
_____
_____
_____

FIGURE 10.1. MMPI-3 Interpretation Worksheet, continued

Thought Dysfunction　　THD ____　RC6 ____　RC8 ____　PSYC ____

_____
_____
_____
_____
_____

Behavioral Dysfunction　　BXD ____　RC4 ____　RC9 ____　CYN ____
　　　　　　　　　　　　　　　　　　　　FML ____　IMP ____　DISC ____
　　　　　　　　　　　　　　　　　　　　JCP ____　ACT ____
　　　　　　　　　　　　　　　　　　　　SUB ____　AGG ____

_____
_____
_____
_____
_____
_____
_____
_____
_____
_____

Interpersonal Functioning　　SFI ____　DOM ____　AGGR ____　DSF ____　SAV ____　SHY ____

_____
_____
_____
_____
_____
_____
_____

FIGURE 10.1. MMPI-3 Interpretation Worksheet, continued

Diagnostic Considerations

_____
_____
_____
_____
_____
_____
_____
_____
_____
_____
_____
_____
_____
_____

Treatment Considerations

_____
_____
_____
_____
_____
_____
_____
_____
_____
_____
_____
_____
_____

FIGURE 10.1. MMPI-3 Interpretation Worksheet, continued

domain does not include an H-O scale, it is treated somewhat differently from the other three domains. If scores on scales in the related (both conceptually and empirically) Emotional Dysfunction domain are interpreted, any elevated scores in the Somatic/Cognitive Dysfunction domain are interpreted in the paragraph immediately following discussion of the Emotional Dysfunction domain. However, if there are no interpretable scores on any of the Emotional Dysfunction scales, elevations on the Somatic/Cognitive Dysfunction scales, if any, are interpreted in the paragraph immediately preceding discussion of the Interpersonal scales.

The sixth and seventh domains in the Substantive Scale Findings section of the framework deal with diagnostic and treatment considerations, which are relevant when the MMPI-3 is administered in clinical settings. These sections may be replaced or augmented with other salient topics in nonclinical settings. For example, in personnel screening, possible risk factors associated with hiring a candidate (e.g., poor impulse control) can be identified; in correctional settings, factors associated with the potential for causing harm to self and others may be suggested for follow-up evaluation.

Use of the worksheet is discussed and illustrated in the following sections, beginning with the Validity Scales.

Validity Scale Interpretation

Figure 10.2 demonstrates use of the Validity Scales page of the worksheet with the profile provided in Figure 10.3. Validity scale scores for CNS and the 10 validity indicators are recorded on the worksheet first. Next, Tables 8.2 to 8.12 in chapter 8 are consulted to generate the typed statements in Figure 10.2. For example, the first statement in the Under-Reporting section, "Under-reporting is indicated by the test taker presenting himself in an extremely positive light by denying many minor faults and shortcomings that most people acknowledge," appears in Table 8.11 under the heading "Protocol Validity Concerns" for L T scores greater than or equal to 80.

The completed worksheet can then serve as a starting point for generating a narrative report of the validity scale findings, which combines the statements in Figure 10.2 with relevant extratest information. For example, if the individual who produced this Validity Scales profile was evaluated in the context of parental capacity evaluation, the following interpretation could be provided:

> Mr. X's scores on the MMPI-3 Validity Scales indicate that he responded to all of the items and did so in a remarkably consistent manner. There is no evidence of overreporting. However, there is very substantial evidence of underreporting. Mr. X portrayed himself in an extremely positive light by denying many minor

MMPI®-3 Interpretation Worksheet

Protocol Validity

Content Nonresponsiveness   CNS 0   CRIN 33   VRIN 35   TRIN 50

The test taker provided scorable responses to all 335 items.
There is no evidence of remarkably consistent responding.
There is no evidence of fixed, content-inconsistent responding.

Over-Reporting   F 41   Fp 50   Fs 47   FBS 45   RBS 39

There is no evidence of over-reporting.

Under-Reporting   L 81   K 62

Under-reporting is indicated by the test taker presenting himself in an extremely positive light by denying many minor faults and shortcomings that most people would acknowledge. Possible under-reporting is also indicated by the test taker presenting himself as very well adjusted. An absence of elevation on the Substantive Scales should be interpreted with caution. Elevated scores on the Substantive Scales may underestimate the problems assessed by those scales.

FIGURE 10.2. MMPI-3 Interpretation Worksheet With Completed Validity Scales Page

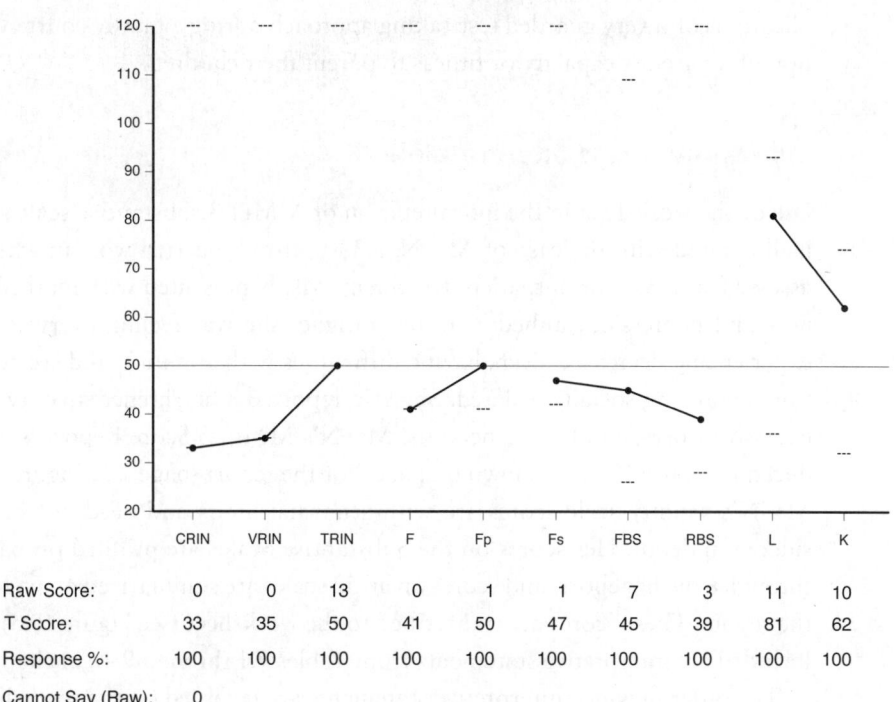

FIGURE 10.3. MMPI-3 Score Report Validity Scales Profile

faults and shortcomings that most people acknowledge. He also presented as being very well adjusted. Owing to substantial findings of marked underreporting, the absence of problematic findings on the Substantive Scales cannot be relied upon to rule out significant psychological dysfunction in Mr. X, which was the purpose of this evaluation. His test-taking approach raises significant concerns about Mr. X's cooperation with this assessment.

In this example, after reporting the test findings, the narrative discusses the implications of a very guarded test-taking approach during a family court evaluation of a parent's capacity or fitness to parent their children.

Substantive Scale Interpretation

Use of the worksheet in the interpretation of MMPI-3 substantive scale scores is illustrated with the case of Ms. N, a 33-year-old married woman who was assessed at intake for outpatient treatment. Ms. N presented with marked sadness and depression, anhedonia, and fatigue; she was feeling overwhelmed, experiencing decreased sleep, having difficulties with attention and concentration, and being socially isolated. She also reported a heightened anxiety level, excessive worry, and feeling nervous. Ms. N's MMPI-3 Score Report is reproduced in Figure 10.4. As shown on page 2 of the report (page 1 of Figure 10.4), Ms. N's validity scale scores are within normal limits and need not be considered in detail. Her scores on the Substantive Scales are profiled on pages 3 through 6 of the report, and scores on all 52 scales are summarized on page 7 of the report. These scores are transcribed to the worksheet (see Figure 10.5); also included are interpretive statements from Tables 9.1 through 9.42 in chapter 9.

The order in which interpretive statements are recorded on the worksheet is determined by the hierarchical structure of the test and relative scale elevations. For each of the first four substantive domains, elevated (or, if relevant, low) scores are interpreted beginning with the broadest measures (RC1, EID, THD, and BXD, respectively), and then incorporating lower-level scale scores according to their relative elevations across subdomains. RC1 is included here because it provides the broadest MMPI-3-based assessment of possible somatoform psychopathology. As described earlier, the H-O Scales are considered first, and in the actual narrative writeup of the results (not the worksheet) these domains are prioritized in order of elevation. The Somatic/Cognitive domain interpretation, if applicable, is included immediately after the emotional domain (if applicable) or immediately before the interpersonal domain.

For example, in Figure 10.5 the statements in the Emotional Dysfunction section begin with an interpretation of the EID score: "Ms. N's responses indicate considerable emotional distress that is likely to be perceived as a crisis."

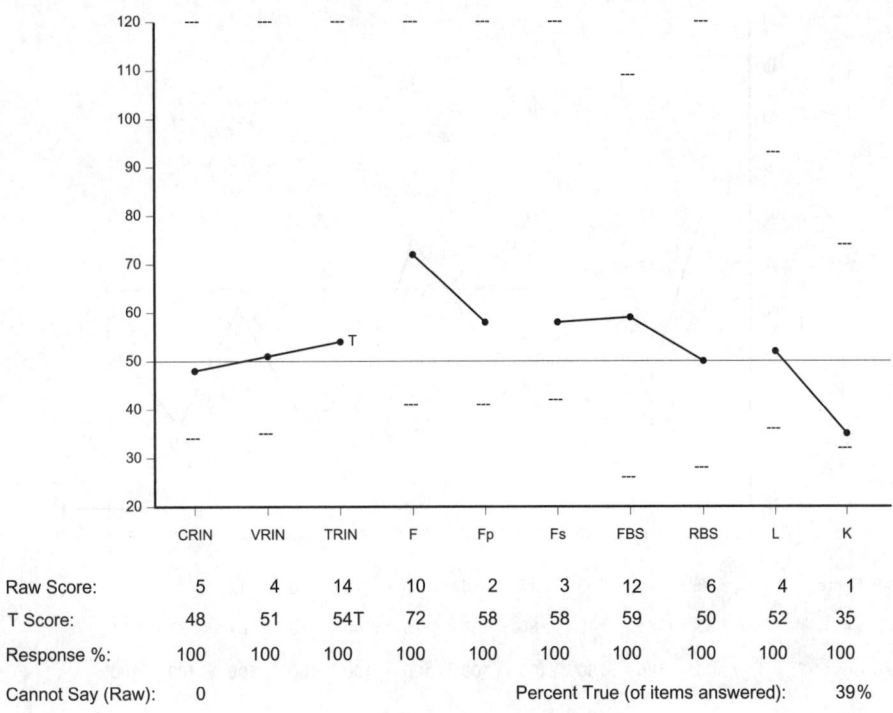

FIGURE 10.4. Ms. N's MMPI-3 Score Report

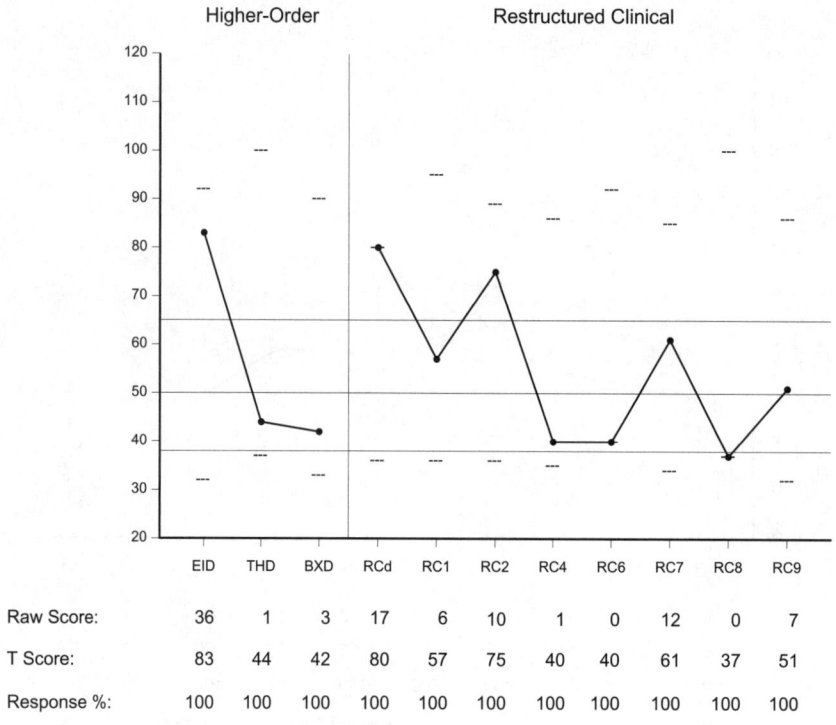

FIGURE 10.4. Ms. N's MMPI-3 Score Report, continued

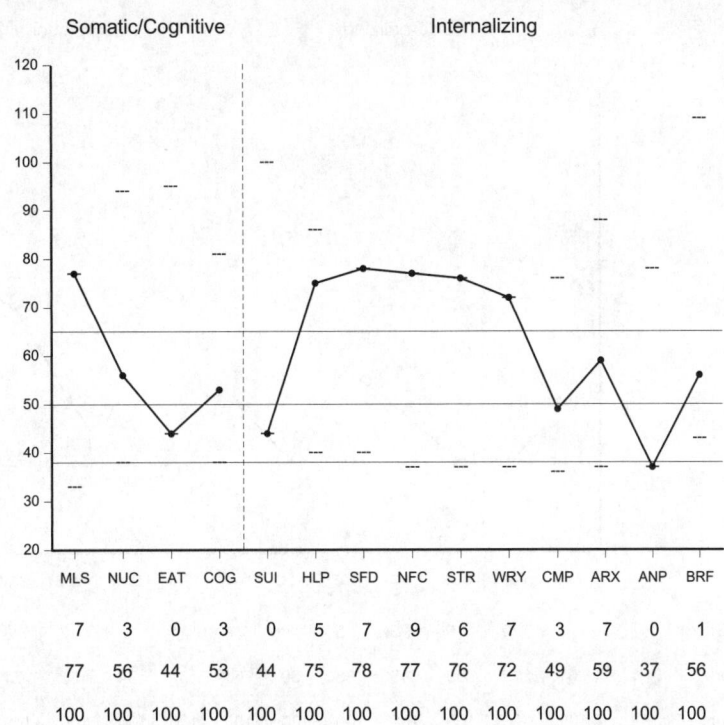

FIGURE 10.4. Ms. N's MMPI-3 Score Report, continued

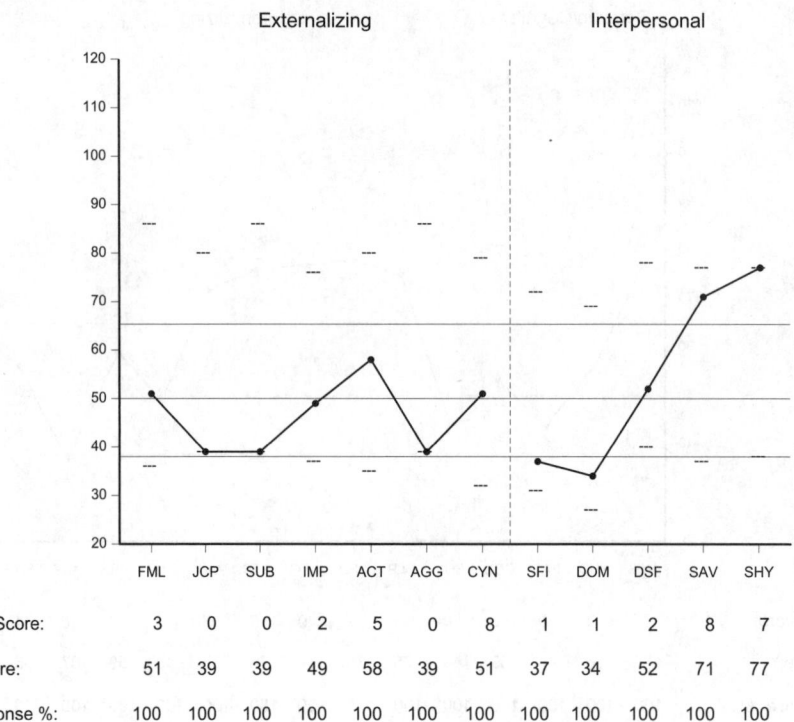

FIGURE 10.4. Ms. N's MMPI-3 Score Report, continued

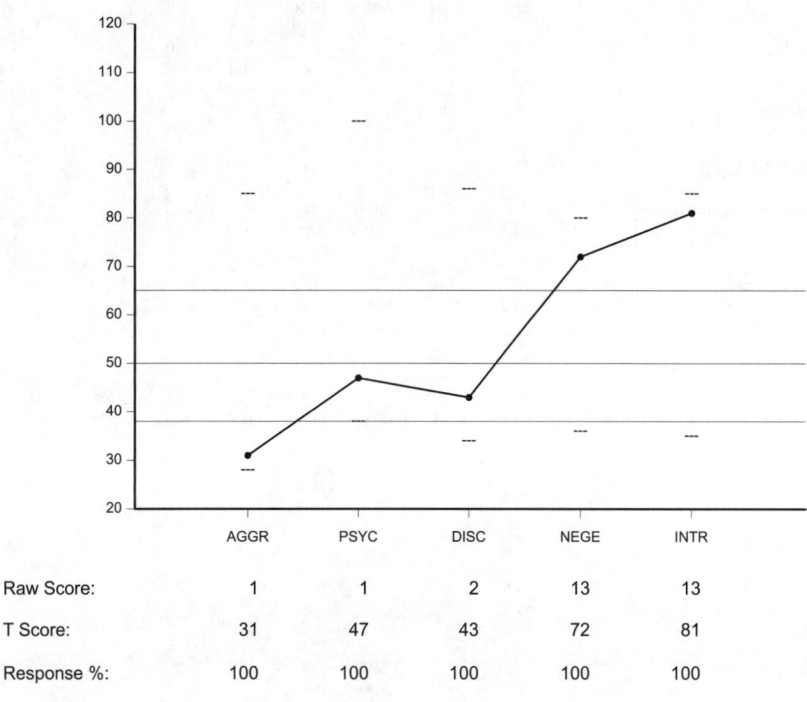

FIGURE 10.4. Ms. N's MMPI-3 Score Report, continued

MMPI-3 T SCORES (BY DOMAIN)

PROTOCOL VALIDITY

Content Non-Responsiveness

0	48	51	54 T
CNS	CRIN	VRIN	TRIN

Over-Reporting

72	58	58	59	50
F	Fp	Fs	FBS	RBS

Under-Reporting

52	35
L	K

SUBSTANTIVE SCALES

Somatic/Cognitive Dysfunction

57	77	56	44	53
RC1	MLS	NUC	EAT	COG

Emotional Dysfunction

83							
EID							

80	44	75	78	77
RCd	SUI	HLP	SFD	NFC

75	81
RC2	INTR

61	76	72	49	59	37	56	72
RC7	STR	WRY	CMP	ARX	ANP	BRF	NEGE

Thought Dysfunction

44
THD

40
RC6

37
RC8

47
PSYC

Behavioral Dysfunction

42
BXD

40	51	39	39
RC4	FML	JCP	SUB

51	49	58	39	51
RC9	IMP	ACT	AGG	CYN

43
DISC

Interpersonal Functioning

37	34	31	52	71	77
SFI	DOM	AGGR	DSF	SAV	SHY

Note. This information is provided to facilitate interpretation following the recommended structure for MMPI-3 interpretation in Chapter 5 of the *MMPI-3 Manual for Administration, Scoring, and Interpretation*, which provides details in the text and an outline in Table 5-1.

FIGURE 10.4. Ms. N's MMPI-3 Score Report, continued

MMPI®-3 Score Report
06/21/2019, Page 8

ID: Ms. N

ITEM-LEVEL INFORMATION

Unscorable Responses

The test taker produced scorable responses to all the MMPI-3 items.

Critical Responses

Seven MMPI-3 scales--Suicidal/Death Ideation (SUI), Helplessness/Hopelessness (HLP), Anxiety-Related Experiences (ARX), Ideas of Persecution (RC6), Aberrant Experiences (RC8), Substance Abuse (SUB), and Aggression (AGG)--have been designated by the test authors as having critical item content that may require immediate attention and follow-up. Items answered by the individual in the keyed direction (True or False) on a critical scale are listed below if her T score on that scale is 65 or higher. However, any item answered in the keyed direction on SUI is listed. The percentage of the MMPI-3 normative sample that answered each item in the keyed direction is provided in parentheses following the item content.

Helplessness/Hopelessness (HLP, T Score = 75)

    Item number and content omitted. (True, 10.9%)
    Item number and content omitted. (True, 8.7%)
    Item number and content omitted. (True, 4.6%)
    Item number and content omitted. (True, 45.4%)
    Item number and content omitted. (True, 8.4%)

End of Report

FIGURE 10.4. Ms. N's MMPI-3 Score Report, continued

MMPI®-3 Interpretation Worksheet

Protocol Validity

Content Nonresponsiveness   CNS 0   CRIN 48   VRIN 51   TRIN 54T

The test taker provided responses to all 335 items with no indications of inconsistent responses.

Over-Reporting   F 72   Fp 58   Fs 58   FBS 59   RBS 50

There is no evidence of over-reporting.

Under-Reporting   L 52   K 35

There is no evidence of under-reporting.

FIGURE 10.5. Ms. N's Completed MMPI-3 Interpretation Worksheet

Substantive Scale Interpretation

Somatic/Cognitive Dysfunction RC1 _57_ MLS _77_ NUC _56_ EAT _44_ COG _53_

Ms. N reports a generalized sense of malaise manifested in poor health and feeling tired, weak, and incapacitated. She very likely is preoccupied with poor health and complains of sleep disturbance, fatigue, low energy, and sexual dysfunction.

Emotional Dysfunction EID _83_ RCd _80_ RC2 _75_ RC7 _61_ NEGE _72_

SUI _44_ STR _76_ INTR _81_

HLP _75_ WRY _72_

SFD _78_ CMP _49_

NFC _77_ ARX _59_

ANP _37_

BRF _56_

Ms. N's responses indicate considerable emotional distress that is likely to be perceived as a crisis. She reports experiencing significant demoralization, feeling overwhelmed, and being extremely unhappy, sad, and dissatisfied with her life. She is very likely at risk for suicidal ideation and very likely complains about feeling depressed, experiences sadness and despair, does not cope well with stress, has difficulty concentrating, feels sad, and is pessimistic. She reports feeling helpless and/or hopeless, and likely feels overwhelmed and that life is a strain, believes she cannot be helped, believes she gets a raw deal from life, and lacks motivation for change. She reports lacking in confidence, feeling worthless, and believing she is a burden to others, and very likely feels inferior and insecure, is self-disparaging, is prone to rumination, is intropunitive, and presents with lack of confidence and feelings of uselessness. She reports being very indecisive and inefficacious, believing she is incapable of making decisions and dealing effectively with crisis situations, and having difficulties when dealing with small, inconsequential matters. She very likely experiences subjective incompetence and shame and lacks perseverance and self-reliance. She reports a lack of positive emotional experiences, significant anhedonia, and lack of interest. She is likely to be pessimistic, socially introverted and disengaged, and to lack energy. She reports multiple problems involving stress and feeling nervous and very likely complains about stress and feels incapable of controlling her anxiety level. She reports excessive worry, including worries about misfortune and finances, as well as preoccupation with disappointments. She likely worries excessively.

FIGURE 10.5. Ms. N's Completed MMPI-3 Interpretation Worksheet, continued

Thought Dysfunction   THD 44   RC6 40   RC8 37   PSYC 47

There are no indications of thought dysfunction in this protocol.

Behavioral Dysfunction   BXD 42   RC4 40   RC9 51   CYN 51

FML 51   IMP 49   DISC 43

JCP 39   ACT 58

SUB 39   AGG 39

There are no indications of behavioral externalizing dysfunction in this protocol.

Interpersonal Functioning   SFI 37   DOM 34   AGGR 31   DSF 52   SAV 71   SHY 77

Ms. N describes herself as lacking in positive qualities. She reports being passive and submissive, not liking to be in charge, and being ready to give in to others. She is likely to be passive and submissive in interpersonal relationships. She reports not enjoying social events and avoiding social situations and is likely introverted, has difficulty forming close relationships, and is emotionally restricted. She reports being shy, easily embarrassed, and uncomfortable around others. She very likely is socially introverted and inhibited, is anxious and nervous in social situations, and is viewed by others as socially awkward.

FIGURE 10.5. Ms. N's Completed MMPI-3 Interpretation Worksheet, continued

Diagnostic Considerations

Evaluate for internalizing disorders, particularly depression-related and anhedonia-related, generalized anxiety disorder, disorders involving excessive worry and rumination, somatic symptom disorder, disorders characterized by passive-submissive behavior such as dependent personality disorder, disorders associated with social avoidance such as avoidant personality disorder, and disorders associated with social anxiety.

Treatment Considerations

Evaluate risk for self-harm, and need for antidepressant medication. Emotional difficulties may motivate her for treatment; however, significant lack of positive emotions may interfere with engagement in treatment. Focus on relief of demoralization, anhedonia, loss of hope and despair, as initial targets for treatment. Focus on low self-esteem, indecisiveness, stress management skills, excessive worry and rumination, passive-submissive behavior, social avoidance, and social anxiety as targets for intervention.

FIGURE 10.5. Ms. N's Completed MMPI-3 Interpretation Worksheet, continued

This is followed by an interpretation of RCd, on which Ms. N has the highest score among the three RC Scales in this domain (RCd, RC2, and RC7). The interpretation of RCd begins with content-based statements reflecting what Ms. N said when responding to the RCd items: "She reports experiencing significant demoralization, feeling overwhelmed, and being extremely unhappy, sad, and dissatisfied with her life." The empirical correlates of her RCd score are then stated: "She is very likely at risk for suicidal ideation and very likely complains about feeling depressed, experiences sadness and despair, does not cope well with stress, has difficulty concentrating, feels sad, and is pessimistic." Probabilistic language (e.g., very likely) is used to reflect the nature of empirical correlates (i.e., as the scale score increases, so does the likelihood that the correlates of a scale will apply in a given case). The RCd correlates are characterized as very likely to apply to Ms. N because of her high score on this scale. In Tables 9.1 to 9.42, correlates for scales scores in the lower T score range can be characterized as likely applying to the test taker, whereas correlates for scale scores in the higher T score range can be characterized with greater certainty as very likely applying to the test taker. In the case of RCd, the higher range begins at T score 74 (see Table 9.4); hence, the RCd correlates are interpreted as very likely to apply to Ms. N.

When interpreting scores on RC Scales that have associated Specific Problems (SP) Scales, the latter can be used to determine which empirical correlates of the RC scale to emphasize or deemphasize in the interpretation. Thus, the SP Scales associated with RCd (listed under RCd on the worksheet), Suicidal Death Ideation (SUI), Helplessness/Hopelessness (HLP), Self-Doubt (SFD), and Inefficacy (NFC), are considered. In Ms. N's case, HLP, SFD, and NFC, but not SUI, are elevated. The full range of RCd correlates is presented in the statements entered on the worksheet, except for content-based statements about suicidal ideation (note that the risk remains considering elevated RCd and HLP scores). Thus, following the RCd score interpretation, the worksheet illustration in Figure 10.5 states, "She reports feeling helpless and/or hopeless, and likely feels overwhelmed and that life is a strain, believes she cannot be helped, believe she gets a raw deal from life, and lacks motivation for change. She reports lacking in confidence, feeling worthless, and believing she is a burden to others, and very likely feels inferior and insecure, is self-disparaging, is prone to rumination, is intropunitive, and presents with lack of confidence and feelings of uselessness. She reports being very indecisive and inefficacious, believing she is incapable of making decisions and dealing effectively with crisis situations, and having difficulties when dealing with small, inconsequential matters. She very likely experiences subjective incompetence and shame and lacks perseverance and self-reliance."

The next set of statements in the Emotional Dysfunction section of the worksheet are based on Ms. N's score on RC2: "She reports a lack of positive emotional experiences, significant anhedonia, and lack of interest. She is likely to be pessimistic, socially introverted and disengaged, and to lack energy." Note that Table 9.6 for RC2 does not include a higher range of interpretive statements; therefore, the correlate statements are characterized as likely applying in this case.

The final statements in the Emotional Dysfunction section of Ms. N's worksheet are based on her score on the Stress (STR) and Worry (WRY) SP Scales: "She reports multiple problems involving stress and feeling nervous and very likely complains about stress and feels incapable of controlling her anxiety level. She reports excessive worry, including worries about misfortune and finances, as well as preoccupation with disappointments. She likely worries excessively." Note that SP scale scores can be interpreted even when the RC Scales with which they are associated (in this case, RC7) are not elevated.

The two PSY-5 Scales associated with Emotional Dysfunction are also elevated in Ms. N's case. The correlates of these scales overlap substantially with statements generated by the other measures and are, therefore, not repeated. Given the nature of the constructs that the PSY-5 Scales measure, it could be worthwhile to note in the interpretative narrative that Ms. N has a dispositional proclivity toward negative emotional experiences, introversion, and anhedonia. Personality disorder features are specifically associated with PSY-5 scale elevations, such as features of dependent or avoidant personality disorder.

The remaining sections of Ms. N's worksheet illustrate other elements of the recommended process for interpreting MMPI-3 substantive scale scores. The highest-level measure in the Somatic/Cognitive Dysfunction domain, RC1, is not elevated. Therefore, the interpretive statements in this section are based on one SP scale, Malaise (MLS), on which Ms. N produced an elevated score. As explained earlier, any interpretation of this domain would immediately follow the emotional domain in a narrative writeup of the results.

Because none of the scales in the Thought Dysfunction domain are elevated, the following statement is entered in that part of the worksheet: "There are no indications of thought dysfunction in this protocol." Ms. N did not produce any elevated scores in the Behavioral Dysfunction domain, and a similar statement is provided in that section of the worksheet. Neither of these statements need to be included in the narrative writeup of Ms. N's results.

Scores on the Interpersonal Functioning scales are interpreted in the order they appear on the worksheet, which was determined by the conceptual consideration of associations between the constructs assessed by these measures. In Ms. N's case, it is noteworthy that a combination of low scores on SFI, DOM, and AGGR and high scores on SAV and SHY combined to form statements reflecting a passive-submissive interpersonal style and significant social anxiety and withdrawal.

As noted earlier, the Diagnostic and Treatment Considerations sections of the worksheet are primarily relevant when the MMPI-3 is used in clinical assessments, as was the case with Ms. N. While interpreting the scales in the first six Substantive Scale subsections of the worksheet, the relevant Diagnostic and Treatment Considerations can be recorded in these final two sections. In Figure 10.5, the statements included in these sections come from several elevated scales, including EID, RCd, RC2, STR, WRY, IPP, SAV, SHY, AGGR, NEGE, and INTR.

Once completed, the worksheet can be used to write a narrative interpretation of the test results. Typically, a narrative report would begin with a discussion of validity scale findings, followed by interpretation of the substantive scale scores. Special circumstances indicating a need to qualify interpretive statements listed in the worksheet would then be considered. For example, if Ms. N had a known serious medical condition that could account for her report of poor health and physical debilitation, and thus understandably psychological preoccupation, her MLS score would likely not be interpreted as indicating a possible somatic symptom disorder.

As noted earlier, the order that the first four substantive areas (Somatic/Cognitive, Emotional, Thought, and Behavioral Dysfunction) are addressed in a narrative report can be based on the relative prominence of dysfunction in these domains. In Ms. N's case, emotional dysfunction is the most prominent finding and would be addressed first (following a discussion of the validity of her test protocol). In most circumstances, a finding of possible risk for self-harm would be mentioned early in the report.

Following the process just described, a narrative report of Ms. N's MMPI-3 results would read as follows:

Ms. N produced a valid and interpretable MMPI-3 protocol. Her scores on the Substantive Scales are likely to provide an accurate portrayal of her psychological functioning, reflecting a cooperative approach to the evaluation.

Ms. N's responses indicate considerable emotional distress that is likely to be perceived as a crisis. She reports experiencing significant demoralization, feeling overwhelmed, and being extremely unhappy, sad, and dissatisfied with her life. Although she did not endorse explicit statements of suicide or death ideation, she is nevertheless very likely at risk for suicidal ideation and very likely complains about feeling depressed, experiences sadness and despair, does not cope well with stress, has difficulty concentrating, feels sad, and is pessimistic. She reports feeling helpless and/or hopeless, and likely feels overwhelmed and that life is a strain, believes she cannot be helped, believe she gets a raw deal from life, and lacks motivation for change. She reports lacking in confidence, feeling worthless, and believing she is a burden to others, and very likely feels inferior and insecure, is self-disparaging, is prone to rumination, is intropunitive, and presents with lack of confidence and feelings of uselessness. She reports being very indecisive and inefficacious, believing she is incapable of making decisions and dealing effectively with crisis situations, and having difficulties when dealing with small, inconsequential matters. She very likely experiences subjective incompetence and shame and lacks perseverance and self-reliance.

Ms. N further reports a lack of positive emotional experiences, significant anhedonia, and lack of interest, and likely presents with anhedonia and low energy. She reports multiple problems involving stress and feeling nervous, and very likely complains about stress and feels incapable of controlling her anxiety level. She reports excessive worry, including worries about misfortune and finances, as well as preoccupation with disappointments. She likely worries excessively. These low positive and high negative emotional experiences are likely of a dispositional nature.

Ms. N reports a generalized sense of malaise manifested in poor health and feeling tried, weak, and incapacitated. She very likely is preoccupied with poor health and complains of sleep disturbance, fatigue, low energy, and sexual dysfunction.

Interpersonally, Ms. N describes herself as lacking in positive qualities. She reports being passive and submissive, not liking to be in charge, and being ready to give in to others. She is likely to be passive and submissive in interpersonal relationships. She reports not enjoying social events and avoiding social situations and is likely introverted, has difficulties forming close relationships, and is emotionally restricted. She reports being shy, easily embarrassed, and uncomfortable around others. She very likely is socially introverted and inhibited, is anxious and nervous in social situations, and is viewed by others as socially awkward.

Ms. N's test results indicate a number of possible diagnoses warranting further consideration. It is recommended that she be evaluated for possible internalizing disorders, particularly depression-related and anhedonia-related disorders, and disorders involving excessive worry and rumination, such as generalized anxiety disorder. Although her reports of feeling physically debilitated and in poor health should be considered in the context of her medical history and possible internalizing problems, the presence of a somatic symptom disorder should also be evaluated. Finally, disorders characterized by passive-submissive behavior, such as dependent personality disorder, and disorders associated with social avoidance and anxiety, such as avoidant personality disorder, should further be considered.

<u>Ms. N's risk for self-harm should be evaluated immediately.</u> The need for antidepressant medication should be assessed. Emotional difficulties may motivate her for treatment; however, significant anhedonia may interfere with engagement in treatment. Initial targets for treatment should be focused on relief of demoralization, anhedonia, loss of hope and despair. Subsequent targets for intervention should include low self-esteem, indecisiveness, stress

management skills, excessive worry and rumination, passive-submissive behavior, social avoidance, and social anxiety.

This report illustrates how a completed worksheet can be used to generate a narrative interpretation of the Substantive Scales. The process of writing a full MMPI-3 interpretation is demonstrated next.

CASE EXAMPLE

The report is based on the case of Mr. I, a 26-year-old single man who presented to a university psychology clinic complaining of significant anxiety, low mood, relationship problems, and behavioral regulation difficulties. He reported daily cannabis use to cope with negative emotions. He also reported that he was exposed to chronic violence in his family growing up, and his symptoms appeared consistent with complex trauma.

Mr. I's MMPI-3 Score Report is reproduced in Figure 10.6. The first step in the interpretation process is to enter Mr. I's MMPI-3 scores onto the worksheet. All scores can be found on page 7 of the Score Report. A worksheet containing Mr. I's scores and the recommended interpretive statements associated with them is presented in Figure 10.7.

Interpretation of Mr. I's MMPI-3 results begins with an examination of his validity scale scores. The CNS score of 0 indicates that Mr. I provided scorable responses to all items. Although Mr. I's CRIN and VRIN scores reach 60T, and thus, one standard deviation above the normative mean, they are nonetheless in the normal range and no concerns are noted. Scores on the overreporting and underreporting Validity Scales are all within normal limits per interpretative guidelines. Therefore, Mr. I's MMPI-3 protocol would be deemed valid for clinical interpretation.

Substantive scale entries on the worksheet for Mr. I begin with statements associated with his elevated scores in the Emotional Dysfunction domain. These entries primarily reflect elevations associated with demoralization (RCd, SUI, SFD, and NFC) as well as an elevated WRY score. Statements in the Thought Dysfunction domain are associated with Mr. I's elevated scores on RC8, though moderate scores on RC6 and PSYC (both at 63T) are noteworthy considering this general context. An extensive list of interpretive statements appears in the Behavioral Dysfunction section of Mr. I's worksheet. They begin with statements associated with an elevated BXD score. Of the two RC Scales in this domain, RC4 is elevated and this score is interpreted next along with elevated scores on SUB, IMP, and DISC. In the Interpersonal Functioning domain, no scores reach the threshold for interpretation.

The next step in interpreting Mr. I's MMPI-3 test results is to generate a narrative report, integrating statements recorded on the worksheet with avail-

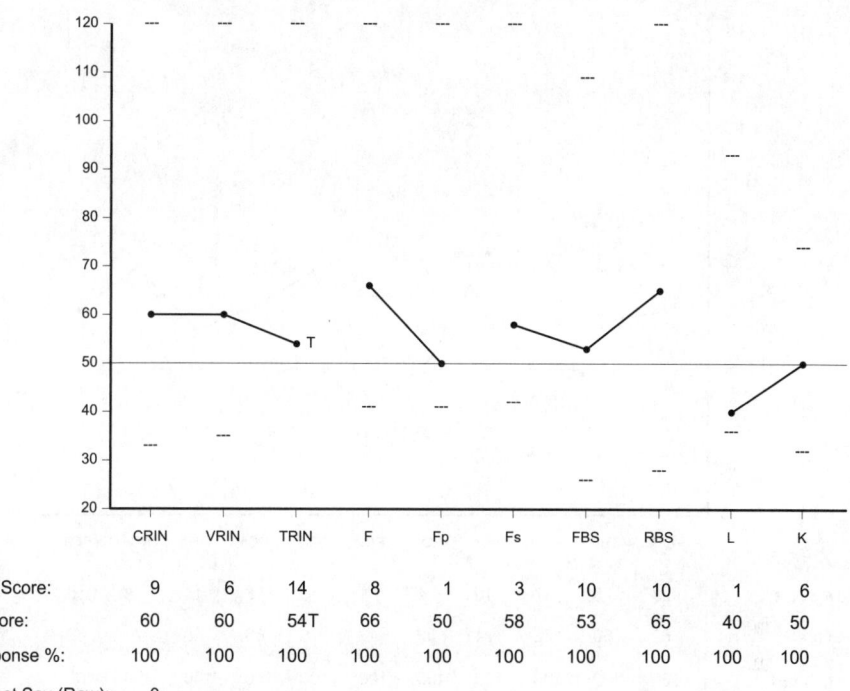

FIGURE 10.6. Mr. I's MMPI-3 Score Report

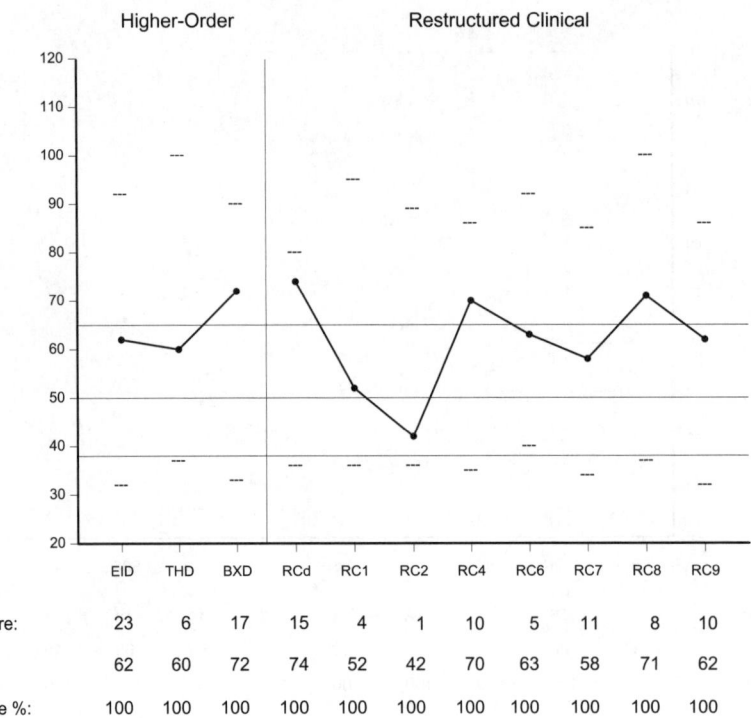

FIGURE 10.6. Mr. I's MMPI-3 Score Report, continued

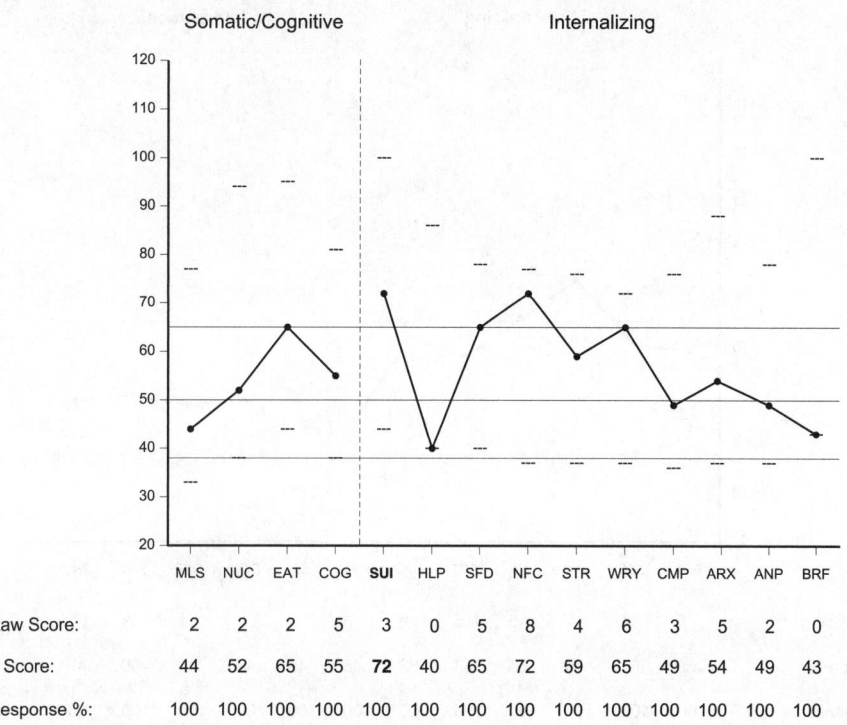

FIGURE 10.6. Mr. I's MMPI-3 Score Report, continued

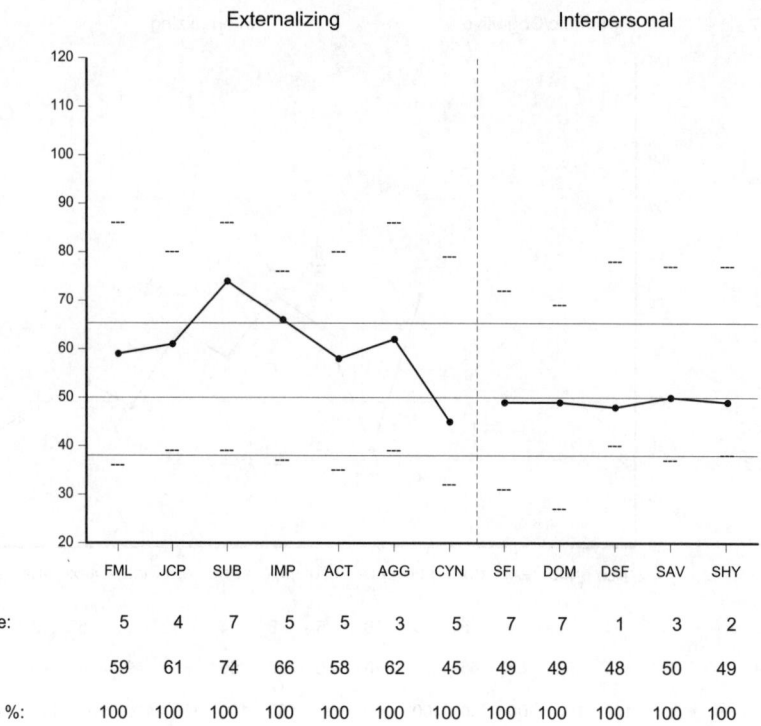

FIGURE 10.6. Mr. I's MMPI-3 Score Report, continued

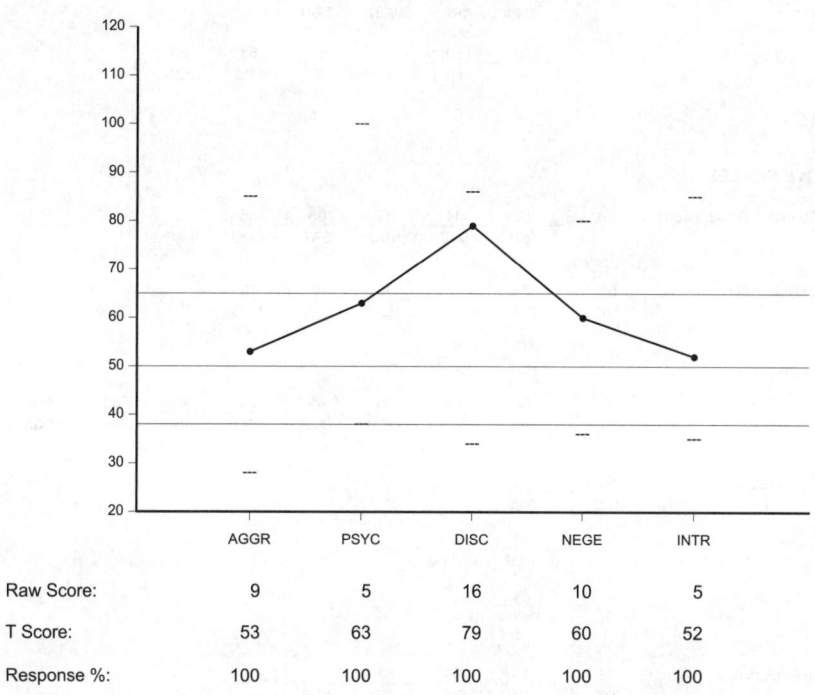

MMPI-3 PSY-5 Scales

	AGGR	PSYC	DISC	NEGE	INTR
Raw Score:	9	5	16	10	5
T Score:	53	63	79	60	52
Response %:	100	100	100	100	100

The highest and lowest T scores possible on each scale are indicated by a "---"; MMPI-3 T scores are non-gendered.

AGGR Aggressiveness
PSYC Psychoticism
DISC Disconstraint
NEGE Negative Emotionality/Neuroticism
INTR Introversion/Low Positive Emotionality

FIGURE 10.6. Mr. I's MMPI-3 Score Report, continued

MMPI-3 T SCORES (BY DOMAIN)

PROTOCOL VALIDITY

Content Non-Responsiveness

0	60	60	54 T
CNS	CRIN	VRIN	TRIN

Over-Reporting

66	50		58	53	65
F	Fp		Fs	FBS	RBS

Under-Reporting

40	50
L	K

SUBSTANTIVE SCALES

Somatic/Cognitive Dysfunction

52	44	52	65	55
RC1	MLS	NUC	EAT	COG

Emotional Dysfunction

62
EID

74	72	40	65	72
RCd	SUI	HLP	SFD	NFC

42	52
RC2	INTR

58	59	65	49	54	49	43	60
RC7	STR	WRY	CMP	ARX	ANP	BRF	NEGE

Thought Dysfunction

60
THD

63
RC6

71
RC8

63
PSYC

Behavioral Dysfunction

72
BXD

70	59	61	74
RC4	FML	JCP	SUB

62	66	58	62	45
RC9	IMP	ACT	AGG	CYN

79
DISC

Interpersonal Functioning

49	49	53	48	50	49
SFI	DOM	AGGR	DSF	SAV	SHY

Note. This information is provided to facilitate interpretation following the recommended structure for MMPI-3 interpretation in Chapter 5 of the *MMPI-3 Manual for Administration, Scoring, and Interpretation*, which provides details in the text and an outline in Table 5-1.

FIGURE 10.6. Mr. I's MMPI-3 Score Report, continued

ITEM-LEVEL INFORMATION

Unscorable Responses

The test taker produced scorable responses to all the MMPI-3 items.

Critical Responses

Seven MMPI-3 scales—Suicidal/Death Ideation (SUI), Helplessness/Hopelessness (HLP), Anxiety-Related Experiences (ARX), Ideas of Persecution (RC6), Aberrant Experiences (RC8), Substance Abuse (SUB), and Aggression (AGG)—have been designated by the test authors as having critical item content that may require immediate attention and follow-up. Items answered by the individual in the keyed direction (True or False) on a critical scale are listed below if his T score on that scale is 65 or higher. However, any item answered in the keyed direction on SUI is listed. The percentage of the MMPI-3 normative sample that answered each item in the keyed direction is provided in parentheses following the item content.

Suicidal/Death Ideation (SUI, T Score = 72)

Item number and content omitted. (True, 22.2%)
Item number and content omitted. (True, 8.1%)
Item number and content omitted. (True, 3.2%)

Aberrant Experiences (RC8, T Score = 71)

Item number and content omitted. (True, 35.7%)
Item number and content omitted. (True, 38.0%)
Item number and content omitted. (True, 8.4%)
Item number and content omitted. (True, 12.7%)
Item number and content omitted. (True, 18.2%)
Item number and content omitted. (True, 11.2%)
Item number and content omitted. (True, 24.3%)
Item number and content omitted. (True, 5.7%)

Substance Abuse (SUB, T Score = 74)

Item number and content omitted. (True, 21.7%)
Item number and content omitted. (True, 43.0%)
Item number and content omitted. (True, 38.2%)
Item number and content omitted. (False, 31.9%)
Item number and content omitted. (True, 8.1%)
Item number and content omitted. (True, 18.7%)
Item number and content omitted. (True, 14.4%)

End of Report

FIGURE 10.6. Mr. I's MMPI-3 Score Report, continued

MMPI®-3 Interpretation Worksheet

Protocol Validity

Content Nonresponsiveness   CNS 0   CRIN 60   VRIN 60   TRIN 54

There are no concerns about content nonresponsive responding.

Over-Reporting   F 66   Fp 50   Fs 58   FBS 53   RBS 65

There are no concerns about over-reporting.

Under-Reporting   L 40   K 50

There are no concerns about under-reporting.

FIGURE 10.7. Mr. I's Completed MMPI-3 Interpretation Worksheet

Substantive Scale Interpretation

Somatic/Cognitive Dysfunction   RC1 _52_   MLS _44_   NUC _52_   EAT _65_   COG _55_

No interpretations are made in the Somatic/Cognitive Dysfunction domain.

Emotional Dysfunction   EID _62_   RCd _74_   RC2 _52_   RC7 _58_   NEGE _60_

SUI _72_   STR _59_   INTR _52_

HLP _40_   WRY _65_

SFD _65_   CMP _49_

NFC _72_   ARX _54_

ANP _49_

BRF _43_

He reports feeling sad and unhappy and being dissatisfied with his current life circumstances. He is at risk for suicidal ideation and for self-harm, including suicide attempts. Complains about being depressed. He reports having low self-esteem and feeling like a burden on others. He is likely self-disparaging. He reports being indecisive, passive, and inefficacious. Feels incapable of changing his life circumstances. He tends to be pessimistic and feel insecure. He is likely to feel subjectively incompetent and shameful. He reports excessive worry, including worries about misfortune and finances, as well as preoccupation with disappointments. He likely ruminates.

FIGURE 10.7. Mr. I's Completed MMPI-3 Interpretation Worksheet, continued

Thought Dysfunction   THD 60   RC6 63   RC8 71   PSYC 63

He reports unusual thoughts and perceptual processes. He may experience thought disorganization and unrealistic thinking. Aberrant experiences may include dissociation. His reported experiences could be substance-induced.

Behavioral Dysfunction   BXD 72   RC4 70   RC9 62   CYN 45

FML 59   IMP 66   DISC 79

JCP 61   ACT 58

SUB 74   AGG 62

His responses indicate significant externalizing, acting-out behavior, which is likely to have gotten him into difficulties. He reports a significant history of antisocial behavior. He likely fails to conform to societal norms and expectations and may have been involved with the criminal justice system. He reports significant past and current substance abuse. He likely has a history of problematic use of alcohol or drugs, including misuse of prescription medication. He may have had legal problems as a result of substance abuse. He reports engaging in problematic impulsive behavior and likely has a history of nonplanful and hyperactive behaviors. He is likely easily bored and engages in sensation seeking behavior. He likely has a dispositional proclivity towards externalizing and disinhibition.

Interpersonal Functioning   SFI 49   DOM 49   AGGR 53   DSF 48   SAV 50   SHY 49

No interpretations are made in the interpersonal functioning domain.

FIGURE 10.7. Mr. I's Completed MMPI-3 Interpretation Worksheet, continued

Diagnostic Considerations

Evaluate for depressive disorders, disorders involving excessive worry and rumination, disorders manifesting psychotic symptoms, personality disorders manifesting in unusual thinking, and disorders of externalizing or disinhibition, including antisocial and/or borderline personality disorder, and substance use disorder.

Treatment Considerations

Immediately evaluate for risk for suicide. Emotional difficulties may motivate him for treatment. However, indecisiveness may interfere with establishing treatment goals and progress in treatment. Impaired thinking may disrupt treatment. He is unlikely to be internally motivated for treatment. Acting-out tendencies, including impulsivity, can result in treatment noncompliance and interfere with the development of a therapeutic relationship. Focus on relief of demoralization, low self-esteem, excessive worry and rumination as an initial target for intervention. Assist him in gaining insight about his thought dysfunction. Inadequate impulse contol should also be a target for intervention. Focus on reduction or cessation of substance misuse should be another target for intervention.

FIGURE 10.7. Mr. I's Completed MMPI-3 Interpretation Worksheet, continued

able information regarding Mr. I's background and referral. As always, the report begins with an analysis of protocol validity. Interpretation of Mr. I's substantive scale scores begins with the Behavioral Dysfunction domain, for which his test results indicate that he is experiencing the greatest dysfunction (per BXD). As no other H-O Scales are elevated, once the Behavioral Dysfunction has been covered, the next level of the interpretative hierarchy (the RC Scales) is considered. As RCd is the most highly elevated RC scale, the emotional domain is addressed next. Further inspection of the RC Scales indicates an elevation on RC8, and thus, the Thought Dysfunction domain is then interpreted. As no scales from the Interpersonal Functioning domain are elevated, no further interpretations are indicated. A narrative report following these procedures would read as follows:

Mr. I responded to all test items and there were no indications of inconsistent responding, overreporting, or underreporting in this protocol. Therefore, scores on the Substantive Scales should provide an accurate indication of Mr. I's functioning. His protocol is valid for clinical interpretation.

His responses indicate that Mr. I engages in significant externalizing, acting out behavior, which is likely to have gotten him into difficulties. He reports a significant history of antisocial behavior; he likely fails to conform to societal norms and expectations and may have been involved with the criminal justice system. He reports significant past and current substance abuse, and likely has a history of problematic use of alcohol or drugs, including misuse of prescription medication. He may have had legal problems as a result of substance abuse. He further reports engaging in problematic impulsive behavior and likely has a history of nonplanful and hyperactive behaviors. He is likely easily bored and engages in sensation-seeking behavior. He likely has a dispositional proclivity towards externalizing and disinhibition.

Mr. I reports feeling sad and unhappy and being dissatisfied with his current life circumstances. He is at risk for suicidal ideation and for self-harm, including suicide attempts. He likely complains about being depressed. He reports having low self-esteem and feeling like a burden on others. He is likely self-disparaging. He reports being indecisive, passive, and inefficacious and likely feels incapable of changing his life circumstances. He tends to be pessimistic and feel insecure. He is likely to feel subjectively incompetent and shameful. He further reports excessive worry, including worries about misfortune and finances, as well as preoccupation with disappointments. He likely ruminates.

Mr. I reports unusual thoughts and perceptual processes. He may experience thought disorganization and unrealistic thinking. Aberrant experiences may include dissociation. His reported experiences could be substance induced.

Mr. I should first and foremost be evaluated for disorders of externalizing or disinhibition, including antisocial and/or personality disorder, and substance use disorder. He should also be evaluated for depressive disorders, disorders involving excessive worry and rumination, disorders manifesting in psychotic symptoms, and personality disorders manifesting in unusual thinking.

Mr. I's MMPI-3 scores identify several areas for follow up and intervention. <u>Risk for suicide should be assessed immediately.</u> Although his general emotional difficulties may motive him for treatment, indecisiveness may interfere with establishing treatment goals and progress in treatment. Impaired thinking may also disrupt treatment. He is unlikely to be internally motivated for treatment. Moreover, acting-out tendencies, including impulsivity, can result in treatment noncompliance and interference with the development of a therapeutic relationship. The treatment goals should initially focus on reduction or cessation of substance misuse, and inadequate impulse control should be a long-term target. Focus should also be placed on relief of demoralization, low self-esteem, and excessive worry and rumination. Treatment should assist him in gaining insight about his thought dysfunction.

After several assessment sessions, Mr. I was diagnosed with borderline personality disorder and cannabis use disorder. His treatment focused initially on reducing self-harm and excessive risk-taking behaviors, including reduction in cannabis use and binge eating behaviors for emotional regulation. Over time, treatment begun to incorporate strategies for adaptive emotional regulation. His treatment compliance was inconsistent and progress was slow.

Conclusion

A recommended framework and process for interpreting scores on the MMPI-3 Validity and Substantive Scales in clinical contexts were detailed and illustrated in this chapter. The case illustrations included were designed to demonstrate use of the MMPI-3 Interpretation Worksheet to organize findings and guide writing of a narrative report of the test results. In a typical psychological evaluation, other sources of information (e.g., collateral contacts, other testing, and interview findings) will be considered along with the MMPI-3 results to address specific referral questions. In many settings where the test is used, interpretation will also involve consideration of comparison group data (described in chapter 7). The case studies presented in the final chapter of this book illustrate these additional aspects of MMPI-3 interpretation.

MMPI-3 Case Studies 11

In this chapter, MMPI-3 interpretation is illustrated with 11 cases representing various settings in which the test is used. Each case description begins with relevant background information, although some nonessential details have been changed to protect test takers' identities. Next, an MMPI-3 interpretation following the format described in chapter 10 is provided for each case, followed by a discussion of how the test findings can assist in addressing specific referral questions. Relevant comparison group data are printed along with the test takers' scores for most of the cases. Some examples also illustrate use of item-level information, although the actual item number and content is redacted to protect the security of MMPI-3 items.

MS. A: CHRONIC FATIGUE SYNDROME

Ms. A, a 63-year-old divorced woman, was referred by her general practitioner physician to a private practice psychologist to help her acquire stress management strategies to assist in coping with chronic fatigue syndrome. Two years prior, she had moved to her current city to be closer to her daughter and grandchild. Ms. A had retired from a very busy work life as a gym owner, and she described herself as "always on the go" and "doing things." Ms. A reported that the morning after moving to the current city she woke up with extreme exhaustion and was unable to engage in normal daily activities, such as walking down a step without assistance. Since that time, Ms. A had also noticed cognitive and sensory processing difficulties, such as difficulties with attention and concentration, and she described subsequent diminished ability to have a normal conversation, watch television, or read a book. She was diagnosed by her physician with chronic fatigue syndrome about 12 months prior to the evaluation.

During her initial clinical interview, Ms. A reported that she was also experiencing anxiety around social situations, general worries about the state of the world, and a specific fear of earthquakes. She displayed an inability to accurately report and reflect on emotional experiences and described every emotion as "anxiety." Her subjective mood was generally incongruent with her affective presentation, especially as she described strong emotions but did not appear distressed during the interview. Ms. A was provisionally diagnosed with a somatic symptom disorder and was administered the MMPI-3 to further assist with case formulation and treatment planning.

MMPI-3 Interpretation

Ms. A responded to all of the MMPI-3 items and her validity scale scores indicate that she did so in a relevant and consistent manner (Figure 11.1). There was no evidence for overreporting in her profile; however, possible underreporting is indicated by Ms. A presenting herself in a very positive light by denying some minor faults and shortcomings that most people would acknowledge. Any absence of scale elevations should therefore be interpreted with some caution. Nevertheless, her MMPI-3 profile was deemed valid for clinical interpretation.

Ms. A's responses indicate that she reports multiple somatic complaints that may include head pain and neurological and gastrointestinal symptoms. She is likely preoccupied with health concerns and is prone to developing physical symptoms in response to stress; these symptoms likely have an underlying psychological component. She likely perceives her symptoms as life-interfering. Ms. A reports experiencing poor health, feeling weak or tired, and presents with vague neurological complaints. She may complain about sleep disturbance and sexual dysfunction as well as dizziness, coordination difficulties, and sensory problems. Ms. A further reports a diffuse pattern of cognitive difficulties including memory problems, difficulties with attention and concentration, and possible confusion. She likely has low frustration tolerance and copes poorly with stress.

Ms. A also reports episodes of heightened excitation and energy level. On the other hand, she reports being decisive and efficacious, and a below average level of worry.

Ms. A's MMPI-3 results indicate the need to evaluate for a somatic symptom disorder and attention-related disorders, particularly if physical health concerns can be ruled out, or if the presentation is in excess of what would be expected from any diagnosed physical health problems. Ms. A should also be evaluated for manic or hypomanic episodes or other conditions associated with excessive energy and activation.

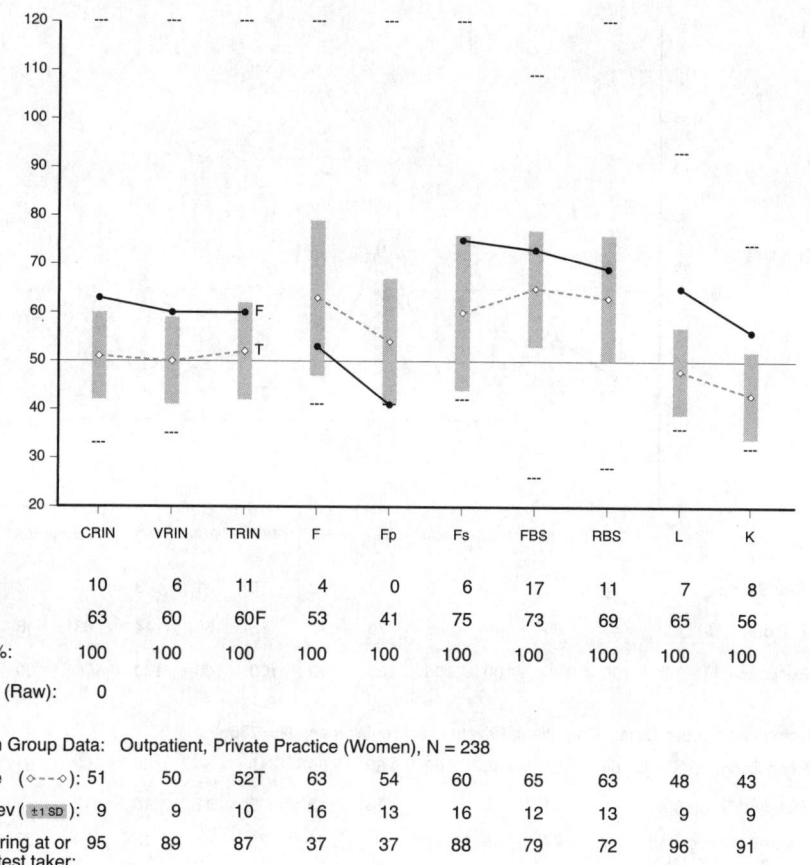

FIGURE 11.1. Ms. A's MMPI-3 Score Report

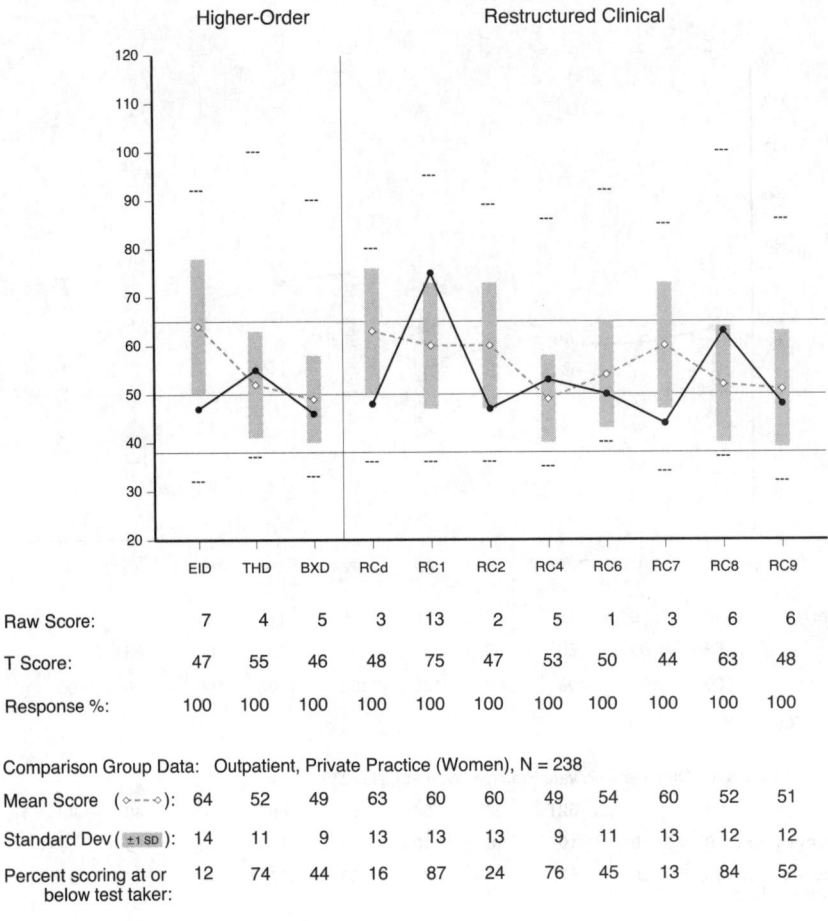

FIGURE 11.1. Ms. A's MMPI-3 Score Report, continued

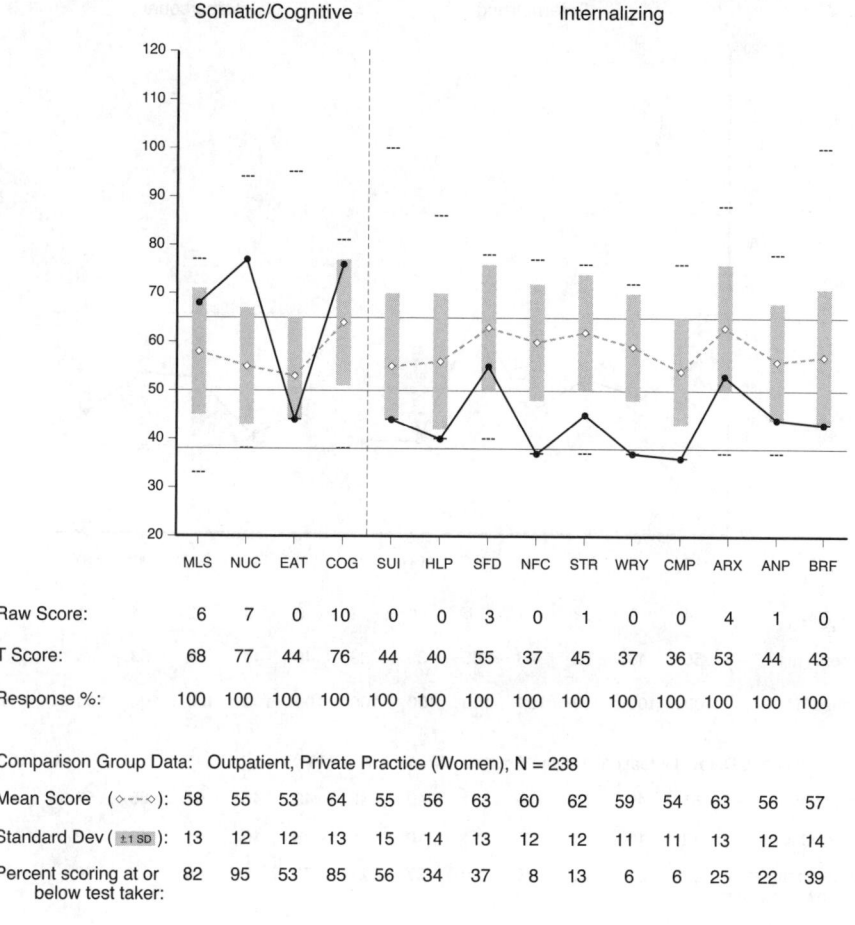

FIGURE 11.1. Ms. A's MMPI-3 Score Report, continued

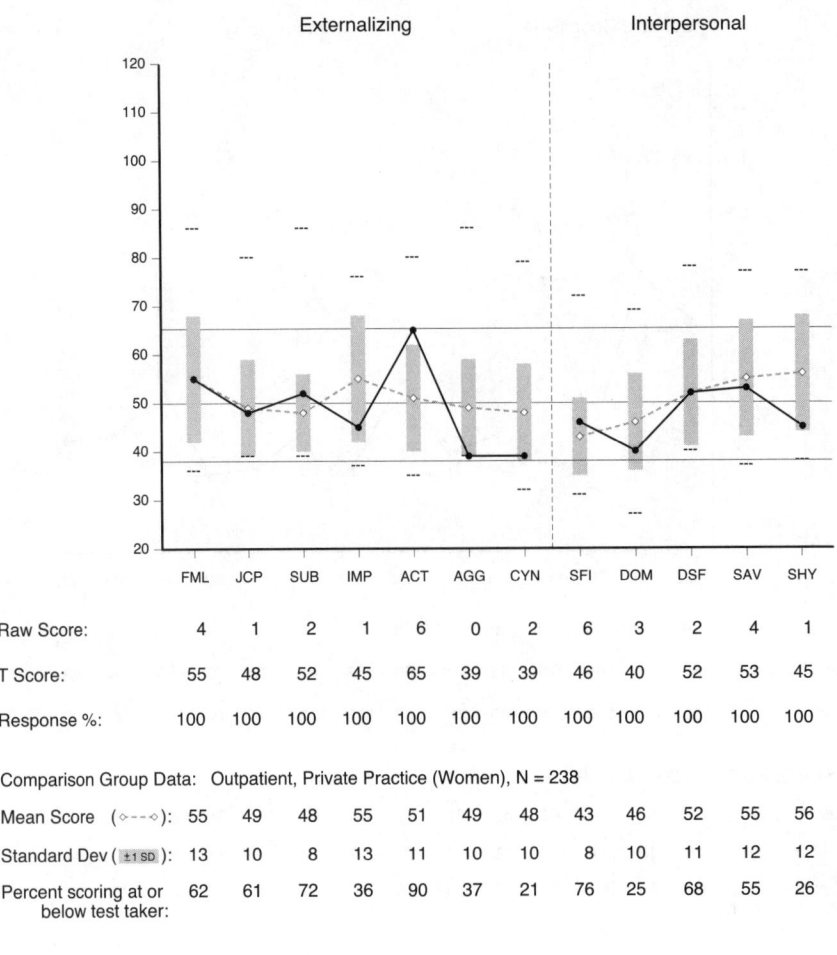

FIGURE 11.1. Ms. A's MMPI-3 Score Report, continued

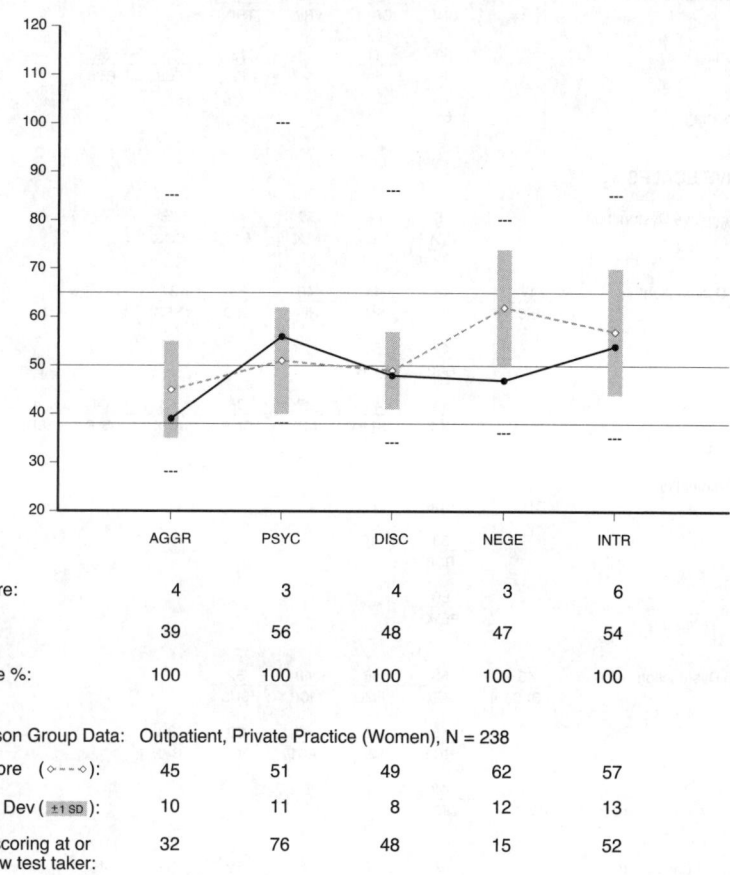

FIGURE 11.1. Ms. A's MMPI-3 Score Report, continued

MMPI-3 T SCORES (BY DOMAIN)

PROTOCOL VALIDITY

Content Non-Responsiveness

0	63	60	60 F
CNS	CRIN	VRIN	TRIN

Over-Reporting

53	41		75	73	69
F	Fp		Fs	FBS	RBS

Under-Reporting

65	56
L	K

SUBSTANTIVE SCALES

Somatic/Cognitive Dysfunction

75	68	77	44	76
RC1	MLS	NUC	EAT	COG

Emotional Dysfunction

47
EID

48	44	40	55	37
RCd	SUI	HLP	SFD	NFC

47	54
RC2	INTR

44	45	37	36	53	44	43	47
RC7	STR	WRY	CMP	ARX	ANP	BRF	NEGE

Thought Dysfunction

55
THD

50
RC6

63
RC8

56
PSYC

Behavioral Dysfunction

46
BXD

53	55	48	52
RC4	FML	JCP	SUB

48	45	65	39	39
RC9	IMP	ACT	AGG	CYN

48
DISC

Interpersonal Functioning

46	40	39	52	53	45
SFI	DOM	AGGR	DSF	SAV	SHY

Note. This information is provided to facilitate interpretation following the recommended structure for MMPI-3 interpretation in Chapter 5 of the *MMPI-3 Manual for Administration, Scoring, and Interpretation*, which provides details in the text and an outline in Table 5-1.

FIGURE 11.1. Ms. A's MMPI-3 Score Report, continued

ITEM-LEVEL INFORMATION

Unscorable Responses

The test taker produced scorable responses to all the MMPI-3 items.

Critical Responses

Seven MMPI-3 scales—Suicidal/Death Ideation (SUI), Helplessness/Hopelessness (HLP), Anxiety-Related Experiences (ARX), Ideas of Persecution (RC6), Aberrant Experiences (RC8), Substance Abuse (SUB), and Aggression (AGG)—have been designated by the test authors as having critical item content that may require immediate attention and follow-up. Items answered by the individual in the keyed direction (True or False) on a critical scale are listed below if her T score on that scale is 65 or higher. However, any item answered in the keyed direction on SUI is listed.

The test taker has not produced an elevated T score ($\geq$ 65) on any of these scales or answered any SUI items in the keyed direction.

End of Report

FIGURE 11.1. Ms. A's MMPI-3 Score Report, continued

Ms. A's test results indicate that she is likely to reject psychological interpretations of somatic and neurological complaints, her level of malaise might impede her willingness or ability to engage in treatment, and the origins of her cognitive and neurological complaints should be explored, possibly through a neuropsychological evaluation. Moreover, excessive behavioral activation may interfere with treatment.

Discussion

Ms. A's MMPI-3 results indicate that her problems lie within the Somatic/Cognitive domain. Comparison group results reported on page 3 of Figure 11.1 indicate that 87% of the 238 women who make up the outpatient, private practice comparison group score the same as or below Ms. A on the Somatic Complaints (RC1) scale. Thus, her clinically significant level of somatic preoccupation (as indicated by a T score of 75 on RC1) substantially exceeds what is found typically in women assessed in similar settings. Similarly, her scores on three of the four Somatic/Cognitive Specific Problems (SP) Scales (see Figure 11.1, page 4), and on the Neurological Complaints (NUC) scale in particular, are also clinically elevated in reference to both the MMPI-3 normative sample and the outpatient, private practice comparison group. Furthermore, Ms. A also has a clinically elevated score on Activation (ACT) as indicated by a T score of 65, with 90% of women in the comparison group scoring at or below this level. This latter scale score might be reflective of Ms. A's desire for, and historical tendency toward, high energy and activation rather than overstimulation, as both her current presentation and other MMPI-3 scale scores are inconsistent with this latter interpretation.

Interestingly, Ms. A's score on several Internalizing SP Scales (Inefficacy [NFC], Worry [WRY], Compulsivity [CMP]; see Figure 11.1, page 4) reach low score levels, and most such scales were substantially lower than would be expected in this context. These scores are also noteworthy given Ms. A's complaints about anxiety and worry during the intake interview; however, any interpretation of these low scale scores needs to be done in light of the caution about potential underreporting. Indeed, her L scale score is 65T and within a range in which underreporting is possible. Both her L and K scores are also substantially higher than is typically observed in this context, with 96% and 91%, respectively, of women in the comparison group scoring at or below this level. These low scores may also reflect Ms. A's difficulties with accurately describing emotional experiences that were discussed earlier.

Considering Ms. A's presenting complaints, the MMPI-3 results are consistent with the intake clinician's preliminary diagnosis of somatic symptom disorder. Although her test results disconfirm reports of subjective anxiety, worry, and fearfulness, it is also possible that she underreported or had difficulty accurately describing such symptoms on the MMPI-3, possibly either because she did not want to acknowledge psychological problems in the context of her physical health problems, or because she lacks insight or self-awareness into her emotional experience. Additional clinical contact provided support for the latter interpretation. Ms. A's difficulties could be formulated from the perspective of alexithymia with significant physical health problems developing because of a substantial life stressor (moving from a high-energy, business life to retiring to a larger city in which she did not know anyone besides her daughter) coupled with a significant inability for emotional identification. Ms. A attended weekly therapy sessions for approximately 1 month before a nationwide lockdown due to Covid-19 interrupted her treatment. She elected not to return to treatment once possible.

MR. B: ADHD OR MANIA?

Mr. B. is a 28-year-old single man who was referred by his workplace to an outpatient community mental health center for an evaluation and possible treatment for attention deficit/hyperactivity disorder (ADHD). For the past several years leading up to the evaluation, he had a successful career as an architect, working at a prestigious firm and was generally viewed by senior management as a "rising star." More recently, his coworkers and supervisor expressed concern about his ability to focus and concentrate and his increasingly disorganized behavior. He had become erratic and hostile toward coworkers and accused them of unprofessional behavior. A counselor at an employee assistance program, to which he was initially referred, was concerned about ADHD interfering with Mr. B's ability to do his job as his work demands were increasing and becoming overwhelming.

Mr. B explained to the intake therapist that he had developed difficulties with concentration and sustaining attention because his thoughts raced constantly. He stated that these difficulties were affecting his performance at work, which was more important than ever, as his coworkers were trying to "steal his ideas" and hinder his success. He would also spend most nights awake in an attempt to "outwork" everyone else but was not bothered from sleep deprivation. The intake therapist noted that Mr. B's general ideas and sense of self were quite expansive in that Mr. B clearly viewed himself as superior to his coworkers and was convinced that he was on the verge of getting assigned a new project coveted by all the top architects in the city. Mr. B claimed, without evidence, that his coworkers were conspiring to prevent him from being assign this project and trying to limit his success and promotion. Mr. B was provisionally diagnosed with a manic episode rather than ADHD and was administered the MMPI-3 to further assist with formulation and treatment recommendations.

MMPI-3 Interpretation

Mr. B responded to all of the MMPI-3 items, and thus, there are no concerns about unscorable responding (Figure 11.2). Although there is no evidence of random or variable inconsistent responding, there is some evidence of fixed, content-inconsistent responding, in the True direction. In other words, he indiscriminately responded True to test items. This degree of fixed responding is insufficient to invalidate the protocol, but it does indicate that some caution should be exercised when interpreting his MMPI-3 results, including scores on other Validity Scales. Indeed, possible overreporting of psychological dysfunction is indicated by a much larger than average number of infrequent responses, but this level of infrequent responding could be due to indiscriminate True responding as well as genuine psychopathology. No other concerns about overreporting or underreporting are noted. Although the MMPI-3 profile can be interpreted, caution should be exercised as scores on most Substantive Scales could be inflated due to indiscriminate True responding.

Mr. B's responses indicate serious thought dysfunction. He reports many unusual thoughts and perceptions, including likely dissociation. He likely experiences thought disorganization, engages in unrealistic thinking, and believes he has unusual sensory-perceptual abilities, which may include auditory and/or visual hallucinations and nonpersecutory delusions such as thought broadcasting and mind reading. It is also possible that Mr. B's reality testing is significantly impaired, and his experiences likely cause significant impairment in occupational and interpersonal functioning. Moreover, Mr. B reports prominent persecutory ideation that may rise to the level of paranoid delusions. He has persecutory beliefs, is suspicious and distrustful of others, and likely experiences interpersonal difficulties as a result of his suspiciousness, including alienation. He also likely lacks insight into these problems and tends to blame others for his difficulties.

Mr. B further reports many behaviors and experiences associated with hypomanic activation, such as excitability, impulsivity, and elevated mood. He is likely restless and easily bored. He tends to be overactivated, as manifested in poor impulse control, nonplanful behavior, sensation seeking, risk-taking and other forms of undercontrolled behavior, aggression, mood instability, excessive euphoria, and general excitability. Mr. B also reports episodes of heightened excitation and energy level, uncontrollable mood swings, and lack of sleep, and may have a history of symptoms associated with manic or hypomanic episodes. He further reports engaging in physically aggressive, violent behavior and losing control. He is likely to have a history of abusive and violent behavior toward others and may experience anger-related problems. Mr. B also reports believing others look out only for their own interests. He is likely self-centered and lacking in empathy. Additionally, he reports conflictual family

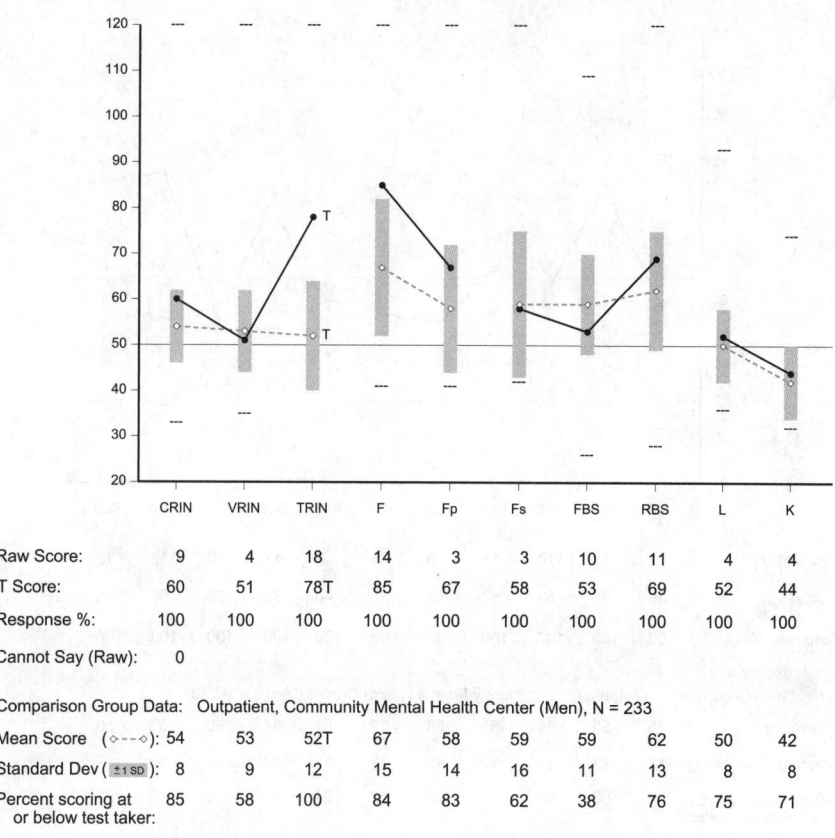

FIGURE 11.2. Mr. B's MMPI-3 Score Report

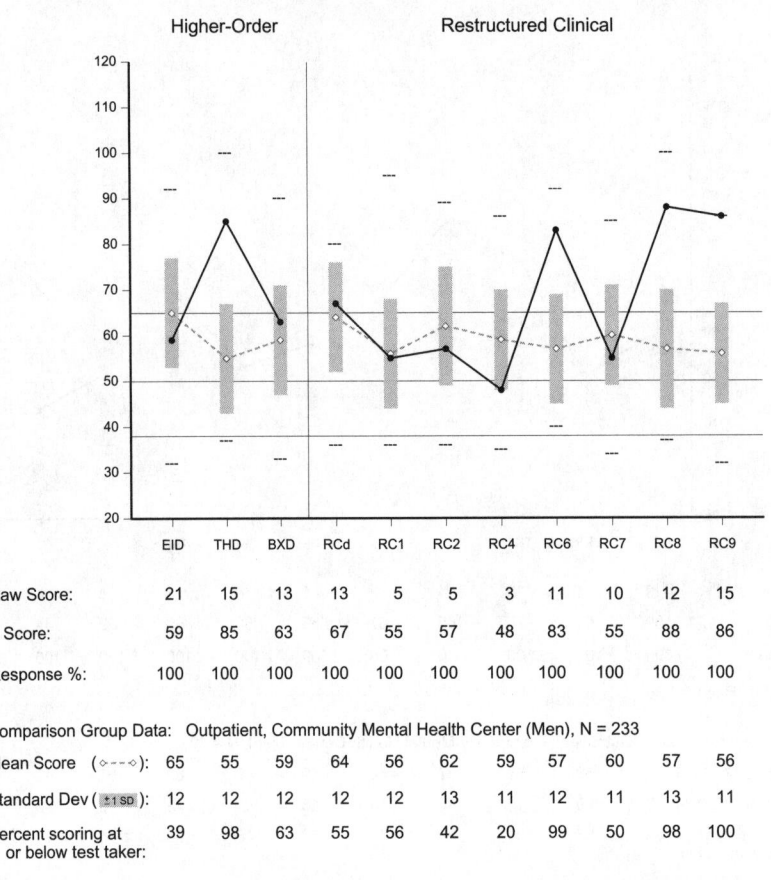

FIGURE 11.2. Mr. B's MMPI-3 Score Report, continued

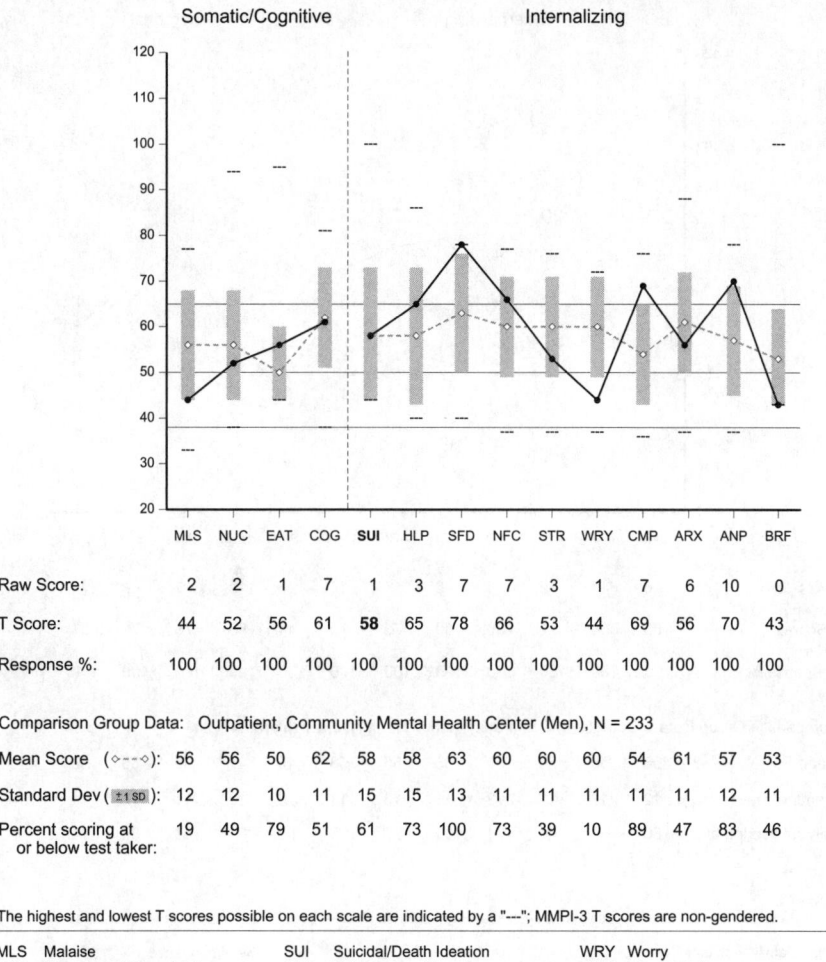

FIGURE 11.2. Mr. B's MMPI-3 Score Report, continued

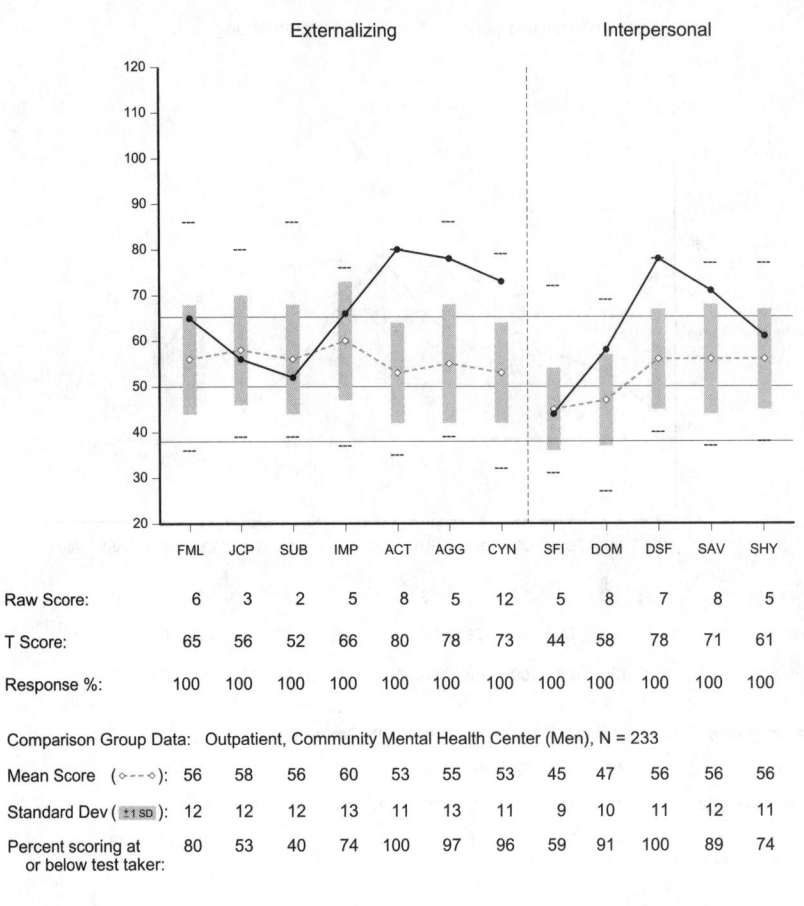

FIGURE 11.2. Mr. B's MMPI-3 Score Report, continued

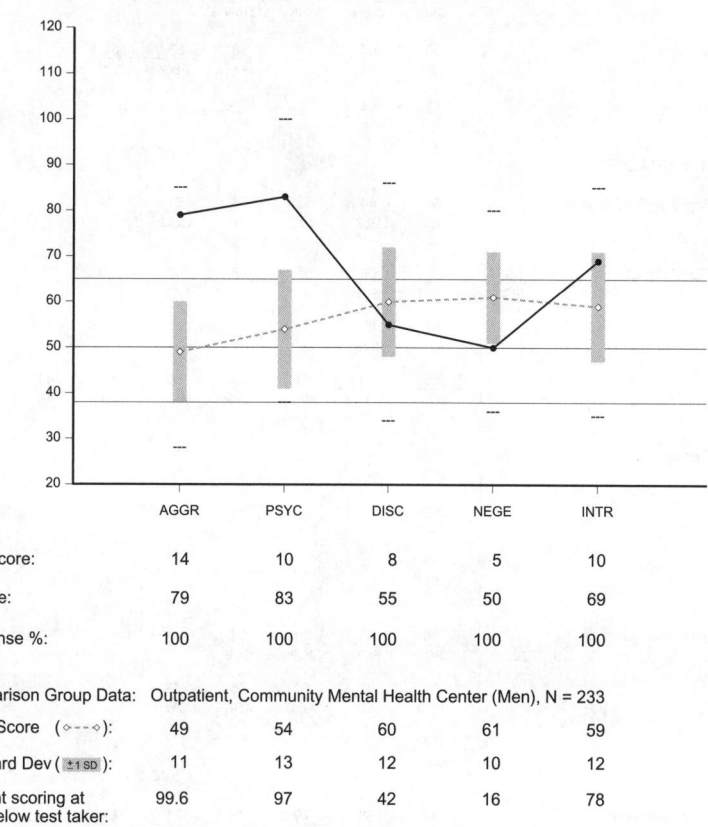

FIGURE 11.2. Mr. B's MMPI-3 Score Report, continued

MMPI-3 T SCORES (BY DOMAIN)

PROTOCOL VALIDITY

Content Non-Responsiveness

0	60	51	78 T
CNS	CRIN	VRIN	TRIN

Over-Reporting

85	67		58	53	69
F	Fp		Fs	FBS	RBS

Under-Reporting

52	44
L	K

SUBSTANTIVE SCALES

Somatic/Cognitive Dysfunction

55	44	52	56	61
RC1	MLS	NUC	EAT	COG

Emotional Dysfunction

59		67	58	65	78	66		
EID		RCd	SUI	HLP	SFD	NFC		
		57	69					
		RC2	INTR					
		55	53	44	69	56	70	43	50
		RC7	STR	WRY	CMP	ARX	ANP	BRF	NEGE

Thought Dysfunction

85		83
THD		RC6
		88
		RC8
		83
		PSYC

Behavioral Dysfunction

63		48	65	56	52	
BXD		RC4	FML	JCP	SUB	
		86	66	80	78	73
		RC9	IMP	ACT	AGG	CYN
		55				
		DISC				

Interpersonal Functioning

44	58	79	78	71	61
SFI	DOM	AGGR	DSF	SAV	SHY

Note. This information is provided to facilitate interpretation following the recommended structure for MMPI-3 interpretation in Chapter 5 of the *MMPI-3 Manual for Administration, Scoring, and Interpretation*, which provides details in the text and an outline in Table 5-1.

FIGURE 11.2. Mr. B's MMPI-3 Score Report, continued

ITEM-LEVEL INFORMATION

Unscorable Responses

The test taker produced scorable responses to all the MMPI-3 items.

Critical Responses

Seven MMPI-3 scales—Suicidal/Death Ideation (SUI), Helplessness/Hopelessness (HLP), Anxiety-Related Experiences (ARX), Ideas of Persecution (RC6), Aberrant Experiences (RC8), Substance Abuse (SUB), and Aggression (AGG)—have been designated by the test authors as having critical item content that may require immediate attention and follow-up. Items answered by the individual in the keyed direction (True or False) on a critical scale are listed below if his T score on that scale is 65 or higher. However, any item answered in the keyed direction on SUI is listed. The percentage of the MMPI-3 normative sample (NS) and of the Outpatient, Community Mental Health Center Comparison Group (CG) that answered each item in the keyed direction are provided in parentheses following the item content.

Suicidal/Death Ideation (SUI, T Score = 58)

    Item and number content omitted. (True; NS 10.1%, CG 18.5%)

Helplessness/Hopelessness (HLP, T Score = 65)

    Item number and content omitted. (True; NS 10.9%, CG 21.9%)
    Item number and content omitted. (True; NS 12.3%, CG 23.6%)
    Item number and content omitted. (True; NS 45.4%, CG 50.6%)

Ideas of Persecution (RC6, T Score = 83)

    Item number and content omitted. (True; NS 26.7%, CG 44.2%)
    Item number and content omitted. (True; NS 20.4%, CG 34.3%)
    Item number and content omitted. (True; NS 7.8%, CG 17.6%)
    Item number and content omitted. (True; NS 8.3%, CG 15.9%)
    Item number and content omitted. (True; NS 30.9%, CG 48.9%)
    Item number and content omitted. (False; NS 16.4%, CG 27.0%)
    Item number and content omitted. (True; NS 11.9%, CG 36.9%)
    Item number and content omitted. (True; NS 12.1%, CG 22.7%)
    Item number and content omitted. (True; NS 19.0%, CG 34.3%)
    Item number and content omitted. (True; NS 5.6%, CG 11.6%)
    Item number and content omitted. (True; NS 7.7%, CG 20.2%)

Aberrant Experiences (RC8, T Score = 88)

    Item number and content omitted. (True; NS 38.0%, CG 51.9%)
    Item number and content omitted. (True; NS 7.8%, CG 13.3%)
    Item number and content omitted. (False; NS 36.5%, CG 44.6%)
    Item number and content omitted. (True; NS 19.1%, CG 33.5%)
    Item number and content omitted. (True; NS 8.4%, CG 27.9%)
    Item number and content omitted. (True; NS 12.7%, CG 30.5%)
    Item number and content omitted. (True; NS 11.2%, CG 26.6%)
    Item number and content omitted. (True; NS 24.3%, CG 54.5%)
    Item number and content omitted. (True; NS 5.7%, CG 9.4%)
    Item number and content omitted. (True; NS 7.0%, CG 5.2%)
    Item number and content omitted. (True; NS 17.1%, CG 22.7%)
    Item number and content omitted. (True; NS 12.5%, CG 23.2%)

FIGURE 11.2. Mr. B's MMPI-3 Score Report, continued

Aggression (AGG, T Score = 78)
> Item number and content omitted. (True; NS 28.8%, CG 56.7%)
> Item number and content omitted. (True; NS 24.3%, CG 34.8%)
> Item number and content omitted. (True; NS 13.3%, CG 23.6%)
> Item number and content omitted. (True; NS 9.4%, CG 11.6%)
> Item number and content omitted. (True; NS 44.6%, CG 47.2%)

End of Report

FIGURE 11.2. Mr. B's MMPI-3 Score Report, continued

relationships and lack of support from family members, and it is likely he has family conflicts and blames family members for his problems.

Mr. B further reports feeling sad, unhappy, and being dissatisfied with his current life circumstances. He is at risk for suicidal ideation and does indeed report having attempted suicide. He likely complains about feeling depressed, feels hopeless and pessimistic about the future, does not cope well with stress, and feels incapable of dealing with current life circumstances. Mr. B likely believes he cannot be helped and that he gets a raw deal from life. He also reports lacking confidence, feeling worthless, and believing he is a burden to others. He is likely intropunitive, prone to rumination, and feels inferior. He further reports being passive, indecisive, and inefficacious, and may lack self-reliance and perseverance. In addition, Mr. B reports engaging in compulsive behavior and may be rigid and perfectionistic. He also reports being anger prone and is likely irritable, argumentative, hostile, holds grudges, and throws temper tantrums.

Interpersonally, Mr. B reports disliking people and being around them, preferring to be alone. He reports not enjoying social events and avoiding social situations. He is likely asocial, introverted, emotionally restricted, and emotionally disconnected from others. Finally, Mr. B reports engaging in instrumentally aggressive behavior and is overly assertive and socially dominant when interacting with others.

Mr. B's MMPI-3 results identify a range of diagnostic considerations. He should be evaluated for disorders associated with thought dysfunction, including those manifesting in psychotic symptoms, such as schizophrenia with paranoid features, paranoid delusional disorder, or obsessive-compulsive-related disorders. If psychosis is ruled out, schizotypal personality disorder should be considered. He should also be evaluated for the presence of a manic or hypomanic episode, including a cycling mood disorder, as well as a combined mood and psychotic disorder, such as schizoaffective disorder. He should also be evaluated for depression, likely in the context of a bipolar mood disorder. Moreover, he should be evaluated for potential personality disorders that involve antagonism, including paranoia, mistrust, and instrumental aggression, as well as impulse-control disorders. Finally, he should be evaluated for disorders that involve excessive social withdrawal, such as avoidant or schizoid personality disorder.

In terms of treatment considerations, there are several implications and barriers that need to be considered based on Mr. B's MMPI-3 results. Although emotional distress may motivate Mr. B for treatment, indecisiveness, behavioral activation, and impulsivity may interfere with establishing treatment goals and progress in treatment. Significantly impaired thinking may disrupt treatment. There are also likely several barriers to establishing a therapeutic relationship, including paranoia and suspiciousness, cynical beliefs, and general social aversion, which might further impact treatment progress.

Several potential targets and needs for invention are identified by Mr. B's MMPI-3 results. First and foremost, risk for self-harm needs to be evaluated. He endorsed one critical item referring to explicit suicidal behavior and evidenced clinical levels of demoralization and hopelessness. Moreover, Mr. B might also require inpatient hospitalization for thought dysfunction, paranoid delusions, and/or disorganized thinking and possible manic or hypomanic episodes. The need for both antipsychotic and mood stabilizing medication should be evaluated, and he might need to be stabilized on medication for other treatment to be effective. Psychotic symptoms, including persecutory ideation, and stabilizing mood should be immediate targets for intervention. Mr. B may need to gain insight about his thought dysfunction. Additional targets of intervention may include relief of demoralization and hopelessness, low self-esteem, and potential obsessive-compulsive behaviors. In addition, anger management, including a reduction in interpersonal aggressive behaviors, should be considered as a target for intervention. This could be part of a broader focus on improved impulse control. Family and other interpersonal difficulties, including social avoidance and mistrust, would likely serve as appropriate targets as well.

Discussion

Mr. B's MMPI-3 findings highlight the potential effects that severe thought dysfunction and mania might have on an individual's response style. He was likely quite disorganized and hyperactive while completing the test and tended to respond in a rather indiscriminately affirmative manner as a result. This responding may have contributed to the F scale score (85T), which raises concerns about overreporting, as many of these items are not only infrequent, but also keyed in the True response direction. Mr. B's other validity scale scores are generally in the range that would be expected in reference to the outpatient, community mental health center comparison group. Overall, whereas the MMPI-3 results are valid for clinical interpretation, Mr. B's indiscriminate True response style could have contributed to some seemingly incongruous scale elevation patterns and some inconsistent findings with his general presentation at intake.

The MMPI-3 Substantive Scales generally confirmed the intake clinician's provisional diagnosis of a manic episode. Both RC9 and ACT reach their respective maximum scores. The MMPI-2-RF counterpart to the MMPI-3 ACT scale has been observed to be a sensitive marker of bipolar disorder (Sellbom, Bagby et al., 2012; Watson et al., 2011) even when patients with schizophrenia are included. However, elevations in the thought dysfunction domain are most pervasive in Mr. B's MMPI-3 protocol. His THD score (85T) is very high even in reference to male community mental health outpatients, as 98% of them would score at or below Mr. B on this scale. The combination of thought dysfunction and possible mania raises the possibility of a schizoaffective disorder, bipolar type, or a bipolar disorder with psychotic features. MMPI-3 scores do not provide sufficient specificity for this level of differential diagnosis. Rather, the clinician would need to determine whether the psychotic symptoms are mood-congruent or occur independently of the manic symptoms.

Scores on the various externalizing scales also highlighted problems with general antagonism, aggression, anger, impulsivity, and mistrust, which could be markers of an underlying personality disorder, but given the externalizing manifestations of individuals in active manic episodes, it would be important to disentangle these characteristics from manic symptom sequela vis-à-vis personality or other pathology when mood has stabilized. Such disentanglement would also have implications for potential treatment considerations as indicated by the MMPI-3 results.

The degree to which Mr. B's social aversion and disaffiliativeness are a product of persecutory ideation would also need to be determined prior to formulating targets for intervention in these domains. Finally, Mr. B's scores on various Emotional/Internalizing scales, especially SFD, are generally inconsistent with his clinical presentation, which was quite energized and grandiose. It is possible that this was part of his general response style or it may reflect past experiences in the context of a bipolar mood disorder.

Ultimately, further assessment of Mr. B revealed that he met diagnostic criteria for an active manic episode with severe mood-congruent psychotic features, which included grandiose and paranoid delusions. He did not exhibit hallucinations but evidenced significant thought disorganization. It was Mr. B's first manic episode, and though he had never sought treatment for mental health problems, further inquiry revealed that he had likely met criteria for a depressive disorder in the past. Because of the severity of his presentation, and risk for suicide, he was hospitalized at a psychiatric inpatient facility and stabilized with antipsychotic and mood stabilizing medication. Mr. B responded well to treatment and once stabilized, there was no evidence of an underlying personality pathology.

MR. C: SEVERE PERSONALITY DISORDER

Mr. C, an 18-year-old man, was referred by his general practitioner to an outpatient community mental health team for assistance with low mood and generalized anxiety.[1] At the time, he was attending a university bridging course that he found "extremely stressful" and had been accepted into an engineering program. Mr. C reported that when he is particularly stressed from coursework, he feels like the world "isn't real," and he becomes especially suspicious of others. Mr. C further reported a general mistrust of other people's intentions, believing that even his close friends cannot be trusted with personal information as they might use it against him. Mr. C discussed that he could determine whether someone has good intentions just by looking at them, which appeared to further contribute to his general mistrust of others.

At the time of the evaluation, Mr. C was experiencing persistent low mood, and reported intense suicidal thoughts that are always present, although he denied any intent to kill himself "at the moment." Three months prior to the intake interview he had been hospitalized for the second time following a suicide attempt, which he said had occurred on impulse. Mr. C reported that he often feels he cannot sufficiently control his emotions, as extreme feelings of depression or anger could be triggered with little reason.

Mr. C described an upbringing with emotionally cold, distant parents who were hypercritical of his perceived lack of academic ability. He reported that his mother had told him he would never pass his engineering degree, which he said was increasing his levels of stress surrounding his coursework. Mr. C reported that he was frequently bullied throughout his school years and therefore found it difficult to connect with his peers.

Mr. C was administered the MMPI-3 to further assist with formulation and treatment recommendations.

MMPI-3 Interpretation

Mr. C responded to all of the MMPI-3 items (Figure 11.3). There are no concerns about inconsistent responding. Possible overreporting of psychological dysfunction is indicated by a much larger than average number of infrequent responses, including in mental health patient populations. However, this level of infrequent responding can be a result of genuine severe psychopathology, rather than an attempt to overreport. This would be consistent with Mr. C's history. There are no signs of underreporting in this protocol. Overall, the MMPI-3 results are deemed valid for clinical interpretation.

Mr. C's responses indicate significant emotional distress. He reports experiencing significant demoralization, being unhappy, sad, and dissatisfied. He also reports feeling overwhelmed and likely does not cope well with stress. He is likely to complain about feeling depressed, anxious, and being incapable of dealing with life circumstances. He further reports current suicidal ideation and a history of suicidal ideation and attempts. He is likely preoccupied with suicide and death, is at significant risk for self-harm, and may recently have attempted suicide. Mr. C also reports lacking confidence, feeling worthless, and believing he is a burden to others. He likely feels inferior and insecure, is self-disparaging, tends to ruminate, be intropunitive, and likely presents to others with low confidence and feelings of uselessness.

Mr. C also reports various negative emotional experiences including anxiety, guilt, and anger. He is likely behaviorally inhibited due to negative emotions. He reports an above-average level of stress, likely complains about stress, and

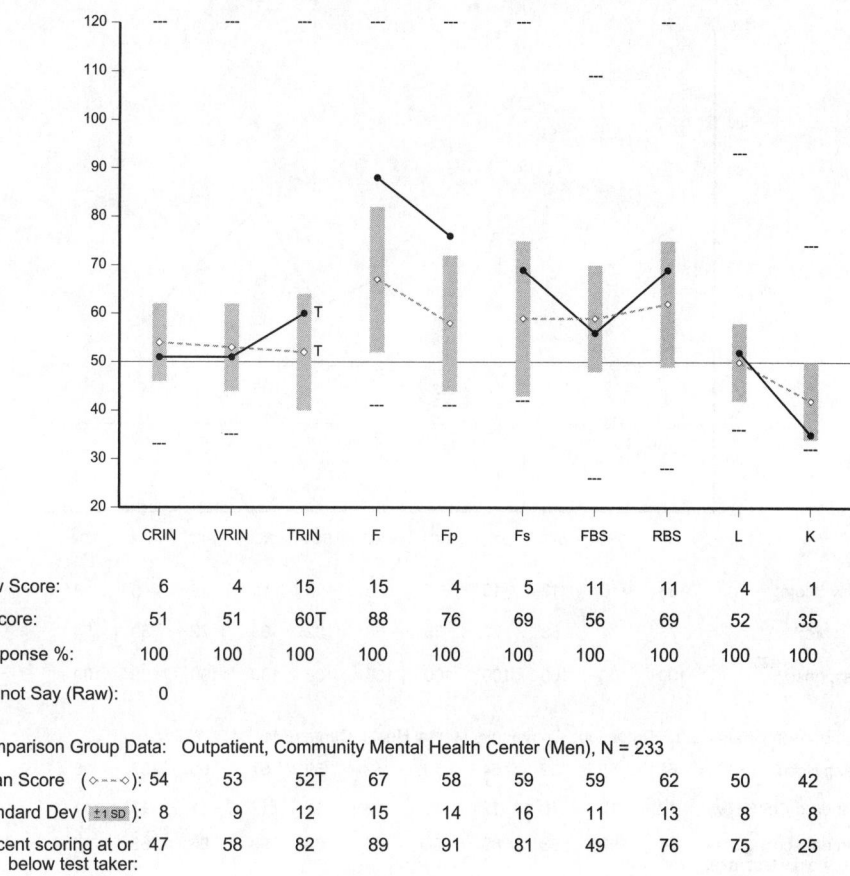

FIGURE 11.3. Mr. C's MMPI-3 Score Report

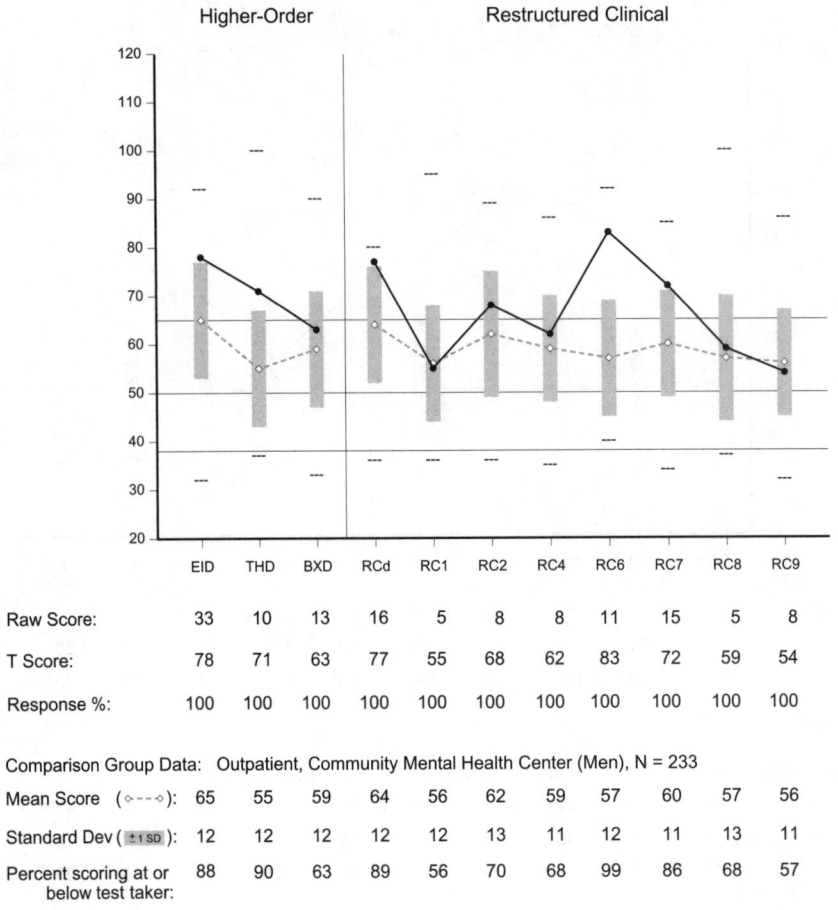

FIGURE 11.3. Mr. C's MMPI-3 Score Report, continued

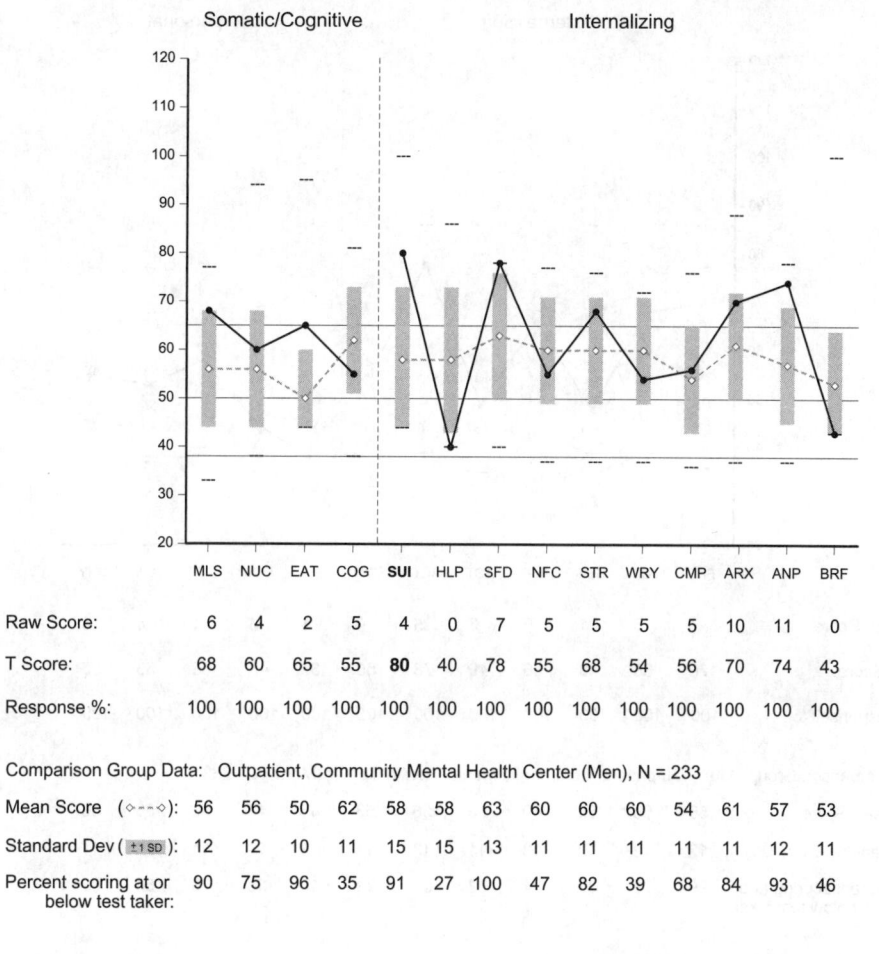

FIGURE 11.3. Mr. C's MMPI-3 Score Report, continued

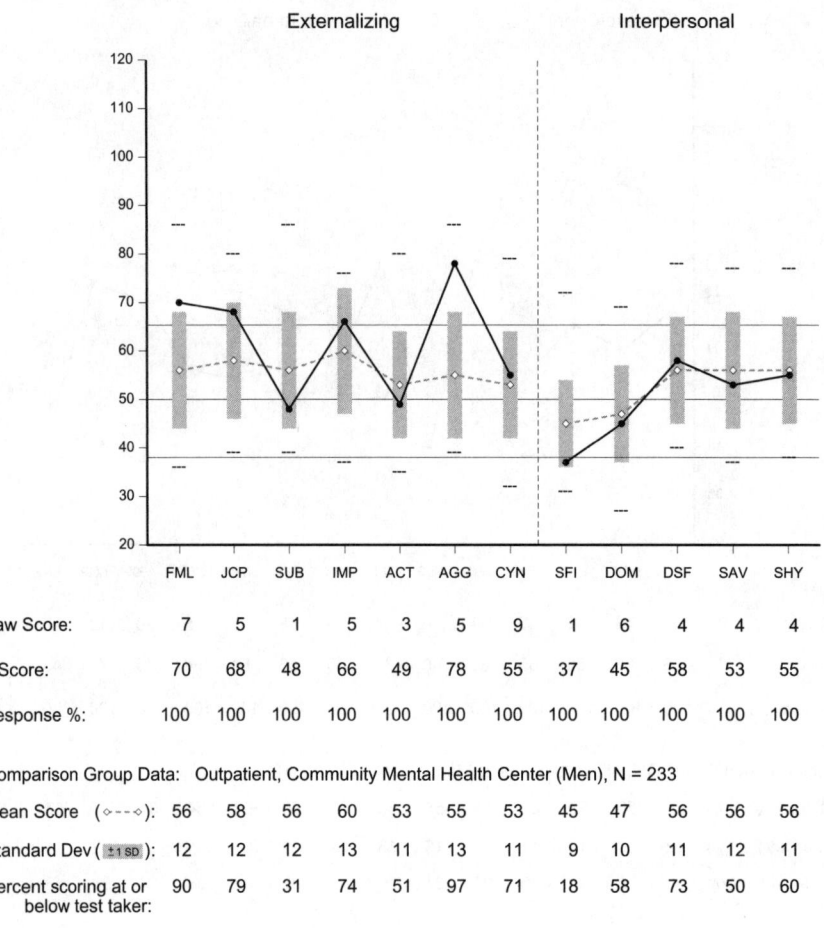

FIGURE 11.3. Mr. C's MMPI-3 Score Report, continued

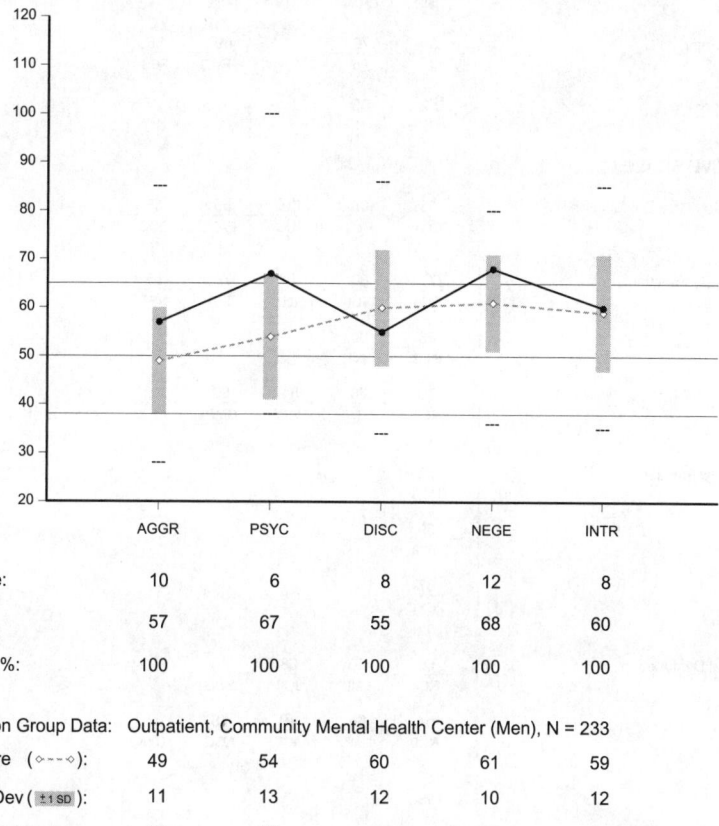

FIGURE 11.3. Mr. C's MMPI-3 Score Report, continued

MMPI-3 T SCORES (BY DOMAIN)

PROTOCOL VALIDITY

Content Non-Responsiveness

0	51	51	60 T
CNS	CRIN	VRIN	TRIN

Over-Reporting

88	76		69	56	69
F	Fp		Fs	FBS	RBS

Under-Reporting

52	35
L	K

SUBSTANTIVE SCALES

Somatic/Cognitive Dysfunction

55	68	60	65	55
RC1	MLS	NUC	EAT	COG

Emotional Dysfunction

78 EID

77	80	40	78	55
RCd	SUI	HLP	SFD	NFC

68	60
RC2	INTR

72	68	54	56	70	74	43	68
RC7	STR	WRY	CMP	ARX	ANP	BRF	NEGE

Thought Dysfunction

71 THD

83
RC6

59
RC8

67
PSYC

Behavioral Dysfunction

63 BXD

62	70	68	48
RC4	FML	JCP	SUB

54	66	49	78	55
RC9	IMP	ACT	AGG	CYN

55
DISC

Interpersonal Functioning

37	45	57	58	53	55
SFI	DOM	AGGR	DSF	SAV	SHY

Note. This information is provided to facilitate interpretation following the recommended structure for MMPI-3 interpretation in Chapter 5 of the *MMPI-3 Manual for Administration, Scoring, and Interpretation*, which provides details in the text and an outline in Table 5-1.

FIGURE 11.3. Mr. C's MMPI-3 Score Report, continued

ITEM-LEVEL INFORMATION

Unscorable Responses

The test taker produced scorable responses to all the MMPI-3 items.

Critical Responses

Seven MMPI-3 scales—Suicidal/Death Ideation (SUI), Helplessness/Hopelessness (HLP), Anxiety-Related Experiences (ARX), Ideas of Persecution (RC6), Aberrant Experiences (RC8), Substance Abuse (SUB), and Aggression (AGG)—have been designated by the test authors as having critical item content that may require immediate attention and follow-up. Items answered by the individual in the keyed direction (True or False) on a critical scale are listed below if his T score on that scale is 65 or higher. However, any item answered in the keyed direction on SUI is listed. The percentage of the MMPI-3 normative sample (NS) and of the Outpatient, Community Mental Health Center (Men) Comparison Group (CG) that answered each item in the keyed direction are provided in parentheses following the item content.

Suicidal/Death Ideation (SUI, T Score = 80)

    Item number and content omitted. (True; NS 22.2%, CG 43.3%)
    Item number and content omitted. (True; NS 8.1%, CG 25.8%)
    Item number and content omitted. (True; NS 2.5%, CG 20.2%)
    Item number and content omitted. (True; NS 2.8%, CG 13.3%)

Anxiety-Related Experiences (ARX, T Score = 70)

    Item number and content omitted. (True; NS 31.2%, CG 77.3%)
    Item number and content omitted. (True; NS 31.4%, CG 67.0%)
    Item number and content omitted. (True; NS 16.9%, CG 44.2%)
    Item number and content omitted. (True; NS 4.7%, CG 12.0%)
    Item number and content omitted. (True; NS 27.3%, CG 30.5%)
    Item number and content omitted. (True; NS 28.6%, CG 59.7%)
    Item number and content omitted. (True; NS 26.0%, CG 73.0%)
    Item number and content omitted. (True; NS 14.9%, CG 36.5%)
    Item number and content omitted. (True; NS 35.8%, CG 75.1%)
    Item number and content omitted. (True; NS 39.8%, CG 39.1%)

Ideas of Persecution (RC6, T Score = 83)

    Item number and content omitted. (True; NS 2.9%, CG 15.9%)
    Item number and content omitted. (True; NS 1.4%, CG 5.2%)
    Item number and content omitted. (True; NS 26.7%, CG 44.2%)
    Item number and content omitted. (True; NS 20.4%, CG 34.3%)
    Item number and content omitted. (True; NS 7.8%, CG 17.6%)
    Item number and content omitted. (True; NS 30.9%, CG 48.9%)
    Item number and content omitted. (False; NS 16.4%, CG 27.0%)
    Item number and content omitted. (True; NS 11.9%, CG 36.9%)
    Item number and content omitted. (True; NS 12.1%, CG 22.7%)
    Item number and content omitted. (True; NS 19.0%, CG 34.3%)
    Item number and content omitted. (True; NS 7.7%, CG 20.2%)

Aggression (AGG, T Score = 78)

    Item number and content omitted. (True; NS 28.8%, CG 56.7%)
    Item number and content omitted. (True; NS 24.3%, CG 34.8%)
    Item number and content omitted. (True; NS 13.3%, CG 23.6%)
    Item number and content omitted. (True; NS 44.6%, CG 47.2%)
    Item number and content omitted. (True; NS 12.6%, CG 31.8%)

End of Report

FIGURE 11.3. Mr. C's MMPI-3 Score Report, continued

tends to feel incapable of controlling his anxiety level. Mr. C reports multiple anxiety-related experiences, including generalized anxiety, reexperiencing, and/or panic. He is likely to experience intrusive ideation, sleep difficulties, including nightmares, and possibly posttraumatic distress. He further reports being anger prone and is likely to have problems with anger, irritability, and frustration tolerance. He likely holds grudges, is argumentative and hostile, and may throw temper tantrums.

Mr. C reports a lack of positive emotional experiences, significant anhedonia, and lack of interest. He is likely pessimistic, socially disengaged, and lacking in energy. Indeed, Mr. C reports experiencing poor health and feeling weak or tired, he may be preoccupied with poor health and is likely to complain about fatigue, sleep disturbance, low energy, and sexual dysfunction.

Mr. C's responses also indicate significant thought dysfunction. He reports prominent persecutory ideation that may rise to the level of paranoid delusions. He likely has persecutory beliefs, is suspicious and distrustful, experiences interpersonal difficulties as a result, lacks insight into his difficulties, and tends to blame others for his problems. He also reports unusual beliefs and perceptions, and he is likely to experience unusual thought processes and perceptual phenomena, feel alienated from others, engage in unrealistic thinking, and present with impaired reality testing.

Mr. C reports engaging in physically aggressive, violent behavior and losing control. He may have a history of violent behavior toward others, be abusive, and experience anger-related problems. He reports conflictual family relationships and lack of support from family members. He is likely to have family conflicts and poor family functioning. He may have strong negative feelings about family members and blame them for his difficulties. Mr. C also reports significant past and current substance abuse and is likely to have a history of problematic alcohol and drug use and may have had legal problems as a result of such use. He further reports engaging in problematic impulsive behaviors and is likely to be nonplanful and have poor impulse control.

Mr. C's MMPI-3 results identify a number of possible diagnostic considerations. He should be evaluated for internalizing disorders, including depressive disorders, anhedonia-related disorders, and anxiety-related disorders (including generalized anxiety disorder and PTSD). If a physical origin for malaise can be ruled out, he should also be evaluated for a somatic symptom disorder. Furthermore, Mr. C should be evaluated for potential externalizing disorders that involve anger, aggression, impulsivity, and substance misuse. Moreover, Mr. C should be evaluated for disorders related to thought dysfunction, and in particular paranoid delusional disorder. If psychosis can be ruled out, paranoid or schizotypal personality disorder should be considered. Other personality disorders that manifest in significant negative emotionality, including borderline and dependent personality disorders, should be considered as well.

In terms of treatment, Mr. C's MMPI-3 results indicate it is likely that his emotional difficulties will motivate him for treatment, though malaise and anhedonia might interfere with engagement. Poor impulse control might also negatively impact treatment compliance. Persecutory ideation may interfere with forming a therapeutic relationship. In terms of recommendations, Mr. C's risk for suicide should be evaluated immediately and steps should be taken to monitor and manage his risk level. The presence of a delusional disorder and the associated need for inpatient hospitalization and antipsychotic medication would need to be evaluated. Furthermore, a treatment protocol is likely necessary to target a range of emotional, behavioral, and interpersonal difficulties. Specifically, relief of demoralization and various negative emotions, including anxiety and anger, should be targets for intervention. There should also be a focus on addressing issues concerning low self-esteem, as well as stress and anger management. Mr. C should be evaluated for need for antidepressant medication. Other treatment foci should involve interpersonal mistrust as well as possible externalizing behaviors, such as substance abuse, aggression, and general impulse control.

Discussion

Mr. C's MMPI-3 results raise several important clinical concerns that should be helpful in formulation and treatment. However, it is important to be mindful of the fact that two scales reflective of overreporting of psychopathology (F and Fp) are in a concerning range. Mr. C also scored at the same level or higher than 89% (F) and 91% (Fp) of males in the outpatient, community mental health center comparison group. He presented with current serious mental health concerns and also had a history of severe psychopathology, including inpatient hospitalizations. It is not uncommon to see high overreporting validity scale scores in such individuals. However, existing psychopathology and overreporting are not mutually exclusive, and therefore, appropriate caution should be taken when weighing his self-report data in light of other available sources of information.

Mr. C's scores on the MMPI-3 Substantive Scales reflect dysfunction in all three broad superspectra of psychopathology: Internalizing, Thought Dysfunction, and Externalizing. There is clear evidence for emotional dysregulation (STR, AXR, ANP) that is likely dispositional in nature (NEGE) and for demoralization, low self-esteem, and thoughts about suicide and self-harm. The SUI critical responses include four explicit statements referring to a loss of will to live and wanting to kill oneself. At the same time, significant thought dysfunction (and persecutory ideation in particular) is prominent in this protocol. Indeed, RC6 has the highest score (83T) in the entire profile. In the case of Mr. C, overt psychosis was eventually ruled out, but he exhibits significant paranoid personality traits as well as other unusual experiences (PSYC), particularly under periods of significant stress. Finally, although not necessarily dispositionally prone to externalizing (DISC = 55T), his test scores reflect significant impulsivity, substance abuse, and aggression as well as family problems consistent with externalizing tendencies. Borderline personality disorder is a severe personality dysfunction that is consistent with all three psychopathology domains (including Psychoticism under periods of stress). Personality disorder research with the MMPI-2-RF has shown that EID, THD, RCd, RC7, SUI, SFD, STR, AXR, ANP, FML, SUB, AGG, PSYC, and NEGE are all reflective of borderline personality disorder, with the only other scales not elevated in the current profile being BXD and DISC (Anderson et al., 2015b; Sellbom & Smith, 2017; Zahn et al., 2017).

Ultimately, the clinician used the MMPI-3 information as well as clinical interview and medical records to diagnose Mr. C with ICD-11 severe personality disorder, with negative affectivity and disinhibition trait qualifiers and borderline pattern, as well as ICD-11 schizotypal disorder (which is not considered a personality disorder in the ICD-11 but rather part of the schizophrenia spectrum). Given Mr. C's age, significant paranoia, unusual thinking, experience of derealization when under stress, and other schizotypal symptoms, concerns about prodromal psychosis were raised as well, with the need for this to be monitored during treatment. Mr. C was prescribed antidepressant and mood stabilizing medication by a psychiatrist and was recommended to undergo Dialectical Behavior Therapy (DBT)-informed psychotherapy with immediate focus on reducing self-harming behaviors.

MX. D: A CASE OF SOCIAL COMMUNICATION DEFICITS

Mx. D is a 19-year-old single individual who is androgynous and prefers the pronoun *they*. They presented to a university-affiliated clinical psychology center upon referral from their general practitioner, who requested that Mx. D be evaluated for atypical social behaviors and for having little empathy. During the interview with their therapist, Mx. D reported difficulties with adapting to standard social norms. Mx. D explained that they saw little reason to use commonplace greetings, such as "hello" or "goodbye," as they were unnecessary. Mx D's male partner, who was also present during the initial interview as a support person, described Mx. D as "socially awkward, but not introverted." He further reported that Mx. D had difficulties with relating to other people's emotional experiences and sometimes "zoned out" when others were discussing personal topics. Mx. D elaborated that they had built a structure and rules for how to interact with others, especially strangers.

Mx. D reported growing up in an emotionally invalidating home. Their father had alcohol problems and was easily angered; their mother was frequently depressed. Both parents were sometimes violent toward their children, including them. Mx. D had previous mental health treatment. Available records forwarded from Mx. D's general practitioner indicated that they had been evaluated for autism spectrum disorder in primary school, but the evaluation did not support such a diagnosis. They had also been evaluated at age 14, and records indicated that Mx. D, who at the time listed their sex as male, which they were assigned at birth, suffered from depression associated with being transgender, and struggled to talk to and relate with other boys in high school. They felt more connected to girls as girls understood them better. At that time, Mx. D's mother had reported to clinic staff that Mx. D was constantly resisting authority and showed no empathy for others getting hurt.

To assist with clinical formulation and treatment recommendations, the student clinician administered the MMPI-3. No provisional diagnoses had been made at this point.

MMPI-3 Interpretation

Mx. D responded to all of the MMPI-3 items (Figure 11.4). There is no concern about inconsistent or content-inconsistent indiscriminate responding, overreporting, or underreporting. The MMPI-3 profile is therefore valid for clinical interpretation.

Mx. D's responses indicate significant externalizing, acting-out behavior, which is likely to have gotten them into difficulties. They report a history of antisocial behavior, which likely includes failure to conform to social norms and standards, difficulty with individuals in positions of authority, conflictual interpersonal relationships, and possible involvement with the criminal justice system (though the latter could be ruled out from Mx. D's history). They further report a history of juvenile conduct problems, including acting-out behaviors as a child.

Mx. D reports a lack of positive emotional experiences, significant anhedonia, and a lack of interest in various activities. They are likely pessimistic, lack energy, are introverted, and generally disengaged. They report a history of suicidal ideation and/or past suicide attempts and provided item responses directly indicative of suicidal behavior. They report feeling helpless and/or hopeless and pessimistic, and they likely feel overwhelmed and that life is a strain, believe that they cannot be helped, that they get a raw deal from life, and they generally lack the motivation to change. They further report self-doubt and likely feel inferior and insecure. They may be self-disparaging and feel worthless. Mx. D further reports being passive, indecisive, and inefficacious. They likely experience shame, subjective incompetence, and tend to feel that they lack perseverance and self-reliance. Moreover, Mx. D reports engaging in compulsive behavior, including repetitive checking and counting. They likely experience obsessive thinking, are rigid, and perfectionistic.

Mx. D reports significant persecutory ideation such as believing that others seek to harm them. They are likely suspicious of the intentions of others,

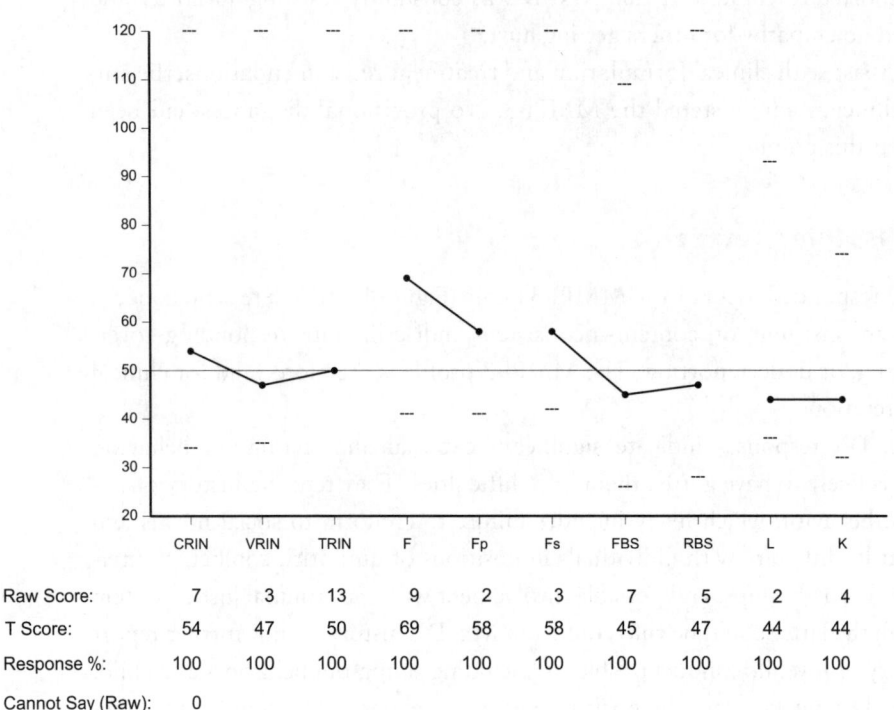

FIGURE 11.4. Mx. D's MMPI-3 Score Report

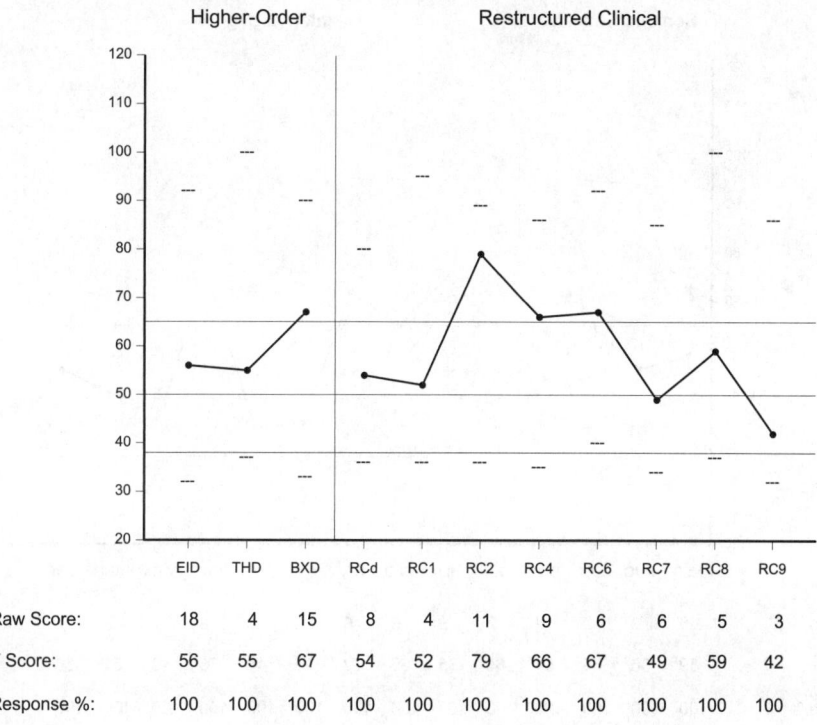

FIGURE 11.4. Mx. D's MMPI-3 Score Report, continued

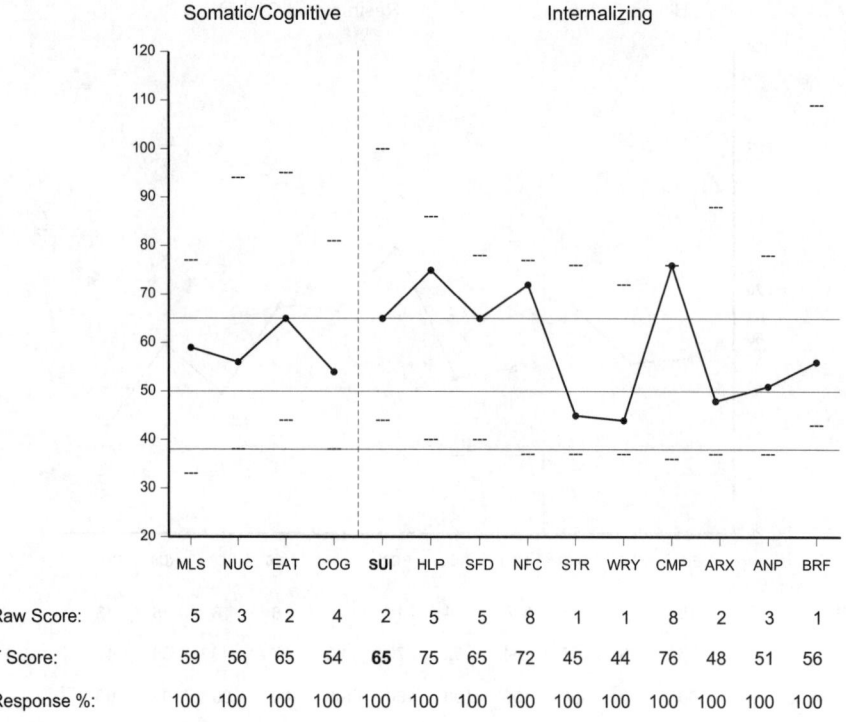

FIGURE 11.4. Mx. D's MMPI-3 Score Report, continued

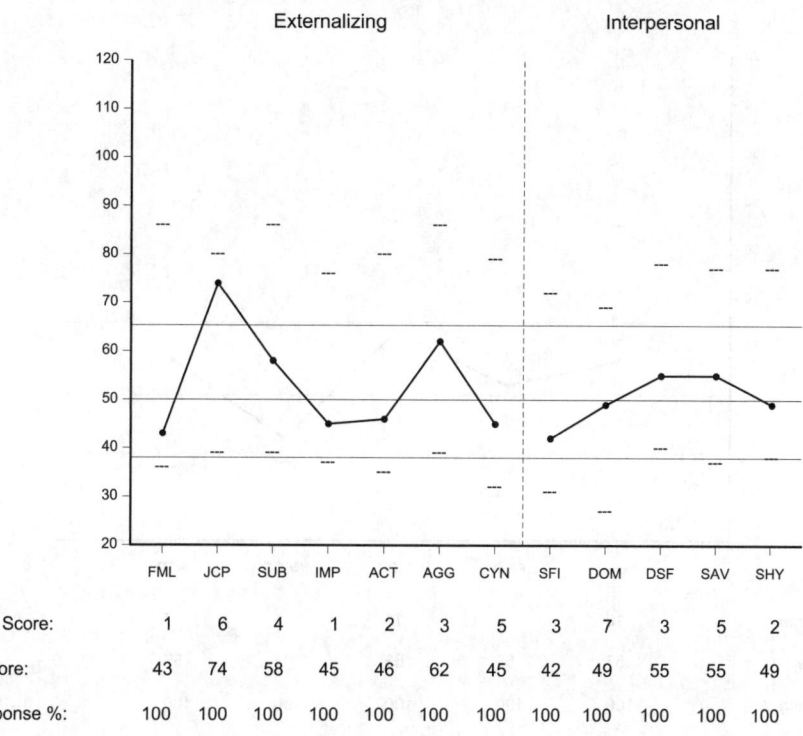

FIGURE 11.4. Mx. D's MMPI-3 Score Report, continued

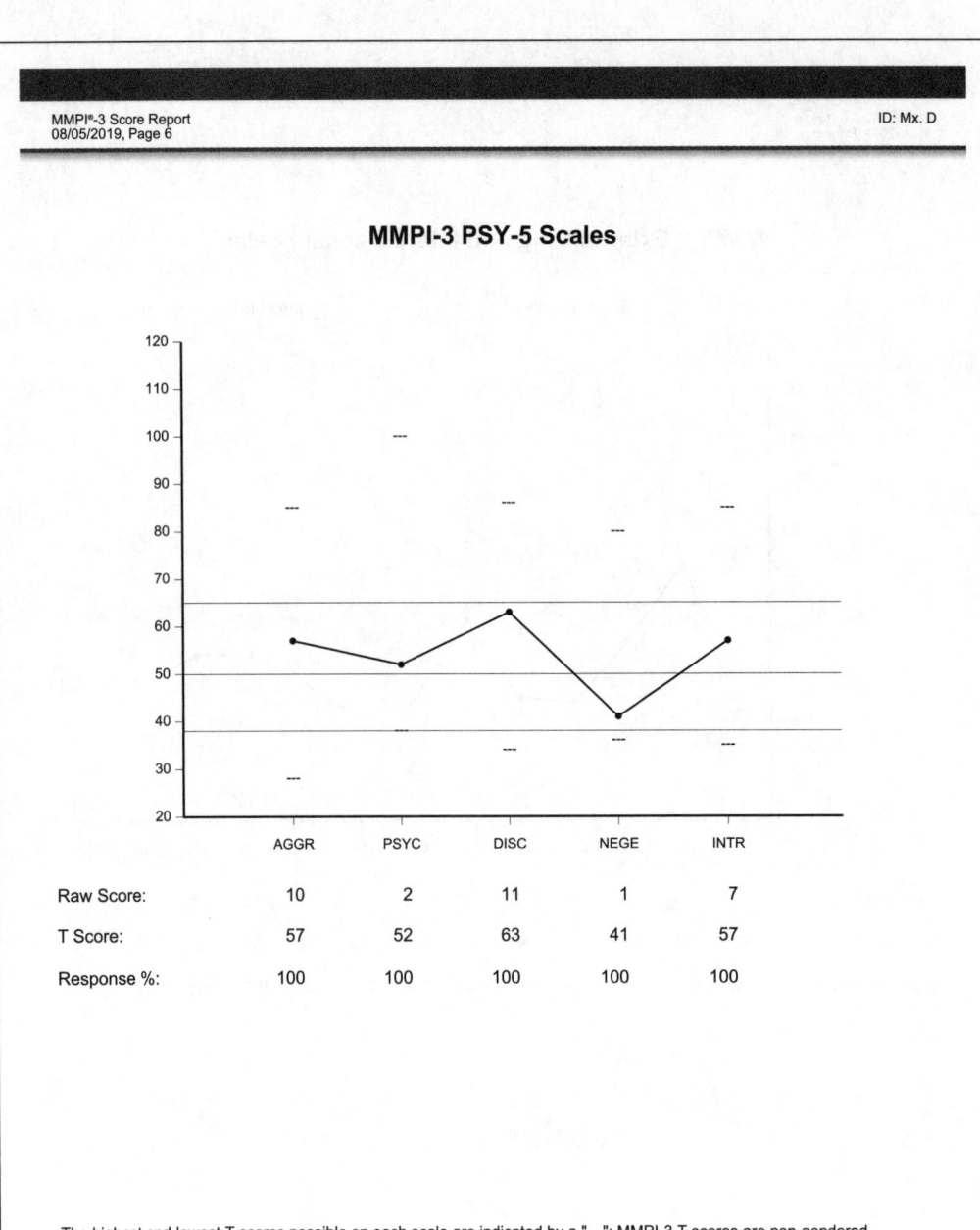

FIGURE 11.4. Mx. D's MMPI-3 Score Report, continued

MMPI-3 T SCORES (BY DOMAIN)

PROTOCOL VALIDITY

Content Non-Responsiveness

0	54	47	50
CNS	CRIN	VRIN	TRIN

Over-Reporting

69	58		58	45	47
F	Fp		Fs	FBS	RBS

Under-Reporting

44	44
L	K

SUBSTANTIVE SCALES

Somatic/Cognitive Dysfunction

52	59	56	65	54
RC1	MLS	NUC	EAT	COG

Emotional Dysfunction: 56 EID

54	65	75	65	72
RCd	SUI	HLP	SFD	NFC

79	57
RC2	INTR

49	45	44	76	48	51	56	41
RC7	STR	WRY	CMP	ARX	ANP	BRF	NEGE

Thought Dysfunction: 55 THD

67
RC6

59
RC8

52
PSYC

Behavioral Dysfunction: 67 BXD

66	43	74	58
RC4	FML	JCP	SUB

42	45	46	62	45
RC9	IMP	ACT	AGG	CYN

63
DISC

Interpersonal Functioning

42	49	57	55	55	49
SFI	DOM	AGGR	DSF	SAV	SHY

Note. This information is provided to facilitate interpretation following the recommended structure for MMPI-3 interpretation in Chapter 5 of the *MMPI-3 Manual for Administration, Scoring, and Interpretation*, which provides details in the text and an outline in Table 5-1.

FIGURE 11.4. Mx. D's MMPI-3 Score Report, continued

ITEM-LEVEL INFORMATION

Unscorable Responses

The test taker produced scorable responses to all the MMPI-3 items.

Critical Responses

Seven MMPI-3 scales—Suicidal/Death Ideation (SUI), Helplessness/Hopelessness (HLP), Anxiety-Related Experiences (ARX), Ideas of Persecution (RC6), Aberrant Experiences (RC8), Substance Abuse (SUB), and Aggression (AGG)—have been designated by the test authors as having critical item content that may require immediate attention and follow-up. Items answered by the individual in the keyed direction (True or False) on a critical scale are listed below if his T score on that scale is 65 or higher. However, any item answered in the keyed direction on SUI is listed. The percentage of the MMPI-3 normative sample that answered each item in the keyed direction is provided in parentheses following the item content.

Suicidal/Death Ideation (SUI, T Score = 65)
  Item number and content omitted. (True, 22.2%)
  Item number and content omitted. (True, 8.1%)

Helplessness/Hopelessness (HLP, T Score = 75)

  Item number and content omitted. (True, 10.9%)
  Item number and content omitted. (True, 8.7%)
  Item number and content omitted. (True, 12.3%)
  Item number and content omitted. (True, 45.4%)
  Item number and content omitted. (False, 22.0%)

Ideas of Persecution (RC6, T Score = 67)

  Item number and content omitted. (True, 26.7%)
  Item number and content omitted. (False, 16.4%)
  Item number and content omitted. (True, 11.9%)
  Item number and content omitted. (True, 12.1%)
  Item number and content omitted. (True, 19.0%)
  Item number and content omitted. (True, 7.7%)

End of Report

FIGURE 11.4. Mx. D's MMPI-3 Score Report, continued

generally distrustful, may experience conflicts with others due to mistrust, tend to lack insight into these difficulties, and often blame others for their problems. However, this interpersonal suspiciousness may also reflect cultural mistrust in a gender nonconforming individual.

Mx. D's MMPI-3 results signal several diagnostic considerations. They should be evaluated for an externalizing disorder, and in particular, antisocial personality disorder. They should further be evaluated for an anhedonia-related disorder as well as obsessive-compulsive-related disorders. Finally, they should be evaluated for a disorder involving persecutory ideation.

Mx. D's MMPI-3 results also indicate considerations for treatment. Specifically, Mx. D might not be internally motivated for treatment and low positive emotionality could further exacerbate such amotivation. Indecisiveness may interfere with establishing treatment goals and progress in treatment, and persecutory ideation and acting-out tendencies may interfere with forming a therapeutic relationship and treatment compliance. Mx. D is at significant risk for treatment noncompliance. With respect to targets for intervention, the assessment of suicide risk should be the most immediate concern. Once such risk is determined and managed, targets for intervention should likely focus on anhedonia, hopelessness, low self-esteem, and obsessive-compulsive behaviors. They might need to be evaluated for need of antidepressant medication and even inpatient treatment for internalizing problems. Persecutory ideation and interpersonal mistrust as well as inadequate self-control should be targeted as well.

Discussion

No comparison group data are provided for Mx. D's MMPI-3 results, as non-gendered comparison groups were unavailable at the time of this writing.

Mx. D provided a valid MMPI-3 protocol, which allows for interpretation of Substantive Scale findings without caveats. The MMPI-3 results provide findings directly relevant to a conceptual formulation. Two broad themes of atypical externalizing and atypical internalizing tendencies can be observed. With respect to the former, the MMPI-3 results reveal a tendency to deviate from social norms and standards, to reject authority, and to have interpersonal conflicts, but at the same time there is no indication of the impulsivity, risk-taking, and aggression typically associated with externalizing problems. In terms of internalizing, there are clear themes of anhedonia, obsessive-compulsivity, inefficacy, hopelessness, low self-esteem, and even suicidal ideation, but without subjective emotional distress. There is also an element of interpersonal suspiciousness and likely alienation from others; though, as Mx. D's partner indicated during their interview, there are no signs of introversion. It is important to consider, however, that this interpersonal suspiciousness might indeed reflect cultural mistrust in a gender nonconforming individual rather than a pathological process. Three of the six RC6 items that Mx. D endorsed in the keyed direction appear on Dixon et al.'s (2023) list (see discussion in chapter 6).

These MMPI-3 results inform a clinical case formulation that centers on a highly rigid and ego-syntonic obsessive-compulsive personality style.[2] Mx. D was conceptualized as an overly self-focused individual who rejected conventional societal rules and norms and had instead internalized their own set of social rules and guidelines with which to conduct themself. They had significant difficulties with identifying subjective emotions but nevertheless struggled with significant anhedonia; disengagement from others, which was in part rooted in interpersonal mistrust from early life experiences; and hopelessness about the future. Mx. D's suicidal ideation was mostly a product of cognitive reasoning about it being better to be dead than alive in a society with rules they struggled to identify. Furthermore, obsessive-compulsive personality disorder is often associated with rigid perfectionism that results in inefficacy and shame, but also self-centeredness, restrictive affectivity, and coldness (Samuel et al., 2012). Ultimately, after the assessment sessions had been completed and Mx. D attended the formulation session, they declined to participate in psychotherapy and instead expressed contentment with learning more about themself.

MS. E: A BARIATRIC SURGERY CANDIDATE

Ms. E is a 32-year-old married woman who presented for a psychological evaluation prior to bariatric surgery. She had completed some college and was employed full time at the time of the assessment. The purpose of the presurgical psychological evaluation was to determine whether psychological factors exist that would interfere with her ability to understand and carry out the lifestyle changes necessary to achieve and maintain weight loss following bariatric surgery.

Ms. E was pursuing surgery for reasons of health and quality of life and to reduce the severity of her weight-related medical comorbidities. These included type 2 diabetes mellitus, nonalcoholic steatohepatitis, kidney stones, and polycystic ovarian syndrome. During her clinical interview, Ms. E reported fair support from her spouse and parents. She demonstrated a fair understanding of the procedure and postoperative eating recommendations but was encouraged to do more independent research to better understand the requirements for bariatric surgery.

At the time she was assessed, Ms. E was approximately 15 pounds below her highest weight. Her eating behaviors were characterized by the assessor as problematic in that she skipped breakfast and lunch daily. Ms. E reported a history of binge eating, which had been in remission since age 16.

Ms. E had previous diagnoses of depression, anxiety, and panic attacks. She reported relative stability in her depression symptoms since a suicide attempt during her early teenage years. In her clinical interview, she reported currently experiencing mild to moderate symptoms of anxiety including occasional panic attacks, social anxiety, and an increase in handwashing due to the Covid-19 pandemic. Ms. E reported that she was prescribed medications to manage her psychiatric symptoms; however, she was not engaged in therapy at the time of her evaluation. She had previously attended therapy and found it helpful. Ms. E reported some ongoing stress in her marital relationship. She denied any current or past problematic alcohol or substance use.

MMPI-3 Interpretation

Ms. E's MMPI-3 findings are reported in Figure 11.5. She produced a valid MMPI-3 protocol. There are no problems with unscorable items. Ms. E responded to the items relevantly based on their content, and there are no indications of overreporting or underreporting.

Ms. E's response to one of the SUI scale items is in the keyed direction, indicating she may be at risk for self-harm, preoccupied with suicide and death, and at risk for current suicidal ideation and attempts. Moreover, Ms. E reports engaging in compulsive behavior. She indeed likely engages in compulsive behavior such as repeated checking, experiences obsessions, and is rigid and perfectionistic.

Ms. E reports multiple somatic complaints including gastrointestinal symptoms and head pain complaints. She likely is preoccupied with physical health concerns, is prone to developing physical symptoms in response to stress, complains of fatigue, and perceives her physical problems as life interfering.

Ms. E reports being shy, easily embarrassed, and uncomfortable around others. She is likely to be socially introverted and inhibited, anxious and nervous in social situations, and viewed by others as socially awkward.

Diagnostically, Ms. E's scores indicate that she should be evaluated for a possible somatic symptom disorder, obsessive-compulsive disorder, and a social anxiety disorder.

Treatment considerations indicated by Ms. E's MMPI-3 results include assessment of suicide risk, further evaluation of the extent to which genuine physical health problems contribute to her elevated RC1 score, and concern that she is likely to reject psychological interpretations of her somatic complaints. Possible targets for intervention include suicide risk, obsessive-compulsive thoughts and behaviors, and anxiety in social situations.

Discussion

Ms. E's MMPI-3 results include several positive findings. Specifically, she was open and cooperative with the assessment, and her scores do not reflect the presence of severe psychopathology. Her scores on most scales associated with features of depression and anxiety are well within normal limits, indicating that these problems remained successfully controlled at the time of her evaluation.

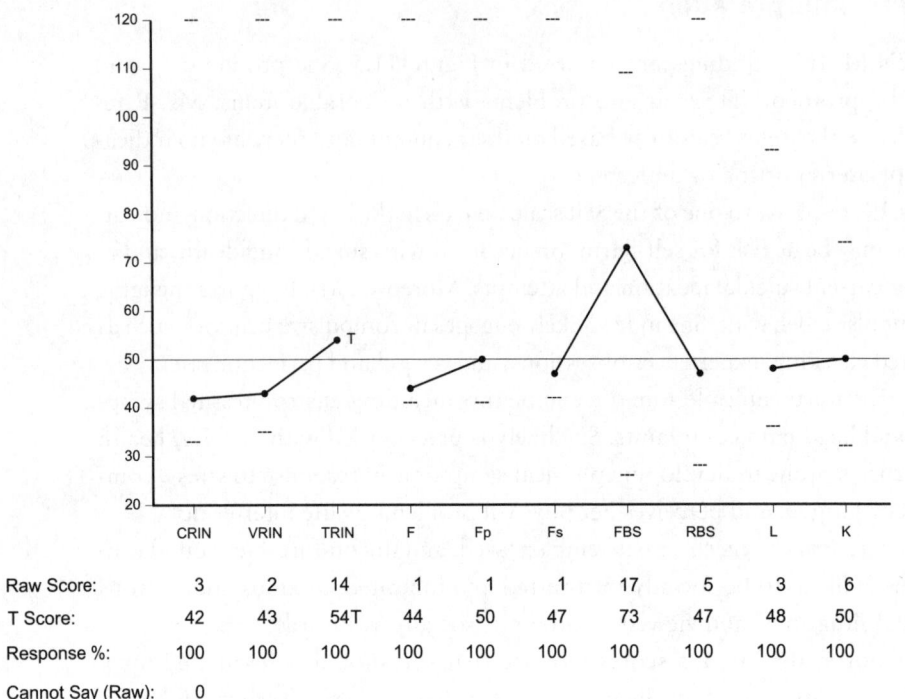

FIGURE 11.5. Ms. E's MMPI-3 Score Report

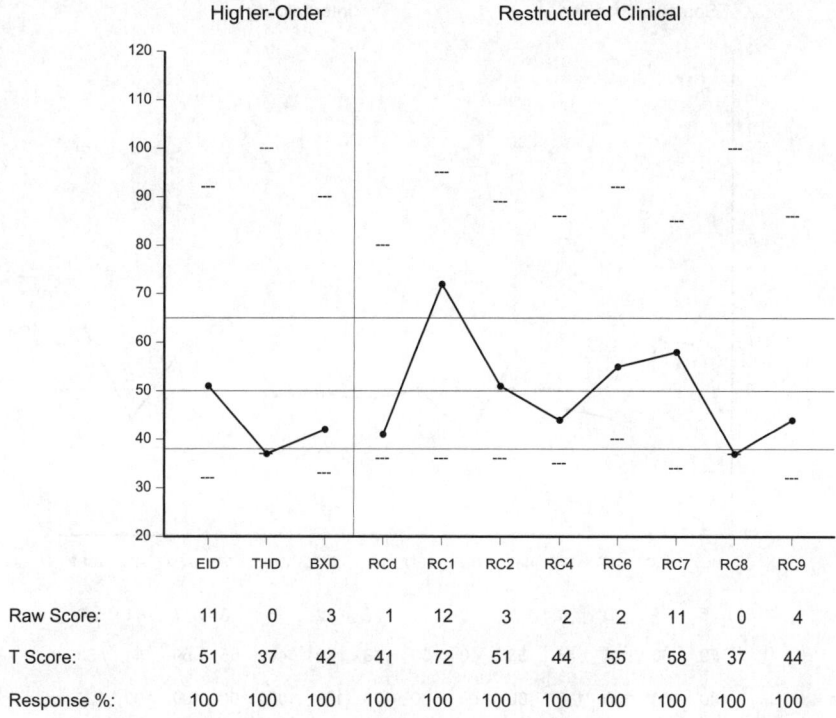

FIGURE 11.5. Ms. E's MMPI-3 Score Report, continued

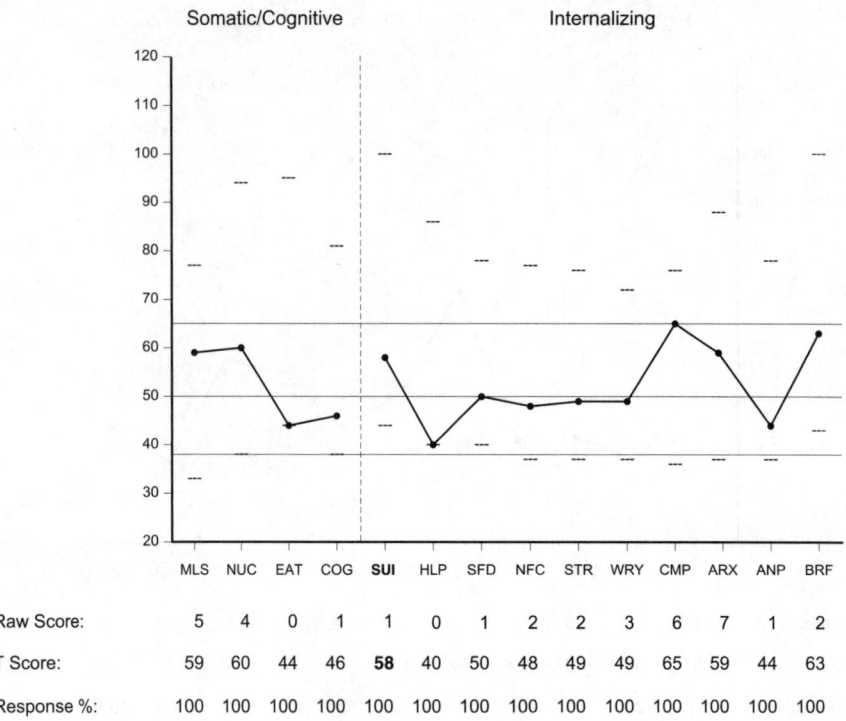

FIGURE 11.5. Ms. E's MMPI-3 Score Report, continued

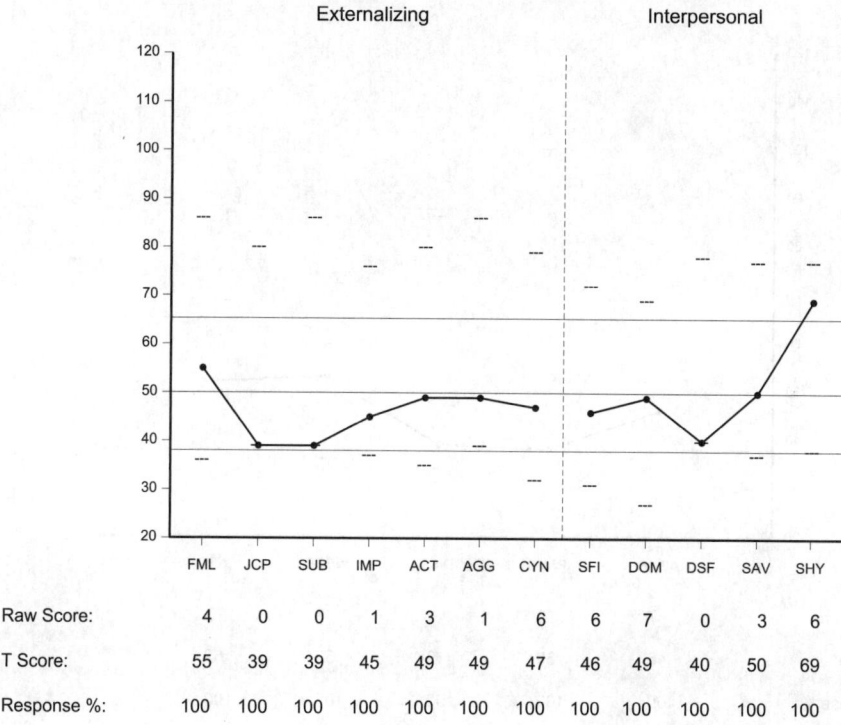

FIGURE 11.5. Ms. E's MMPI-3 Score Report, continued

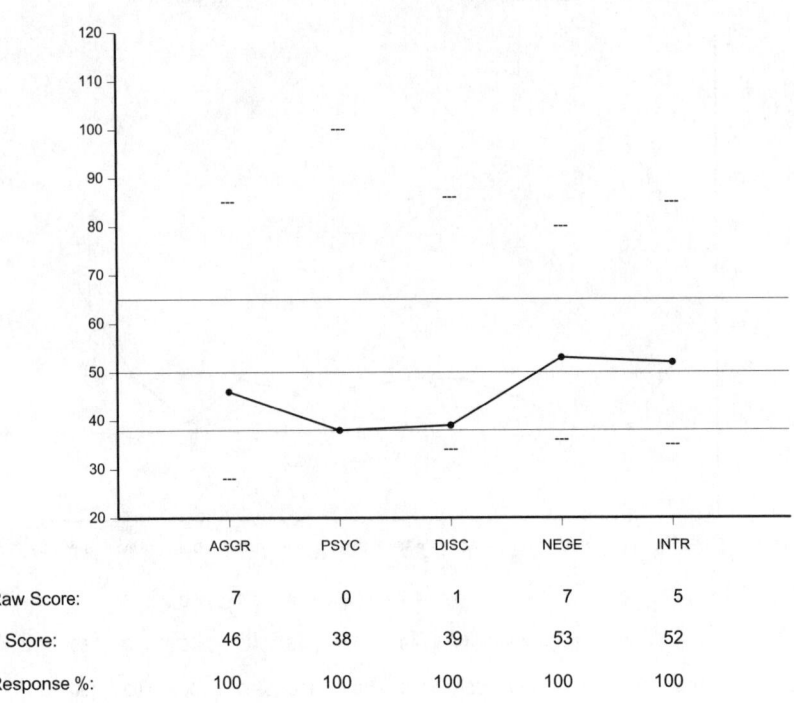

FIGURE 11.5. Ms. E's MMPI-3 Score Report, continued

MMPI-3 T SCORES (BY DOMAIN)

PROTOCOL VALIDITY

Content Non-Responsiveness

0	42	43	54 T
CNS	CRIN	VRIN	TRIN

Over-Reporting

44	50		47	73	47
F	Fp		Fs	FBS	RBS

Under-Reporting

48	50
L	K

SUBSTANTIVE SCALES

Somatic/Cognitive Dysfunction

72	59	60	44	46
RC1	MLS	NUC	EAT	COG

Emotional Dysfunction

51					
EID					

41	58	40	50	48
RCd	SUI	HLP	SFD	NFC

51	52
RC2	INTR

58	49	49	65	59	44	63	53
RC7	STR	WRY	CMP	ARX	ANP	BRF	NEGE

Thought Dysfunction

37
THD

55
RC6

37
RC8

38
PSYC

Behavioral Dysfunction

42
BXD

44	55	39	39
RC4	FML	JCP	SUB

44	45	49	49	47
RC9	IMP	ACT	AGG	CYN

39
DISC

Interpersonal Functioning

46	49	46	40	50	69
SFI	DOM	AGGR	DSF	SAV	SHY

Note. This information is provided to facilitate interpretation following the recommended structure for MMPI-3 interpretation in Chapter 5 of the *MMPI-3 Manual for Administration, Scoring, and Interpretation*, which provides details in the text and an outline in Table 5-1.

FIGURE 11.5. Ms. E's MMPI-3 Score Report, continued

ITEM-LEVEL INFORMATION

Unscorable Responses

The test taker produced scorable responses to all the MMPI-3 items.

Critical Responses

Seven MMPI-3 scales—Suicidal/Death Ideation (SUI), Helplessness/Hopelessness (HLP), Anxiety-Related Experiences (ARX), Ideas of Persecution (RC6), Aberrant Experiences (RC8), Substance Abuse (SUB), and Aggression (AGG)—have been designated by the test authors as having critical item content that may require immediate attention and follow-up. Items answered by the individual in the keyed direction (True or False) on a critical scale are listed below if her T score on that scale is 65 or higher. However, any item answered in the keyed direction on SUI is listed. The percentage of the MMPI-3 normative sample that answered each item in the keyed direction is provided in parentheses following the item content.

Suicidal/Death Ideation (SUI, T Score = 58)
  Item number and content omitted. (True, 4.1%)

End of Report

FIGURE 11.5. Ms. E's MMPI-3 Score Report, continued

Several areas of concern can also be identified. Foremost among these is Ms. E's response in the keyed direction to an item on the SUI scale, which required a follow-up suicide risk assessment that did not point to current risk for self-harm. Her most prominent MMPI-3 elevation was on the Somatic Complaints (RC1) scale. An examination of the 12 items Ms. E answered in the keyed direction on this scale (details omitted for the purpose of protecting test security) indicates that her elevated score on this scale cannot be attributed to physical health experiences related to the medical morbidities described earlier. Tarescavage, Wygant, Boutacoff, and Ben-Porath (2013) reported that higher RC1 scores among bariatric surgery candidates are associated with limited insight at the time of their evaluation. Marek, Ben-Porath, Merrell, Ashton, and Heinberg (2014) found that higher presurgical RC1 scores were associated with greater reporting of dehydration, vomiting, nausea, and pain at 1 and 3 months following surgery. Ms. E's clinical elevated score on the Compulsivity (CMP) scale indicates that her increased handwashing (described earlier), which she attributed to the Covid-19 pandemic, may reflect a pattern of compulsive behavior that could present challenges following surgery. Finally, her elevated Shyness (SHY) scale score indicates that Ms. E may have difficulty seeking social support postsurgery.

Ms. E was referred to a therapist to address a possible somatic symptoms disorder and a disorder marked by compulsive behavior, to improve stress management, and to address concerns related to social anxiety. She agreed to return to clinic after 3 months, at which time her functioning in these areas of concern would be further assessed.

MR. F: A SPINAL CORD STIMULATOR CANDIDATE

Mr. F is a 52-year-old man seen for presurgical psychological evaluation for a spinal cord stimulator. He had had two previous spine surgeries: a microdiscectomy 2 years earlier, then a fusion at vertebrae L2-L5 one year earlier. Neither surgery provided lasting pain relief. Mr. F reported being unable to stand for more than 10 minutes, being unable to walk more than 40 yards, and having to sleep in a recliner chair. Mr. F also indicated that because of his chronic pain, he was unable to work at his job as a mechanic and he was receiving workers compensation benefits. He was prescribed opiate-based pain medication.

Mr. F had undergone a spinal cord stimulator trial prior to the present presurgical psychological evaluation. He indicated experiencing about 50% reduction in pain during this trial. He was ambivalent about the permanent implant because of the variability in the effectiveness of the trial stimulator. He also reported experiencing some significant stress and distress related to his wife's medical problems.

MMPI-3 Interpretation

Mr. F's MMPI-3 results can be found in Figure 11.6. He produced a valid MMPI-3 protocol. There are no problems with unscorable items. Mr. F responded to the items relevantly based on their content, and there are no indications of overreporting or underreporting. His scores on the MMPI-3 Substantive Scales would be expected to provide an accurate picture of his psychological functioning.

Mr. F reports experiencing poor health and feeling weak or tired. He is likely preoccupied with poor health and complains of sleep disturbance, fatigue, low energy, and sexual dysfunction. Mr. F reports feeling helpless and/or hopeless and pessimistic. He likely feels overwhelmed, and that life is a strain, believes he cannot be helped and gets a raw deal from life, and lacks motivation for change. His responses indicate a higher-than-average level of behavioral constraint. He is unlikely to engage in externalizing, acting-out behavior. He reports a below average level of past antisocial behavior. In addition, he describes others as well-intentioned and trustworthy and disavows cynical beliefs about them. He is possibly overly trusting.

Diagnostically, Mr. F's MMPI-3 results indicate the need to evaluate him further for a possible somatic symptom disorder if physical origins for his malaise-related complaints can be ruled out. Treatment considerations include the need to further evaluate the origin of his malaise-related complaints, concern that his level of malaise could impeded his willingness to engage in treatment, and loss of hope and feelings of despair as early targets for intervention.

Discussion

Mr. F's open and cooperative approach to the assessment, as reflected in his MMPI-3 validity scale scores can be viewed as a positive finding of his presurgical evaluation. The absence of severe psychopathology is also a positive indicator.

The primary area of concern identified in Mr. F's MMPI-3 findings is related to his elevated MLS scale score. Examination of Figure 11.6, which includes comparison group data for spine surgery candidates, indicates that Mr. F's MLS score falls at the 95th percentile for this population. MLS elevations have consistently been identified among the strongest predictors of negative outcomes in spine surgery and spinal cord stimulator candidates. Block, Ben-Porath, and Marek (2012) reported that elevated MLS scores were associated with reports of pain-related disability and difficulties coping with stress, and of particular concern, opioid medication misuse in individuals assessed presurgically. Block, Marek, Ben-Porath, and Kukal (2017) found higher presurgical MLS scores to be associated with poorer outcome and greater dysfunction several months postimplant. Block, Marek, Ben-Porath, and Ohnmeiss (2014) found elevated

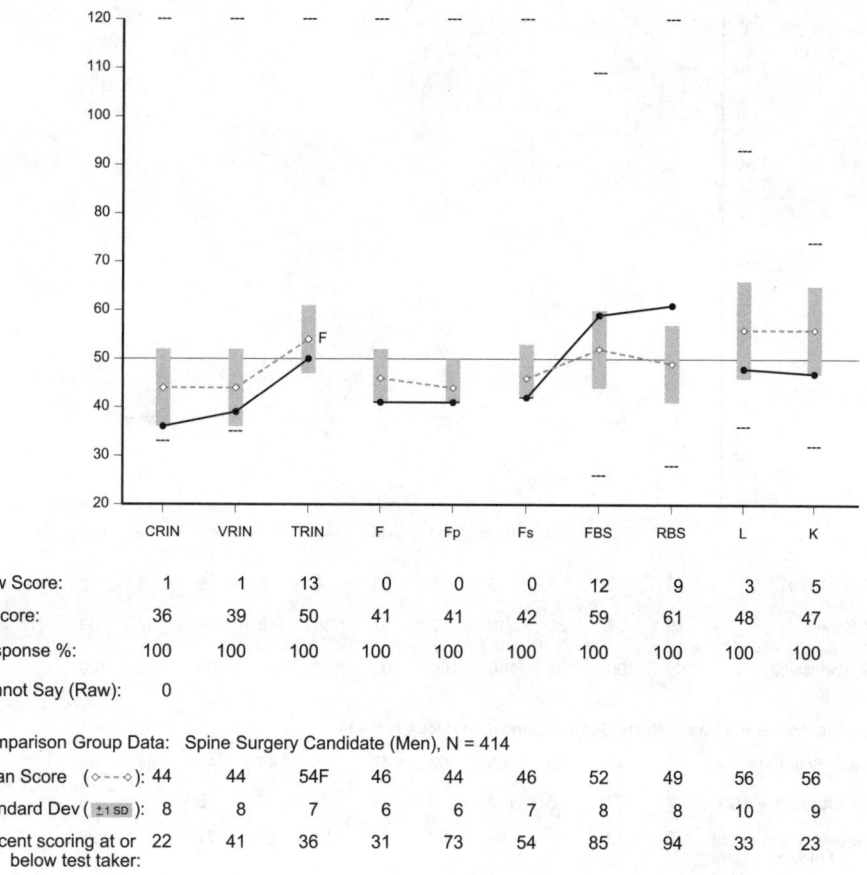

FIGURE 11.6. Mr. F's MMPI-3 Score Report

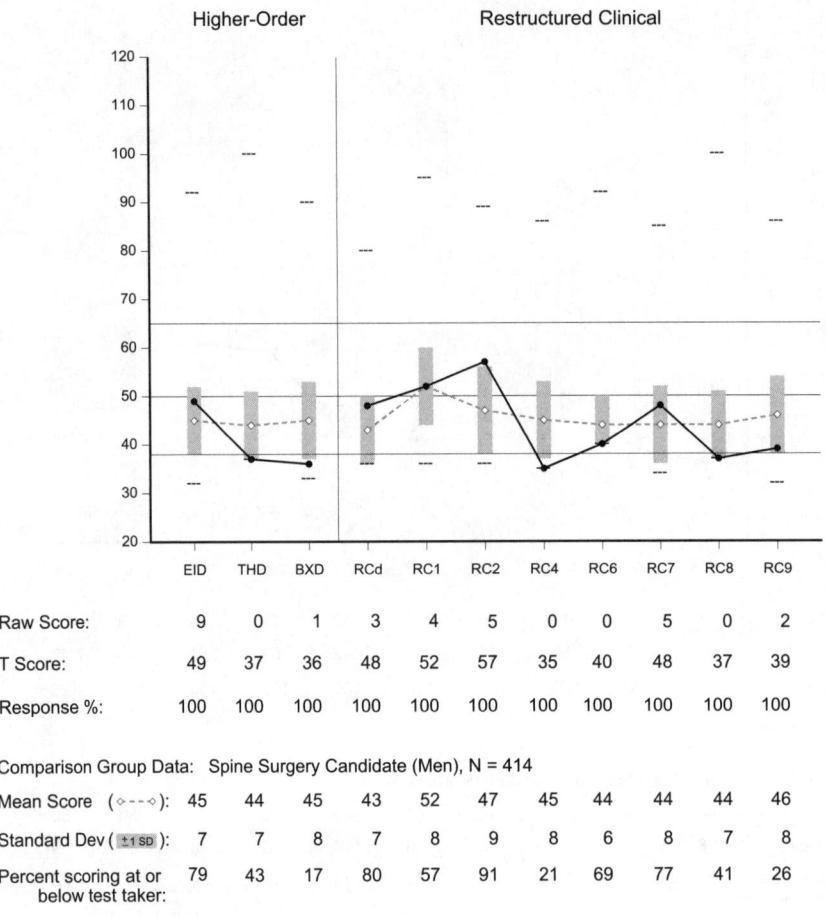

FIGURE 11.6. Mr. F's MMPI-3 Score Report, continued

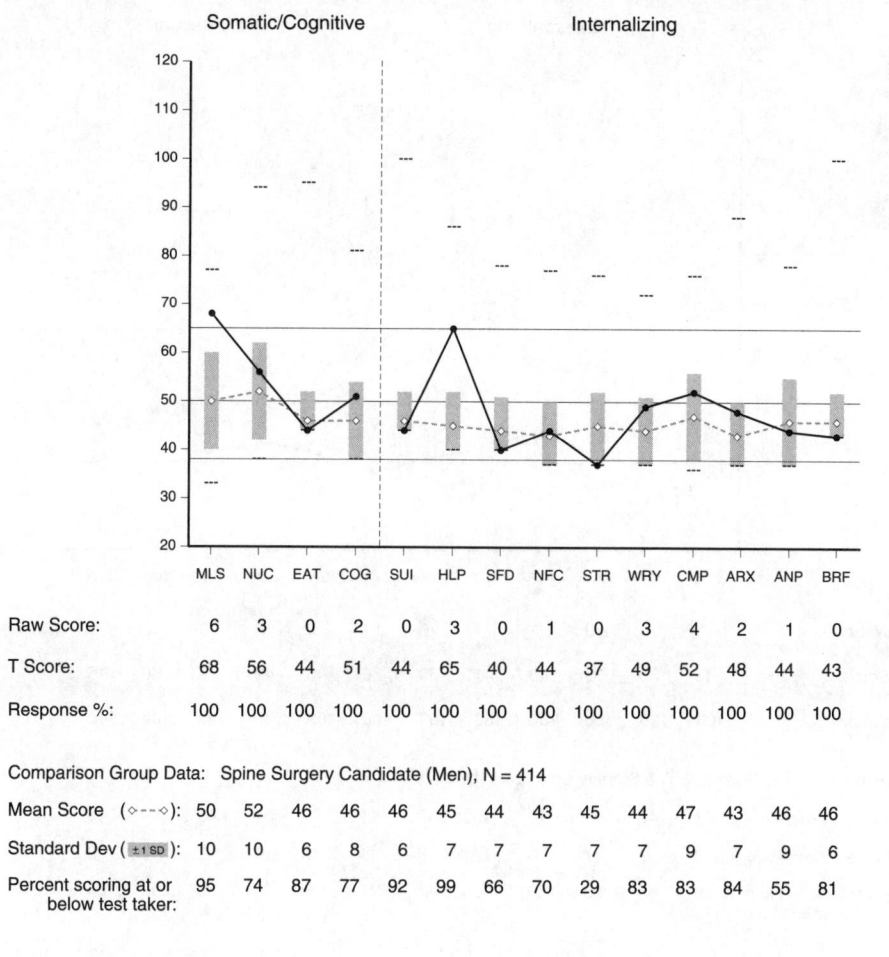

FIGURE 11.6. Mr. F's MMPI-3 Score Report, continued

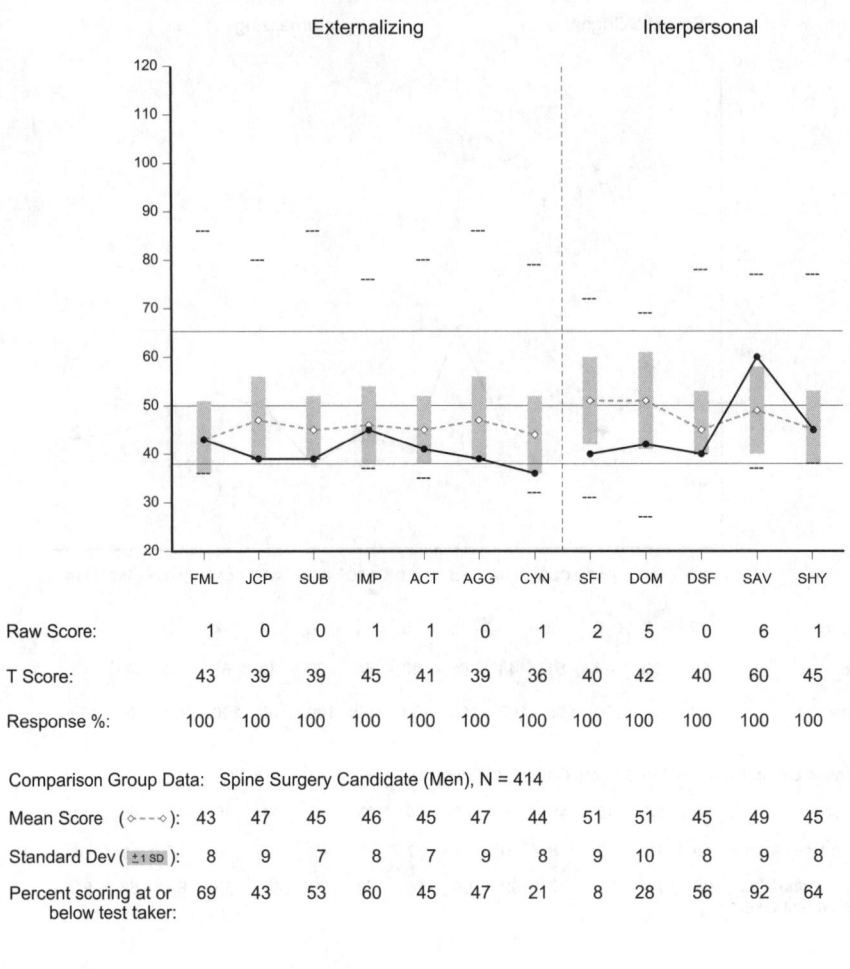

FIGURE 11.6. Mr. F's MMPI-3 Score Report, continued

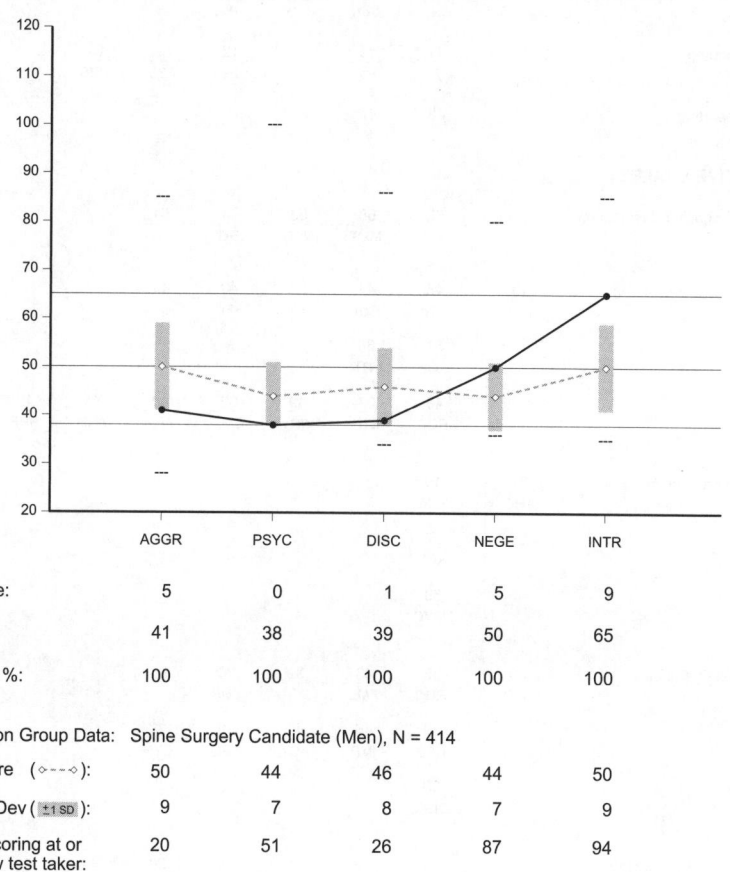

FIGURE 11.6. Mr. F's MMPI-3 Score Report, continued

MMPI-3 T SCORES (BY DOMAIN)

PROTOCOL VALIDITY

Content Non-Responsiveness

0	36	39	50
CNS	CRIN	VRIN	TRIN

Over-Reporting

41	41		42	59	61
F	Fp		Fs	FBS	RBS

Under-Reporting

48	47
L	K

SUBSTANTIVE SCALES

Somatic/Cognitive Dysfunction

52	68	56	44	51
RC1	MLS	NUC	EAT	COG

Emotional Dysfunction

49							
EID							

48	44	65	40	44
RCd	SUI	HLP	SFD	NFC

57	65
RC2	INTR

48	37	49	52	48	44	43	50
RC7	STR	WRY	CMP	ARX	ANP	BRF	NEGE

Thought Dysfunction

37
THD

40
RC6

37
RC8

38
PSYC

Behavioral Dysfunction

36
BXD

35	43	39	39
RC4	FML	JCP	SUB

39	45	41	39	36
RC9	IMP	ACT	AGG	CYN

39
DISC

Interpersonal Functioning

40	42	41	40	60	45
SFI	DOM	AGGR	DSF	SAV	SHY

Note. This information is provided to facilitate interpretation following the recommended structure for MMPI-3 interpretation in Chapter 5 of the *MMPI-3 Manual for Administration, Scoring, and Interpretation*, which provides details in the text and an outline in Table 5-1.

FIGURE 11.6. Mr. F's MMPI-3 Score Report, continued

ITEM-LEVEL INFORMATION

Unscorable Responses

The test taker produced scorable responses to all the MMPI-3 items.

Critical Responses

Seven MMPI-3 scales—Suicidal/Death Ideation (SUI), Helplessness/Hopelessness (HLP), Anxiety-Related Experiences (ARX), Ideas of Persecution (RC6), Aberrant Experiences (RC8), Substance Abuse (SUB), and Aggression (AGG)—have been designated by the test authors as having critical item content that may require immediate attention and follow-up. Items answered by the individual in the keyed direction (True or False) on a critical scale are listed below if his T score on that scale is 65 or higher. However, any item answered in the keyed direction on SUI is listed. The percentage of the MMPI-3 normative sample (NS) and of the Spine Surgery Candidate (Men) Comparison Group (CG) that answered each item in the keyed direction are provided in parentheses following the item content.

Helplessness/Hopelessness (HLP, T Score = 65)
    Item number and content omitted. (True; NS 10.9%, CG 3.4%)
    Item number and content omitted. (True; NS 45.4%, CG 28.5%)
    Item number and content omitted. (False; NS 22.0%, CG 10.4%)

End of Report

FIGURE 11.6. Mr. F's MMPI-3 Score Report, continued

MLS scores to be predictive of poorer response to spine surgery above and beyond receipt of workers compensation benefits. Mr. F's clinically elevated HLP scale score raises concerns related to his motivation for change.

Based on the diagnostic interview and the MMPI-3 findings, as well as Mr. F's stress level and ambivalence about the stimulator, the evaluator opined that his overall level of psychosocial risk was moderate to high. The surgeon went ahead with the permanent implant; however, despite working with the manufacturer's representative to obtain a stimulation pattern sufficient for pain control, Mr. F never felt satisfactory results were achieved, and the stimulator was eventually explanted.

MS. G: PSYCHOLOGICAL SEQUELA OF HEAD TRAUMA

Ms. G is a 29-year-old woman who was referred for a neuropsychological disability evaluation following a mild traumatic brain injury sustained a year prior.[3] Ms. G had slipped and fallen in her kitchen at night and hit her head on the tiled floor. She did not lose consciousness but recalled intense head pain as her head hit the floor. She went to sleep following the fall and went to work the next day. She felt unwell, however, and her colleagues encouraged her to leave as she was slurring her words, was unable to speak correctly, and made simple errors during routine tasks. She took a few days off, slept for most of the time, and went to her general practitioner 3 days after the accident. Her general practitioner ordered her off work for several weeks, then she gradually returned. Since the injury, Ms. G has experienced ongoing concerns with fatigue, headaches, irritability, tearfulness, and a range of cognitive symptoms, including memory problems, "slowed" thinking, distractibility, concentration problems, word-finding difficulties, and frequent annoying mistakes in usual tasks, which increase her distress. Her anxiety has remained high postinjury, and her mood has been low. Ms. G has also undergone a range of rehabilitation efforts, including vestibular rehabilitation and physical rehabilitation to improve exercise tolerance, and she has been prescribed medication for headaches. At the time of the evaluation, Ms. G was on a "stay at work plan" with a gradual return to full work hours over the next 6 months.

In terms of psychosocial background history, Ms. G's parents both drank heavily throughout her life. She witnessed intimate partner violence between them while growing up, and her parents eventually separated acrimoniously when she was still young. Her stepfather was also a heavy drinker and was sexually abusive toward her. She became very attached to a relative who lived nearby, as this became a place of safety for her. Ms. G was academically gifted and eventually obtained a law degree. She reported a good relationship with her current romantic partner; although, they had only been together for a few months prior to her injury, which she feels has affected the relationship somewhat. Ms. G reported a history of low mood and high anxiety through adolescence, and then again in her early twenties during and after a verbally and physically abusive romantic relationship.

Ms. G was administered the MMPI-3 as part of the neuropsychological evaluation to assess her psychological functioning. She passed performance validity tests and scored in the high average range of intelligence as well as in all other areas of cognitive functioning. There were no marked strengths or weaknesses identified in cognitive testing.

MMPI-3 Interpretation

Ms. G responded to all of the MMPI-3 items (Figure 11.7).[4] There are no concerns about inconsistent responding. However, possible overreporting of psychological dysfunction and somatic symptoms is indicated by a larger than average number of infrequent responses and in the assertion of a much larger than average number of somatic symptoms rarely described by individuals with genuine medical problems. Ms. G also provided an unusual combination of responses that is associated with noncredible reporting of somatic and/or cognitive symptoms. Although these concerns are noted, genuine psychopathology can also elevate these scales. There is no evidence of underreporting. Overall, with caution, her profile is deemed valid for clinical interpretation.

Ms. G's responses indicate significant emotional distress. She reports being sad and unhappy, as well as being dissatisfied with life. She is likely to complain about feeling depressed. She reports a history of suicidal ideation and/or past suicide attempts, may be preoccupied with suicide and death, and may be at risk for self-harm. Her critical responses indicate explicit thoughts about how to die by suicide and having secretly attempted suicide in the past. She also reports feeling helpless and/or hopeless and pessimistic, likely feels overwhelmed and that life is a strain. She likely also believes that she cannot be helped and that she gets a raw deal from life. She may have little motivation to change. Ms. G further reports lacking confidence, feeling worthless, and believing she is a burden to others. She likely feels inferior and insecure, is self-disparaging, intropunitive, and tends to present with lack of confidence and feelings of uselessness. In addition, Ms. G reports a lack of positive emotional experiences, significant anhedonia, and a lack of interest in various activities. She is likely pessimistic, lacking in energy, introverted, and generally disengaged; she might have a dispositional proclivity toward anhedonia and social disengagement. Ms. G further reports being prone to negative emotional experiences, including multiple anxiety-related experiences, such as generalized anxiety, reexperiencing, and/or panic symptoms. She is likely to experience intrusive ideation, sleep difficulties, and possible posttraumatic distress. She might be stress-reactive, engage in excessive rumination, and be self-critical and guilt-prone. She may be inhibited behaviorally because of negative emotions.

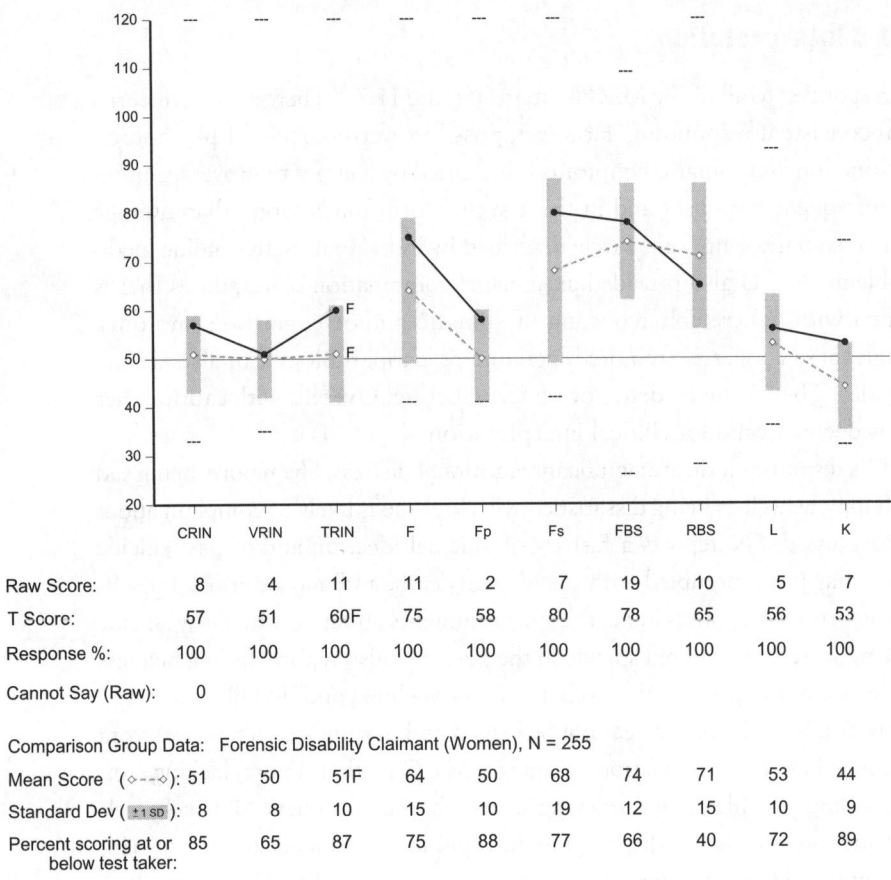

FIGURE 11.7. Ms. G's MMPI-3 Score Report

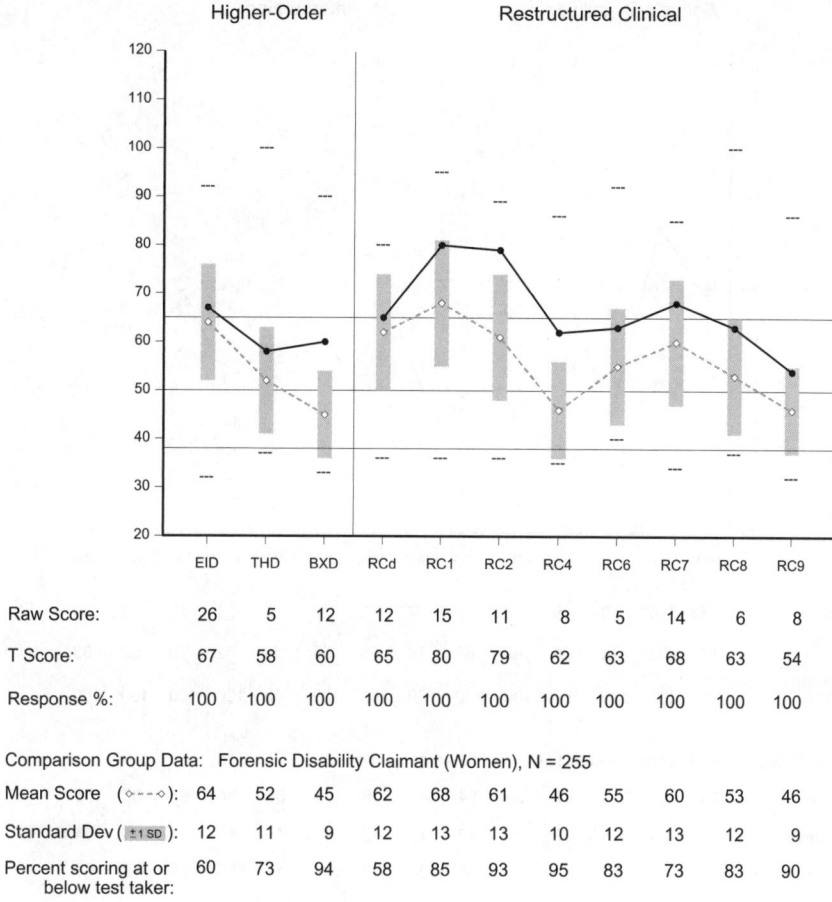

FIGURE 11.7. Ms. G's MMPI-3 Score Report, continued

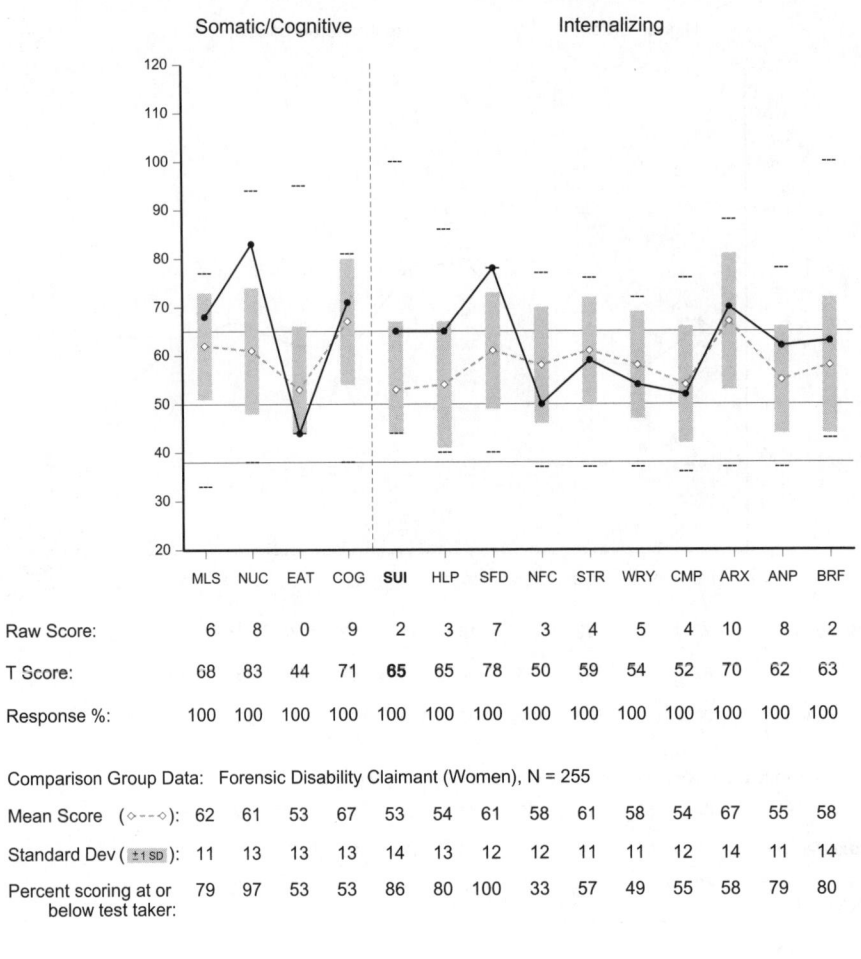

FIGURE 11.7. Ms. G's MMPI-3 Score Report, continued

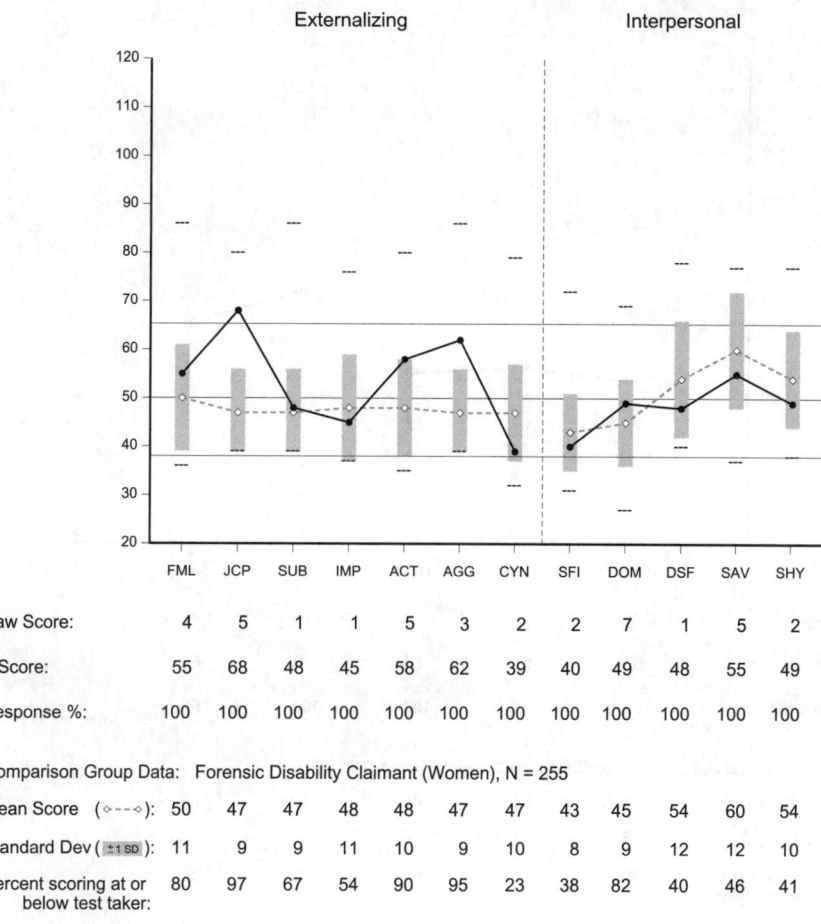

FIGURE 11.7. Ms. G's MMPI-3 Score Report, continued

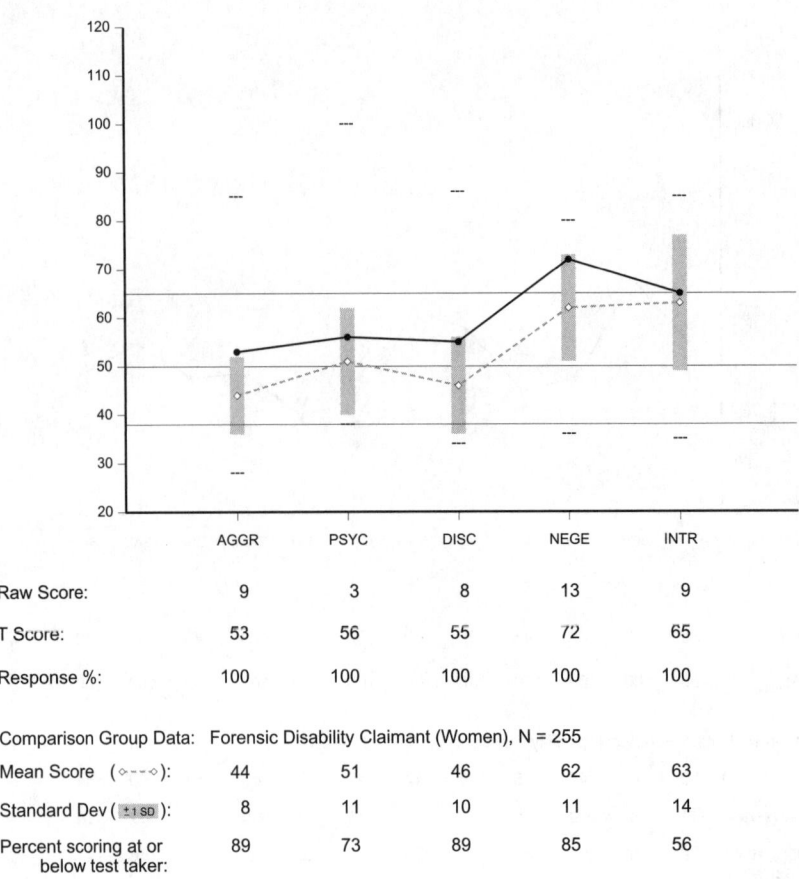

FIGURE 11.7. Ms. G's MMPI-3 Score Report, continued

MMPI-3 T SCORES (BY DOMAIN)

PROTOCOL VALIDITY

Content Non-Responsiveness

0	57	51	60 F
CNS	CRIN	VRIN	TRIN

Over-Reporting

75	58		80	78	65
F	Fp		Fs	FBS	RBS

Under-Reporting

56	53
L	K

SUBSTANTIVE SCALES

Somatic/Cognitive Dysfunction

80	68	83	44	71
RC1	MLS	NUC	EAT	COG

Emotional Dysfunction

67
EID

65	65	65	78	50
RCd	SUI	HLP	SFD	NFC

79	65
RC2	INTR

68	59	54	52	70	62	63	72
RC7	STR	WRY	CMP	ARX	ANP	BRF	NEGE

Thought Dysfunction

58
THD

63
RC6

63
RC8

56
PSYC

Behavioral Dysfunction

60
BXD

62	55	68	48
RC4	FML	JCP	SUB

54	45	58	62	39
RC9	IMP	ACT	AGG	CYN

55
DISC

Interpersonal Functioning

40	49	53	48	55	49
SFI	DOM	AGGR	DSF	SAV	SHY

Note. This information is provided to facilitate interpretation following the recommended structure for MMPI-3 interpretation in Chapter 5 of the *MMPI-3 Manual for Administration, Scoring, and Interpretation,* which provides details in the text and an outline in Table 5-1.

FIGURE 11.7. Ms. G's MMPI-3 Score Report, continued

ITEM-LEVEL INFORMATION

Unscorable Responses

The test taker produced scorable responses to all the MMPI-3 items.

Critical Responses

Seven MMPI-3 scales—Suicidal/Death Ideation (SUI), Helplessness/Hopelessness (HLP), Anxiety-Related Experiences (ARX), Ideas of Persecution (RC6), Aberrant Experiences (RC8), Substance Abuse (SUB), and Aggression (AGG)—have been designated by the test authors as having critical item content that may require immediate attention and follow-up. Items answered by the individual in the keyed direction (True or False) on a critical scale are listed below if her T score on that scale is 65 or higher. However, any item answered in the keyed direction on SUI is listed. The percentage of the MMPI-3 normative sample (NS) and of the Forensic Disability Claimant (Women) Comparison Group (CG) that answered each item in the keyed direction are provided in parentheses following the item content.

Suicidal/Death Ideation (SUI, T Score = 65)

    Item number and content omitted. (True; NS 22.2%, CG 29.4%)
    Item number and content omitted. (True; NS 10.1%, CG 10.2%)

Helplessness/Hopelessness (HLP, T Score = 65)

    Item number and content omitted. (True; NS 45.4%, CG 36.9%)
    Item number and content omitted. (False; NS 22.0%, CG 36.5%)
    Item number and content omitted. (True; NS 8.4%, CG 21.2%)

Anxiety-Related Experiences (ARX, T Score = 70)

    Item number and content omitted. (True; NS 31.2%, CG 78.8%)
    Item number and content omitted. (True; NS 31.4%, CG 58.8%)
    Item number and content omitted. (True; NS 4.7%, CG 30.6%)
    Item number and content omitted. (True; NS 27.3%, CG 62.4%)
    Item number and content omitted. (True; NS 28.6%, CG 69.8%)
    Item number and content omitted. (True; NS 26.0%, CG 74.1%)
    Item number and content omitted. (True; NS 41.7%, CG 71.8%)
    Item number and content omitted. (True; NS 14.9%, CG 54.5%)
    Item number and content omitted. (True; NS 8.6%, CG 39.6%)
    Item number and content omitted. (True; NS 39.8%, CG 72.9%)

End of Report

FIGURE 11.7. Ms. G's MMPI-3 Score Report, continued

Ms. G reports a diffuse pattern of somatic complaints involving different bodily systems that probably include head pain and neurological and gastrointestinal symptoms. She is likely preoccupied with poor health and various physical health concerns, which likely have a psychological component. She may be prone to developing physical symptoms in response to stress. She tends to perceive her physical problems as life-interfering. Ms. G further reports experiencing poor health and feeling weak or tired. She is likely to complain about fatigue, sleep problems, low energy, and sexual dysfunction. She also reports vague neurological complaints, and is likely to present with dizziness, coordination difficulties, and sensory problems. She reports a diffuse pattern of cognitive difficulties and likely complains about attention, concentration, and memory problems.

Ms. G also reports a history of juvenile conduct problems and may have a history of juvenile delinquency and criminal or antisocial behavior. She may experience conflictual interpersonal relationships and have difficulties with people in authority positions.

Ms. G's MMPI-3 results identify several possible diagnostic considerations. She should be evaluated for an internalizing disorder, including depressive disorders, anxiety disorders, and trauma-related disorders. Ms. G should also be evaluated for a somatic symptom disorder if a physical explanation for her symptom presentation can be ruled out. She should also be evaluated for disorders affecting attention and memory.

Discussion

A critical question when considering Ms. G's MMPI-3 results relates to the implications of her validity scale scores. Three scales (F, Fs, and FBS) are at a level that triggers interpretations about possible overreporting of psychopathology and somatic and cognitive complaints. In a disability case such as this, where a significant financial incentive to overreport exists, the possibility of malingering is raised. As mentioned earlier, however, Ms. G did have long-standing difficulties with depressed mood and anxiety, which she reported were intensified by her accident, and there are no other indicators of overreporting (she passed performance validity tests).

In this case, it can be particularly helpful to also consider the forensic, disability claimant comparison group. Indeed, Ms. G scored comparably to women in this setting, as she is within one standard deviation from the mean of this group on F, Fs, and RBS. Also, 75%, 77%, and 66% of comparison group members obtained the same or lower scores as Ms. G on these respective scales. Moreover, available MMPI-2-RF research has indicated that individuals with somatic symptom disorders tend to score at these levels on these scales (Sellbom, Wygant, & Bagby, 2012), with somatic overreporters typically obtaining substantially higher scores. Therefore, all things considered, Ms. G's MMPI-3 Validity Scales profile is not considered indicative of overreporting but rather likely a reflection of genuine psychopathology.

Ms. G's scores on the MMPI-3 Substantive Scales are quite helpful in understanding her presentation. Although there is no objective evidence for actual cognitive dysfunction associated with her head injury, the MMPI-3 results point to prominent internalizing and psychosomatic difficulties. Her NUC, RC2, and SFD scores in particular were higher than typical for women in the forensic, disability claimant comparison group. Indeed, in the case of Ms. G, her injury was a significant destabilizer for her mental health, as it triggered automatic core beliefs about her vulnerability. She became hyperattentive to physical symptoms, which in turn perpetuated and intensified previous low mood and anxiety symptoms. Thus, her injury had a more substantial functional impact than reasonably anticipated, but given its significant psychological component, long-term changes to cognitive functioning were ultimately deemed less likely. Ms. G was referred for psychotherapy for treatment of her underlying emotional disorder.

MS. H: PERSONALITY DISORDER OR COMPLEX PTSD?

Ms. H is a 38-year-old woman referred by an insurance agency for a mental injury disability evaluation. Her primary and undisputed complaint was that she had experienced chronic recurrent sexual abuse as a child and adolescent. Indeed, sexual abuse had been perpetrated by several family members, including her grandfather, adoptive father, and sister's boyfriend when Ms. H was between ages 4 and 15. She also reported multiple instances of inappropriate sexual behavior with same-aged relatives (including her half-brother) and that she had been sexually assaulted by most romantic partners in adulthood.

Ms. H had a history of complex trauma. In addition to sexual abuse, she also reported, and records verified, multiple instances of physical and emotional abuse as well as neglect. For instance, her stepmother called her a liar and physically punished her after Ms. H made complaints of sexual abuse by her father and half-brother to a school counselor. Ms. H started living on the streets on and off at age 13 to escape sexual abuse perpetrated by her family members. She was adopted into a gang, formed connections with antisocial peers who influenced her to sell drugs for them, and she frequently shoplifted to feed herself. She also started smoking marijuana to numb emotions associated with her traumatic experiences. She dropped out of school around the same age. Ms. H has five children (ages 22 to 4) fathered by four different partners, including one from a one-night stand. She had received limited mental health treatment that consisted mainly of intervention for PTSD from a mental health counselor for 2 years prior to the evaluation.

The government-operated insurance agency had accepted that she met criteria for PTSD but initially denied her claim because a psychiatrist opined that her mental injury and current impairment were not connected. In other words, a personality disorder, rather than PTSD, was causing her functional impairment. Upon appeal, she saw a second psychiatrist who deemed (based on a defensive Personality Assessment Inventory [Morey, 2007] profile) that there was no evidence for personality disorder, but rather that she should be diagnosed with complex PTSD. The government-operated insurance agency therefore commissioned the current evaluation to address whether Ms. H has a personality disorder or complex PTSD, and regardless of diagnosis, the degree to which her mental disorder is linked to her functional impairment.

MMPI-3 Interpretation

Ms. H provided responses to all but five MMPI-3 items (Figure 11.8).[5] Therefore, the absence of elevation on individual scales with excessive unscorable responding cannot be interpreted. There is no evidence of content-inconsistent responding. Possible overreporting is indicated by assertion of a larger than average number of symptoms rarely described by individuals with genuine, severe psychopathology, as well as an unusual combination of responses that is associated with noncredible memory complaints. However, these scores can also be found in an individual who experiences genuine mental health problems. There is no evidence of underreporting.

Ms. H's MMPI-3 results indicate considerable externalizing, acting-out behavior that is very likely to result in marked dysfunction and to have gotten her into difficulties. She reports serious past and current antisocial behavior. She likely fails to conform to societal norms and expectations and has been involved with the criminal justice system. She may have difficulty with individuals in positions of authority and experience conflictual interpersonal relationships. She reports a history of juvenile conduct problems such as problematic behavior at school, stealing, and being arrested. She also reports significant past and current substance abuse. She is likely to have a history of problematic use of alcohol or drugs, including misuse of prescription medication, and may have had legal problems as a result of such use. She further reports engaging in problematic impulsive behavior, is likely nonplanful, and may have a history of hyperactive behavior. In addition, she reports engaging in physically aggressive, violent behavior and losing control; has a history of violent behavior toward others, is possibly abusive, and likely has anger-related problems. She also reports a pattern of disconstrained behavior, which is likely dispositional in nature, and she is also likely sensation and excitement seeking.

Ms. H reports experiencing significant demoralization, feeling overwhelmed, and being extremely unhappy, sad, and dissatisfied with her life. She likely

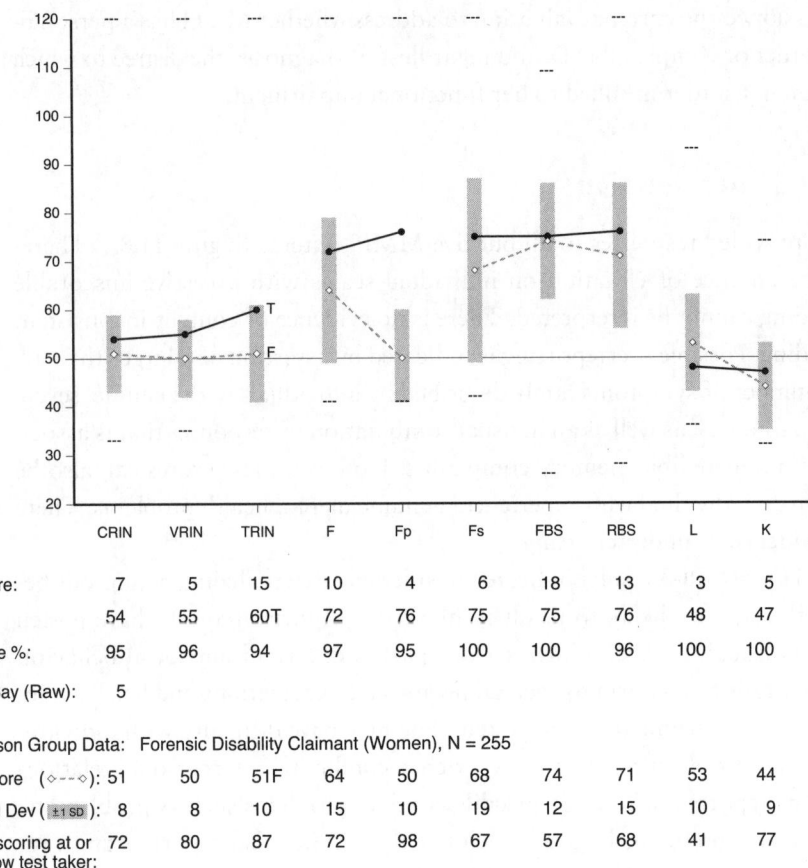

FIGURE 11.8. Ms. H's MMPI-3 Score Report

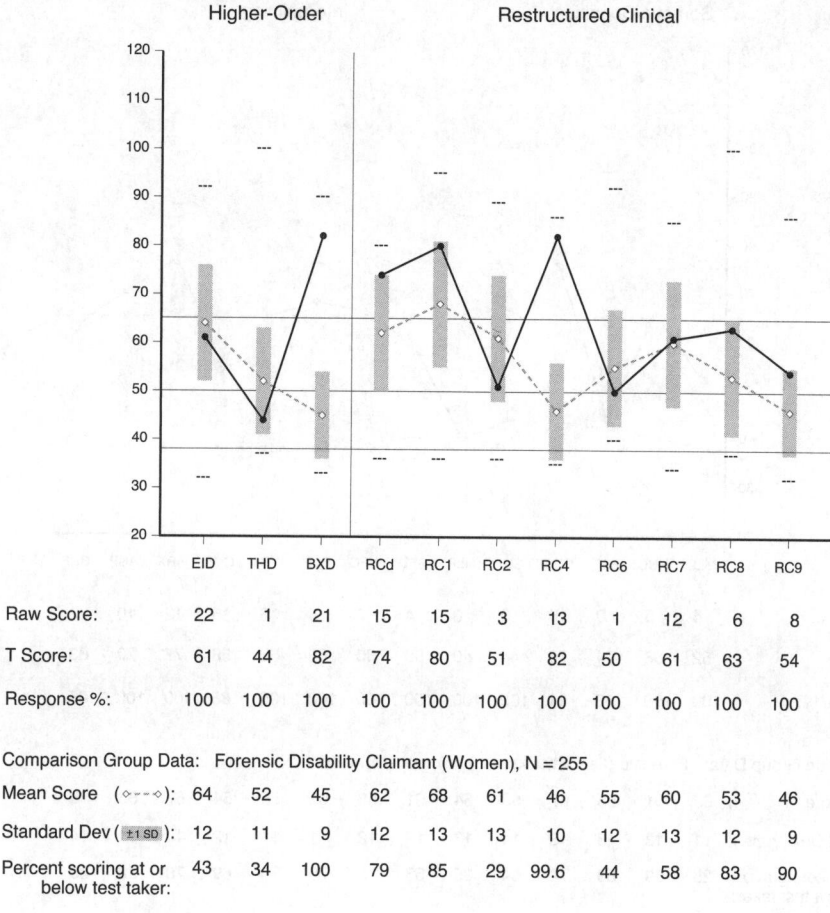

FIGURE 11.8. Ms. H's MMPI-3 Score Report, continued

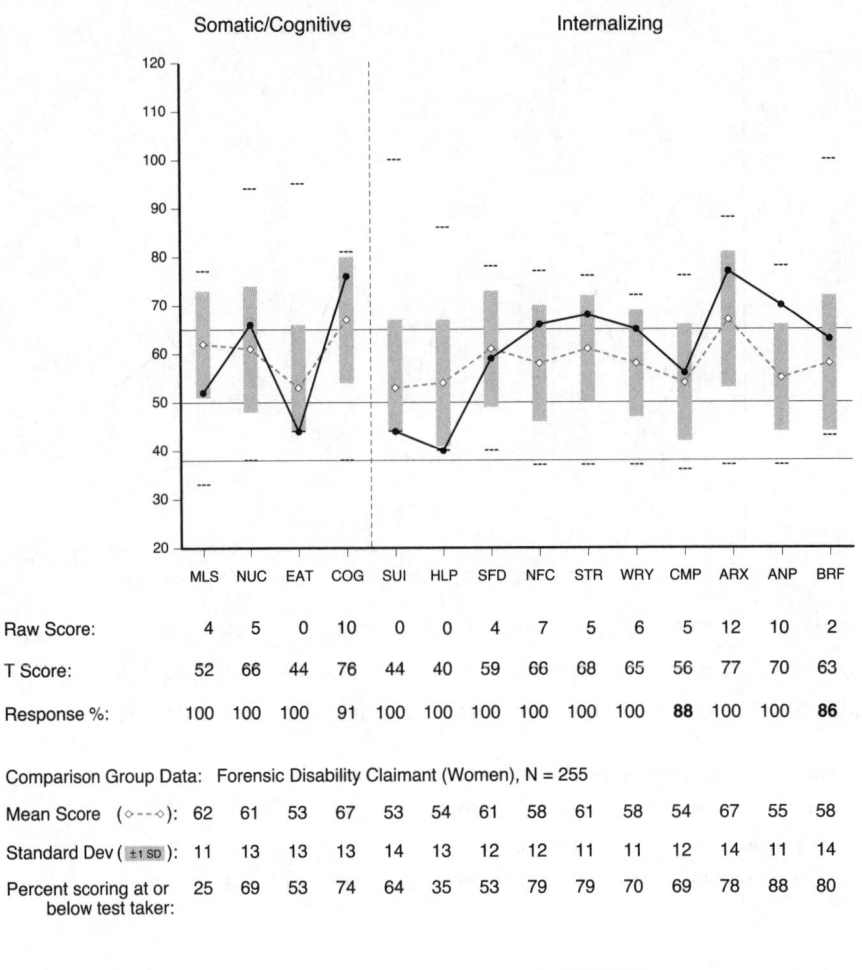

FIGURE 11.8. Ms. H's MMPI-3 Score Report, continued

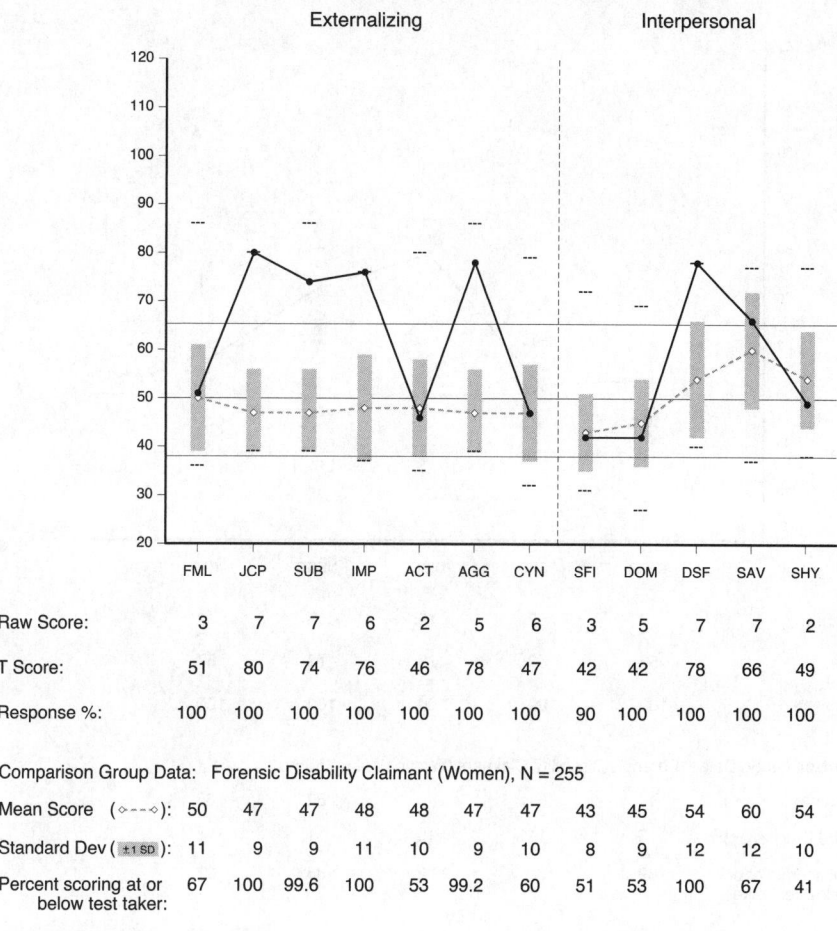

FIGURE 11.8. Ms. H's MMPI-3 Score Report, continued

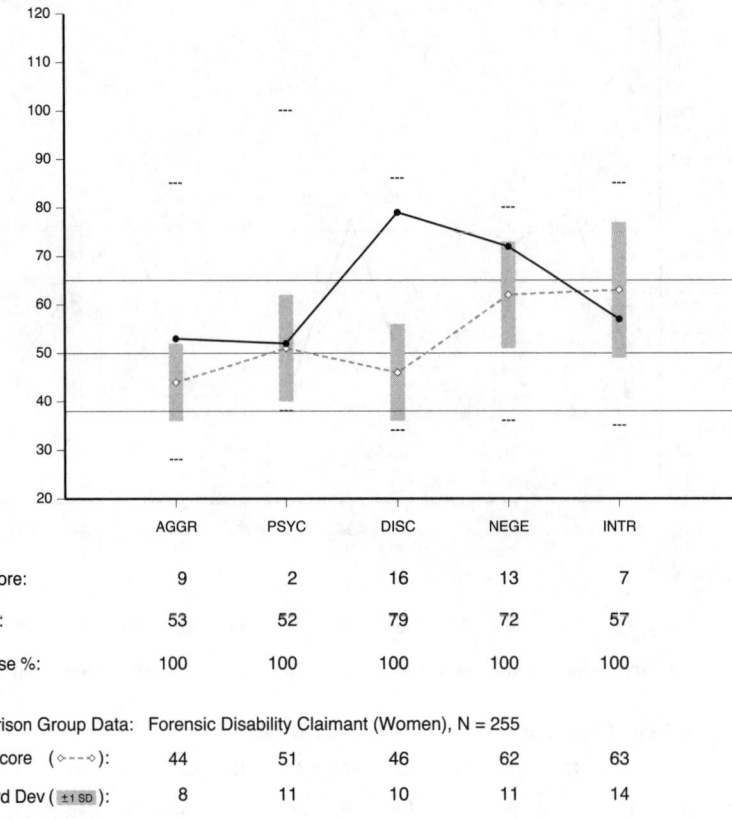

FIGURE 11.8. Ms. H's MMPI-3 Score Report, continued

MMPI®-3 Score Report
07/19/2019, Page 7
ID: Ms. H

MMPI-3 T SCORES (BY DOMAIN)

PROTOCOL VALIDITY

Content Non-Responsiveness	5	54	55	60 T
	CNS	CRIN	VRIN	TRIN

Over-Reporting	72	76		75	75	76
	F	Fp		Fs	FBS	RBS

Under-Reporting	48	47
	L	K

SUBSTANTIVE SCALES

Somatic/Cognitive Dysfunction		80	52	66	44	76
		RC1	MLS	NUC	EAT	COG

Emotional Dysfunction	61	74	44	40	59	66		
	EID	RCd	SUI	HLP	SFD	NFC		
		51	57					
		RC2	INTR					
		61	68	65	56*	77	70	63*	72
		RC7	STR	WRY	CMP	ARX	ANP	BRF	NEGE

Thought Dysfunction	44	50
	THD	RC6
		63
		RC8
		52
		PSYC

Behavioral Dysfunction	82	82	51	80	74	
	BXD	RC4	FML	JCP	SUB	
		54	76	46	78	47
		RC9	IMP	ACT	AGG	CYN
		79				
		DISC				

Interpersonal Functioning	42	42	53	78	66	49
	SFI	DOM	AGGR	DSF	SAV	SHY

*The test taker provided scorable responses to less than 90% of the items scored on this scale. See the relevant profile page for the specific percentage.

Note. This information is provided to facilitate interpretation following the recommended structure for MMPI-3 interpretation in Chapter 5 of the *MMPI-3 Manual for Administration, Scoring, and Interpretation*, which provides details in the text and an outline in Table 5-1.

FIGURE 11.8. Ms. H's MMPI-3 Score Report, continued

MMPI®-3 Score Report
07/19/2019, Page 8

ID: Ms. H

ITEM-LEVEL INFORMATION

Unscorable Responses

Following is a list of items to which the test taker did not provide scorable responses. Unanswered or double answered (both True and False) items are unscorable. The scale(s) on which the items appear are in parentheses following the item content.

   Item number and content omitted. (TRIN, F, RBS, COG)
   Item number and content omitted. (VRIN, CMP)
   Item number and content omitted. (VRIN, TRIN, SFI)
   Item number and content omitted. (Fp)
   Item number and content omitted. (BRF)

Critical Responses

Seven MMPI-3 scales—Suicidal/Death Ideation (SUI), Helplessness/Hopelessness (HLP), Anxiety-Related Experiences (ARX), Ideas of Persecution (RC6), Aberrant Experiences (RC8), Substance Abuse (SUB), and Aggression (AGG)—have been designated by the test authors as having critical item content that may require immediate attention and follow-up. Items answered by the individual in the keyed direction (True or False) on a critical scale are listed below if her T score on that scale is 65 or higher. However, any item answered in the keyed direction on SUI is listed. The percentage of the MMPI-3 normative sample (NS) and of the Forensic Disability Claimant (Women) Comparison Group (CG) that answered each item in the keyed direction are provided in parentheses following the item content.

Anxiety-Related Experiences (ARX, T Score = 77)

   Item number and content omitted. (True; NS 31.2%, CG 78.8%)
   Item number and content omitted. (True; NS 31.4%, CG 58.8%)
   Item number and content omitted. (True; NS 16.9%, CG 52.5%)
   Item number and content omitted. (True; NS 10.9%, CG 54.9%)
   Item number and content omitted. (True; NS 4.7%, CG 30.6%)
   Item number and content omitted. (True; NS 27.3%, CG 62.4%)
   Item number and content omitted. (True; NS 28.6%, CG 69.8%)
   Item number and content omitted. (True; NS 26.0%, CG 74.1%)
   Item number and content omitted. (True; NS 41.7%, CG 71.8%)
   Item number and content omitted. (True; NS 35.8%, CG 67.5%)
   Item number and content omitted. (True; NS 39.8%, CG 72.9%)
   Item number and content omitted. (True; NS 15.2%, CG 48.6%)

Substance Abuse (SUB, T Score = 74)

   Item number and content omitted. (True; NS 21.7%, CG 14.5%)
   Item number and content omitted. (True; NS 43.0%, CG 27.1%)
   Item number and content omitted. (True; NS 38.2%, CG 27.5%)
   Item number and content omitted. (True; NS 15.0%, CG 12.2%)
   Item number and content omitted. (True; NS 8.1%, CG 5.9%)
   Item number and content omitted. (True; NS 18.7%, CG 13.7%)
   Item number and content omitted. (True; NS 6.7%, CG 2.4%)

Aggression (AGG, T Score = 78)

   Item number and content omitted. (True; NS 28.8%, CG 33.7%)
   Item number and content omitted. (True; NS 13.3%, CG 11.8%)
   Item number and content omitted. (True; NS 9.4%, CG 5.5%)
   Item number and content omitted. (True; NS 44.6%, CG 26.7%)
   Item number and content omitted. (True; NS 12.6%, CG 5.5%)

End of Report

FIGURE 11.8. Ms. H's MMPI-3 Score Report, continued

complains about feeling depressed, does not cope well with stress, and may feel incapable of dealing with current life circumstances. She further reports being passive, indecisive, and inefficacious. She likely experiences subjective incompetence, shame, and tends to lack perseverance and self-reliance. Moreover, she reports an above-average level of stress, likely complains about feeling stressed, and may feel incapable of controlling her anxiety level. She also reports excessive worry, including worries about misfortune and finances, as well as preoccupation with disappointments. She is likely to ruminate. Ms. H reports multiple anxiety-related experiences, including generalized anxiety, reexperiencing, and/or panic. She is likely to experience significant anxiety and anxiety-related problems, intrusive ideation, sleep difficulties, including nightmares, and possible posttraumatic distress. Ms. H further reports being anger-prone and is likely to have experienced problems with irritability, low tolerance of frustration, holding grudges, temper tantrums, and being hostile and argumentative. Her tendency to experience a wide range of negative emotions is likely dispositional in nature.

Ms. H reports a diffuse pattern of somatic complaints involving different bodily systems that probably include head pain and neurological and gastrointestinal symptoms. She is likely preoccupied with physical health concerns, is prone to developing physical symptoms in response to stress, to perceive her physical problems as life-interfering, and to have a psychological component to her physical problems. She also likely complains of fatigue. Ms. H reports vague neurological complaints and is likely to present with dizziness, coordination difficulties, and sensory problems. She also reports a diffuse pattern of cognitive difficulties including memory problems, difficulties with attention and concentration, and possible confusion.

In terms of interpersonal functioning, Ms. H reports disliking people and being around them, preferring to be alone. She is likely to be asocial, socially introverted, and emotionally disconnected. She also reports not enjoying social events and avoiding social situations, and likely has difficulties forming close relationships and tends to be emotionally restricted.

Ms. H's MMPI-3 results indicate various diagnostic considerations. She should be evaluated for disorders that include disinhibition and poor impulse control, aggression, and other externalizing tendencies, including antisocial personality disorder, borderline personality disorder, and substance use disorders. Ms. H should also be evaluated for various internalizing disorders, including depressive disorder, generalized anxiety disorder, and posttraumatic stress disorder, as well as dependent personality disorder. If a physical explanation for her somatic complaints can be ruled out, she should also be evaluated for a somatic symptom disorder and an attention- or memory-related disorder. Finally, she should be evaluated for disorders that involve extreme social disaffiliation, including schizoid or avoidant personality disorders.

Discussion

Ms. H's Validity Scale results warrant further scrutiny. She provided unscorable responses to five items. The Unscorable Responses section of the MMPI-3 Score Report did not identify a clear theme among these items. Two scales, CMP and BRF, fell below the 90% threshold for scorable responding (one item was missing from each). As such, the absence of elevation on neither scale could be interpreted, as it is unknown what these scores would have been had she responded to the items. The Validity Scales also indicated possible overreporting of both severe psychopathology (Fp = 76T) and cognitive complaints (RBS = 76T). However, the RBS scale score is well within what is generally expected in this context, though the weight placed on the COG scale score would be lowered. Ms. H's Fp score at or above that of 98% of women undergoing forensic disability evaluations. However, because she had a well-documented and long-standing history of PTSD resulting from recurrent and severe trauma, excessive overreporting was ruled out.

Ms. H's MMPI-3 results are helpful in documenting her mental health functioning and addressing the referral questions. The referral agency had already accepted PTSD as a specific diagnosis and the MMPI-3 results are consistent with such psychopathology. Indeed, research on PTSD in forensic disability contexts has indicated that scales such as RCd, STR and WRY, ARX, ANP, and SAV uniquely predict the range of PTSD symptoms (Sellbom, Lee et al., 2012). The MMPI-2-RF counterpart of ARX has been found to be the best marker of PTSD on the entire test (Sellbom, 2019b). Her MMPI-3 scores capture the intrusive ideation, avoidance, negative alterations in cognition and mood (COG = 76T), and hyperarousal symptoms associated with the disorder. Furthermore, Ms. H also has a very high score on DSF, indicating significant detachment from others, which is found in many trauma survivors. Finally, although her scores on the Somatic/Cognitive Scales might suggest a somatic symptom disorder, such a diagnosis would be inconsistent with extratest information. Ms. H does, however, report considerable physiological symptoms in response to stress and anxiety, which in this case is likely better linked to her hyperarousal symptoms.

There is also considerable support for the potential of a personality disorder diagnosis in Ms. H's MMPI-3 scores. The diagnostic considerations, for instance, indicate antisocial, borderline, schizoid, avoidant, and dependent personality disorders as possibilities. A more nuanced examination of the results, in light of available MMPI-2-RF research on the topic, points to two diagnoses in particular. First, the combination of negative emotionality and emotional dysregulation (NEGE, RCd, STR, WRY, AXR, ANP) along with pervasive externalizing tendencies (BXD, DISC, RC4, JCP, SUB, IMP, and AGG) suggests a strong likelihood of borderline personality disorder (Anderson, Sellbom, Pymont et al., 2015; Finn et al., 2014; Sellbom, Smid, De Saeger, Smit, & Kamphuis, 2014; Sellbom & Smith, 2017; Zahn et al., 2017). Indeed, such personality pathology would be consistent with her recurrent and complex traumatic experiences and history of interpersonal functioning. In addition, a diagnosis of antisocial personality disorder would also require consideration based on the externalizing domain scales being the most elevated in the protocol and would be highly consistent with the literature on personality pathology (Anderson, Sellbom, Pymont et al., 2015; Finn et al., 2014; Sellbom, Smid, de Saeger, Smit, & Kamphuis, 2014; Sellbom & Smith, 2017; Zahn et al., 2017). Consistent with this diagnosis, Ms. H has a longstanding history of antisocial conduct, including shoplifting and drug sales from a very early age.

Ultimately, the issue of complex PTSD was deemed inconsequential. Contemporary formulations and proposals for complex PTSD in the ICD-11 (Brewin et al., 2017) essentially combine the criteria for "simple" PTSD and the general criteria for personality disorder. Therefore, complex PTSD is a matter of labeling a particular psychopathology profile rather than providing incremental understanding about the clinical phenomenon. In the case of Ms. H, the clinician diagnosed her with both PTSD and personality disorder, with borderline and antisocial features. However, unlike the initial psychiatrist whose evaluation had resulted in Ms. H's claim being denied, the clinician provided a clinical formulation, rooted in the science of both PTSD and personality disorder, which articulated how her recurrent sexual abuse (i.e., her mental injury), invalidating family environment, and learned environmental adaptation to survive could account for the comprehensive psychopathology profile including her current psychosocial impairment.

MR. I: A CASE OF DIMINISHED RESPONSIBILITY?

Mr. I is a 39-year-old man who was referred by his lawyer for a diminished responsibility evaluation in the context of criminal assault and reckless driving charges. The primary basis for his complaint was PTSD from a previous assault, which led him to commit assault in the instant matter. The general circumstances of the alleged offense were as follows. Mr. I had a disagreement with his (now) ex-partner while driving at 4 a.m. in an urban area. The argument resulted in him allegedly punching his former partner after they had pulled over to the side of the road. She escaped the vehicle, waved down another car, who stopped and let her in. Mr. I subsequently intercepted the vehicle and intentionally crashed into it. The man who was driving that car exited the vehicle to confront Mr. I, who also exited his car carrying a metal pipe. Mr. I allegedly bludgeoned the other man with this pipe, then got back into his vehicle and drove away.

Mr. I claimed during the diminished responsibility evaluation that he felt threatened by the other man and that he reacted out of extreme fear and assaulted the man in self-defense because he had developed PTSD from a stabbing assault several years prior. Mr. I stated that he had seen a therapist as a result of the past assault, during which he was treated for PTSD, but no records were available to corroborate this information. Mr. I denied that he carried a metal pipe out of the car but rather claimed he found it on the ground and grabbed it. What could be confirmed was that Mr. I has a very lengthy criminal history, which includes carjacking, previous assaults, drug possession, and drug trafficking. He had been incarcerated multiple times.

The forensic examiner administered the Clinician-Administered PTSD Scale for *DSM-5* (CAPS-5; Weathers et al., 2018), which is a structured clinical interview. It was negative for PTSD. The examiner also administered the MMPI-3 to further evaluate for any potential mental health problems that could address the psycho-legal question at hand.

MMPI-3 Interpretation

Mr. I responded to all but three of the MMPI-3 items (Figure 11.9).[6] Therefore, the absence of elevation on individual scales with excessive unscorable responding cannot be interpreted. There is no evidence of content-inconsistent responding. Possible overreporting is indicated by assertion of a larger than average number of symptoms rarely described by individuals with genuine, severe psychopathology. However, these responses can also be consistent with an individual who experiences genuine mental health problems. There is no evidence of underreporting.

Mr. I's MMPI-3 results indicate considerable externalizing, acting-out behavior that is very likely to result in marked dysfunction and to have gotten him into difficulties. He reports serious past and current antisocial behavior. He likely fails to conform to societal norms and expectations and is likely to have been involved with the criminal justice system. He may have difficulty with individuals in positions of authority and experience conflictual interpersonal relationships. He reports a history of juvenile conduct problems such as problematic behavior at school, stealing, and being arrested. He also reports a significant history of substance abuse, current substance abuse, frequent use of alcohol and drugs, using alcohol to "relax and open up," and inappropriate use of prescription medication; and he may have a legal history as a result of drug and alcohol use.

Mr. I further reports behaviors and experiences associated with hypomanic activation, such as excitability, impulsivity, and elevated mood. He is likely to experience mood lability and excitability and to be restless and bored. Indeed, he specifically reports engaging in problematic impulsive behavior, is likely

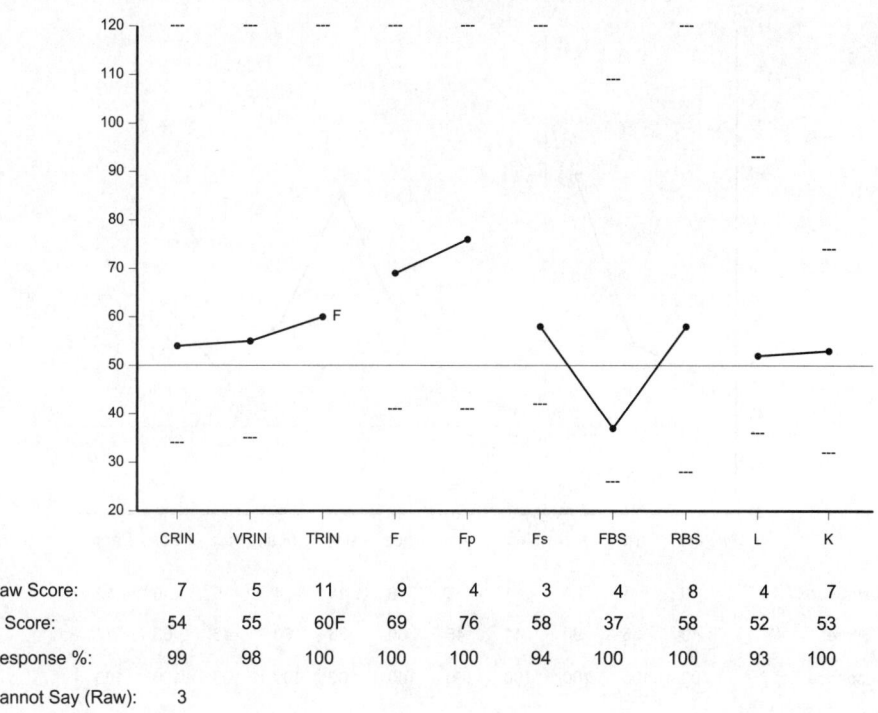

FIGURE 11.9. Mr. I's MMPI-3 Score Report

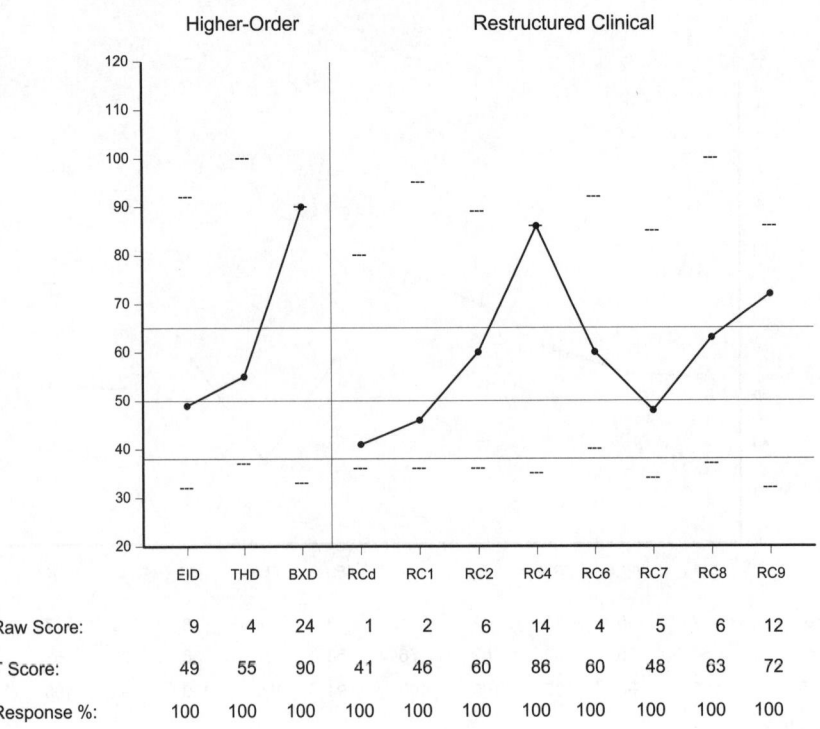

FIGURE 11.9. Mr. I's MMPI-3 Score Report, continued

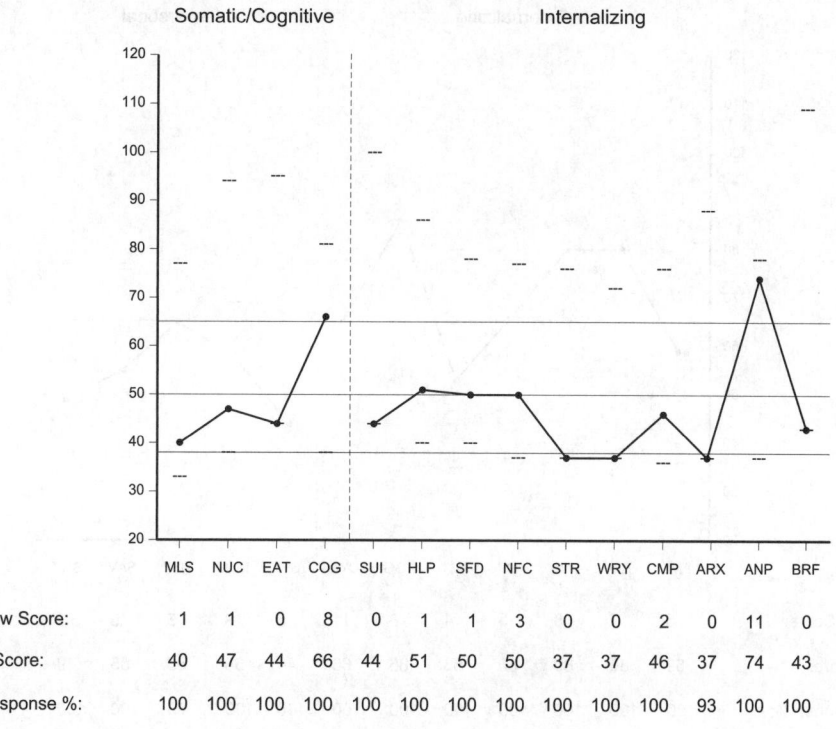

FIGURE 11.9. Mr. I's MMPI-3 Score Report, continued

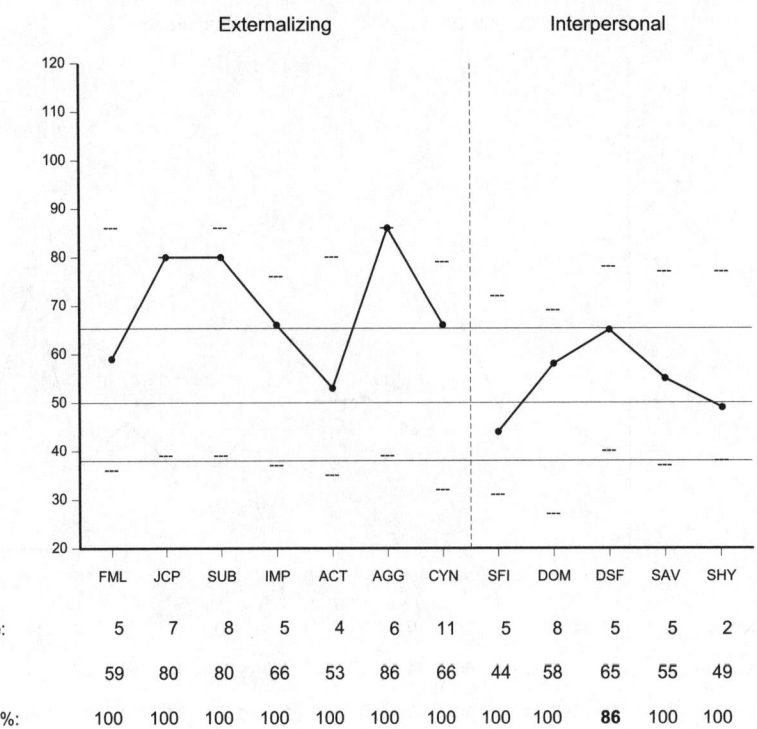

FIGURE 11.9. Mr. I's MMPI-3 Score Report, continued

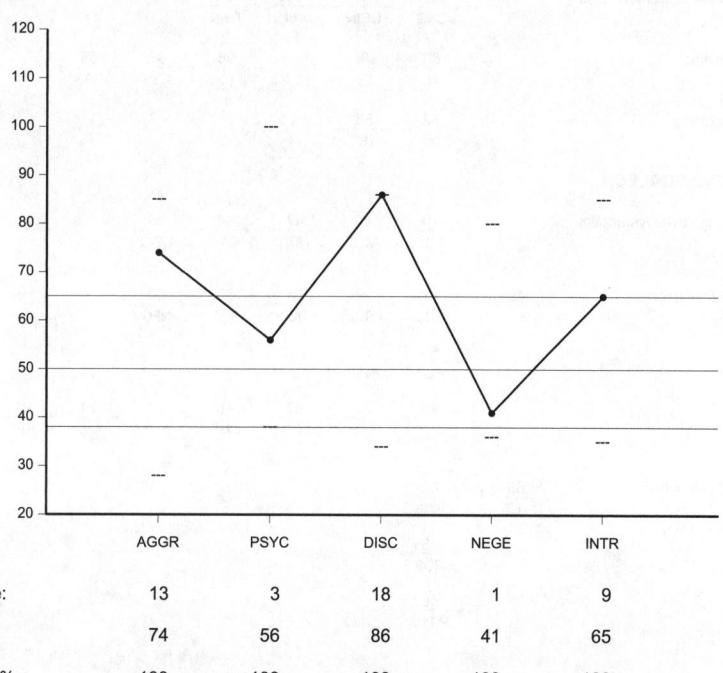

FIGURE 11.9. Mr. I's MMPI-3 Score Report, continued

MMPI-3 T SCORES (BY DOMAIN)

PROTOCOL VALIDITY

Content Non-Responsiveness	3	54	55	60 F		
	CNS	CRIN	VRIN	TRIN		

Over-Reporting	69	76		58	37	58
	F	Fp		Fs	FBS	RBS

Under-Reporting	52	53
	L	K

SUBSTANTIVE SCALES

Somatic/Cognitive Dysfunction		46	40	47	44	66			
		RC1	MLS	NUC	EAT	COG			

Emotional Dysfunction	49	41	44	51	50	50			
	EID	RCd	SUI	HLP	SFD	NFC			
		60	65						
		RC2	INTR						
		48	37	37	46	37	74	43	41
		RC7	STR	WRY	CMP	ARX	ANP	BRF	NEGE

Thought Dysfunction	55	60							
	THD	RC6							
		63							
		RC8							
		56							
		PSYC							

Behavioral Dysfunction	90	86	59	80	80				
	BXD	RC4	FML	JCP	SUB				
		72	66	53	86	66			
		RC9	IMP	ACT	AGG	CYN			
		86							
		DISC							

Interpersonal Functioning		44	58	74	65*	55	49
		SFI	DOM	AGGR	DSF	SAV	SHY

*The test taker provided scorable responses to less than 90% of the items scored on this scale. See the relevant profile page for the specific percentage.

Note. This information is provided to facilitate interpretation following the recommended structure for MMPI-3 interpretation in Chapter 5 of the *MMPI-3 Manual for Administration, Scoring, and Interpretation*, which provides details in the text and an outline in Table 5-1.

FIGURE 11.9. Mr. I's MMPI-3 Score Report, continued

ITEM-LEVEL INFORMATION

Unscorable Responses

Following is a list of items to which the test taker did not provide scorable responses. Unanswered or double answered (both True and False) items are unscorable. The scale(s) on which the items appear are in parentheses following the item content.

    Item number and content omitted. (L)
    Item number and content omitted. (VRIN, DSF)
    Item number and content omitted. (Fs, ARX)

Critical Responses

Seven MMPI-3 scales—Suicidal/Death Ideation (SUI), Helplessness/Hopelessness (HLP), Anxiety-Related Experiences (ARX), Ideas of Persecution (RC6), Aberrant Experiences (RC8), Substance Abuse (SUB), and Aggression (AGG)—have been designated by the test authors as having critical item content that may require immediate attention and follow-up. Items answered by the individual in the keyed direction (True or False) on a critical scale are listed below if his T score on that scale is 65 or higher. However, any item answered in the keyed direction on SUI is listed. The percentage of the MMPI-3 normative sample that answered each item in the keyed direction is provided in parentheses following the item content.

Substance Abuse (SUB, T Score = 80)

    Item number and content omitted. (True, 21.7%)
    Item number and content omitted. (True, 43.0%)
    Item number and content omitted. (True, 38.2%)
    Item number and content omitted. (False, 31.9%)
    Item number and content omitted. (True, 8.1%)
    Item number and content omitted. (True, 18.7%)
    Item number and content omitted. (True, 6.7%)
    Item number and content omitted. (True, 14.4%)

Aggression (AGG, T Score = 86)

    Item number and content omitted. (True, 28.8%)
    Item number and content omitted. (True, 24.3%)
    Item number and content omitted. (True, 13.3%)
    Item number and content omitted. (True, 9.4%)
    Item number and content omitted. (True, 44.6%)
    Item number and content omitted. (True, 12.6%)

End of Report

FIGURE 11.9. Mr. I's MMPI-3 Score Report, continued

nonplanful, and has a possible history of hyperactive behavior. In addition, he reports engaging in physically aggressive, violent behavior, including explosive behavior and physical altercations, and enjoying intimidating others. He likely has a history of violent behavior toward others, is possibly abusive, and likely has anger-related problems. He reports having cynical beliefs, being distrustful of others, and believing others look out only for their own interests. He is likely self-centered and lacking in empathy, distrustful and alienated from others, and has negative interpersonal experiences. He also reports a pattern of disconstrained behavior, which is likely dispositional in nature, and is also likely sensation and excitement seeking.

Mr. I reports being anger prone and likely has problems with irritability, low tolerance for frustration, holding grudges, temper tantrums, and being hostile and argumentative. He reports a below average level of stress, worry, and other anxiety-related experiences. Mr. I further reports a diffuse pattern of cognitive difficulties and is likely to complain about memory problems and difficulties with attention and concentration.

Interpersonally, Mr. I reports disliking people and being around them and is likely asocial and emotionally disconnected. He reports engaging in instrumentally aggressive behavior and is likely overly assertive and socially dominant.

Mr. I's MMPI-3 results point to some diagnostic considerations. He should be evaluated for antisocial personality disorder, substance use disorders, and other externalizing disorders, including those associated with poor impulse control, anger, hostility, aggression, and mistrust. He should be evaluated for other personality disorders that include antagonistic personality traits, including narcissistic personality disorder. Mr. I should further be considered for an attention-deficit disorder, and given the high impulsivity, attention-deficit hyperactivity disorder. Finally, it should be evaluated whether these symptoms and behaviors can be accounted for by a manic episode.

Discussion

Mr. I did not provide a scorable response to three items. It is helpful to determine if there is an underlying theme by reviewing the list of Unscorable Responses in the MMPI-3 Score Report, but in this case, there is no theme present. Examination of the individual MMPI-3 scales reveals that DSF is the only scale affected to a degree at which the score might be unduly attenuated because of unscorable responding. In this case, however, the scale score is 65T, which is the threshold for clinical elevation. The scale is therefore interpreted, but with some caution, as the interpretation might reflect an underestimate of the score had Mr. I responded to all the DFS items.

Overreporting is always a concern in a diminished responsibility evaluation, as the defendant has an external incentive to portray themselves as having more problems or more severe difficulties than they actually do. Mr. I's score on Fp (76T) is just above threshold to trigger the possibility for overreporting of severe psychopathology; however, at this level, his score could also reflect genuine psychopathology. Although Mr. I is claiming that PTSD reduced his moral culpability in this case, no emotional or other severe psychopathology indicators are elevated. The only potential marker of major mental illness, RC9 (72T) is likely elevated in the context of severe externalizing proclivities more so than signaling a manic episode. Ultimately, there is no other contextual information to support that Mr. I might have been malingering, as his MMPI-3 results are generally consistent with documented history.

As just mentioned, despite his claim of PTSD, Mr. I's MMPI-3 results are not reflective of this disorder. Indeed, ARX, which is the best marker of PTSD symptoms, indicates below average anxiety-related experiences. Therefore, between the CAPS-5 and the MMPI-3 scores, this diagnosis is readily ruled out. Instead, Mr. I responded in a manner that is more reflective of psychopathic personality traits. He obtained a clinically elevated score on almost every externalizing scale, including the two PSY-5 Scales, AGGR and DISC, which have been well-validated as indicators of antisocial and psychopathic personality traits. Indeed, Sellbom has shown in Appendix B of the *MMPI-3 Technical Manual* that the externalizing scales cover a breadth of both disinhibited and antagonistic externalizing tendencies germane to this personality pathology. It is also worth noting that the AGG scale score, which reaches the ceiling, has items reflective of callousness, and research has indicated that elevated AGG scores are correlated with such tendencies (Ben-Porath & Tellegen, 2020b; Klein Haneveld et al., 2017). The CYN scale also covers antagonistic attitudes and correlates with a lack of empathy (Appendix B; Ben-Porath & Tellegen, 2020b). In addition, Mr. I scored below average on numerous internalizing scales (especially, STR, WRY, ARX), indicating that he is stress immune and feels little guilt over his externalizing conduct. The only negative emotion that Mr. I reports experiencing at all is anger. In addition, his score on DSF, which might be an underestimate, likely signals a dislike for others, misanthropic attitudes, and failing to emotionally connect with others.

Research on the MMPI-2-RF and psychopathic personality traits has revealed a pattern of scales associated with this multidimensional construct (Klein Haneveld et al., 2017; Sellbom et al., 2005; Sellbom, Ben-Porath et al., 2007; Sellbom, Ben-Porath et al., 2012; Wygant & Sellbom, 2012). The *Technical Manual* indicates similar correlates for the MMPI-3 versions of these scales in prison, community-externalizing, and university samples (Ben-Porath & Tellegen, 2020b). More specifically, the literature has revealed that externalizing scales reflective of more antagonism tendencies, such as AGGR, AGG, CYN, but also DSF tend to be associated with affective-interpersonal psychopathy traits (e.g., manipulation, deceitfulness, callousness, lack of empathy and remorse). Externalizing scales that reflect more disinhibitory traits, such as DISC, RC4, JCP, SUB, IMP tend to be better aligned with the more behavioral/lifestyle psychopathy traits (e.g., impulsivity, irresponsibility, risk-taking). Several studies have indicated that low scores of negative emotionality scales, especially those measuring anxiety and fear, are also associated with affective-interpersonal and boldness psychopathy traits (e.g., fearlessness, social dominance).

In the case of Mr. I, his MMPI-3 results are quite consistent with the literature just briefly reviewed. The forensic examiner opined that no mental disorder was present that could have reduced Mr. I's moral culpability for the alleged offenses, but rather, the acts with which he was charged were entirely consistent with his personality pathology.

MR. J: A POLICE CANDIDATE

Mr. J is a 40-year-old male who applied for a state law enforcement position. He reported a developmental history characterized by multiple adverse childhood experiences, including frequent conflict with his abusive father and older brother and being assaulted with a knife by a teenager when he was 10 years old. He had never married nor had children, but he had a partner of 5 years. He earned an online bachelor's degree in criminal justice. At the time of the evaluation, he was in federal employment in a non-law enforcement position. During the interview, he presented as confused and had difficulty following instructions and interpreting simple questions. He was unsmiling and dour. He admitted to having made racial remarks at work but defended them as "just for joking purposes. . . . You're there all day and you've got to have fun." He was previously disciplined for making an offensive remark to a customer, as well as for abuse of sick leave. He failed two previous preemployment evaluations for police officer positions that were conducted elsewhere. He said he has had recurring thoughts of "not being good enough" since failing his previous examinations.

MMPI-3 Findings

Figure 11.10 provides an MMPI-3 Police Candidate Interpretive Report (PCIR) generated based on Mr. J's responses to the test items. Described in detail by Corey and Ben-Porath (2022), the PCIR provides a detailed, annotated interpretation of Mr. J's MMPI-3 findings. Pages 2–6 of the report provide Mr. J's scores on the 42 MMPI-3 scales and how they compare with those generated by a sample of 2,036 police candidates. The open diamonds represent the comparison group means and the shaded bars a range of plus and minus one standard deviation from the mean. The last row of numbers on these pages indicates the percent of comparison group members whose scores fell at or below that of Mr. J. The values can be interpreted similarly to percentiles.

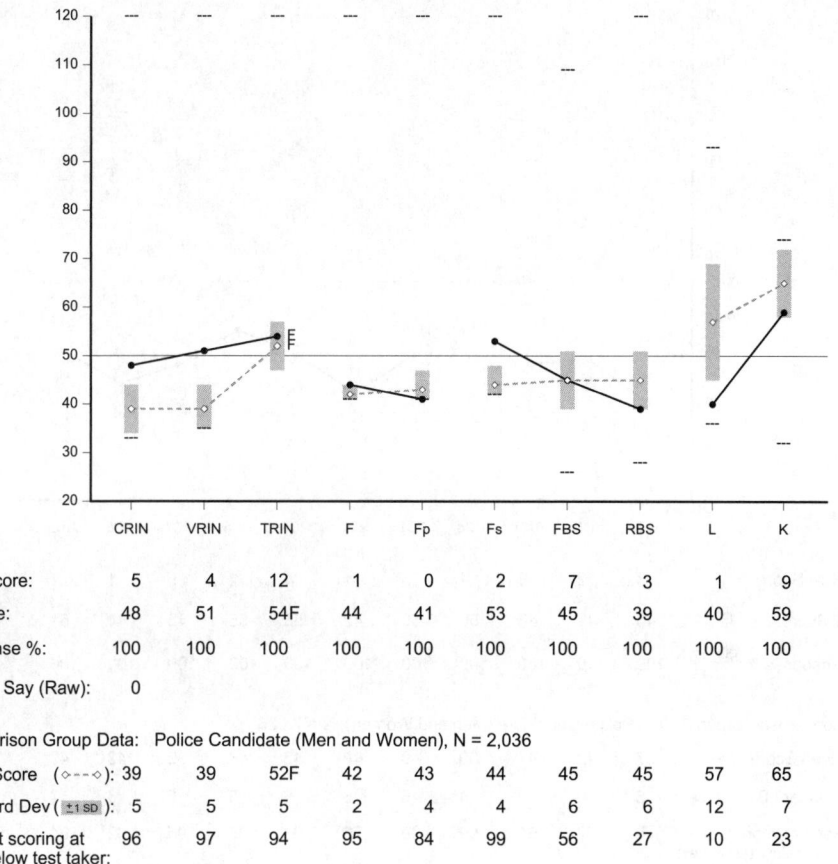

FIGURE 11.10. Mr. J's MMPI-3 Police Candidate Interpretive Report

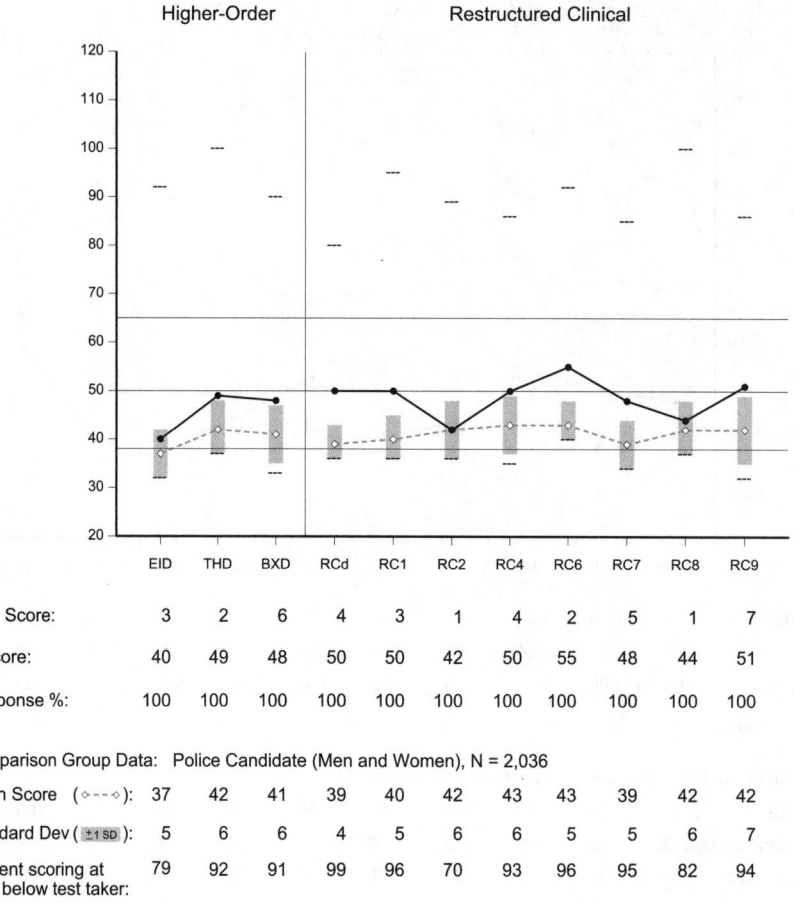

FIGURE 11.10. Mr. J's MMPI-3 Police Candidate Interpretive Report, continued

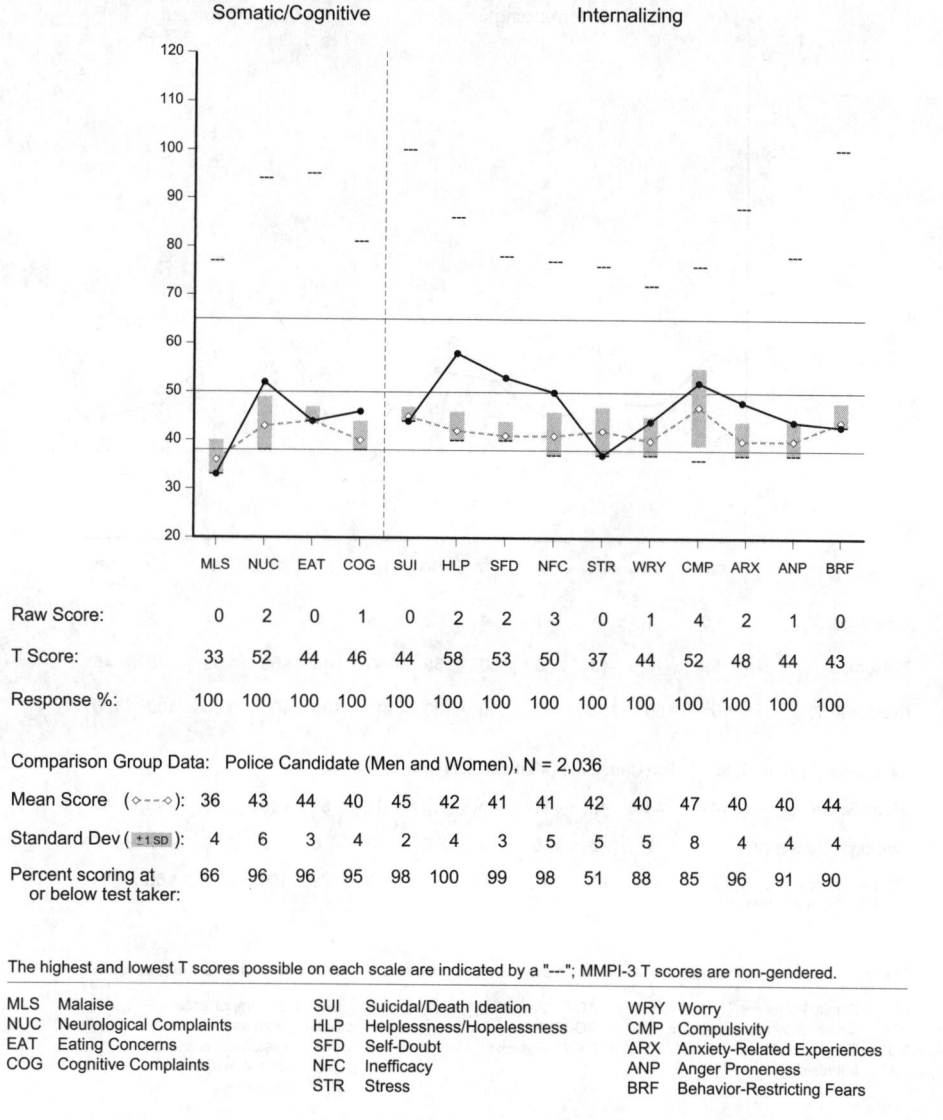

FIGURE 11.10. Mr. J's MMPI-3 Police Candidate Interpretive Report, continued

MMPI-3 Externalizing and Interpersonal Scales

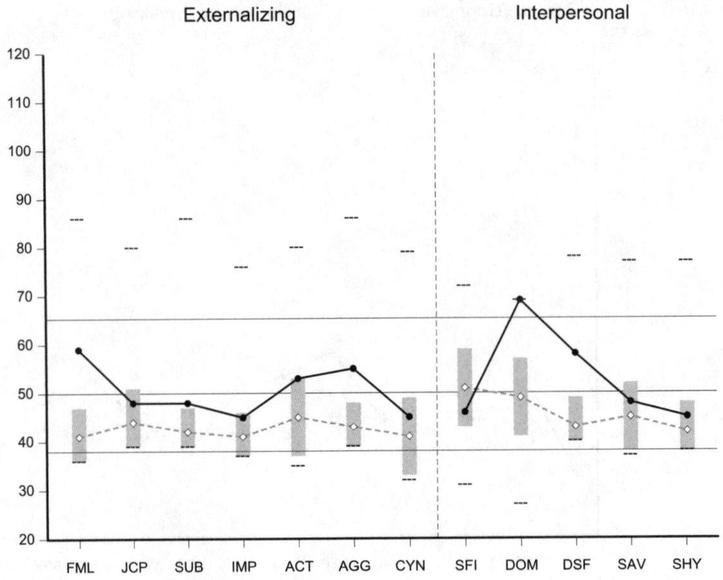

	Externalizing							Interpersonal				
	FML	JCP	SUB	IMP	ACT	AGG	CYN	SFI	DOM	DSF	SAV	SHY
Raw Score:	5	1	1	1	4	2	5	6	9	4	2	1
T Score:	59	48	48	45	53	55	45	46	69	58	48	45
Response %:	100	100	100	100	100	100	100	100	100	100	100	100

Comparison Group Data: Police Candidate (Men and Women), N = 2,036

	FML	JCP	SUB	IMP	ACT	AGG	CYN	SFI	DOM	DSF	SAV	SHY
Mean Score (◇---◇):	41	44	42	41	45	43	41	51	49	43	45	42
Standard Dev (±1 SD):	6	7	5	5	8	5	8	8	8	6	7	6
Percent scoring at or below test taker:	99.6	81	91	87	90	98	75	39	100	99.2	68	85

The highest and lowest T scores possible on each scale are indicated by a "---"; MMPI-3 T scores are non-gendered.

FML	Family Problems	ACT	Activation
JCP	Juvenile Conduct Problems	AGG	Aggression
SUB	Substance Abuse	CYN	Cynicism
IMP	Impulsivity		
		SFI	Self-Importance
		DOM	Dominance
		DSF	Disaffiliativeness
		SAV	Social Avoidance
		SHY	Shyness

FIGURE 11.10. Mr. J's MMPI-3 Police Candidate Interpretive Report, continued

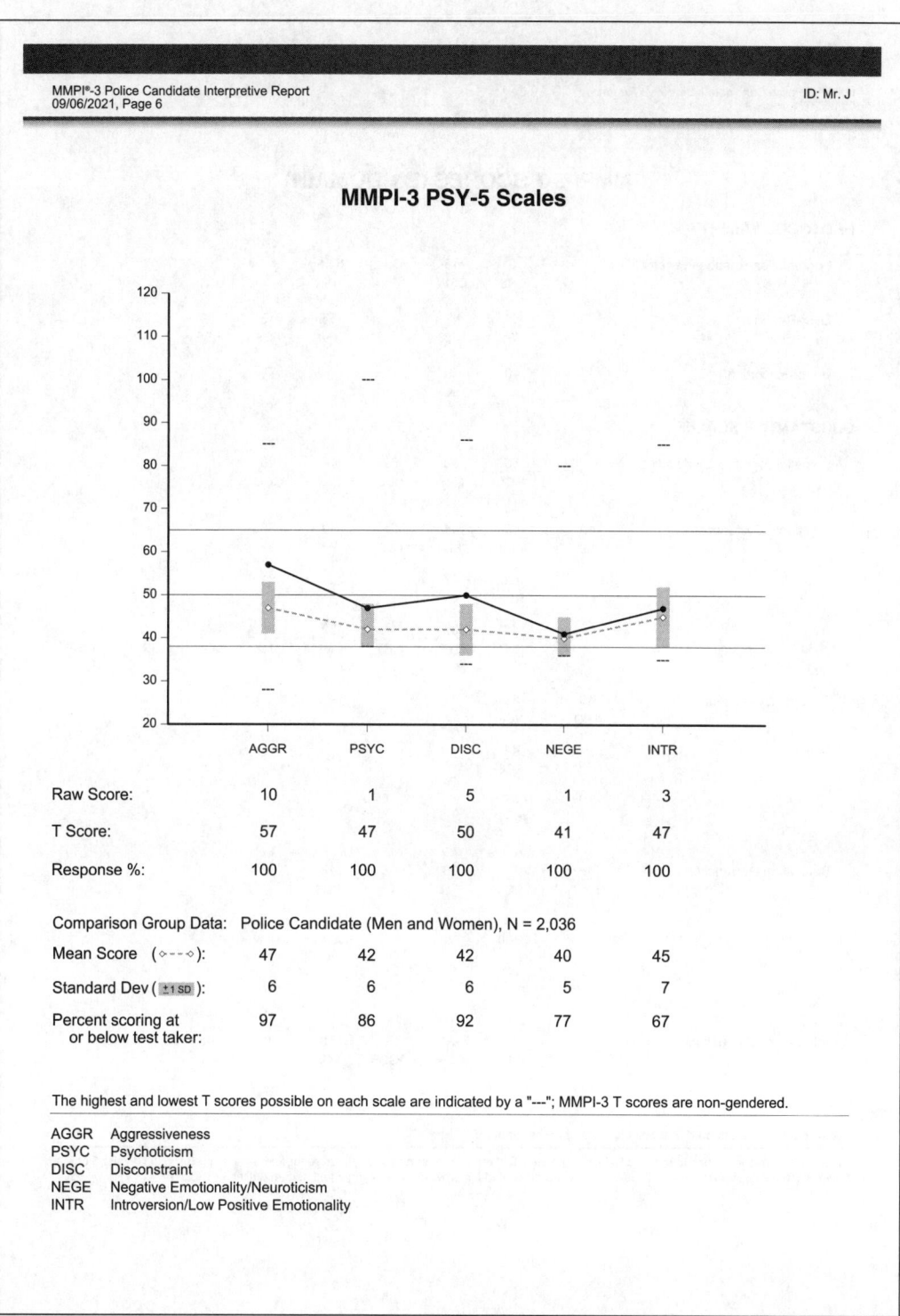

FIGURE 11.10. Mr. J's MMPI-3 Police Candidate Interpretive Report, continued

MMPI-3 T SCORES (BY DOMAIN)

PROTOCOL VALIDITY

Content Non-Responsiveness

0	48	51	54 F
CNS	CRIN	VRIN	TRIN

Over-Reporting

44	41	53	45	39
F	Fp	Fs	FBS	RBS

Under-Reporting

40	59
L	K

SUBSTANTIVE SCALES

Somatic/Cognitive Dysfunction

50	33	52	44	46
RC1	MLS	NUC	EAT	COG

Emotional Dysfunction

40					
EID					
	50	44	**58**	**53**	50
	RCd	SUI	**HLP**	**SFD**	NFC
	42	47			
	RC2	INTR			

48	37	44	52	48	44	43	41
RC7	STR	WRY	CMP	ARX	ANP	BRF	NEGE

Thought Dysfunction

49	
THD	
	55
	RC6
	44
	RC8
	47
	PSYC

Behavioral Dysfunction

48				
BXD				
	50	**59**	48	48
	RC4	**FML**	JCP	SUB
	51	45	53	**55**	45
	RC9	IMP	ACT	**AGG**	CYN
	50				
	DISC				

Interpersonal Functioning

46	**69**	57	**58**	48	45
SFI	**DOM**	AGGR	**DSF**	SAV	SHY

Scale scores shown in bold font are interpreted in the report.

Note. This information is provided to facilitate interpretation following the recommended structure for MMPI-3 interpretation in Chapter 5 of the *MMPI-3 Manual for Administration, Scoring, and Interpretation*, which provides details in the text and an outline in Table 5-1.

FIGURE 11.10. Mr. J's MMPI-3 Police Candidate Interpretive Report, continued

This interpretive report is intended for use by a professional qualified to interpret the MMPI-3 in the context of preemployment psychological evaluations of police and other law enforcement candidates. **It focuses on identifying problems; it does not convey potential strengths.** The information it contains should be considered in the context of the test taker's background, the demands of the position under consideration, the clinical interview, findings from supplemental tests, and other relevant information.

The interpretive statements in the Protocol Validity section of the report are based on T scores derived from the general MMPI-3 normative sample, as well as scores obtained by the multisite sample of 2,036 individuals that make up the Police Candidate Comparison Group.

The interpretive statements in the Clinical Findings and Diagnostic Considerations sections of the report are based on T scores derived from the general MMPI-3 normative sample. Following recommended practice, only T scores of 65 and higher (with a few exceptions) are considered clinically significant. Scores at this clinical level are generally rare among police candidates.

Statements in the Comparison Group Findings and Job-Relevant Correlates sections are based on comparisons with scores obtained by the Police Candidate Comparison Group. Statements in these sections may be based on T scores that, although less than 65, are nevertheless uncommon in reference to the comparison group.

The report includes extensive annotation, which appears as superscripts following each statement in the narrative, keyed to Endnotes with accompanying Research References, which appear in the final two sections of the report. Additional information about the annotation features is provided in the headnotes to these sections and in the MMPI-3 User's Guide for the Public Safety Candidate Interpretive Reports.

SYNOPSIS

This is a valid MMPI-3 protocol. Scores on the Substantive Scales indicate clinically significant interpersonal dysfunction. Interpersonal difficulties relate to overly domineering behavior.

Comparison group findings point to additional possible concerns about helplessness, self-doubt, family conflict, physically aggressive behavior, and disaffiliativeness.

Possible job-relevant problems are identified in the following domains: Emotional Control and Stress Tolerance, Routine Task Performance, Decision-Making and Judgment, Feedback Acceptance, Assertiveness, Social Competence and Teamwork, Conscientiousness and Dependability, and Impulse Control.

PROTOCOL VALIDITY

This is a valid MMPI-3 protocol. There are no problems with unscorable items. The test taker responded to the items relevantly on the basis of their content, and there are no indications of over- or under-reporting.

FIGURE 11.10. Mr. J's MMPI-3 Police Candidate Interpretive Report, continued

CLINICAL FINDINGS

Clinical-level symptoms, personality characteristics, and behavioral tendencies of the test taker are described in this section and organized according to an empirically guided framework. (Please see Chapter 5 of the MMPI-3 Manual for Administration, Scoring, and Interpretation *for details.) Statements containing the word "reports" are based on the item content of MMPI-3 scales, whereas statements that include the word "likely" are based on empirical correlates of scale scores. Specific sources for each statement can be viewed with the annotation features of this report.*

The test taker describes himself as having strong opinions, as standing up for himself, as assertive and direct, and as able to lead others[1]. He likely believes he has leadership capabilities, but is viewed by others as overly domineering[2].

There are no indications of clinically significant somatic, cognitive, emotional, thought, or behavioral dysfunction in this protocol.

DIAGNOSTIC CONSIDERATIONS

This section provides recommendations for psychodiagnostic assessment based on the test taker's MMPI-3 results. It is recommended that he be evaluated for the following:

Interpersonal Disorders
- Disorders characterized by excessively domineering behavior[3]

COMPARISON GROUP FINDINGS

This section describes the MMPI-3 substantive scale findings in the context of the Police Candidate Comparison Group. Specific sources for each statement can be accessed with the annotation features of this report. **Job-related correlates of these results, if any, are provided in the subsequent Job-Relevant Correlates section.**

Emotional/Internalizing Problems
The test taker reports a high level of beliefs that he cannot solve problems and reach important goals compared to other police candidates[4]. Only 0.7% of comparison group members convey this level of helplessness. He also reports a comparatively high level of self-doubt for a police candidate[5]. Only 3.0% of comparison group members convey this or a greater lack of confidence.

Behavioral/Externalizing Problems
The test taker reports a comparatively high level of physically aggressive behavior for a police candidate[6]. Only 6.0% of comparison group members convey this or a greater level of inappropriately aggressive behavior.

Interpersonal Problems
The test taker reports a comparatively high level of family conflict for a police candidate[7]. Only 1.0% of comparison group members convey this or a greater level of family problems.

His responses indicate a level of dominance that may be incompatible with public safety requirements for good interpersonal functioning[3]. This level of domineering behavior is uncommon among police candidates. Only 6.0% of comparison group members give evidence of this level of dominance.

FIGURE 11.10. Mr. J's MMPI-3 Police Candidate Interpretive Report, continued

The test taker reports a comparatively high level of disaffiliativeness for a police candidate[8]. Only 2.0% of comparison group members convey this or a greater level of disinterest in interacting with others.

JOB-RELEVANT CORRELATES

Job-relevant personality characteristics and behavioral tendencies of the test taker are described in this section and organized according to ten problem domains commonly identified in the professional literature as relevant to public safety candidate suitability. (Please see MMPI-3 User's Guide for the Public Safety Candidate Interpretive Reports *for details.) Statements that begin with "Compared with other police candidates" are based on correlations with other self-report measures obtained in police candidate samples that included individuals who were subsequently hired as well as those who were not. Statements that begin with "He is more likely than most police officers or trainees" are based on correlations with outcome data obtained in samples of hired candidates during academy or field training, probation, and/or the postprobation period. Specific sources for each statement can be accessed with the annotation features of this report.*

Emotional Control and Stress Tolerance Problems

Compared with other police candidates, the test taker is more likely to have difficulty coping with stress[9]; to develop physical symptoms in response to stress and worry about his health[10]; and to have a history of adverse childhood experiences[11].

He is more likely than most police officers or trainees to exhibit difficulties performing under stressful conditions[12].

Routine Task Performance Problems

The test taker is more likely than most police officers or trainees to exhibit cognitive adaptation problems[13] and report writing problems[14].

Decision-Making and Judgment Problems

The test taker is more likely than most police officers or trainees to exhibit difficulties using tactical thinking, legal knowledge, and awareness of ethics to reach decisions quickly[15]. He is also more likely to exhibit difficulties with seeking assistance in complex situations as needed[16] and with performing duties in a manner conducive to the safety of others[17].

Feedback Acceptance Problems

Compared with other police candidates, the test taker is less likely to reflect on his behavior[18] and more likely to brush off criticism and other negative feedback[18].

He is more likely than most police officers or trainees to exhibit difficulties accepting and responding to constructive performance feedback[19].

Assertiveness Problems

Compared with other police candidates, the test taker is more likely to be ill at ease in dealing with others[20] and to lack assertiveness[10].

He is more likely than most police officers or trainees to exhibit difficulties engaging or confronting subjects in circumstances in which an officer would normally approach or intervene[21]. He is also more likely to exhibit difficulties in demonstrating a command presence and controlling situations requiring order or resolution[22].

Social Competence and Teamwork Problems

Compared with other police candidates, the test taker is more likely to be self-centered[23]; to have a history of problems getting along with others[24]; and to be opinionated and outspoken[18]. He is also more likely to be demanding[18]; to have a limited social support network[25]; and to prefer to work out problems alone[26]. In addition, he is more likely to be seen by others as socially detached and emotionally distant[26] and to have problems with social

FIGURE 11.10. Mr. J's MMPI-3 Police Candidate Interpretive Report, continued

competence[27].

He is more likely than most police officers or trainees to exhibit difficulties stemming from rude and/or overbearing behavior that results in complaints from the public[28]; cooperating with peers and/or supervisors[29]; and interacting effectively with others in a variety of contexts[17].

Conscientiousness and Dependability Problems
The test taker is more likely than most police officers or trainees to exhibit difficulties with reliable work behavior and dependable follow-through[30].

Impulse Control Problems
The test taker is more likely than most police officers or trainees to exhibit problems controlling and de-escalating conflict[16].

The candidate's test scores are not associated with problems in the following domains:
- Integrity
- Substance Use

ITEM-LEVEL INFORMATION

Unscorable Responses

The test taker produced scorable responses to all the MMPI-3 items.

Critical Responses

Seven MMPI-3 scales—Suicidal/Death Ideation (SUI), Helplessness/Hopelessness (HLP), Anxiety-Related Experiences (ARX), Ideas of Persecution (RC6), Aberrant Experiences (RC8), Substance Abuse (SUB), and Aggression (AGG)—have been designated by the test authors as having critical item content that may require immediate attention and follow-up. Items answered by the individual in the keyed direction (True or False) on a critical scale are listed below if his T score on that scale is 65 or higher. However, any item answered in the keyed direction on SUI is listed.

The test taker has not produced an elevated T score ($\geq$ 65) on any of these scales or answered any SUI items in the keyed direction.

User-Designated Item-Level Information

The following item-level information is based on the report user's selection of additional scales, and/or of lower cutoffs for the critical scales from the previous section. Items answered by the test taker in the keyed direction (True or False) on a selected scale are listed below if his T score on that scale is at the user-designated cutoff score or higher. The percentage of the MMPI-3 normative sample (NS) and of the Police Candidate Comparison Group (CG) that answered each item in the keyed direction are provided in parentheses following the item content.

Dominance (DOM, T Score = 69)
    Item number and content omitted. (False; NS 85.2%, CG 96.5%)
    Item number and content omitted. (True; NS 78.7%, CG 78.2%)
    Item number and content omitted. (True; NS 68.8%, CG 40.8%)
    Item number and content omitted. (True; NS 74.7%, CG 73.7%)
    Item number and content omitted. (True; NS 74.3%, CG 90.2%)
    Item number and content omitted. (True; NS 60.7%, CG 74.0%)

FIGURE 11.10. Mr. J's MMPI-3 Police Candidate Interpretive Report, continued

Item number and content omitted. (False; NS 80.6%, CG 97.6%)
Item number and content omitted. (True; NS 66.5%, CG 87.1%)
Item number and content omitted. (True; NS 39.8%, CG 12.1%)

Critical Follow-up Items

This section contains a list of items to which the test taker responded in a manner warranting follow-up. The items were identified by public safety candidate screening experts as having critical content. Clinicians are encouraged to follow up on these statements with the candidate by making related inquiries, rather than reciting the item(s) verbatim. Each item is followed by the candidate's response, the percentage of Police Candidate Comparison Group members who gave this response, and the scale(s) on which the item appears.

Item number and content omitted. (True; 19.4%; BXD, RC9, IMP, DISC)
Item number and content omitted. (True; 0.0%; VRIN, F, HLP)
Item number and content omitted. (True; 12.7%; ARX)

FIGURE 11.10. Mr. J's MMPI-3 Police Candidate Interpretive Report, continued

MMPI®-3 Police Candidate Interpretive Report
09/06/2021, Page 13

ID: Mr. J

ENDNOTES

This section lists for each statement in the report the MMPI-3 score(s) that triggered it. In addition, each statement is identified as a <u>Test Response</u>, if based on item content, a <u>Correlate</u>, if based on empirical correlates, or an <u>Inference</u>, if based on the report authors' judgment. (This information can also be accessed on-screen by placing the cursor on a given statement.) For correlate-based statements, research references (Ref. No.) are provided, keyed to the consecutively numbered reference list following the endnotes.

[1] Test Response: DOM=69
[2] Correlate: DOM=69, Ref. 1, 2, 4, 5, 6, 14
[3] Inference: DOM=69
[4] Test Response: HLP=58
[5] Test Response: SFD=53
[6] Test Response: AGG=55
[7] Test Response: FML=59
[8] Test Response: DSF=58
[9] Correlate: SFD=53, Ref. 8, 16
[10] Correlate: SFD=53, Ref. 16
[11] Correlate: FML=59, Ref. 15
[12] Correlate: DSF=58, Ref. 2
[13] Correlate: HLP=58, Ref. 2; DSF=58, Ref. 2
[14] Correlate: HLP=58, Ref. 2
[15] Correlate: HLP=58, Ref. 10
[16] Correlate: DOM=69, Ref. 7
[17] Correlate: AGG=55, Ref. 7
[18] Correlate: DOM=69, Ref. 2
[19] Correlate: AGG=55, Ref. 10
[20] Correlate: DSF=58, Ref. 2, 3
[21] Correlate: HLP=58, Ref. 10; DSF=58, Ref. 10
[22] Correlate: HLP=58, Ref. 10; DSF=58, Ref. 9, 10
[23] Correlate: FML=59, Ref. 2
[24] Correlate: DSF=58, Ref. 13
[25] Correlate: DSF=58, Ref. 3, 13
[26] Correlate: DSF=58, Ref. 3
[27] Correlate: DSF=58, Ref. 16
[28] Correlate: AGG=55, Ref. 12
[29] Correlate: AGG=55, Ref. 10, 11, 12; DOM=69, Ref. 7; DSF=58, Ref. 2
[30] Correlate: DSF=58, Ref. 9, 10

FIGURE 11.10. Mr. J's MMPI-3 Police Candidate Interpretive Report, continued

RESEARCH REFERENCE LIST

The following studies are sources for empirical correlates identified in the Endnotes section of this report.

1. Ayearst, L. E., Sellbom, M., Trobst, K. K., & Bagby, R. M. (2013). Evaluating the interpersonal content of the MMPI-2-RF Interpersonal Scales. *Journal of Personality Assessment, 95*(2), 187–196. https://doi.org/10.1080/00223891.2012.730085

2. Ben-Porath, Y. S., & Tellegen, A. (2020). *The Minnesota Multiphasic Personality Inventory-3 (MMPI-3): Technical manual.* University of Minnesota Press.

3. Corey, D. M., & Ben-Porath, Y. S. (2022). *Minnesota Multiphasic Personality Inventory-3 (MMPI-3): User's guide for the public safety candidate interpretive reports.* University of Minnesota Press.

4. Cox, A., Courrégé, S. C., Feder, A. H., & Weed, N. C. (2017). Effects of augmenting response options of the MMPI-2-RF: An extension of previous findings. *Cogent Psychology, 4*(1), 1323988. https://doi.org/10.1080/23311908.2017.1323988

5. Kastner, R. M., Sellbom, M., & Lilienfeld, S. O. (2012). A comparison of the psychometric properties of the Psychopathic Personality Inventory full-length and short-form versions. *Psychological Assessment, 24*(1), 261–267. https://doi.org/10.1037/a0025832

6. Menton, W. H., Crighton, A. H., Tarescavage, A. M., Marek, R. J., Hicks, A. D., & Ben-Porath, Y. S. (2019). Equivalence of laptop and tablet administrations of the Minnesota Multiphasic Personality Inventory-2 Restructured Form. *Assessment, 26*(4), 661–669. https://doi.org/10.1177/1073191117714558

7. Roberts, R. M., Tarescavage, A. M., Ben-Porath, Y. S., & Roberts, M. D. (2018). predicting post-probationary job performance of police officers using CPI and MMPI-2-RF test data obtained during preemployment psychological screening. *Journal of Personality Assessment, 101*(5), 544–555. https://doi.org/10.1080/00223891.2018.1423990

8. Sellbom, M., Corey, D. M., & Ben-Porath, Y. S. (2021). Incremental validity of the Multidimensional Personality Questionnaire in the preemployment assessment of police officer candidates. *Criminal Justice and Behavior.* Advance online publication. https://doi.org/10.1177/00938548211033630

9. Tarescavage, A. M., Brewster, J., Corey, D. M., & Ben-Porath, Y. S. (2015). Use of pre-hire Minnesota Multiphasic Personality Inventory-2-Restructured Form (MMPI-2-RF) police candidate scores to predict supervisor ratings of post-hire performance. *Assessment, 22*(4), 411–428. https://doi.org/10.1177/1073191114548445

10. Tarescavage, A. M., Corey, D. M., & Ben-Porath, Y. S. (2015). Minnesota Multiphasic Personality Inventory-2-Restructured Form (MMPI-2-RF) predictors of police officer problem behavior. *Assessment, 22*(1), 116–132. https://doi.org/10.1177/1073191114534885

11. Tarescavage, A. M., Corey, D. M., & Ben-Porath, Y. S. (2016). A prorating method for estimating MMPI-2-RF scores from MMPI responses: Examination of score fidelity and illustration of empirical utility in the PERSEREC police integrity study sample. *Assessment, 23*(2), 173–190. https://doi.org/10.1177/1073191115575070

12. Tarescavage, A. M., Corey, D. M., Gupton, H. M., & Ben-Porath Y.S. (2015). Criterion validity and practical utility of the Minnesota Multiphasic Personality Inventory-2-Restructured Form (MMPI-2-RF) in assessments of police officer candidates. *Journal of Personality Assessment, 97*(4), 382–394. https://doi.org/10.1080/00223891.2014.995800

FIGURE 11.10. Mr. J's MMPI-3 Police Candidate Interpretive Report, continued

13. Tarescavage, A. M., Fischler, G. L., Cappo, B. M., Hill, D. O., Corey, D. M., & Ben-Porath, Y. S. (2015). Minnesota Multiphasic Personality Inventory-2-Restructured Form (MMPI-2-RF) predictors of police officer problem behavior and collateral self-report test scores. *Psychological Assessment, 27*(1), 125–137. https://doi.org/10.1037/pas0000041

14. Tellegen, A., & Ben-Porath, Y. S. (2008/2011). *Minnesota Multiphasic Personality Inventory-2-Restructured Form (MMPI-2-RF): Technical manual.* University of Minnesota Press.

15. Whitman, M. R., Corey, D. M., & Ben-Porath, Y. S. (2021). Associations between MMPI-3 and psychosocial history findings obtained in preemployment evaluations of public safety candidates [Manuscript under review].

16. Whitman, M. R., Elias, L. S., Cappo, B. M., & Ben-Porath, Y. S. (2021). Criterion validity of MMPI-3 scores in preemployment evaluations of public safety candidates. *Psychological Assessment.* Advance online publication. https://doi.org/10.1037/pas0001042

End of Report

FIGURE 11.10. Mr. J's MMPI-3 Police Candidate Interpretive Report, continued

Page 7 summarizes all of Mr. J's scores following the recommended structure for MMPI-3 interpretation described in detail in chapter 9. As indicated at the bottom of the page, scale scores shown in bold on page 7 are interpreted in the report. The interpretation found on pages 8–10 begins with a synopsis of the findings in this case, followed by a section labeled Protocol Validity that interprets the validity scale scores, another section that begins on the top of page 9 titled Clinical Findings that focuses on clinically elevated scores, and then a list of diagnostic considerations indicated by Mr. J's clinically elevated MMPI-3 scores. Also depicted on page 9 is the section titled Comparison Group Findings, which describes the MMPI-3 Substantive Scale findings in the context of the Police Candidate Comparison Group. Importantly, nonclinically elevated scores that deviate substantially from the comparison group mean are interpreted in this and the subsequent Job-Relevant Correlates section, which identifies job-relevant personality characteristics and behavioral tendencies associated empirically with Mr. J's scores. The next section, which begins on page 11, provides item-level information that is redacted from Figure 11.10 to protect test security. Superscripted numbers following each statement in the report link to endnotes found on page 13, which annotate what scale(s) generated the statement and whether the statement is based on item content or empirical correlates or is an inference of the report authors. Statements identified as being based on correlates include reference numbers linked to the Research Reference List on pages 14–15 of this report.

Page 2 of Mr. J's report shows his MMPI-3 validity scale scores and how they compare with a sample of 2,036 police candidates. His scores on the inconsistency scales, CRIN, VRIN, and TRIN, indicate that Mr. J provided consistent responses to the MMPI-3. His scores on the underreporting scales, L and K, stand out as being uncommonly low for a police candidate, raising questions about his motivation to be hired. On page 7, bolding indicates that six of Mr. J's scores reached interpretable levels: his clinically elevated DOM score and his nonclinically elevated scores on HLP, SFD, FML, AGG, and DSF. Comparison group data reported on page 9 of the report illustrate that though his SFD T score of 53 falls well below the cutoff for clinically significant elevation, this score is quite uncommon among police candidates, falling at the 99th percentile for the comparison group. Interpretation of Mr. J's scores on the six scales highlighted on page 7 can be found on pages 8–11 of the report.

Discussion

Mr. J's MMPI-3 results were consistent with findings of the examiner during the clinical interview, reflecting a combination of unusually low self-regard and a sense of helplessness on one hand and domineering and possibly overaggressive behavior on the other. As detailed on pages 10–11, Mr. J's MMPI-3 scores are associated with a range of counterproductive behaviors in police officers. Based on these converging findings, the examiner recommended against hiring Mr. J.

MS. K: NEUROPSYCHOLOGICAL ASSESSMENT OF A SPANISH SPEAKER

Ms. K, a 64-year-old Latina woman, was referred by her neurologist for a neuropsychological consultation in connection with increasing neurocognitive difficulties she was experiencing. Ms. K had been under the care of this neurologist for Parkinson's disease, which was under good control with medication. In the months leading to the referral, Ms. K began complaining of word-finding difficulties and memory deficits (initially short term, but now also long term) as well as headaches and disrupted sleep. A brain MRI and blood work were interpreted as yielding normal findings.

In addition to the difficulties just described, Ms. K reported to the Spanish-speaking neuropsychologist that she was experiencing periodic unexplained bouts of depression, marked by having no energy or motivation and substantial dysphoria. The examiner described Ms. K as pleasant and cooperative during the evaluation and indicated that she presented with flat affect but no deficits in expressive or receptive language and no evidence of psychosis. She was administered three performance validity tests and scored at a level indicating good effort. She scored 21/30 on the Montreal Cognitive Assessment (MoCA), demonstrating deficits in fluency and delayed recall. Intelligence testing yielded a score that fell within the average range and a memory score that fell at the 17th percentile. As part of the evaluation, the neuropsychologist administered the Spanish-language MMPI-3.

MMPI-3 Interpretation

Ms. K's MMPI-3 results can be found in Figure 11.11. She answered at least 90% of the items on each of the MMPI-3 scales. She also responded relevantly to the items based on their content. Ms. K provided an unusual combination of responses that is associated with noncredible reporting of somatic and/or cognitive symptoms. This combination of responses may occur in individuals with substantial medical problems who report credible symptoms, but it could also reflect exaggeration. Scores on the RC1, MLS, NUC, and COG scales should be interpreted in light of this caution. There are no indications of underreporting in her protocol.

Ms. K reports various negative emotional experiences and likely is self-critical and guilt prone. More specifically, she reports multiple anxiety-related experiences, including generalized anxiety and reexperiencing and/or panic. She indeed likely experiences significant anxiety and anxiety-related problems

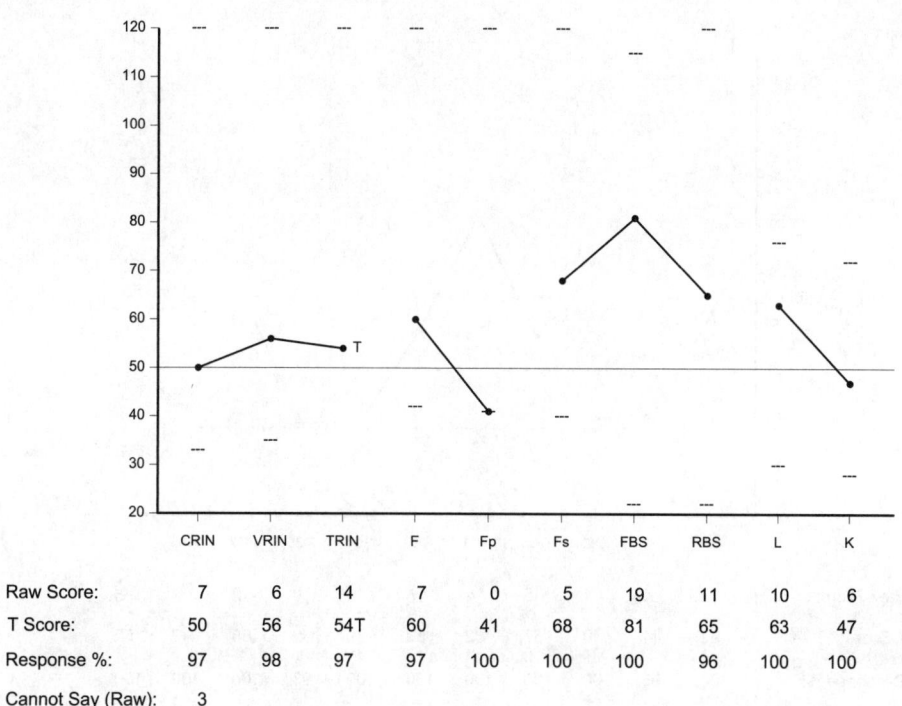

FIGURE 11.11. Ms. K's MMPI-3 Score Report

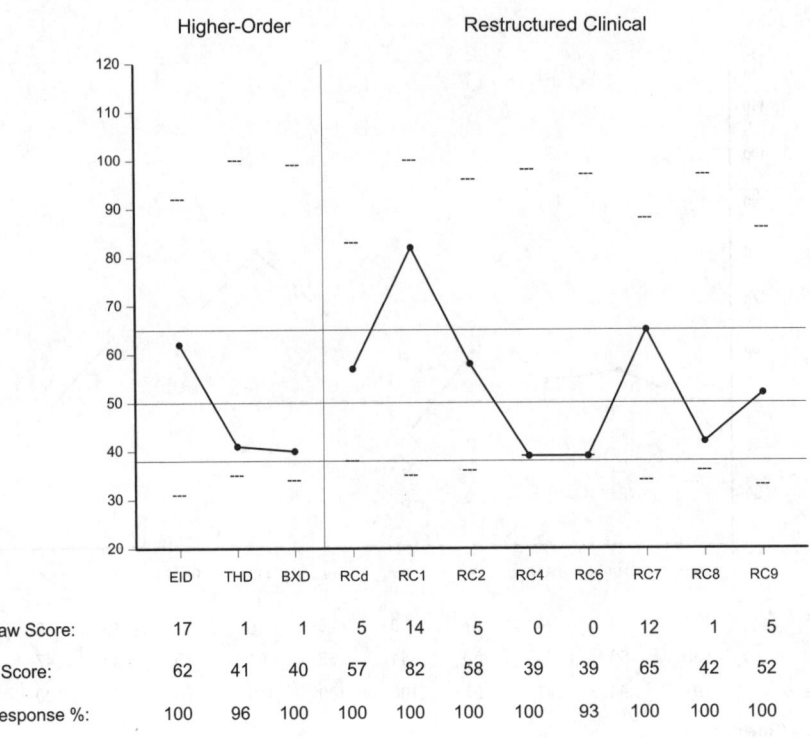

FIGURE 11.11. Ms. K's MMPI-3 Score Report, continued

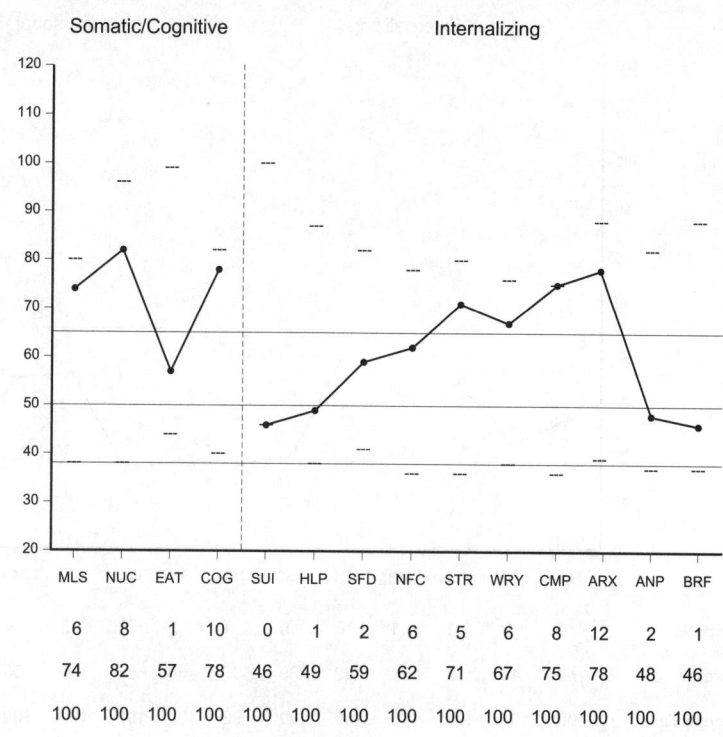

FIGURE 11.11. Ms. K's MMPI-3 Score Report, continued

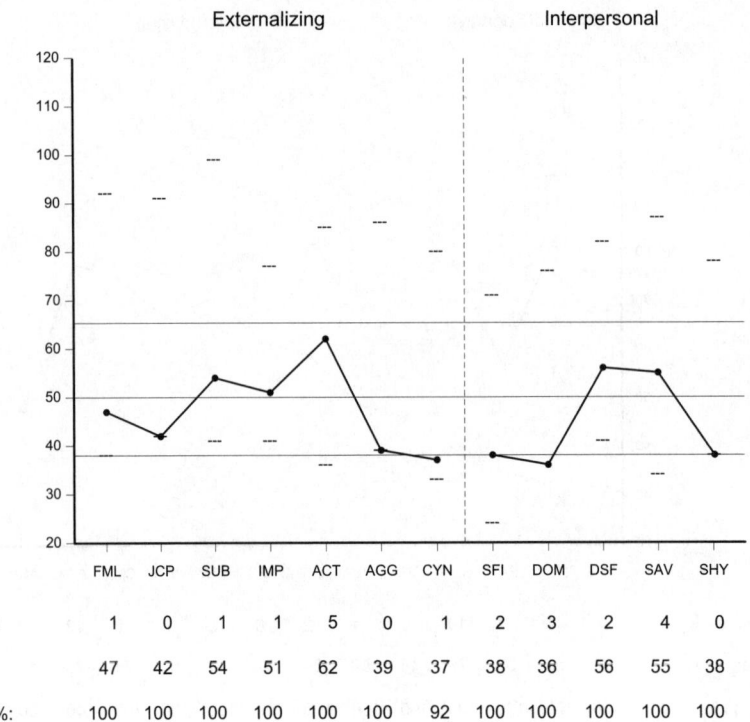

FIGURE 11.11. Ms. K's MMPI-3 Score Report, continued

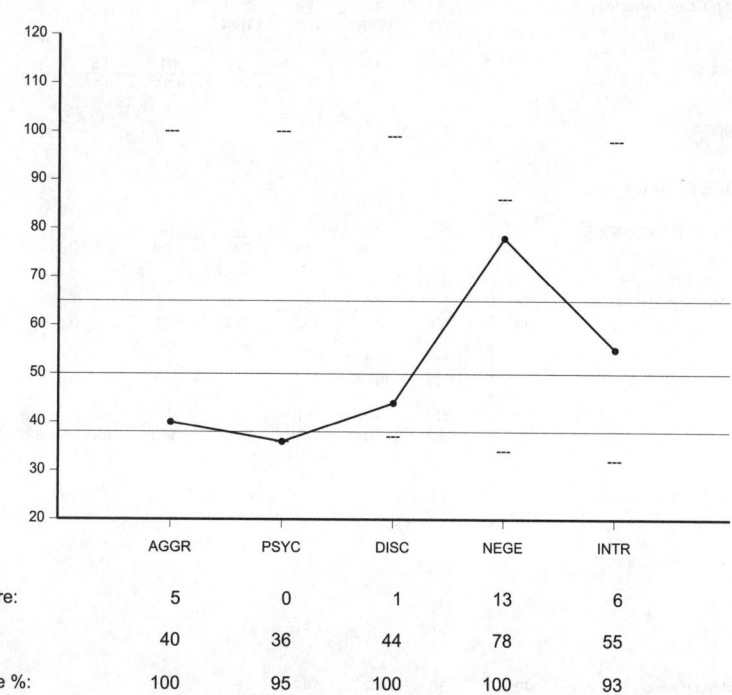

FIGURE 11.11. Ms. K's MMPI-3 Score Report, continued

MMPI-3 T SCORES (BY DOMAIN)

PROTOCOL VALIDITY

Content Non-Responsiveness

3	50	56	54 T
CNS	CRIN	VRIN	TRIN

Over-Reporting

60	41		68	81	65
F	Fp		Fs	FBS	RBS

Under-Reporting

63	47
L	K

SUBSTANTIVE SCALES

Somatic/Cognitive Dysfunction

82	74	82	57	78
RC1	MLS	NUC	EAT	COG

Emotional Dysfunction

62					
EID					

57	46	49	59	62
RCd	SUI	HLP	SFD	NFC

58	55
RC2	INTR

65	71	67	75	78	48	46	78
RC7	STR	WRY	CMP	ARX	ANP	BRF	NEGE

Thought Dysfunction

41
THD

39
RC6

42
RC8

36
PSYC

Behavioral Dysfunction

40
BXD

39	47	42	54
RC4	FML	JCP	SUB

52	51	62	39	37
RC9	IMP	ACT	AGG	CYN

44
DISC

Interpersonal Functioning

38	36	40	56	55	38
SFI	DOM	AGGR	DSF	SAV	SHY

Note. This information is provided to facilitate interpretation following the recommended structure for MMPI-3 interpretation in Chapter 5 of the *MMPI-3 Manual for Administration, Scoring, and Interpretation*, which provides details in the text and an outline in Table 5-1.

FIGURE 11.11. Ms. K's MMPI-3 Score Report, continued

as well as PTSD features including intrusive ideation, nightmares, and panic. She also reports an above average level of stress. She likely complains about stress and feels incapable of controlling her anxiety level. In addition, she reports excessive worry, including worries about misfortune and finances, as well as preoccupation with disappointments. She indeed likely worries excessively and ruminates. She reports engaging in compulsive behavior. She indeed likely engages in compulsive behavior such as repeated checking, experiences obsessions, and is rigid and perfectionistic.

Ms. K also reports a diffuse and pervasive pattern of somatic complaints involving different bodily systems, including head pain complaints, and a number of vague neurological complaints. She very likely has a psychological component to her somatic complaints and perceives her physical problems as life interfering. She also very likely is prone to developing physical symptoms in response to stress. She also reports experiencing poor health and feeling weak or tired. Indeed, she is likely preoccupied with poor health and complains of sleep disturbance, fatigue, low energy, and sexual dysfunction. She also reports a diffuse pattern of cognitive difficulties including memory problems, difficulties with attention and concentration, and possible confusion. She very likely complains about memory problems, has low tolerance for frustration, does not cope well with stress, and experiences difficulties in attention and/or concentration.

There are no indications of disordered thinking in this protocol. There also are no indications of maladaptive externalizing behavior. Ms. K describes others as well-intentioned and trustworthy and disavows cynical beliefs about them. She is possibly overly trusting. She describes herself as lacking in positive qualities. She also reports being passive and submissive, not liking to be in charge, and being ready to give in to others. She indeed likely is passive and submissive in interpersonal relationships.

Diagnostic considerations indicated by Ms. K's MMPI-3 findings include somatic symptom disorder, if physical origins for malaise and neurological complaints have been ruled out; disorders related to attention difficulties; features of personality disorders involving negative emotionality such as dependent and obsessive-compulsive; anxiety-related disorders, including generalized anxiety disorder, posttraumatic stress disorder, and panic disorder; and obsessive-compulsive disorder.

Areas for further evaluation indicated by Ms. K's scores include the extent to which genuine physical health problems contribute to her scores RC1 and NUC, the origin of her malaise complaints, and the origin of her cognitive complaints, bearing in mind possible overreporting.

Psychotherapy process issues to consider should Ms. K be referred for treatment include that she is likely to reject psychological interpretations of her somatic complaints and that malaise may impede her willingness or ability to engage in treatment, but emotional difficulties may also motivate her for treatment.

Possible targets for intervention include dysfunctional negative emotions, anxiety, developing stress management skills, excessive worry and rumination, obsessive-compulsive thoughts and behaviors, and reducing passive, submissive behavior.

Discussion

The first issue to be considered in Ms. K's case is whether her elevated FBS scores indicate overreporting. Considering her long-standing diagnosis of Parkinson's disease and findings of memory deficits with no indication of poor effort on performance validity tests, the examiner concluded that her moderately elevated FBS score did not indicate overreporting.

The referring neurologist was interested in feedback regarding Ms. K's self-reported depression and specifically whether antidepressant medication should be considered. The absence of elevation on the RCd and RC2 scales was not consistent with a diagnosis of depression. Rather, informed in part by MMPI-3 findings, the neuropsychologist concluded that Ms. K's self-reported depression was related to her experience of malaise, secondary to her Parkinson's disease and that, to some extent, this malaise manifested in physical health complaints that went beyond experiences related to her Parkinson's disease, rising to the level of a somatic symptom disorder.

An unexpected finding, considering Ms. K's presenting complaints and the neurologist's referral questions, was the broad range of problems related to negative emotionality and anxiety. The neuropsychologist followed up on these findings with diagnostic interviewing that indicated Ms. K likely had an anxiety disorder marked by excessive worry and rumination and an obsessive-compulsive disorder. They recommended that medication be considered for these conditions and for her sleep-related difficulties and that she be referred for psychotherapy to address her anxiety-related dysfunction.

Based on non-MMPI testing, the neuropsychologist concluded that Ms. K's memory complaints were the result of a mild neurocognitive disorder due to Parkinson's disease and that she be referred for follow-up evaluation in 6 months (or as necessary) to assess for further deterioration of her cognitive functioning.

Notes

1. HISTORICAL FOUNDATIONS OF THE MMPI-3

1. As a consequence of this decision, the psychometric shortcomings of the Clinical Scales were carried over to the MMPI-2 and addressed subsequently with the restructuring of the Clinical Scales, which was the first step toward developing the MMPI-2-RF. The shortcomings and the solutions adopted to address them are discussed in chapter 2.

3. DEVELOPING THE MMPI-3

1. Outside the United States, postsecondary institutions are more typically called universities rather than colleges.

6. DIVERSITY-SENSITIVE ASSESSMENT WITH THE MMPI-3

1. As used by Prichard and Rosenblatt (1980) and throughout this chapter, "bias" refers to systematic psychometric error as reflected in differential associations with external criteria across groups (slope bias) and/or differential overprediction or underprediction of external criteria (intercept bias). Subsequently introduced latent variable methods assessing construct equivalence through measurement invariance (see e.g., Han et al., 2019) also speak to the concept of test bias. We return to this issue in the final part of this chapter.
2. We recognize that "Hispanic" is one of several terms used by individuals whose origins or ancestral origins are Spanish-speaking countries and that there are differences in preferred terminology across and within subgroups of these individuals. We use the term "Hispanic" because it is the one presently used by the U.S. Census Bureau.

3. In a comprehensive review of associations between MMPI scores and race/ethnicity, Greene (1987) recommended that a minimum 5 T score point difference (corresponding to half an *SD* in normative T score units) be required for mean scores to be considered clinically significant, noting that smaller differences are unlikely to have any clinical relevance. This standard, which was adopted in future reviews of this topic, corresponds roughly to the median *SEM* estimated for MMPI-3 scales in the normative sample.

7. ADMINISTERING AND SCORING THE MMPI-3

1. To protect test security, item numbers and content are redacted from this and all other case examples in this book but are included in the actual reports.

8. INTERPRETING THE MMPI-3 VALIDITY SCALES

1. This would not necessarily be the case when the MMPI-3 is used in preemployment evaluations of public safety candidates (see Corey and Ben-Porath [2024] for details).
2. These cases focus on interpretation of underreporting scale scores in the context of clinical assessments. In preemployment evaluations, where test takers are more likely to be morally virtuous and well-adjusted than individuals assessed in a clinical context, Corey and Ben-Porath (2024) recommend using cutoffs different from the ones listed in Tables 8.11 and 8.12.

10. INTERPRETING THE MMPI-3

1. A copy of the MMPI-3 Interpretation Worksheet can be downloaded at the website for this book (https://www.upress.umn.edu/book-division/books/interpreting-the-mmpi-3).

11. MMPI-3 CASE STUDIES

1. The authors thank Tiffany Brown for her assistance with this case illustration.
2. Although the clinical picture as well as some elements of the MMPI-3 profile (e.g., RC2, CMP) may reflect symptoms of autism spectrum disorder, such a diagnosis had been ruled out in childhood, and there was no reason to doubt or otherwise overrule that assessment based on the current findings.
3. The authors thank Elizabeth Waugh for her assistance with this case illustration.
4. Treatment considerations are not listed in this interpretation because they were not the focus of this forensic evaluation.
5. Treatment considerations are not listed in this interpretation because they were not the focus of this forensic evaluation.
6. Treatment considerations are not listed in this interpretation because they were not the focus of this forensic evaluation.

References

Aaronson, A. L., Dent, O. B., & Kline, C. D. (1996). Cross-validation of MMPI and MMPI-2 predictor scales. *Journal of Clinical Psychology, 52,* 311–315.

Achenbach, T. M. (1966). The classification of children's psychiatric symptoms: A factor-analytic study. *Psychological Monographs, 80,* 1–37.

Achenbach, T. M., & Edelbrock, C. S. (1978). The classification of child psychopathology: A review and analysis of empirical efforts. *Psychological Bulletin, 85,* 1275–1301.

Ackerman, M. J., Kane, A. W., Gould, J., & Dale, M. D. (2015). *Psychological experts in divorce actions.* Wolters Kluwer.

Adams, D. K., & Horn, J. L. (1965). Non-overlapping keys for the MMPI Scales. *Journal of Consulting Psychology, 29,* 284.

Adler, T. (1990). Does the "new" MMPI beat the "classic"? *APA Monitor,* pp. 18–19.

Aguerrevere, L. E., Calamia, M. R., Greve, K. W., Bianchini, K. J., Curtis, K. L, & Ramirez, V. (2018). Clusters of financially incentivized chronic pain patients using the Minnesota Multiphasic Personality Inventory-2 Restructured Form (MMPI-2-RF). *Psychological Assessment, 30*(5), 634–644. https://doi.org/10.1037/pas0000509

Allard, G., & Faust, D. (2000). Errors in scoring objective personality tests. *Assessment, 7*(2), 119–131.

Allen, L., Conder, R. L., Green, P., & Cox, D. R. (1997). *CARB' 97 manual for the computerized assessment of response bias.* CogniSyst.

American Educational Research Association, American Psychological Association, & National Council on Measurement in Education (Eds.). (2014). *Standards for educational and psychological testing.* American Educational Research Association.

American Psychiatric Association (2013). *Diagnostic and statistical manual of mental disorders* (5th ed.). https://doi.org/10.1176/appi.books.9780890425596

American Psychiatric Association (2022). *Diagnostic and statistical manual of mental disorders* (5th ed.), Text Revision.

American Psychological Association. (2020). *Publication manual of the American Psychological Association* (7th ed.). https://doi.org/10.1037/0000165-000

Anderson, J. L., Brockhaus, R., Kloefer, J., & Sellbom, M. (2020). Utility of the MMPI-2-RF in sexual violence risk assessment. *International Journal of Forensic Mental Health, 19*(4), 403–415. https://doi.org/10.1080/14999013.2020.1805648

Anderson, J. L., Burchett, D., Glassmire, D. M., Wygant, D. B., Kamphuis, J. H., Smid, W., & Sellbom, M. (2021). Differentiating borderline and antisocial personality disorders in forensic settings. *Psychology, Crime & Law*. Advance online publication. https://doi.org/10.1080/1068316X.2021.1880586

Anderson, J. L., Sellbom, M., Ayearst, L., Quilty, L. C., Chmielewski, M., & Bagby, R. M. (2015a). Associations between *DSM-5* Section III personality traits and the Minnesota Multiphasic Personality Inventory 2-Restructured Form (MMPI-2-RF) scales in a psychiatric patient sample. *Psychological Assessment, 27*(3), 801–815. https://doi.org/10.1037/pas0000096

Anderson, J. L., Sellbom, M., Bagby, R. M., Quilty, L. C., Veltri, C. O. C., Markon, K. E., & Krueger, R. F. (2013). On the convergence between PSY-5 domains and PID-5 domains and facets: Implications for assessment of *DSM-5* personality traits. *Assessment, 20*(3), 286–294. https://doi.org/10.1177/1073191112471141

Anderson, J. L., Sellbom, M., Ayearst, L., Quilty, L. C., Chmielewski, M., & Bagby, R. M. (2015b). Associations between *DSM-5* Section III personality traits and the Minnesota Multiphasic Personality Inventory 2-Restructured Form (MMPI-2-RF) Scales in a psychiatric patient sample. *Psychological Assessment, 27*, 801–815.

Anderson, J. L., Sellbom, M., Pymont, C., Smid, W., De Saeger, H., & Kamphuis, J. H. (2015c). Measurement of *DSM-5* Section II personality disorder constructs using the MMPI-2-RF in clinical and forensic samples. *Psychological Assessment, 27*(3), 786–800. https://doi.org/10.1037/pas0000103

Anderson, J. L., & Sellbom, M. (2021). Assessing ICD-11 personality trait domain qualifiers with the MMPI-2-RF. *Journal of Clinical Psychology, 77*(4), 1090–1105. https://doi.org/10.1002/jclp.23099

Andrews, D. A., & Bonta, J. (2010). *The psychology of criminal conduct* (5th ed.). Routledge.

Anestis, J. C., Finn, J. A., Gottfried, E. D., Arbisi, P. A., & Joiner, T. E. (2015). Reading the road signs: The utility of the MMPI-2 Restructured Form Validity Scales in prediction of premature termination. *Assessment, 22*(3), 279–288. https://doi.org/10.1177/1073191114541672

Anestis, J. C., Finn, J. A., Gottfried, E. D., Hames, J. L., Bodell, L. P., Hagan, C. R., Arnau, R. C., Anestis, M. D., Arbisi, P. A., & Joiner, T. E. (2018). Burdensomeness, belongingness, and capability: Assessing the interpersonal-psychological theory of suicide with MMPI-2-RF scales. *Assessment, 25*(4), 415–431. https://doi.org/10.1177/1073191116652227

Anestis, J. C., Preston, O. C., Rodriguez, T. R., & Harrop, T. M. (2022). MMPI-3 scale predictors of reactions to ostracism in a sample of racially diverse college students. *Psychological Assessment, 34*(6), 503–516. https://doi.org/10.1037/pas0001113

Aragona, M., Tarsitani, L., De Nitto, S., & Inghilleri, M. (2008). *DSM-IV-TR* "pain disorder associated with psychological factors" as a nonhysterical form of somatization. *Pain Research and Management, 13*, 13–18.

Arbisi, P. A., & Ben-Porath, Y. S. (1995). An MMPI-2 infrequent response scale for use with psychopathological populations: The Infrequency-Psychopathology Scale, F(p). *Psychological Assessment, 7*, 424–431.

Arbisi, P. A., Ben-Porath, Y. S., & McNulty, J. (2002). A comparison of MMPI-2 validity in African American and Caucasian psychiatric inpatients. *Psychological Assessment, 14*(1), 3–15. https://doi.org/10.1037/1040-3590.14.1.3

Arbisi, P. A., Ben-Porath, Y. S., & McNulty, J. L. (2003). Refinement of the MMPI-2 F(p) Scale is not necessary: A response to Gass and Luis. *Assessment, 10,* 123–128.

Arbisi, P. A., Polusny, M. A., Erbes, C. R., Thuras, P., & Reddy, M. K. (2011). The Minnesota Multiphasic Personality Inventory 2 Restructured Form in National Guard soldiers screening positive for posttraumatic stress disorder and mild traumatic brain injury. *Psychological Assessment, 23,* 203–214.

Arbisi, P. A., Sellbom, M., & Ben-Porath, Y. S. (2008). Empirical correlates of the MMPI-2 Restructured Clinical (RC) Scales in psychiatric inpatients. *Journal of Personality Assessment, 90,* 122–128.

Archer, R. P., Handel, R. W., & Couvadelli, B. (2004). An evaluation of the incremental validity of the MMPI-2 Superlative (S) Scale in an inpatient psychiatric sample. *Assessment, 11,* 102–108.

Archer, R. P., Handel, R. W., Ben-Porath, Y. S., & Tellegen, A. (2016). *Minnesota Multiphasic Personality Inventory-Adolescent-Restructured Form (MMPI-A-RF): Administration, scoring, interpretation, and technical manual*. University of Minnesota Press.

Armistead-Jehle, P., Cooper, D. B., Grills, C. E., Cole, W. R., Lippa, S. M., Stegman, R. L., & Lange, R. T. (2018). Clinical utility of the mBIAS and NSI Validity-10 to detect symptom over-reporting following mild TBI: A multicenter investigation with military service members. *Journal of Clinical and Experimental Neuropsychology, 40*(3), 213–223. https://doi.org/10.1080/13803395.2017.1329406

Avdeyeva, T. V., Tellegen, A., & Ben-Porath, Y. S. (2011). Empirical correlates of low scores on MMPI-2/MMPI-2-RF Restructured Clinical Scales in a sample of university students. *Assessment, 19*(3), 388–393. https://doi.org/10.1177/1073191111411675

Ayearst, L. E., Sellbom, M., Trobst, K. K., & Bagby, R. M. (2013). Evaluating the interpersonal content of the MMPI-2-RF Interpersonal Scales. *Journal of Personality Assessment, 95*(2), 187–196. https://doi.org/10.1080/00223891.2012.730085

Azan, A. (1989). The MMPI version Hispanic: Standardization and cross-cultural personality study with a population of Cuban refugees (Doctoral dissertation, University of Minnesota, 1988). *Dissertation Abstracts International, 50,* 2144B.

Bach, B., & First, M. B. (2018). Application of the ICD-11 classification of personality disorders. *BMC psychiatry, 18*(1), 1–14.

Bach, B., Sellbom, M., Kongerslev, M., Simonsen, E., Krueger, R. F., & Mulder, R. (2017). Deriving ICD-11 personality disorder domains from DSM-5 traits: Initial attempt to harmonize two diagnostic systems. *Acta Psychiatrica Scandinavica, 136*(1), 108–117.

Baer, R. A., & Miller, J. (2002). Underreporting of psychopathology on the MMPI-2: A meta-analytic review. *Psychological Assessment, 41,* 16–26.

Baer, R. A., Wetter, M. W., Nichols, D., Greene, R., & Berry, D. T. R. (1995). Sensitivity of MMPI-2 Validity Scales to underreporting of symptoms. *Psychological Assessment, 7,* 419–423.

Baez, M. E., Miller, S. N., & Banou, E. (2018). Psychological and personality differences between male and female veterans in an inpatient interdisciplinary chronic pain program. *Journal of Applied Behavioral Research, 24*(1). https://doi.org/10.1111/jabr.12146

Bagby, R. M., & Marshall, M. B. (2004). Assessing underreporting response bias on the MMPI-2. *Assessment, 11*, 115–126.

Bagby, R. M., Marshall, M. B., & Bacchiochi, J. R. (2005). The validity and clinical utility of the MMPI-2 Malingering Depression Scale. *Journal of Personality Assessment, 85*, 304–311.

Bagby, R. M., Nicholson, R. A., Buis, T., Radovanovic, H., & Fidler, B. J. (1999). Defensive responding on the MMPI-2 in family custody and access evaluations. *Psychological Assessment, 11*, 24–28.

Bagby, R. M., Onno, K. A., Mortezaei, A., & Sellbom, M. (2020). Examining the "Traditional Background Hypothesis" for the MMPI-2-RF L-r scores in a Muslim faith-based sample. *Psychological Assessment, 32*(10), 991–995. https://doi.org/10.1037/pas0000941

Bagby, R. M., Rogers, R., Nicholson, R. A., Buis, T., Seeman, M. V., & Rector, N. A. (1997). Effectiveness of the MMPI-2 validity indicators in the detection of defensive responding in clinical and nonclinical samples. *Psychological Assessment, 9*, 406–413.

Bagby, R. M., Ryder, A. G., Ben-Dat, D., Bacchiochi, J., & Parker, J. D. (2002). Validation of the dimensional factor structure of the Personality Psychopathology Five in clinical and nonclinical samples. *Journal of Personality Disorders, 16*(4), 304–316.

Bagby, R. M., Sellbom, M., Ayearst, L. E., Chmielewski, M. S., Anderson, J. L., & Quilty, L. C. (2014). Exploring the hierarchical structure of the MMPI-2-RF Personality Psychopathology Five in psychiatric patient and university student samples. *Journal of Personality Assessment, 96*(2), 166–172. https://doi.org/10.1080/00223891.2013.825623

Bagby, R. M., Sellbom, M., Costa, P. T., & Widiger, T. A. (2008). Predicting *Diagnostic and Statistical Manual of Mental Disorders–IV* personality disorders with the Five-Factor Model of personality and the Personality Psychopathology Five. *Personality and Mental Health, 2*(2), 55–69.

Ball, J. C. (1960). Comparison of MMPI profile differences among Negro-white adolescents. *Journal of Clinical Psychology, 16*, 304–307.

Bandura, A. (1994). Social cognitive theory of mass communication. In J. Bryant & D. Zillmann (Eds.), *Media effects: Advances in theory and research* (pp. 61–90). Lawrence Erlbaum Associates.

Bandura, A. (2001). Social cognitive theory: An agentic perspective. *Annual Review of Psychology, 52*, 1–26.

Barber-Rioja, V., Zottoli, T. M., Kucharski, L. T., & Duncan, S. (2009). The utility of the MMPI-2 criminal offender Infrequency (Fc) Scale in the detection of malingering in criminal defendants. *International Journal of Forensic Mental Health, 8*, 16–24.

Barlow, K., Grenyer, B., & Ilkiw-Lavalle, O. (2000). Prevalence and precipitants of aggression in psychiatric inpatient units. *Australian and New Zealand Journal of Psychiatry, 34*, 967–974.

Barron, F. (1953). An ego-strength scale which predicts response to psychotherapy. *Journal of Consulting Psychology, 17*, 327–333.

Barthlow, D. L., Graham, J. R., Ben-Porath, Y. S., Tellegen, A., & McNulty, J. L. (2002). The appropriateness of the MMPI-2 K correction. *Assessment, 9*, 219–229.

Beauchaine, T. P., Zisner, A. R., & Sauder, C. L. (2017). Trait impulsivity and the externalizing spectrum. *Annual Review of Clinical Psychology, 13*(1), 343–368.

Beck, A. T., Epstein, N., Brown, G., & Steer, R. A. (1988). An inventory for measuring clinical anxiety: Psychometric properties. *Journal of Consulting and Clinical Psychology, 56*(6), 893–897. https://doi.org/10.1037/0022-006X.56.6.893

Beck, A. T., Weissman, A., Lester, D., & Trexler, L. (1974). The measurement of pessimism: The Hopelessness Scale. *Journal of Consulting and Clinical Psychology, 42,* 861–865.

Bender, D. S., Morey, L. C., & Skodol, A. E. (2011). Toward a model for assessing level of personality functioning in *DSM–5,* part I: A review of theory and methods. *Journal of Personality Assessment, 93,* 332–346.

Ben-Porath, Y. S. (2013). Self-report inventories: Assessing personality and psychopathology. In J. R. Graham & J. Naglieri (Eds.), Vol X: *Handbook of assessment psychology (2nd Edition,* pp. 622–644). Wiley.

Ben-Porath, Y. S., & Butcher, J. N. (1989a). The comparability of MMPI and MMPI-2 scales and profiles. *Psychological Assessment: A Journal of Consulting and Clinical Psychology, 1,* 345–347.

Ben-Porath, Y. S., & Butcher, J. N. (1989b). The psychometric stability of rewritten MMPI items. *Journal of Personality Assessment, 53,* 645–653.

Ben-Porath, Y. S., & Butcher, J. N. (1991). The historical development of personality assessment. In C. E. Walker (Ed.), *Clinical psychology: Historical and research roots* (pp. 121–156). Plenum.

Ben-Porath, Y. S., Butcher, J. N., & Graham, J. R. (1991). Contribution of the MMPI-2 Content Scales to the differential diagnosis of psychopathology. *Psychological Assessment: A Journal of Consulting and Clinical Psychology, 3,* 634–640.

Ben-Porath, Y. S., Graham, J. R., & Tellegen, A. (2009). *The MMPI-2 Symptom Validity (FBS) Scale: Development, research findings, and interpretive recommendations.* University of Minnesota Press.

Ben-Porath, Y. S., Greve, K. W., Bianchini, K. J., & Kaufmann, P. M. (2009). The MMPI-2 Symptom Validity Scale (FBS) is an empirically-validated measure of over-reporting in personal injury litigants and claimants: Reply to Butcher et al. (2008). *Psychological Injury and the Law, 1,* 62–85.

Ben-Porath, Y. S., & Sherwood, N. E. (1993). *The MMPI-2 Content Component Scales: Development, psychometric characteristics, and clinical applications.* University of Minnesota Press.

Ben-Porath, Y. S., & Tellegen, A. (2008/2011). *Minnesota Multiphasic Personality Inventory-2-Restructured Form (MMPI-2-RF): Manual for administration, scoring, and interpretation.* University of Minnesota Press.

Ben-Porath, Y. S., & Tellegen, A. (2020a). *Minnesota Multiphasic Personality Inventory-3 (MMPI-3): Manual for administration, scoring, and interpretation.* University of Minnesota Press.

Ben-Porath, Y. S., & Tellegen, A. (2020b). *Minnesota Multiphasic Personality Inventory-3 (MMPI-3): Technical manual.* University of Minnesota Press.

Ben-Porath, Y. S., & Tellegen, A. (2020c). *Minnesota Multiphasic Personality Inventory-3 (MMPI-3): User's guide for the score and clinical interpretive reports.* University of Minnesota Press.

Ben-Porath, Y. S., Tellegen, A., & Puente, A. E. (2020). *Minnesota Multiphasic Personality Inventory-3 (MMPI-3): Manual supplement for the U.S. Spanish translation.* University of Minnesota Press.

Bentall, R. P., Corcoran, R., Howard, R., Blackwood, N., & Kinderman, P. (2001). Persecutory delusions: a review and theoretical integration. *Clinical Psychology Review, 21*(8), 1143–1192.

Bentall, R. P., Kinderman, P., & Kaney, S. (1994). The self, attributional processes and abnormal beliefs: Towards a model of persecutory delusions. *Behavior Research and Therapy, 32*(3), 331–341.

Bernreuter, R. J. (1933). Theory and construction of the personality inventory. *Journal of Social Psychology, 4*, 387–405.

Bernstein, D., Arntz, A., & Travaglini, L. (2009). Schizoid and avoidant personality disorders. In T. Millon (Ed.), *Oxford textbook of psychopathology* (2nd ed., pp. 586–601). Oxford University Press.

Bhar, S. S., Ghahramanlou-Holloway, M., Brown, G. K., & Beck, A. T. (2008). Self-esteem and suicide ideation in psychiatric outpatients. *Suicide and Life Threatening Behavior, 38*, 511–516.

Bianchini, K. J., Aguerrevere, L. E., Curtis, K. L., Roebuck-Spencer, T. M., Frey, F. C., Greve, K. W., & Calamia, M. (2018). Classification accuracy of the Minnesota Multiphasic Personality Inventory-2 (MMPI-2)-Restructured Form Validity Scales in detecting malingered pain-related disability. *Psychological Assessment, 30*(7), 857–869. https://doi.org/10.1037/pas0000532

Bianchini, K. J., Greve, K. W., & Glynn, G. (2005). Review article: On the diagnosis of malingered pain-related disability: Lessons from cognitive malingering research. *The Spine Journal, 5*, 404–417.

Bigos, S., Battie, M., Spengler, D., Fisher, L., Fordyce, W., Hansson, T. et al. (1991). A prospective study of work perceptions and psychosocial factors affecting the report of back injury. *Spine, 16*, 1–6.

Binder, R. L., & McNeil, D. E. (1988). Effects of diagnosis and context on dangerousness. *American Journal of Psychiatry, 145*, 728–732.

Binford, A., & Liljequist, L. (2008). Behavioral correlates of selected MMPI-2 Clinical, Content, and Restructured Clinical Scales. *Journal of Personality Assessment, 60*, 608–614.

Blackwood, N. J., Howard, R. J., Bentall, R. P., & Murray, R. M. (2001). Cognitive neuropsychiatric models of persecutory delusions. *American Journal of Psychiatry, 158*(4), 527–539.

Blais, M. A. (2010). The common structure of normal personality and psychopathology: Preliminary exploration in a non-patient sample. *Journal of Personality and Individual Differences, 48*, 322–326.

Blanchard, J. L., Horan, W. P., & Brown, S. A. (2001). Diagnostic differences in social anhedonia: A longitudinal study of schizophrenia and major depressive disorder. *Journal of Abnormal Psychology, 110*, 363–371.

Blasco Saiz, J. L., & Pallardó Durá, L. (2013). Detección de exageración de síntomas mediante el SIMS y el MMPI-2-RF en pacientes diagnosticados de trastorno mixto ansioso-depresivo y adaptativo en el contexto medicolegal: Un estudio preliminar [Symptom exaggeration detection by the SIMS and the MMPI-2-RF in patients diagnosed of mixed anxiety-depressive disorder and adjustment disorder in the medico-legal context: A preliminary study]. *Clínica y Salud, 24*(3), 177–183. https://doi.org/10.1016/S1130-5274(13)70019-7

Block, A. R., Ben-Porath, Y. S., & Marek, R. J. (2012). Psychological risk factors for poor outcome of spine surgery and spinal cord stimulator implant: A review of the literature and their assessment with the MMPI-2-RF. *The Clinical Neuropsychologist, 27*(1), 81–107. https://doi.org/10.1080/13854046.2012.721007

Block, A. R., Marek, R. J., Ben-Porath, Y. S., & Kukal, D. (2017). Associations between pre-implant psychosocial factors and spinal cord stimulation outcome: Evaluation using the MMPI-2-RF. *Assessment, 24*(1), 60–70. https://doi.org/10.1177/1073191115601518

Block, A. R., Marek, R. J., Ben-Porath, Y. S, & Ohnmeiss, D. D. (2014). Associations between Minnesota Multiphasic Personality Inventory-2-Restructured Form (MMPI-2-RF) scores, workers' compensation status, and spine surgery outcome. *Journal of Applied Biobehavioral Research, 19*(4), 248–267. https://doi.org/10.1111/jabr.12028

Block, J. (1965). *The challenge of response sets: Unconfounding meaning, acquiescence, and social desirability in the MMPI*. Appleton-Century-Crofts.

Blonigen, D. M., Hicks, B. M., Krueger, R. F., Patrick, C. J., & Iacono, W. G. (2005). Psychopathic personality traits: Heritability and genetic overlap with internalizing and externalizing psychopathology. *Psychological Medicine: A Journal of Research in Psychiatry and the Allied Sciences, 35*, 637–648.

Bolinskey, P. K., Trumbetta, S. L., Hanson, D. R., & Gottesman, I. I. (2010). Predicting adult psychopathology from adolescent MMPIs: Some victories. *Personality and Individual Differences, 49*, 324–330.

Bornstein, R. F. (2005). Context-specific deficits and strengths. *The Dependent Patient*. 57–72.

Brewin, C. R., Cloitre, M., Hyland, P., Shevlin, M., Maercker, A., Bryant, R. A., & Reed, G. M. (2017). A review of current evidence regarding the ICD-11 proposals for diagnosing PTSD and complex PTSD. *Clinical Psychology Review, 58*, 1–15.

Bridges, S. A., & Baum, L. J. (2013). An examination of MMPI-2-RF L-r Scale in an outpatient Protestant sample. *Journal of Psychology and Christianity, 32*, 115–123.

Briere, J. (2001). *Detailed assessment of posttraumatic stress (DAPS)*. Psychological Assessment Resources.

Broadbent, D. E., Cooper, P. F., Fitzgerald, P., & Parkers, K. R. (1982). The cognitive failure questionnaire and its correlates. *British General of Clinical Psychology, 21*, 1–16.

Brown, J. R., Hicks, A.D., Sellbom, M., & McCord, D. M. (2023). Further mapping of the MMPI-3 onto HiTOP in a primary medical care sample. *Psychological Assessment*. Advance online publication. https://dx.doi.org/10.1037/pas0001218.

Brown, S. A. (2008). The reality of persecutory beliefs: Base rate information for clinicians. *Ethical Human Psychology and Psychiatry: An International Journal of Critical Inquiry, 10*, 163–178.

Brown, T. A. (2007). Temporal course and structural relationships among dimensions of temperament and *DSM-IV* anxiety and mood disorder constructs. *Journal of Abnormal Psychology, 116*(2), 313–328.

Brown, T. A., Chorpita, B. F., & Barlow, D. H. (1998). Structural relationships among dimensions of the *DSM–IV* anxiety and mood disorders and dimensions of negative affect, positive affect, and autonomic arousal. *Journal of Abnormal Psychology, 107*, 179–192.

Brown, T. A., & Sellbom, M. (2020). The utility of the MMPI-2-RF Validity Scales in detecting underreporting. *Journal of Personality Assessment, 102*(1), 66–74. https://doi.org/10.1080/00223891.2018.1539003

Brown, T. A., & Sellbom, M. (2021). Associations between MMPI-3 scale scores and the *DSM-5* personality disorders. *Journal of Clinical Psychology, 77*(12), 2943–2964. https://doi.org/10.1002/jclp.23230

Brown, T. A., & Sellbom, M. (2022). Associations between MMPI-3 scale scores and the *DSM-5* AMPD and ICD-11 dimensional personality traits. *Assessment*. Advance online publication. https://doi.org/10.1177/10731911221075724

Bruns, D. (2014). Clinical and forensic standards for the psychological assessment of patients with chronic pain. *Psychological Injury and Law, 7*, 297–316.

Bryant, W. T. (2020). A transgender sample for the Minnesota Multiphasic Personality Inventory-2-Restructured Form (MMPI-2-RF). *Dissertation Abstracts International: Section B: The Sciences and Engineering, 82*(3-B).

Bryant, W. T., Livingston, N. A., McNulty, J. L., Choate, K. T., & Brummel, B. J. (2021). Examining Minnesota Multiphasic Personality Inventory-2-Restructured Form (MMPI-2-RF) scale scores in a transgender and gender diverse sample. *Psychological Assessment, 33*(12), 1239–1246. https://doi.org/10.1037/pas0001087

Bryant, W. T., Livingston, N. A., McNulty, J. L., Choate, K.T., Santa Ana, E. J., & Ben-Porath, Y. S. (2023). Exploring the MMPI-3 in a transgender and gender diverse sample. Manuscript under review.

Budtz-Lilly, A., Fink, P., Ørnbøl, E., Vestergaard, M., Moth, G., Christensen, K. S., & Rosendal, M. (2015). A new questionnaire to identify bodily distress in primary care: the "BDS checklist." *Journal of Psychosomatic Research, 78*(6), 536–545.

Buckley, P. F., Miller, B. J., Lehrer, D. S., & Castle, D. J. (2009). Psychiatric comorbidities and schizophrenia. *Schizophrenia Bulletin, 35*, 383–402.

Burchett, D. L., & Ben-Porath, Y. S. (2010). The impact of overreporting on MMPI-2-RF substantive scale score validity. *Assessment, 17*, 497–516.

Burchett, D., Dragon, W. R., Smith Holbert, A. M., Tarescavage, A. M., Mattson, C. A., Handel, R. W., & Ben-Porath, Y. S. (2016). "False feigners": Examining the impact of non-content-based invalid responding on the Minnesota Multiphasic Personality Inventory-2 Restructured Form content-based invalid responding indicators. *Psychological Assessment, 28*(5), 458–470. https://doi.org/10.1037/pas0000205

Burke, J. D., Loeber, R., & Lahey, B. B. (2007). Adolescent conduct disorder and interpersonal callousness as predictors of psychopathy in young adults. *Journal of Clinical Child and Adolescent Psychology, 36*, 334–346.

Butcher, J. N. (1972a). *Objective personality assessment: Changing perspectives*. Academic Press.

Butcher, J. N. (1972b). Personality assessment: Problems and perspectives. In J. N. Butcher (Ed.), *Objective personality assessment: Changing perspectives* (pp. 1–20). Academic Press.

Butcher, J. N. (1985). Personality assessment in industry: Theoretical issues and illustrations. In H. J. Bernardin (Ed.), *Personality assessment in organizations* (pp. 277–310). Praeger.

Butcher, J. N. (2011). *MMPI-2: A beginner's guide* (3rd ed.). American Psychological Association.

Butcher, J. N., Aldwin, C. L., Levenson, M. R., Ben-Porath, Y. S., Spiro, A., & Bosse, R. (1991). Personality and aging: A study of the MMPI-2 aging elderly men. *Psychology of Aging, 6,* 361–370.

Butcher, J. N., Arbisi, P. A., Atlis, M. M., & McNulty, J. L. (2003). The construct validity of the Lees-Haley Fake-Bad Scale (FBS): Does this scale measure somatic malingering and feigned emotional distress? *Archives of Clinical Neuropsychology, 18,* 473–485.

Butcher, J. N., Ball, B., & Ray, E. (1964). Effects of socioeconomic level on MMPI differences in Negro-white college students. *Journal of Counseling Psychology, 11,* 83–87.

Butcher, J. N., Braswell, L., & Raney, D. (1983). A cross-cultural comparison of American Indian, Black, and White inpatients on the MMPI and presenting symptoms. *Journal of Consulting and Clinical Psychology, 51*(4), 587–594. https://doi.org/10.1037/0022-006X.51.4.587

Butcher, J. N., Cabiya, J., Lucio, E., & Garrido, M. (2007). *Assessing Hispanic clients using the MMPI-2 and MMPI-A.* American Psychological Association. https://doi.org/10.1037/11585-00

Butcher, J. N., Dahlstrom, W. G., Graham, J. R., Tellegen, A. & Kaemmer, B. (1989). *Minnesota Multiphasic Personality Inventory-2 (MMPI-2): Manual for administration and scoring.* University of Minnesota Press.

Butcher, J. N., Gass, C. S., Cumella, E., Kally, Z., & Williams, C. L. (2008). Potential for bias in MMPI-2 assessments using the Fake Bad Scale (FBS). *Psychological Injury and Law, 1,* 191–209.

Butcher, J. N., Graham, J. R., Ben-Porath, Y. S., Tellegen, A., Dahlstrom, W. G., & Kaemmer, B. (2001). *Minnesota Multiphasic Personality Inventory-2 (MMPI-2): Manual for administration, scoring, and interpretation* (Rev. ed.). University of Minnesota Press.

Butcher, J. N., Graham, J. R., Dahlstrom, W. G., & Bowman, E. (1990). The MMPI-2 with college students. *Journal of Personality Assessment, 54,* 1–15.

Butcher, J. N., Graham, J. R., Williams, C. L., & Ben-Porath, Y. S. (1990). *Development and use of the MMPI-2 Content Scales.* University of Minnesota Press.

Butcher, J. N., Hamilton, C. K., Rouse, S. V., & Cumella, E. J. (2006). The deconstruction of the Hy Scale of MMPI-2: Failure of RC3 in measuring somatic symptom expression. *Journal of Personality Assessment, 87,* 186–192.

Butcher, J. N., & Han, K. (1995). Development of an MMPI-2 scale to assess the presentation of self in a superlative manner: The S Scale. In J. N. Butcher & C. D. Spielberger (Eds.), *Advances in personality assessment* (Vol. 10, pp. 25–50). Lawrence Erlbaum Associates.

Butcher, J. N., Jeffrey, T., Cayton, T. G., Colligan, S., DeVore, J., & Minnegawa, R. (1990). A study of active duty military personnel with the MMPI-2. *Military Psychology, 2,* 47–61.

Butcher, J. N., & Pancheri, P. (1976). *A handbook of cross-national MMPI research.* University of Minnesota Press.

Cady, V. M. (1923). The estimation of juvenile incorrigibility. *Journal of Juvenile Delinquency, Monographs No. 2.*

Caldwell, A. B. (1969). *MMPI critical items.* Unpublished manuscript.

Caldwell, A. B. (2006). Maximal measurement or meaningful measurement: The interpretive challenges of the MMPI-2 Restructured Clinical (RC) Scales. *Journal of Personality Assessment, 87,* 193–201.

Campbell, D. P. (1972). The practical problems of revising an established psychological test. In J. N. Butcher (Ed.), *Objective personality assessment: Changing perspectives* (pp. 117–130). Academic Press.

Campos, L. P. (1989). Adverse impact, unfairness, and bias in the psychological screening of Hispanic peace officers. *Hispanic Journal of Behavioral Sciences, 11*(2), 122–135. https://doi.org/10.1177/07399863890112002

Canul, G. D., & Cross, H. J. (1994). The influence of acculturation and racial identity attitudes on Mexican-Americans' MMPI-2 performance. *Journal of Clinical Psychology, 50*(5), 736–745. https://doi.org/10.1002/1097-4679(199409)50:5<736::AID-JCLP2270500511>3.0.CO;2-Z

Capilla Ramírez, P., González Ordi, H., Santamaría Fernández, P., Pérez Nieto, M. A., & Casado Morales, M. I. (2013). Fibromialgia: ¿Exageración o simulación? [Fibromyalgia: Exaggeration or malingering?]. *Clínica y Salud, 24*(3), 185–195. https://doi.org/10.5093/cl2013a20

Carnovale, M., Sellbom, M., & Bagby, R. M. (2020). The Personality Inventory for ICD-11: Investigating reliability, structural and concurrent validity, and method variance. *Psychological Assessment, 32*(1), 8–17. https://doi.org/10.1037/pas0000776

Caron, G. R., & Archer, R. P. (1997). MMPI and Rorschach characteristics of individuals approved for gender reassignment surgery. *Assessment, 4*(3), 229–241. https://doi.org/10.1177/107319119700400303

Caspi, A., Houts, R. M., Belsky, D. W., Goldman-Mellor, S. J., Harrington, H., Israel, S., . . . & Moffitt, T. E. (2014). The p factor: one general psychopathology factor in the structure of psychiatric disorders? *Clinical Psychological Science, 2*(2), 119–137.

Castro, Y., Gordon, K. H., Brown, J. S., Anestis, J. C., & Joiner, T. E. (2008). Examination of racial differences on the MMPI-2 Clinical and Restructured Clinical Scales in an outpatient sample. *Assessment, 15,* 277–286.

Cattell, R. B. (1965). *The scientific analysis of personality*. Penguin Books.

Cattell, R. B. (Ed.). (1966). *Handbook of multivariate experimental psychology*. Rand McNally.

Cattell, R. B., Eber, H. W., & Tatsuoka, M. (1970). *Handbook for the Sixteen Personality Factor Questionnaire*. Institute of Personality and Ability Testing.

Chapman, L. J., & Chapman, J. P. (1980). Scales for rating psychotic and psychotic-like experiences as continua. *Schizophrenia Bulletin, 6,* 476–489.

Chapman, L. J., Chapman, J. P., & Raulin, M. L. (1976). Scales for physical and social anhedonia. *Journal of Abnormal Psychology, 85,* 374–382.

Chapman, L. J., Chapman, J. P., & Raulin, M. L. (1978). Body-image aberration in schizophrenia. *Journal of Abnormal Psychology, 87,* 399–407.

Chmielewski, M., Zhu, J., Burchett, D., Bury, A. S., & Bagby, R. M. (2017). The comparative capacity of the Minnesota Multiphasic Personality Inventory-2 (MMPI-2) and MMPI-2 Restructured Form (MMPI-2-RF) Validity Scales to detect malingering in a disability claimant sample. *Psychological Assessment, 29*(2), 199–208. https://doi.org/10.1037/pas0000328

Choi, J. Y. (2017). Posttraumatic stress symptoms and dissociation between childhood trauma and two different types of psychosis-like experience. *Child Abuse and Neglect, 72,* 404–410. https://doi.org/10.1016/j.chiabu.2017.08.023

Choi, J. Y., Gim, M. S., & Lee, J. Y. (2020). Predictability of temperaments and negative experiences in higher-order symptom-based subtypes of depression. *Journal of Affective Disorders, 265*, 18–25. https://doi.org/10.1016/j.jad.2020.01.028

Choi, J. Y., & Park, E.-H. (2021). Psychological characteristics of suicide attempters with major depressive disorder using the Minnesota Multiphasic Personality Inventory-2 Restructured Form. *Korean Journal of Psychosomatic Medicine, 29*(1), 1–10. https://doi.org/10.22722/KJPM.2021.29.1.1

Chu, C. M., & Ogloff, J. R. P. (2012). Assessing child sexual abusers in non-criminal contexts: Proposed practice guidelines. *Psychiatry, Psychology, and Law, 19*, 464–481.

Clark, L. A. (1993). *Manual for the Schedule for Nonadaptive and Adaptive Personality (SNAP)*. University of Minnesota Press.

Clark, L. A., & Watson, D. (1991). Tripartite model of anxiety and depression: Psychometric evidence and taxonomic implications. *Journal of Abnormal Psychology, 100*, 316–336.

Clark, M. E. (1996). MMPI-2 negative treatment indicators Content and Content Component Scales: Clinical correlates and outcome prediction for men with chronic pain. *Psychological Assessment, 8*, 32–38.

Clarke, D. M., & Kissane, D. W. (2002). Demoralization: Its phenomenology and importance. *Australian and New Zealand Journal of Psychiatry, 6*, 733–742.

Cleckley, H. (1941). *The mask of sanity: An attempt to reinterpret the so-called psychopathic personality*. Mosby.

Cockram, C. A., Doros, G., & de Figueiredo, J. M. (2009). Diagnosis and measurement of subjective incompetence: The clinical hallmark of demoralization. *Psychotherapy and Psychosomatics, 78*, 342–345.

Cofer, C. N., Chance, J. E., & Judson, A. J. (1949). A study of malingering on the MMPI. *Journal of Psychology, 27*, 491–499.

Colligan, R. C., Osborne, D., Swenson, W. M., & Offord, K. P. (1983). *The MMPI: A contemporary normative study*. Praeger.

Combs, D. R., & Mueser, K. T. (2007). Schizophrenia. In M. Hersen, S. Turner, & D. Beidel (Eds.), *Adult psychopathology and diagnosis* (5th ed., pp. 234–285). John Wiley.

Conway, C. C., Forbes, M. K., Forbush, K. T., Fried, E. I., Hallquist, M. N., Kotov, R., . . . & Eaton, N. R. (2019). A hierarchical taxonomy of psychopathology can transform mental health research. *Perspectives on Psychological Science, 14*(3), 419–436.

Cook, W. W., & Medley, D. M. (1954). Proposed hostility and Pharisaic-virtue scales for the MMPI. *Journal of Applied Psychology, 38*, 414–418.

Corey, D. M., & Ben-Porath, Y. S. (2018). *Assessing police and other public safety personnel using the MMPI-2-RF: A practical guide*. University of Minnesota Press.

Corey, D. M., & Ben-Porath, Y. S. (2020). Practical guidance on the use of the MMPI instruments in remote psychological testing. *Professional Psychology: Research and Practice, 51*(3), 199–204. https://doi.org/10.1037/pro0000329

Corey, D. M., & Ben-Porath, Y. S. (2022). *Minnesota Multiphasic Personality Inventory-3 (MMPI-3): User's guide for the Public Safety Candidate Interpretive Reports*. University of Minnesota Press.

Corey, D. M., & Ben-Porath, Y. S. (2024). *Assessing police and other public safety candidates with the MMPI-3: A practical guide*. University of Minnesota Press.

Corey, D. M., Sellbom, M., & Ben-Porath, Y. S. (2018). Risks associated with overcontrolled behavior in police officer recruits. *Psychological Assessment, 30*(12), 1691–1702.

Costa, P. T., Jr., & McCrae, R. R. (1985). *The NEO personality inventory manual*. Psychological Assessment Resources.

Costa, P. T., & McCrae, R. R. (1992). *NEO PI-R professional manual*. Psychological Assessment Resources.

Craske, M., Wittchen, U., Bogels, S., Stein, M., Andrews, G., & Lebeu, R. (2013). *Severity measure for generalized anxiety disorder-adult*. American Psychiatric Association.

Crawford, M. J., Koldobsky, N., Mulder, R., & Tyrer, P. (2011). Classifying personality disorder according to severity. *Journal of Personality Disorders, 25*(3), 321–330.

Crighton, A. H., Marek, R. J., Dragon, W. R., & Ben-Porath, Y. S. (2017). Utility of the MMPI-2-RF Validity Scales in the detection of simulated underreporting: Implications of incorporating a manipulation check. *Assessment, 24*(7), 853–864.

Cronbach, L. J., & Meehl, P. E. (1955). Construct validity in psychological tests. *Psychological Bulletin, 52*, 281–302.

Cuadra, C. A. (1953). *A psychometric investigation of control factors in psychological adjustment*. Unpublished doctoral dissertation, University of California, Berkeley.

Dahlstrom, L. E. (1986). MMPI findings on other minority groups. In W. G. Dahlstrom, D. Lachar, & L. E. Dahlstrom (Eds.), *MMPI patterns of American minorities* (pp. 50–86). University of Minnesota Press.

Dahlstrom, W. G. (1972). Wither the MMPI? In J. N. Butcher (Ed.), *Objective personality assessment: Changing perspectives* (pp. 85–115). Academic Press.

Dahlstrom, W. G. (1992). The growth in acceptance of the MMPI. *Professional Psychology: Research and Practice, 23*, 345–348.

Dahlstrom, W. G., Archer, R. P., Hopkins, D. G., Jackson, E., & Dahlstrom, L. E. (1994). *Assessing the readability of the Minnesota Multiphasic Personality Inventory Instruments: The MMPI, MMPI-2, MMPI-A*. University of Minnesota Press.

Dahlstrom, W. G., & Gynther, M.D. (1986). Previous MMPI research on Black Americans. In W. G. Dahlstrom, D. Lachar, & L. E. Dahlstrom (Eds.), *MMPI patterns of American minorities* (pp. 24–49). University of Minnesota Press.

Dahlstrom, W. G., Lachar, D., Gynther, M. D., & Webb, J. T. (1986). Community samples of Black and White adults. In W. G. Dahlstrom, D. Lachar, & L. E. Dahlstrom (Eds.). *MMPI patterns of American minorities* (pp. 87–103). University of Minnesota Press.

Dahlstrom, W. G., & Welsh, G. S. (1960). *An MMPI handbook: A guide to use in clinical practice and research*. University of Minnesota Press.

Dahlstrom, W. G., Welsh, G. S., & Dahlstrom, L. E. (1972). *An MMPI handbook: Vol. I. Clinical interpretation* (Rev. ed.). University of Minnesota Press.

Dahlstrom, W. G., Welsh, G. S., & Dahlstrom, L. E. (1975). *An MMPI handbook: Vol. II. Research applications*. University of Minnesota Press.

de Figuiredo, J. M. (1993). Depression and demoralization: Phenomenological differences and research perspectives. *Comprehensive Psychiatry, 34*, 308–311.

De Saeger, H., Kamphuis, J. H., & Anderson, J. L. (2020). Clinical utility of the MMPI-2-RF hierarchical description: An illustration in Cluster C personality disorder patients. *European Journal of Psychological Assessment, 36*(5), 907–912. https://doi.org/10.1027/1015-5759/a000560

Derogatis, L. R. (1994). *Symptom Checklist-90-R: Administration, scoring, and procedures manual*. NCS Pearson.

Detrick, P., Ben-Porath, Y. S., & Sellbom, M. (2016). Associations between MMPI-2-RF (Restructured Form) and Inwald Personality Inventory (IPI) scale scores in a law enforcement preemployment screening sample. *Journal of Police and Criminal Psychology, 31*, 81–95.

Detrick, P., & Chibnall, J. T. (2014). Underreporting on the MMPI-2-RF in a high-demand police officer selection context: An illustration. *Psychological Assessment, 26*(3), 1044–1049. https://doi.org/10.1037/pas0000013

Detrick, P., Chibnall, J. T., & Rosso, M. (2001). Minnesota Multiphasic Personality Inventory–2 in police officer selection: Normative data and relation to the Inwald Personality Inventory. *Professional Psychology: Research and Practice, 32*, 484–490.

Dixon, J. N., Caddell, T. M., Alexander, A. A., Burchett, D., Anderson, J. L., Marek, R. J., & Glassmire, D. M. (2023). Adapting assessment processes to consider cultural mistrust in forensic practices: An example with the MMPI instruments. *Law and Human Behavior, 47*(1), 292–306. https://doi.org/10.1037/lhb0000504

Dohrenwend, B. P., Shrout, P. E., Egri, G., & Mendelsohn, F. S. (1980). Nonspecific psychological distress and other dimensions of psychopathology. *Archives of General Psychiatry, 3*(7), 1229–1236.

Donders, J., Lefebre, N., & Goldsworthy, R. (2021). Patterns of performance and symptom validity test findings after mild traumatic brain injury. *Archives of Clinical Neuropsychology, 36*(3), 394–402.

Dragon, W. R., Ben-Porath, Y. S., & Handel, R. W. (2012). Examining the impact of unscorable item responses on the validity and interpretability of MMPI-2/MMPI-2-RF Restructured Clinical (RC) Scale Scores. *Assessment, 19*(1), 101–113. https://doi.org/10.1177/1073191111415362

Duits, A., Munnecom, T., van Heugten, C., & van Oostenbrugge, R. J. (2008). Cognitive complaints in the early phase after stroke are not indicative of cognitive impairment. *Journal of Neurology, Neurosurgery and Psychiatry, 79*, 143–146.

Dunkley, D. M., & Grilo, C. M. (2007). Self-criticism, low self-esteem, depressive symptoms, and over-evaluation of shape and weight in Binge Eating Disorder patients. *Behaviour Research and Therapy, 45*, 139–149.

Eckblad, M., & Chapman, L. J. (1983). Magical ideation as an indicator of Schizotypy. *Journal of Consulting and Clinical Psychology, 51*, 215–225.

Eckblad, M., & Chapman, L. J. (1986). Development and validation of a scale for hypomanic personality. *Journal of Abnormal Psychology, 95*, 214–222.

Eckhardt, C. I., Norlander, B., & Deffenbacher, J. L. (2004). The assessment of anger and hostility: A critical review. *Aggression and Violent Behavior: A Review Journal, 9*, 17–43.

Edwards, A. L. (1957). Social desirability and probability of endorsement of items in the interpersonal check list. *Journal of Abnormal and Social Psychology, 55*, 394–396.

Edwards, A. L. (1963). A factor analysis of experimental social desirability and response set scales. *Journal of Applied Psychology, 47*, 308–316.

Edwards, A. L. (1964). Social desirability and performance on the MMPI. *Psychometrika, 29*, 295–308.

Egger, J. I. M., De Mey, H. R. A., Derksen, J. J. L., & van der Staak, C. P. F. (2003). Cross-cultural replication of the five-factor model and comparison of the NEO-PI-R and MMPI-2 PSY-5 scales in a Dutch psychiatric sample. *Psychological Assessment, 15*, 81–88.

Egland, B., Erickson, M., Butcher, J. N., & Ben-Porath, Y. S. (1991). MMPI-2 profiles of women at risk for child abuse. *Journal of Personality Assessment, 57*, 254–263.

Englert, D. R., Weed, N. C., & Watson, G. S. (2000). Convergent, discriminant, and internal properties of the Minnesota Multiphasic Personality Inventory (2nd ed.) Low Self-Esteem Content Scale. *Measurement and Evaluation in Counseling and Development, 33*, 42–49.

Epker, J., & Block, A. R. (2014). Psychological screening before spine surgery: Avoiding failed surgery syndrome. *Psychological Injury and Law, 7*, 317–324.

Evans, L., Cowlishaw, S., & Hopwood, M. (2009). Family functioning predicting outcomes for veterans in treatment for Posttraumatic Stress Disorder. *Journal of Family Psychology, 23*, 531–539.

Eysenck, H. J. (1953). *The structure of human personality*. John Wiley.

Eysenck, H. J. (1977). *Crime and personality*. Routledge & Kegan Paul.

Eysenck, H. J., & Eysenck, S. B. G. (1964). *Manual of the Eysenck Personality Inventory*. University London Press.

Eysenck, H. J., & Eysenck, S. B. G. (1975). *Eysenck Personality Questionnaire*. Educational and Industrial Testing Service.

Fairbank, J. A., McCaffrey, R. J., & Keane, T. M. (1985). Psychometric detection of fabricated symptoms of Posttraumatic Stress Disorder. *American Journal of Psychiatry, 42*, 501–503.

Fairburn, C. G., & Beglin, S. J. (1994). Assessment of eating disorders: Interview or self-report questionnaire?. *International Journal of Eating Disorders, 16*(4), 363–370.

Fava, G. A., Freyberger, H. J., Bech, P., Christodoulou, G., Sensky, T., Theorell, T. et al. (1995). Diagnostic criteria for use in psychosomatic research. *Psychotherapy and Psychosomatics, 63*, 1–8.

Fazel, S., Langstrom, N., Hjern, A., Grann, M., & Lichtenstein, P. (2009). Schizophrenia, substance abuse, and violent crime. *Journal of the American Medical Association, 301*, 2016–2023.

Fenig, S., & Levav, I. (1991). Demoralization and social supports among Holocaust survivors. *Journal of Nervous and Mental Disease, 179*, 167–172.

Ferrier-Auerbach, A. G., Kehle, S. M., Erbes, C. R., Arbisi, P. A., Thuras, P., & Polusny, M. A. (2009). Predictors of alcohol use prior to deployment in National Guard soldiers. *Addictive Behaviors, 34*, 625–631.

Finger, M. S., & Ones, D. S. (1999). Psychometric equivalence of the computer and booklet forms of the MMPI: A meta-analysis. *Psychological Assessment, 11*(1), 58–66. https://doi.org/10.1037/1040-3590.11.1.58

Fink, P. (2017). Syndromes of bodily distress or functional somatic syndromes—Where are we heading. Lecture on the occasion of receiving the Alison Creed award 2017. *Journal of Psychosomatic Research, 97*, 127–130.

Fink, P., & Schröder, A. (2010). One single diagnosis, bodily distress syndrome, succeeded to capture 10 diagnostic categories of functional somatic syndromes and somatoform disorders. *Journal of Psychosomatic Research, 68*(5), 415–426.

Finn, J. A., Arbisi, P. A., Erbes, C. R., Polusny, M. A., & Thuras, P. (2014). The MMPI-2 Restructured Form Personality Psychopathology Five Scales: Bridging *DSM-5* Section 2 personality disorders and *DSM-5* Section 3 personality trait dimensions. *Journal of Personality Assessment, 96*(2), 173–184. https://doi.org/10.1080/00223891.2013.866569

Finn, J. A., Ben-Porath, Y. S., & Tellegen, A. (2015). Dichotomous versus polytomous response options in psychopathology assessment: Method or meaningful variance? *Psychological Assessment, 27*(1), 184–193. https://doi.org/10.1037/pas0000044

Finney, J. C. (1968). Correction for unwanted variance. *Psychological Reports, 23,* 1231–1235.

Finney, J. C., Brandsma, J. M., Tondow, M., & LeMaistre, G. (1975). A study of transsexuals seeking gender reassignment. *The American Journal of Psychiatry, 132*(9), 962–964. https://doi.org/10.1176/ajp.132.9.962

Forbes, D., Elhai, J. D., Miller, M. W., & Creamer, M. (2010). Internalizing and externalizing classes in posttraumatic stress disorder: A latent class analysis. *Journal of Traumatic Stress, 23*(3), 340–349.

Forbes, M. K., Kotov, R., Ruggero, C. J., Watson, D., Zimmerman, M., & Krueger, R. F. (2017). Delineating the joint hierarchical structure of clinical and personality disorders in an outpatient psychiatric sample. *Comprehensive Psychiatry, 79,* 19–30.

Forbey, J. D., & Ben-Porath, Y. S. (2007). A comparison of the MMPI-2 RC Scales and Clinical Scales in a substance abuse treatment sample. *Psychological Services, 4,* 46–58.

Forbey, J. D., & Ben-Porath, Y. S. (2008). Empirical correlates of the MMPI-2 Restructured Clinical (RC) Scales in a nonclinical setting. *Journal of Personality Assessment, 90,* 136–141.

Forbey, J. D., Ben-Porath, Y. S., & Gartland, D. (2009). Validation of the MMPI-2 Computerized Adaptive version (MMPI-2-CA) in a correctional intake facility. *Psychological Services, 6,* 279–292.

Forbey, J. D., Lee, T. T. C., & Handel, R. W. (2010). Correlates of the MMPI-2-RF in a college setting. *Psychological Assessment, 22,* 734–744.

Forbey, J. D., Lee, T. T. C., Ben-Porath, Y. S., Arbisi, P. A., & Gartland, D. (2013). Associations between MMPI-2-RF Validity Scale scores and extra-test measures of personality and psychopathology. *Assessment, 20*(4), 448–461. https://doi.org/10.1177/1073191113478154

Forbush, K. T., South, S. C., Krueger, R. F., Iacono, W. G., Clark, L. A., Keel, P. K., Legrand, L. N., & Watson, D. (2010). Locating eating pathology within an empirical diagnostic taxonomy: Evidence from a community-based sample. *Journal of Abnormal Psychology, 119*(2), 282–292.

Forbush, K. T., Wildes, J. E., Pollack, L. O., Dunbar, D., Luo, J., Patterson, K., Petruzzi, L., Pollpeter, M., Miller, H., Stone, A., Bright, A., & Watson, D. (2013). Development and validation of the Eating Pathology Symptoms Inventory (EPSI). *Psychological Assessment, 25*(3), 859–878.

Fordyce, W. E. (1998). Environmental issues in disability status. *Canadian Journal of Rehabilitation, 11,* 170–171.

Fordyce, W. E., Bigos, S., Battie, M., & Fisher, L. (1992). MMPI Scale 3 as a predictor of back pain report: What does it tell us? *Clinical Journal of Pain, 8,* 222–226.

Frank, J. D. (1974). Psychotherapy: The restoration of morale. *American Journal of Psychiatry, 131,* 271–274.

Frank, J. D. (1985). Further thoughts on the anti-demoralization hypothesis of psychotherapeutic effectiveness. *Integrative Psychiatry, 3,* 17–20.

Frank, J. D., & Frank, J. B. (1996). Demoralization and unexplained illness in two cohorts of American soldiers overseas. *Journal of Nervous and Mental Disease, 184,* 445–446.

Franz, A. O., Harrop, T. M., & McCord, D. M. (2017). Examining the construct validity of the MMPI-2-RF Interpersonal Functioning Scales using the Computerized Adaptive Test of Personality Disorder as a comparative framework. *Journal of Personality Assessment,* 99(4), 416–423. https://doi.org/10.1080/00223891.2016.1222394

Freeman, D. (2007). Suspicious minds: The psychology of persecutory delusions. *Clinical Psychology Review, 27,* 425–457.

Freeman, D., & Garety, A. (2000). Comments on the content of persecutory delusions: Does the definition need clarification? *British Journal of Clinical Psychology, 39,* 407–414.

Freeman, D., Gittins, M., Pugh, K., Antley, A., Slater, M., & Dunn, G. (2008). What makes one person paranoid and another persona anxious? The differential prediction of social anxiety and persecutory ideation in an experimental situation. *Psychological Medicine, 38,* 1121–1132.

Freeman, D., Pugh, K., Green, C., Valmaggia, L., Dunn, G., & Garety, P. (2007). A measure of state persecutory ideation for experimental studies. *Journal of Nervous and Mental Disease, 195,* 781–784.

Friedman, A. F., Bolinskey, K. P., Levak, R. W., & Nichols. D. S. (2015). *Psychological assessment with the MMPI-2/MMPI-2-RF.* Routledge.

Gallo, F. J., & Halgin, R. P. (2011). A Guide for Establishing a Practice in Police Preemployment Postoffer Psychological Evaluations. *Professional Psychology: Research and Practice.* https://doi.org/10.1037/a0022493

Galton, F. (1888). Co-relations and their measurement. *Proceedings of the Royal Society, London Series, 45,* 135–145.

Garcia, R., Azan, A., Hoffman, N., & Butcher, J. N. (1983). *Spanish translation of the MMPI for Hispanic Americans.* University of Minnesota Press.

Garcia-Peltoniemi, R., & Azan Chaviano, A. (1993). *MMPI-2: Inventario Multifasico de la Personalidad-2-Minnesota, Version Hispana.* Available from National Computer Systems, P.O. Box 1416, Minneapolis, MN 55440.

Gard, D. E., Kring, A. M., Gard, M. G., Horan, W. P., & Green, M. F. (2007). Anhedonia in Schizophrenia: Distinctions between anticipatory and consummatory pleasure. *Schizophrenia Research, 93,* 253–260.

Garner, D. M., Olmsted, M. P., Bohr, Y., & Garfinkel, P. E. (1982). The eating attitudes test: psychometric features and clinical correlates. *Psychological Medicine,* 12(4), 871–878.

Gass, C. S., & Luis, C. A. (2001). MMPI-2 Scale F(p) and feigning: Scale refinement. *Assessment, 8,* 425–429.

Gatchel, R. J., Polatin, P. B., & Kinney, R. K. (1995). Predicting outcome of chronic back pain using clinical predictors of psychopathology: A prospective analysis. *Health Psychology, 14,* 415–420.

Gervais, R. O., Ben-Porath, Y. S., & Wygant, D. B. (2009). Empirical correlates and interpretation of the MMPI-2-RF Cognitive Complaints Scale. *Clinical Neuropsychologist, 23,* 996–1015.

Gervais, R. O., Ben-Porath, Y. S., Wygant, D. B., & Green, P. (2007). Development and validation of a Response Bias Scale (RBS) for the MMPI-2. *Assessment, 14,* 196–208.

Gervais, R. O., Ben-Porath, Y. S., Wygant, D. B., & Green, P. (2008). Differential sensitivity of the Response Bias Scale (RBS) and MMPI-2 Validity Scales to memory complaints. *The Clinical Neuropsychologist, 22*(6), 1061–1079. https://doi.org/10.1080/13854040701756930

Gervais, R. O., Ben-Porath, Y. S., Wygant, D. B., & Sellbom, M. (2010). Incremental validity of the MMPI-2-RF over-reporting scales and RBS in assessing the veracity of memory complaints. *Archives of Clinical Neuropsychology, 25,* 274–284.

Gervais, R. O., Tarescavage, A. M., Greiffenstein, M. F., Wygant, D. B., Deslauriers, C., & Arends, P. (2018). Inconsistent responding on the MMPI-2-RF and uncooperative attitude: Evidence from cognitive performance validity measures. *Psychological Assessment, 30*(3), 410–415. https://doi.org/10.1037/pas0000506

Gervais, R. O., Wygant, D. B., Sellbom, M., & Ben-Porath, Y. S. (2011). Associations between Symptom Validity Test failure and scores on the MMPI-2-RF Validity and Substantive Scales. *Journal of Personality Assessment, 93*(5), 508–517. https://doi.org/10.1080/00223891.2011.594132

Gilberstadt, H., & Duker, J. (1965). *A handbook for clinical and actuarial MMPI interpretation.* Saunders.

Glassmire, D. M., Jhawar, A., Burchett, D., & Tarescavage, A. M. (2017). Evaluating item endorsement rates for the MMPI-2-RF F-r and Fp-r scales across ethnic, gender, and diagnostic groups with a forensic inpatient sample. *Psychological Assessment, 29*(5), 500–508. https://doi.org/10.1037/pas0000366

Glassmire, D. M., Stolberg, R. A., Greene, R. L., & Bongar, B. (2001). The utility of MMPI-2 suicide items for assessing suicidal potential: Development of a suicidal potential scale. *Assessment, 8,* 281–290.

Glassmire, D. M, Tarescavage, A. M., Burchett, D., Martinez, J., & Gomez, A. (2016). Clinical utility of the MMPI-2-RF SUI items and scale in a forensic inpatient setting: Association with interview self-report and future suicidal behavior. *Psychological Assessment, 28*(11), 1502–1509. https://doi.org/10.1037/pas0000220

Glenn, A. L., & Sellbom, M. (2015). Theoretical and empirical concerns regarding the dark triad as a construct. *Journal of Personality Disorders, 29*(3), 360–377. https://doi.org/10.1521/pedi_2014_28_162

Goldberg, L. R. (1965). Diagnosticians vs. diagnostic signs: The diagnosis of psychosis versus neurosis for the MMPI. *Psychological Monographs, 79.*

Goldberg, L. R. (1968). *The diagnosis of psychosis and neurosis from the MMPI.* Paper presented at the Third Annual Symposium on Use of the MMPI, Minneapolis, MN.

Goldberg, L. R. (1969). The search for configural relationships in personality assessment: The diagnosis of psychosis vs. neurosis from the MMPI. *Multivariate Behavioral Research, 4,* 523–536.

Goldberg, L. R. (1971). A historical survey of personality scales and inventories. In P. McReynolds (Ed.), *Advances in psychological assessment* (Vol. 2, pp. 293–336). Science and Behavior Books.

Goldberg, L. R. (2006). Doing it all bass-ackwards: The development of hierarchical factor structures from the top down. *Journal of Research in Personality, 40*(4), 347–358.

Goodwin, B. E., Sellbom, M., & Arbisi, P. A. (2013). Posttraumatic stress disorder in veterans: The utility of the MMPI-2-RF Validity Scales in detecting overreported symptoms. *Psychological Assessment, 25*(3), 671–678. https://doi.org/10.1037/a0032214

Gottfried, E., Bodell, L. M., Carbonell, J., & Joiner, T. (2014). The clinical utility of the MMPI-2-RF Suicidal/Death Ideation scale. *Psychological Assessment, 26*(4), 1205–1211. https://doi.org/10.1037/pas0000017

Gough, H. G. (1946). Diagnostic patterns on the MMPI. *Journal of Clinical Psychology, 2*, 23–37.

Gough, H. G. (1947). Simulated patterns on the Minnesota Multiphasic Personality Inventory. *Journal of Abnormal and Social Psychology, 42*, 215–255.

Gough, H. G. (1948). A new dimension of status: I. Development of a personality scale. *American Sociology Review, 13*, 401–409.

Gough, H. G. (1951). Studies of social intolerance: I. Psychological and sociological correlates of anti-Semitism. *Journal of Social Psychology, 33*, 237–246.

Gough, H. G. (1957). *Manual for the California Psychological Inventory*. Consulting Psychologists Press.

Gough, H. G., McClosky, H., & Meehl, P. E. (1951). A personality scale for dominance. *Journal of Abnormal and Social Psychology, 46*, 360–366.

Graham, J. R. (1977). *The MMPI: A practical guide*. Waverly Press.

Graham, J. R. (2011). *MMPI-2: Assessing personality and psychopathology* (5th ed.). Oxford University Press.

Graham, J. R. (2012). *MMPI-2: Assessing personality and psychopathology*. Oxford University Press.

Graham, J. R., Ben-Porath, Y. S., & McNulty, J. L. (1999). *MMPI-2 correlates for outpatient mental health settings*. University of Minnesota Press.

Graham, J. R., & Butcher, J. N. (1988). *Differentiating Schizophrenia and major affective disorders with the revised form of the MMPI*. Paper presented at the 23rd annual symposium on Recent Developments in the Use of the MMPI, St. Petersburg Beach, FL.

Graham, J. R., Timbrook, R. E., Ben-Porath, Y. S., & Butcher, J. N. (1991). Congruence between MMPI and MMPI-2: Separating fact from artifact. *Journal of Personality Assessment, 57*, 205–215.

Granieri, A., Tamburello, S., Tamburello, A., Casale, S., Cont, C., Guglielmucci, F., & Innamorati, M. (2013). Quality of life and personality traits in patients with malignant pleural mesothelioma and their first-degree caregivers. *Neuropsychiatric Disease and Treatment, 9*, 1193–1202. https://doi.org/10.2147/NDT.S48965

Grassi, L., Rossi, E., Sabato, S., Cruciani, G., & Zambelli, M. (2004). Diagnostic criteria for psychosomatic research and psychosocial variables in breast cancer patients. *Psychosomatics: Journal of Consultation Liaison Psychiatry, 45*, 483–491.

Gray, J. A. (1970). The psychophysiological basis of introversion–extraversion. *Behaviour Research and Therapy, 8*, 249–266.

Gray, J. A., & McNaughton, N. (2000). *The neuropsychology of anxiety: An enquiry into the functions of the septo-hippocampal system*. Oxford University Press.

Grayson, H. M. (1951). *A psychological admissions testing program and manual*. Veterans Administration Center, Neuropsychiatric Hospital.

Green, C., Garety, P. A., Freeman, D., Fowler, D., Bebbington., P., Dunn, G. et al. (2006). Content and affect in persecutory delusions. *British Journal of Clinical Psychology, 45*, 561–577.

Green, D. P., Goldman, S. L., & Salovey, P. (1993). Measurement error masks bipolarity in affect ratings. *Journal of Personality and Social Psychology, 64*, 1029–1041.

Green, P., Allen, L., & Astner, K. (1996). *Manual for Computerised Word Memory Test.* CogniSyst.

Greene, R. L. (1980). *The MMPI: An interpretive manual.* Grune & Stratton.

Greene, R. L. (1987). Ethnicity and MMPI performance: A review. *Journal of Consulting and Clinical Psychology, 55*(4), 497–512. https://doi.org/10.1037/0022-006X.55.4.497

Greene, R. L. (2011). *The MMPI-2/MMPI-2-RF: An interpretive manual* (3rd ed.). Pearson.

Greene, R. L., Robin, R. W., Albaugh, B., Caldwell, A., & Goldman, D. (2003). Use of the MMPI-2 in American Indians: II. Empirical Correlates. *Psychological Assessment, 15*(3), 360–369. https://doi.org/10.1037/1040-3590.15.3.360

Greene, R. L., Weed, N. C., Butcher, J. N., Arredondo, R., & Davis, H. G. (1992). A cross validation of the MMPI-2 substance abuse scales. *Journal of Personality Assessment, 58,* 405–410.

Gregory, S. D., Newmeyer, M., Baum, L. J., & Lichi, D. A. (2021). Marital distress in missionaries as measured by the MMPI-2-RF Interpersonal Scales. *Journal of Psychology and Theology, 49*(4), 374–386. https://doi.org/10.1177/0091647120968312

Greiffenstein, M. F., Baker, W. J., Axelrod, B., Peck, E. A., & Gervais, R. (2004). The Fake Bad Scale and MMPI-2 F-family in detection of implausible psychological trauma claims. *Clinical Neuropsychologist, 18,* 573–590.

Greiffenstein, M. F., Fox, D., & Lees-Haley, P. R. (2007). The MMPI-2 Fake Bad Scale in detection of noncredible brain injury claims. In K. Boone (Ed.), *Assessment of feigned cognitive impairment: A neuropsychological perspective* (pp. 210–235). Guilford Press.

Greve, K. W., & Bianchini, K. J. (2004). Response to Butcher et al., The construct validity of the Lees-Haley Fake-Bad Scale. *Archives of Clinical Neuropsychology, 19,* 337–339.

Greve, K. W., Bianchini, K. J., Love, J. M., Brennan, A., & Heinly, M. T. (2006). Sensitivity and specificity of MMPI-2 Validity Scales and indicators to malingered neurocognitive dysfunction in traumatic brain injury. *Clinical Neuropsychologist, 20,* 491–512.

Gros, D. F., Simms, L. J., & Acierno, R. (2010). Specificity of posttraumatic stress disorder symptoms: an investigation of comorbidity between posttraumatic stress disorder symptoms and depression in treatment-seeking veterans. *The Journal of Nervous and Mental Disease, 198*(12), 885–890.

Grossi, L. M., Green, D., Belfi, B., McGrath, R. E., Griswold, H., & Schreiber, J. (2015). Identifying aggression in forensic inpatients using the MMPI-2-RF: An examination of MMPI-2-RF scale scores and estimated psychopathy indices. *International Journal of Forensic Mental Health, 14*(4), 231–244. https://doi.org/10.1080/14999013.2015.1108943

Grunebaum, M . F., Galfalvy, H. C., Nichols, C. M., Caldeira, N. A., Sher, L., Dervic, K. et al. (2006). Aggression and substance abuse in Bipolar Disorder. *Bipolar Disorders, 8,* 496–502.

Gu, W., Reddy, H. B., Green, D., Belfi, B., & Einzig, S. (2017). Inconsistent responding in a criminal forensic setting: An evaluation of the VRIN-r and TRIN-r scales of the MMPI-2-RF. *Journal of Personality Assessment, 99*(3), 286–296. https://doi.org/10.1080/00223891.2016.1149483

Guetta, R. E., Wilcox, E. S., Stoop, T. B., Maniates, H., Ryabchenko, K. A., Miller, M. W., & Wolf, E. J. (2019). Psychometric properties of the Dissociative Subtype of PTSD Scale: Replication and extension in a clinical sample of trauma-exposed veterans. *Behavior Therapy, 50*(5), 952–966.

Guilford, J. P. (1939). *General psychology.* Van Nostrand.

Guilford, J. P. (1959). *Personality*. McGraw-Hill.

Guilford, J. P. (1977). *Way beyond the IQ*. Creative Education Foundation.

Gutkovich, Z., Rosenthal, R. N., Galynker, I., Muran, C., Batchelder, S., & Itskhoki, E. (1999). Depression and demoralization among Russian-Jewish immigrants in primary care. *Psychosomatics: Journal of Consultation Liaison Psychiatry, 40*, 117–125.

Gynther, M.D. (1972). White norms and Black MMPIs: A prescription for discrimination? *Psychological Bulletin, 78*, 386–402.

Gynther, M.D. (1979). Aging and personality, In J. N. Butcher (Ed.), *New developments in use of the MMPI*. University of Minnesota Press.

Haber, J. C., & Baum, L. J. (2014). Minnesota Multiphasic Personality Inventory-2 Restructured Form (MMPI-2-RF) Scales as predictors of psychiatric diagnoses. *South African Journal of Psychology, 44*(4), 439–453. https://doi.org/10.1177/0081246314532788

Halevy, A., Moos, R. H., & Soloman, G. F. (1965). A relationship between blood serotonin concentrations and behavior in psychiatric patients. *Journal of Psychiatric Research, 3*, 1–10.

Hall, G. C. N., Bansal, A., & Lopez, I. R. (1999). Ethnicity and psychopathology: A meta-analytic review of 31 years of comparative MMPI/MMPI-2 research. *Psychological Assessment, 11*(2), 186–197. https://doi.org/10.1037/1040-3590.11.2.186

Hall, J. T., Lee, T. T. C., Ajayi, W., Friedhoff, L. A., & Graham, J. R. (2021). Associations between MMPI-2-RF Internalizing RC Scales and positive characteristics. *Journal of Personality Assessment, 103*(1), 1–9.

Han, K., Weed, N. C., Calhoun, R. F., & Butcher, J. N. (1995). Psychometric characteristics of the MMPI-2 Cook–Medley Hostility Scale. *Journal of Personality Assessment, 65*, 567–585.

Han, K., Colarelli, S. M., & Weed, N. C. (2019). Methodological and statistical advances in the consideration of cultural diversity in assessment: A critical review of group classification and measurement invariance testing. *Psychological Assessment, 31*(12), 1481–1496. https://doi.org/10.1037/pas0000731

Handel, R. W., & Archer, R. P. (2008). An investigation of the psychometric properties of the MMPI-2 Restructured Clinical (RC) Scales with mental health inpatients. *Journal of Personality Assessment, 90*, 239–249.

Handel, R. W., Ben-Porath, Y. S., Tellegen, A., & Archer, R. P. (2010). Psychometric Functioning of the MMPI-2-RF VRIN-r and TRIN-r scales with varying degrees of randomness, acquiescence, and counter-acquiescence. *Psychological Assessment, 22*, 87–95.

Hanvik, L. J. (1951). MMPI profiles in patients with low-back pain. *Journal of Consulting Psychology, 15*, 350–353.

Hare, R. D. (1985). Comparison of procedures for the assessment of psychopathy. *Journal of Consulting and Clinical Psychology, 53*(1), 7–16.

Hare, R. D. (1991). *The revised psychopathy checklist*. Multi-Health Systems.

Hare, R. D. (2003). *Hare Psychopathy Checklist–Revised (PCL-R), Technical manual* (2nd ed.). Multi-Health Systems.

Harkness, A. R. (1992). Fundamental topics in the personality disorders: Candidate trait dimensions from lower regions of the hierarchy. *Psychological Assessment, 4*, 251–259.

Harkness, A. R., Finn, J. A., McNulty, J. L., & Shields, S. M. (2012). The Personality Psychopathology Five (PSY-5): Recent constructive replication and assessment literature review. *Psychological Assessment, 24*(2), 432–443. https://doi.org/10.1037/a0025830

Harkness, A. R., & McNulty, J. L. (1994). The Personality Psychopathology Five (PSY-5): Issues from the pages of a diagnostic manual instead of a dictionary. In S. Strack & M. Lorr (Eds.), *Differentiating normal and abnormal personality* (pp. 291–315). Springer.

Harkness, A. R., & McNulty, J. L. (2007). *Restructured versions of the MMPI-2 Personality Psychopathology Five (PSY-5) Scales.* Paper presented at the meeting of the American Psychological Association, San Francisco, CA.

Harkness, A. R., McNulty, J. L., & Ben-Porath, Y. S. (1995). The Personality Psychopathology Five (PSY-5): Constructs and MMPI-2 scales. *Psychological Assessment, 7,* 104–114.

Harkness, A. R., McNulty, J. L., Ben-Porath, Y. S., & Graham, J. R. (2002). *MMPI-2 Personality Psychopathology Five (PSY-5) Scales: Gaining an overview for case conceptualization and treatment planning.* University of Minnesota Press.

Harkness, A. R., Reynolds, S. M., & Lilienfeld, S. O. (2014). A review of systems for psychology and psychiatry: Adaptive systems, Personality Psychopathology Five (PSY-5), and *DSM-5*. *Journal of Personality Assessment, 96*(2), 121–139. https://doi.org/10.1080/00223891.2013.823438

Harp, J. P., Jasinski, L. J., Shandera-Ochsner, A. L., Mason, L. H., & Berry, D. T. R. (2011). Detection of malingered ADHD using the MMPI-2-RF. *Psychological Injury and Law, 4,* 32–43.

Harris, R., & Lingoes, J. (1955). *Subscales for the Minnesota Multiphasic Personality Inventory.* Unpublished manuscript.

Hart, S., Cox, D., & Hare, R. (1995). *The Hare PCL: SV Psychopathy Checklist: Screening version.* Multi-Health Systems.

Hartshorne, H., May, M. A., & Shuttleworth, F. K. (1930). *Studies in the nature of character: Vol. 3. Studies in the organization of character.* Macmillan.

Hathaway, S. R. (1947). A coding system for MMPI profiles. *Journal of Consulting Psychology, 11,* 334–337.

Hathaway, S. R. (1956). Scale 5 (Masculinity–Femininity), Scale 6 (Paranoia) and Scale 8 (Schizophrenia). In G. S. Welsh & W. G. Dahlstrom (Eds.), *Basic readings on the MMPI in psychology and medicine* (pp. 104–111). University of Minnesota Press.

Hathaway, S. R. (1960). Foreword. In W. G. Dahlstrom & G. S. Welsh (Eds.), *An MMPI handbook: A guide to use in clinical practice and research* (pp. vii–xi). University of Minnesota Press.

Hathaway, S. R. (1972a). Foreword. In W. G. Dahlstrom, G. S. Welsh, & L. E. Dahlstrom (Eds.), *An MMPI handbook: Vol. 1. Clinical interpretation* (pp. xiii–iv). University of Minnesota Press.

Hathaway, S. R. (1972b). Where have we gone wrong? The mystery of the missing progress. In J. N. Butcher (Ed.), *Objective personality assessment: Changing perspectives* (pp. 21–43). Academic Press.

Hathaway, S. R., & McKinley, J. C. (1940). A multiphasic personality schedule (Minnesota): I. Construction of the schedule. *Journal of Psychology, 10,* 249–254.

Hathaway, S. R., & McKinley, J. C. (1942). A multiphasic personality schedule (Minnesota): III. The measurement of symptomatic depression. *Journal of Psychology, 14,* 73–84.

Hathaway, S. R., & McKinley, J. C. (1943). *The Minnesota Multiphasic Personality Inventory.* University of Minnesota Press.

Hathaway, S. R., & McKinley, J. C. (1951). *Manual for the Minnesota Multiple Personality Inventory*. Psychological Corporation.

Hathaway, S. R., & McKinley, H. C. (1967). *Minnesota Multiphasic Personality Inventory Manual—Revised*. Psychological Corporation.

Haut, K. M., & MacDonald III, A. W. (2010). Persecutory delusions and the perception of trustworthiness in unfamiliar faces in schizophrenia. *Psychiatry Research, 178*(3), 456–460.

Hawk, G. L., & Cornell, D. G. (1989). MMPI profiles of malingerers diagnosed in pretrial forensic evaluations. *Journal of Clinical Psychology, 45,* 673–678.

Heilbrun, A. B. J. (1961). Male and female personality correlates of early termination in counseling. *Journal of Counseling Psychology, 8,* 31–36.

Heiser, N. A., Turner, S. M., Beidel, D. C., & Roberson-Nay, R. (2009). Differentiating social phobia from shyness. *Journal of Anxiety Disorders, 23,* 469–476.

Helmes, E., & Reddon, J. R. (1993). A perspective on developments in assessing psychopathology: A critical review of the MMPI and MMPI-2. *Psychological Bulletin, 113,* 453–471.

Henry, G. K., Heilbronner, R. L., Mittenberg, W., Enders, C., & Stanczal, S. R. (2008). Comparison of the Lees-Haley Fake Bad Scale, Henry–Heilbronner Index, and Restructured Clinical Scale 1 in identifying noncredible symptom reporting. *Clinical Neuropsychologist, 22,* 919–929.

Heymans, G., & Wiersma, E. (1906). Beitrage zur spezillen psychologie auf grund einer massen-unterschung. *Zeitschrift fur Psychologie, 43,* 81–127.

Hjemboe, S., Almagor, M., & Butcher, J. N. (1992). Empirical assessment of marital distress: The Marital Distress Scale (MDS) for the MMPI-2. In C. D. Spielberger & J. N. Butcher (Eds.), *Advances in personality assessment* (Vol. 9, pp. 141–152). Lawrence Erlbaum Associates.

Hill, J. S., Pace, T. M., & Robbins, R. R. (2010). Decolonizing personality assessment and honoring indigenous voices: A critical examination of the MMPI-2. *Cultural Diversity and Ethnic Minority Psychology, 16*(1), 16–25. https://doi.org/10.1037/a0016110

Himsl, K., Burchett, D., Tarescavage, A. M., & Glassmire, D. M. (2017). Assessing reading ability for psychological testing in forensic assessments: An investigation with the WRAT-4 and MMPI-2-RF. *International Journal of Forensic Mental Health, 16*(3), 239–248. https://doi.org/10.1080/14999013.2017.1330293

Hirschel, D., Hutchison, I. W., & Shaw, M. (2010). The interrelationship between substance abuse and the likelihood of arrest, conviction, and re-offending in cases of intimate partner violence. *Journal of Family Violence, 25,* 81–90.

Hoch, A., & Amsden, G. S. (1913). A guide to the descriptive study of the personality. With special reference to the taking of anamneses of cases with psychoses. *Review of Neurology and Psychiatry, 11,* 577–587.

Hoelzle, J. B., & Meyer, G. J. (2008). The factor structure of the MMPI-2 Restructured Clinical (RC) Scales. *Journal of Personality Assessment, 90*(5), 443–455. https://doi.org/10.1080/00223890802248711

Hoelzle, J. B., & Meyer, G. J. (2009). The invariant component structure of the Personality Assessment Inventory (PAI) full scales. *Journal of Personality Assessment, 91,* 175–186.

Hofmann, S. G., Richey, J. A., Sawyer, A., Ansaani, A., & Rief, W. (2009). Social Anxiety Disorder and the *DSM-V*. In D. McKay, J. S. Abramowitz, S. Taylor, & G. J. G. Asmundson (Eds.), *Current perspectives on the anxiety disorders: Implications for DSM-V and beyond* (pp. 411–429). Springer.

Hokanson, J. E., & Calden, G. (1960). *Negro-white differences on the MMPI*. Journal of Clinical Psychology, 16, 32–33.

Home Office. (2002). *Offender Assessment System: OASys Manual V2*. Home Office.

Horan, W. P., Kring, A. M., & Blanchard, J. J. (2006). Anhedonia in Schizophrenia: A review of assessment strategies. *Schizophrenia Bulletin, 32,* 259–273.

Horst, P. (1941). The role of predictor variables which are independent of the criterion. *Social Science Research Bulletin, 48,* 431–436.

Hughes, M. E., Alloy, L. B., & Cogswell, A. (2008). Repetitive thought in psychopathology: The relation of rumination and worry to depression and anxiety symptoms. *Journal of Cognitive Psychotherapy: An International Quarterly, 22,* 273–291.

Humm, D. G., & Wadsworth, G. W. (1935). The Humm–Wadsworth temperament scale. *American Journal of Psychiatry, 92,* 163–200.

Hunt, H. F. (1948). The effect of deliberate deception on Minnesota Multiphasic Personality Inventory performance. *Journal of Consulting Psychology, 12,* 396–402.

Ingram, P. B., Golden, B. L., & Armistead-Jehle, P. J. (2020). Evaluating the Minnesota Multiphasic Personality Inventory-2-Restructured Form (MMPI-2-RF) over-reporting scales in a military neuropsychology clinic. *Journal of Clinical and Experimental Neuropsychology, 42*(3), 263–273. https://doi.org/10.1080/13803395.2019.1708271

Ingram, P. B., Kelso, K. M., & McCord, D. M. (2011). Empirical correlates and expanded interpretation of the MMPI-2-RF Restructured Clinical Scale 3 (Cynicism). *Assessment, 18,* 95–101.

Ingram, P. B., Tarescavage, A. M., Ben-Porath, Y. S., Oehlert, M. E., & Bergquist, B. K. (2021). External correlates of the MMPI-2-Restructured Form across a national sample of veterans. *Journal of Personality Assessment, 103*(1), 19–26. https://doi.org/10.1080/00223891.2020.1732995

Ingram, P. B., & Ternes, M. S. (2016). The detection of content-based invalid responding: A meta-analysis of the MMPI-2-Restructured Form's (MMPI-2-RF) over-reporting validity scales. *The Clinical Neuropsychologist, 30*(4), 473–496. https://doi.org/10.1080/13854046.2016.1187769

Insel, T., Cuthbert, B., Garvey, M., Heinssen, R., Pine, D. S., Quinn, K., . . . & Wang, P. (2010). Research domain criteria (RDoC): toward a new classification framework for research on mental disorders. *American Journal of psychiatry, 167*(7), 748–751.

Inwald, R. (1992). *Inwald Personality Inventory technical manual* (Rev. ed.). Hilson Research.

Jackson, D. N. (1970). A sequential system for personality scale development. In C. D. Spielberger (Ed.), *Current practices in clinical and community psychology* (Vol. 2, pp. 60–96). Academic Press.

Jackson, D. N. (1971). The dynamics of structured personality tests. *Psychological Review, 78,* 229–248.

Jackson, D. N., Fraboni, M., & Helmes, E. (1997). MMPI-2 Content Scales: How much content do they measure? *Assessment, 4,* 111–117.

Jackson, D. N., & Messick, S. (1962). Response styles on the MMPI: Comparison of clinical and normal samples. *Journal of Abnormal and Social Psychology, 65,* 285–299.

James, L., & Taylor, J. (2008). Revisiting the structure of mental disorder: Borderline Personality Disorder and the internalizing/externalizing spectra. *British Journal of Clinical Psychology, 47,* 361–380.

Janca, A., Burke, J. D., Jr., Isaac, M., Burke, K. C., Costa, J., Silva, E., Acuda, S. W. et al. (1995). The World Health Organization Somatoform Disorders schedule: A preliminary report on design and reliability. *European Psychiatry, 10,* 373–378.

Jiménez-Gómez, F., Sánchez-Crespo, G., & Ampudia-Rueda, A. (2013). Is there a social desirability scale in the MMPI-2-RF? *Clínica y Salud, 24(3),* 161–168. https://doi.org/10.1016/S1130-5274(13)70017-3

Johnson, S. L., Leedom, L. J., & Muhtadie, L. (2012). The dominance behavioral system and psychopathology: Evidence from self-report, observational, and biological studies. *Psychological Bulletin, 138(4),* 692–743.

Joiner, T. E., Walker, R. L., Pettit, J. W., Perez, M., & Cukrowicz, K. C. (2005). Evidence-based assessment of depression in adults. *Psychological Assessment, 17,* 267–277.

Jones, A. (2016). Cutoff scores for MMPI-2 and MMPI-2-RF cognitive-somatic validity scales for psychometrically defined malingering groups in a military sample. *Archives of Clinical Neuropsychology, 31(7),* 786–801. https://doi.org/10.1093/arclin/acw035

Judge, T. A., Erez, A., Bono, J. E., & Thoresen, C. J. (2002). Discriminant and incremental validity of four personality traits: Are measures of self-esteem, neuroticism, locus of control, and generalized self-efficacy indicators of a common core construct? *Journal of Personality and Social Psychology, 83,* 693–710.

Jurick, S. M., Crocker, L. D., Keller, A. V., Hoffman, S. N., Bomyea, J., Jacobson, M. W., & Jak, A. J. (2019). The Minnesota Multiphasic Personality Inventory-2-RF in treatment-seeking veterans with history of mild traumatic brain injury. *Archives of Clinical Neuropsychology, 34(3),* 366–380. https://doi.org/10.1093/arclin/acy048

Kashdan, T. B., Elhai, J. D., & Frueh, B. C. (2006). Anhedonia and emotional numbing in combat veterans with PTSD. *Behaviour Research and Therapy, 44,* 457–467.

Kashdan, T. B., Uswatte, G., Steger, M. F., & Julian, T. (2006). Fragile self-esteem and affective instability in Posttraumatic Stress Disorder. *Behaviour Research and Therapy, 44,* 1609–1619.

Kaslow, N. J., Thompson, M. P., Brooks, A. E., & Twomey, H. B. (2000). Ratings of family functioning of suicidal and nonsuicidal African American women. *Journal of Family Psychology, 14,* 585–599.

Kassebaum, G. G., Couch, A. S., & Slater, P. E. (1959). The factorial dimensions of the MMPI. *Journal of Consulting Psychology, 23,* 226–236.

Katz, M. M., & Lyerly, S. B. (1963). Methods for measuring adjustment and social behavior in the community. *Psychological Reports, 13,* 503–535.

Keane, T. M., Malloy, P. F., & Fairbank, J. A. (1984). Empirical development of an MMPI subscale for the assessment of combat-related posttraumatic stress disorder. *Journal of Consulting and Clinical Psychology, 52(5),* 888–891.

Keane, T. M., Taylor, K. L., & Penk, W. E. (1997). Differentiating Posttraumatic Stress Disorder (PTSD) from Major Depression (MDD) and Generalized Anxiety Disorder (GAD). *Journal of Anxiety Disorders, 11,* 317–328.

Keo-Meier, C. L., Herman, L. I., Reisner, S. L., Pardo, S. T., Sharp, C., & Babcock, J. C. (2015). Testosterone treatment and MMPI-2 improvement in transgender men: A prospective controlled study. *Journal of Consulting and Clinical Psychology, 83*(1), 143–156. https://doi.org/10.1037/a0037599

Keller, L. S., & Butcher, J. N. (1991). *Use of the MMPI-2 with chronic pain patients.* University of Minnesota Press.

Khazem, L. R., Anestis, J. C., Erbes, C. R., Ferrier-Auerbach, A. G., Schumacher, M. M., & Arbisi, P. A. (2021). Assessing the clinical utility of the MMPI-2-RF in detecting suicidal ideation in a high acuity, partially-hospitalized veteran sample. *Journal of Personality Assessment, 103*(1), 10–18. https://doi.org/10.1080/00223891.2020.1739057

Klein, D. F. (1974). Endogenomorphic depression: A conceptual and terminological revision. *Archives of General Psychiatry, 31,* 447–454.

Klein Haneveld, E., Kamphuis, J. H., Smid, W., & Forbey, J. D. (2017). Using MMPI-2-RF correlates to elucidate the PCL-R and its four facets in a sample of male forensic psychiatric patients. *Journal of Personality Assessment, 99*(4), 398–407. https://doi.org/10.1080/00223891.2016.1228655

Kline, J. A., Rozynko, V. V., Flint, G., & Roberts, A. C. (1973). Personality characteristics of male native American alcoholic patients. *International Journal of the Addictions, 8*(4), 729–732. https://doi.org/10.3109/10826087309057498

Klonsky, E. D., Oltmanns, T. F., Turkheimer, E., & Fiedler, E. (2000). Recollections of conflict with parents and family support in the personality disorders. *Journal of Personality Disorders, 14,* 311–322.

Knop, J., Penick, E. C., Nickel, E. J., Mortensen, E. L., Sullivan, M. A., Murtaza, S. et al. (2009). Childhood ADHD and Conduct Disorder as independent predictors of male alcohol dependence at age 40. *Journal of Studies on Alcohol and Drugs, 70,* 169–177.

Koss, M. P., & Butcher, J. N. (1973). A comparison of psychiatric patients' self-report with other sources of clinical information. *Journal of Research in Personality, 7,* 225–236.

Koss, M. P., Butcher, J. N., & Hoffman, N. G. (1976). The MMPI critical items: How well do they work? *Journal of Consulting and Clinical Psychology, 44,* 921–928.

Kotelnikova, Y., Weaver, C. A., & Clark, L. A. (2019). The joint structure of maladaptive personality traits and psychopathology. *Journal of Research in Personality, 81,* 64–71. https://doi.org/10.1016/j.jrp.2019.05.007

Kotov, R., Chang, S.-W., Fochtmann, L. J., Mojtabai, R., Carlson, G. A., Sedler, M. J., & Bromet, E. J. (2011). Schizophrenia in the internalizing-externalizing framework: A third dimension? *Schizophrenia Bulletin, 37,* 1168–1178.

Kotov, R., Jonas, K. G., Carpenter, W. T., Dretsch, M. N., Eaton, N. R., Forbes, M. K., . . . & HiTOP Utility Workgroup. (2020). Validity and utility of hierarchical taxonomy of psychopathology (HiTOP): I. Psychosis superspectrum. *World Psychiatry, 19*(2), 151–172.

Kotov, R., Krueger, R. F., Watson, D., Achenbach, T. M., Althoff, R. R., Bagby, R. M., Brown, T. A., Carpenter, W. T., Caspi, A., Clark, L. A., Eaton, N. R., Forbes, M. K., Forbush, K. T., Goldberg, D., Hasin, D., Hyman, S. E., Ivanova, M. Y., Lynam, D. R., Markon, K., . . . Zimmerman, M. (2017). The Hierarchical Taxonomy of Psychopathology (HiTOP): A dimensional alternative to traditional nosologies. *Journal of Abnormal Psychology, 126*(4), 454–477.

Kotov, R., Krueger, R. F., Watson, D., Cicero, D. C., Conway, C. C., DeYoung, C. G., . . . & Wright, A. G. (2021). The Hierarchical Taxonomy of Psychopathology (HiTOP): A quantitative nosology based on consensus of evidence. *Annual Review of Clinical Psychology, 17,* 83–108.

Kraepelin, E. (1921). Ueber Entwurtzelung. *Zeitschrift fur die Gesamte Neurologie und Psychiatrie, 63,* 1–8.

Kramer, M. D., Krueger, R. F., & Hicks, B. M. (2008). The role of internalizing and externalizing liability factors in accounting for gender differences in the prevalence of common psychopathological syndromes. *Psychological Medicine: A Journal of Research in Psychiatry and the Allied Sciences, 38,* 51–61.

Kremyar, A. J., & Lee, T. T. C. (2021). MMPI-3 predictors of anxiety sensitivity and distress intolerance. *Assessment.* Advance online publication. https://doi.org/10.1177/10731911211001948

Kring, A. M., & Germans, M. K. (2000). Anhedonia. In A. E. Kazdin (Ed.), *Encyclopedia of psychology* (Vol. 1, pp. 174–175). Washington, DC: American Psychological Association.

Kroll, J. (2003). Posttraumatic symptoms and the complexity of responses to trauma. *Journal of the American Medical Association, 290,* 667–670.

Kroll, J., & McDonald, C. (2003). A diverse refugee population requires complex solutions. *Psychiatric Times, 20*(10). http://www.psychiatrictimes.com/display/article/10168/48371

Krueger, R. F., Derringer, J., Markon, K. E., Watson, D., & Skodol, A. E. (2012). Initial construction of a maladaptive personality trait model and inventory for DSM-5. *Psychological Medicine, 42,* 1879–1890.

Krueger, R. F., Hobbs, K. A., Conway, C. C., Dick, D. M., Dretsch, M. N., Eaton, N. R., . . . & HiTOP Utility Workgroup. (2021). Validity and utility of hierarchical taxonomy of psychopathology (HiTOP): II. Externalizing superspectrum. *World Psychiatry, 20*(2), 171–193.

Krueger, R. F., & Markon, K. E. (2006). Reinterpreting comorbidity: A model-based approach to understanding and classifying psychopathology. *Annual Review of Clinical Psychology, 2,* 111–133.

Krueger, R. F., Markon, K. E., Patrick, C. J., Benning, S. D., & Kramer, M. D. (2007). Linking antisocial behavior, substance use, and personality: An integrative quantitative model of the adult externalizing spectrum. *Journal of Abnormal Psychology, 116,* 645–666.

Kwapil, T. R., Gross, G. M., Burgin, C. J., Raulin, M. L., Silvia, P. J., & Barrantes-Vidal, N. (2018). Validity of the Multidimensional Schizotypy Scale: Associations with schizotypal traits and normal personality. *Personality Disorders: Theory, Research, and Treatment, 9*(5), 458–466.

Kwapil, T. R., Miller, M. B., Zinser, M. C., Chapman, L. J., Chapman, J., & Eckblad, M. (2000). A longitudinal study of high scorers on the Hypomanic Personality Scale. *Journal of Abnormal Psychology, 109,* 222–226.

Lachar, D., & Wrobel, T. A. (1979). Validating clinicians' hunches: Construction of a new MMPI critical item set. *Journal of Consulting and Clinical Psychology, 47,* 277–284.

Lamberty, G. (2008). *Understanding somatization in the practice of clinical neuropsychology.* Oxford University Press.

Landis, C., & Katz, S. E. (1934). The validity of certain questions which purport to measure neurotic tendencies. *Journal of Applied Psychology, 18,* 343–356.

Landis, C., Zubin, J., & Katz, S. E. (1935). Empirical validation of three personality adjustment inventories. *Journal of Educational Psychology, 26*, 321–330.

Lange, R. T., Brickell, T. A., & French, L. M. (2015). Examination of the Mild Brain Injury Atypical Symptom scale and the Validity-10 scale to detect symptom exaggeration in US military service members. *Journal of Clinical and Experimental Neuropsychology, 37*(3), 325–337. https://doi.org/10.1080/13803395.2015.1013021

Langwerden, R. J., van der Heijden, P. T., Egger, J. I. M., & Derksen, J. J. L. (2021). Robustness of the maladaptive personality plaster: An investigation of stability of the PSY-5-r in adults over 20 years. *Journal of Personality Assessment, 103*(1), 27–32. https://doi.org/10.1080/00223891.2020.1729772

Lanyon, R. I., & Thomas, M. L. (2013). Assessment of global psychiatric categories: The PSI/PSI-2 and the MMPI-2-RF. *Psychological Assessment, 25*(1), 227–232. https://doi.org/10.1037/a0030313

Larrabee, G. J. (2007). *Assessment of malingered neuropsychological deficits*. Oxford University Press.

Larrabee, G. J., & Rohling, M. L. (2013). Neuropsychological differential diagnosis of Mild Traumatic Brain Injury. *Behavioral Sciences and the Law, 31*, 686–701.

Laurinaitytė, I., Laurinavičius, A., Ustinavičiūtė, L., Wygant, D. B., & Sellbom, M. (2017). Utility of the MMPI-2 Restructured Form (MMPI-2-RF) in a sample of Lithuanian male offenders. *Law and Human Behavior, 41*(5), 494–505. https://doi.org/10.1037/lhb0000254

Lee, T. T. C., Graham, J. R., & Arbisi, P. A. (2018). The utility of MMPI-2-RF scale scores in differential diagnosis of schizophrenia and major depressive disorder. *Journal of Personality Assessment, 100*(3), 305–312. https://doi.org/10.1080/00223891.2017.1300906

Lee, T. T. C., Graham, J. R., Sellbom, M., & Gervais, R. O. (2012). Examining the potential for gender bias in the prediction of symptom validity test failure by MMPI-2 symptom validity scale scores. *Psychological Assessment, 24*(3), 618–627. https://doi.org/10.1037/a0026458

Lee, T. T. C., Taylor, A. M., Holbert, A. M., & Graham, J. R. (2019). MMPI-2-RF predictors of interpersonal relationship characteristics in committed couples. *Psychological Assessment, 31*(9), 1118–1124. https://doi.org/10.1037/pas0000735

Lees-Haley, P. R. (1984). Detecting the psychological malingerer. *American Journal of Forensic Psychology, 2*, 165–169.

Lees-Haley, P. R. (1989). Malingering Post-traumatic Stress Disorder on the MMPI. *Forensic Reports, 2*, 89–91.

Lees-Haley, P. R. (1992). Efficacy of MMPI-2 Validity Scales and MCMI-II modifier scales for detecting spurious PTSD claims: F, F–K, Fake Bad Scale, Ego Strength, Subtle–Obvious subscales, DIS, and DEB. *Journal of Clinical Psychology, 48*, 681–689.

Lees-Haley, P. R., English, L. T., & Glenn, W. J. (1991). A fake bad scale on the MMPI-2 for personal injury claimants. *Psychological Reports, 68*, 203–210.

Lees-Haley, P. R., & Fox, D. D. (2004). Commentary on Butcher, Arbisi, Atlis, and McNulty (2003) on the Fake Bad Scale. *Archives of Clinical Neuropsychology, 19*, 333–336.

Leon, G. R., Gillum, B., Gillum, R., & Gouze, M. (1979). Personality stability and change over a 30-year period—middle age to old age. *Journal of Consulting and Clinical Psychology, 47*(3), 517–524. https://doi.org/10.1037/0022-006X.47.3.517

Lessenger, L. H. (1997). Acculturation and MMPI-2 scale scores of Mexican American substance abuse patients. *Psychological Reports, 80*(3, Pt 2), 1181–1182. https://doi.org/10.2466/pr0.1997.80.3c.1181

Levenson, M. R., Kiehl, K. A., & Fitzpatrick, C. M. (1995). Assessing psychopathic attributes in a noninstitutionalized population. *Journal of Personality and Social Psychology, 68,* 151–158.

Lewinsohn, P. M., Pettit, J. W., Joiner, T., & Seeley, J. R. (2003). The symptomatic expression of Major Depressive Disorder in adolescents and young adults. *Journal of Abnormal Psychology, 112,* 244–252.

Lewis, A. (1970). Paranoia and paranoid: A historical perspective. *Psychological Medicine: A Journal of Research in Psychiatry and the Allied Sciences, 1,* 2–12.

Lezak, M. D. (1987). Norms for growing older. *Developmental Neuropsychology, 3*(1), 1–12. https://doi.org/10.1080/87565648709540360

Lightsey, O. R., Burke, M., Ervin, A., Henderson, D., & Lee, C. (2006). Generalized self-efficacy, self-esteem, and negative effect. *Canadian Journal of Behavioural Science, 38,* 72–80.

Lilienfeld, S. O., & Andrews, P. (1996). Development and preliminary validation of a self-report measure of psychopathic personality traits in noncriminal populations. *Journal of Personality Assessment, 66,* 488–524.

Lim, J., & Butcher, J. N. (1996). Detection of faking on the MMPI-2: Differentiating among faking-bad, denial, and claiming extreme virtue. *Journal of Personality Assessment, 67,* 1–25.

Lincourt, T. M., Tarescavage, A. M., Burchett, D., & Glassmire, D. M. (2020). Association between MMPI-2-RF SUB items/scale and interview-reported substance abuse history among forensic psychiatric inpatients. *Psychological Assessment, 32*(2), 132–139. https://doi.org/10.1037/pas0000769

Locke, D. E. C., Kirlin, K. A., Thomas, M. L., Osborne, D., Hurst, D. F., Drazkowsi, J. F. et al. (2010). The Minnesota Multiphasic Personality Inventory–Restructured Form in the epilepsy monitoring unit. *Epilepsy and Behavior, 17,* 252–258.

Loevinger, J. (1957). Objective tests as instruments of psychological theory. *Psychological Reports, 3,* 635–694.

Loevinger, J. (1972). Some limitations of objective personality tests. In J. N. Butcher (Ed.), *Objective personality assessment: Changing perspectives* (pp. 45–58). Academic Press.

Lord, F. M., & Novick, M. R. (1968). *Statistical theories of mental test scores.* Addison-Wesley.

Lubin, B., Wallis, R. R., & Paine, C. (1971). Patterns of psychological test usage in the United States: 1935–1969. *Professional Psychology, 2,* 70–74.

Lynum, L. I., Wilberg, T., & Karterud, S. (2008). Self-esteem in patients with Borderline and Avoidant Personality disorders. *Scandinavian Journal of Psychology, 49,* 469–477.

MacAndrew, C. (1965). The differentiation of male alcoholic outpatients from nonalcoholic psychiatric outpatients by means of the MMPI. *Quarterly Journal of the Studies on Alcohol, 26,* 238–246.

MacCorquodale, K., & Meehl, P. E. (1948). On a distinction between hypothetical constructs and intervening variables. *Psychological Review, 55,* 95–107.

Maher, B. A. (1974). Delusional thinking and perceptual disorder. *Journal of Individual Psychology, 30,* 98–113.

Maller, J. B. (1932). *Character sketches.* Teachers College, Columbia University.

Mangelli, L., Fava, G. A., Grandi, S., Grassi, L., Ottolini, F., & Porcelli, P. (2005). Assessing demoralization and depression in the setting of medical disease. *Journal of Clinical Psychiatry, 66,* 391–394.

Manschreck, T. C. (1979). The assessment of paranoid features. *Comprehensive Psychiatry, 20,* 370–377.

Marek, R. J., & Anderson, J. L. (2022). Measurement of eating pathology using the Minnesota Multiphasic Personality Inventory-3 (MMPI-3). *Journal of Personality Assessment, 104*(5), 674–679. https://doi.org/10.1080/00223891.2021.1991361

Marek, R. J., Ben-Porath, Y. S., Epker, J. T., Kreymar, J. K., & Block, A. R. (2020). Reliability and validity of the Minnesota Multiphasic Personality Inventory-2-Restructured Form (MMPI-2-RF) in spine surgery and spinal cord stimulator samples. *Journal of Personality Assessment, 102*(1), 22–35. https://doi.org/10.1080/00223891.2018.1488719

Marek, R. J., Ben-Porath, Y. S., Merrell, J., Ashton, K., & Heinberg, L. J. (2014). Predicting one and three month post-operative somatic concerns, psychological distress, and maladaptive eating behavior in bariatric surgery candidates with the Minnesota Multiphasic Personality Inventory-2 Restructured Form (MMPI-2-RF). *Obesity Surgery, 24*(4), 631–639. https://doi.org/10.1007/s11695-013-1149-y

Marek, R. J., Block, A. R., & Ben-Porath, Y. S. (2015). The Minnesota Multiphasic Personality Inventory-2-Restructured Form (MMPI-2-RF): Incremental validity in predicting early postoperative outcomes in spine surgery candidates. *Psychological Assessment, 27*(1), 114–124. https://doi.org/10.1037/pas0000035

Marek, R. J., Martin-Fernandez, K., Ben-Porath, Y. S., & Heinberg, L. J. (2021a). Psychosocial functioning of bariatric surgery patients 6-years postoperative. *Obesity Surgery, 31,* 712–724. https://doi.org/10.1007/s11695-020-05025-x

Marek, R. J., Martin-Fernandez, K., Heinberg, L. J., & Ben-Porath, Y. S. (2021b). An investigation of the Eating Concerns scale of the Minnesota Multiphasic Personality Inventory–3 (MMPI-3) in a postoperative bariatric surgery sample. *Obesity Surgery, 31,* 2335–2338. https://doi.org/10.1007/s11695-020-05113-y

Markon, K. E., Krueger, R. F., & Watson, D. (2005). Delineating the structure of normal and abnormal personality: An integrative hierarchical approach. *Journal of Personality and Social Psychology, 88,* 139–157.

Marks, P. A., & Seeman, W. (1963). *The actuarial description of abnormal personality: An atlas for use with the MMPI.* Williams & Wilkins.

Marsella, A. J., Sanborn, K. O., Kameoka, V., Shizuru, L., & Brennan, J. (1975). Cross-validation of self-report measures of depression among normal populations of Japanese, Chinese, and Caucasian ancestry. *Journal of Clinical Psychology, 31*(2), 281–287.

Martin, P. K., Schroeder, R. W., & Odland, A. P. (2015). Neuropsychologists' validity testing beliefs and practices: A survey of North American professionals. *The Clinical Neuropsychologist, 29*(6), 741–776. https://doi.org/10.1080/13854046.2015.1087597

Martínez, Ú., Fernández del Río, E., López-Durán, A., & Becoña, E. (2017). The utility of the MMPI-2-RF to predict the outcome of a smoking cessation treatment. *Personality and Individual Differences, 106*(1), 172–177. https://doi.org/10.1016/j.paid.2016.11.019

Martínez, Ú., Fernández del Río, E., López-Durán, A., Martínez-Vispo, C., & Becoña, E. (2018). Types of smokers who seek smoking cessation treatment according to psychopathology. *Journal of Dual Diagnosis, 14*(1), 50–59. https://doi.org/10.1080/15504263.2017.1398360

Mason, L. H., Shandera-Ochsner, A. L., Williamson, K. D., Harp, J. P., Edmundson, M., Berry, D. T. R., & High, W. M. (2013). Accuracy of MMPI-2-RF Validity Scales for identifying feigned PTSD symptoms, random responding, and genuine PTSD. *Journal of Personality Assessment, 95*(6), 585–593. https://doi.org/10.1080/00223891.2013.819512

Mattson, C. A., Powers, B. K., Halfaker, D., Akeson, S. T., & Ben-Porath, Y. S. (2012). Predicting drug court treatment completion using the MMPI-2-RF. *Psychological Assessment, 24*(4), 937–943. https://doi.org/10.1037/a0028267

Mazza, C., Monaro, M., Orrù, G., Burla, F., Colasanti, M., Ferracuti, S., & Roma, P. (2019). Introducing machine learning to detect personality faking-good in a male sample: A new model based on Minnesota Multiphasic Personality Inventory-2 Restructured Form scales and reaction times. *Frontiers in Psychology.* https://doi.org/10.3389/fpsyt.2019.00389

McBride, W. F., Crighton, A. H., Wygant, D. B., & Granacher, R. P. (2013). It's not all in your head (or at least your brain): Association of traumatic brain lesion presence and location with performance on measures of response bias in forensic evaluation. *Behavioral Sciences and the Law, 31*(6), 779–788. https://doi.org/10.1002/bsl.2083

McCord, D. M. (2018). *Assessment using the MMPI-2-RF.* American Psychological Association.

McCord, D. M., & Drerup, L. C. (2011). Relative practical utility of the Minnesota Multiphasic Personality Inventory–2 Restructured Clinical Scales versus the Clinical Scales in a chronic pain patient sample. *Journal of Clinical and Experimental Neuropsychology, 33,* 140–146.

McDevitt-Murphy, M. E., Weathers, F. W., Flood, A. M., Eakin, D. E., & Benson, T. A. (2007). The utility of the PAI and the MMPI-2 for discriminating PTSD, depression, and social phobia in trauma-exposed college students. *Assessment, 14,* 181–195.

McDonald, R. L., & Gynther, M. D. (1962). MMPI norms for southern adolescent negros. *Journal of Social Psychology, 58,* 277–282.

McDonald, R. L., & Gynther, M. D. (1963). MMPI differences associated with sex, race, and class in two adolescent samples. *Journal of Consulting Psychology, 27,* 112–116.

McGrath, R. E., Mitchell, M., Kim, B. H., & Hough, L. (2010). Evidence for response bias as a source of error variance in applied assessment. *Psychological Bulletin, 136*(3), 450–470.

McKay, R., Langdon, R., & Coltheart, M. (2006). The Persecutory Ideation Questionnaire. *Journal of Nervous and Mental Disease, 194,* 628–631.

McKenna, T., & Butcher, J. N. (1987). *Continuity of the MMPI with alcoholics.* Paper presented at the 22nd annual symposium on Recent Developments in the Use of the MMPI, Seattle, WA.

McKinley, J. C., & Hathaway, S. R. (1940). A multiphasic personality schedule (Minnesota): II. A differential study of hypochondriasis. *Journal of Psychology, 10,* 255–268.

McKinley, J. C., & Hathaway, S. R. (1942). A multiphasic personality schedule (Minnesota): IV. Psychasthenia. *Journal of Applied Psychology, 26,* 614–624.

McKinley, J. C., & Hathaway, S. R. (1944). A multiphasic personality schedule (Minnesota): V. Hysteria, hypomania, and psychopathic deviate. *Journal of Applied Psychology, 28,* 153–174.

McKinley, J. C., Hathaway, S. R., & Meehl, P. E. (1948). The MMPI: VI. The K scale. *Journal of Consulting Psychology, 12,* 20–31.

McMillan, D., Gilbody, S., Beresford, E., & Neilly, L. (2007). Can we predict suicide and nonfatal self-harm with the Beck Hopelessness Scale? A meta-analysis. *Psychological Medicine, 37*, 769–778.

McNeil, D. E., Binder, R. L., & Greenfield, T. K. (1988). Predictors of violence in civilly committed acute psychiatric patients. *American Journal of Psychiatry, 145*, 965–970.

McNulty, J. L., Ben Porath, Y. S., & Graham, J. R. (1998). An empirical examination of the correlates of well-defined and not defined MMPI-2 code types. *Journal of Personality Assessment, 71*, 393–410.

McNulty, J. L., Graham, J. R., Ben-Porath, Y. S., & Stein, L. A. R. (1997). Comparative validity of MMPI-2 scores of African American and Caucasian mental health center clients. *Psychological Assessment, 9*(4), 464–470. https://doi.org/10.1037/1040-3590.9.4.464

McNulty, J. L., & Overstreet, S. R. (2014). Viewing the MMPI-2-RF structure through the Personality Psychopathology Five (PSY-5) lens. *Journal of Personality Assessment, 96*(2), 151–157. https://doi.org/10.1080/00223891.2013.840305

Meehl, P. E. (1945a). The dynamics of "structured" personality tests. *Journal of Clinical Psychology, 1*, 296–303.

Meehl, P. E. (1945b). An investigation of a general normality or control factor in personality testing. *Psychological Monographs, 59* (4; Whole no. 274).

Meehl, P. E. (1946). Profile analysis of the MMPI in differential diagnosis. *Journal of Applied Psychology, 30*, 517–524.

Meehl, P. E. (1954). *Clinical versus statistical prediction: A theoretical analysis and a review of the evidence.* University of Minnesota Press.

Meehl, P. E. (1956). Wanted—a good cookbook. *American Psychologist, 11*, 263–272.

Meehl, P. E. (1962). Schizotaxia, Schizotypy, Schizophrenia. *American Psychologist, 17*, 827–838.

Meehl, P. E. (1972). Reactions, reflections, projections. In J. N. Butcher (Ed.), *Objective personality assessment: Changing perspectives* (pp. 131–189). Academic Press.

Meehl, P. E. (1975). Hedonic capacity: Some conjectures. *Bulletin of the Menninger Clinic, 39*, 295–307.

Meehl, P. E. (1978). Theoretical risks and tabular asterisks: Sir Karl, Sir Ronald, and the slow progress of soft psychology. *Journal of Consulting and Clinical Psychology, 46*, 806–834.

Meehl, P. E. (1987). "Hedonic capacity" ten years later: Some clarifications. In D. C. Clark & J. Fawcett (Eds.), *Anhedonia and affect deficit states* (pp. 47–50). PMA.

Meehl, P. E. (2001). Primary and secondary hypohedonia. *Journal of Abnormal Psychology, 110*, 188–193.

Meehl, P. E., & Dahlstrom, W. G. (1960). Objective configural rules for discriminating psychotic from neurotic MMPI profiles. *Journal of Consulting Psychology, 24*, 375–387.

Meehl, P. E., & Hathaway, S. R. (1946). The K factor as a suppressor variable in the MPI. *Journal of Applied Psychology, 30*, 525–564.

Mendez, B., Bozzay, M., & Verona, E. (2021). Internalizing and externalizing symptoms and aggression and violence in men and women. *Aggressive behavior, 47*(4), 439–452.

Menton, W. H., Crighton, A. H., Tarescavage, A. M., Marek, R. J., Hicks, A. D., & Ben-Porath, Y. S. (2019). Equivalence of laptop and tablet administrations of the Minnesota Multiphasic Personality Inventory–2 Restructured Form. *Assessment, 26*(4), 661–669. https://doi.org/0.1177/1073191117714558

Miach, P. P., Berah, E. F., Butcher, J. N., & Rouse, S. (2000). Utility of the MMPI-2 in assessing gender dysphoric patients. *Journal of Personality Assessment, 75*(2), 268–279. https://doi.org/10.1207/S15327752JPA7502_7

Michaelis, B. H., Goldberg, J. F., Davis, G. P., Singer, T. M., Garno, J. L., & Wenze, S. J. (2004). Dimensions of impulsivity and aggression associated with suicide attempts among bipolar patients: A preliminary study. *Suicide and Life-Threatening Behavior, 34,* 172–186.

Miller, M. W., Fogler, J. M., Wolf, E. J., Kaloupek, D. G., & Keane, T. M. (2008). The internalizing and externalizing structure of psychiatric comorbidity in combat veterans. *Journal of Traumatic Stress, 21,* 58–65.

Miller, M. W., Kaloupek, D. G., Dillon, A. L., & Keane, T. M. (2004). Externalizing and internalizing subtypes of combat-related PTSD: A replication and extension using the PSY-5 scales. *Journal of Abnormal Psychology, 113,* 636–645.

Miller, K. E., Koffel, E., Kramer, M. D., Erbes, C. R., Arbisi, P. A., & Polusny, M. A. (2018). At-home partner sleep functioning over the course of military deployment. *Journal of Family Psychology, 32*(1), 114–122. https://doi.org/10.1037/fam0000262

Miller, M. W., Vogt, D. S., Mozley, S. L., Kaloupek, D. G., & Keane, T. M. (2006). PTSD and substance-related problems: The mediating roles of disconstraint and negative emotionality. *Abnormal Psychology, 115,* 369–379.

Miller, M. W., Wolf, E. J., Harrington, K. M., Brown, T. A., Kaloupek, D. G., & Keane, T. M. (2010). An evaluation of competing models for the structure of PTSD symptoms using external measures of comorbidity. *Journal of Traumatic Stress, 23,* 631–638.

Millon, T. (1981). *Disorders of personality.* John Wiley.

Mineka, S., Watson, D., & Clark, L. A. (1998). Comorbidity of anxiety and unipolar mood disorders. *Annual Review of Psychology, 49,* 377–412.

Miranda, R., Fontes, M., & Marroquin, B. (2008). Cognitive content-specificity in future expectancies: Role of hopelessness and intolerance of uncertainty in depression and GAD symptoms. *Behaviour Research and Therapy, 46,* 1151–1159.

Monaghan, C., Bizumic, B., & Sellbom, M. (2016). The role of Machiavellian views and tactics in psychopathology. *Personality and Individual Differences, 94,* 72–81.

Monnot, M. J., Quirk, S. W., Hoerger, M., & Brewer, L. (2009). Racial bias in personality assessment: Using the MMPI-2 to predict psychiatric diagnoses of African American and Caucasian chemical dependency patients. *Psychological Assessment, 21,* 137–151.

Moran, P. (1999). The epidemiology of Antisocial Personality Disorder. *Social Psychiatry and Psychiatric Epidemiology, 34,* 231–242.

Morey, L. C. (1991). *Personality Assessment Inventory professional manual.* Psychological Assessment Resources.

Morey, L. C. (2007). *Personality Assessment Inventory professional manual* (2nd ed.). Psychological Assessment Resources.

Morey, L. C. (2012). Detection of response bias in applied assessment: Comment on McGrath et al. (2010). *Psychological Injury and Law, 5*(3), 153–161.

Morey, L. C., Warner, M. B., & Hopwood, C. J. (2007). The Personality Assessment Inventory. In A. Goldstein (Ed.), *Forensic psychology: Advanced Topics for forensic mental experts and attorneys* (pp. 97–126). John Wiley.

Moultrie, J. K., & Engel, R. R. (2017). Empirical correlates for the Minnesota Multiphasic Personality Inventory-2-Restructured Form in a German inpatient sample. *Psychological Assessment, 29*(10), 1273–1289.

Najt, P., Perez, J., Sanches, M., Peluso, M. A. M., Glahn, D., & Soares, J. C. (2007). Impulsivity and Bipolar Disorder. *European Neuropsychopharmacology, 17,* 313–320.

Naragon-Gainey, K., Watson, D., & Markon, K. E. (2009). Differential relations of depression and social anxiety symptoms to the facets of extraversion/positive emotionality. *Journal of Abnormal Psychology, 118*(2), 299–310.

Neiss, M. B., Stevenson, J., Legrand, L. N., Iacono, W. G., & Sedikides, C. (2009). Self-esteem, negative emotionality, and depression as a common temperamental core: A study of mid-adolescent twin girls. *Journal of Personality, 77,* 327–346.

Nelson, N., Hoelzle, J., Sweet, J., Arbisi, P., & Demakis, G. (2010). Updated meta-analysis of the MMPI-2 Symptom Validity Scale (FBS): Verified utility in forensic practice. *Clinical Neuropsychologist, 24,* 701–724.

Nelson, N. W., Sweet, J. J., & Demakis, G. J. (2006). Meta-analysis of the MMPI-2 Fake Bad Scale: Utility in forensic practice. *Clinical Neuropsychologist, 20,* 39–58.

Neo, P. S., McNaughton, N., & Sellbom, M. (2021). Early and late signals of unexpected reward contribute to low extraversion and high disinhibition, respectively. *Personality Neuroscience, 4,* e5.

Nguyen, C. T., Green, D., & Barr, W. B. (2015). Evaluation of the MMPI-2-RF for detecting over-reported symptoms in a civil forensic and disability setting. *The Clinical Neuropsychologist, 29*(2), 255–271. https://doi.org/10.1080/13854046.2015.1033020

Nichols, D. S. (2006). The trials of separating bath water from baby: A review and critique of the MMPI-2 Restructured Clinical Scales. *Journal of Personality Assessment, 87,* 121–138.

Noordhof, A., Kamphuis, J. H., Sellbom, M., Eigenhuis, A., & Bagby, R. M. (2018). Change in self-reported personality during major depressive disorder treatment: A reanalysis of treatment studies from a demoralization perspective. *Personality Disorders: Theory, Research, and Treatment, 9*(1), 93–100.

Noordhof, A., Sellbom, M., Eigenhuis, A., & Kamphuis, J. H. (2015). Distinguishing between demoralization and specific personality traits in clinical assessment with the NEO-PI-R. *Psychological Assessment, 27*(2), 645–656. https://doi.org/10.1037/pas0000067

Norman, W. (1972). Psychometric considerations for a revision of the MMPI. In J. N. Butcher (Ed.), *Objective personality assessment: Changing perspectives* (pp. 59–83). Academic Press.

Novaco, R. W. (1994). *Novaco Anger Scale and Provocation Inventory (NAS-PI)*. Western Psychological Services.

Novaco, R. W., & Taylor, J. L. (2004). Assessment of anger and aggression among male offenders with developmental disabilities. *Psychological Assessment, 16,* 42–50.

Nunnally, J. C. (1967). *Psychometric theory*. McGraw-Hill.

O'Connor, B. P. (2002). The search for dimensional structure differences between normality and abnormality: A statistical review of published data on personality and psychopathology. *Journal of Personality and Social Psychology, 83,* 962–982.

Oltmanns, J. R., & Widiger, T. A. (2018). A self-report measure for the ICD-11 dimensional trait model proposal: The Personality Inventory for ICD-11. *Psychological Assessment, 30*(2), 154–169.

Orth, U., Robins, R. W., Trzesniewski, K. H., Maes, J., & Schmitt, M. (2009). Low self-esteem is a risk factor for depressive symptoms from young adulthood to old age. *Journal of Abnormal Psychology, 118,* 472–478.

Osberg, T. M., Haseley, E. N., & Kamas, M. M. (2008). The MMPI-2 Clinical Scales and Restructured Clinical (RC) Scales: Comparative psychometric properties and relative diagnostic efficiency in young adults. *Journal of Personality Assessment, 90,* 81–92.

Osberg, T. M., & Poland, D. L. (2002). Comparative accuracy of the MMPI-2 and the MMPI-A in the diagnosis of psychopathology in 18-year-olds. *Psychological Assessment, 14,* 164–169.

Overall, J. E., & Gorham, D. R. (1988). Introduction: The Brief Psychiatric Rating Scale (BPRS): recent developments in ascertainment and scaling. *Psychopharmacology Bulletin, 24,* 97–98.

Pace, T. M., Robbins, R. R., Choney, S. K., Hill, J. S., Lacey, K., & Blair, G. (2006). A cultural-contextual perspective on the validity of the MMPI-2 with American Indians. *Cultural Diversity and Ethnic Minority Psychology, 12*(2), 320–333. https://doi.org/10.1037/1099-9809.12.2.320

Page, R. D., and Bozlee, S. (1982). A cross-cultural MMPI comparison of alcoholics. *Psychological Reports, 50*(2), 639–646. https://doi.org/10.2466/pr0.1982.50.2.639

Papakostas, G. I., Crawford, C. M., Scalia, M. J., & Fava, M. (2007). Timing of clinical improvement and symptom resolution in the treatment of Major Depressive Disorder: A replication of findings with the use of a double-blind, placebo-controlled trial of *Hypericum perforatum* versus fluoxetine. *Neuropsychobiology, 56,* 132–137.

Pardis, A. D., Reinherz, H. Z., Giaconia, R. M., Beardslee, W. R., Ward, K. E., & Fitzmaurice, G. M. (2009). The long-term impact of family arguments and physical violence on adult functioning at age 30. *Journal of the American Academy of Child and Adolescent Psychiatry, 48,* 291–299.

Parwatikar, S. D., Holcomb, W. R., & Menninger, K. A. (1985). The detection of malingered amnesia in accused murderers. *Bulletin of the American Academy of Psychiatry and the Law, 13,* 97–103.

Patel, K. D., & Suhr, J. A. (2019). The relationship of MMP-2-RF scales to treatment engagement and alliance. *Journal of Personality Assessment, 102*(5), 594–603. https://doi.org/10.1080/00223891.2019.1635488

Patrick, C. J. (2007). Affective processes in psychopathy. In J. Rottenberg & S. L. Johnson (Eds.), *Emotion and psychopathology: Bridging affective and clinical science* (pp. 215–239). American Psychological Association.

Patrick, C. J. (2010). Operationalizing the triarchic conceptualization of psychopathy: Preliminary description of brief scales for assessment of boldness, meanness, and disinhibition. *Unpublished test manual, Florida State University, Tallahassee, FL,* 1110–1131.

Paulhus, D. L. (1984). Two-component models of socially desirable responding. *Journal of Personality and Social Psychology, 46,* 598–609.

Pearson, K., & Filon, L. (1898). Mathematical contributions to the theory of evolution, iv. On the probable errors of frequency constants and on the influence of random selection on variation and correlation. *Philosophical Transactions, Series A, 191*, 229–311.

Peck, C. P., Schroeder, R. W., Heinrichs, R. J., VonDran, E. J., Brockman, C. J., Webster, B. K., & Baade, L. E. (2013). Differences in MMPI-2 FBS and RBS scores in brain injury, probable malingering, and conversion disorder groups: A preliminary study. *The Clinical Neuropsychologist, 27*(4), 693–707. https://doi.org/10.1080/13854046.2013.779032

Pedersen, S. S., Denollet, J., Erdman, R. A. M., Serruys, P. W., & van Domburg, R. T. (2009). Co-occurrence of diabetes and hopelessness predicts adverse prognosis following percutaneous coronary intervention. *Journal of Behavioral Medicine, 32*, 294–301.

Penk, W. E., Bell, W., Robinowitz, R., Dolan, M., Black, J., Dorsett, D., & Noriega, L. (1986). Ethnic differences in personality adjustment of black and white male Vietnam combat veterans seeking treatment for substance abuse. Unpublished manuscript.

Petersen, M. W., Schröder, A., Jørgensen, T., Ørnbøl, E., Dantoft, T. M., Eliasen, M., . . . & Fink, P. (2020). The unifying diagnostic construct of bodily distress syndrome (BDS) was confirmed in the general population. *Journal of Psychosomatic Research, 128*, 109868.

Petroskey, L., Ben-Porath, Y. S., & Stafford, K. P. (2003). Correlates of the Minnesota Multiphasic Personality Inventory–2 (MMPI-2) Personality Psychopathology Five (PSY-5) scales in a forensic assessment setting. *Assessment, 10*, 393–399.

Phillips, T. R., Sellbom, M., Ben-Porath, Y. S., & Patrick, C. J. (2014). Further development and construct validation of MMPI-2-RF indices of global psychopathy, fearless-dominance, and impulsive-antisociality in a sample of incarcerated women. *Law and Human Behavior, 38*(1), 34–46. https://doi.org/10.1037/lhb0000040

Pilkonis, P. A., Choi, S. W., Reise, S. P., Stover, A. M., Riley, W. T., Cella, D., & PROMIS Cooperative Group. (2011). Item banks for measuring emotional distress from the Patient-Reported Outcomes Measurement Information System (PROMIS®): depression, anxiety, and anger. *Assessment, 18*(3), 263–283.

Pilowsky, D. J., Wickramartine, P., Nomura, Y., & Weissman, M. M. (2006). Family discord, parental depression, and psychopathology in offspring: 20-year follow-up. *Journal of the American Academy of Child and Adolescent Psychiatry, 45*, 452–460.

Pollack, D. R., & Grainey, T. F. (1984). A comparison of MMPI profiles for state and private disability insurance applicants. *Journal of Personality Assessment, 48*, 121–125.

Pollack, D., & Shore, J. H. (1980). Validity of the MMPI with Native Americans. *The American Journal of Psychiatry, 137*(8), 946–950. https://doi.org/10.1176/ajp.137.8.946

Pope, K. S., Butcher, J. N., & Seelen, J. (1993). *The MMPI, MMPI-2 & MMPI-A in court: A practical guide for expert witnesses and attorneys.* American Psychological Association.

Prichard, D. A., & Rosenblatt, A. (1980). Racial bias in the MMPI: A methodological review. *Journal of Consulting and Clinical Psychology, 48*(2), 263–267. https://doi.org/10.1037/0022-006X.48.2.263

Priebe, S., Fakhoury, W. K., & Henningsen, P. (2008). Functional incapacity and physical and psychological symptoms: How they interconnect in chronic fatigue syndrome. *Psychopathology, 41*, 339–345.

Priest, W., & Meunier, G. F. (1993). MMPI-2 performance of elderly women. *Clinical Gerontologist: The Journal of Aging and Mental Health, 14*(2), 3–11. https://doi.org/10.1300/J018v14n02_02

Rado, S. (1956). *Psychoanalysis of behavior; collected papers*. Grune & Stratton.

Rafanelli, C., Roncuzzi, R., Milaneschi, Y., Tomba, E., Colistro, M. C., Pancaldi, L. G. et al. (2005). Stressful life events, depression and demoralization as risk factors for acute coronary heart disease. *Psychotherapy and Psychosomatics, 74*, 179–184.

Reed, G. M., First, M. B., Kogan, C. S., Hyman, S. E., Gureje, O., Gaebel, W., . . . Saxena, S. (2019). Innovations and changes in the ICD-11 classification of mental, behavioural and neurodevelopmental disorders. *World Psychiatry, 18*, 3–19.

Reeves, C. K., Brown, T. A., & Sellbom, M. (2022). An Examination of the MMPI-3 Validity Scales in Detecting Overreporting of Psychological Problems. *Psychological Assessment, 34*, 517–527.

Reid, R. C., & Carpenter, N. (2009). Exploring relationships of psychopathology in hypersexual patients using the MMPI-2. *Journal of Sex and Marital Therapy, 35*, 294–310.

Restifo, K., Harkavy-Friedman, J. M., & Shrout, P. E. (2009). Suicidal behavior in Schizophrenia: A test of the demoralization hypothesis. *Journal of Nervous and Mental Disease, 197*, 147–153.

Røysamb, E., Kendler, K. S., Tambs, K., Ørstavik, R. E., Neale, M. C., Aggen, S. H., Torgersen, S., & Reichborn-Kjennerud, T. (2011). The joint structure of DSM-IV Axis I and Axis II disorders. *Journal of Abnormal Psychology, 120*(1), 198–209.

Roback, H. B., McKee, E., Webb, W., Abramowitz, C. V., & Abramowitz, S. I. (1976). Psychopathology in female sex-change applicants and two help-seeking controls. *Journal of Abnormal Psychology, 85*(4), 430–432. https://doi.org/10.1037/0021-843X.85.4.430

Robin, R. W., Greene, R. L., Albaugh, B., Caldwell, A., & Goldman, D. (2003). Use of the MMPI-2 in American Indians: I. Comparability of the MMPI-2 Between Two Tribes and With the MMPI-2 Normative Group. *Psychological Assessment, 15*(3), 351–359. https://doi.org/10.1037/1040-3590.15.3.351

Robinson, E. V., & Rogers, R. (2018). Detection of feigned ADHD across two domains: MMPI-2-RF and CAARS for faked symptoms and TOVA for simulated attention deficits. *Journal of Psychopathology and Behavioral Assessment, 40*(3), 376–385. https://doi.org/10.1007/s10862-017-9640-8

Rogers, M. L., Anestis, J. C., Harrop, T. M., Schneider, M., Bender, T. W., Ringer, F. B., & Joiner, T. E. (2017). Examination of MMPI-2-RF substantive scales as indicators of acute suicidal affective disturbance components. *Journal of Personality Assessment, 99*(4), 424–434. https://doi.org/10.1080/00223891.2016.1222393

Rogers, R., Gillard, N. D., Berry, D. T. R., & Granacher, R. P. (2011). Effectiveness of the MMPI-2-RF Validity Scales for feigned mental disorders and cognitive impairment: A known-groups study. *Journal of Psychopathology and Behavioral Assessment*. Advance online publication. https://doi.org/10.1007/s10862-011-9222-0

Rogers, R., Sewell, K. W., Harrison, K. S., & Jordan, M. J. (2006). The MMPI-2 Restructured Clinical Scales: A paradigmatic shift in scale development. *Journal of Personality Assessment, 87*, 139–147.

Rogers, R., Sewell, K. W., Martin, M. A., & Vitacco, M. J. (2003). Detection of feigned mental disorders: A meta-analysis of the MMPI-2 and malingering. *Assessment, 10*, 160–177.

Rohling, M. L., Larrabee, G. J., Greiffenstein, M. F., Ben-Porath, Y. S., Lees-Haley, P., Green, P., & Greve, K. W. (2011). A misleading review of response bias: Comment on McGrath, Mitchell, Kim, and Hough (2010). *Psychological Bulletin, 137*(4), 708–712.

Roma, P., Verrocchio, M. C., Mazza, C., Marchetti, D., Burla, F., Cinti, M. E., & Ferracuti, S. (2018). Could time detect a faking-good attitude? A study with the MMPI-2-RF. *Frontiers in Psychology.* https://doi.org/10.3389/fpsyg.2018.01064

Rosen, A. C. (1974). Brief report of MMPI characteristics of sexual deviation. *Psychological Reports, 35*(1, Pt 1), 73–74. https://doi.org/10.2466/pr0.1974.35.1.73

Rouse, S. V. (2007). Using reliability generalization methods to explore measurement error: An illustration using the MMPI-2 PSY-5 scales. *Journal of Personality Assessment, 88,* 264–275.

Rouse, S. V., Butcher, J. N., & Miller, K. B. (1999). Assessment of substance abuse in psychotherapy clients: The effectiveness of the MMPI-2 substance abuse scales. *Psychological Assessment, 11,* 101–107.

Rouse, S. V., Finger, M. S., & Butcher, J. N. (1999). Advances in clinical personality measurement: An item response theory analysis of the MMPI-2 PSY-5 scales. *Journal of Personality Assessment, 72,* 282–307.

Ruch, F. L. (1942). A technique for detecting attempts to fake performance on the self-inventory type of personality test. In Q. McNemar & M. A. Merrill (Eds.), *Studies in personality* (pp. 229–234). McGraw-Hill.

Ruggero, C. J., Kotov, R., Hopwood, C. J., First, M., Clark, L. A., Skodol, A. E., Mullins-Sweatt, S. N., Patrick, C. J., Bach, B., Cicero, D. C., Docherty, A., Simms, L. J., Bagby, R. M., Krueger, R. F., Callahan, J. L., Chmielewski, M., Conway, C. C., De Clercq, B., Dornbach-Bender, A., . . . Zimmermann, J. (2019). Integrating the Hierarchical Taxonomy of Psychopathology (HiTOP) into clinical practice. *Journal of Consulting and Clinical Psychology, 87*(12), 1069–1084.

Ruggero, C. J., Kotov, R., Watson, D., Kilmer, J. N., Perlman, G., & Liu, K. (2014). Beyond a single index of mania symptoms: Structure and validity of subdimensions. *Journal of Affective Disorders, 161,* 8–15.

Ruiz, M. A., & Edens, J. F. (2008). Recovery and replication of internalizing and externalizing dimensions within the Personality Assessment Inventory. *Journal of Personality Assessment, 90,* 585–592.

Russo, A. C. (2018). A practitioner survey of Department of Veterans Affairs psychologists who provide neuropsychological assessments. *Archives of Clinical Neuropsychology, 33*(8), 1046–1059.

Sacks, S., Cleland, C. M., Melnick, G., Flynn, P. M., Knight, K., Friedmann, P. D. et al. (2009). Violence associated with co-occurring substance use and mental health problems: Evidence from CJDATS. *Behavioral Sciences and the Law, 27,* 51–69.

Sammut, S., Bethus, I., Goodall, G., & Muscat, R. (2002). Antidepressant reversal of interferon-a–induced anhedonia. *Physiology and Behavior, 75,* 765–772.

Samuel, D. B., Riddell, A. D., Lynam, D. R., Miller, J. D., & Widiger, T. A. (2012). A five-factor measure of obsessive–compulsive personality traits. *Journal of Personality Assessment, 94*(5), 456–465.

Sánchez, G., Ampudia, A., Jiménez, F., & Amado, B. G. (2017). Contrasting the efficacy of the MMPI-2-RF overreporting scales in the detection of malingering. *The European*

Journal of Psychology Applied to Legal Context, 9(2), 51–56. https://doi.org/10.1016/j.ejpal.2017.03.002

Sansone, R. A., Wiederman, M. W., & Sansone, L. A. (1998). The self-harm inventory (SHI): Development of a scale for identifying self-destructive behaviors and borderline personality disorder. *Journal of Clinical Psychology, 54*(7), 973–983.

Santor, D. A., & Coyne, J. C. (2001). Evaluating the continuity of symptomatology between depressed and nondepressed individuals. *Journal of Abnormal Psychology, 110,* 216–225.

Sawrie, S. M., Kabat, M. H., Dietz, C. B., Greene, R. L., Arrendondo, R., & Mann, A. W. (1996). Internal structure of the MMPI-2 Addiction Potential Scale in alcoholic and psychiatric inpatients. *Journal of Personality Assessment, 66,* 177–193.

Scarpa, A., & Raine, A. (1997). Psychophysiology of anger and violent behavior. *Psychiatric Clinics of North America, 20,* 375–394.

Schinka, J. A., & Borum, R. (1993). Readability of adult psychopathology inventories. *Psychological Assessment, 5,* 384–386.

Schinka, J. A., & Lalone, L. (1997). MMPI-2 norms: Comparisons with a census-matched subsample. *Psychological Assessment, 9,* 307–311.

Schlaepfer, T. E., Cohen, M. X., Frick, C., Kosel, M., Brodesser, D., Axmacher, N. et al. (2008). Deep brain stimulation to reward circuitry alleviates anhedonia in refractory major depression. *Neuropsychopharmacology, 33,* 368–377.

Schmidt, H. O. (1945). Test profiles as a diagnostic aid: The Minnesota Multiphasic Inventory. *Journal of Applied Psychology, 29,* 115–131.

Schneider, K. (1959). *Clinical psychopathology* (5th ed.). Grune & Stratton.

Schretlen, D., & Arkowitz, H. (1990). A psychological test battery to detect prison inmates who fake insanity or mental retardation. *Behavioral Sciences and the Law, 8,* 75–84.

Schroeder, R. W., Baade, L. E., Peck, C. P., VonDran, E., Brockman, C. J., Webster, B. K., & Heinrichs, R. J. (2012). Validation of MMPI-2-RF Validity Scales in criterion group neuropsychological samples. *The Clinical Neuropsychologist, 26*(1), 129–146. https://doi.org/10.1080/13854046.2011.639314

Schroeder, R.W., Martin, P. K., & Odland, A. P. (2016). Expert beliefs and practices regarding neuropsychological validity testing. *The Clinical Neuropsychologist,* 30, 515–535.

Sellbom, M. (2011). Elaborating on the construct validity of the Levenson Self-Report Psychopathy Scale in incarcerated and non-incarcerated samples. *Law and Human Behavior, 35*(6), 440–451. https://doi.org/10.1007/s10979-010-9249-x

Sellbom, M. (2016). Elucidating the validity of the externalizing spectrum of psychopathology in correctional, forensic, and community samples. *Journal of Abnormal Psychology, 125*(8), 1027–1038. https://doi.org/10.1037/abn0000171

Sellbom, M. (2017a). Mapping the MMPI–2–RF specific problems scales onto extant psychopathology structures. *Journal of Personality Assessment, 99*(4), 341–350.

Sellbom, M. (2017b). Using the MMPI-2-RF to characterize defendants evaluated for competency to stand trial and criminal responsibility. *International Journal of Forensic Mental Health, 16*(4), 304–312. https://doi.org/10.1080/14999013.2017.1371259

Sellbom, M. (2019a). Antagonism's Place in Psychiatric Nosology. In D. R. Lynam & J. D. Miller (Eds.), *The Handbook of Antagonism: Conceptualizations, Assessment, Consequences, and Treatment of the Low End of Agreeableness* (pp. 171–184). Academic Press.

Sellbom, M. (2019b). The MMPI-2-Restructured Form (MMPI-2-RF): Assessment of personality and psychopathology in the twenty-first century. *Annual Review of Clinical Psychology, 15*(1), 149–177. https://doi.org/10.1146/annurev-clinpsy-050718-095701

Sellbom, M. (2021). Examining the criterion and incremental validity of the MMPI-3 Self-Importance scale. *Psychological Assessment, 33*(4), 363–368.

Sellbom, M. (2022). *Minnesota Multiphasic Personality Inventory-3 (MMPI-3): Manual supplement for the Australia and New Zealand Community comparison groups.* University of Minnesota Press.

Sellbom, M., Anderson, J. L., & Bagby, R. M. (2013). Assessing DSM-5 Section III personality traits and disorders with the MMPI-2-RF. *Assessment, 20*(6), 709–722. https://doi.org/10.1177/1073191113508808

Sellbom, M., & Bagby, R. M. (2008). Validity of the MMPI-2-RF (Restructured Form) L-r and K-r scales in detecting underreporting in clinical and nonclinical samples. *Psychological Assessment, 20*, 370–376.

Sellbom, M., Bagby, R. M., Kushner, S., Quilty, L. C., & Ayearst, L. E. (2012). Diagnostic construct validity of the MMPI-2 Restructured Form (MMPI-2-RF) scale scores. *Assessment, 19*(2), 176–186. https://doi.org/10.1177/1073191111428763

Sellbom, M., & Ben-Porath, Y. S. (2005). Mapping the MMPI-2 Restructured Clinical Scales onto normal personality traits: Evidence of construct validity. *Journal of Personality Assessment, 85*, 179–187.

Sellbom, M., Ben-Porath, Y. S., & Bagby, R. M. (2008a). On the hierarchical structure of mood and anxiety disorders: Confirmatory evidence and elaboration of a model of temperament markers. *Journal of Abnormal Psychology, 117*, 576–590.

Sellbom, M., Ben-Porath, Y. S., & Bagby, R. M. (2008b). Personality and psychopathology: Mapping the MMPI-2 Restructured Clinical (RC) Scales onto the Five Factor Model of personality. *Journal of Personality Disorders, 22*, 291–312.

Sellbom, M., Ben-Porath, Y. S., Baum, L. J., Erez, E., & Gregory, C. (2008c). Predictive validity of the MMPI-2 Restructured Clinical (RC) Scales in a batterers' intervention program. *Journal of Personality Assessment, 90*, 129–135.

Sellbom, M., Ben Porath, Y. S., & Graham, J. R. (2006). Correlates of the MMPI-2 Restructured Clinical (RC) Scales in a college counseling setting. *Journal of Personality Assessment, 86*, 89–99.

Sellbom, M., Ben-Porath, Y. S., Lilienfeld, S. O., Patrick, C. J., & Graham, J. R. (2005). Assessing psychopathic personality traits with the MMPI-2. *Journal of Personality Assessment, 85*, 334–343.

Sellbom, M., Ben-Porath, Y. S., McNulty, J. L., Arbisi, P. A., & Graham, J. R. (2006). Elevation differences between MMPI-2 Clinical and Restructured Clinical (RC) Scales: Frequency, origins, and interpretative implications. *Assessment, 13*(4), 430–441. https://doi.org/10.1177/1073191106293349

Sellbom, M., Ben-Porath, Y. S., Patrick, C. J., Wygant, D. B., Gartland, D. M., & Stafford, K. P. (2012). Development and construct validation of MMPI-2-RF measures assessing global psychopathy, fearless-dominance, and impulsive-antisociality. *Personality Disorders: Theory, Research, and Treatment, 3*(1), 17–38. https://doi.org/10.1037/a0023888

Sellbom, M., Ben-Porath, Y. S., & Stafford, K. P. (2007). A comparison of MMPI-2 measures of psychopathic deviance in a forensic setting. *Psychological Assessment, 19*, 430–436.

Sellbom, M., Brown, T. A., & Vaňousová, M. (2021, March). *Construct validity of four new MMPI-3 specific problems scales.* Paper presented at the 2021 Annual Meeting for the Society of personality Assessment, virtual conference.

Sellbom, M., Carragher, N., Sunderland, M., Calear, A. L., & Batterham, P. J. (2020). The role of maladaptive personality domains across multiple levels of the HiTOP structure. *Personality and Mental Health, 14*(1), 30–50.

Sellbom, M., Fischler, G. L., & Ben-Porath, Y. S. (2007). Identifying MMPI-2 predictors of police officer integrity and misconduct. *Criminal Justice and Behavior, 34,* 985–1004.

Sellbom, M., Forbush, K. T., Gould, S. R., Markon, K. E., Watson, D., & Witthöft, M. (2022). HiTOP assessment of the somatoform spectrum and eating disorders. *Assessment, 29*(1), 62–74.

Sellbom, M., Graham, J. R., & Schenk, P. W. (2006). Incremental validity of the MMPI-2 Restructured Clinical (RC) Scales in a private practice sample. *Journal of Personality Assessment, 86,* 196–205.

Sellbom, M., Kremyar, A. J., & Wygant, D. B. (2021). Mapping MMPI-3 scales onto the hierarchical taxonomy of psychopathology. *Psychological Assessment, 33*(12), 1153–1168.

Sellbom, M., Laurinavičius, A., Ustinavičiūtė, L., & Laurinaitytė, I. (2018). The Triarchic Psychopathy Measure: An examination in a Lithuanian Inmate Sample. *Psychological Assessment, 30,* e10-e20.

Sellbom, M., Lee, T. T. C., Ben-Porath, Y. S., Arbisi, P. A., & Gervais, R. O. (2012). Differentiating PTSD symptomatology with the MMPI-2-RF (Restructured Form) in a forensic disability sample. *Psychiatry Research, 197*(1–2), 172–179. https://doi.org/10.1016/j.psychres.2012.02.003

Sellbom, M., Smid, W., De Saeger, H., Smit, N., & Kamphuis, J. H. (2014). Mapping the Personality Psychopathology Five domains onto *DSM-IV* personality disorders in Dutch clinical and forensic samples: Implications for *DSM-5*. *Journal of Personality Assessment, 96*(2), 185–191. https://doi.org/10.1080/00223891.2013.825625

Sellbom, M., & Smith, A. (2017). Assessment of *DSM-5* Section II personality disorders with the MMPI-2-RF in a nonclinical sample. *Journal of Personality Assessment, 99*(4), 384–397. https://doi.org/10.1080/00223891.2016.1242074

Sellbom, M., Solomon-Krakus, S., Bach, B., & Bagby, R. M. (2020). Validation of Personality Inventory for *DSM-5* (PID-5) Algorithms to Assess ICD-11 Personality Trait Domains in a Psychiatric Sample. *Psychological Assessment, 32,* 40–49.

Sellbom, M., Toomey, J. A., Wygant, D. B., Kucharski, L. T., & Duncan, S. (2010). Utility of the MMPI-2-RF (Restructured Form) Validity Scales in detecting malingering in a criminal forensic setting: A known-groups design. *Psychological Assessment, 22,* 22–31.

Sellbom, M., & Wygant, D. B. (2018). *Forensic applications of the MMPI-2-RF: A casebook.* University of Minnesota Press.

Sellbom, M., Wygant, D. B., & Bagby, R. M. (2012). Utility of the MMPI-2-RF in detecting non-credible somatic complaints. *Psychiatry Research, 197*(3), 295–301. https://doi.org/10.1016/j.psychres.2011.12.043

Sellbom, M., Wygant, D. B., & Ben-Porath, Y. S. (2018). *Forensic applications of the MMPI-2-RF: A casebook.* University of Minnesota Press.

Shaevel, B., & Archer, R. P. (1996). Effects of MMPI-2 and MMPI-A norms on T-score elevations for 18-year-olds. *Journal of Personality Assessment, 67,* 72–78.

Sharf, A. J., Rogers, R., Williams, M. M., & Henry, S. A. (2017). The effectiveness of the MMPI-2-RF in detecting feigned mental disorders and cognitive deficits: A meta-analysis. *Journal of Psychopathology and Behavioral Assessment, 39,* 441–455. https://doi.org/10.1007/s10862-017-9590-1

Sharland, M. J., & Gfeller, D. (2007). A survey of neuropsychologists' beliefs and practices with respect to the assessment of effort. *Archives of Clinical Neuropsychology, 22,* 213–223.

Sharpe, J. P., & Desai, S. (2001). The revised NEO Personality Inventory and the MMPI-2 Psychopathology Five in the prediction of aggression. *Personality and Individual Differences, 31,* 505–518.

Shayegan, D. K., & Stahl, S. M. (2005). Emotion processing, the amygdala, and outcome in schizophrenia. *Progress in Neuro-Psychopharmacology and Biological Psychiatry, 29*(5), 840–845.

Shkalim, E. (2015). Psychometric evaluation of the MMPI-2/MMPI-2-RF Restructured Clinical Scales in an Israeli sample. *Assessment, 22*(5), 607–618. https://doi.org/10.1177/1073191114555884

Shkalim, E., Almagor, M., & Ben-Porath, Y. S. (2017). Examining current conceptualizations of psychopathology with the MMPI-2/MMPI-2-RF Restructured Clinical Scales: Preliminary findings from a cross-cultural study. *Journal of Personality Assessment, 99*(4), 375–383. https://doi.org/10.1080/00223891.2016.1189429

Shkalim, E., Ben-Porath, Y. S., Handel, R. W., Almagor, M., & Tellegen, A. (2016). Psychometric examination, adaptation, and evaluation of the Hebrew translation of the MMPI-2-RF VRIN-r and TRIN-r Validity Scales. *Journal of Personality Assessment, 98*(6), 608–615. https://doi.org/10.1080/00223891.2016.1174705

Shure, G. H., & Rogers, M. S. (1965). Note of caution on the factor analysis of the MMPI. *Psychological Bulletin. 63,* 14–18.

Simms, L. J., Casillas, A., Clark, L .A., Watson, D., & Doebbeling, B. I. (2005). Psychometric evaluation of the Restructured Clinical Scales of the MMPI-2. *Psychological Assessment, 17,* 345–358.

Simms, L. J., Goldberg, L. R., Roberts, J. E., Watson, D., Welte, J., & Rotterman, J. H. (2011). Computerized adaptive assessment of personality disorder: Introducing the CAT–PD project. *Journal of Personality Assessment, 93*(4), 380–389.

Simon, R., Goddard, R., & Patton, W. (2002). Hand-scoring error rates in psychological testing. *Assessment, 9,* 292–300.

Skinner, H. A., & Jackson, D. N. (1978). A model of psychopathology based on an integration of MMPI actuarial systems. *Journal of Consulting and Clinical Psychology, 46,* 231–238.

Slater, P. E., & Scarr, H. A. (1964). Personality in old age. *Genetic Psychology Monographs, 70*(2), 229–269.

Sleep, C. E., Crowe, M. L., Carter, N. T., Lynam, D. R., & Miller, J. D. (2021). Uncovering the structure of antagonism. *Personality Disorders: Theory, Research, and Treatment, 12*(4), 300–311.

Slick, D. J., Sherman, E. M. S., & Iverson, G. L. (1999). Diagnostic criteria for malingered neurocognitive dysfunction: Proposed standards for clinical practice and research. *The Clinical Neuropsychologist, 13*, 545–561.

Smart, C. M., Nelson, N. W., Sweet, J. J., Bryant, F. B., Berry, D. T. R., Granacher, R. P. et al. (2008). Use of MMPI-2 to identify cognitive effort: A hierarchically optimal classification tree analysis. *Journal of the International Neuropsychological Society, 14*, 842–852.

Smith, E. E. (1959). Defensiveness, insight, and the K scale. *Journal of Consulting Psychology, 23*, 275–277.

Smith, S. R., & Krishnamurthy, R. (2018). *Diversity-sensitive personality assessment*. Routledge.

Snibe, J. R., Peterson, P. J., & Sosner, B. (1980). Study of psychological characteristics of a workers compensation sample using the MMPI and Millon Clinical Multiaxial Inventory. *Psychological Reports, 47*, 959–966.

Spanier, G. B. (1976). Measuring dyadic adjustment: New scales for assessing the quality of marriage and similar dyads. *Journal of Marriage and the Family, 38*(1), 15–28. https://doi.org/10.2307/350547

Spielberger, C. D., Jacobs, G., Russell, S., & Crane, R. S. (1983). Assessment of anger: The State–Trait Anger Scale. *Advances in Personality Assessment, 2*, 161–189.

Spitzer, R. L., Endicott, J., & Robins, E. (1978). Research diagnostic criteria: Rationale and reliability. *Archives of General Psychiatry, 35*, 773–782.

Stanley, I. H., Yancey, J. R., Patrick, C. J., & Joiner, T. E. (2018). A distinct configuration of MMPI-2-RF scales RCd and RC9/ACT is associated with suicide attempt risk among suicide ideators in a psychiatric outpatient sample. *Psychological Assessment, 30*(9), 1249–1254. https://doi.org/10.1037/pas0000588

Steenhaut, P., Rossi, G., Demeyer, I., & De Raedt, R. (2019). How is personality related to wellbeing in older and younger adults? The role of psychological flexibility. *International Psychogeriatrics, 31*(9), 1355–1365. https://doi.org/10.1017/s1041610218001904

Stein, L. A. R., Graham, J. R., Ben-Porath, Y. S., & McNulty, J. L. (1999). Using the MMPI-2 to detect substance abuse in an outpatient mental health setting. *Psychological Assessment, 11*, 94–100.

Stenner, A. J., Horabin, I., Smith, D. R., & Smith, M. (1988, June). Most comprehension tests do measure reading comprehension: A response to McLean and Goldstein. *Phi Delta Kappan*, pp. 765–769.

Stern, S. L., Dhanda, R., & Hazuda, H. P. (2009). Helplessness predicts the development of hypertension in older Mexican and European Americans. *Journal of Psychosomatic Research, 67*, 333–337.

Stevens, M. J., Kwan, K.-l., & Graybill, D. F. (1993). Comparison of MMPI-2 scores of foreign Chinese and Caucasian-American students. *Journal of Clinical Psychology, 49*(1), 23–27. https://doi.org/10.1002/1097-4679(199301)49:1<23::AID-JCLP2270490104>3.0.CO;2-O

Stice, E., Telch, C. F., & Rizvi, S. L. (2000). Development and validation of the Eating Disorder Diagnostic Scale: a brief self-report measure of anorexia, bulimia, and binge-eating disorder. *Psychological Assessment, 12*(2), 123–131.

Stones, M. J., Clyburn, L. D., Gibson, M. C., & Woodbury, M. G. (2006). Predicting diagnosed depression and anti-depressant treatment in institutionalized older adults by symptom profiles: A closer look at anhedonia and dysphoria. *Canadian Journal on Aging, 25,* 153–159.

Strada, E. A. (2009). Grief, demoralization, and depression: Diagnostic challenges and treatment modalities. *Primary Psychiatry, 16,* 49–55.

Strassberg, D. S., Clutton, S., & Korboot, P. (1991). A descriptive and validity study of the Minnesota Multiphasic Personality Inventory-2 (MMPI-2) in an elderly Australian sample. *Journal of Psychopathology and Behavioral Assessment, 13*(4), 301–311. https://doi.org/10.1007/BF00960443

Strong, E. K. (1938). *Manual for vocational interest blank for men.* University Press.

Strupp, H. H. (1973). Specific versus nonspecific factors in psychotherapy and the problem of control. In H. H. Strupp (Ed.), *Psychotherapy: Clinical, research, and theoretical issues* (pp. 103–212). Jason Aronson.

Stulemeijer, M., Vos, P., Bleijenberg, G., & van der Werf, S. (2007). Cognitive complaints after mild traumatic brain injury: Things are not always what they seem. *Journal of Psychosomatic Research, 63,* 637–645.

Sue, S., Keefe, K., Enomoto, K., Durvasula, R. S., & Chao, R. (1996). Asian American and White college students' performance on the MMPI-2. In J. N. Butcher (Ed.), *International adaptations of the MMPI-2: Research and clinical applications* (pp. 206–218). University of Minnesota Press.

Sue, S., & Sue, D. W. (1974). MMPI comparisons between Asian-American and non-Asian students utilizing a student health psychiatric clinic. *Journal of Counseling Psychology, 21*(5), 423–427. https://doi.org/10.1037/h0037074

Sundberg, N. D. (1961). The practice of psychological testing in clinical services in the United States. *American Psychologist, 16,* 79–83.

Svanum, S., McGrew, J., & Ehrmann, L. (1994). Validity of the substance abuse scales of the MMPI-2 in a college student sample. *Journal of Personality Assessment, 62,* 427–439.

Swanson, S. C., Templer, D. I., Thomas-Dobson, S., Cannon, W. G., Streiner, D. L., Reynolds, R. M. et al. (1995). Development of a three-scale MMPI: The MMPI-TRI. *Journal of Clinical Psychology, 51,* 361–374.

Swenson, W. M., Pearson, J. D., & Osborne, D. (1973). *An MMPI source book: Basic item, scale, and pattern data on 50,000 medical patients.* University of Minnesota Press.

Taft, R. (1957). A cross-cultural comparison of the MMPI. *Journal of Consulting Psychology, 21*(2), 161–164.

Tandon, R., & Jibson, M. D. (2003). Suicidal behavior in Schizophrenia: Diagnosis, neurobiology, and treatment implications. *Current Opinion in Psychiatry, 16,* 193–197.

Tarescavage, A. M., Azizian, A. Broderick, C., & English, P. (2019). Associations between MMPI-2-RF scale scores and institutional violence among patients detained under sexually violent predator laws. *Psychological Assessment, 31*(5), 707–713. https://doi.org/10.1037/pas0000682

Tarescavage, A. M., Brewster, J., Corey, D. M., & Ben-Porath, Y. S. (2015). Use of pre-hire MMPI-2-RF police candidate scores to predict supervisor ratings of post-hire performance. *Assessment, 22*(4), 411–428.

Tarescavage, A. M., Cappo, B. M., & Ben-Porath, Y. S. (2018). Assessment of sex offenders with the Minnesota Multiphasic Personality Inventory-2-Restructured Form. *Sexual Abuse, 30*(4), 413–437. https://doi.org/10.1177/1079063216667921

Tarescavage, A. M., Corey, D. M., & Ben-Porath, Y. S. (2015). Minnesota Multiphasic Personality Inventory-2-Restructured Form (MMPI-2-RF) predictors of police officer problem behavior. *Assessment, 22*(1), 116–132.

Tarescavage, A. M., Corey, D. M., & Ben-Porath, Y. S. (2016). A prorating method for estimating MMPI-2-RF scores from MMPI responses: Examination of score fidelity and illustration of empirical utility in the PERSEREC Police Integrity Study sample. *Assessment, 23*(2), 173–190. https://doi.org/10.1177/1073191115575070

Tarescavage, A. M., Corey, D. M., Gupton, H. M., & Ben-Porath, Y. S. (2015). Criterion validity and clinical utility of the Minnesota Multiphasic Personality Inventory-2-Restructured Form (MMPI-2-RF) in assessments of police officer candidates. *Journal of Personality Assessment, 97*(4), 382–394. https://doi.org/10.1080/00223891.2014.995800

Tarescavage, A. M., Fischler, G. L., Cappo, B. M., Hill, D. O., Corey, D. M., & Ben-Porath, Y. S. (2015). Minnesota Multiphasic Personality Inventory-2-Restructured Form (MMPI-2-RF) predictors of police officer problem behavior and collateral self-report test scores. *Psychological Assessment, 27*(1), 125–137. https://doi.org/10.1037/pas0000041

Tarescavage, A. M., Forner, E. H., & Ben-Porath, Y. S. (2021). Construct validity of *DSM-5* Level 2 Assessments (PROMIS Depression, Anxiety, and Anger): Evidence from the MMPI-2-RF. *Assessment, 28*(3), 788–795.

Tarescavage, A. M., Glassmire, D. M., & Burchett, D. (2016). Introduction of a conceptual model for integrating the MMPI-2-RF into HCR-20^{V3} violence risk assessments and associations between the MMPI-2-RF and institutional violence. *Law and Human Behavior, 40*(6), 626–637. https://doi.org/10.1037/lhb0000207

Tarescavage, A. M., Glassmire, D. M., & Burchett, D. (2018). Minnesota Multiphasic Personality Inventory-2-Restructured Form markers of future suicidal behavior in a forensic psychiatric hospital. *Psychological Assessment, 30*(2), 170–178. https://doi.org/10.1037/pas0000463

Tarescavage, A. M., Luna-Jones, L., & Ben-Porath, Y. S. (2014). Minnesota Multiphasic Personality Inventory-2-Restructured Form (MMPI-2-RF) predictors of violating probation after felonious crimes. *Psychological Assessment, 26*(4), 1375–1380.

Tarescavage, A. M., & Menton, W. H. (2020). Construct validity of the Personality Inventory for ICD-11 (PiCD): Evidence from the MMPI-2-RF and CAT-PD-SF. *Psychological Assessment, 32*(9), 889–895. https://doi.org/10.1037/pas0000914

Tarescavage, A. M., Scheman, J., & Ben-Porath, Y. S. (2015). Reliability and validity of the Minnesota Multiphasic Personality Inventory-2-Restructured Form (MMPI-2-RF) in evaluations of chronic low back pain patients. *Psychological Assessment, 27*(2), 433–446. https://doi.org/10.1037/pas0000056

Tarescavage, A. M., Scheman, J., & Ben-Porath, Y. S. (2018). Prospective comparison of the Minnesota Multiphasic Personality Inventory-2 (MMPI-2) and MMPI-2-Restructured Form (MMPI-2-RF) in predicting treatment outcomes among patients with chronic low back pain. *Journal of Clinical Psychology in Medical Settings, 25,* 66–79. https://doi.org/10.1007/s10880-017-9535-6

Tarescavage, A. M., Wygant, D. B., Boutacoff, L. I., & Ben-Porath, Y. S. (2013). Reliability, validity, and utility of the Minnesota Multiphasic Personality Inventory-2-Restructured Form (MMPI-2-RF) in assessments of bariatric surgery candidates. *Psychological Assessment, 25*(4), 1179–1194. https://doi.org/10.1037/a0033694

Taylor, C. T., Laposa, J. M., & Alden, L. E. (2004). Is Avoidant Personality Disorder more than just social avoidance? *Journal of Personality Disorders, 18,* 573–597.

Tellegen, A. (1982). *Brief manual of the Multidimensional Personality Questionnaire.* Unpublished manuscript.

Tellegen, A. (1985). Structures of mood and personality and their relevance to assessing anxiety, with an emphasis on self-report. In A. H. Tuna & J. D. Maser (Eds.), *Anxiety and the anxiety disorders* (pp. 681–706). Lawrence Erlbaum Associates.

Tellegen, A. (1988). The analysis of consistency in personality assessment. *Journal of Personality, 56,* 621–663.

Tellegen, A. (1993). Folk concepts and psychological concepts of personality and personality disorder. *Psychological Inquiry, 4,* 122–130. https://doi.org/10.1207/s15327965pli0402_12

Tellegen, A. (1995/2003). *Multidimensional Personality Questionnaire–276 (MPQ-276) test booklet.* University of Minnesota Press.

Tellegen, A., & Ben-Porath, Y. S. (1992). The new uniform T-scores for the MMPI-2: Rationale, derivation, and appraisal. *Psychological Assessment, 4,* 145–155.

Tellegen, A., & Ben-Porath, Y. S. (1993). Code-type comparability of the MMPI and MMPI-2: Analysis of recent findings and criticisms. *Journal of Personality Assessment, 61,* 489–500.

Tellegen, A., & Ben-Porath, Y. S. (2005, April). *Restructured MMPI-2 Scales: A progress report on further developments.* Paper presented at the 40th annual symposium on Recent Research with the MMPI-2/MMPI-A, Fort Lauderdale, FL.

Tellegen, A., & Ben-Porath, Y. S. (2008/2011). *MMPI-2-RF (Minnesota Multiphasic Personality Inventory–2 Restructured Form) technical manual.* University of Minnesota Press.

Tellegen, A., Ben-Porath, Y. S., McNulty, J. L., Arbisi, P. A., Graham, J. R., & Kaemmer, B. (2003). *The MMPI-2 Restructured Clinical Scales: Development, validation, and interpretation.* University of Minnesota Press.

Tellegen, A., Ben-Porath, Y. S., Sellbom, M., Arbisi, P. A., McNulty, J. L., & Graham, J. R. (2006). Further evidence on the validity of the MMPI-2 Restructured Clinical (RC) Scales: Addressing questions raised by Rogers, Sewell, Harrison, and Jordan and Nichols. *Journal of Personality Assessment, 87,* 148–171.

Tellegen, A., Butcher, J. N., & Hoeglund, T. (1993). *Are unisex norms for the MMPI-2 needed? Would they work?* Paper presented at the 28th annual symposium on Recent Developments in the Use of the MMPI/MMPI-2/MMPI-A, St. Petersburg, FL.

Tellegen, A., Sellbom, M., Kamp, J., & Handel, R. W. (2023). *Mulitdimensional Personality Questionnaire (MPQ): Manual for administration, scoring, and interpretation.* University of Minnesota Press.

Tellegen, A., & Waller, N. G. (2008). Exploring personality through test construction: Development of the Multidimensional Personality Questionnaire. In S. R. Briggs & J. M. Cheek (Eds.), *Personality measures: Development and evaluation* (pp. 261–292). JAI Press.

Tellegen, A., Watson, D., & Clark, L. A. (1999a). Further support for a hierarchical model of affect: Reply to Green and Salovey. *Psychological Science, 10,* 307–309.

Tellegen, A., Watson, D., & Clark, L. A. (1999b). On the dimensional and hierarchical structure of affect. *Psychological Science, 10*, 297–303.

Thomas, M. L., & Locke, D. E. C. (2010). Psychometric properties of the MMPI-2-RF Somatic Complaints (RC1) Scale. *Psychological Assessment, 22*, 492–503.

Thomas, M. L., & Youngjohn, J. R. (2010). Let's not get hysterical: Comparing the MMPI-2 Validity, Clinical, and RC Scales in TBI litigants tested for effort. *Clinical Neuropsychologist, 23*, 1067–1084.

Thornton, V. A., Dodd, C. G., & Weed, N. C. (2020). Assessment of prescription stimulant misuse among college students using the MMPI-2-RF. *Addictive Behaviors, 110*. https://doi.org/10.1016/j.addbeh.2020.106511

Timbrook, R. E., & Graham, J. R. (1994). Ethnic differences on the MMPI-2? *Psychological Assessment, 6*(3), 212–217. https://doi.org/10.1037/1040-3590.6.3.212

Timbrook, R. E., Graham, J. R., Keiller, S. W., & Watts, D. (1993). Comparison of the Wiener–Harmon Subtle–Obvious scales and the standard Validity Scales in detecting valid and invalid MMPI-2 profiles. *Psychological Assessment, 5*, 53–61.

Tombaugh, T. N. (1997). The Test of Memory Malingering (TOMM): Normative data from cognitively intact and cognitively impaired individuals. *Psychological Assessment, 9*, 260–268.

Trimble, M. (2004). *Somatoform Disorders: A medicolegal guide*. Cambridge University Press.

Trull, T. J., Useda, J. D., Costa, P. T., & McCrae, R. R. (1995). Comparison of the MMPI-2 Personality Psychopathology Five (PSY-5), the NEO-PI, and NEO-PI-R. *Psychological Assessment, 7*, 508–516.

Tsai, D. C., & Pike, P. L. (2000). Effects of acculturation on the MMPI-2 scores of Asian American students. *Journal of Personality Assessment, 74*(2), 216–230. https://doi.org/10.1207/S15327752JPA7402_4

Tsushima, W. T., & Onorato, V. A. (1982). Comparison of MMPI scores of White and Japanese-American medical patients. *Journal of Consulting and Clinical Psychology, 50*(1), 150–151. https://doi.org/10.1037/0022-006X.50.1.150

Tsushima, W. T., & Wedding, D. (1979). MMPI results of male candidates for transsexual surgery. *Journal of Personality Assessment, 43*(4), 385–387. https://doi.org/10.1207/s15327752jpa4304_8

Tuohy, A., & McVey, C. (2008). Subscales measuring symptoms of non-specific depression, anhedonia, and anxiety in the Edinburgh Postnatal Depression Scale. *British Journal of Clinical Psychology, 47*, 153–169.

Tweed, D. L., Shern, D. L., & Ciarlo, J. A. (1988). Disability, dependency, and demoralization. *Rehabilitation Psychology, 33*, 143–154.

Tylicki, J. L., Gervais, R. O., & Ben-Porath, Y. S. (2020). Examination of the MMPI-3 overreporting scales in a forensic disability sample. *The Clinical Neuropsychologist, 36*, 1878–1901.

Tylicki, J. L., Martin-Fernandez, K. W., & Ben-Porath, Y. S. (2019). Predicting therapist ratings of treatment progress and outcomes with the MMPI-2-RF. *Journal of Clinical Psychology, 75*(9), 1673–1683. https://doi.org/10.1002/jclp.22795

Tylicki, J. L., Phillips, T. R., Ben-Porath, Y. S., & Sellbom, M. (2020). Construct validity of Minnesota Multiphasic Personality Inventory-2-Restructured Form scale scores in correctional settings. *Personality and Mental Health, 14*(4), 319–335.

Uecker, A. E., Boutilier, L. R., & Richardson, E. H. (1980). "Indianism" and MMPI scores of men Alcoholics. *Journal of Studies in Alcohol and Drugs, 41,* 357–362.

U.S. Census Bureau. (2017a). *Table 2. Projected population by single year of age, sex, race, and Hispanic origin for the United States: 2016 to 2060* [Data file]. https://www2.census.gov/programs-surveys/popproj/datasets/2017/2017-popproj/np2017_d1.csv

Valtonen, H. M., Suominen, K., Haukka, J., Mantere, O., Arvilommi, P., Leppämäki, S. et al. (2009). Hopelessness across phases of Bipolar I or II Disorder: A prospective study. *Journal of Affective Disorders, 115,* 11–17.

Valtonen, H. M., Suominen, K., Haukka, J., Mantere, O., Leppämäki, S., Arvilommi, P. et al. (2008). Differences in incidence of suicide attempts during phases of Bipolar I and II Disorders. *Bipolar Disorders, 10,* 588–596.

Van der Heijden, P. T., Egger, J. I. M., & Derksen, J. J. L. (2008). Psychometric evaluation of the MMPI-2 Restructured Clinical Scales in two Dutch samples. *Journal of Personality Assessment, 90*(5), 456–464. https://doi.org/10.1080/00223890802248745

Van der Heijden, P. T., Egger, J. I., Rossi, G. M., & Derksen, J. J. (2012). Integrating psychopathology and personality disorders conceptualized by the MMPI–2–RF and the MCMI–III: A structural validity study. *Journal of Personality Assessment, 94*(4), 345–357.

Van der Heijden, P. T., Egger, J. I., Rossi, G. M., Grundel, G., & Derksen, J. J. (2013a). The MMPI-2-Restructured Form and the standard MMPI-2 clinical scales in relation to *DSM-IV*. *European Journal of Psychological Assessment, 29,* 182–188. https://doi.org/10.1027/1015-5759/a000140

Van der Heijden, P. T., Egger, J. I. M., Rossi, G. M. P., van der Veld, W. M., & Derksen, J. J. L. (2013b). Personality and psychopathology: Mapping the MMPI-2-RF on Cloninger's psychobiological model of personality. *Assessment, 20*(5), 576–584. https://doi.org/10.1177/1073191113490791

Van der Heijden, P. T., Rossi, G. M. P., van der Veld, W. M., Derksen, J. J. L., & Egger, J. I. M. (2013c). Personality and psychopathology: Higher order relations between the Five Factor Model of personality and the MMPI-2 Restructured Form. *Journal of Research in Personality, 47*(5), 572–579. https://doi.org/10.1016/j.jrp.2013.05.001

Vaňousová, N., Brown, T. A., & Sellbom, M. (2021). Criterion and incremental validity of the MMPI-3 Eating Concerns Scale in a university sample. *Journal of Clinical Psychology in Medical Settings.* Advance online publication. https://doi.org/10.1007/s10880-021-09772-6

Velissaris, S. L., Wilson, S. J., Newton, M. R., Berkovic, S. F., & Saling, M. M. (2009). Cognitive complaints after a first seizure in adulthood: Influence of psychological adjustment. *Epilepsia, 50,* 1012–1021.

Vendrig, A. A. (1999). Prognostic factors and treatment-related changes associated with return to work in the multimodal treatment of chronic back pain. *Journal of Behavioral Medicine, 22,* 217–232.

Vendrig, A. A., Derksen, J. J. L., & de Mey, H. R. (1999). Utility of selected MMPI-2 scales in the outcome prediction for patients with chronic back pain. *Psychological Assessment, 11,* 381–385.

Vendrig, A. A., Derksen, J. J. L., & de Mey, H. R. (2000). MMPI-2 Personality Psychopathology Five (PSY-5) and prediction of treatment outcome for patients with chronic back pain. *Journal of Personality Assessment, 74,* 423–438.

Viken, R. J., & Rose, R. J. (2007). Genetic variation and covariation in the original and Restructured Clinical Scales of the MMPI. *Journal of Abnormal Psychology, 116,* 842–847.

Vize, C. E., Collison, K. L., & Lynam, D. R. (2020). The importance of antagonism: Explaining similarities and differences in psychopathy and narcissism's relations with aggression and externalizing outcomes. *Journal of Personality Disorders, 34*(6), 842–854.

Vize, C. E., Miller, J. D., & Lynam, D. R. (2019). Antagonism in the dark triad. In D. R. Lynam & J. D. Miller (Eds.), *The Handbook of Antagonism: Conceptualizations, Assessment, Consequences, and Treatment of the Low End of Agreeableness* (pp. 253–267). Academic Press.

Votruba, K., Marshall, D., Finks, J, & Giordani, B. (2014). Neuropsychological factors in bariatric surgery: A review. *Current Psychiatry Reports,* 16:448, 1–7.

Waddell, G., McCulloch, J. A., Kummel, E. D., & Venner, R. M. (1980). Nonorganic physical signs in low-back pain. *Spine, 5*(2), 117–125.

Waldman, I. D., & Slutske, S. (2000). Antisocial behavior and alcoholism: A behavioral genetic perspective on comorbidity. *Clinical Psychology Review, 20,* 255–287.

Walker, E. F., Bollini, A., Hochman, K., Kestler, L., & Mittal, V. A. (2007). Schizophrenia. In J. E. Maddox & B. A. Winstead (Eds.), *Psychopathology: Foundations for a contemporary understanding* (2nd ed.). Lawrence Erlbaum Associates.

Walters, G. D., White, T. W., & Greene, R. L. (1988). Use of the MMPI to identify malingering and exaggeration of psychiatric symptomatology in male prison inmates. *Journal of Consulting and Clinical Psychology, 56,* 111–117.

Wang, J., Han, K., Ketterer, H. L., Weed, N. C., Ben-Porath, Y. S., Kim, J., & Moon, K. (2021). Evaluating the measurement invariance of MMPI-2-RF Restructured Clinical Scale 4 (Antisocial Behavior) between American and Korean clinical samples: Exploring cultural and translation issues affecting item responding. *Journal of Personality Assessment, 103*(4), 465–475. https://doi.org/10.1080/00223891.2020.1769111.

Walvoort, S. J. W., van der Heijden, P. T., Wester, A. J., Kessels, R. P. C., & Egger, J. I. M. (2016). Self-awareness of cognitive dysfunction: Self-reported complaints and cognitive performance in patients with alcohol-induced mild or major neurocognitive disorder. *Psychiatry Research, 245,* 291–296. https://doi.org/10.1016/j.psychres.2016.08.007

Wasyliw, O. E., Grossman, L. S., Haywood, T. W., & Cavanaugh, J. L. (1988). The detection of malingering in criminal forensic groups: MMPI Validity Scales. *Journal of Personality Assessment, 52,* 321–333.

Watanabe, N., Hasegawa, K., & Yoshinaga, Y. (1995). Suicide in later life in Japan: Urban and rural differences. *International Psychogeriatrics, 7,* 253–261.

Watson, D. (2005). Rethinking the mood and anxiety disorders: A quantitative hierarchical model for *DSM-V. Journal of Abnormal Psychology, 114,* 522–536.

Watson, D., & Clark, L. A. (1984). Negative affectivity: The disposition to experience aversive emotional states. *Psychological Bulletin, 96,* 465–490.

Watson, D., Levin-Aspenson, H. F., Waszczuk, M. A., Conway, C. C., Dalgleish, T., Dretsch, M. N., . . . & Zinbarg, R. E. (2022). Validity and utility of Hierarchical Taxonomy of Psychopathology (HiTOP): III. Emotional dysfunction superspectrum. *World Psychiatry, 21*(1), 26–54.

Watson D., O'Hara M. W., Naragon-Gainey K., Koffel E., Chmielewski M., Kotov R., Stasik S. M., & Ruggero C. J. (2012). Development and validation of new anxiety and bipolar symptom scales for an expanded version of the IDAS (the IDAS-II). *Assessment 19*, 399–420.

Watson, D., & Tellegen, A. (1985). Toward a consensual structure of mood. *Psychological Bulletin, 98*, 219–235.

Watson, D., Wiese, D., Vaidya, J., & Tellegen, A. (1999). The two general activation systems of affect: Structural findings, evolutionary considerations, and psychobiological evidence. *Journal of Personality and Social Psychology, 76*, 820–838.

Watson, D., & Wu, K. D. (2005). Development and validation of the Schedule of Compulsions, Obsessions, and Pathological Impulses (SCOPI). *Assessment, 12*(1), 50–65.

Watson, L. C., Quilty, L. C., & Bagby, R. M. (2011). Differentiating bipolar disorder from major depressive disorder using the MMPI-2-RF: A receiver operating characteristics (ROC) analysis. *Journal of Psychopathology and Behavioral Assessment, 33*(3), 368–374. https://doi.org/10.1007/s10862-010-9212-7

Watters, C. A., & Bagby, R. M. (2018). A meta-analysis of the five-factor internal structure of the Personality Inventory for *DSM–5*. *Psychological Assessment, 30*(9), 1255–1260.

Weathers, F. W., Bovin, M. J., Lee, D. J., Sloan, D. M., Schnurr, P. P., Kaloupek, D. G., Keane, T. M., & Marx, B. P. (2018). The Clinician-Administered PTSD Scale for DSM–5 (CAPS-5): Development and initial psychometric evaluation in military veterans. *Psychological Assessment, 30*(3), 383–395.

Webb, J. T., Levitt, E. E., & Rojdev, R. (1993). *After three years: A comparison of the clinical use of the MMPI and MMPI-2*. Paper presented at the 53rd annual meeting of the Society for Personality Assessment, San Francisco, CA.

Wechsler, D. (2008). *Wechsler Adult Intelligence Scale–fourth edition*. Pearson.

Weed, N. C., Ben-Porath, Y. S., & Butcher, J. N. (1990). Failure of the MMPI Wiener and Harmon subtle scales as measures of personality and as validity indicators. *Psychological Assessment: A Journal of Consulting and Clinical Psychology, 2*, 281–285.

Weed, N. C., Butcher, J. N., McKenna, T., & Ben-Porath, Y. S. (1992). New measures for assessing alcohol and drug abuse with the MMPI-2: The APS and AAS. *Journal of Personality Assessment, 58*, 389–404.

Wells, F. L. (1914). The systematic observation of the personality in its relation to the hygiene of mind. *Psychological Review, 21*, 295–333.

Welsh, G. S. (1948). An extension of Hathaway's MMPI profile coding system. *Journal of Consulting Psychology, 12*, 343–344.

Welsh, G. S. (1956). Factor dimensions A and R. In G. S. Welsh & W. G. Dahlstrom (Eds.), *Basic readings on the MMPI in psychology and medicine* (pp. 264–281). University of Minnesota Press.

Welsh, G. S., & Dahlstrom, W. G. (Eds.). (1956). *Basic readings on the MMPI in psychology and medicine*. University of Minnesota Press.

Whitman, M. R., & Ben-Porath, Y. S. (2021). Distinctiveness of the MMPI-3 Self-Importance and Self-Doubt Scales. *Journal of Personality Assessment, 103*(5), 613–620. https://doi.org/10.1080/00223891.2021.1883628

Whitman, M. R., Burchett, D. L., Tarescavage, A. M., Ben-Porath, Y. S., & Sellbom, M. (2020). Predictive Validity of Minnesota Multiphasic Personality Inventory-2-Restructured Form scale scores in an intimate partner violence intervention program. *Criminal Justice and Behavior, 47*(8), 978–995. https://doi.org/10.1177/0093854820918003

Whitman, M. R., Tarescavage, A. M., Glassmire, D. M., Burchett, D., & Sellbom, M. (2019). Examination of differential validity of MMPI-2-RF scores by gender and ethnicity in predicting future suicidal and violent behaviors on a forensic sample. *Psychological Assessment, 31*(3), 404–409. https://doi.org/10.1037/pas0000677

Whitman, M. R., Tylicki, J. L., & Ben-Porath, Y. S. (2021a). Utility of the MMPI-3 Validity Scales for detecting overreporting and underreporting and their effects on substance scale validity: A simulation study. *Psychological Assessment, 33*(5), 411–426. https://doi.org/10.1037/pas0000988

Whitman, M. R., Tylicki, J. L., Mascioli, R., Pickle, J., & Ben-Porath, Y. S. (2021b). Psychometric properties of the Minnesota Multiphasic Personality Inventory-3 (MMPI-3) in a clinical neuropsychology setting. *Psychological Assessment, 33*(2), 142–155. https://doi.org/10.1037/pas0000969

Whitworth, R. H., & McBlaine, D. D. (1993). Comparison of the MMPI and MMPI-2 administered to Anglo- and Hispanic-American university students. *Journal of Personality Assessment, 61*(1), 19–27. https://doi.org/10.1207/s15327752jpa6101_2

Whitworth, R. H., & Unterbrink, C. (1994). Comparison of MMPI-2 clinical and content scales administered to Hispanic and Anglo-Americans. *Hispanic Journal of Behavioral Sciences, 16*(3), 255–264. https://doi.org/10.1177/07399863940163004

Widiger, T. A., & Costa, P. T. (2002). Five Factor Model personality disorder research. In P. T. Costa & T. A. Widiger (Eds.), *Personality disorders and the Five Factor Model of personality* (2nd ed., pp. 59–87). American Psychological Association.

Widiger, T. A. (2020). Bruno Klopfer Award address: Five-factor Model personality disorder scales. *Journal of Personality Assessment, 102*(1), 1–9.

Wiener, D. N. (1948). Subtle and obvious keys for the MMPI. *Journal of Consulting Psychology, 12*, 164–170.

Wiener, D. N. (1952). Personality characteristics of selected disability groups. *Genetic Psychology Monographs, 45*, 175–255.

Wiener, D. N., & Harmon, L. R. (1946). Subtle and obvious keys for the MMPI: Their development. *VA Advisement Bulletin, 16*.

Wiggins, J. S. (1959). Interrelationships among MMPI measures of dissimulation under standard and social desirability instructions. *Journal of Consulting Psychology, 23*, 419–427.

Wiggins, J. S. (1966). Substantive dimensions of self-report in the MMPI item pool. *Psychological Monographs: General and Applied, 80*(22), 1–42. https://doi.org/10.1037/h0093901.

Wiggins, J. S. (1968). Personality structure. *Annual Review of Psychology, 19*, 293–350.

Wiggins, J. S. (1990). Foreword. In J. N. Butcher, J. R. Graham, C. L. Williams, & Y. S. Ben-Porath (Eds.), *Development and use of the MMPI-2 Content Scales* (pp. vii–ix). University of Minnesota Press.

Wiggins, C. W., Wygant, D. B., Hoelzle, J. B., & Gervais, R. O. (2012). The more you say the less it means: Over-reporting and attenuated criterion validity in a forensic disability sample. *Psychological Injury and Law, 5*, 162–173. https://doi.org/10.1007/s12207-012-9137-4

Wilde, E. A., Whiteneck, G. G., Bogner, J., Bushnik, T., Cifu, D. X., Dikmen, S., French, L., Giacino, J. T., Hart, T., Malec, J. F., Millis, S. R., Novack, T. A., Sherer, M., Tulsky, D. S., Vanderploeg, R. D., & von Steinbuechel, N. (2010). Recommendations for the use of common outcome measures in traumatic brain injury research. *Archives of*

Physical Medicine and Rehabilitation, 91(11), 1650–1660.e17. https://doi.org/10.1016/j.apmr.2010.06.033.

Williams, C. B., Galanter, M., Dermatis, H., & Schwartz, V. (2008). The importance of hopelessness among university students seeking psychiatric counseling. *Psychiatric Quarterly, 79,* 311–319.

Williams, H. L. (1952). The development of a caudality scale for the MMPI. *Journal of Clinical Psychology, 8,* 293–297.

Williams, L. M., Das, P., Harris, A. W., Liddell, B. B., Brammer, M. J., Olivieri, G., . . . & Gordon, E. (2004). Dysregulation of arousal and amygdala-prefrontal systems in paranoid schizophrenia. *American Journal of Psychiatry, 161*(3), 480–489.

Wingate, L., Joiner, T., Walker, R., Rudd, M. D., & Jobes, D. (2004). Empirically informed approaches to topics in suicide risk assessment. *Behavioral Sciences and the Law, 22,* 1–15.

Wittenborn, J. R. (1951). Symptom patterns in a group of mental hospital patients. *Journal of Consulting Psychology, 15,* 290–302.

Wolf, E. J., Miller, M. W., Orazem, R. J., Weierich, M. R., Castillo, D. T., Milford, J., Kaloupek, D.G., & Keane T. M. (2008). The MMPI-2 Restructured Clinical Scales in the assessment of posttraumatic stress disorder and comorbid disorders. *Psychological Assessment, 20*(4), 327–340.

Woodworth, R. S. (1920). *Personal data sheet.* Stoelting.

World Health Organization. (2022). *ICD-11 Clinical Descriptions and Diagnostic Guidelines for Mental and Behavioural Disorders.*

Wright, A. G. C., Krueger, R. F., Hobbs, M. J., Markon, K. E., Eaton, N. R., & Slade, T. (2013). The structure of psychopathology: Toward an expanded quantitative empirical model. *Journal of Abnormal Psychology, 122*(1), 281–294.

Wright, A. G., & Simms, L. J. (2015). A metastructural model of mental disorders and pathological personality traits. *Psychological Medicine, 45*(11), 2309–2319.

Wright, A. G. C., Thomas, K. M., Hopwood, C. J., Markon, K. E., Pincus, A. L., & Krueger, R. F. (2012). The hierarchical structure of *DSM-5* pathological personality traits. *Journal of Abnormal Psychology, 121*(4), 951–957.

Wu, C. (2009). Factor analysis of the general self-efficacy scale and its relationship with individualism/collectivism among twenty-five countries: Application of multilevel confirmatory factor analysis. *Personality and Individual Differences, 46,* 699–703.

Wygant, D. B., Anderson, J. L., Sellbom, M., Rapier, J. L., Algeier, L. M., & Granacher, R. P. (2011). Association of MMPI-2 Restructured Form (MMPI-2-RF) Validity Scales with structured malingering criteria. *Psychological Injury and Law, 4,* 13–23.

Wygant, D. B., Arbisi, P. A., Bianchini, B. J., Umlauf, R. L. (2017). Waddell non-organic signs: New evidence suggests somatic amplification among outpatient chronic pain patients. *The Spine Journal, 17*(4), 505–510. https://doi.org/10.1016/j.spinee.2016.10.018

Wygant, D. B., Ben-Porath, Y. S., & Arbisi, P. A. (2004, May). *Development and initial validation of a scale to detect infrequent somatic complaints.* Poster presented at the 39th annual symposium on Recent Developments of the MMPI-2/MMPI-A, Minneapolis, MN.

Wygant, D. B., Boutacoff, L. I., Arbisi, P. A., Ben-Porath, Y. S., Kelly, P. H., & Rupp, W. M. (2007). Examination of the MMPI-2 Restructured Clinical (RC) Scales in a sample of bariatric surgery candidates. *Journal of Clinical Psychology in Medical Settings, 14,* 197–205.

Wygant, D. B., & Sellbom, M. (2012). Viewing psychopathy from the perspective of the Personality Psychopathology Five model: Implications for *DSM-5*. *Journal of Personality Disorders, 26*(5), 717–726.

Wygant, D. B., Sellbom, M., Ben-Porath, Y. S., Stafford, K. P., Freeman, D. B., & Heilbronner, R. I. (2007). The relation between symptom validity testing and MMPI-2 scores as a function of forensic evaluation context. *Archives of Clinical Neuropsychology, 22*, 488–499.

Wygant, D. B., Sellbom, M., Graham, J. R., & Schenk, P. W. (2006). Incremental validity of the MMPI-2 PSY-5 scales in assessing self-reported personality disorder criteria. *Assessment, 13*, 178–186.

Ying, Y., & Akutsu, D. (1997). Psychological adjustment of Southeast Asian refugees: The contribution of sense of coherence. *Journal of Community Psychology, 25*, 125–139.

Young, J. C., & Gross, A. M. (2011). Detection of response bias and noncredible performance in adult Attention-Deficit/Hyperactivity Disorder. *Archives of Clinical Neuropsychology, 26*(3), 165–175. https://doi.org/10.1093/arclin/acr013

Zahn, N., Sellbom, M., Pymont, C., & Schenk, P. W. (2017). Associations between MMPI-2-RF scale scores and self-reported personality disorder criteria in a private practice sample. *Journal of Psychopathology and Behavioral Assessment, 39*(4), 723–741. https://doi.org/10.1007/s10862-017-9616-8

Index

Aberrant Experiences (RC8) scale, 65, 66, 115, 164, 176, 184, 231, 232, 250, 290, 327, 458; conceptualizing, 190–92; described, 190–94, 391–92; empirical findings with, 192–93; interpretation, 394 (table); RC6 and, 190; scores on, 141, 193

abnormality, 36, 63

acculturation, 242, 246, 247

Achenbach, T. M., 63

ACT. *See* Activation (ACT) scale

acting out, 62, 65, 161, 162, 404, 407, 417, 458, 495, 514

Activation (ACT) scale, 116, 196, 211, 215, 217, 231, 232, 252, 393, 406, 407, 470, 482; described, 409–10; interpretation, 410 (table); items, 213–14

Activity, 61, 62

Addiction Acknowledgment Scale (AAS), 31

Addiction Potential Scale (APS), 31

ADHD. *See* attention deficit/hyperactivity disorder

Adjustment Scale, 25, 26

Adjustment Validity (K) scale, 5, 15, 82, 84, 93, 95, 113, 139, 246, 303; constructing, 78; scores, 79, 80, 87, 153, 154, 353, 362, 375, 380, 382, 470; underreporting and, 80, 94

Adjustment Validity (K-r) scale, 113, 149, 150, 151, 277; described, 95, 353–54; interpretation, 353 (table)

administration, 27, 73, 105, 239, 269–75, 277, 334; abbreviated, 28, 82; booklet/computer, 274–75

Adult Basic Education, 119

Aesthetic/Literary Interests (AES) scale, 107

Affective Lability, 159, 162, 226

AGG. *See* Aggression (AGG) scale

AGGR. *See* Aggressiveness (AGGR) scale

AGGR-r. *See* Aggressiveness-Revised (AGGR-r) scale

aggression, 63, 64, 161, 162, 198, 472, 483, 492, 493, 503, 552; instrumental, 481; interpersonal, 213, 482; physical, 213, 492, 533

Aggression (AGG) scale, 116, 196, 212, 213, 214, 215, 216, 231, 232, 252, 290, 327, 393, 404, 406, 407, 494, 542, 553, 569; described, 410; interpretation, 411 (table)

aggressiveness, 162, 177, 181, 206, 213, 223, 230

633

Aggressiveness (AGGR) scale, 71, 116, 127, 225, 226, 303, 443, 444, 553; Antagonism and, 227; described, 416; Dissociality and, 228; interpretation, 417 (table)
Aggressiveness-Revised (AGGR-r) scale, 251
agoraphobia, 230, 231
agreeableness, 163; low, 179, 218
Agreeableness, 197, 416
Aguerrevere, L. E., 171
alcohol abuse, 63, 162, 177, 458, 492, 494, 505, 533, 544; correlations with, 179
alcoholism, 242
alienation, 49, 184, 185, 211, 214, 217, 472, 503
Allard, G., 276
alternative *DSM-5* model for personality disorders (AMPD), 193, 225, 226, 228, 229, 233, 235–36, 237, 415, 417, 418, 420; antagonism domain of, 416; ICD-11/PSY-5 Scales and, 235 (table); personality disorders and, 222; PSY-5 Scales and, 223, 235 (table); Psychoticism domain of, 416; trait model, 227
American Indians, 247, 264; assessments of, 249; scores of, 242
American Psychological Association (APA), 225, 240
AMPD. *See* alternative *DSM-5* model for personality disorders
Amsden, G. S., 61
Anankastia, 209, 235; DISC and, 228
Anderson, J. L., 203, 217, 228
anger, 179, 226, 472, 483, 484, 492, 552; assessing, 206; management, 198, 482, 493; symptoms/self-reported, 210
Anger Proneness (ANP) scale, 115, 117, 206, 207, 252, 391, 398, 493, 494, 542; described, 404; interpretation, 405 (table); scores, 210
anhedonia, 159, 190, 192, 203, 221, 226, 231, 393, 420, 430, 492, 493, 503, 504, 523; depression and, 173, 174, 175; disorders of, 445, 492; literature on, 176; PTSD and, 174; schizophrenia and, 174, 175; social, 174, 175; term, 172
anorexia nervosa (AN), 200

ANP. *See* Anger Proneness (ANP) scale
antagonism, 116, 177, 178, 180, 212, 213, 219, 223, 226, 227, 228, 230, 232, 233, 481, 483, 553; agreeableness and, 163; detachment and, 218
Antagonism, 228, 416; AGGR and, 227
Antagonism/Dissociality, 197
antidepressant medication, 166, 174, 203, 493, 494
antipsychotic medication, 161, 482, 483, 493
antisocial behavior, 51, 63, 68, 162, 177, 211, 212, 216, 389, 531
Antisocial Behavior (RC4) scale, 59, 65, 66, 68, 115, 116, 127, 164, 211, 250, 260, 385, 386, 406, 407, 446; ASPD and, 180, 181; conceptualization of, 177–78; described, 177–81, 389; empirical findings with, 178–81; interpretation, 391 (table); PPI and, 180; psychopathy and, 180
Antisocial Characteristics, 245
antisocial personality disorder (ASPD), 162, 177, 178, 212, 215, 417, 459, 503, 543; RC4 and, 180, 181; RC9 and, 197
anxiety, 43, 44, 62, 63, 159, 160, 161, 166, 173, 186, 187, 188, 245, 415, 484, 493, 505, 570; cognitive components of, 205; controlling, 443, 577; depression and, 260; disorders, 159, 177, 205, 209, 492, 531, 577, 578; experiencing, 462; generalized, 168, 205, 230, 523; health, 200; level of, 541; subjective, 470; symptoms of, 504, 532. *See also* generalized anxiety disorder
Anxiety (AXY) scale, 9, 41, 62, 116, 205, 207, 209, 210, 252, 253
Anxiety-Related Experiences (ARX) scale, 117, 176, 205, 207, 209, 290, 327, 391, 398, 399, 493, 494, 542, 553; described, 404; interpretation, 405 (table)
Anxiousness, 209, 222, 226
APA. *See* American Psychological Association
APA Monitor, 32
Aragona, M., 199
Arbisi, Paul, 69, 85, 245; Clinical Scales and, 99; Fp and, 84; Fp-r and, 93; Fs and, 93; RC Scales and, 99

Archer, R. P., 56, 248, 270; gender diversity and, 247; RC9 and, 196; S and, 87
Areas for Further Evaluation, 327
Army Specialized Training Program, 77, 79
ARX. *See* Anxiety-Related Experiences (ARX) scale
Ashton, K., 513
Asian participants, 243, 247
ASPD. *See* antisocial personality disorder
assertiveness, 51, 412, 413, 416, 481, 552; low, 218
attention, 200; difficulties with, 201, 345, 430, 461, 471, 531, 541, 552, 577
attention deficit/hyperactivity disorder (ADHD), 136, 161, 177, 212, 215, 471–72, 481–83, 552; dissimulation scale for, 147; feigning, 147, 148; overreporting, 147
Authority Problems, 43
autism spectrum disorder, 495
Avdeyeva, T. V., 192
avoidant personality disorders, 208, 219, 220, 221, 222, 443, 541
Axis II disorders, 70, 71, 223
AXY. *See* Anxiety (AXY) scale
Ayearst, L., 220, 221
Azán Chaviano, A., 106
Azizian, A., 216

Bacchiochi, J. R., 224
Baer, R. A., 94, 152
Baez, M. E., 170
Bagby, R. M., 95, 146, 150, 160, 167, 168, 173, 175, 183, 231; ACT and, 217; PSY-5 Scales and, 224; RC7 and, 188; RC9 and, 197
Balanced Inventory for Desirable Responding Impression Management (IM), 152
Bandura, A., 204
bariatric surgery, 163, 171, 175, 181, 201, 253, 504–5, 513; Black/Hispanic, 251
Barlow, D. H., 173, 196
Barratt Impulsivity Scale, 216
Basic Readings (Welsh and Dahlstrom), 6
Baum, L. J., 151, 184
BDS. *See* bodily distress syndrome
Beck Anxiety Inventory, 210

Beck Depression Inventory, 243
behavior, 416; control, 179; problems with, 47, 63, 163, 375
Behavior Activation, 186
Behavior-Restricting Fears (BRF) scale, 115, 127, 206, 207, 210, 391, 398, 542; described, 404, 406; interpretation, 406 (table)
Behavioral Dysfunction, 65, 325, 407, 422, 443, 444, 446, 458
Behavioral/Externalizing Dysfunction (BXD) scale, 65, 67, 97, 116, 117, 126, 127, 158, 177, 210, 326, 383, 385, 407, 430, 446, 458, 494, 542; described, 162–63; interpretation, 386 (table)
Behavioral Inhibition System (BIS), 186, 188, 190
Ben-Dat, D., 224
Ben-Porath, Yossef S., 30, 31, 36, 59, 65, 90, 135, 157, 160, 162, 164, 168, 173, 175, 178, 180, 181, 184, 188, 192, 202, 207, 208, 220, 231, 274; anxiety and, 210; DISC scores and, 225; eating disorders and, 200; Externalizing Scales and, 214; FBS and, 89; Fp and, 84; Fp-r and, 93; Fs and, 93; Internalizing Scales and, 206; overreporting scales and, 146; protocol validity and, 73; RC1 and, 170; RC3 and, 217; RC6 and, 185; RC7 and, 188; RC9 and, 196–98; Somatic/Cognitive Dysfunction and, 427; Static-99 and, 215–16; Validity Scales and, 137–38, 333–34
Benson, T. A., 189
Bernal dek Riesgo, Ildefonso, 257
Bernreuter Personality Inventory (BPI), 4, 74
Bernstein, D., 219
Bhar, S. S., 204
bias, 185, 250; intercept, 245, 579n1; negative response, 73, 337; positive response, 73, 337; predictive, 253; slope, 245, 250, 253; test, 242, 265
Bigos, S., 199
Binder, R. L., 196
binge eating, 200, 504
binge-eating disorder (BED), 200

bipolar disorder, 35, 160, 162, 194, 197, 214, 217, 220, 481, 482, 483; diagnosis of, 198; suicide attempts and, 196; symptoms of, 213
BIS. *See* Behavioral Inhibition System
Black men: cultural mistrust and, 255; T score and, 251; violent behavior and, 252
Black and White comparisons, 241–42, 244–45, 249–50
blame externalization, 180, 184, 217
Blanchard, J. L., 174
Block, A. R., 34, 514, 522; MMPI factors and, 18; theoretical framework of, 18
bodily distress syndrome (BDS), 169, 199, 200, 201
Bollini, A., 190
borderline features, 159, 161, 235
Borderline Features scale, 216
borderline personality disorder (BPD), 162, 208, 213, 235, 417, 492, 494, 543
Bornstein, R. F., 218
Borum, R., 271, 272
Boston Normative Aging Study, 26, 248
Boutacoff, L. I., 153, 175, 180; RC6 and, 185
BPD. *See* borderline personality disorder
BPI. *See* Bernreuter Personality Inventory
Braswell, L., 242
BRF. *See* Behavior-Restricting Fears (BRF) scale
Bridges, S. A., 151
Brief Psychiatric Rating Scale (BPRS), 192
Briquet, Paul, 168–69
Brockhaus, R., 180, 197, 215; RC3 and, 217
Brown, Tiffany, 150, 151, 173, 183, 209, 216, 227, 228, 233, 580n1; maladaptive personality traits and, 226
Bryant, W. T., 243, 253, 254, 255; MMPI-2-RF Substantive Scales and, 252; TGD and, 256
Budtz-Lilly, A., 201
bulimia nervosa (BN), 200
Burchett, D., 141, 168, 170, 181; RC9 and, 196; suicide and, 207; Validity Scales and, 137–38

Butcher, James, 23, 86, 98, 99, 130, 242, 272; FBS and, 89; item pool and, 3; MMPI and, 258; RC3 and, 59
BXD. *See* Behavioral/Externalizing Dysfunction (BXD) scale

Cady, V. M., 74
Caldwell, A. B., 10, 59
California Psychological Inventory (CPI), 62
callousness, 116, 163, 177, 212, 213, 216, 553
Callousness, 221
Campbell, D. P., 23
Cannot Say (CNS) score, 74–75, 81, 87, 90, 120, 135, 153, 288, 303, 339, 354, 427; described, 340–41; score interpretation, 341 (table)
Canul, G. D., 246
Cappo, B. M., 215–16, 217
CAPS-5, 544, 553
cardiovascular disease, 204
Carefree Nonplanfulness, 180
Carnovale, M., 228
Caron, G. R., 247, 248
Carpenter, N., 57
Carragher, N., 173
Castro, Y., 245, 249, 250
CAT-PD. *See* Comprehensive Assessment of Traits relevant to Personality Disorders
Cattell, R. B., 44–45
CG. *See* comparison group
Chapman, Jean, 191, 192
Chapman, Loren, 174, 191, 192, 213
Character Sketches, 74
Charcot, Jean-Martin, 169
Chibnall, J. T., 151, 154
Chinese men, Clinical Scale 0 and, 247
Chorpita, B. F., 173
chronic fatigue syndrome, 168, 461–62, 470–71
chronic pain, 96, 163, 167, 225; evaluations for, 170
Clark, L. A., 187; Negative Temperament and, 188; SNAP and, 193
Clarke, D. M., 165
Claustrophobia, 210

Cleckley, H., 71
Clinical Scale 0, 54, 243, 247; described, 51–52; Seed scale for, 67
Clinical Scale 1, 54, 243, 248; described, 50
Clinical Scale 2, 40, 43, 49, 54, 172, 186; demoralization and, 50; described, 50; scores on, 243
Clinical Scale 3, 54, 67, 199, 243, 246, 248; described, 50
Clinical Scale 4, 40, 43, 47–48, 54, 59, 178, 246, 248; demoralization and, 50–51; described, 50
Clinical Scale 5, 54, 243; demoralization and, 51; described, 51; Seed scale for, 67
Clinical Scale 6, 54; demoralization and, 51; described, 51
Clinical Scale 7, 40, 49, 54, 65, 80, 186, 189, 245, 247, 248; described, 51
Clinical Scale 8, 40, 54, 65, 80, 200, 241, 247; described, 51
Clinical Scale 9, 54, 241; described, 51
Clinical Scales, 7–10, 14, 15, 19, 22, 24, 26, 28, 29, 33, 36, 56–60, 62, 64, 67, 68, 79, 80, 83, 84, 92, 97, 99, 130–33, 229, 246; code types of, 65; components of, 50–52; as configural indicators, 16; correlations between, 40–41, 46–48, 51, 53; development of, 11, 42, 47, 48, 229; items on, 41–44; Kraepelinian diagnoses in, 17; methodological considerations for, 44–45; original, 3, 6, 164; pre-restructured solutions to, 42–44; problems with, 23, 25, 32, 39, 40, 579n1; revising, 3, 40, 42, 44–54, 55; structural problems with, 37
Clinician-Administered PTSD Scale, 544
Cluster C personality disorders, 208, 221, 222
Cluster D symptoms, 167
CMP. *See* Compulsivity (CMP) scale
CNS. *See* Cannot Say (CNS) score
code types, 4, 7–8, 17, 23, 33, 43, 44, 64, 65, 66
COG. *See* Cognitive Complaints (COG) scale
cognitive complaints, 135, 144, 200, 201, 222, 262, 327, 354, 366, 552

Cognitive Complaints (COG) scale, 115, 117, 199, 200, 202, 232, 253, 349, 350, 388, 470, 531, 542, 570; described, 398; interpretation, 399; pain ratings and, 201; scores, 252, 370
Cognitive Dysfunction, 380, 444, 532
Cognitive and Lack of Ego Mastery, Conative, 200
Cognitive Problems, 226
cognitive symptoms, 208, 345, 396, 522, 523; overreporting, 370
Combined Response Inconsistency (CRIN) scale, 111, 113, 135, 136, 139, 141, 142, 153, 273, 277, 303, 330, 338, 339, 340, 354, 362, 366, 375; described, 341–42; interpretation, 342 (table); scores, 292, 358
Combs, D. R., 190
common factor, 43, 49, 50, 53, 55, 58, 164; defining/capturing, 46–48
comorbidity, 52, 56, 64, 178, 181, 187; depression, 175; phenotypic, 163, 190
comparison group (CG), 303–4; described, 291–92, 329
Comparison Group Findings, 569
Comprehensive Assessment of Traits relevant to Personality Disorders (CAT-PD), 208, 209, 210, 216, 221, 222, 226, 228
compulsive behavior, 209, 481, 495, 505, 513, 577
Compulsivity (CMP) scale, 116, 117, 153, 157, 205, 207, 232, 235, 289, 391, 398, 470, 542; described, 403; interpretation, 404 (table); scores, 209
Computerized Assessment of Response Bias (CARB), 94
concentration, 461, 522, 531
confounds, 265; consideration of, 338–40; extratest, 339; terminological, 187–88
conscientiousness, 163, 179, 417
Constraint factor, 64
Content Component Scales, 70; described, 30–31
content nonresponsiveness, 73, 76, 77, 87, 150, 324; scales, 340–44

Content Scales, 26, 28, 29, 30, 34, 36, 37, 68, 98, 82, 132, 246; described, 28–29; research on, 37
Corey, D. M., 160, 162, 180, 274, 331, 381, 554, 580n2; RC6 and, 185
Correction (K), 77–81
Correctional Candidate Interpretive Report (CCIR), 330
Covid-19, 417, 505, 513
Coyne, J. C., 173
Crighton, A. H., 149, 150, 151
criminal behavior, 177, 181, 531
criminal justice system, 495, 533, 544
CRIN. *See* Combined Response Inconsistency (CRIN) scale
critical items, 290, 303, 327, 482; lists of/described, 10
Critical Responses, 291, 327, 330; described, 289–90
Cross, H. J., 246
Cukrowicz, K. C., 173
CYN. *See* Cynicism (CYN) scale
cynicism, 59, 67, 481
Cynicism (CYN) scale, 97, 115, 116, 117, 206, 212, 213, 214, 215, 216, 232, 246, 393, 396, 406, 407, 553; described, 410–11; interpretation, 412 (table)
Cynicism (RC3) scale, 59, 68, 97, 116, 117, 149, 164, 213, 214, 215, 216, 217, 250

Dahlstrom, L. E., 244
Dahlstrom, W. Grant, 6, 23, 24, 33, 79, 81, 257, 271–72; malingering and, 154; MMPI and, 3–4, 12, 13; review by, 241
data: analyses, 56; biographical, 25; clinical, 259; collecting, 12, 118–20, 259; comparison group, 303; demographic, 25; descriptive, 292; empirical, 19; extratest, 344, 345, 348; sets, 13, 69, 72
de Figuiredo, J. M., 165
de Mey, H. R., 225
de Saeger, H., 221, 222
deceitfulness, 177, 181, 213
delusions, 184, 190, 192, 218, 493; paranoid, 185, 472, 481, 482, 483, 492; persecutory, 182, 183, 190; somatic, 153, 171, 348
demoralization, 167, 174, 183, 186, 187, 188, 190, 204, 217; conceptualizing, 165; depression and, 166, 173, 203; psychological problems and, 165; self-reported, 166; term, 172
Demoralization (RCd) scale, 41, 46, 47, 50, 51, 58, 65, 66, 67, 68, 69, 108, 113, 164, 173, 176, 187, 190, 193, 231, 251, 289, 291, 385, 389, 390, 398; capturing, 4849; described, 165–68, 386–87; empirical findings with, 166–68; experiencing, 444; interpretation, 387 (table); markers of, 49; RCI and, 168; scores, 167, 386; variance, 52–53
denial, 72, 73, 337, 338
dependent personality disorders, 207, 208, 218, 221, 443, 492
depression, 43, 44, 63, 159, 161, 165, 167, 168, 186, 197, 204, 205, 209, 230, 231, 245, 430, 484, 495; anhedonia and, 173, 174, 175, 203; anxiety and, 260; bouts of, 570; demoralization and, 166, 173, 203; diagnoses of, 504, 578; endogenomorphic, 172; major, 188, 389; neurotic, 172, 173, 217; nonspecific, 173; risk for, 50, 172; self-reported, 578; suicide attempters with, 260; symptoms, 504
depressive disorders, 79, 204, 208, 217, 389, 445, 459, 483, 492, 531, 541
Depressivity, 159, 188, 226
Derksen, H. R. A., 225
Desai, S., 224
Desirable Responding Impression Management (IM), scores, 152
despair, 47, 159, 290, 442, 444, 445, 514
detachment, 173, 174, 188, 206, 219, 223, 230, 231, 232, 235, 542; antagonism and, 218; avoidant, 220; emotional, 221, 226, 236; low, 218; schizoid, 220; social, 159, 236
Detachment, 232, 420; INTR and, 227, 228
Detailed Assessment of PTSD (Briere), 159
Detrick, P., 15, 80, 151, 154

development samples: demographic characteristics of, 105; described, 104–5
Diagnostic Considerations, 324, 326, 382, 422, 541
Diagnostic Criteria for Psychosomatic Research (DCPR), 165
Dialectical Behavior Therapy (DBT), 494
diminished responsibility, 543–44, 552–54
Disaffiliativeness (DSF) scale, 116, 117, 127, 217, 219, 220, 221, 232, 289, 411, 542, 552, 553, 569; described, 413; interpretation, 414 (table)
disappointments: preoccupation with, 402, 443, 445, 458, 541, 577; severe, 172
DISC. *See* Disconstraint (DISC) scale
disconstraint, 223, 230, 552
Disconstraint (DISC) scale, 72, 116, 127, 225, 226, 235, 407, 446, 494, 542, 553, 554; Anankastia and, 228; described, 417; Disinhibition and, 227, 228; interpretation, 418 (table)
discrimination, 183, 247, 265
disinhibition, 163, 198, 213, 232
Disinhibition, DISC and, 227, 228
disorganization, 190, 192, 335, 459, 472, 483
Dispatcher Candidate Interpretive Report (DCIR), 330–31
Dissimulation scale, 147
Dissociality, AGGR and, 228
distress, 232, 522; disorders, 205, 231
diversity-sensitive assessments, 261–65
Diversity-Sensitive Personality Assessment (Smith and Krishnamurthy), 240
Dixon, J. N., 255, 265, 504
dizziness, 531, 541
"Does the 'New' MMPI Beat the 'Classic'?" (*APA Monitor*), 32
Dohrenwend, B. P., 48, 165
Dominance (DOM) scale, 116, 213, 217, 220, 221, 232, 289, 303, 393, 411, 443, 569; described, 218, 412–13; interpretation, 414 (table)
Domineering, 221, 226
Dragon, W. R., 140
Drerup, L. C., 57, 175

drug abuse. *See* substance abuse
DSF. *See* Disaffiliativeness (DSF) scale
DSM, 178, 226, 228, 230, 233
DSM-III, 23, 165
DSM-III-R, 70, 248, 250; criteria, 71, 223; gender identity disorder and, 248
DSM-IV, 194
DSM-5, 37, 169, 178, 193, 200, 205, 206, 225, 233, 383, 415, 544; ASPD and, 177; disorders, 219; malingering and, 337
DSM-5 Alternative Model of Personality Disorders, 70
Dyadic Adjustment Scale, 25, 26
dysfunction, 67, 113, 218, 345, 444, 481; anxiety-related, 578; dimensions of, 66; level of, 338; marked, 544; reporting, 344
Dysfunctional Negative Emotions (RC7) scale, 53, 65, 66, 68, 108, 115, 176, 205, 231, 385, 386, 398, 442, 443; conceptualizing, 186–88; described, 186–90, 390–91; empirical findings with, 188–89; interpretation, 393 (table); PTSD and, 189, 190; scores on, 188, 189, 252, 391
dysphoria, 167, 176, 248, 389; acute, 172, 217
dysthymia, 168, 230

Eakin, D. E., 167, 189
EAT. *See* Eating Concerns (EAT) scale
Eating Attitudes Test-26 (EAT-26), 202
Eating Concerns (EAT) scale, 117, 157, 199, 200, 201, 202, 388, 446, 458; described, 396; interpretation, 396, 398 (table)
Eating Disorder Examination Questionnaire (EDE-Q), 202
eating disorders, 160, 200, 204, 458
Eating Pathology Symptom Inventory (EPSI), 202
Eccentric Perceptions, 192–93
Eckblad, M., 191, 213
Edelbrock, C. S., 63
Edens, J. F., 53
education, 118, 120, 122, 246, 277; participant level of, 250
Edwards, A. L., 17, 56
ego strength, 16, 18, 187

Ego Strength (Es), 97
Egri, G., 48
EID. *See* Emotional/Internalizing Dysfunction (EID) scale
electroencephalography (EEG), 216
Elhai, J. D., 174
Emotional Detachment, 221, 226
emotional disorder, 172, 208, 217, 445, 532
emotional distress, 166, 484, 523
Emotional Dysfunction, 65, 66, 160, 327, 346, 366, 422, 427, 430, 442, 444, 446, 493, 542, 554
emotional lability, 230, 236
Emotional/Internalizing Disorders, 113, 326
Emotional/Internalizing Dysfunction (EID) scale, 67, 158, 159–60, 289, 304, 383, 430, 444, 483, 494; described, 384; interpretation, 384 (table); literature on, 160; scale score utility of, 160
Emotionality, 61, 62
energy: excessive, 462; low, 445, 514, 531
English language, 258; fluency, 242. *See also* target language
English-language MMPI-3 Norms, and Spanish-language norms compared, 127
English-language MMPI-3 Norms—Externalizing and Interpersonal Scales, Spanish-language MMPI-3 Normative Sample scored using, 129 (fig.)
English-language MMPI-3 Norms—Higher-Order and Restructured Clinical Scales, Spanish-language MMPI-3 Normative Sample scored using, 128 (fig.)
English-language MMPI-3 Norms—Personality Psychopathology Five (PSY-5) Scales, Spanish-language MMPI-3 Normative Sample scored using, 130 (fig.)
English-language MMPI-3 Norms—Somatic/Cognitive and Internalizing Scales, Spanish-language MMPI-3 Normative Sample scored using, 129 (fig.)
English-language MMPI-3 Norms—Validity Scales, Spanish-language MMPI-3 Normative Sample scored using, 128 (fig.)

English-language studies, review of, 241–57
epilepsy, 57, 170
ethnic groups, 119, 246–47, 251; score differences for, 242–43
ethnicity, 240, 241, 249–52, 263, 580n3
euphoria, 196, 472
EurekaFacts, 118, 119, 120, 122
Exhibitionism, 221, 222, 226
Externalizing, 3, 63, 64, 198, 394, 493
externalizing behaviors, 222, 493
Externalizing SP Scales, 115, 115 (table), 116, 117, 127, 288; constructs of, 211–14; described, 211–17, 406; reliability estimates for, 214
extraversion, 62, 71, 174, 175, 218
Extraversion/Positive Emotionality, 61
Eysenck, H. J., 71
Eysenck Personality Inventory, 61, 62
Eysenck Personality Questionnaire (EPQ), 62

F. *See* Infrequent Responses (F) scale
F-r. *See* Infrequent Responses (F-r) scale
Fairbank, J. A., 30
fake bad, 73, 77, 79, 85, 344
fake good, 73, 79, 337, 350
False, 11, 75, 76, 82, 85, 102, 289, 334, 336, 340, 343, 344; responding, 34, 83, 136, 338, 362, 382
False-False (FF), 83, 91, 110, 342
False-True (FT), 91, 110, 342
Family Problems (FML) scale, 116, 161, 211, 214, 215, 246, 256, 289, 389, 407 (table), 494, 569; described, 406–7
Fantasy Proneness, 226
fatigue, 430, 445, 514, 522, 531
Faust, D., 276
FBS. *See* Symptom Validity (FBS) scale
FBS-r. *See* Symptom Validity (FBS-r) scale
fear, 159, 231
fear disorders, 189, 205, 206
Ferrier-Auerbach, A. G., 225
FF. *See* False-False
fibromyalgia, 260
Fifth Annual Symposium on Recent Development in the Use of the MMPI, 14

Fink, P., 169, 199–200
Finn, J. A., 102, 103, 227
Firefighter Interpretive Report (FCIR), 331
Fischler, G. L., 180, 185
fixed responding, 73, 334; described, 335–36
Flesch-Kincaid index, 272, 273
Flint, G., 242
Flood, A. M., 189
FML. *See* Family Problems
Forbes, M. K., 189
Forbey, J. D., 138, 170, 175, 202, 272
Fordyce, W., 199
Forner, E. H., 210
40th Annual Symposium on Recent MMPI Research, 69
Fp. *See* Infrequent Psychopathology (Fp) scale
Fp-r. *See* Infrequent Psychopathology Responses (Fp-r) scale
Frank, Jerome, 46, 172; demoralization and, 47, 48, 165, 167; RCd and, 168
Freeman, D., 182, 183
Freud, Sigmund, 169, 186
Frueh, B. C., 174
Fs. *See* Infrequent Somatic Responses (Fs) scale
FT. *See* False-True

GAD. *See* generalized anxiety disorder
Galton, Francis, 61
García-Peltoniemi, R., 106
Gard, D. E., 176
Garety, A., 182, 183
Gartland, D. M., 180
Gastrointestinal Complaints (GIC) scale, 107, 115, 252
gastrointestinal symptoms, 169, 462, 505, 531
Gatchel, R. J., 199
gender, 183, 246, 277; binary, 263; differences, 64; identity, 248, 264
gender affirming surgery, 247, 248, 249
gender diversity, 247–48, 252–53, 263; mental health challenges of, 252; psychopathology levels and, 243
Gender Role-Feminine, 29, 51
Gender Role-Masculine, 29, 51

gender-identity disorder of adolescence and adulthood, nontranssexual type (GIDAANT), 248
gender-neutral language, 263, 330
General Educational Development (GED), 119
General Maladjustment, 41
generalized anxiety disorder (GAD), 205, 210, 231, 492, 541, 577
Germans, M. K., 172
Gervais, R. O., 94, 142, 146, 202
Gfeller, D., 89
GIC. *See* Gastrointestinal Complaints (GIC) scale
Glassmire, D. M., 168, 176, 181, 207, 251; SUI and, 203
Goldberg, L. R., 14, 22, 61, 232
Goldman, S. L., 186, 187
Gottesman, Irving, 32
Gottfried, E. D., 207
Gough, H. G., 7, 62
Graham, John, 24, 33, 69, 80, 89, 154, 155, 192, 243; Black and White comparisons and, 244–45; Clinical Scales and, 99; RC Scales and, 99; RC1 and, 170
Gray, J. A.: BIS and, 186, 188, 190
Grayson, H. M., 10
Green, P., 183, 186, 187
Greene, R. L., 31, 80, 97, 155, 246; MMPI-2 and, 98
Greenfield, T. K., 196
Gregory, S. D., 185, 215
Grenyer, B., 196
Greve, K. W., 89
Gross, A. M., 148
Grunebaum, M. F., 196
Gu, W., 142
Guilford-Zimmerman Temperament Survey, 61
guilt, 167, 253, 484, 523, 553, 570
Gupton, H. M., 160, 185
Gynther, M. D., 241

Hall, G. C. N., 246
hallucinations, 161, 184, 190, 191, 210

Han, K., 86, 265
Handel, R. W., 56, 140, 141, 202; RC9 and, 196
Happiness/Unhappiness, 49, 165, 187
Happy-Unhappy, 166
Hare, R. D., 59
Harkness, Allan, 31, 60, 70, 225; PSY-5 Scales and, 71, 72, 109, 224, 383, 415; systems theory and, 223
Harmon, L. R., 8, 30
Harp, J. P., 147, 148
Harris, R., 10
Harris-Lingoes Lassitude-Malaise (Hy3) scale, 199, 200
Harris-Lingoes subscales, 30, 42, 43, 44, 70; described, 10
Hartshorne, H., 75
Hathaway, Starke, 11, 17, 20, 23, 42, 79, 80, 81, 153, 271; appraisal by, 8, 13–14; Clinical Scales and, 4, 6, 15, 40; CNS and, 74, 75; F scale and, 76–77, 84; F-r and, 92; item pool and, 3; K scale and, 78; L and, 75; on measuring device, 22; MMPI development and, 4, 7–8, 90, 257; overreporting and, 87; personality theory and, 15; protocol validity and, 74; underreporting and, 94; Validity Scales and, 73, 74
head pain, 505, 522, 531
Head Pain Complaints (HPC) scale, 107, 115
head trauma, psychological sequela of, 522–24, 531–32
Health Anxiety, 226
health concerns, 388, 471, 541
Heilbrun, A. B. J., 80
Heinberg, L. J., 513
Heiser, N. A., 219
Helmes, E., 55, 56; review by, 3337
helplessness, 168, 204
Helplessness/Hopelessness (HLP) scale, 98, 115, 117, 203, 206, 207, 208, 289, 290, 327, 387, 398, 442, 522, 569; described, 400; interpretation, 401 (table)
Henry, G. K., 171
Heymans, G., 61, 62, 66

Hierarchical Taxonomy of Psychopathology (HiTOP), 199, 229–33; scale mapping, 234 (fig.)
Higher-Order (H-O) Scales, 40, 60, 61–70, 109, 113, 114 (table), 116, 126, 158–63, 198, 230, 289, 354, 422, 430, 458; construct-relevant criteria for, 163; described, 383–85; development of, 66–67; personality disorders and, 160; psychometric properties of, 158–59; psychopathology domains and, 158
Hill, J. S., 247
Himsl, K., 273
Hippocrates, 168, 182
Hispanic individuals, 121, 246; L-r and, 251; score validity for, 242; violent behavior and, 252
histrionic personality disorder, 216, 218, 221, 227, 420
HiTOP. *See* Hierarchical Taxonomy of Psychopathology
Hjemboe, S., 31
HLP. *See* Helplessness/Hopelessness (HLP) scale
Hoch, A., 61
Hochman, K., 190
Hofmann, S. G., 219
hopelessness, 159, 168, 203, 204, 482, 503
Horman, Warren, 15
Horst, P., 78
H-O Scales. *See* Higher-Order (H-O) Scales
Hostile Aggression, 221, 226
hostility, 31, 97, 162, 177, 197, 206, 209, 212, 213, 216, 236, 552
Hostility (Ho) Scale, 31
HPC. *See* Head Pain Complaints (HPC) scale
Humm, D. G., 74
Humm-Wadsworth Temperament Scales, 4, 74
hyperactive behavior, 168, 458, 552
hypertension, 204
hypochondriasis, 6, 47, 169
Hypochondriasis (Hs), 7
hypomania, 195, 198, 217
hypomanic activation, 196, 198, 544

Hypomanic Activation (RC9) scale, 53, 65, 66, 108, 115, 116, 117, 149, 164, 192, 214, 250, 385, 386, 406, 407, 472; conceptualization of, 194–96; described, 194–98, 392–93; empirical findings with, 196–98; interpretation, 395 (table); RCd and, 168; scores, 196–97, 198, 325, 393
hypomanic episodes, 198, 462, 472, 481
Hypomanic Personality (HYP) scale, 213
hysteria, 4, 168
Hysteria (Hy) scale, 199

ICD-11. *See* International Classification of Diseases 11th Revision
IDAS-II. *See* Inventory for Depression and Anxiety Symptoms-II
Ideas of Persecution (RC6) scale, 65, 66, 115, 117, 126, 148, 164, 208, 231, 232, 250, 266, 290, 327, 411, 493; conceptualizing, 181–84; described, 181–85, 389; empirical findings with, 184–85; examination of, 183; interpretation, 392 (table); RC8 and, 190; scores on, 141, 184, 185
Ilkiw-Lavalle, O., 196
Ill Temper, 210
IMP. *See* Impulsivity (IMP) scale
impulse control, 472, 481, 492, 493
impulsive behavior, 177, 544, 552
Impulsive Nonconformity, 180, 191
impulsivity, 43, 179, 181, 198, 483, 492, 494, 503
Impulsivity (IMP) scale, 116, 117, 157, 212, 213, 214, 215, 216, 232, 393, 406, 407, 446, 542, 554; described, 408; interpretation, 409 (table)
Inclusive Language Guidelines (APA), 240
Inconsistent Responding, 330
Inconsistent Response Indicators, described, 110–11
Indigenous groups, 246, 264
Inefficacy (NFC) scale, 98, 115, 207, 208, 289, 291, 387, 398, 399, 442, 446, 470; described, 400–401; interpretation, 402 (table); scale, 204–5
inferiority, 481, 484

Infrequent Responses (F) scale, 5, 76–77, 81, 82, 87, 92, 112, 113, 120, 135, 136, 137, 145, 148, 153, 241, 289, 324, 325, 347, 349, 370, 531; overreporting and, 88; score, 84, 85, 127, 292, 330, 362, 366, 482
Infrequent Psychopathology Responses (Fp) scale, 30, 84–86
Infrequent Psychopathology Responses (Fp-r) scale, 84, 86, 87, 92, 94, 112, 113, 120, 136, 141, 143, 144, 145, 148, 153, 277; described, 93, 345–48; interpretation, 347 (table); items, 93; score, 37, 135, 292, 330, 346, 347, 358, 366, 370, 542, 553
Infrequent Responses (F-r) scale, 105, 277, 324; described, 345; indicators, 348; interpretation, 346 (table)
Infrequent Somatic Responses (Fs) scale, 92, 95, 112, 113, 135, 141, 143, 147, 148, 153, 277, 366, 370, 395, 396; described, 93–94, 348; interpretation, 348 (table); overreporting and, 144, 145; scores, 292
Ingram, P. B., 145, 193; AXY and, 210; overreporting and, 143, 144; RC3 and, 217
insanity, 88, 182, 194, 251
Institutional Review Board, 120
instrument validity, understanding, 333–34
intentionality, 73, 153, 344, 351, 396
intercorrelations, 41, 42, 46, 108
Interest Scales, 127, 253; SP and, 67–70
Internalizing, 63, 64, 198, 232, 394
internalizing disorders, 160, 222, 541
Internalizing SP Scales, 114–15 (table), 115, 126, 288, 398, 399; constructs of, 203, 206; described, 203–10
International Classification of Diseases 11th Revision (ICD-11), 227, 229, 230, 233, 235–36, 237, 543; personality disorders and, 222, 223, 494; personality models of, 197; PSY-5 Scales and, 228, 235 (table); schizotypal disorder, 494
International Society for the Study of Personality Disorders, 235
Interpersonal, 198, 394
interpersonal behaviors, 482, 503

Interpersonal Disorders, 326
Interpersonal Functioning, 222, 422, 443, 458; history of, 543; measuring, 219
Interpersonal Passivity (IPP) scale, 116, 218, 220–21, 444
interpersonal relationships, 531, 544; passive/submissive in, 445
Interpersonal Scales, 115 (table), 116, 127, 213, 288, 289, 411–13, 415; constructs of, 217–20; described, 217–22
interpretive guidelines, 29, 82, 87, 90, 153, 239, 288, 340, 325, 333, 358, 366, 381, 382; described, 340–54
Interview for Mood and Anxiety Disorders (IMAS), 196
INTR. *See* Introversion/Low Positive Emotionality (INTR) scale
introversion, 231, 505
Introversion/Low Positive Emotionality (INTR) scale, 72, 223, 226, 289, 444; described, 420; Detachment and, 227, 228; interpretation, 419 (table)
Introversion/Low Positive Emotions-Revised (INTR-r) scale, 251
Invalid Protocols, 329–30
invalid responding, 340; content-based, 73, 336–38; non-content-based, 73, 140–42, 334–36
Inventory for Depression and Anxiety Symptoms-II (IDAS-II), 209, 210, 222
Inwald Personality Inventory (IPI), 80
IPP. *See* Interpersonal Passivity (IPP) scale
Irresponsibility, 181, 216, 226
irritability, 195, 196, 492, 522, 541, 552
IRT. *See* item response theory
item modification, described, 103
item response theory (IRT), 170, 224
Item-Level Information, 290–92, 303–4, 324; described, 289, 327–28

Jackson, Douglas, 15, 17–18, 21, 22, 34, 42, 55, 58, 65, 336; Block and, 18; Clinical Scales and, 37, 44; Meehl and, 18–19; social desirability and, 56; Tellegen and, 45

Janet, Pierre, 169
JCP. *See* Juvenile Conduct Problems (JCP) scale
Job-Relevant Correlates, 569
Joiner, T. E., 173
Journal of Personality Assessment, 57
Judge, T. A., 204
Juvenile Conduct Problems (JCP) scale, 116, 212, 213, 214, 216, 231, 232, 389, 406, 542, 554; described, 407–8; interpretation, 408 (table); violent/nonviolent offenses and, 215
juvenile misconduct, 177, 181, 212, 531

K. *See* Adjustment Validity (K) scale
K-r. *See* Adjustment Validity (K-r) scale
Kaemmer, Beverly, 23, 24
Kahlbaum, Karl, 182
Kaloupek, D. G., 225
Kashdan, T. B., 174
Kaslow, N. J., 211
Kassebaum, G. G., 62
Katz, M. M., 25
Keane, T. M., 30, 225
Kelso, K. M., 217
Kent State University, 102, 103, 104, 120
Keo-Meier, C. L., 248
Kestler, L., 190
Khazem, L. R., 207
Kissane, D. W., 165
Klein, D. F., 172, 173
Klein Haneveld, E., 180
Kline, J. A., 242
Klonsky, E. D., 211
Koss, M. P., 10
Kraepelin, E., 4, 190, 194, 195, 198
Kraepelinian nosology, 4, 5, 7, 14, 16, 17, 23, 198; reliance on, 20, 22
Kremyar, A. J., 214, 232
Kring, A. M., 172
Krishnamurthy, R., 240
Krueger, R. F., 178, 231
Kukal, D., 514
Kwapil, T. R., 192, 213

L. *See* Uncommon Virtues (L) scale
L-r. *See* Uncommon Virtues (L-r) scale
Lack of Ego Mastery, 200
lack of interest, 445, 492
Lalone, L., 32
Lamberty, G., 168, 171
language comprehension, 265, 273, 341
Langwerden, R. J., 225
Lanyon, R. I., 160
Laurinavičius, A., 180, 210
Lee, T. T. C., 160, 167, 202, 214; FBS and, 89
Lees-Haley, P. R., 88
Levels of Personality Functioning, 237
Levels of Service Inventory–Revised (LSI-R), 210, 216, 217
Levenson Self-Report Psychopathy scale, 180
Lewinsohn, P. M., 173
Lie (L) scale, 75
Lightsey, O. R., 204
Lingoes, J., 10
Locke, D. E. C., 57, 170, 202
Loevinger, Jane, 16, 19, 22, 55; Clinical Scales and, 37; promising constructs and, 15
Low Positive Emotions (RC2) scale, 65, 66, 115, 186, 188, 191, 192, 198, 231, 250, 291, 383–84, 386, 411, 442–43, 444, 532, 578; conceptualizing, 172–75; described, 172–76, 388–89; empirical findings with, 175–76; interpretation, 390 (table); scores, 141, 175, 176, 393
LSI-R. *See* Levels of Service Inventory-Revised
Lubin, B., 12
Luna-Jones, L., 181, 216
Lyerly, S. B., 25

MacAndrew Alcoholism Scale-Revised (MAC-R), 31, 97
Machiavellian Egocentricity, 180
Machiavellianism, 213, 217
Magical Ideation Scale (MIS), 184, 191, 193
Maher, B. A., 182
maladaptive personality, 161, 218, 233
malaise, 493, 514

Malaise (MLS) scale, 115, 127, 199, 202, 232, 253, 348, 349, 388, 443, 444, 514, 522, 570; described, 396; interpretation, 397 (table); NUC and, 201; pain ratings and, 201
malingering, 73, 143, 144, 146, 362, 396; detecting, 154–55; diagnosis of, 344; positive, 73, 337, 351
malingering neurocognitive dysfunction (MND), 146
Maller, J. B., 74
Malloy, P. F., 30
mania, 161, 195, 196, 218, 245, 471–72, 481–83; literature on, 214; symptoms, 210
manic episodes, 194, 198, 462, 472, 482, 483, 553
manic symptoms, 209, 217, 483
Manipulativeness, 226
Manschreck, T. C., 181–82
Marek, R. J., 153, 160, 171, 203, 231, 251, 514, 522; MMPI-2-RF and, 253
Marital Distress Scale (MDS), 31
Markon, K. E., 63, 64
Marshall, D., 95
Masculinity/Femininity scale, 7
Mason, L. H., 141
Mattson, C. A., 181
McBlaine, D. D., 246
McCord, David, 57, 175, 217
McDevitt-Murphy, M. E., 189
McGrath, R. E., 138
McKay, R., 183
McKinley, J. C., 11, 13, 42, 79, 80, 81, 153, 271; assessment and, 8; Clinical Scales and, 6, 15; CNS and, 74, 75; F scale and, 76, 84; F-r and, 92; item pool and, 3; L and, 75; on measuring device, 22; MMPI development and, 90; scale development and, 4; Validity Scales and, 73, 74
McNaughton, N., 216
McNeil, D. E., 196
McNulty, John, 31, 60, 214, 230, 245; Clinical Scales and, 99; PSY-5 Scales and, 71, 72, 109, 383, 415; RC Scales and, 99

McVey, C., 173
Mechanical/Physical Interests (MEC) scale, 107
Meehl, Paul, 6, 15, 17, 18–22, 45, 55, 56, 64, 65, 76–77, 79, 81, 153, 174, 191; anhedonia and, 172; article by, 4; Clinical Scales and, 37; configural scoring and, 22; criterion keying and, 21; F and, 77; Jackson and, 18–19; K scale and, 78; MMPI and, 5, 11, 19, 23; on Norman, 20; overreporting and, 87; protocol validity and, 74; RC2 and, 172; schizotypic personality construct and, 191; underreporting and, 94; melancholia, 194
memory problems, 350, 398, 462, 522, 531, 541, 552, 577
Mendelsohn, F. S., 48
mental disorders, 64, 144, 177, 206, 554
mental health, 105, 158, 159, 160, 163, 167, 175, 193, 235, 493; history, 264; problems, 256, 346, 533, 544; testosterone and, 248; TGD and, 256, 257; treatment, 494, 532
mental illness, 182, 183, 553
mental injury, 532, 533, 543
Menton, W. H., 228
Merrell, J., 153
Messick, S., 17, 336
Meunier, G. F., 249
Miach, P. P., 248
Michaelis, B. H., 196
Midwestern Psychological Association, 7
Miller, M. W., 94, 224, 225
Millon, T., 219
Minnesota Multiphasic Personality Schedule (Hathaway and McKinley), publication of, 72
MIS. *See* Magical Ideation Scale (MIS)
mistrust, 221, 226, 481, 483, 552; cultural, 181, 255, 503; interpersonal, 184, 493, 503, 504; social, 482
Mittal, V. A., 190
MLS. *See* Malaise (MLS) scale
MMPI: appraisals of, 12–14, 31, 32, 41–42, 55, 96; development of, 4, 6, 14–15, 239–40, 241; future of, 265–66; international adaptations for, 257–60; interpretation of, 11, 13, 289; original, 3–4, 12, 43; revision of, 12–14, 15, 1920, 24, 25–26, 26–29, 32; studies on, 155, 248, 257; translations for, 257–60, 261, 262
MMPI First Factor, 41
MMPI Handbook (Dahlstrom and Welsh), 8, 13, 155, 257
MMPI Handbook (Dahlstrom, Welsh, and Dahlstrom), 258
MMPI Hispania, 106
MMPI Restandardization Committee, 24, 30, 33, 36, 37; goals for, 25; T scores and, 32
MMPI Restandardization Project, 3, 24, 25, 28, 68; new norms and, 2627
MMPI Validity Scales, 5, 8, 20, 26, 73, 74, 90, 113, 114 (table), 242, 247, 259, 277–78, 329–30, 340, 444; described, 28, 110; development of, 11, 135; functions of, 152–55; interpretation, 427, 430; introduction of, 82–84; nature of, 139; need for, 137–38; revised profile for, 87
MMPI-2, 23–24, 29, 54, 56, 66, 70; acculturation and, 246; appraisals of, 31–37, 55; FBS and, 89–90; Hispanic participants and, 246; normative sample for, 26, 27, 28, 248, 261–64, 270; older individuals and, 249; PAI and, 272; predictive validity of, 245; production of, 24–37, 39; reading level for, 271–72; studies on, 155; translation of, 259
MMPI-2 booklet, 28, 271
MMPI-2 manual, 29–31, 90; Validity Scales in, 82–84
MMPI-2 Validity Scales, 37, 40, 60, 84–87, 88, 93, 95; described, 81; development of, 90; revision of, 30
MMPI-2-RF, 26, 28, 29, 31, 34, 36, 54, 64, 66, 68, 69, 93, 115, 117, 126, 138, 141, 155, 157; appraisals of, 96–99; completing, 59–60; correlate data in, 399; development of, 3, 37, 39, 101, 102;

goals of, 157; interpretive guidance for, 96; literature, 135–37, 139, 158, 160, 216, 226, 233, 249, 254; MMPI-2 and, 98; norms of, 261, 262; overreporting scales, 142–48; predictive validity of, 253; protocols, 105; PSY-5 Scales and, 72; psychological assessments and, 99; RC Scales and, 40; scoring, 102, 106, 251, 253, 254; studies on, 72, 155, 235, 249–54, 531, 553; summary of findings with, 253–54; translation of, 259

MMPI-2-RF booklet, 103, 104, 106, 140, 148

MMPI-2-RF Manual for Administration, Scoring, and Interpretation (Ben-Porath and Tellegen), 97

MMPI-2-RF Restructured (RC) Scales, 140

MMPI-2-RF Substantive Scales, 60–72, 99, 107, 112, 138, 252, 254

MMPI-2-RF Technical Manual, 69, 70, 72, 94, 97, 98, 254, 261, 262, 382

MMPI-2-RF Validity Scales, 60, 110, 138, 155, 254; psychometric findings with, 139–52; publication of, 72–95

MMPI-2-RF-EX, 105106, 109, 120, 122, 138, 151, 255

MMPI-2-RF-EX booklet, 105, 106

MMPI-3, 28, 34, 36, 37, 103, 111, 112, 113, 117, 137, 141, 157, 158, 164; administration of, 27, 121, 269–75; assessments with, 261–65; census projections and, 262; cultures/languages and, 266; development of, 3, 101, 104, 105, 107, 229, 239, 261; goals of, 157; interpretation of, 264, 421, 422, 461, 462, 470, 472, 481482, 484, 492–94, 495, 503–4, 505, 513, 570, 577–78; literature on, 158, 161, 162; measurement invariance and, 266; norms of, 117–21, 122, 261–64, 270, 277; psychopathology models, 229–33; research on, 235; scale mapping, 234 (fig.); Spanish-language, 127, 261, 262, 570; standard scores for, 130–33; translations of, 260, 274

MMPI-3 Interpretation Worksheet, 289, 421, 423–26 (fig.), 427, 430, 438–41 (fig.), 442–46, 454–57 (fig.), 459; with completed Validity Scales page, 428 (fig.)

MMPI-3 Interpretive Report for Clinical Settings, 276, 291, 327, 328, 389, 392, 399, 400, 408, 410, 421; described, 304, 324; features of, 329–30

MMP-3 Manual for Administration, Scoring, and Interpretation (Ben-Porath and Tellegen), 104, 123, 133, 145, 146, 151, 325, 382

MMPI-3 Manual Supplement for the U.S. Spanish Translation (Ben-Porath, Tellegen, and Puente), 104–5, 106, 122, 257, 262

MMPI-3 Normative Sample Men and Women—Externalizing, Interpersonal, and Interest Scales, MMPI-2-RF scores of, 125 (fig.)

MMPI-3 Normative Sample Men and Women—Higher-Order and Restructured Clinical Scales, MMPI-2-RF scores of, 124 (fig.)

MMPI-3 Normative Sample Men and Women—Personality Psychopathology Five Scales, MMPI-2-RF scores of, 125 (fig.)

MMPI-3 Normative Sample Men and Women—Somatic/Cognitive and Internalizing Scales, MMPI-2-RF scores of, 124 (fig.)

MMPI-3 Normative Sample Men and Women—Validity Scales, MMPI-2-RF scores of, 123 (fig.)

MMPI-3 Police Candidate Interpretive Report (PCIR), 330, 554, 555–68 (fig.)

MMPI-3 Public Safety Candidate Interpretive Reports (PSCIRs), 330–31

MMPI-3 scales, 104, 107, 113, 114–15 (table), 115–17, 123, 138, 237, 339; reliability of, 139; scores on, 254–57, 266

MMPI-3 Substantive Scales, 105, 107, 109, 110, 153, 157, 229, 230, 257, 288, 330, 358, 370, 382; described, 126–27; interpretation, 344, 383, 430, 442–46; scores on, 351, 354, 375, 381

MMPI-3 Technical Manual (Ben-Porath and Tellegen), 102, 104, 105, 106, 116, 117, 118, 120, 121, 122, 136, 139, 157, 158, 159, 164, 193, 201, 202, 205, 209, 214, 215, 216, 217, 221, 223, 225, 228; maladaptive personality traits and, 226; SP Scales and, 394; validation analyses and, 107; validity data and, 140

MMPI-3 User's Guide for the Public Safety Candidate Interpretive Reports (Corey and Ben-Porath), 331

MMPI-3 User's Guide for the Score and Clinical Interpretive Reports (Ben-Porath and Tellegen), 271, 277, 291, 303, 304, 329

MMPI-3 Validity Scales, 32, 34, 95, 137, 254, 270, 273, 277, 288, 326–27, 330, 345, 386, 422, 427, 430, 446, 462, 469, 472, 482, 493, 514, 531, 532, 542, 569; described, 126; development of, 73, 135, 333; functioning of, 152–55; guidelines for, 340; interpretation, 333, 354; protocol validity assessment of, 338; psychometric findings with, 139–52; scores on, 325, 339 (table), 340, 381; threats to protocol validity and confounds, 339 (table)

MMPI-A, 270, 271

MMPI-A-RF, 270

MMPI-AX, 25, 26

Monnot, M. J., 189, 192, 245, 250

Montreal Cognitive Assessment (MoCA), 570

mood, 204, 484; disorders, 177, 481; instability, 472; psychopathology and, 186; sad/anxious, 194; structure of, 48; symptoms, 532; variance, 186–87

mood disorders, 177, 481

mood stabilizing medication, 482, 483, 494

Morey, L. C., 137, 272

MPQ. *See* Multidimensional Personality Questionnaire

MSF. *See* Multiple Specific Fears (MSF) scale

Mueser, K. T., 190

Multidimensional Measure of Islamic Spirituality (MMS), 152

Multidimensional Personality Questionnaire (MPQ), 28, 45, 62, 82, 83, 166, 175, 192

Multidimensional Schizotypy Scales, 192

multiple chemical sensitivities (MCSs), 171

Multiple Specific Fears (MSF) scale, 107, 116, 126, 251, 252

NA. *See* Negative Activation (NA); Negative Affect (NA)

Najt, P., 196

Naragon-Gainey, K., 174

narcissism, 43, 212, 233

narcissistic personality disorder, 197, 218, 220, 221, 227

National Computer Systems, 24

Negative Activation (NA), 166, 168; PA and, 49

Negative Affect (NA), 48, 186, 187, 232

Negative Affectivity (NA), 187, 190, 418; NEGE and, 227, 228

Negative Affectivity (Watson and Clark), 188

Negative Appraisals, 56, 57–59

negative emotionality, 187, 204, 205, 223, 230–31, 445

Negative Emotionality (NEM), 49, 51, 53, 62, 64, 187, 188, 189, 190, 204, 542, 554; described, 186; PEM and, 186

Negative Emotionality/Neuroticism (NEGE) scale, 61, 66, 71, 225, 226, 235, 291, 444, 493, 494, 542; described, 417–18; interpretation, 419 (table); Negative Affectivity and, 227, 228

Negative Emotionality/Neuroticism-Revised (NEGE-r) scale, 252, 253

negative emotions, 446, 484, 493, 523; dysfunctional, 188; strong, 492

Negative Temperament, 188

Negative Treatment Indicators (TRT), 29, 98

NEGE. *See* Negative Emotionality/ Neuroticism (NEGE) scale

NEGE-r. *See* Negative Emotionality/ Neuroticism-Revised (NEGE-r) scale

NEM. *See* Negative Emotionality

Neo, P. S., 216

NEO Personality Inventory-Revised (NEO PI-R), 63, 166, 175, 188, 224
nervousness, 71, 205
neurocognitive dysfunction, 169, 260, 578
Neurological Complaints (NUC) scale, 115, 126, 199, 200, 202, 206, 232, 348, 349, 388, 470, 532, 541, 570, 577; described, 396; interpretation, 397 (fig.); MLS and, 201; pain ratings and, 201
neurological symptoms, 192, 462, 531
neurophysiological evaluations, 207
neuropsychological assessment, of Spanish speakers, 570, 577–78
neuropsychological evaluations, 88–89, 162, 208, 209, 210
neuropsychology, 161, 167, 175, 179, 210, 522, 570
neuroticism, 62, 71, 166, 187, 188
Neuroticism dimension, NEGE and, 417–18
NFC. *See* Inefficacy (NFC) scale
Nichols, D. S., 58
nonalcoholic steatohepatitis, 504
Non-Perseverance, 216, 226
nonplanful behavior, 180, 458, 472
Non-Planfulness, 216
Non-Planning, 226
nonresponding, 334, 336, 339
nonresponsiveness, 340
Noordhof, A., 166
Norm Violation, 162, 216, 226
normal personality, 65, 224; inventory, 45, 64; models of, 70; structure of, 61, 63–64
Norman, W., 22, 44, 53, 55; Clinical Scales and, 15–17, 37; Kraepelinian nosology and, 20
normative samples (NS), 26, 101, 152, 244, 245, 248, 303; assembling, 120–21; composition of, 121–23; English-language, 118, 120, 121; Spanish-language, 118, 120–21, 122–23, 126–27
norms: clinical scale scores and, 29; concerns about, 32–33; gender-specific, 264–65; group-specific, 264–65; language-specific, 264; MMPI versus MMPI-2, 33; MMPI-2-RF versus MMPI-3, 123; new, 26–28; social, 181, 495
nosology, 4, 5, 16, 17, 20, 22, 198, 237
Novaco, R. W., 206
NS. *See* normative samples
NUC. *See* Neurological Complaints (NUC) scale

obsessions, 209, 505
obsessive-compulsive disorder (OCD), 159, 205, 481, 482, 503, 505, 577, 578; self-reported, 209
obsessive-compulsive personality, 209, 221, 227, 504
OCD. *See* obsessive-compulsive disorder
O'Connor, B. P., 63
Offender Assessment System, 215
Ohnmeiss, D. D., 514, 522
older adults, 119, 122, 174, 260, 262; scores of, 243, 248–49, 253
Onorato, V. A., 243
opioid medication, 513, 514
Osberg. T. M., 57, 270
Other, 122, 330
Overcontrolled/Internalizing Syndromes, 63
overreporting, 73, 76, 85, 86, 87, 88, 89, 105, 138, 142 148, 260, 277, 324, 330, 336, 340, 346, 350, 351, 358, 370, 375, 380, 396; cognitive, 146; described, 337; indicators, 92–94, 112, 143, 153; intentional, 77, 337; scales, 112, 142–48, 344–45; somatic, 146; unintentional, 77, 337
Overstreet, S. R., 214, 230

PA. *See* Positive Activation; Positive Affect
Pace, T. M., 246, 247
PAI. *See* Personality Assessment Inventory
pain disorder, 169, 171, 199
pain medication, opiate-based, 513
panic, 189, 205, 209, 230, 231, 492, 523, 577
panic attacks, 205, 504–5
Papakostas, G. I., 203
paranoia, 159, 161, 182, 183, 184, 210, 212, 481
Paranoia-Persecution, 161

Pardis, A. D., 211, 221
Parker, J. D., 224
Parkinson's disease, 570, 578
PAS. *See* Perceptual Aberration Scale
passive-submissive behavior, 218, 445, 446, 578
Patient-Reported Outcomes Measurement Information System (PROMIS), 210
Patrick, C. J., 180
Paulhus, D. L., 153
PCIR. *See* MMPI-3 Police Candidate Interpretive Report
PCL-R. *See* Psychopathy Checklist-Revised
PCL-SV. *See* Psychopathy Checklist-Screening Version
Pearson, Karl, 61
Pearson Assessments, 24
Pearson scoring, 271, 275, 276, 329, 381
PEM. *See* Positive Emotionality
People of Color (POC), 254, 255
Perceptual Aberration Scale (PAS), 191, 193
Perceptual Dysregulation, 193
Perez, M., 173
perfectionism, 209, 505
performance validity tests (PVTs), 350, 531, 578
persecutory ideation, 183, 185, 483, 493, 495, 503
Persecutory Ideation Questionnaire (PIQ), 183
perseverance, 442, 445, 481, 495, 541
Personal Data Sheet, 61, 74
personality, 34, 55, 97, 157, 179, 187, 219, 245, 260; adult, 61; characteristics, 163, 194; clinical assessments of, 5; measures of, 12, 351; psychopathology and, 49, 61, 163, 212, 218, 228; research in, 37; structure of, 60; studying, 13. *See also* normal personality
personality assessment, 3, 11, 12, 14, 24, 258
Personality Assessment Inventory (PAI), 63, 64, 66, 161, 162, 216, 533; MMPI-2 and, 272
personality disorders, 160, 172, 177, 197, 217, 222, 228, 443, 445, 459, 532–33, 541–43, 577; dimensional models of, 233, 235–36, 483–84, 492–94; severe, 483–84, 492–94
Personality Inventory for *DSM-5* (PID-5), 187, 188, 228
personality pathology, 211, 219, 225, 483, 543, 554
Personality Psychopathology Five (PSY-5) Scales, 37, 50, 69, 109, 115 (table), 117, 132, 220, 222–29, 235, 237, 251, 255, 288, 383, 384, 385, 386; AMPD and, 223, 235 (table); described, 31, 415; development of, 70–72; factor analyses and, 224; ICD-11 and, 228, 235 (table); measures on, 71; original, 70–72; personality disorders and, 222; personality trait domains and, 228; psychometric findings with, 225–29; revising, 60, 72, 415
personality traits, 216, 228; adaptive, 161; antagonistic/disinhibited, 198; pathological, 222
pessimism, 43, 203, 207
Petersen, M. W., 201
Petroskey, L., 225
Pettit, J. W., 173
phobias, 63, 189, 205, 206, 210, 230; social, 187, 188, 230, 231
Physical Anhedonia, 191
physical disabilities, 262, 270–71
PID-5. *See* Personality Inventory for *DSM-5*
Pike, P. L., 247
Pilowsky, D. J., 211
Pleasantness/Unpleasantness (PU), 49, 165, 166, 187
POC. *See* People of Color
Poland, D. L., 270
Pollack, D. R., 242
polycystic ovarian syndrome, 504
Pope, K. S., 32
Positive Activation (PA), 166, 168; NA and, 49
Positive Affect (PA), 48, 186, 187
positive emotional responsiveness, lack of, 175
Positive Emotionality (PEM), 49, 62, 64; demoralization and, 186; low, 71, 173, 175; NEM and, 186

Positive Emotionality/Extraversion, 66, 71
Possible Targets for Treatment, 327
posttraumatic stress disorder (PTSD), 28, 29, 56, 64, 141, 143, 145, 160, 161, 168, 170, 175, 176, 180, 193, 204, 205, 211, 224, 230, 231, 492, 523; anhedonia and, 174; ARX and, 404; complex, 533; Detailed Assessment of, 159; diagnosis of, 174, 189, 210, 225; predictors of, 167, 209; RC7 and, 189, 190; self-reporting, 210; symptoms of, 209, 542
PPI. *See* Psychopathic Personality Inventory
Prichard, D. A., 241, 242, 579n1
Priest, W., 249
Primary versus Secondary Function, 61, 62
Protocol Validity, 334, 427, 569; assessing threats to, 73–81, 153–54; described, 324–25; threats to, 73, 333–40
PSCIRs. *See* MMPI-3 Public Safety Candidate Interpretive Reports
PSY-5 Scales. *See* Personality Psychopathology Five Scales
PSYC. *See* Psychoticism (PSYC) scale
psychiatric disorders, 48, 149, 182, 200
psychodiagnosis, 61, 173
psychological adjustment (K), 95, 135
psychological assessment, 12, 61, 96, 99, 101, 105, 153, 459, 504, 523
psychological dysfunction, 48, 171, 185, 190, 246, 249, 251, 345, 346, 351, 366, 375, 430, 484, 523; increase in, 265; overreporting, 380
psychological functioning, 190, 191, 245, 338, 514
Psychological Screening Inventory Discomfort scale, 160
psychological tests, 12, 22, 41
psychometric findings, 54, 71, 139152, 190, 191, 201–3, 206–10, 214–17, 220–22
psychometric properties, 19, 56, 158–59, 164
psychomotor activation/increased energy, 195
psychomotor retardation, 190
Psychopathic Deviate, Clinical Scale 4, 178
Psychopathic Personality Inventory (PPI), 180
psychopathology, 10, 34, 36, 47, 48, 55, 67, 70, 85, 97, 104, 131, 135, 138, 147, 148, 153, 157, 158, 165, 173, 178, 190, 205, 220, 231, 233, 243, 258, 337, 543, 553; adult, 61; assessing, 3, 24; classification of, 23; concealment of, 154–55; detachment, 218; domains of, 65, 66; externalizing, 56, 211–12; factor, 177; hierarchical nature of, 163; measures of, 12, 58, 59, 61, 63, 230, 351; models of, 4, 229; mood and, 186; personality and, 49, 61, 163, 212, 218, 228; physiological correlates of, 12; research in, 12, 13, 37; screen instrument for, 4; severe, 87, 88, 136, 143, 366, 505, 533, 544; somatoform, 169; structure of, 60, 63–64, 205, 206, 218; subgroup differences in, 241–42; symptoms, 163, 345, 366; understanding, 22
psychopathy, 47, 179, 181, 218, 225, 415; acute primary, 273; aspects of, 219; measures of, 40; RC4 and, 180; RC9 and, 197
Psychopathy Checklist-Revised (PCL-R), 59, 180
Psychopathy Checklist-Screening Version (PCL-SV), 59, 180, 215
psychosis, 62, 64, 65, 183–84, 218, 570; positive, 192; prodromal, 494; proneness, 191, 194
psychotherapy, 66, 166, 187, 494, 504; literature, 46; modes of, 47; process, 327, 577–78; psychodynamic orientations to, 46
Psychotherapy Process Issues, 327
psychotic symptoms, 161, 191, 346, 459, 481, 482, 483
Psychoticism (PSYC) scale, 62, 71, 193, 223, 225, 226, 228, 230, 446, 493, 494; described, 416; interpretation, 418 (table); PSY-5 and, 227
PTSD. *See* posttraumatic stress disorder
PU. *See* Pleasantness/Unpleasantness
public safety personnel, 137, 154, 290, 421, 580n1; assessments of, 331

Publication Manual of the American Psychological Association, 330
Puente, Antonio E., 106
PVTs. *See* performance validity tests

Q Local, 105, 330
Question Score, 74
Quilty, L. C., 197, 217

R. *See* Repression (R)
race, 118, 183, 240, 241, 249–252, 263, 580n3
racial groups, 246–47; score differences for, 242–43
Raine, A., 206
random responding, 73, 77, 334, 335, 336
random variance hypothesis, 42
Raney, D., 242
RBS. *See* Response Bias Scale
RC Scales. *See* Restructured Clinical Scales
RC1. *See* Somatic Complaints (RC1) scale
RC2. *See* Low Positive Emotions (RC2) scale
RC3. *See* Cynicism (RC3) scale
RC4. *See* Antisocial Behavior (RC4) scale
RC6. *See* Ideas of Persecution (RC6) scale
RC7. *See* Dysfunctional Negative Emotions (RC7) scale
RC8. *See* Aberrant Experiences (RC8) scale
RC9. *See* Hypomanic Activation (RC9) scale
RCd. *See* Demoralization (RCd) scale
Reddon, J. R., 55, 56; review by, 33–37
Reeves, C. K., 138, 145
Reid, R. C., 57
Relationship Insecurity, 159, 226
reporting, computer-generated, 276–77, 288–92, 303–4, 324–31
Repression (R), 9, 62
Research Domain Criteria, 223
Research References, 304, 328, 569
responding measures: content-based invalid, 92–95; non-content-based invalid, 90–92
Response Bias Scale (RBS), 92, 93, 95, 112, 113, 126, 135, 136, 137, 143, 146, 147, 277, 292, 347, 358, 366, 395, 396, 398, 470; described, 94, 350; interpretation, 350 (table); overreporting and, 144, 145; scale, 148
Restructured Clinical (RC) Scales, 3, 37, 39–44, 59–60, 66–70, 97, 99, 108–9, 113–14, 114 (table), 126, 140, 149, 203, 216, 232, 249, 289, 354, 383, 384, 385–93, 394; analytic studies of, 65; appraisals of, 55–59, 96; construction of, 49; deriving final, 53–54; developing, 40, 42, 44–54, 56; descriptions of, 164–98; factor analyses of, 230; personality/psychopathology and, 55; predictive value of, 250; psychometric properties of, 164, 260
Ribot, T. H., 172
risk taking, 163, 226, 459, 472, 503
Roberts, J. E., 242
Robinson, E. V., 147
Rogers, M. L., 207
Rogers, R., 57–58, 147
Rohling, M. L., 137
Roma, P., 150–51
Rose, R. J., 57
Rosenblatt, A., 241, 242, 579n1
Rozynko, V. V., 242
Ruch, F. L., 74
Rudeness, 216, 221, 226
Ruggero. C. J., 195, 196
Ruiz, M. A., 63
rumination, 208, 458, 481, 523, 578; disorders involving, 445; excessive, 446, 459; proneness to, 444
Ryder, A. G., 224

Salovey, P., 186, 187
Sammut, S., 174
Santor, D. A., 173
SAV. *See* Social Avoidance (SAV) scale
scale development, 11, 21, 46–48, 50, 58, 68, 101–2, 109; alternative, 44–45; described, 107; stages of, 23; targets for, 4, 45
scale keying, unbalanced, 34–35
Scarpa, A., 206
Scheman, J., 160, 161, 170–71, 201

Schenk, P. W., 170, 192
Schedule of Compulsions, Obsessions, and Pathological Impulses (SCOPI), 209
Schinka, J. A., 32, 272
schizoid personality disorder, 219, 221, 481, 541
schizophrenia, 63, 79, 159, 160, 161, 166, 176, 184, 190, 192, 212, 217, 482; anhedonia and, 174, 175; developing, 191; with paranoid features, 481; spectrum, 494
Schizophrenia-Psychotic Experiences, 161
schizotypal personality disorder, 193, 222, 223, 226, 227, 481, 492, 494
schizotypy, 191, 192
Schlaepfer, T. E., 174
Schlenger PTSD scale, 29, 30
Schneider, M., 190–91
Schroeder, R. W., 96
SCL-90-4, Somatization scale of, 170
Score Report, 276, 278–87 (fig.), 289, 291, 292, 327, 389, 392, 399, 400, 408, 410, 430, 431–37 (fig.), 446, 447–53 (fig.), 463–69 (fig.), 473–80 (fig.), 485–91 (fig.), 496–502 (fig.), 506–12 (fig.), 515–21 (fig.), 524–30 (fig.), 534–40 (fig.), 542, 545–51 (fig.), 571–76 (fig.); Clinical Settings, 305–23 (fig.); With Comparison Group Data, 293–302 (fig.); described, 277, 288; Fixed, Validity Scales/Content-Inconsistent True Responding, 361 (fig.); information in, 304; Scales Profile, 429 (fig.); unscorable responses in, 552; Validity Scales/Combined Inconsistent Responding, 357 (fig.); Validity Scales/ Elevated F and L Scores Reflecting Overreporting While, Claiming Uncommon Virtues, 378 (fig.); Validity Scales/ Elevated F and L Scores Reflecting Overreporting While, Claiming Uncommon Virtues, 378 (fig.); Validity Scales/ Elevated FBS Score and Moderately Elevated RBS Score, 371 (fig.); Validity Scales/Elevated Fp Score Reflecting Overreporting of Severe, Psychopathology, 365 (fig.); Validity Scales/Elevated Fs Score Reflecting Overreporting of Somatic Symptoms, 369 (fig.); Validity Scales/Elevated K Score With Low L Score, 376 (fig.); Validity Scales/Elevated L and K Scores, 377 (fig.); Validity Scales/ Elevated L Score, 374 (fig.); Validity Scales/Elevated RBS Score and Moderately Elevated FBS Score, 372 (fig.); Validity Scales/Fixed, Content-Inconsistent False Responding, 363 (fig.); Validity Scales/Highly Elevated F and Fp Scores, 367 (fig.); Validity Scales/Highly Elevated F Score Reflecting Overreporting, 364 (fig.); Validity Scales/Highly Elevated Scores on All Overreporting Scales, 373 (fig.); Validity Scales/Moderately Elevated F Score, 368 (fig.); Validity Scales/Nonresponding, 355 (fig.), 356 (fig.); Validity Scales/Valid Protocol, 379 (fig.); Validity Scales/ Variable Inconsistent Responding, 359 (fig.), 360 (fig.)
scoring, 7, 30, 237, 244, 269, 271, 273; computer, 90, 275, 276, 341; configural, 12, 17, 22, 23; keys, 35; linear, 12. *See also* Pearson scoring
Seed Scales, 52, 53, 67, 69
Seeley, J. R., 173
seizures, 57, 202; epileptic/nonepileptic, 170
Self-Alienation (Pd5) scale, 44
self-concept, 208, 338
self-doubt, 204, 495
Self-Doubt (SFD) scale, 115, 117, 204, 207–8, 220, 289, 291, 387, 398, 442, 483, 494, 532, 569; described, 400; interpretation, 401 (table)
self-esteem, 176; low, 168, 172, 204, 208, 211, 217, 445, 458, 459, 482, 503
self-harm, 159, 226, 290, 444, 513; reducing, 459; risk for, 445, 484, 505, 523
Self-Harm Inventory (SHI), 207
Self-Importance (SFI) scale, 116, 117, 157, 208, 213, 217, 218, 220, 232, 393, 411, 443; described, 412; interpretation, 412 (table), 413 (table)

self-presentation (S), 5, 86–87, 344, 350, 353, 375, 380
self-reliance, 442, 445, 481, 495, 541
self-reporting, 137, 333, 334, 337, 351, 392; susceptibility of, 81
Sellbom, Martin, 23, 59, 65, 146, 150, 151, 160, 167, 168, 171, 173, 175, 184, 192, 193, 209, 214, 227, 228, 232, 264, 553; ACT and, 213, 217; ANP and, 210; Clinical Scales and, 99; DISC scores and, 225; IMP and, 216; L-r/K-r and, 149; maladaptive personality traits and, 226; MMPI-2-RF and, 231; RC Scales and, 99, 170, 180, 185, 188, 197; SFI and, 220
SEMs. *See* standard errors of measurement
sensation seeking, 197, 458, 472
sensory problems, 531, 541
SES. *See* socioeconomic status
Severity Measure for Panic Disorder-Adult, 209
sexual abuse, 522, 532
sexual diversity, mental health challenges of, 252
sexual dysfunction, 445, 462, 492, 514, 531
sexual offenders, 197, 215, 216, 217
Sexual Violence Risk (SVR), 215
SFD. *See* Self-Doubt (SFD) scale
SFI. *See* Self-Importance (SFI) scale
Shaevel, B., 270
shame, 442, 445, 495, 504, 541
Sharf, A. J., 144, 145
Sharland, M. J., 89
Sharpe, J. P., 224
Sherwood, N. E., 30, 31
Shkalim, E., 141, 168, 170, 189, 231
Shore, J. H., 242
Shrout, P. E., 48
shy, 176, 218, 220, 221, 222, 232, 291, 396, 443, 444
Shyness (SHY) scale, 116, 206, 219, 411, 513; described, 413, 415; interpretation, 416 (table)
Simms, L. J., 57, 170
16PF (Sixteen Personality Factor Questionnaire). *See* Sixteen Personality Factor Questionnaire (16PF)

Sixteen Personality Factor Questionnaire (16PF), 44, 61, 224
Skinner, H. A., 65
sleep disturbance, 445, 462, 514, 531, 577
Slick, D. J., 146
Smith, A., 227
Smith, E. E., 80
Smith, S. R., 240
SNAP, 175, 193
Social Anhedonia scale, 174, 191
social anxiety, 183, 189, 205, 222, 413, 415, 443, 446, 513; anhedonia and, 175; disorder, 219, 220, 231, 505
Social Avoidance (SAV) scale, 116, 176, 218, 219, 220, 232, 289, 411, 443, 444, 446, 482, 542; described, 413; interpretation, 415 (table); scores, 221
social communication deficits, 494–95, 503–4
social desirability, 16, 17, 56, 58, 260, 336; described, 34
Social Desirability (Sd) scale, 94
Social Deviance, 179
Social Discomfort, 245
Social Introversion scale, 7, 420
social situations, 415, 462; anxiousness/nervousness in, 445
social withdrawal, 219, 221, 222, 226
socioeconomic status (SES), 32, 264
Solomon-Krakus, S., 228
somatic complaints, 47, 50, 59, 69, 135, 143, 144, 161, 202, 222, 254, 265, 327, 366, 370, 382; noncredible, 348
Somatic Complaints (RC1) scale, 57, 65, 68, 107, 115, 126, 199, 200, 250, 348, 349, 382, 385, 386, 430, 443, 505, 570, 577; conceptualizing, 168–69; described, 168–71, 388; empirical findings with, 169–70; interpretation, 388 (table); pain disability and, 171; scores on, 141, 170
somatic dysfunction, 380
somatic scales, 200, 366, 396
somatic symptoms, 200, 345, 523; disorders, 169, 201, 396, 462, 470, 505, 513, 531; overreporting, 366, 370

Somatic/Cognitive Scales, 114 (table), 115, 198, 256, 288, 394, 444, 458, 470, 542; constructs of, 199–201; described, 395–96; presurgical evaluations and, 202; reliability of, 201
Somatic/Cognitive Dysfunction, 422, 443, 446; H-O scale and, 427
Somatic/Cognitive Specific Problems (SP) Scales, 68, 69, 70, 98, 108, 176, 198–222, 384, 385, 386, 387, 388, 389, 391, 393, 394, 443, 470; described, 199–203; externalizing, 231; new, 109
somatization, 63, 67, 169, 170
somatoform disorders, 12, 65, 146, 147, 169–70, 230, 232
SP Scales. *See* Somatic/Cognitive Specific Problems (SP) Scales
Spanier, G. B., 25
Spanish speakers, 106; neuropsychological assessment of, 570, 577–78
Spanish-language MMPI-3, 274; Norms, and English-language norms compared, 127–28
Spearman-Brown formula, 35, 36
Specific Problems (SP) Scales, 40, 60, 67–70, 108, 114 (table), 157, 196, 383; described, 393–96, 398–404, 406–13, 415
Spielberger, C. D., 206
spinal cord stimulation, 513–14, 522
Spitzer, R. L., 165
S scale: subscales for, 86, 87; underreporting and, 94; validity of, 87
Stafford, K. P, 178, 180, 225
Standard Compliant, Underreporting Compliant versus, 150
standard errors of measurement (SEMs), 35–36, 98, 139, 207, 214, 225
Standards for Educational and Psychological Testing (AERA), 239, 274, 275, 328
Stanley, I. H., 168
State Social Paranoia scale, described, 183
Static-99, JCP/AGG and, 215–16
Stevens, M. J., 247
Stones, M. J., 174

STR. *See* Stress (STR) scale
stress, 159, 483, 493, 494, 505, 531, 541
Stress (STR) scale, 117, 157, 205, 207, 208, 291, 391, 398, 399, 443, 493, 494, 542, 553; described, 402; interpretation, 403 (table)
stress management skills, 445–46, 461, 578
Stress/Worry (STW) scale, 116, 157, 207, 253
Strong Engagement/Disengagement (SD), 49
structural models, 198, 229
structural studies, 169, 177
structure of personality, search for, 61–66
Structured Clinical Interview for the DSM-III (SCID), 250
Structured Interview of Reported Symptoms (SIRS), 142
STW. *See* Stress/Worry (STW) scale
SUB. *See* Substance Abuse (SUB) scale
subjective incompetence, 442, 541
Subjective Incompetence Scale, 208
submissiveness, 21, 221, 230, 578
subscales, 4, 10; obvious/subtle, 8, 9, 42
substance abuse, 31, 63, 162, 177, 178, 181, 189, 198, 211, 212, 215, 458, 492, 493, 494, 505, 533; correlations with, 179; history of, 544; rates of, 213
Substance Abuse (SUB) scale, 21, 26, 116, 212, 213, 214, 215, 231, 232, 252, 290, 327, 389, 406, 407, 411, 446, 494, 542, 554; described, 408; interpretation, 409 (table)
substance use disorders (SUD), 177, 178, 215, 459
Substantive Scale Interpretation, 324, 325
Substantive Scales, 64, 75, 87, 139, 229, 326, 327, 342, 352, 443, 444, 446, 458, 459, 493, 503, 532, 569; described, 107; development of, 72, 290; underreporting on, 153
SUD. *See* substance use disorders
Sue, S., 247
SUI. *See* Suicidal/Death Ideation (SUI) scale
suicidal ideation, 63, 68, 69, 159, 168, 176, 203, 204, 207, 209, 251, 252, 482

Suicidal/Death Ideation (SUI) scale, 115, 117, 203, 256, 288, 289, 290, 303, 327, 328, 387, 398, 442, 446, 493, 494, 505, 513; described, 399; interpretation, 400 (table); scores, 207, 252
suicide: depression and, 260; interpersonal theory of, 208; preoccupation with, 303, 505; risk for, 203, 207, 290, 327, 459, 483, 513
suicide attempts, 168, 203, 481, 484, 495, 504; bipolar disorder and, 196; family problems and, 211
Sundberg, N. D., 13
Superlative Self-Presentation (S), 30, 84
Supplementary Scales, 8, 24, 30, 31, 44, 82, 132
Sydenham, Thomas, 168
Symptom Validity (FBS) scale, 92, 94, 113, 135, 136, 137, 139, 144, 146, 148, 153, 277, 292, 347, 354, 366, 370, 395, 396, 398; described, 88–90, 349; false positives and, 89; interpretation, 349, 349 (table); MMPI-2 and, 89–90
Symptom Validity-Revised (FBS-r) scale, 112, 126, 143, 144, 146, 147, 148; described, 94
syndromes: measurement of, 41; multifaceted, 41; psychiatric, 160, 229. *See also* bodily distress syndrome; chronic fatigue syndrome; polycystic ovarian syndrome
Synopsis, 324

Tarescavage, A. M., 160, 162, 168, 180, 181, 201, 228, 513; anxiety and, 210; RC1 and, 170–71; RC3 and, 217; RC6 and, 185; Static-99 and, 215–16; suicide and, 207
target language, 258, 259
Taylor, A. M., 214
Taylor, J. L., 206, 219
TBI. *See* traumatic brain injury
Tellegen, Auke, 24, 27, 36, 40, 51, 52, 53, 54, 55, 57, 62, 64, 65, 84, 89, 90, 137, 157, 164, 170, 176; "big seven" model and, 218; Clinical Scales and, 3, 37, 39, 42, 44, 165; demoralization and, 47, 48, 166; Externalizing Scales and, 214; Internalizing Scales and, 206; Jackson and, 45; model by, 50; mood variance and, 186–87; MPQ and, 28, 45, 82, 83, 166, 192; NEM and, 71, 186, 187, 189, 190; PA/NA and, 49, 187; PEM and, 186; Pleasant versus Unpleasant and, 187; Positive Emotionality and, 71; PSY-5 Scales and, 225; psychopathology and, 165; RC Scales and, 58–59, 164, 168, 172, 188; Seed Scales and, 67; Somatic/Cognitive Dysfunction and, 427; structure of mood and, 48
temper tantrums, 481, 492
Ternes, M. S., 143, 144, 145
Test of Memory Malingering (TOMM), 94
test results, 55, 72, 265, 266, 270, 304, 324, 326, 327, 338, 344, 381; comparability of, 120; interpretation of, 421, 422, 444, 445, 446, 458, 459, 470
test takers, 6, 7, 10, 11, 24, 27, 28, 43, 71, 74–75, 79, 85; age of, 270; Hispanic, 121; reading level of, 271–72, 273; testability of, 270–73
testosterone, mental health and, 248
TF. *See* True-False
TGD. *See* transgender and gender diverse
THD. *See* Thought Dysfunction (THD) scale
Thomas, M. L., 57, 160, 170
thought disorders, 160, 326
thought dysfunction, 181, 182, 185, 232
Thought Dysfunction (THD) scale, 64–65, 66, 67, 158, 160–62, 210, 232, 370, 383, 422, 430, 443, 444; assessing, 214; described, 384–85; domain, 482; interpretation, 385 (table); symptoms of, 347
Timbrook, R. E.: Black and White comparisons and, 244–45
transgender and gender diverse (TGD), 252, 253, 254, 255; mental health services and, 256, 257; nontreatment-receiving, 256; suicide risk and, 256

transgender issues, 248, 495
trauma, 165, 193, 446, 531, 532, 542, 543.
  See also head trauma; posttraumatic stress disorder
traumatic brain injury (TBI), 57, 96, 143, 144
Treatment Considerations, 324, 382, 580n4, 580n5, 580n6; described, 326–27
treatment noncompliance, 327, 459, 503
treatment planning, 382, 462
Treatment Recommendations, 422, 484
Triarchic Psychopathy Measure, 180
TRIN. *See* True Response Inconsistency (TRIN) scale
TRIN-r. *See* True Response Inconsistency-Revised (TRIN-r) scale
TRT. *See* Negative Treatment Indicators
True, 34, 75, 76, 82, 85, 102, 289, 334, 336, 340, 344, 354, 358, 382; responding, 83, 136, 338, 362, 472, 482
True-False (TF), 91, 102, 110, 342
True Response Inconsistency (TRIN) scale, 28, 37, 87, 90, 91, 110, 111, 113, 120, 121, 135, 136, 139, 141, 142, 153, 276, 277, 292, 303, 330, 338, 341, 342–44, 354, 358, 362, 366; described, 82–84; interpretation, 343 (table); MMPI-2 version of, 83; MPQ, 82, 83
True Response Inconsistency-Revised (TRIN-r) scale, 110, 120, 126, 136, 140, 141, 142, 273; described, 91–92; invalid responding and, 11
True-True (TT), 83, 91, 92, 110, 111, 342
Trull, T. J., 224
Tsai, D. C., 247
T scores, 6, 9, 27, 33, 44, 75, 81, 85, 87, 104, 120, 123, 126, 130–33, 139, 141, 206, 207, 214, 244, 245, 246, 250, 251, 6, 263, 270, 273; by domain, 277, 288–92, 303–4; deflated, 32; linear, 259, 277; overreporting, 145; percentile equivalents of, 132 (table); prototype distribution for, 132 (fig.); uniform, 28, 36, 132, 133
Tsushima, W. T., 243
TT. *See* True-True
Tuohy, A., 173
Tylicki, J. L., 146

Uncommon Virtues (L) scale, 5, 82, 84, 93, 95, 113, 137, 139, 241, 242, 277, 358, 381; described, 351–52; interpretation, 352 (table); scores, 75, 87, 127, 153, 154, 246, 352, 362, 370, 375, 470; underreporting and, 94
Uncommon Virtues (L-r) scale, 113, 137, 150, 151, 152; described, 95; validity of, 149
Undercontrolled/Externalizing Syndromes, 63
underreporting, 73, 80, 87, 105, 137, 149–52, 154, 277, 324, 330, 340, 344, 350–51, 352, 353, 354, 375, 380; described, 113, 337–38; indicators of, 94–95, 113, 149; intentional, 338; speed/response latency and, 150; unintentional, 153, 338
Underreporting Compliant, Standard Compliant versus, 150
Underreporting Noncompliant, 150
University of Minnesota, MMPI and, 23, 258
University of Minnesota Hospital, 6, 24, 241
University of Minnesota Press, 23, 30, 84, 89, 258, 259
Unscorable Responses, 140, 324, 327, 329–30, 542, 552; described, 289
Unterbrink, C., 246
U.S. Census Bureau, 120, 261, 579n2

VA. *See* Veterans Administration
Validating Scores. *See* MMPI Validity Scales
validity indicators, 30, 81, 84, 87, 90, 93, 95, 110, 137, 139, 291, 333, 339, 427; development of, 155; function of, 154
Van der Heijden, P. T., 170
Vaňousová, M., 202
Variable Response Inconsistency (VRIN) scale, 28, 37, 87, 91, 110, 111, 113, 120, 121, 135, 136, 139, 141, 142, 273, 276, 277, 303, 330, 338, 341, 354, 362, 366, 375; described, 82–84, 342; interpretation, 343 (table); MMPI-2 version of, 83, 85, 90; MPQ, 82, 83; T scores on, 292, 358

Variable Response Inconsistency-Revised (VRIN-r) scale, 110, 120, 126, 136, 140, 141, 273; described, 91–92; invalid responding and, 142
Vendrig, A. A., 199, 225
Veterans Administration (VA), 8, 85, 141, 170, 197, 207, 250
Viken, R. J., 57
violence, 64, 162, 163, 196, 206, 207, 210, 214, 215, 216; chronic, 446; domestic, 197, 212, 522; institutional, 251, 252, 410
violent behavior, 64, 161, 252, 492, 533, 552
Vogt, D. S., 225
VRIN. See Variable Response Inconsistency (VRIN) scale
VRIN-r. See Variable Response Inconsistency-Revised (VRIN-r) scale

Waddell, G., 147
Wadsworth, G. W., 74
Walker, E. F., 190
Walker, R. L., 173
Waller, N. G., 45, 62
Watson, D., 166, 169, 217, 231; mood variance and, 186–87; NEM/PEM and, 186; PA/NA and, 49; Pleasant versus Unpleasant and, 187; RC9 and, 197; structure of mood and, 48
Watters, C. A., 188
Weathers, F. W., 189
Wechsler Adult Intelligence Scale-Fourth Edition (WAIS-IV), 383
Weed, N. C., 42
Wells, F. L., 61
Welsh factor scales, 9
Welsh, George S., 6, 7, 62, 79, 257; Anxiety and, 187; malingering and, 154; MMPI and, 12, 13

White participants, 246, 247, 250, 255; Clinical Scale 0 and, 247; L-r and, 251; scores of, 242, 243, 254; violent behavior and, 252
Whitman, M. R., 151, 159, 168, 170, 189, 208, 214, 216, 222; BRF and, 210; EAT and, 202; MMPI-2-RF scores and, 251; overreporting and, 145; SFI and, 220
Whitworth, R. H., 246
WHO, 222, 233
Wiener, D. N., 8, 9, 30, 42
Wiener-Harmon Subscales, 8–9, 30, 42
Wiersma, E., 61, 62, 66
Wiggins, J. S., 10–11, 29, 61, 62, 94; empiricists manifesto and, 11; scale development and, 11; Validity Scales and, 138
Wiggins content scales, described, 10–11
Wittenborn, J. R., 195
Wolf, E. J., 56, 170, 193
Woodworth, R. S., 61, 74
Woodworth Psychometric Inventory, 74
Word Memory Test (WMT), 94
Work Interference (WRK), 98
worry: disorders involving, 445; excessive, 446, 459, 578
Worry (WRY) scale, 117, 157, 205, 207, 208, 291, 391, 398, 399, 443, 444, 446, 470, 542, 553; described, 402; interpretation, 403 (table)
worthlessness, 167, 176, 204
WRY. See Worry (WRY) scale
Wygant, D. B., 93, 146, 147, 171, 175, 180, 202, 214, 224, 232, 513; RC6 and, 185

Young, J. C., 148
Youngjohn, J. R., 57

Zahn, N., 227

YOSSEF S. BEN-PORATH, PHD, is a professor of psychological sciences at Kent State University. He received his doctoral training at the University of Minnesota and has been involved extensively in MMPI research since 1986. He is a codeveloper of the MMPI-3, MMPI-2-RF, and MMPI-A-RF and coauthor of test manuals, books, book chapters, and articles on the MMPI instruments. Dr. Ben-Porath is a board-certified clinical psychologist (American Board of Professional Psychology-Clinical) whose clinical practice involves supervision of assessments at Kent State's Psychological Clinic, consultation to agencies that screen candidates for public safety positions, and provision of consultation and expert witness services in forensic cases.

MARTIN SELLBOM, PHD, is a professor in clinical psychology at the University of Otago, Dunedin, New Zealand. He received his PhD in clinical psychology from Kent State University. His research focuses on psychopathy and other personality disorders, the integration of personality and psychopathology, and personality assessment with the MMPI instruments. Dr. Sellbom's work has been featured in more than three hundred publications, and he is coauthor of *Forensic Applications of the MMPI-2-RF: A Case Book* (Minnesota). He serves as the editor-in-chief for the *Journal of Personality Assessment* and specializes in forensic psychological evaluations in his clinical practice.